The French Revolutionary Tradition in Russian and Soviet Politics, Political Thought, and Culture

The French Revolutionary Tradition in Russian and Soviet Politics, Political Thought, and Culture

JAY BERGMAN

OXFORD
UNIVERSITY PRESS

OXFORD
UNIVERSITY PRESS

Great Clarendon Street, Oxford, OX2 6DP,
United Kingdom

Oxford University Press is a department of the University of Oxford.
It furthers the University's objective of excellence in research, scholarship,
and education by publishing worldwide. Oxford is a registered trade mark of
Oxford University Press in the UK and in certain other countries

Published in the United States of America by Oxford University Press
198 Madison Avenue, New York, NY 10016, United States of America

British Library Cataloguing in Publication Data
Data available

Library of Congress Control Number: 2019938179

ISBN 978-0-19-884270-5

Printed and bound in Great Britain by
Clays Ltd, Elcograf S.p.A.

Links to third party websites are provided by Oxford in good faith and
for information only. Oxford disclaims any responsibility for the materials
contained in any third party website referenced in this work.

For Marshall Shatz
teacher, mentor, scholar, critic, friend
exemplary in every respect

Preface

As revolutionaries, the Bolsheviks in Russia were intent on creating a new society superior in every way to all those that preceded it. This might suggest that history had no purpose for them, that, like the Jacobins in France, who introduced a new calendar to indicate that time began with the French Revolution, they considered the past devoid of any relevance and value.[1] But the Bolsheviks, in this respect, were not like the Jacobins. History was useful to them; instead of devising a new calendar, in 1918 they adopted a different existing one.[2] Professing a Marxist world view that considered history a linear process in which seemingly discrete events were actually a part of a larger and unifying development and design, the Bolsheviks could no more disregard what had preceded them than they could ignore what Marx had written, however sketchily, about the communism the future would bring, and in doing so bring history to an end. Contained within the sequential dichotomies Marxism posited of the powerful oppressing the powerless—in slave societies, under feudalism, and under industrial capitalism—there was, in fact, transcendent meaning: the unfolding over time of a saga of human suffering that, in its negation, foreshadowed the emancipation of the individual personality that would occur after history ended, when people would be prosperous, enjoy their labour, and have the leisure to realize, at last, their full potential as human beings.

History, therefore, was meaningful to the Bolsheviks. But one must be precise about the benefits it provided. Was the past something they mined selectively for guidance as to how the communist society they intended to bring about should be constructed? Could the template of such a society, the way it would be organized, be found in history—if not in full, then as an adumbration of its actual arrangements? Or was the past useful in an entirely different way, as a source of the inspiration and moral legitimacy that revolutions, precisely because they are disruptive, violent, illegal, and almost always unexpected, usually require? These are some of the questions this study tries to answer.

---

[1] The first day of the Jacobin calendar, which was introduced in 1793, was 22 September 1792, the day on which the Convention first met in Paris. By adopting it the Jacobins helped to change the very meaning of 'revolution' from returning to something old to creating something new: Lynn Hunt, *Politics, Culture and Class in the French Revolution* (Berkeley CA, 2004), p. 34.

[2] By replacing the Julian Calendar with the Gregorian (or Western) one, which in the twentieth century was thirteen days ahead of it, the Bolsheviks subsequently celebrated the October Revolution in November.

Because they were Marxists, the Bolsheviks believed that the past was prologue: that embedded in history there was a Holy Grail, a series of mysterious but nonetheless accessible and comprehensible universal laws that explained the course of history, in all of its multifarious manifestions, from beginning to end; those who understood these laws would be able to mould the future to conform to their own expectations. But what should the Bolsheviks do if their Marxist ideology proved to be either erroneous or insufficient—if it could not explain, or explain fully, the course of events that followed the revolution they carried out? Something else would have to perform this essential function. The underlying argument of this book is that the Bolsheviks saw the revolutions in France in 1789, 1830, 1848, and 1871 as supplying practically everything their Marxism lacked. The English Revolution and the Puritan Commonwealth of the seventeenth century were not without utility—the Bolsheviks would cite them occasionally and at times utilize them as propaganda—but these paled in comparison to what the revolutions in France a century later provided.[3]

One must bear in mind that in any revolution carried out for the purpose of establishing socialism and communism, Marxism postulated that the proletariat would have to play a leading role, and that, absent its doing so, any revolution carried out in its name and on its behalf was ideologically illegitimate. The problem for the Bolsheviks was that by every measure of economic and political development, Russia in the late nineteenth and early twentieth centuries was not ready for a proletarian revolution. Its proletariat was simply too small and politically immature. When it would be was anyone's guess. But the anarchy and chaos in Russia in 1917 opened a window of opportunity that might quickly close and never open again. Fortunately, the leader of the Bolsheviks, Vladimir Lenin, was as tactically flexible as he was unswerving in his ultimate objectives, and he took full advantage of this unique constellation of forces in the Russian capital, and in a few other cities of Russia, to take power in an insurrection that would not be challenged seriously for almost a year; by the end of it the Bolsheviks had created an army capable of fighting the forces that had formed against them. But this did not mean that Lenin's ideological conundrum had

---

[3] In the early 1920s, A. V. Lunacharskii's play about Oliver Cromwell achieved considerable notoriety, particularly in Moscow, where the Maly Theatre produced it as a costume drama rather than as a play about ideas, thus obscuring the comparison Lunacharskii, who served as commissar of education in Lenin's first government, had hoped audiences would draw between Lenin and Cromwell: Sheila Fitzpatrick, *The Commissariat of Enlightenment: Soviet Organization of Education and the Arts under Lunacharsky, October 1917-21* (Cambridge, 1970), pp. 152–3, 158. Neither Lenin nor any of the other leading Bolsheviks tried to explain Cromwell or the commonwealth he established in any serious or systematic fashion, though some Marxist historians of Russia have drawn analogies between the Puritans and the Bolsheviks; the most enthusiastic, Isaac Deutscher, even compared Cromwell to Stalin, in *Stalin: A Political Biography* (New York, 1967), pp. 569–70. The leader of the Socialist Revolutionary Party, Viktor Chernov, stated in his recollections of 1917, *Rozhdenie revoliutsionnoi Rossii* (Paris, 1934), p. 405, that the Puritan Revolution, while respected in Russia at the time, was nonetheless 'more distant and more foreign' than the French.

disappeared. On the contrary, it required intellectual gymnastics of world-class caliber to resolve. In taking power in Russia in 1917 Lenin and the Bolsheviks had reversed the orthodox Marxist relationship between base and superstructure. Instead of economic conditions determining politics, in 1917 politics prevailed. Paraphrasing Grigorii Piatakov's much-quoted comment in 1928, Lenin made a proletarian revolution and then set about creating the objective conditions necessary for it to occur.[4]

In the light of this reversal of Marxist cause and effect, Lenin and the Bolsheviks needed revolutions prior to the October Revolution, preferably proximate to it temporally and geographically, to justify it and to provide guidance in construct-ing the new society that would follow it. Revolutions in countries where capitalism had already emerged would be especially suitable. It would seem, at first glance, that there was a plethora of revolutions to choose from, even if these were limited to Europe because it was there that capitalism first existed. But many European revolutions were not suitable for thoroughgoing Marxists like the Bolsheviks to utilize, either because these were too liberal (as was the case for Spain in 1820), too national (Greece in 1821 and Lombardy in 1848), or too liberal and too national simultaneously (the German states in 1848).[5] Instead, the Bolsheviks turned for the antecedents they needed—one presumes with a collective sigh of relief—to France. Marx, many years earlier, had located the beginning of modernity and modern history in the French Revolution. And since additional revolutions, according to Marx, were needed after the Bourbon restoration in 1814 to finish what the French Revolution began, the subsequent revolutions in France in 1830, 1848, and 1871 became milestones in a revolutionary teleology, a dialectical unfolding of history, that originated in 1789 and would culminate in socialism and communism. As a result, by the time they emerged in 1903 as an identifiable faction in Russian Social Democracy, the Bolsheviks had all the components of a revolutionary tradition—one that began in France in 1789 and ended in France in 1871—at their disposal.

Of course the relationship between Russian revolutionaries—not just the Bolsheviks—and their French equivalents in 1789, 1830, 1848, and 1871 was a dynamic one. It changed over time. In fact, there developed between the French revolutions and the Russians who reacted to them a mutually reinforcing rela-tionship: the conclusions Russian revolutionaries drew about France's revolutions affected what they thought about their own prospective revolution, while the notions they had about their own revolution coloured their evaluation of France's. Within the mental universe Russian revolutionaries inhabited, France and Russia were the polarities in a dialectical process yielding lessons about the history of

---

[4] N. Valentinov, 'Sut' bol'shevizma v izobrazhenii Iu. Piatakov', *Novyi zhurnal*, 52 (1958): p. 149.
[5] Godfrey Elton, *The Revolutionary Idea in France 1789–1871* (New York, 1971), p. 180.

both countries that, when used properly and to good advantage, would change the course of history in Russia, and perhaps even the course of history in France.

In brief, my book explores the role French revolutions in 1789, 1830, 1848, and 1871—which together comprised what can fairly be called a Revolutionary Tradition—played in the history of Bolshevism and Soviet Communism. It also sheds light on how these revolutions influenced the evolving mythology of the new Soviet regime. These are large topics, which can be considered within the rubric of an even larger one, namely the interaction between two national histories and culture, in this case those of Russia and France. The specific issues the book is concerned with, and the conclusions that are stated at the end of it, clearly suggest that the causal arrow in this interaction travelled mostly eastward—that Russia received from France more than it gave in return.[6] As it happens, this view is consistent with the rough consensus among historians who have concerned themselves with the relationship between Russia and the West generally that a similar disparity obtains. Like it or not, Europe influenced Russia more than Russia influenced Europe.[7]

It is important to bear in mind what this book is not. It is not a study in comparative revolution, and it certainly is not concerned with developing a generic template of revolution, in which the factors common to all revolutions—their origins, evolution, and eventual end—are defined and described. This has been done by historians and political scientists since Crane Brinton's pioneering study, *The Anatomy of Revolution*, appeared in 1938.[8] Nor is it concerned with establishing typologies of revolutions, an endeavour that, instead

---

[6] Historians are not the only ones who have come to this conclusion. Pëtr Chaadaev, in his 'First Philosophical Letter', composed in 1829, and accessible in P. Ia. Chaadaev, *Polnoe sobranie sochinenii i izbrannye pis'ma* (Moscow, 1991), vol. I, pp. 90–3, argued—with the grandiloquence and propensity for taking the most extreme position on every issue, to which the Russian intelligentsia was naturally inclined—that Russia had contributed nothing of value to the world, and to the West in particular. Other Russians, not surprisingly, disagreed.

[7] None of this is meant to suggest that Russia's influence on France is not worth exploring and that a book that does what this one does 'in reverse' is not worth writing. In fact, Martin Malia has written on the influence of Russia on Europe from the early seventeenth century to the early twentieth century in *Western Eyes from the Bronze Horseman to the Lenin Mausoleum* (New York, 2000). And David Caute, in *Communism and the French Intellectuals* (New York, 1964), and Paul Hollander, in *Political Pilgrims: Travels of Western Intellectuals in Search of the Good Society* (New York, 1981), have explored the attraction the Soviet Union had for intellectuals in the West. But both ascribed it to the attributes of intellectuals generally, rather than to factors particular to France or Russia. For that reason this lacuna in the historical literature on the two countries and the relationship between them remains, regrettably, unfilled.

[8] Critiques of Brinton's thesis can be found in Bailey Stone, *The Anatomy of Revolution Revisited: A Comparative Analysis of England, France, and Russia* (New York, 2014), especially pp. 1–44; Martin Malia, *History's Locomotives: Revolutions and the Making of the Modern World* (New Haven CT, 2006), pp. 302–5; and from the perspective of Marxism–Leninism, Iu. A. Krasin, *Revoliutsiei ustrashennye. Kriticheskii ocherk burzhuaznykh kontseptsii sotsial'noi revoliutsii* (Moscow, 1975), pp. 278–82. An approach more congenial to political scientists than to historians is to distinguish revolutions not by the ideologies and objectives of the individuals who carry them out, but by the structural differences in the institutions of governance in the countries where revolutions occur. The result, perhaps unavoidable, is a universally applicable theory or scenario of revolution in which 'the realm of the state is likely to be

of stressing commonalities among revolutions, as Brinton's did, emphasizes differences. Chalmers Johnson and Barrington Moore have written extensively on this; whether the taxonomies they constructed are accurate and useful remains a matter of debate.[9]

Nor does my book deal with the generic phenomenon of what is sometimes called 'thinking by analogy'—although the analogies the Bolsheviks drew with French revolutions are closely analysed for the purpose of ascertaining the lessons the Bolsheviks believed they contained.[10] Nor, for that matter, does it purport to resolve the question of whether thinking by analogy is useful for policymakers, and it plainly does not evaluate different kinds of analogies for the purpose of determining their reliability. Richard Neustadt and Ernest May have written cogently on the former; Robert Jervis has done so on the latter.[11] Nor, finally, is the book a retrospective comparison of French revolutions and the October Revolution in Russia, much less an attempt to prove a causal relationship between them; too often this leads to ahistorical absurdities, such as the assertion that the Convention of the French Revolution was 'in embryo . . . something resembling Stalinism'.[12]

---

central': Theda Skocpol, *States and Social Revolutions: A Comparative Analysis of France, Russia, and China* (New York, 1979), p. 293.

---

[9] In *Revolution and the Social System* (Stanford CA, 1964), Johnson distinguishes six types of revolution: peasant, millenarian, anarchistic, Jacobin Communist, conspiratorial, and militarized. These are analysed succinctly in Lawrence Stone, 'Theories of Revolution', *World Politics*, 18 (1965-6): pp. 159–76, and Eugene Kamenka, 'Revolution – The History of an Idea', in *A World in Revolution?* edited by Eugene Kamenka (Canberra, 1970), pp. 7–8. In *Social Origins of Dictatorship and Democracy: Lord and Peasant in the Making of the Modern World* (Boston, MA, 1967), Moore considers revolutions—which he believes can originate peacefully 'from above' as well as through violence 'from below'—a way of navigating the transition from a predominantly peasant society to a modern industrialized one, and argues that how this transition is managed determines whether the governments that issue from revolutions will be democratic or dictatorial.

[10] An intelligent analysis of this kind of thinking is Michel de Coster, *L'analogie en sciences humaines* (Paris, 1978).

[11] Richard Neustadt and Ernest May, *Thinking in Time: The Uses of History for Decision Makers* (New York, 1986); Ernest May, *Lessons of the Past* (New York, 1973); Robert Jervis, *Perception and Misperception in International Affairs* (Princeton NJ, 1976). A useful taxonomy of the errors policymakers are prone to when they look to history, and specifically to historical analogies, for guidance is provided in Yaacov Y. I. Vertzberger, 'Foreign Policy Decision-Makers as Practical-Intuitive Historians: Applied History and its Shortcomings', *International Studies Quarterly*, no. 30 (1986): pp. 223–47. Much has been written on how specific historical analogies have influenced history. A prime example is that between the appeasement embodied in the Munich agreement in 1938 and failing to stop communist expansionism in South East Asia. On how this contributed to American involvement in the Vietnam War in the 1960s, see Foong Khong Yuen, 'From Rotten Apples to Falling Dominoes to Munich: The Problem of Reasoning by Analogy about Vietnam' (PhD dissertation, Harvard University, 1987).

[12] Philippe de Villiers quoted in Steven Laurence Kaplan, *Farewell Revolution: Disputed Legacies: France 1789/1989* (Ithaca NY, 1995), p. 55. Even more audacious were the efforts of Jacob Talmon, in *The Origins of Totalitarian Democracy* (New York, 1952), to locate the intellectual origins of 'totalitarianism' in the Enlightenment and the French Revolution. Incisive criticism of Talmon's thesis can be found in Peter Gay, *The Party of Humanity: Essays in the French Enlightenment* (New York, 1963), pp. 279–86.

What the book is is a study of what the Bolsheviks themselves believed about these revolutions in France, and of the roles their beliefs played in the mythology they constructed that would legitimize the nascent Soviet state and justify the entire enterprise of constructing socialism in the Soviet Union.[13] In this endeavour the Bolsheviks of course invoked Marxist doctrine, which long before the October Revolution had acquired the status of holy writ. But as a guide to actual policy Marxism was sadly deficient, in large part because it looked to Western Europe, rather than to Russia, as the place where socialist revolutions would first occur.

The Bolsheviks were well aware of this, and for that reason many of them—though not Lenin—thought that any revolution they attempted would be premature: it would either fail or prove so problematical that even if the Bolsheviks took power, they would not be able to hold onto it. But in 1917 the Bolsheviks did take power in Russia and ruled it for the next seventy-four years. This did not mean, however, that, in creating the Soviet state, the problem of reconciling their ideology with empirical reality was any less forbidding than it was in 1917. The Bolsheviks had to improvise at many junctures in their rule, and without Marxist ideology to guide them, for many of them their impulse was to look to France and its tradition of revolution to provide at least a modicum of assistance. The result was that large swatches of French history informed a good deal of what the Bolsheviks did while ruling Russia—from the early disputations over Robespierre and the Jacobins, through the heated polemics during the NEP over the Soviet Union's ostensible 'growing over' into Thermidor, to the alleged danger of 'Bonapartism' in the Stalin era and then, under Khrushchev, in the person of Marshal Zhukov. In the last years of the Soviet Union, the French Revolution and the Paris Commune were occasionally invoked by the Gorbachev regime to sanction its policy of *perestroika* (reconstruction).

The reader should know at the outset that the four French revolutions that comprise this revolutionary tradition are treated separately and in chronological order. The result, to take just one example, is that what Russians thought about the French Revolution from the time it began in 1789 all the way to the Soviet Union's collapse in 1991 is followed (in a separate chapter) by what many of these same Russians thought about the French revolution that occurred in 1830. In other words, there is in the book 'a jumping back and forth' in Russian history—though

---

[13] To be sure, one historian of Russia and the Soviet Union, Dmitry Shlapentokh, has produced works that, taken as a whole, constitute a study similar to mine: *The French Revolution in Russian Intellectual Life 1865–1905* (New Brunswick NJ, 2009); *The French Revolution and the Russian Anti-Democratic Tradition: A Case of False Consciousness* (New Brunswick NJ, 1997); *The Counter-Revolution in Revolution: Images of Thermidor and Napoleon at the Time of the Russian Revolution and Civil War* (New York, 1999); and 'The Images of the French Revolution in the February and Bolshevik Revolutions', *Russian History*, 16, no. 1 (1989): pp. 31–54. But none of these works go much beyond the Bolshevik Revolution in 1917 and in any event were written no later than two decades ago. Perusal of the source material in my own book will show that it takes into account the scholarship both in the West and in the former Soviet Union that has been produced since then on many of the issues Shlapentokh addressed.

not in French history—that may, for some readers, be disconcerting. But the only alternative to this approach—tracing chronologically from 1789 to 1991 what Russians thought of all four French revolutions—would be untenable: readers would have to keep separate in their minds what, say, Lenin was thinking about four revolutions at any particular time, while simultaneously remembering how his views on one, some, or all of them changed from one period in his life to the next.

The last thing the reader might want to bear in mind before proceeding to the actual text of the book is that definitions of revolutions in history and politics—in contrast to how the word is used and understood in science as a form of spin or rotation—are legion, and no single definition is immune to criticism or falsification. Every definition, in other words, is either incomplete or deficient in one way or another. But analysing revolutions without defining the phenomenon itself, as it has manifested itself in history, would be unwise. The result would not be clarity but rather even greater confusion. What seems the least objectionable definition— and the one that informs the analysis in this book—is Samuel Huntington's: 'a rapid, fundamental, and violent domestic change in the dominant values and myths of a society, in its political institutions, social structure, leadership, and government activity and politics'.[14] To this definition one might object that it underestimates the ambitions of modern revolutions like the French and the Bolshevik that were driven by ideologies promising the transformation not only of the entities Huntington mentions, but of humanity itself. In fact, the very magnitude of what these revolutions intended required not just a radical break with the status quo, but the conviction that the past had meaning primarily for what it revealed, in embryonic form, of what the future, in all of its salubrious manifestations, would bring not just to the French and the Russians, but to everyone. Although the Bolsheviks, unlike the Jacobins in France, chose not to alter their calendar, they were, if anything, even more committed to the radical transformation of humanity. But one of history's many ironies is that, in attempting to achieve this grandiose objective, the Bolsheviks often found themselves looking backwards to a series of revolutions in France that had ended before almost all of them were born.

To be sure, the French Revolutionary Tradition, by providing legitimacy, inspiration and, not least, a vocabulary useful in *ad hominem* polemics intended to gain political advantage, proved helpful to the Bolsheviks. But it also hampered them, at times severely. The analogies the Bolsheviks drew with the four revolutions comprising this tradition usually generated more heat than light, not only in

[14] Samuel Huntington, *Political Order in Changing Societies* (New Haven CT, 1968), p. 264. Other works concerned with revolutions that provide a working definition are, among others, Jack Goldstone, *Revolution and Rebellion in the Early Modern World* (Berkeley CA, 1991); Charles Tilly, *European Revolutions, 1492–1992* (New York, 1996); John Dunn, *Modern Revolutions: An Introduction to the Analysis of a Political Phenomenon* (Cambridge, 1989); and Noel Parker, *Revolutions and History: An Essay in Interpretation* (Cambridge, 1999).

explaining the course of events in the Soviet Union, but also in the Bolsheviks'
understanding of the original revolutions in France to which these events were
analogized. For that reason the Bolsheviks would have been better off either
ignoring the French Revolutionary Tradition entirely, or at least drawing analogies while bearing in mind the stubborn refusal of historical events to corroborate
facile comparisons that belie, or seriously minimize, their singularity. To the
extent that my book demonstrates that reality, it may have utility for all historians,
not just those of Russia and France.

Acknowledgements

Writing a book is not an entirely solitary task. In ways large and small, many people helped me.

The idea for this book originated in discussions with Eric Edelman, my roommate and closest friend in graduate school, who encouraged me to write it. Years later, my colleague at Central Connecticut State University, Bolek Biskupski, prodded me first to start the project, and later on to finish it. In between, he was always willing to read passages I sent him and to comment on them perceptively. Other colleagues, in different ways, were just as generous with their time and assistance. Paul Karpuk provided guidance on the finer points of Russian–English translation, and Glenn Sunshine, whose knowledge of the *ancien régime* in France I could never hope to match, patiently answered my many questions about its demise. Perhaps my most valuable resource at the university was Sarah White, the Interlibrary Loan Manager at the Elihu Burritt Library, who responded to my seemingly interminable requests for obscure documents in a language she did not understand with unfailing good humour and impeccable efficiency. I could not have written this book without her assistance.

I was also fortunate in the historians elsewhere who assisted me. Marisa Linton of Kingston University kindly answered queries about the Jacobins and the Girondins; Jonathan Sperber of the University of Missouri clarified the provenance of Marx's writings on the French revolutions with which my book is concerned. Matthew Rendle of the University of Exeter read an early version of the manuscript and made valuable suggestions for improvement. Christopher Read of the University of Warwick did the same and even proposed a title—which I quickly adopted—that reflected his belief that what Russian revolutionaries prior to the Bolsheviks thought of the French Revolutionary Tradition should constitute the opening chapters of the book. Finally, I will be forever grateful to Martin Conway of Balliol College, University of Oxford, who selflessly took time away from his own scholarship to read and comment on the original manuscript insightfully and at considerable length, thereby demonstrating that the Atlantic Ocean is no impediment to collegiality. His quip in the evaluation he sent me that the French held their revolutions so that Russians could comment on them seems from my perspective to contain a truth more profound than he may have imagined.

All books, irrespective of their authors, are in many ways only as good as their publishers. In this regard I was exceedingly fortunate; the editors I dealt with at Oxford University Press easily met my expectations. The consideration Christina

Perry and Cathryn Steele unfailingly showed me at various junctures in the multistage process of transforming my manuscript into a book was exceeded only by their professionalism and cool efficiency. Happily, the same was true of Saranya Jayakumar, the Senior Project Manager for SPi Global, one of the partner production companies of Oxford University Press, who oversaw the copyediting, which was done by Brian North with maximal precision and kind understanding of my *cris de coeur* when a function on Microsoft Word proved recalcitrant. His 'jeweller's eye' for the errant citation and the wrongly-worded bibliographical entry was remarkable. No less so was the deftness with which Christopher Summerville prepared the index.

Others made this book possible without even knowing it. Mary and Gerry Crean kept my spirits up when the drudgery of research and revision would otherwise have left me too tired and depressed to persevere. Geraldine Lenz was a source of much-needed moral support, and her insights on matters far removed from the French Revolutionary Tradition had the surprising effect of enhancing my understanding of it. My cousins Neil Corday and Paul Stanzler kept my mind sharp with probing questions about the objectives and larger purpose of the project, while my oldest and closest friend, Scott Seminer, provided an example of quiet courage in the face of adversity that showed my own occasional difficulties in writing chapters to be trivial by comparison. He and his wife Diana opened their home to me whenever I needed to get away from my notes and rough drafts with the same hospitality his late parents, Edith and Maxwell Seminer, showed me earlier in my life. And I would be remiss if I did not thank Drs Jeffrey Laut and Stuart Kesler for saving my life.

Whatever virtues inhere in this book are traceable ultimately to inspiring teachers in college and graduate school. As an undergraduate at Brandeis University many years ago I had the good fortune to take a course on civil liberties in America taught by Jerold Auerbach. The analytical rigour he demanded of his students became for me a standard of academic excellence that I have tried to uphold in my own scholarship and teaching. As a doctoral candidate at Yale University I learned from both Barbara Malament and Firuz Kazemzadeh the skills that writing history requires; the latter ably directed my doctoral dissertation. In the lucidity and concision with which he boiled down complex issues of historical interpretation to their essentials, another of my teachers at Yale, Robert Crummey, impressed me to the point where I almost abandoned modern Russian history for its pre-Petrine antecedent, which was his specialty. And it was at Yale that Henry A. Turner, Jr., in a marvellous course on fascism informed by his insistence on rigorous argument and scrupulous analysis of empirical evidence, became for me the embodiment of the professional historian at his best; the wisdom he imparted has remained vivid in my mind to this day. One of my few regrets about this book is that he did not live to see it.

The same, unfortunately, is true for my parents, Moe and Hannah Bergman, who passed away not long after I had begun my research. But their unstinting support of my earlier academic endeavours, and their conviction that I could overcome all obstacles and achieve whatever goals I set for myself, still resonate. For that reason I believe that my writings help to honour and perpetuate their blessed memory.

My wife Julie has been my most helpful critic while sharing her life with me. She endured with remarkable equanimity the long hours on weekends when I was away from home, ensconced in my office attending to something about which she had little reason to care other than for the fact of our marriage. I could not have completed this project without her love, forbearance, and encouragement. Of all the joys we have experienced together, by far the greatest has been to watch the development of our son Aaron from childhood into a wonderfully empathic and highly ethical adult. In ways too numerous to mention, he also reminded me while I was researching and writing that there is more to life than Jacobins and Bolsheviks.

Marshall Shatz was my first teacher of Russian history. It was his example at Brandeis that inspired me to follow him into his profession, and throughout the many years since our paths diverged he has remained, in some sense, at my side, commentating on my work with the lucidity and critical intelligence that inform his own impeccable scholarship. My dedication of this book to him, no matter how profuse and all-encompassing it may appear, cannot capture the full extent of my indebtedness.

Of course I alone am responsible for any errors and omissions readers may discover.

Jay Bergman

January 2019

Contents

PART IV. 1871

PART V. CONCLUSION

Note on Transliteration

Transliteration of Russian words follows the Library of Congress system. The only exceptions are to render the 'ks' in, for example, Aleksei, as 'x'—hence, Alexei—and the names of persons well known in the West in the way they are spelled in the West—hence 'Trotsky' instead of 'Trotskii', 'Kerensky' instead of 'Kerenskii', and 'Mikoyan' instead of 'Mikoian'.

'The chief practical use of history is to deliver us from plausible historical analogies'

James Bryce, *The American Commonwealth* (1908)

PART I

1789

1

The Initial Reception of the French Revolution

The French Revolutionary Tradition began in 1789 with the commencement of the French Revolution.[1] In Russia the reaction to it, by supporters and opponents alike, was vehement, unequivocal, and often unconstrained by accurate information about it. Long after it ended in 1799 in Napoleon's *coup d'état*, the revolution, for many Russians, was more the expression of subjective needs long predating the revolution than a sequence of objective events informed by the political and ideological requirements of the individuals who carried it out. For this reason, instead of changing minds, the French Revolution froze them, turning assumptions into beliefs, and beliefs into dogma. Supporters of the Russian monarchy and its autocratic rule became even more supportive once they realized that what was happening in France might happen in Russia. That the execution of Louis XVI might serve as a precedent for regicides elsewhere in Europe was too horrible a prospect to ignore. At the same time, Russians who found in the revolution confirmation of the rationalism and the belief in progress and man's perfectibility that had earlier characterized the Enlightenment were emboldened by the revolution to deny the moral and political legitimacy of the very same autocracy, with its conservatism, paternalism, and penchant for acting capriciously and arbitrarily. This was precisely what motivated the Decembrists—who had learned about the revolution while serving as army officers stationed in Paris following Napoleon's abdication in 1814—to mount in 1825 the first challenge to the existing order in Russia that was based on moral principle, rather than by a desire merely to substitute one ruling elite, drawn from the nobility, for another.

Of course to many Russians the French Revolution remained unknown or was of no interest. Peasants, who comprised the majority of the population, were

---

[1] Although historians generally agree on when the French Revolution began, there is no consensus on when it ended. Here it is assumed, admittedly arbitrarily, that the latter occurred in 1799 with the *coup d'état* that brought Napoleon to power. For that reason the history of 'Bonapartism', as it pertained to Soviet politics and culture, will not be described and analysed in any of the chapters on the French Revolution; instead, it will be dealt with in the section on the revolution in France in 1848 that follows it. It was not until Louis Napoleon had taken power in the aftermath of that later revolution that the concept even existed, largely as a result of Marx's belief that it helped to explain the second Bonaparte's rise to power, which he considered a parody, rather than an actual replication, of that of the first. And only much later than that—specifically in 1917—was the term first used in Russia as a synonym for a military dictatorship or a dictatorship that required the military's support to survive.

mostly illiterate, and too concerned with physical survival to care about, much less to imitate, events that were unfolding hundreds of miles away. But those who worked in towns and villages, or had reason, in the course of their daily lives, to visit them might pick up bits and pieces of information from soldiers or government officials. And while Soviet historians understandably exaggerated peasant unrest in Russia after 1789, and also the extent to which the French Revolution prompted it, dissatisfaction in the Russian countryside and among the masses generally was nonetheless real, and the revolution's contribution to it not nonexistent.[2]

As for the educated elite in Russia, its knowledge of the revolution was exceeded only by the degree to which it was influenced by it. One is hard pressed to think of another foreign event or series of events in Russia's history, in a pre-industrial age, when modern means of communication did not exist, that was as profound and long-lasting in its consequences as the French Revolution. To be sure, Russians' infatuation with all things French predated it. During the reign of the Empress Elizabeth (1741–62), French fashions spread widely, and by the time the revolution began, the Russian nobility had already adopted French as its language *du jour*; even Peter III, who remarked that serving as a private in the Prussian army would be preferable to being tsar, spoke French very well.[3] But it was the French Revolution, even more than the Enlightenment that preceded it, that polarized opinions about France itself. Indeed, it mattered greatly, in terms of the personal politics of many Russians, whether they applauded the French Revolution or abhorred it, or were able to evaluate it with an equanimity conducive to a mixed evaluation. Among the first group, France remained the country to which they first looked for guidance because they found their own country's politics and culture so deficient. On the emerging intelligentsia of the early nineteenth century, which enlarged principles largely traceable to France and the French Revolution into moral and philosophical absolutes, the influence of French socialism was equalled only by that of German philosophical idealism. Indeed, by the mid-nineteenth century, Russians pursued for their politics by the tsarist police were often drawn to France, and to Paris in particular, by its large *émigré* community of radicals and revolutionaries, which provided sustenance, support, and a subculture not altogether different from their own; no doubt many of them would have agreed with Engels' comment that Paris in the nineteenth century was 'the head and the

---

[2] K. E. Dzhedzhula, *Rossiia i velikaia frantsuzskaia burzhuaznaia revoliutsiia kontsa 18 veka* (Kiev, 1972), p. 160. For a largely 'lexical' analysis utilizing French 'loanwords' of this at times seemingly mindless reverence for French culture, see the PhD dissertation of Adam Nathaniel Coker, 'French Influences in Russia, 1780s to 1820s: The Origins of Permanent Cultural Transfer' (University of Exeter, 2015).

[3] See, for example, Dzhedzhula, *Rossiia i velikaia frantsuzskaia burzhuaznaia revoliutsiia*, especially pp. 97–126; Michael T. Florinsky, *Russia: A History and Interpretation* (New York, 1953), vol. I, p. 497.

heart of the world'.[4] But Russian revolutionaries, who tended to dichotomize the world on the basis of moral principles they considered timeless, universal, and absolute, were enamoured of the French capital also because it seemed to them the geographical embodiment of moral virtue itself.[5] It was hardly a coincidence that the Okhrana, a separate and largely autonomous police force established in 1881 to fight revolutionaries, had its principal foreign headquarters in the French capital.[6] Writing in 1880, P. V. Annenkov described the almost hypnotic effect Paris had on Russians who came to consider the city the antithesis of everything that was antediluvian in St Petersburg and Moscow:

> Owing to various aspects of its political life, Paris had a captivating effect on Russians who made their way there always in a more or less secret, stealthy way, since it was officially forbidden in those days to have the word France inscribed in one's passport. The impression Paris produced on the travellers from the North was something like what ensues upon a sudden windfall; they flung themselves on the city with the passion and enthusiasm of a wayfarer who comes out of a desert wasteland and finds the long-expected fountainhead.[7]

For most of the nineteenth century, England was actually more hospitable than France to exiles and *émigrés* because the individual liberties it provided its own people benefitted foreigners as well. But England did not have a legacy of revolution as compelling as the French, and throughout the nineteenth century (excepting only 1848) a revolution there seemed unlikely. The Glorious Revolution lacked the drama of the French Revolution, and arguably was not a revolution at all, while the protests of the Chartists and the anarchic violence of the Luddites two

---

[4] Quoted in Edmund Wilson, *To the Finland Station: A Study in the Writing and Acting of History* (New York, 1972), p. 203.

[5] For insights into the mentality of the Russian intelligentsia, from which the Russian revolutionary movement emerged in the late nineteenth century, see Marshall Shatz, *Soviet Dissent in Historical Perspective* (New York, 1980), pp. 12–63, and Isaiah Berlin's four essays, collectively titled 'A Remarkable Decade', that appeared in *Encounter* in 1955 and 1956, and are reprinted in Isaiah Berlin, *Russian Thinkers* (New York, 1978), pp. 114–209.

[6] Richard Pipes, *Russia under the Old Regime* (New York, 1974), 301–2. In the 1920s Paris would again be the destination of many Russians, this time mostly opponents of the new Soviet regime; among those who settled in the French capital were Alexander Kerensky, Pavel Miliukov, the wife of Viktor Chernov, and, in the early 1930s, Trotsky's son, Leon Sedov, whom the People's Commissariat for Internal Affairs (NKVD) murdered in 1938. Orlando Figes, *Natasha's Dance: A Cultural History of Russia* (New York, 2002), p. 531. Marc Raeff, in *Russia Abroad: A Cultural History of the Russian Emigration 1919–1939* (New York, 1990), p. 37, calls Paris 'the true political and cultural capital of Russia Abroad'.

[7] P. V. Annenkov, *Extraordinary Decade* (Ann Arbor MI, 1968), p. 165. To be sure, Russian revolutionary *émigrés* generally did not assimilate into the countries where they took up residence, preferring self-contained communities instead. They did so not necessarily out of any political or philosophical rejection of Europe and the West, but rather because they never relinquished their original objective of fomenting revolution in Russia. Martin A. Miller, *The Russian Revolutionary Emigres 1825–1870* (Baltimore MD, 1986), p. 4. This was also true of those who, after leaving Russia in 1917, thought the new Soviet regime would soon collapse, thereby rendering assimilation unnecessary.

centuries later were hardly the work of revolutionaries seeking the overthrow of the existing order in its entirety.

The degree to which Russian writers and intellectuals were fascinated by all things French even after the revolution ended should not be underestimated. Russian nobles who admired and idealized France appeared frequently in Russian literature and theatre. The character Chatskii in Griboedov's 'Woe from Wit' is a prime example. In addition, Russian writers who bemoaned the absence in the Russian language of words for concepts they deemed important, such as privacy, sympathy, and imagination, often adopted the French equivalents.[8] And while Napoleon's Russian campaign diminished this Francophilia considerably, it did not extinguish it. In keeping with the traditions of the Russian nobility, Leo Tolstoy learned French as a child, and possibly replicated his own experience in *Anna Karenina* by including a scene in which Dolly Oblonskaia forces her daughter to speak French instead of Russian.[9] How successful this forcible immersion in French could be is implicit in the confession of Vladimir Nabokov's uncle—on whom the character of Humbert Humbert in *Lolita* may have been based—that while as an adult he spoke French fluently, he still made grammatical mistakes in Russian.[10] But France was attractive and appealing for more than its language. For many Russians it was an exact antithesis of their own country. Mikhail Saltykov-Shchedrin's description of the alienation he and others experienced in the 1840s—and of its amelioration by their identification with France— makes this point clearly and simply:

> We existed only in a factual sense.... We went to the office, we wrote letters to our relatives, we dined in restaurants, we conversed with one another, and so on. But spiritually we were all inhabitants of France.[11]

One must bear in mind that the French Revolution spoke so directly to the whole issue of Russia's national identity because the debate about it had begun well before the revolution did. Countries just beginning to modernize, as Russia was under Peter the Great in the early eighteenth century, often define themselves in relation to others that are technologically and militarily superior. For Russia, this meant that Europe—particularly England, Holland, and Sweden—became the standard by which its military prowess and its scientific and technological advancement were judged.[12] Later in the century, during the reign of Empress Elizabeth, the comparison

---

[8] V. Vinogradov, *Ocherki po istorii russkogo literaturnogo iazyka XVII–XIX vv.* (Leiden, 1949), p. 239.

[9] Figes, *Natasha's Dance*, p. 57; Leo Tolstoy, *Anna Karenina* (New York, 1961), p. 279.

[10] Vladimir Nabokov, *Speak, Memory: An Autobiography Revisited* (New York, 1999), p. 71.

[11] Quoted in Figes, *Natasha's Dance*, p. 55. He also stated that Russians have two fatherlands: Russia and France. John Keep, 'The Tyranny of Paris over Petrograd', *Soviet Studies* 20, no. 1 (July 1968): p. 22.

[12] These were precisely the countries in Europe Peter looked to for the technology from which he thought Russia could greatly benefit, and for the institutional arrangements he considered transferable to Russia. Lindsey Hughes, *Russia in the Age of Peter the Great* (New Haven CT, 1998).

came to include cultural matters and social institutions; under Catherine the Great, the Enlightenment itself, with its models of governance based on reason and natural law, contrasted sharply with the conservatism and paternalism that for centuries had served to justify Russian autocracy. The result, when the French Revolution began, was that it served as a surrogate for Western Europe as a whole: Russians who wanted their own country to pursue the historical path Europe was following were likely to approve of the revolution, while those who rejected the West and thought Russia's future best informed by the principles of Orthodox Christianity considered the revolution the ultimate degradation of another and very different culture in a country hundreds of miles from Russia's western border; for that reason Russians should ignore the French Revolution or, if that was not possible, try to minimize its deleterious effects. Not surprisingly, no synthesis of these two diametrically opposite views of the revolution—and of Russia's national culture and historical destiny— proved to be possible until the Soviet era, when Russia was ruled by leaders espousing a Western ideology that nonetheless rejected the West.

The French Revolution, of course, was not monolithic. All sorts of distinctions could be drawn between its phases, and one could even argue plausibly that the revolution was actually several revolutions combined into one. Depending on one's point of view, these 'revolutions within the revolution' could be simultan-eous or sequential. In arguing for the simultaneity of these separate revolutions, one could reasonably claim, for example, that while the urban bourgeoisie worked with the peasantry and the *sans-culottes* to overthrow the monarchy, its objectives were fundamentally different from those of its allies—and could thus be said to be engaged in a revolution of its own. In arguing, instead, that these revolutions were actually sequential, one could praise the original revolution of 1789 while distin-guishing it from subsequent events, such as the Jacobin Terror, that could be considered largely or entirely malevolent.

But however one interpreted it, the French Revolution divided Russia's educated elite like nothing else since Peter the Great's reforms nearly a century earlier. Every educated Russian in the nineteenth and twentieth centuries had to express an opinion of it. It is true that in the thirty-six years separating the outbreak of the revolution and the Decembrist Revolt in 1825 there were no street demonstrations in Russia like those of the *sans-culottes*, no political clubs like the Jacobins, nor any cottage industry producing pamphlets resembling Sieyès's that openly advocated the transformation of the country as a whole. Alexander Radishchev's *Journey from St. Petersburg to Moscow*, written in 1790 and rightly seen by Catherine as subver-sive of the existing social order, was intended as a warning to the nobility of the nefarious consequences that would follow its refusal to emancipate the serfs, rather than as an exhortation to revolution.[13] But the French Revolution changed the way

---

[13] Alexander Radishchev, *A Journey from St. Petersburg to Moscow*, ed. Roderick Page Thaler (Cambridge MA, 1966). This of course was how the Bolsheviks interpreted the book, and at least

opponents of the Russian monarchy condemned it—not just by accentuating the monarchy's moral illegitimacy, but also by helping them conceptualize the institutions and the principles of governance that would replace it. In just the way the French Revolution made subsequent revolutions seem necessary for Frenchmen of later generations who for whatever reason found it insufficient, so, too, in Russia were there revolutionaries who believed that the French Revolution, while laudable, was incomplete; that it failed to address fundamental issues of class and economic deprivation; and that it required an additional revolution, or several additional revolutions, to achieve the universal social justice—in Russia as well as in France— that was beyond the imagination and power of the original revolutionaries of 1789; while succeeding in some respects, the French Revolution failed in others. But however one evaluated its accomplishments, the moral gloss Russians placed on the revolution affected profoundly their view not only of their own society and culture but also, to a significant degree, of themselves.

In the minds of many of its participants, the French Revolution was seen as the first step in the emancipation of humanity. This was certainly true for Jacques-Pierre Brissot, the Girondin who, in December 1791, called for 'a crusade for universal liberty'.[14] In June 1794, Maximilien Robespierre, the leader of the Jacobins, lauded the revolution for what it had already accomplished. 'A new world', he said, 'has appeared that exceeds the limits of the old one. Half of the revolution in the world is already done.' But he cautioned that 'the other half' remained unfinished.[15] In Russia statements like Robespierre's were taken seriously. Opponents of the autocracy obviously welcomed the possibility of the revolution's replication in their own country. But what for the autocracy's opponents was a promise of better things to come was received by its supporters as a threat. Although until Napoleon's campaign in 1812 Russia seemed too far away from France for any revolutionary army to attack it, its government was vulnerable to the notion implicit in the revolution that any political system like the Russian that denied its people liberty and equality was irrational and therefore morally and politically indefensible.

*   *   *

Of those in Russia who opposed the French Revolution, the empress herself, Catherine the Great, who ruled during all but the last three years of it, had the

---

one delegate to the Estates General. Jean-Louis Kapp did so as well, even including five pages of it, in translation, in a revolutionary pamphlet he had written. M. M. Shtrange, *Russkoe obshchestvo i frantsuzskaia revoliutsiia 1789–1974 gg.* (Moscow, 1956), p. 78.

[14] J. P. Brissot, *Second discours sur la nécessité de faire la guerre aux Princes allemands* (Paris, 1791), p. 27. See also Marisa Linton, *Choosing Terror: Virtue, Friendship and Authenticity in the French Revolution* (New York, 2013), p. 109.

[15] Quoted in Albert Mathiez, 'Robespierre et le culte de l'être suprême', *Annales révolutionnaires* 3, no. 2 (April–June, 1910): p. 219.

most to lose from its replication in Russia. Long after Louis XVI went to the guillotine, she realized that that would be her fate should anything like what was engulfing France occur in Russia.[16] Accordingly, in 1794 she forbade the teaching of the French Revolution in schools, which effectively made studying it a crime.[17] Even works like Radishchev's *Journey* that did not call explicitly for revolution were banned and their authors punished, in Radishchev's case because by depicting Russian serfs as human beings, he provided moral justification not just to free them, but to grant them legal and political rights that no autocrat, not even one as enamoured of the Enlightenment as Catherine, could provide without jeopardizing her own security and perhaps even the monarchy itself. For this reason it made sense for her to consign Radishchev to Siberian exile, and to call his friend P. I. Chelishchev, whom she suspected of assisting him in producing the book, the 'second propagandist' in Russia of the French Revolution.[18]

Not surprisingly the French Revolution awakened memories of the Pugachev Revolt in 1773, the greatest upheaval in Russia since the Time of Troubles in the early seventeenth century. Despite their obvious differences, Catherine condemned the deputies to the National Assembly established in 1789 as little more than 'Pugachevs'—a comment that by seeming to Russify the French Revolution made it more threatening.[19] That Pugachev's army had come close to toppling the autocracy only heightened the danger the French Revolution seemed to pose not only to Catherine, but to Russia and to the Russian nobility in particular. Count Vorontsov was hardly the only noble to consider the objectives of the French revolution identical to Pugachev's, and one might legitimately wonder if his fears, and those of his class, were heightened by the presence in Russia of nationalities, such as the Poles, who resented their minority status and sought moral and political justification for changing it.[20] As if in anticipation of this, Catherine, in a letter to Baron von Grimm in 1792, vowed 'to fight Jacobinism in Poland and to defeat it'.[21] The Poles were proving notoriously difficult to assimilate following the first partition of Poland in 1772, and with additional ones likely to follow—as they did in 1793 and 1795—Catherine understandably considered them especially receptive to a revolution carried out in the name of universal liberty. In 1791 she claimed the new constitution that had been drafted in Poland to redress the deficiencies of its political system to be the work of Jacobins.[22]

[16] John T. Alexander, *Catherine the Great: Life and Legend* (New York, 1989), p. 305.

[17] B. S. Itenberg, *Rossiia i velikaia frantsuzskaia revoliutsiia* (Moscow, 1988), p. 89. Because the Third Section, the institution Nicholas created in 1826 that was tasked with enforcing the ban, was so incompetent, it was easily circumvented.

[18] Paul Dukes, 'Russia and the Eighteenth Century Revolution', *History* 118 (1971): p. 384.

[19] Paul Avrich, *Russian Rebels: 1600–1800* (New York, 1976), p. 253.

[20] Shtrange, *Russkoe obshchestvo i frantsuzskaia revoliutsiia*, p. 71.

[21] Quoted in B. Lesnodorski, *La Pologne au X-ieme Congrès International des Sciences Historiques à Rome* (Warsaw, 1955), p. 216.

[22] William Doyle, *The Oxford History of the French Revolution* (New York, 2002), p. 166. In the minds of many of those serving in Catherine's government, Jacobinism infected her own subjects as

But self-interest and an instinct for self-preservation cannot by themselves explain the lengths to which Catherine was willing to go to seal off Russia hermetically from the contagion in France. Catherine's hostility to the French Revolution also reflected her belief that it was a repudiation of the Enlightenment rather than an affirmation of it. Catherine had once tried to bring to Russia a form of governance informed by the rationalism of the Enlightenment, only to conclude in the late 1760s that doing so might jeopardize her own prerogatives as an autocrat. The Pugachev Revolt a half-decade later confirmed the wisdom of her decision. But she never denied the abstract validity of ruling on the basis of rational principles. Writing to Grimm in February 1790, Catherine said she saw in the French Revolution 'the destruction of everything that has been linked with the system of ideas of the beginning and middle of this century, which brought forth rules and principles without which, however, it is impossible to live one day'.[23] As Catherine viewed them, the revolutionaries in France were not merely wrong or misguided. They were 'full of the French madness', and 'filled with venom'.[24] In her mind, they were not just evil. Far worse than that was their irrationality. At bottom, the revolution was a form of collective hysteria and insanity, a mass delusion 'infecting with fury twenty million people in the name of "freedom", of which they do not possess even the shadow, after which these madmen rush forward to ensure that it will never be achieved'.[25] For that reason, those leading the revolution, such as Mirabeau, should be hung 'not once, but many times over'.[26]

Unlike Catherine, who opposed the French Revolution from its inception, there were Russians who, after praising the revolution for its moderation, turned against it as it became more radical; no doubt the execution of Louis XVI played a significant role in this transformation. Some who did so were influenced by the French émigrés who had settled in Russia; others had actually participated in the revolution before it became, in their estimation, too extreme.[27] For example, Dmitrii Golitsyn and his older brother Alexander, who as young men had joined the Parisian sans-culottes in storming the Bastille, years later made their peace with autocracy in their homeland and actively worked on its behalf: after serving as an officer in the Russian army, Dmitrii accepted the position of Military Governor-General of Moscow in 1820, while Alexander served as Procurator of the Holy Synod, which oversaw the Orthodox Church, and then as Minister of

---

well, namely those who read newspapers. Dzhedzhula, *Rossiia i velikaia frantszuskaia burzhuaznia revoliutiia*, pp. 272–3.

[23] Quoted in Dukes, 'Russia and the Eighteenth Century Revolution', p. 381.

[24] These were among the many comments she made on Radishchev's *Journey*, pp. 239, 242.

[25] Quoted in Paul Dukes, *World Order in History: Russia and the West* (London, 2002), pp. 31–2.

[26] Radishchev, *Journey*, p. 249.

[27] N. I. Kazakov, 'Napoleon glazami ego russkikh sovremennikov', *Novaia i novaeishaia istoriia*, no 3 (1970): pp. 36–7.

Education, in which capacity he directed a purge in Russian universities of everything deemed subversive of the state.[28]

The political views of Nicholas Karamzin, the future author of a multi-volume history of Russia stressing the necessity of an autocratic government, followed a similar trajectory. In the winter and spring of 1790, he spent three months in Paris, during which he came to consider France 'the most pleasing country in the world', largely because he found much to admire in the political arrangements that had been put in place in the country in the year before.[29] To Karamzin, the National Assembly closely resembled the republican oligarchy he then considered the best form of government, in which the percentage of the population that elected it did so on the basis of rationality and reasoned judgement. For a time, Karamzin even admired Robespierre; reading one account of his execution caused him to cry.[30] But he soured on the revolution as it seemed increasingly driven by emotion rather than reason. This, in turn, caused him to stress the necessity, if anarchic violence like that of the *sans-culottes* was to be avoided, for ordinary people to relinquish sovereignty voluntarily to their intellectual superiors. From that conclusion it seemed to follow that in Russia, no less than in France, a political system run by a single individual was even better than an oligarchy because the policies it produced would be implemented more efficiently and obeyed without any protests or even objections. As for the French Revolution itself, Karamzin suggested that, by submerging the Enlightenment principles it inherited in a miasma of 'blood and flames', it risked plunging not only France but humanity itself into 'the depths of barbarism'.[31]

Another Russian who turned against the revolution after initially welcoming it was the aforementioned Alexander Radishchev, who has been called, with justification, 'the first Russian radical' and 'the father of the Russian intelligentsia'.[32] In light of these laudatory appellations, one would expect his admiration of the French Revolution to be boundless or, at the very least, considerable. But that was not the case. During his Siberian exile in the 1790s, Radishchev was so impressed by the vastness of the territory that surrounded him that he became a Russian nationalist and imperialist. This, in turn, caused him to view autocratic government more favourably: in such a system the country's resources could be mobilized more easily and applied against its enemies more effectively. For that

[28] Dukes, 'Russia and the Eighteenth Century Revolution', p. 380; Émile Haumant, *La culture française en Russie (1700–1900)* (Paris, 1913), p. 172; Janet M. Hartley, Paul Keenan, and Dominic Lieven, eds, *Russia and the Napoleonic Wars: War, Culture and Society, 1750–1850* (New York, 2015), p. 217.
[29] N. M. Karamzin, 'Lettre au spectateur sur la littérature Russe', in *Pis'ma N. M. Karamzina k I. I. Dmitrievu* (St Petersburg, 1886), p. 480.
[30] Dzhedzhula, *Rossiia i velikaia frantsuzskaia burzhuaznaia revoliutsiia*, p. 148.
[31] Figes, *Natasha's Dance*, p. 67.
[32] David Marshall Lang, *The First Russian Radical: Alexander Radishchev 1749–1802* (London, 1959); Marshall Shatz and Judith Zimmerman, eds, *Vekhi/Landmarks: A Collection of Articles about the Russian Intelligentsia* (Armonk NY, 1994), p. 166.

reason Ivan III was Radishchev's model of an effective ruler, responsibly 'laying the foundation for Russia's subsequent greatness'.[33] To be sure, Radishchev continued to find the rationalism of the Enlightenment attractive even as he regretted what he considered its political perversion in the French Revolution. It was precisely Ivan's careful calculus, based on reason, of all the variables he had to consider before taking action that made him so effective an imperialist, and thus so attractive to Radishchev. But by 1802, Radishchev's conservatism had deepened to the point where he felt compelled to explain precisely what it was about the French Revolution he found objectionable. Shortly before his suicide later in the same year, he composed what he called a *Historical Song*, in which, inter alia, he reiterated his admiration for the revolution in its earliest stages, but argued that it lost its moral virtue with the establishment in 1792 of the Convention, which he condemned as a collective dictatorship that eliminated the freedoms Frenchmen had previously enjoyed. Like the *philosophes* of the Enlightenment, Radishchev found much in the Ancient World that was admirable, but he also found in it instances of irrationality and moral depravity; some of these were strikingly similar to the worst excrescences of the French Revolution. For example, he analogized Robespierre both to Sulla, the Roman general who, as consul, violated the existing constitution and killed many innocent people, and to Caligula, the Roman emperor notorious for his capriciousness, despotism, and psychological instability.[34]

In assessing the role the French Revolution played in Radishchev's life, it is impossible to determine the degree to which the French Revolution affected the conclusions he drew about events he observed in Russia, and conversely the degree to which events he witnessed in Russia influenced what he thought of the French Revolution. What can be said with some assurance is that Radishchev was driven to suicide in 1802 partly by the realization that the reforms he proposed as a member of a commission tasked with devising a new law code for Russia were too radical for Tsar Alexander I and other members of the commission. One cannot help but note how many of these reforms corresponded to the ideals of the French Revolution: freedom of the press, religious toleration, a more equitable and fair means of assessing different levels of taxation, the equality of all classes before the law, and the abolition of the table of ranks, which by the late eighteenth century had degenerated from a hierarchy based on merit, which was how Peter the Great intended it, to one dependent on favouritism and seniority.[35] For all of his appreciation of the practical advantages of autocracy, in the end Radishchev remained faithful to the mostly liberal political principles that revolutionaries in

[33] Allen McConnell, *A Russian Philosophe: Alexander Radishchev, 1749–1802* (The Hague, 1964), p. 149.
[34] V. G. Revunenkov, 'Problem Iakobinskoi diktatury v noveishikh rabotakh sovetskikh istorikov', in V. G. Revunenkov, *Problemy vseobshchei istorii: istoriograficheskii sbornik* (Leningrad, 1967), p. 90.
[35] Thaler, Introduction to Radishchev, *Journey*, p. 17.

France advocated before the establishment of the Convention. But to what happened in France after that critical event he remained unalterably opposed.

Of course there were Russians who opposed the French Revolution for less lofty reasons. Among them, in the late 1790s, was Paul, Catherine's (almost certainly illegitimate) son and successor, one of whose more ridiculous orders forbade his subjects from uttering the word *grazhdanin* ('citizen') because its French equivalent, *citoyen*, was the preferred term of address during the revolution; they were expected to use *zhitel'*, the Russian word for 'inhabitant', instead.[36] In addition, Paul's government considered reading newspapers, irrespective of their content, evidence of 'Jacobinism'.[37] It attached the same stigma to anyone who believed either that Russia's army under Suvorov's command was incapable of defeating the French in the War of the Second Coalition, or that France's army was a good one.[38] In the late 1790s, during the performance of a play, a member of the audience applauded an actor who stated that 'without equality there cannot be friendship'; for his apostasy he was arrested for his ostensibly Jacobin convictions.[39] Paul's murder in 1801, while diminishing hostility to the revolution, did not extinguish it. Paul's successor, Alexander I, initially contemplated reforms similar to some of those the French had carried out, and even after the tsar abandoned plans to implement them, the presence among his ministers of Mikhail Speranskii, who sought a government ruled by law, with interpersonal relationships mediated by a Russian facsimile of the Code Napoleon, was enough to revive the spectre of Jacobinism. Speranskii never contemplated an end to the monarchy, and even with its powers limited by the vertical hierarchy of assemblies he favoured, it would bear no resemblance to the Committee of Public Safety, the only government in the French Revolution run solely by the Jacobins.[40] But none of this prevented Alexander's other advisors and prominent figures in St Petersburg whose opinions Alexander took seriously from stigmatizing Speranskii as a Jacobin, and three months before Napoleon's army entered Russia, which retroactively lent the charge a certain credence, the tsar dismissed him.[41]

Alexander's fear that he would suffer the fate of his father was real, and it contributed to his unwillingness to reform Russia more than he did. A similar apprehension consumed his successor, his youngest brother, Nicholas I, who saw the French Revolution and the Decembrist Revolt—which he thought the revolution had made possible—not only injurious of Russian autocracy. The threat the revolution posed, even long after it ended, was also, for Nicholas, intensely

---

[36] Dukes, 'Russia and the Eighteenth Century Revolution', p. 384.

[37] Dzhedzhula, *Rossiia i velikaia frantsuzskaia burzhuaznaia revoliutsiia*, p. 272.

[38] Ibid.   [39] Ibid.

[40] Marc Raeff, *Michael Speransky: Statesman of Imperial Russia, 1772–1839* (The Hague, 1957), pp. 119–227.

[41] Anatole Mazour, *The First Russian Revolution 1825: The Decembrist Movement* (Berkeley CA, 1937), p. 27.

personal. One cannot help but suspect that Nicholas had himself in mind when he berated Louis XVI, a quarter-century after his execution, for acquiescing, from 1789 to 1791, to the demands of the revolution; by doing so, he 'betrayed his holy duty', and for that reason God imposed the ultimate punishment.[42] Indeed, with the emergence during Nicholas' reign of an intelligentsia bent on the radical transformation of Russian government and society, supporters of the monarchy and the status quo thought some *intelligenty* bore a striking resemblance to the principal figures of the French Revolution. This was the case for Vissarion Belinskii in the 1840s and Nicholas Chernyshevskii in the early 1860s.[43] In the case of the latter, several of those in the government who were demanding his arrest called him 'Marat' and 'a Russian Saint-Just'.[44] In 1865, the censor noted that contributors to the illegal journal *Russkoe slovo*—of which Dmitrii Pisarev was among the most influential—were 'desperate radicals and nihilists [who were] consciously imitating French revolutionaries in the 1790s'.[45] In much the same way, the prominent conservative and supporter of autocracy, Mikhail Pogodin, expressed in 1854 his fear that Russia might soon experience a revolution resembling the French—with results he believed would be catastrophic.[46] A few years later, after Nicholas' successor, Alexander II, had made clear his intention to emancipate the serfs, another conservative, P. V. Dolgorukov, believed emancipation would be the catalyst for the conflagration he feared as much as Pogodin did even if the freed serfs received parcels of land.[47]

Alexander's reforms, far from destroying the autocracy, prolonged its existence, even though the tsar himself fell victim to a terrorist's bomb in 1881. By that time everyone who was alive during the revolution was dead, and one would think it would no longer provoke heated and often intemperate criticism and condemnation. But that was not the case. Alexander allowed discussion of the French Revolution in Russian schools and universities—perhaps because he thought it had lost its ability to inspire radical opinions—and it figured prominently in the lectures of historians such as Vasilii Kliuchevskii, Vladimir Ger'e, and N. I. Kareev, whose influence exceeded the limits of Russian universities.[48] In addition, French histories of the revolution could now be published in

---

[42] Quoted in B. S. Itenberg, *Rossiia i velikaia frantsuzskaia revoliutsiia*, (Moscow, 1988), p. 139.

[43] V. Kuleshov, *'Otechestvennye zapiski' i literatura 40-kh godov XIX veka* (Moscow, 1959), pp. 184–5.

[44] Quoted in V. A. Gavrilichev, 'Velikaia frantsuzskaia revoliutsiia v publitsistike revoliutsionnykh demokratov A. I. Gertsena, V. P. Popova, D. I. Pisareva (konets 50-x-60-e gody XIX v.)', *Frantsuzskii ezhegodnik: stat'i i materialy po istorii Frantsii 1989* (Moscow, 1989), p. 374.

[45] F. F. Kuznetsov, *Russkoe slovo'* (Moscow, 1965), p. 232; A. V. Nikitenko, *Dnevnik* (Moscow, 1955), vol. II, pp. 545–6.

[46] M. P. Pogodin, *Istoriko-politicheskie pis'ma i zapiski v prodolzhenie Krymskoi voiny* (Moscow, 1874), p. 250.

[47] P. V. Dolgorukov, *Petersburgskie ocherki: Pamflety emigranta. 1860–1867* (Moscow, 1934), p. 54.

[48] Tamara Kondratieva, *Bol'sheviki-iakobintsy i prizrak termidora* (Moscow, 1993), p. 61; Robert F. Byrnes, 'Kliuchevskii's View of the Flow of Russian History', in Thomas Sanders, ed.,

translation, and read freely by potential supporters and opponents. As was the case in France itself, some came to oppose the revolution after initially supporting it; Taine's and Tocqueville's works' proved especially influential in changing readers' minds in that direction.[49] By reading their works, Russians previously sympathetic to Alexander's moderate reforms could easily see how reforming another country's government, even absent any desire to transform it, could set in motion a sequence of events resulting in its downfall. Others, who never believed reforms of any kind could have salubrious effects, found in the histories Taine and Tocqueville had written additional corroboration of their opinion. Alexander Pobedonostsev, the head of the Holy Synod and tutor of the last two tsars, Alexander III and Nicholas II, rejected Loris-Melikov's proposal for a consultative assembly in Russia—which Alexander II agreed to mere hours before his assassination—partly because he thought the institution would resemble the Estates General, the establishment of which, in Pobedonostev's jaundiced opinion, would lead inexorably, as the Estates General did in France, to the execution of the monarch.[50]

Pobedonostsev never formally explained his objections to the French Revolution—though from his casual remarks one can easily infer what they were. The same can be said, more or less, for Dostoevsky, Vladimir Soloviev, and Konstantin Leontiev.[51] But other opponents of the French Revolution took the trouble to explain precisely what it was about the revolution they found abhorrent. Nikolai Danilevskii, in 1885, argued that the French Revolution, in the evils it produced, was indivisible. It could not be considered to have had a salubrious beginning, a malevolent middle, and an inconclusive end. By producing uninterrupted 'anti-social anarchy', it was a monstrosity and a horror from its inception—even though, paradoxically, the reforms it carried out were largely inconsequential, hardly ameliorating the social ills afflicting France before the revolution began. Its most abhorrent expression, the Jacobin Terror of the mid-1790s, evolved organically from the original objectives of 1789.[52] Other opponents of the Russian revolutionary movement, such as Nicholas Fedorov, Nicholas Strakhov, and Ivan Aksakov, located the origins of the French Revolution in the

---

Historiography of Imperial Russia: The Profession and Writing of History in a Multinational State (New York, 1999), p. 252.

[49] Kondratieva, *Bol'shevik-iakobintsy*, p. 215, 149–50. Alexander's reform-minded Minister of War, Dmitrii Miliutin, read the works of both historians in retirement, and in his diary commented on the similarities he saw between Russia and the *ancien régime* in France. *Dnevnik D. A. Miliutina, 1881–1882* (Moscow, 1950), vol. III, p. 103.
[50] Ironically, Alexander had long resisted the proposal for the same reason Pobedonostsev did. Itenberg, *Rossiia i velikaia frantsuzskaia revoliutsiia*, pp. 144.
[51] Dmitry Shlapentokh, *The French Revolution in Russian Intellectual Life 1865–1905* (New Brunswick NJ, 2009), pp. 53–71.
[52] Nikolai Danilevskii, *Rossiia i Evropa. Vzgliad na kulturnye i politicheskie otnosheniia slavianskogo mira k germano-romanskomu* (St Petersberg, 1995), pp. 156, 415–16 and *passim*.

Enlightenment, specifically in its rationalism and secularism, which not only substituted man for God as the repository of all moral principles, but presumed their universality while ignoring everything that distinguished Russians (or Slavs) from other peoples.[53]

* * *

Russians who in Western terminology would be considered liberals had a more favourable opinion of the French Revolution. They approved of its objectives and believed that the abolition of the monarchy was required to achieve them. But in Russia the latter would not be necessary because the monarchy was stronger there than in Western Europe. In fact, to Russian liberals who lived through the revolution, Alexander I seemed precisely the monarch they desired, because he had spoken favourably of reform before becoming tsar in 1801—he even hinted that serfdom might be eliminated, or at least significantly restricted; in some cases, they even served in his administration. Pavel Stroganov, for example, had joined a Jacobin Club in Paris in August 1790 and attended its meetings when he was not in Versailles observing the proceedings of the National Assembly. He even dreamed of becoming the Russian equivalent of Mirabeau, whom he admired greatly, and of leading a revolution in Russia no less virtuous than the French.[54] Just before leaving France to return to Russia, he wrote that 'the cry of freedom rings in my ears and the best day of my life will be that when I see Russia regenerated by such a revolution'.[55] But Alexander's liberal rhetoric prior to becoming tsar convinced Stroganov that a revolution was no longer necessary, and after 1801 he served on the 'unofficial committee' Alexander created to reform Russia in ways Stroganov believed would be consistent with the principles of the French Revolution and the Enlightenment. Another member of the committee, Viktor Kochubei, had once referred to himself as 'a true partisan' of the French Revolution.[56] Although in the end the committee produced little of lasting value, the sobriquet that was applied to it—it was known collectively as 'the Jacobin gang'— captured very nicely the enormous influence the French Revolution had on the policies its members favoured, which included the emancipation of the serfs.[57]

Russians liberals generally responded to the revolution with a mixture of nuance and ambivalence, the precise proportions of which fluctuated with changing conditions in Russia. The Russian who most personified this inconsistency, borne out of ambivalence, was Alexander Pushkin, generally considered Russia's

[53] Shlapentokh, *French Revolution in Russian Intellectual Life*, pp. 13–52.
[54] Avrahm Yarmolinsky, *Roots of Revolution* (New York, 1971), p. 19; Haumant, *La culture française en Russie*, p. 172.
[55] Quoted in Dukes, 'Russia and the Eighteenth Century Revolution', p. 380.
[56] Dzhedzhula, *Rossiia i velikaia frantsuzskaia burzhuaznaia revoliutsiia*, p. 149.
[57] Yarmolinsky, *Roots of Revolution*, p. 25. Allen McConnell, *Tsar Alexander I: Paternalistic Reformer* (Northbrook IL, 1970), p. 75.

greatest writer. A measure of the universality of his appeal is that in the twentieth century he would be praised by figures as dissimilar as Trotsky and Nicholas II. But the range of Pushkin's admirers was not just the result of the fact that his works raised issues of universal importance and appeal. It also reflected the fact that his politics were extraordinarily elusive. One finds in his works views that could be fairly characterized as liberal or even radical, such as his championing intellectual and artistic freedom. One also finds, however, much that could be considered conservative, such as his paeans to Nicholas I. Moreover, Pushkin's views changed over the course of his life, and one senses that his beliefs were at least partly the result of indecision, of an innate inability to reduce the complexities he saw in politics to certitudes like those of persons both to his left and to his right politically.

This was certainly true of his views on the French Revolution. Pushkin intended to write a history of the revolution. But the project was unfinished at the time of his death in 1837; all that existed were drafts, apparently of specific chapters, bearing the titles 'On the French Revolution' and 'On the Estates General'.[58] Nevertheless, it is clear that he was genuinely horrified by aspects of it, such as the Terror, and that he strongly identified with those of its victims who believed in individual liberty, such as the poet, André Chernier, who was guillotined in 1794, just a few days before Robespierre suffered the same fate.[59] It may, in fact, have been senseless murders such as Chernier's and that of the Girondins, whom Pushkin admired, that caused him to call Sodom 'the Paris of the Old Testament'.[60] But he also on one occasion termed Robespierre 'a sentimental tiger'— which suggested that the Jacobin executioner was not entirely without praiseworthy qualities. Moreover, he befriended several of the Decembrists, before they tried to overthrow the government in 1825, after their return from France a decade earlier.[61] In light of all this it seems reasonable to believe that Pushkin had the Decembrists in mind when he called certain critics of Karamzin's defence of autocracy 'young Jacobins'—because they were appalled by the 'barbarism and destruction' for which the autocracy was responsible—and that at least in this instance he did not mean his description to be pejorative, but rather a reflection of his (qualified) admiration and respect.[62]

A similar ambivalence pervaded what Russian liberals believed about the French Revolution in the late nineteenth and early twentieth centuries. The jurist and political philosopher Boris Chicherin was upbraided by revolutionaries for what they considered his unconscionable moderation, a prime example of which was his

[58] A. Z. Manfred, *Velikaia frantsuzskaia revoliutsiia* (Moscow, 1983), p. 392.
[59] D. S. Mirskii, *Pushkin* (Moscow, 1926), pp. 57–60.
[60] Ibid; Shlapentokh, *French Revolution in Russian Intellectual Life*, p. 63.
[61] Manfred, *Velikaia frantsuzskaia revoliutsiia*, p. 392.
[62] A. S. Pushkin, *Polnoe sobranie sochinenii* (Moscow, 1965) vol. VIII, pp. 67–8.

preference for the Girondins over the Jacobins.[63] Like Pushkin, Pavel Miliukov, the most influential Russian liberal despite the defeat liberalism suffered when the Bolsheviks took power in 1917, had trouble deciding what to think of the French Revolution. Prior to the 1905 Revolution, when violence and force appeared to him to be the only means by which liberal objectives might be achieved in Russia, Miliukov seemed to justify the terror the Jacobins inflicted, or at least to consider it understandable. However, once a *duma*, or parliament, had convened in 1906, he changed his mind. Convinced that his liberal goals, which included individual rights and the rule of law, could now be achieved peacefully, through negotiation and compromise, he accordingly found the Jacobins less attractive, and even dangerous, their dictatorship sounding the death knell in the French Revolution for the liberal principles that had previously informed it.[64]

Perhaps the most celebrated liberal in Russia in the entire nineteenth century was the novelist Ivan Turgenev, who during his lifetime was far better known in Western Europe than either Dostoevsky or Tolstoy, and for many of his Western readers was their only source of information about the mysterious and seemingly limitless empire to the East. Turgenev's references to the French Revolution were few and, as befitting a novelist, mainly elliptical. Unlike Pushkin, he seemed not to have thought deeply about the revolution. The most one can glean from his comments, which he offered when Russian terrorists in *Narodnaia Volia* were acting on their belief that regicide was the only means of inspiring peasants to overthrow the monarchy, was that whatever one might think of the French Revolution, conditions in France when it began in 1789 bore little resemblance to those in Russia almost a century later. The latter was more heterogeneous ethnically, and opponents of autocracy too few and fragmented politically for a mass revolution, presumably with its liberal principles intact, to succeed.[65] More-over, France, for all its virtues, which included the charm of its people and the refinement of its culture, was hardly the model to which Russians of goodwill who sought a more humane society and government should aspire. The French people, he implied, lacked emotional and intellectual depth; that that particular quality disqualified their country from moral and political leadership might have been the critical consideration behind the cool detachment with which Turgenev viewed the increasingly perfervid efforts of the *narodovol'tsy* to assassinate the tsar.[66]

*   *   *

Further left on the political spectrum, opinions about the French Revolution were based more on ideology and political philosophy than on aesthetic

---

[63] Kondratieva, *Bol'sheviki-iakobintsy*, pp. 31–2, 209. In his memoirs, Herzen condemned Chicherin as 'this Saint-Just of bureaucracy'. Alexander Herzen, *My Past and Thoughts* (New York, 1974), p. 534.

[64] Shlapentokh, *French Revolution and the Russian Anti-Democratic Tradition*, pp. 94–5.

[65] Itenberg, *Rossiia i velikaia frantsuzskaia revoliutsiia*, pp. 130–1.

[66] Ivan Turgenev, *A Nest of Gentlefolk and Other Stories* (London, 1959), *passim*.

sensibility. They were also, for Russians who were experiencing the revolution contemporaneously, informed by emotional attachments and allegiances. The French Revolution polarized opinion in Europe like no other event since the Protestant Reformation in the sixteenth century, and in Russia, where political opinions and theories could not be tested empirically, it was especially easy to apply to politics generally, and to the French Revolution in particular, a moral and political absolutism. Ideologies were adopted, and revolutions supported, either totally or not at all. According to F. V. Rostophchin, the mayor of St Petersburg during the reign of Alexander I and hardly sympathetic to the revolution, 'hundreds of [Russian] youth want[ed] to be called the sons of Robespierre and Danton'.[67] This sentiment was particularly evident in St Petersburg. In memoirs written nearly forty years after the fall of the Bastille, the French ambassador to Russia at the time recalled his own surprise on seeing in Russia 'the enthusiasm which was excited among the merchants, the tradesmen, the citizens, and some young men of a more elevated rank by the destruction of that state prison, and the first triumph of a stormy liberty'.[68] Ekaterina Vorontsova-Dashkova exaggerated only slightly when she stated that there was hardly an aristocratic family in Russia without a member of it sent to Siberia for words or deeds displeasing Catherine II; among them were many whose crimes included praising the French Revolution.[69] Among the few nobles capable of rendering a measured opinion of it was A. M. Saltykov, who, while expressing a preference for the Girondins, admitted that because their differences with the Jacobins were small, he could support the latter should they defeat the Girondins—as they did in 1793—and take power themselves.[70]

By the time of the Decembrist Revolt in 1825, much of the passion the revolution had engendered had dissipated. For that reason the Decembrists—Pavel Pestel in the Southern Society no less than the more 'moderate' revolutionaries in the Northern Society—were able to separate the aspects of the revolution they admired and intended to replicate in Russia from those they found irrelevant, unattainable, or even abhorrent. To be sure, their admiration of the Enlightenment remained strong. For A. A. Bestuzhev, Voltaire and the *philosophes* who produced the *Encyclopedie* were 'tribunes of their century', their message one that in its universality transcended national boundaries, while to Pestel it was axiomatic that 'without understanding Voltaire and Helvétius one could not be useful to oneself, to society, or to one's fatherland'.[71] But when it came to the revolution itself,

<hr>

[67] Quoted in *Arkhiv Vorontsova* (Moscow, 1876), vol. VIII, p. 297. The same might have been true of Marat, whose fiery oratory and subsequent murder by Charlotte Corday were well-known in Russia contemporaneously.

[68] Count Ségur, *Memoirs and Recollections* (London, 1827), vol. III, p. 420.

[69] *Zapiski Dashkova* (St Petersburg, 1907), p. 234.

[70] Dzhedzhula, *Rossiia i velikaia frantsuzskaia burzhuaznaia revoliutsiia*, p. 150.

[71] A. V. Semenova, 'D. Diderot i dekabristy', *Frantsuzskii ezhegodnik: stat'i i materialy po istorii Frantsii 1989* (Moscow, 1989), p. 369.

opinions among the Decembrists were mixed. For one thing, the revolution was of dubious value tactically. Nothing about it, with the possible exception of Babeuf's Conspiracy of Equals, conformed to the Decembrists' vision of a revolution in which the Russian people were the beneficiaries, but not the instruments, of their own emancipation. The Decembrist Revolt, in the end, was a *coup d'état*, rather than an actual revolution, its tactical inspiration more the palace coups in Russia in 1730, 1741, and 1762 than the mass politics of the French Revolution, to which the Decembrists were oblivious. For another, the Decembrists looked to England and the United States, even more than to France, for guidance in devising the political system that would replace the autocracy.[72] Several of them, in fact, considered constitutional government like the American the only safeguard against 'the horrors of the French Revolution'.[73]

Of course there was much about the revolution that Decembrists like Muraviev and Nikolai Turgenev admired. But it is worth recalling that a good deal of what they knew was transmitted through the works of Benjamin Constant, whom the former had actually met and conversed with in 1815.[74] Both men found Constant's liberalism attractive, and there is every reason to believe that the other Decembrists who were cognizant of his politics found them appealing as well.[75] In Turgenev's opinion, it was Constant who, along with the actual events of the French Revolution, did more than any other single individual to introduce to the Decembrists the fundamental concept of 'political rights'.[76] And looking back on the revolution with the benefit of hindsight, Turgenev concluded in 1818 that while 'England forced Europe to love freedom, France forced Europe to hate it'.[77]

A similar ambivalence pervaded Pestel's views. While he considered the Committee of Public Safety easily transferable to Russia, and frequently expressed his admiration of Napoleon, he stated under interrogation prior to his execution in 1826 that he had hoped to avoid in Russia 'the horrors that [had] occurred in France'—by which he meant the Jacobin Terror.[78] One wonders, of course, whether in his testimony Pestel downplayed his admiration of the Jacobins, and of the French Revolution as a whole, to avoid the death penalty. But the government he intended to establish was modelled closely on the Jacobin constitution,

---

[72] See, for example, the arrangements Nikita Muraviev proposed in the constitution he prepared for the Northern Society, which like the American Constitution stressed the separation of powers, even including the impeachment of government officials among the legislature's prerogatives. The influence of English political practice is obvious in the retention of the monarchy, albeit with restrictions like those in England after the Glorious Revolution. Marc Raeff, ed., *The Decembrist Revolt* (Englewood Cliffs NJ, 1966), pp. 101–18.

[73] *Vosstanie dekabristov:materialy* (Moscow/Leningrad, 1925), vol. I, p. 34.

[74] N. M. Druzhinin, *Dekabrist Nikita Murav'ev* (Moscow, 1933), p. 74.

[75] Kondratieva, *Bol'sheviki-iakobintsy*, p. 14.

[76] Nikolai Turgenev, *Rossiia i russkie* (Moscow, 1915), vol. I, pp. 60–1.

[77] Quoted in V. A. Diakov, *Osvoboditel'noe dvizhenie v Rossii 1825–1861 gg.* (Moscow, 1979), p. 25.

[78] M. Pokrovskii, ed., *Vosstanie dekabristov; materialy po istorii vosstania dekabristov* (Moscow, 1925–31), vol. IV, p. 90.

with its rationalism and rigid centralization of authority. Moreover, the amalgam of imperialism and political radicalism that informed *Russkaia pravda*, Pestel's uncompleted compendium of the policies he would pursue on taking power, bore an uncanny resemblance to the Jacobins' goal of radicalizing the revolution at home while exporting it to the rest of Europe. The terminology Pestel adopted to describe what he intended was drawn to a large degree from the distant semi-mythology of Kievan Rus'.[79] But the political and philosophical imperatives it reflected were at least partly traceable to Pestel's estimation of the French Revolution.

Nicholas I, whose accession to the throne triggered the Decembrist Revolt, did his best during the thirty years of his reign to suppress the expression of anything he considered subversive of the status quo; not long before his death he even considered ellipses in mathematics politically dangerous because of their irregular shape.[80] For that reason the revolutionary *intelligenty* of this period, lacking any opportunity to test their ideas empirically, defended them with a ferocity uncommon in more open societies or even during the reign of Alexander I. This was certainly true of Vissarion Belinskii, who apotheosized Marat as a 'lover of humanity' and considered Robespierre worthy of emulation.[81] Even during a brief 'Hegelian' phase in the late 1830s, when he rejected the notion the Jacobins had embraced that the French Revolution should be the first step in the emancipation of humanity, Belinskii still considered 'Robespierrism' a genuine expression of the idealism and German nationalism of Johann Fichte, which he then found profoundly admirable.[82] On most of the other occasions when Belinskii invoked the revolution, he made sure to justify both morally and politically the Jacobins' physical destruction of their enemies. In a letter to Vasilii Botkin in April 1842, he proclaimed his preference for 'the sharp sword of Robespierre and Saint-Just [to] the saccharine and rapturous phraseology of the high-minded Girondins'.[83] Only through the ruthless application of force and coercion, Belinskii concluded, could 'the thousand year reign of God'—Belinskii's synonym for socialism—be established and defended against its implacable enemies.[84]

Belinskii seems to have been spurred to his moral absolutism by Timofei Granovskii, with whom he carried on a lively correspondence in which they disagreed on many issues in addition to the French Revolution. But it was

---

[79] I. Shchipanov, ed., *Izbrannye sotsial'no-politicheskie i filosofskie proizvedeniia Dekabristov* (Moscow, 1951), vol. I, pp. 295–329.

[80] Nicholas Riasanovsky, *Nicholas I and Official Nationality in Russia, 1825-1855* (Berkeley CA, 1969), p. 222.

[81] George Steiner, *Tolstoy or Dostoevsky: An Essay in the Old Criticism* (New Haven CT, 1996), p. 336; V. G. Revunenkov, *Marksizm i problema iakobinskoi diktatury* (Leningrad, 1966), p. 19.

[82] V. G. Belinskii, 'Pis'mo M. Bakuninu ot 12–24 oktiabia 1838', in V. G. Belinskii, *Sobranie sochinenii* (Moscow, 1982), vol. IX, p. 201.

[83] V. G. Belinskii, 'Pis'mo k V. P. Botkinu (15–20 April 1842)', in Belinskii, *Sobranie sochinenii*, vol. IX, p. 511.

[84] Ibid.

Granovskii's comments on the revolution, in particular his preference for the Girondins' moderation, in comparison to the fanaticism of the Jacobins, that Belinskii found not merely disquieting but morally abhorrent and even offensive. No doubt Belinskii would have had no objection to A. Z. Manfred, a prominent Soviet historian of the French Revolution, upbraiding Granovskii for what Manfred termed his 'bourgeois liberalism'.[85] Responding to Belinskii's aforementioned letter to Botkin after its contents became known to him, Granovskii began by chiding its author for seeming to prefer Robespierre to the other Jacobins; if anyone should be praised for 'narrow-minded fanaticism', as Belinskii did Robespierre, it should be Saint-Just.[86] What is more, Granovskii continued, both Mirabeau and the Girondins were more eloquent than any of the Jacobins, especially Robespierre; whatever their failures politically, Mirabeau and the Girondins understood that a political revolution had to be accompanied by a social revolution, without which revolutionaries would be tempted to justify self-serving policies by appealing to abstract and universal moral principles. Unlike Belinskii, Granovskii sensed danger in the moral absolutism to which he believed revolutions and revolutionaries especially susceptible, and he admired the Girondins because they eschewed this kind of rhetoric—and thus the terror it can easily legitimize—more than most of the revolution's other principal actors.[87] In short, the Girondins did not take the revolution beyond what its moral and political principles permitted. For that reason, Granovskii concluded, the Girondins 'went to their graves pure and holy'.[88]

However much they differed on the French Revolution, Granovskii and Belinskii—with the exception of the latter's brief infatuation with Hegel—were quite consistent in their respective opinions of it. Very different, in this respect, was Nikolai Ogarev, who is remembered mostly as Herzen's intellectual companion and confidant, but whose views on many issues, including the French Revolution, were distinctive. In brief, Ogarev mostly praised the revolution before the failure of the 1848 Revolutions in Europe caused him to repudiate certain aspects of it. As a young man, Ogarev wrote a poem expressing his admiration of Robespierre and the Jacobins, the willingness of whom to inflict terror to achieve their objectives he found so laudable and impressive that he wanted to do the same thing himself: 'My heart is filled with love of the masses and with the rage of a Robespierre. I yearn to erect the guillotine anew as an instrument of justice.'[89] To Ogarev the terror the Jacobins inflicted was an expression, rather than a repudiation, of public opinion in France, and for that reason it advanced the revolution, which had the virtue of being popular politically. But Ogarev drew

---

[85] Manfred, *Velikaia frantsuzskaia revoliutsiia*, p. 394.
[86] 'Pis'mo T. H. Granovskogo opublikovano v kommentariiakh k perepiske Belinskogo', in V. G. Belinskii, *Pis'ma*, edited by E. A. Liatskago (St Petersburg, 1914), vol. II, p. 424.
[87] Ibid.   [88] Ibid.
[89] E. L. Rudnitskaia, *N. P. Ogarev v russkom revoliutsionnom dvizhenii* (Moscow, 1969), p. 58.

from the failures in 1848 the conclusion that the centralization of power in France he had previously praised the Jacobins for advancing in fact had had the effect of diminishing, or even, perhaps, of eliminating political freedom in France entirely. In short, Ogarev now condemned what he had previously praised:

> The French Revolution of 1789 long ago destroyed freedom on the European continent by destroying those aspects of life that had been swallowed up by the monolithic state. Everything was, as it were, subordinated to a voluntary centralization. The centralised republic advocated freedom by means of the guillotine...and engaged in genuinely imperialistic centralization. From that time onward, France has been faithless to its own ideal of civic freedom.[90]

By phrasing his criticism as he did, Ogarev made clear that he was rejecting not only the Jacobins for using terror, but also the masses for their complicity in it—though in fairness it is hard to see how ordinary people could have toppled a regime that was waging war on them. In fact, the only way in which the promise of the original revolution could have been fulfilled after the Jacobins betrayed it was if Babeuf and his fellow conspirators had come to power. Babeuf, according to Ogarev, was not like the Jacobins because the conspiratorial tactics he adopted were dictated by political necessity, which Ogarev now believed had not been the case for the Jacobins, who chose to avail themselves of tactics that required the application of terror.[91] Through Buonarroti's *Conspiration pour l'égalité*, Ogarev was well aware of Babeuf, and the glowing portrait Buonarroti painted of the hunted conspirator probably enhanced Ogarev's opinion, which S. V. Utechin has argued strongly influenced Lenin's.[92]

The archetypical *intelligent* and revolutionary of the mid-nineteenth century was Alexander Herzen, who from early childhood was not only cognizant of the French Revolution but aware, if only vaguely at first, of its centrality in history, which he came to believe was a process of moral improvement leading to the liberation of the individual personality.[93] The very first sentence of his memoir and autobiography, *My Past and Thoughts*, makes clear the frequency with which, as a child, he asked his nurse to tell him 'how the French came to Moscow'.[94]

---

[90] Quoted in N. P. Ogarev, *Konstitutsiia i zemskii sobor. Izbrannye sotsial'no-politicheskie i filosofskie proizvedeniia* (Moscow, 1952), vol. I, p. 635.

[91] S. V. Utechin, 'Who Taught Lenin?' *Twentieth Century* (July 1960): pp. 9–10.

[92] Ibid. There is reason to reject Utechin's conclusion. Lenin's knowledge of the intelligentsia was as broad as it was deep, and he surely learned about Babeuf and the utility of conspiratorial tactics from many *intelligenty* in addition to Ogarev, among them Tkachev and the *narodovol'tsy*.

[93] In his biography of Herzen, Martin Malia astutely observes that for socialists like Herzen the French Revolution was admirable for its professions of individualism, which its principal actors believed was part of natural law and therefore universally applicable. Only later would socialists like Marx—and critics of Marxist socialism like Bakunin—consider socialism an ideology conferring primacy on a collective entity such as the proletariat, rather than the individual and his inherent worth and dignity. Martin Malia, *Alexander Herzen and the Birth of Russian Socialism* (New York, 1965), pp. 112–13.

[94] Herzen, *Past and Thoughts*, p. 3.

Herzen's tutor, in fact, was a former Jacobin who had left France and emigrated to Russia after Robespierre's fall on 9 Thermidor. He often described for the boy, no doubt in lurid detail, the execution of Louis XVI.[95] Later in life, Herzen read the works of Michelet, Thiers, Blanc, Lamartine, Tocqueville, and Guizot that concerned or included the French Revolution, and he probably learned of Babeuf from Buonarroti's *Conspiration*, which provided European radicals and socialists in the nineteenth century with a model of revolutionary organization emphasizing the necessity of conspiracy and the centralization of political authority— requirements that were especially appropriate in a country such as Russia, where politics of any kind was forbidden.[96] That Buonarroti's political roots and ideology (as opposed to his tactical models) were Jacobin and Rousseauean, rather than Babouvist, may explain Herzen's early apotheosis of Robespierre, whom he described as 'truly one of the great figures of the French Revolution', while 'steeped in blood, [Robespierre] was not stained by it'.[97] In contrast to Babeuf, whose communism Herzen then considered laudable but well beyond what France and Western Europe were ready for in the late eighteenth century (and what Russia was capable of in the mid-nineteenth century), Robespierre combined unimpeachable idealism with practicality.[98] Indeed, Herzen's belief that at no other time in history were hopes for the future higher than in France in the 1790s was at least partly the result of his seemingly limitless admiration for *l'Incorruptible*.

To be entirely successful, a revolution like that which France experienced had to change the moral character of people as well as the institutional arrangements under which they lived. This, at any rate, was a conviction Herzen retained irrespective of changes in his view of particular revolutions. But he professed it especially emphatically in the early 1840s, and his high opinion of the French Revolution was a factor, after his leaving Russia in 1847 and settling in Italy, in his decision to continue on to France in 1848, fully expecting the revolution that had begun there in February to meet this particular requirement of his. To Herzen, writing in 1843, the French Revolution was 'a completely logical second negation—after the Reformation—of feudalism, and by demonstrating that authority was not of divine origin, it closed the preparatory stage of the transition to the new world'.[99] But Herzen's admiration of the revolution was not just a

---

[95] Gavrilichev, 'Velikaia frantsuzskaia revoliutsiia v publitsistike revoliutsionnykh demokratov', p. 375. '9 Thermidor' was how 27 July 1794 was rendered in the Jacobin calendar.

[96] Elizabeth Eisenstein, *The First Professional Revolutionist: Filippo Michele Buonarroti (1761–1837)* (Cambridge MA, 1959), pp. 81–92; Arthur Lehning, 'Buonarroti's Ideas on Communism and Dictatorship', *International Review of Social History* 2, no. 2 (1957): p. 286; Shlapentokh, *French Revolution in Russian Intellectual Life*, p. 109.

[97] Herzen's friend, Nikolai Ketscher, preferred Marat to Robespierre: 'Instead of praying for a radiant future, he read Marat's speeches'. Quoted in Manfred, *Velikaia frantsuzskaia revoliutsiia*, p. 376.

[98] Herzen viewed the atheism and extreme hostility to Christianity of Anacharsis Cloots and the Hébertists more critically. Herzen, *Past and Thoughts*, p. 510.

[99] Quoted in Malia, *Alexander Herzen*, p. 317.

matter of logic or the application of reason. The exhilaration he felt on arriving in Paris showed that the revolution's moral virtue was, for him, an article of faith, and the socialism that was already germinating in his mind reflected a commitment that was as much psychological as it was cerebral. Paris was where the most iconic moments of the revolution had occurred, and for that reason Herzen's arrival there was as much a coming home, like that which people in the Ancient World experienced when they entered Rome or Jerusalem, as it was an act of carefully calculated self-protection.[100] In his memoirs, he elaborated on what it was precisely about the French capital that he found so captivating and enchanting:

> In Paris—the word meant scarcely less to me than the word 'Moscow!' Of that minute I had been dreaming since my childhood. If I might only see the Hôtel de Ville, the Café Foy in the Palais Royal, where Camille Desmoulins picked a green leaf, stuck it on his hat for a cockade and shouted *à la Bastille!*[101]

The trouble with this kind of euphoria was that when circumstances changed, it could dissipate completely and turn into its opposite. This was what happened to Herzen. Even before the 1848 Revolution, he began berating the Parisians for their bourgeois corruption, and explained his preference for Italy after arriving there for a visit in December 1847 on the grounds that it was not nearly as centralized politically as France.[102] Nevertheless, as Martin Malia has emphasized, it is too simple to ascribe Herzen's disillusionment with France, the French Revolution, and the West to what happened in France and in Europe in 1848.[103] One finds in his writings in the decade that followed an ambivalence that was not resolved until the 1860s, when he finally turned against the revolution irrevocably—though even in these last years of his life he retained an affection for the *sans-culottes* of Paris because they were 'urban peasants', no less hostile to private property and capitalism than the peasants in Russia, whose *obshchina* (the peasant commune) he now considered a microcosm of the socialist society he desired.

One can quote selectively from Herzen's writings to show that even after the cruel disappointment occasioned by the June Days, his approval of the French Revolution did not diminish. In 1849, he compared the so-called revolutionaries of 1848, whom he considered 'short-sighted and weak-willed dilettantes [who

---

[100] Alexander Herzen, 'Pis'mo deviatoe (10 June 1848)', in A. I. Herzen, *Sobranie sochinenii*, edited by M. K. Lemke (Moscow, 1964–5), vol. V, p. 141.

[101] Herzen, *Past and Thoughts*, p. 323. Of course it is also possible that Herzen, writing many years after the fact, exaggerated the positive reaction he had on entering Paris for the first time to underscore his later disillusionment. If that was indeed the case, only what he wrote contemporaneously about his arrival can be considered truly descriptive of his feelings at the time.

[102] A. I. Herzen, 'Pis'mo k E. O. Korshu, T. N. Granovskomu i K.D. Kavelinu (31 January 1848)', in A. I. Herzen, *Polnoe sobranie sochinenii i pisem*, edited by M. K. Lemke (St Petersburg, 1915–25), vol. V, pp. 181–2.

[103] Malia, *Alexander Herzen*, p. 336.

wanted] to freeze the wheel of history', to the original revolutionaries of 1789, whom he judged to be their polar opposites.[104] Marat, in particular, continued to please him: the great orator felt the people's suffering acutely, and the absence of leaders like him in the revolution in France in 1848 helped to explain why it ended with the French people just as oppressed as they were when it began.[105] Looking back at the Jacobin Terror, Herzen proclaimed it 'majestic in its somber lack of mercy' and credited it with saving the revolution from destruction at the hands of its enemies inside France and in the rest of Europe.[106] Also in 1850, Herzen made clear that the admiration he had earlier expressed for the Jacobins should now be enlarged to include the revolution as a whole, which he deemed one of the most consequential events in history, its purpose nothing less than showing humanity how to proceed to the state of moral perfection that will exist when history ends:

> [The French Revolution] accompanies humanity from generation to generation, proving instruction, an example to emulate, advice, comfort, and consolation, support in case of misfortune and, still more, in case of happiness. Only the Homeric heroes of antiquity, great in their purity and in the beauty of their entire persona ... share these attributes with the heroes of the revolution.[107]

In 1854, in an article written while living in London, Herzen called 'the cult of the French Revolution ... the first religion of a young Russian', and asked his readers rhetorically if there are any 'who do not possess portraits of Robespierre and Danton'.[108] Shortly after the Crimean War ended in 1856, he wrote an essay entitled simply '1789', in which he predicted that 'we will soon see an *États Généraux* on the Neva'.[109]

But Herzen's writings after 1848 also include passages that suggest the opposite: that Louis Napoleon's new regime embodied all that was rapacious and fanatical in Jacobinism, and that Anarcharsis Cloots and the Hébertists, notwithstanding their pretensions of rationality, were no less fanatical than medieval priests who burned sorcerers at the stake.[110] The French people, in fact, were incapable of moral improvement, and the ideals not only of 1848 but of 1789 were realizable not in a country like France, where its paradigmatic revolution occurred mainly in cities and towns, but in a predominantly agrarian country like Russia, the peasants of which embodied precisely the virtues of egalitarianism and altruism that townspeople in France, with the notable exception of the *sans-culottes*, conspicuously lacked. But the deficiencies Herzen diagnosed actually afflicted the French

[104] A. I. Herzen, 'Pis'ma iz Frantsii i Italii', in Herzen, *Sobranie sochinenii*, vol. V, p. 427.
[105] A. I. Herzen, 'Sharlotta Korde', ibid., vol. VI, pp. 244–6.
[106] A. I. Herzen, 'Opiat' v Parizhe', ibid., vol. II, p. 347.
[107] Herzen, 'Sharlotta Korde', ibid., vol. VI, p. 243.
[108] A. I. Herzen, 'Au Citoyen redacteur de l'homme (7 February 1854)', ibid., vol. XXX, p. 502.
[109] A. I. Herzen, '1789', ibid., vol. XIX, p. 46.
[110] Herzen, *Past and Thoughts*, pp. 455–6, 510.

people as a whole. In his opinion, they suffered from 'a veritable passion for police and authority. Every Frenchman is at heart a police sergeant; he loves parade and discipline.... Place any sort of military insignia on a Frenchman's cap and he becomes an oppressor.'[111]

In the 1860s this dichotomy seemed to Herzen even more stark and unyielding. In 1862, he criticized *Molodaia Rossia*, a proclamation of the younger and even more radical revolutionary, Pëtr Zaichnevskii, for adopting 'the metaphysics of the French Revolution'—by which Herzen meant a mindset conducive to the ideological fanaticism to which the Jacobins, in particular, had shown themselves susceptible; the terror they practised caused their passions to be freed from all constraints.[112] Essentially conflating the Jacobin Terror and the French Revolution as a whole, Herzen seemed now to be calling into question the moral legitimacy of the revolution itself, arguing that it was corrupt from its inception and that despite its many laudable consequences, it was, on balance, a bad thing for France and a bad thing for the West. Moreover, the revolution distracted attention from Russia, where peasants should not be instructed in 'the writings of Feuerbach or Babeuf', but instead encouraged to develop 'a religion of the land' it can comprehend.[113] In 1864 Herzen clarified the objections he had articulated two years earlier, arguing now that the French Revolution was 'too aristocratic' in its leadership, even under the Convention and the Committee of Public Safety, and that that was why it did not provide 'genuine equality' for the masses, who failed to resist the counter-revolution that began on 9 Thermidor.[114] Even the Jacobins, Herzen wrote in his memoirs, hardly resembled the Spartans and the Romans, whom he greatly admired; rather, they were mere murderers, ill-equipped ethically and politically to address the needs and aspirations of the masses.[115] In 1867 Herzen observed matter-of-factly that, whatever their original relevance, 'the principles of 1789', had become, for him, 'mere words, like the liturgy and the words of a prayer'.[116]

By this time in Herzen's life, just three years before his death, the French Revolution had become a cautionary tale, a warning to the current generation of revolutionaries in Russia that, because it was Western, the revolution was at best irrelevant, and at worst an example of everything in word and deed they should avoid if they did not want their own revolution to degenerate into mindless terror, and in doing so benefit only themselves. Still, it is hard to avoid the conclusion that Herzen was not entirely convinced of this, and that at no time in his long career as

---

[111] Quoted in Malia, *Alexander Herzen*, pp. 377–8.

[112] A. I. Herzen, 'Molodaia i staraia Rossia (15 July 1862)', in Herzen, *Sobranie sochinenii*, vol. XVI, p. 203; A. I. Herzen, 'Zhurnalisty i terroristy (15 August 1862)', ibid., vol. XVI, p. 221.

[113] Herzen, 'Zhurnalisty i terroristy', ibid., vol. XVI, p. 225.

[114] A. I. Herzen, 'Cho zhe dal'she', ibid., vol. XVIII, p. 308.

[115] Herzen, *Past and Thoughts*, p. 387. Earlier Herzen had said that the revolution was led by *meshchane* (the Russian term used pejoratively by revolutionaries for the petit-bourgeoisie). Gavrili-chev, 'Velikaia frantsuzskaia revoliutsiia v publitsistike revoliutsionnykh demokratov', p. 380.

[116] Herzen, *Past and Thoughts*, p. 616.

a revolutionary was he ever entirely sure about what the French Revolution was and what he should think of it. Perhaps the only thing one can say with assurance is that, in an age of romanticism, Herzen's thoughts were shaped considerably by his emotions, and by an aesthetic sensibility more appropriate in an artist or writer than a revolutionary.

Very different from Herzen temperamentally was his contemporaneous and fellow 'gentry revolutionary', Mikhail Bakunin. In an early, 'conservative' phase of his life, in which he expressed admiration for Russian autocracy, Bakunin, not surprisingly, was hostile to the French Revolution. But he quickly changed his mind when his politics were radicalized to the point where he became the most cosmopolitan of all the Russian revolutionaries prior to the October Revolution, managing to appear, as an observer or a participant, at many of the European revolutions from 1848 to 1871. For Bakunin revolution was something from which all nations benefitted, and his new-found opinion of the French Revolution reflected this conviction. In both its actions and its rhetoric, he saw 'the spirit of pure humanity', which would inform everything people did once they had rid themselves of their parochial prejudices and preconceptions.[117] The result would be a world made virtuous by 'the holy spirit of freedom and equality' which first manifested itself in France in 1789.[118] Liberté, égalité, and fraternité, he wrote in 1873, were 'great words' that in their universality transcended the temporal and geographical limits of the revolution that had given rise to them.[119]

But Bakunin tempered his praise with severe and unrelenting criticism. As an anarchist, he could not help but condemn the Jacobins for their authoritarianism. However much he admired them for their personal qualities—their energy, enthusiasm, and passion—the Jacobins fostered 'a cult of state control' that facilitated Napoleon's dictatorship and in doing so cost the French people their freedom.[120] At best misguided, at worst immoral, the Jacobins may have supported rhetorically the noble objectives of the revolution, but by centralizing political authority to the extent that they did they drained the revolutionary triad of liberty, equality, and fraternity of its meaning. Only Danton, for whose melodramatic oratory Bakunin might have had harboured a special fondness, escaped the Russian anarchist's rhetorical wrath.[121]

As Bakunin described it, the French Revolution was virtuous precisely to the extent to which it kept political power from being exercised exclusively from Paris until the Jacobins, in 1793, betrayed the revolution by doing precisely the reverse.

---

[117] M. A. Bakunin, 'Kommunizm (June 1843)', in M. A. Bakunin, Sobranie sochineniia i pisem, 1828–1876, edited by Y. M. Steklov (Moscow, 1934–6), vol. III, p. 230.

[118] Ibid.

[119] Mikhail Bakunin, Statism and Anarchy, edited by Marshall Shatz (New York, 1990), p. 18.

[120] Arthur P. Mendel, Michael Bakunin: Roots of Apocalypse (New York, 1981), pp. 357, 371.

[121] P. Péchoux, 'Bakunin et la Révolution française', Revue des Études Slaves lxi, no. 1–2 (1989): p. 168. Bakunin may also have admired' a special fondness for Danton because after advocating and practising terror, he fell victim to it.

The French Revolution was originally an 'anarchist' revolution, and as such it successfully avoided, if only for a time, the centralization of power that was anarchism's antithesis. But one must bear in mind that in his own career as a revolutionary, Bakunin's rhetoric was sometimes contradictory, and his actions sometimes contradicted his rhetoric. While condemning the Jacobins for their authoritarianism, he also praised Blanqui and the Blanquists in France, who favoured the centralization of political authority, as genuine socialists.[122] Moreover, Bakunin ran the so-called World Revolutionary Alliance he established in the late 1860s much the way the Jacobins had ruled France. To be sure, the alliance was a chimera concocted mostly to impress Sergei Nechaev, at the time his young disciple and putative successor; Bakunin may also have conjured it to convince himself that he had not lost his relevance politically. But he said enough about its (mostly non-existent) organization to reveal a genuinely authoritarian streak in his personality that directly contradicted his anarchist principles and might well have caused him to run dictatorially any political party or genuine organization he established. In that respect Bakunin was more of a Jacobin than he ever imagined.[123]

* * *

The multiplicity and variety of opinions in Russia on the French Revolution show the degree to which Russians in the educated elite, from Karamzin and Catherine the Great at one end of the political spectrum to Herzen and Bakunin at the other, considered the revolution sufficiently relevant to conditions in their own country to write about it. Even more significantly, the severity with which these opinions were expressed suggested that any consensus, any 'regression to the mean', was unlikely to occur for the foreseeable future. This was indeed the case. Indeed, this polarization of opinion continued into the late nineteenth century, when the revolutionary intelligentsia gave rise to a genuine revolutionary movement. Moderates still existed. But many felt compelled to choose sides. This was largely the result of a political system repressive enough to prevent ideas from being tested

---

[122] Arthur Lehning, ed., *Archives Bakounine* (Leiden, 1977), vol. VI, p. 50. Because the Bolsheviks, like Bakunin, so often contrasted Blanquism and Jacobinism, usually as a means of illuminating what they disliked about the former and admired in the latter, the role Blanqui and the Blanquists played in the history of Bolshevism and of the Soviet Union will be considered in a later chapter, also concerned with the French Revolution, even though Blanqui would not be born, and Blanquism would not exist, until long after the revolution had ended.

[123] Citing previously unknown private correspondence, the Soviet historian, Viacheslav Polonskii, made the same argument in 'Bakunin–Iakobinets', *Vestnik Kommunisticheskoi akademii*, no. 18 (1926): pp. 42–62. Bakunin, he wrote, should be judged by the tactics he said he would use to achieve his objectives, as well as by the objectives themselves. And because his tactics entailed conspiracy and the centralization of power—both of them attributes of Jacobinism—Bakunin could fairly be called a Jacobin. One would have thought that, since Lenin and the Bolsheviks centralized political authority in their underground party before doing the same after taking power in Russia in 1917, Polonskii would have called Bakunin a proto-Bolshevik or a proto-Leninist. But because Marx had been so hostile to Bakunin (though no more than Bakunin had been hostile to Marx), Polonskii could not do this, at least not in print.

empirically, but not repressive enough simply to exterminate its enemies, as its Soviet successor would be willing and able to do. Absent empirical corroboration, ideas, especially as they pertained to politics, were adhered to with a ferocity equalled only by their increasingly radical (or reactionary) content.

It is this fractionalization of opinion on the French Revolution, within this revolutionary movement in particular, on which our attention will now be focused.

2

The French Revolution in the Russian Revolutionary Movement

The Russian revolutionaries who came of age in the late nineteenth century were different from Herzen and Bakunin. Most were of non-noble origin and could not subsidize their activities, as Herzen was able to do even while in exile in Western Europe, using income on properties he had inherited in Russia. The result was a more severe and ascetic temperament, quite dissimilar from Herzen's, that stressed the absolute necessity of 'moral wholeness', according to which a revolutionary's life was indivisible. Every aspect of it, even those that might seem extraneous to politics, was open to scrutiny, and revolutionaries could be deemed morally deficient if their private life was not as virtuous as their public one. In short, nothing was off limits because everything mattered.[1]

For that reason the French Revolution, as a subjective idea as much as an objective external event, assumed even greater significance for this new generation of revolutionaries than it had for earlier ones. Not only were ideas a substitute for action in an autocracy in which politics of any kind was forbidden, but because of this insistence on moral wholeness, every idea a person expressed was considered revelatory of personal character. What a revolutionary thought of the Jacobins and the National Assembly and the Convention showed nothing less than the kind of person, and the kind of revolutionary, he was. In the opinion of N. V. Shelgunov, himself an active participant in the revolutionary movement at the time, what distinguished the new generation from earlier ones was that 'the spirit' it manifested resembled that which had existed in France in 1789 and thereafter.[2]

Evidence of the tenacity, even the fanaticism, with which these younger revolutionaries expressed and defended their views on the French Revolution is abundant. Sergei Nechaev, while writing nothing about it, nevertheless read Robespierre's *Memoires*, attended discussions of Buonarroti's *Conspiration* in

---

[1] In one of the essays that were published serially in *Encounter* in 1955–6 under the title 'A Remarkable Decade', Isaiah Berlin argues, in my view correctly, that this insistence on moral wholeness was one of the defining features of the Russian intelligentsia as a whole. The essay, entitled 'The Birth of the Russian Intelligentsia', is reprinted in Berlin, *Russian Thinkers*, pp. 114–35. That the Bolsheviks possessed many of the attributes of the intelligentsia and can fairly be considered its heir and successor is shown conclusively in Shatz, *Soviet Dissent*, pp. 64–92.

[2] N. V. Shelgunov, 'Vnutrenee obozrenie', *Delo*, no. 3 (1881): pp. 161–2.

St Petersburg in 1868, and included among his meagre possessions pictures of Robespierre and Saint-Just; one can reasonably infer from this that Nechaev considered the fall of the Jacobins proof that revolutionaries everywhere, including and especially in Russia, would be safe only after their enemies had been obliterated.[3] To another revolutionary of that era, A. V. Nikitenko, there seemed a strong resemblance between Louis XVI and Alexander II; fires raging in St Petersburg in the 1860s were one of several reasons he believed Russia to be on the verge of a revolution comparable to the French.[4] In the same decade, D. F. Shelgunov (not to be confused with N. V. Shelgunov) praised the Jacobins as 'passionate to the point of being extremists, but consistent and pure in their convictions'.[5] Robespierre, he said, was a fanatic, but not evil or bloodthirsty.[6] Pëtr Zaichnevskii, whose pamphlet, *Molodaia rossiia* ('Young Russia'), best captured the *weltanshauung* of the new generation, evidently vacillated in deciding which Jacobin he most admired: Robespierre, Saint-Just, or Marat.[7] Perhaps his considerable knowledge of the French Revolution—Lamartine's and Michelet's histories recounting it were apparently his favourites—made it hard for him to make up his mind. But about his passion for the subject, and his praise for most of its participants, there cannot be any doubt. Zaichnevskii so admired the French Revolution that he deliberately pronounced Russian words particular to it, such as *burzhuaziia*, the way they were in French.[8] And as far as the Jacobins were concerned, he apotheosized them in *Molodaia rossiia* for their willingness to shed blood to achieve their objectives. But since the forces opposing the revolutionaries in Russia were more intractable than those the Jacobins encountered, Zaichnevskii pledged to exceed them should that be necessary: 'we will not shrink from shedding twice as much blood as the Jacobins did'.[9]

Rare among these revolutionaries was the opinion, expressed by N. I. Utin, that the Jacobins betrayed the revolution and thereby paved the way for Napoleon's dictatorship. However effectively the Jacobins advanced their ideological objectives, the Girondins were actually the more practical of the two factions in organizational matters and thus immune to the temptation to centralize political power to the extent the Jacobins did, which Utin considered the reason for their demise.[10] Far more representative of his generation, indeed its secular saint in the minds of

---

[3] Zemfir Ralli-Arbore, 'Sergei Gennadevich Nechaev (Iz moikh vospominanii)', *Byloe*, no. 7 (July 1906): pp. 137, 142, 144. Kondratieva, *Bol'sheviki-iakobintsy*, p. 200; Paul Avrich, *Bakunin and Nechaev* (London, 1987), p. 5.

[4] Nikitenko, *Dnevnik*, vol. II, p. 279.

[5] *N. A. Dobroliubov v vospominaniakh sovremennikov* (Moscow, 1986), p. 240.

[6] Ibid.

[7] M. P. Golubeva, 'Vospominaniia o P. G. Zaichnevskom', *Proletarskaia revoliutsiia*, no. 18/19 (1923): p. 29; N. S. Rusanov, *Na rodine 1859–1882* (Moscow, 1931), p. 99.

[8] Rusanov, *Na rodine*, p. 99.

[9] Quoted in Itenberg, *Rossiia i velikaia frantsuzskaia revoliutsiia*, p. 76.

[10] N. I. Utin, 'Staraia i novaia Frantsii', *Vestnik evropy* (March 1871): pp. 16, 33–8.

many who belonged to it, was Nicholas Chernyshevskii, a bust of whom would adorn Lenin's desk in the Kremlin after 1917 and whose novel, *What is to be Done?*, provided the title for Lenin's seminal essay, which has justly been called 'the Bible of Bolshevism'.[11] Chernyshevskii was well acquainted with the French Revolution. In *Sovremennik*, the journal he edited until it was shuttered by the government for its incendiary articles and editorials, Chernyshevskii included articles on Napoleon and on the *ancien régime*, relying mainly on Guizot's for information on the revolution itself.[12]

Chernyshevskii's admiration for France and its revolutions, however, had its limits. He worried that an unsuccessful bourgeois revolution in Russia, like that in France in 1848, would lead to a Bonapartist dictatorship, as it did in France shortly afterwards—but also that a successful bourgeois revolution, like that in France in 1789, would yield the same result.[13] Nevertheless, Chernyshevskii identified personally with Robespierre, to the point, according to some contemporaneous accounts, of worshipping him.[14] In a sense, this personal identification with Robespierre and the Jacobins, which exceeded his admiration of their tactics and objectives, and even their principles, was consistent with Chernyshevskii's principal contribution to the Russian revolutionary movement, which was to provide a composite of the individual attributes revolutionaries needed in addition to a coherent vision of the society they favoured and of how it should be organized and governed. In *What is to be Done?* the reader is meant to recognize one character in particular, named simply Rakhmetov, who sleeps on a bed of nails and eats huge quantities of beef to toughen himself for the struggles ahead, as the prototype of the professional revolutionary; one can easily imagine him operating the guillotine in 1794. In light of Chernyshevskii's admiration for the Jacobins, and for Robespierre in particular, it seems reasonable to suggest that, in his mind, irrespective of their differences in appearance and personality, Robespierre was a French Rakhmetov, and Rakhmetov a Russian Robespierre.[15]

---

[11] V. I. Lenin, *What is to be Done? Burning Questions of our Movement* (New York, 1969); Adam B. Ulam, *The Bolsheviks: The Intellectual, Personal and Political History of the Triumph of Communism in Russia* (New York, 1965), p. 167.

[12] Shlapentokh, *French Revolution in Russian Intellectual Life*, p. 128.

[13] E. G. Plimak and V. G. Khoros, 'Velikaia frantsuzskaia revoliutsiia i revoliutsionnaia traditsiia v Rossii'. In *Frantsuzskii ezhegodnik: stat'i i materialy po istorii Frantsii 1989* (Moscow, 1989), pp. 222–72, p. 243.

[14] Nikolai Valentinov, *The Early Years of Lenin* (Ann Arbor MI, 1969), p. 128; S. G. Stakhevich, 'Sredi politicheskykh prestupnikov', in V. Ye. Vatsuro, ed., *N. G. Chernyshevski v vospominanii sovremennikov* (Moscow, 1982), p. 336, cited in Kondratieva, *Bol'sheviki-iakobintsy*, p. 31.

[15] That the Jacobins, along with several others prominent in the French Revolution, were the first in Europe to consider revolution their profession would seem to corroborate this particular analogy. R. R. Palmer, *Twelve Who Ruled: The Year of the Terror in the French Revolution* (Princeton NJ, 1971), p. 20.

Chernyshevskii's contemporary and fellow revolutionary, Dmitrii Pisarev, viewed the French Revolution with a degree of detachment of which Cherny-shevskii was incapable. The achievements of the revolution, as Pisarev enumerated them, were considerable: ending feudalism, redistributing land equitably, and introducing 'bourgeois rights'.[16] Neither the Thermidorians nor Napoleon vitiated these salubrious effects significantly. But the revolution should have gone further, and the reason it did not Pisarev ascribed to a failure of leadership. Lafayette, Mirabeau, and Barnave, in his jaundiced opinion, were hypocrites promising to serve the French people while enacting legislation, such as the *Loi le Chapelier* of 1791, passed by the National Assembly in 1791, that, by abolishing the guilds of merchants and artisans, severely restricted their rights.[17] The Jacobins, after they came to power, certainly did the best they could. Robespierre was an especially effective spokesman for what they favoured. But because the French people remained apolitical and apathetic, he lacked popular support, and in the summer of 1794, dangerously unprotected politically, he suffered a martyr's death.[18] In Pisarev's words, 'the poverty of the French people, and as a consequence, the poverty of the French government, formed the basis, directly or obliquely, for the tragic events of the French Revolution'.[19] As Pisarev imagined it, the revolution was a limited one because its original leaders and the people they claimed to lead suffered from personal failings—hypocrisy in the case of the former, apathy in the case of the latter—that ensured that the Jacobins, the only leaders of the revolution who deserved to lead it, were unable to do so for more than a very limited time.

Russian populists, like Russian revolutionaries generally in the late nineteenth century, radicalized what they understood to be the meaning and the lessons of the French Revolution. But the populists were especially insistent that the revolu-tion was predominantly an urban affair and that the industrial capitalism it (supposedly) fostered was harmful to peasants everywhere, not just in Russia and in France, destroying all that was admirable in their unique culture and way of life. For that reason the French Revolution had to be handled carefully. In the propagandistic possibilities of its central events, the French Revolution was unsur-passed by any other European revolution. Many populists casually referred to the Schlusselberg Fortress in St Petersburg, where many of them were incarcerated, as 'the Russian Bastille'.[20] Like their predecessors, these Russian revolutionaries,

---

[16] D. I. Pisarev, 'Doklad o Genrikhe Geine', in D. I. Pisarev, *Sochineniia* (St Petersburg, 1867), vol. IV, p. 71; Plimak and Khoros, 'Velikaia frantsuzskaia revoliutsiia i revoliutsionnaia traditsiia v Rossii', p. 246.

[17] D. I. Pisarev, 'Istoricheskie eskizy', *Russkoe slovo: zhurnal literaturno-politicheskii*, no. 2, sect. 1 (January 1864): pp. 32, 39.

[18] Ibid., p. 22.   [19] Ibid., p. 56.

[20] Instead of seeking the fortress's destruction, N. N. Morozov, who was confined there for twenty years, wanted it preserved as a symbol of tsarist repression. In 1917 a rampaging mob, probably cognizant of its functional resemblance to the Bastille, tore it down. Richard Stites, *Revolutionary Dreams: Utopian Vision and Experimental Life in the Russian Revolution* (New York, 1989), p. 67.

both in Russia and in emigration in Western Europe, read the works of French historians of the revolution such as Louis Blanc; according to O. V. Aptekman, Russian populists knew enough from their reading about 'Robespierre, Danton, and Marat' to recognize that uncritical praise for their achievements obscured their undeniable defects, which included the application of otherwise laudable principles in ways that harmed the very people whose interests they claimed so loudly to represent.[21] One Populist, I. I. Mainov, even went so far as to claim audaciously, after stating that 'we were raised on the teachings of the French Revolution', that he and the revolutionaries in his circle knew these teachings better than the French did.[22] For other revolutionaries it was not the ideas and ideologies of the revolution that made it attractive, but the personal qualities of its principal actors. To students in Kiev professing allegiance to the virtues they saw in peasants and the peasant commune, the ideas and objectives of Mirabeau and Robespierre—how they were similar, how they were different, and whether or not they were relevant to Russia a century later—were unimportant; what they were drawn to was their bravery and commitment to principle. Nor were these students terribly interested, when they were looking to the revolution for inspiration, in distinguishing winners from losers; the Kievans admired Desmoulins and Danton just as much as they did Saint-Just.[23] For that reason the centenary of the revolution in 1889 was cause in Russian revolutionary circles for celebration and affirmations of solidarity with the French people. Even revolutionaries exiled to Siberia tried to send them a congratulatory message.[24]

But these same revolutionaries remained cognizant that France and Russia were different, that the Romanovs, with few exceptions, were more repressive and hostile to change than the Bourbons, and that in any event the French Revolution simply did not go far enough for it to serve as a precedent for what Russian revolutionaries intended in their own country. Russian populists, in particular, because they believed that the legacy of the French Revolution included industrial capitalism, which they loathed but thought Russia could avoid if its peasant communes became the principal institution of governance, generally qualified their admiration for the revolution. While some populists, in particular the followers of Nicholas Chaikovskii, hoped that any *zemskii sobor* (Council of the Land) peasants established would resemble the National Assembly in France, most populists coupled praise for the achievements of the revolution with a

---

[21] Itenberg, *Rossiia i velikaia frantsuzskaia revoliutsiia*, pp. 106, 240. The example Aptekman cites to support his contention is that the Jacobins' perfectly proper commitment to ending all 'monopolies' in France caused them simultaneously to oppose the formation of guilds for urban artisans, which in the Jacobins' unfortunate estimation by their mere existence somehow stifled political freedom. O. V. Aptekman, 'Pis'mo k byvshim tovarishcham (8 December 1879)', *Chernyi peredel*, no. 1 (16 January 1880): p. 125.

[22] Saratovets [I. I. Mainov], quoted in Itenberg, *Rossiia i velikaia frantsuzskaia revoliutsiia*, p. 212.

[23] Ibid., p. 110.   [24] Ibid., pp. 212–13.

recognition of its insufficiency and even, from their perspective as Russians, its irrelevance.[25] The French Revolution stressed political freedom; the populists considered economic freedom more essential. The French Revolution was carried out in towns and cities, leaving the peasantry as passive beneficiaries of its benevolence; the populists considered peasants the agents of their own liberation. And in contrast to the role the populists believed the revolution played in stimulating industrial capitalism in France, the revolution they intended in Russia would avoid it.

Among the conclusions the populists drew from the French Revolution was that without economic freedom, political freedom was not only worthless, but actually conducive to dictatorship and tyranny. Nikolai Mikhailovskii, who was perhaps the archetypal populist, expressed this conviction succinctly:

> The Great French Revolution did not lead Europe to the Promised Land of Brotherhood, Equality, and Freedom. Rather, the constitutional regime it created delivered political authority to the bourgeoisie, which used the political freedom it possessed to oppress the people economically.[26]

Chernyi Peredel, a loose organization of populists that rejected terrorism in favour of mass agitation among the peasantry, shared Mikhailovskii's belief that the political freedom the Revolution provided was illusory, at least under the Jacobins. Pavel Axelrod, who before converting to Marxism was a populist and a member of *Chernyi Peredel*, wrote in 1878 that Robespierre was an idealist who, by centralizing political power excessively, became a tyrant.[27] Five years later, he went further, arguing that while the revolution deserved praise for ending feudalism, which oppressed peasants more than it did any other class, its rhetoric about assuaging the masses' suffering was meaningless because the revolution was driven by a class, the bourgeoisie, the urban identity of which rendered it oblivious to the French people as a whole. Representing little more than itself, by the early 1790s the bourgeoisie had become an oppressive force, the Committee of Public Safety its principal instrument.[28] But Russian Jacobins like Pëtr Tkachev were no better than the French originals. In his memoirs Axelrod condemned Tkachev and his followers—who 'loved to cite Robespierre and Saint-Just and with pride called themselves "Jacobins"'—for making 'the merciless elimination of enemies the alpha and omega of revolutionary politics'.[29]

---

[25] P. A. Kropotkin, *Zapiski revoliutsionera* (Moscow, 1966), p. 280. Kropotkin himself analogized the assembly to the consultative body Alexander II agreed to on the day of his assassination. Ibid., p. 391.
[26] Quoted in Itenberg, *Rossiia i velikaia frantsuzskaia revoliutsiia*, p. 129.
[27] Abraham Ascher, *Pavel Axelrod and the Development of Menshevism* (Cambridge MA, 1972), pp. 35–9.
[28] P. B. Axelrod, 'Sotsializm i melkaia burzhuaziia', *Vestnik narodnoi voli*, no. 1 (1883): p. 163.
[29] P. B. Axelrod, *Perezhitoe i peredumannoe* (Berlin, 1923), p. 197.

Like other Russian populists, Pëtr Lavrov believed that the French Revolution transcended its geographical and temporal limits. But Lavrov was the only one who considered the lessons of the revolution relevant irrespective of whether one admired the revolution, condemned it, admired it while cautioning against its mistakes and failures, or considered it largely irrelevant. The French Revolution had a message for everyone. For Lavrov himself the French Revolution was more than something the French began and that Russians like himself would finish— although it was certainly that. On one occasion he repeated the reigning ortho-doxy in revolutionary circles that while the French Revolution was mostly a political revolution, and thus incapable of achieving the social justice that was ostensibly one of its principal objectives, in Russia revolutionaries would bring about an economic transformation; Lavrov made clear how essential this trans-formation was by including in his description the requirement that it be 'com-plete'.[30] For Lavrov the French Revolution was really part of a larger phenomenon both temporally and geographically—part of a veritable Age of Revolution that included not only European revolutions but the American Revolution as well.[31]

That said, Lavrov honed in on the French Revolution as the most relevant of these revolutions—and his evaluation of it was decidedly mixed. Prior to the emergence of the Jacobins, the revolution met with his qualified approval: though more political than economic, it at least had popular support. But the Jacobins introduced an element of ambiguity, and after taking power they rendered the revolution untenable. No longer was it, nor could it ever again become, a ben-evolent and progressive phenomenon. In both 1874 and 1876 Lavrov expressed his objections indirectly, by invoking Tkachev, almost an exact contemporary of his who, unlike Lavrov and the populists, preferred conspiracy to mass propa-ganda and agitation as the means by which to rouse the peasantry to revolution. Tkachev and his supporters, several Russian populists wrote pejoratively, were 'Jacobin-socialists'—a sobriquet suggesting that while Tkachev's objectives went beyond those of the French Revolution, the means he chose to achieve them emanated from the revolution generally, and from the Jacobins specifically.[32] What the Jacobins created in France was 'a revolutionary dictatorship of a minority', and Tkachev, by emulating them, would bring the same thing to Russia.[33] Such a dictatorship, he wrote, would be inherently exploitative, and by its nature could not be anything else. For the Russian revolutionary movement, Lavrov insisted, Russian Jacobinism, as he and others termed it, was an alluring

---

[30] P. L. [Lavrov], 'Zametki o novykh knigakh', *Vestnik narodnaia volia*, no. 3 (1884): p. 17.

[31] By considering the French Revolution one component of a larger, transatlantic phenomenon, Lavrov adumbrated by nearly a century the thesis R. R. Palmer advanced in *The Age of Democratic Revolution*, 2 vols (Princeton NJ, 1959–64).

[32] P. L. Lavrov, 'Rol' naroda i rol' intelligentsii', *Vpered'*, no. 34 (1 June 1876): p. 318.

[33] P. L. Lavrov, 'Russkoi sotsial'no-revoliutsionnoi molodezhi po povodu broshiury "Zadachi revoliutsionnoi propagandy v Rossii (1874)"', in P. L. Lavrov, *Izbrannye sochineniia no sotsial'no-politicheskie temy v vos'mi tomakh* (Moscow, 1934), vol. III, p. 360.

but ultimately disastrous cul-de-sac, a dangerous diversion from the task of making a mass revolution. To Tkachev's protestations that conspiracy would yield to mass politics once the peasants had been properly radicalized—a claim that prefigured Lenin's after being attacked in 1903 and 1904 by many of his fellow socialists as a Russian Robespierre—Lavrov responded with disbelief. The Russian Jacobins, he wrote in 1876, might lead what initially would be a broad coalition, but once they had seized power they would jettison their allies and rule dictatorially. The result would be something very different from the worker's socialism the Russian Jacobins said they favoured.[34]

To be sure, Lavrov changed his mind in the early 1880s about the efficacy of conspiracy. The political terrorism he had previously rejected he now considered morally admissible. But the reason for his reappraisal was tactical, not political or philosophical. The mass agitation he had long advocated had simply yielded unimpressive results. Should circumstances change, he would happily realign means and ends to conform to the scenario he had previously conjured of mass agitation producing a mass revolution.[35] Moreover, nothing in Lavrov's tactical improvisations caused him to change his original view of the French Revolution as a partially positive and progressive phenomenon that provided political freedom, but because of the Jacobins' penchant for authoritarianism, did not provide economic freedom.[36]

According to Pëtr Kropotkin, who with Bakunin was the most prominent exemplar of Russian anarchism, the French Revolution accomplished little for the class that needed it most: French peasants may even have been worse off as a result of it. But he considered the revolution significant in so many other ways that he wrote an entire history of it.[37] In this work and in others, Kropotkin interpreted the revolution in a way that was consistent with both his hostility to centralized authority and his belief, which he shared with the populists, that the peasantry was the repository of moral virtue in every society it inhabited. But it was in his writings on the French Revolution that he stated most clearly his belief that being a peasant was more a matter of temperament and inclination than of where one lived and the kind of work one performed. In fact, in the revolution it was often hard to distinguish the urban poor—the *sans-culottes* and *les enragés*—from the peasantry in their desires, needs, and aspirations.

In Kropotkin's estimation, the French Revolution was 'above all a peasant insurrection, a movement of the people to regain possession of the land and to free it from the feudal obligations which burdened it'.[38] Despite their urban

---

[34]   Lavrov, 'Rol' naroda i rol' intelligentsii', p. 318.
[35]   P. L. Lavrov, *Vzgliad ha proshedshee i nastoiashchee russkago sotsializma* (St Petersburg, 1906), especially pp. 26–7. The essay was first published in 1883 in *Kalendar' Narodnoi Voli.*
[36]   See, e.g. Lavrov, 'Zametki o novykh knigakh', p. 17.
[37]   P. A. Kropotkin, *The Great French Revolution 1789–1793* (New York, 1909).
[38]   Ibid., p. 97.

surroundings, the lower classes in Paris and other towns and cities in France were sufficiently similar to the peasantry to lend it the support it needed to force an otherwise unyielding and recalcitrant urban middle class to abolish feudalism in France. In fact, these 'urban peasants' even established an institution, the Paris Commune, to ensure that the middle class did not repudiate the reforms it promised to carry out. To Kropotkin the Commune was the urban equivalent of the peasant commune in Russia and thus would have prevented the emergence in France of the hypertrophied state Kropotkin's anarchism considered conducive to tyranny.[39] But once the objective of eliminating feudalism had been achieved, the middle classes either dropped out of politics, rejected any further radicalization of the revolution, or supported leaders like the Girondins and the Jacobins who remained true to their class interests, selfishly betraying the French people while fighting one another for political supremacy.[40] In this endeavour the Jacobins proved more competent, and beginning in 1793 they ruled France illegitimately as a politically centralized dictatorship. In that way a revolution committed initially to social and economic equality and the decentralization of political power ended with neither of these objectives achieved.[41]

For Kropotkin the French Revolution was more praiseworthy for what it promised than for what it delivered. Its aspirations were more laudable than its results. With that in mind, he could write, as he did in his history of the revolution, that the French Revolution served the legitimate function of eliminating old, anachronistic economic relationships while failing to make permanent more progressive ones.[42] Not surprisingly, Kropotkin seriously minimized the September Massacres of 1792 while claiming simultaneously that the Paris Commune should not be blamed for them.[43] But while largely absolving the peasants and townspeople who drove the revolution of responsibility for its crimes and moral transgressions, Kropotkin strongly criticized virtually all of its leaders, thereby implying that the mere act of leading a revolution—which required the centralization of political authority—was itself morally corrupting, and would cause the revolution eventually to repudiate many, or even all, of its presumably laudable objectives. Excepting the proto-communist Jacques Roux and the Jacobin Marat, whom Kropotkin called 'the people's most devoted friend', none of the principal personages of the revolution escaped his wrath: the Girondins, because of their passivity and moderation, were crypto-royalists; for falsely proclaiming themselves ardent tribunes of the people, the Jacobins were not much better.[44]

[39] Ibid., pp. 180–1.   [40] Ibid., pp. 258, 263–4, 273.
[41] Kropotkin reiterated his condemnation of the Jacobins in an article on anarchism he contributed to the *Encyclopedia Britannica*, reprinted in Peter Kropotkin, *The Conquest of Bread and Other Writings*, edited by Marshall S. Shatz (New York, 1995), pp. 237–8.
[42] Kropotkin, *Great French Revolution*, p. 97.   [43] Ibid., p. 298.
[44] Ibid., pp. 450, 484–92; Kropotkin, *Conquest of Bread*, pp. 53, 59. Kropotkin may have preferred Marat to the other Jacobins because he was murdered before the Jacobin Terror gained momentum.

Jacques Hébert, whose radicalism one would think sufficient to gain Kropotkin's approval, he nonetheless dismissed as too easygoing in temperament to be effective, while even Babeuf, whose communism was surely no less genuine than Roux's, was in reality a crypto-authoritarian who preferred conspiracy to mass action not just as a political necessity but as a matter of principle.[45]

Kropotkin lived to see the October Revolution, which only confirmed his view of the corruptibility of its ostensible precursor in France. Indeed, in Kropotkin's mind the evils of the two revolutions were remarkably similar, although the Russian one, by 'striking deeper into the soul of Russia, into the hearts and minds [of the Russian people]' than its counterpart did in France, had far less to recommend it.[46] That the French Revolution left all sorts of pressing social issues unresolved should not blind one, as Kropotkin admitted not long after the Bolsheviks took power in Russia, to its very real and lasting achievements. In place of the feudalism it rightfully destroyed, it introduced to Europe and the world the concept and the practice of legal equality and representative government. By contrast the October Revolution lacked a spiritual dimension, principally because its economic materialism had produced among its leaders a selfish individualism that was already generating tyranny. In fact, the regime the Bolsheviks had created reminded Kropotkin, in the last years of his life, of what he had once called 'the Jacobin endeavor of Babeuf'—a formulation that linked together the actors in the French Revolution he despised the most: the Jacobins for using the power they possessed to create a dictatorship, and Babeuf, who lacked power, for resorting to conspiracy to obtain it.[47]

In spite of the vitriol Kropotkin directed at the Bolsheviks, Lenin's respect for the Russian anarchist surprisingly remained intact. He always considered Kropotkin's history of the French Revolution 'remarkable', and sometime between 1917 and 1921 asked and received his permission to publish it, which the Soviet government did.[48] Given Lenin's penchant for reserving his harshest rhetoric for critics who attacked him from the left, his exclusion of Kropotkin, in this respect, was remarkable. According to his secretary, V. D. Bonch-Bruevich, the reason was that, for all his disagreements with the old anarchist, Lenin thought the latter's history of the French Revolution would 'enlighten the masses'.[49] Bonch-Bruevich may not be the most reliable witness in this particular instance, but whatever the reason, Lenin's forbearance would be more than compensated by criticism of Kropotkin in the Soviet Union that continued well into the 1960s, when the Soviet

[45] Kropotkin, *Great French Revolution*, pp. 491, 501.
[46] Quoted in Emma Goldman, *My Disillusionment in Russia* (Garden City NY, 1923), p. 155.
[47] Roger S. Baldwin, ed., *Kropotkin's Revolutionary Pamphlets* (New York, 1927), p. 254.
[48] V. M. Dalin, 'K istorii izucheniia Velikoi frantsuzskoi revoliutsii v SSSR'. In *Frantsuzskii ezhegodnik: stat'i i materialy po istorii Frantsii 1989* (Moscow, 1989), p. 106.
[49] V. D. Bonch-Bruevich, *Izbrannye sochineniia: Vospominaniia V. I. Lenine 1917–1924 gg.* (Moscow, 1963), vol. III, p. 405.

historian V. G. Revunenkov took issue with Kropotkin's characterization of *les enragés* as both anarchist and communist in their ideology, arguing that while they qualified as communists, they could hardly be considered anarchists.[50]

*   *   *

Prior to the Bolsheviks, virtually all revolutionaries in Russia believed, not implausibly given the predominantly agrarian nature of its population, that the autocracy would be destroyed in a cataclysmic conflagration in which peasants played the dominant role. But beginning in the late 1870s, after revolutionaries earlier in the decade had failed to convince peasants that their needs could not be satisfied unless they became revolutionaries themselves and acted as the agents of their own liberation, disagreement over tactics emerged. Some continued to dispense propaganda among the peasants. Others, including the *chernoperedel'tsy*, who soon would become Marxists, drew from the peasants' apathy the conclusion that Russian workers were far more likely than peasants to see revolution as the only solution to their own oppression, and that any workers' revolution should be made by workers themselves—not by professional revolutionaries like Robespierre, Marat, and Danton, all of whom in 1880 they condemned as frauds only pretending to care about the French people.[51] Still others advocated terrorism as the only tactic that could incite a peasant revolution. By killing persons in positions of authority, the terrorists would demonstrate the government's weakness, which would cause the peasants finally to revolt. The principal organization that, beginning in the late 1870s, actually practised terrorism was a group numbering at no time more than 500 members and active supporters. It called itself, misleadingly, the *Narodnaia Volia* (The People's Will). At first it limited its targets to government officials it considered sadistic and cruel. But when peasants remained inert, it attacked officials indiscriminately. And when that did not achieve its objective, the group targeted the ultimate source of the oppression it decried—Tsar Alexander II himself. On 1 March 1881, it succeeded in killing him.

The role of the French Revolution in the genesis of all of this was more complex than one might imagine. There was no equivalent in the revolution to the terrorism the *narodovol'tsy* practised. The Jacobins, when they killed people, did so while in power and in control of the state, and for that reason what they did is best referred to as 'terror'.[52] The *narodovol'tsy*, by contrast, did what they did as

[50] Revunenkov, *Marksizm i problema iakobinskoi diktatury*, p. 72. In 1923 Max Eastman criticized Kropotkin for suggesting that the origins of the Soviet Union, which Eastman called 'the world-shattering Communist experiment', were traceable to Babeuf, whose failed attempts at revolution Eastman dismissed as a 'petty fiasco': Max Eastman, 'Jacobinism and Bolshevism', *Queen's Quarterly* 31 (1923): p. 73.

[51] Kondratieva, *Bol'sheviki-iakobintsy*, p. 37.

[52] One of the few acts of terrorism in the French Revolution was Charlotte Corday's murder of Marat on 13 July 1793. What many Russian revolutionaries did not know, or chose to ignore, about the murder was that the assassin was a Girondin disenchanted with Marat's justification of terror, not a

enemies of the government, and calling it 'terrorism' distinguishes it from 'terror', while also making clear that the Jacobins and the *narodovol'tsy* shared the objective of striking fear in all those who did not die or suffer in the killings they carried out. The purpose of both terror and terrorism, as the words themselves suggest, is not to kill, but to terrorize sufficiently so that those who remain alive do what the terrorists want.

Russian revolutionaries generally did not distinguish terror from terrorism, and therefore drew analogies between the Jacobin Terror and Russian revolutionary terrorism. For many of them the purpose of the analogy was a positive one. To justify the former was to justify the latter. Vera Figner, herself a *narodovolets*, once compared Alexander Mikhailov, one of the leaders of *Narodnaia Volia*, and for whom she felt genuine admiration, to Robespierre.[53] On another occasion, shortly after Mikhailov's arrest in 1880, she expressed regret that 'the narrow limits of Russian life do not allow us to deploy our forces on a large scale and to play the outstanding role in history that Robespierre did in revolutionary France in the eighteenth century'.[54] It was true that Figner changed her mind and sought to distance *Narodnaia Volia* from the Jacobins after the assassination of Alexander II, which resulted in the arrest and execution of the leading *narodovol'tsy* and the virtual disintegration of the organization as a whole:

> [We] never called ourselves Jacobins. At no time among us were there speeches on the imposition of the will of the minority over the majority, or about instituting revolutionary socialist and political reforms that were based on Jacobin theory.[55]

Of course it was entirely possible that Figner still admired the Jacobins for the personal qualities they revealed while acknowledging that the tactics they used were conducive to authoritarianism and elitism.

Some *narodovol'tsy* rendered a mixed verdict. N. I. Kibalchich, whose specialty in the organization was the preparation of explosives, credited the Convention, when the Jacobins controlled it, for expropriating nobles' land, but he criticized it

---

royalist or counter-revolutionary, and that the moral and political polarity many claimed implicit in the murder was nonexistent. In Russia many revolutionaries analogized Vera Zasulich's attempted murder of the mayor of St Petersburg in 1878 to Corday's killing Marat even though the mayor and Marat were at opposite ends of the political spectrum. That the analogy was drawn anyway showed the importance the French Revolution played in how events in Russia that were relevant to it were conceptualized. Jay Bergman, *Vera Zasulich: A Biography* (Stanford CA, 1983), p. 43.

[53] V. N. Figner, *Zapechatlennyi trud* (Moscow, 1932), vol. I, p. 172.
[54] Ibid., p. 194.
[55] Ibid., pp. 163–4. The letter itself, in its tone and content, was far from conciliatory. It threatened future acts of violence against the monarchy, and included a demand for amnesty for revolutionaries convicted of political crimes, and a convocation of representatives of the Russian people 'to examine the existing framework of social and governmental life, and to remodel it in accordance with the people's wishes': 'Letter of the Revolutionary Committee to Alexander III (1881)', in *Readings in Modern European History*, edited by James Harvey Robinson and Charles Beard (Boston MA, 1909), vol. II, p. 367.

for transferring the land to the bourgeoisie, rather than to the masses.[56] Others condemned the Jacobins, inside and outside the Convention, entirely. To Lev Tikhomirov Jacobinism at least in Russia, was 'befouled by idle chatter'—a pejorative that nonetheless failed to capture Tikhomirov's more serious and considered criticism of the Jacobins in France, who he believed were intent on transforming the country far more than he considered necessary, and as a result retained power long after the point at which they should have relinquished it. In short, the Jacobins did too much and took too long to do it. But the *narodo-vol'tsy*, Tikhomirov assured his readers, would be different. They would transfer immediately whatever power they had acquired by overthrowing the monarchy to a *zemskii sobor*, thereby avoiding the 'a native despotism' that for Tikhomirov was the Russian equivalent of Jacobinism. In Tikhomirov's opinion the *narodovol'tsy* were actually the antithesis of the Jacobins, and for that reason their accepting the appellation or even just not rejecting it would only give credence to false and pernicious charges of despotism.[57] Ironically, Tikhomirov himself would be upbraided by Nicholas Morozov, also a *narodovolets*, for his 'Jacobin' proclivities.[58]

Other Russian revolutionaries of Figner's generation not only shared her admiration for the Jacobins as individuals. They also did not have the qualms she had about their ruling dictatorially and their using terror to ensure that their dictatorship endured. Sergei Kravchinskii, who in St Petersburg in 1878 stabbed to death in broad daylight the chief of the police force that hunted down revolution-aries, said once that he regretted the reluctance of Russian terrorists to recognize their resemblance, of which he was immensely proud in his own case, to 'the men of 1789 and 1793'.[59] It was obvious to him that the Executive Committee of *Narodnaia Volia* resembled the organizations the Jacobins had earlier established; presumably these included both the Jacobin Clubs and the Committee of Public Safety. But it was the Jacobins' exemplary energy and willpower, more than anything else, that, in Kravchinskii's opinion, explained their triumphs over their enemies.[60] Moreover, Kravchinskii was not the only Russian terrorist to believe this. Maria Oshanina, who served on the executive committee, stated that the disintegration of *Narodnaia Volia* in the late 1880s was especially regrettable because by that time all of its leaders, however much their numbers had dimin-ished due to earlier arrests, were effectively Jacobins.[61]

[56] 'A. Doroshenko', 'Politicheskaia revoliutsiia i ekonomicheskii vopros'. *Narodnaia volia* (5 February 1881), quoted in Itenberg, *Rossiia i velikaia frantsuzskaia revoliutsiia*, p. 132.
[57] 'Pis'mo Izpolitel'nogo Komiteta "Narodnoi voli" zagranichnym tovarishcham', in S. M. Volk, *Revoliutsionnoe narodnichestvo: 70-x godov xix veka* (Moscow/Leningrad, 1965), vol. II, pp. 320–1.
[58] Olga Liubatovich, 'Dalekoe i nedavnee: vospominaniia iz zhizni revoliutsionerov 1878–81 gg.' *Byloe*, no. 6 (1906): p. 122.
[59] 'Otvet S. M. Kravchinskogo na pis'mo ispolnitel'nogo komiteta Narodnoi voli (March 1882)', in Volk, *Revoliutsionnoe narodnichestvo*, vol. II, p. 345.
[60] Itenberg, *Rossiia i velikaia frantsuzskaia revoliutsiia*, p. 109.
[61] Yarmolinsky, *Roots of Revolution*, p. 300.

For all the similarities many *narodovol'tsy* saw between themselves and the Jacobins, the Russian revolutionary for whom the resemblance seemed most obvious—as much to adversaries seeking grounds for condemning him as to supporters seeking reasons to praise him—was Pëtr Tkachev.[62] To his critics, Tkachev's Jacobinism was informed by a brutality and ruthlessness not seen in Europe—not even in Russia—since the original Jacobins practised terror nearly a century earlier. Pavel Axelrod's enmity did not diminish with the passage of time, and in his memoirs, which were written nearly a half-century after the events concerning Tkachev had occurred, he flagellated Tkachev and his supporters for seeing 'the elimination of enemies of the revolution . . . as the highest obligation of any revolutionary organization. There is merit in Alexrod's denunciation. In 1866, at the age of 22, Tkachev made clear his belief that the only way an oppressive and powerful regime could be toppled was by revolutionaries practising conspiracy and then overthrowing it in an urban insurrection bearing all the hallmarks of a *coup d'état*.[63] By 1869 he had decided that the French Revolution was the most relevant and obvious example of this, and made clear his belief that Russians who shared his hatred of the monarchy should imitate the Jacobins and create conspiratorial circles in which power and authority were concentrated in an elite of professional revolutionaries. But only if this elite had no compunctions about using force and violence would it have any chance of success. Here, too, the precedent of the French Revolution and the Jacobins was instructive: 'In France the destruction of the monarchy required the application of terror by the bourgeoisie [because] as a general rule, no radical social reforms have come about without blood-letting and the use of force.'[64] Appealing to the larger body politic, Tkachev believed, would be counterproductive—which was why he excluded Babeuf from the litany of French revolutionaries he admired: while practising conspiracy, Babeuf nonetheless tried to publicize the activities of his co-conspirators for the purpose of gaining popular support, which to Tkachev was a waste of time. Preferable in that respect were Jacobins like Robespierre, whose asceticism and selflessness found their highest expression in conspiracy.[65] For Tkachev the revolutionary tactics he chose were as much a reflection of his temperament and personality as of his goals, and if these tactics were appropriate to the external circumstances that pertained at any particular time, success was not only possible, but highly likely. Revolutionaries should adopt tactics consistent

---

[62] Tkachev's most recent biographer in the West makes clear in the subtitle of her book that she considers him to have been a Jacobin: Deborah Hardy, *Petr Tkachev, the Critic as Jacobin* (Seattle WA, 1977).

[63] P. N. Tkachev, 'Retsenziia no knigu A. Rokhau, "Istoriia Frantsii ot nizverzheniia Napoleona I do vosstanovleniia imperii (1866)"', Axelrod, *Perezhitoe i peredmmannoe*, p. 197; in P. N. Tkachev, *Izbrannye sochineniia na sotsial'no-politicheskie temy*, edited by B. F. Kozmin (Moscow, 1932–6), vol. V, pp. 190–6.

[64] P. N. Tkachev, 'Zhenskii vopros', ibid., vol. I, p. 428.

[65] Hardy, *Petr Tkachev*, p. 265, 274.

with their personalities, and the clear implication in virtually all of Tkachev's many references to the French Revolution was that by marrying these two variables the Jacobins greatly facilitated the task of taking power. For that reason, Tkachev could admire Robespierre and the other members of the Committee of Public Safety while, as a socialist, considering their programmatic objectives insufficiently radical to meet the needs of the masses. In short, Tkachev and his followers should adopt the Jacobins' tactics, but in the pursuit of goals well beyond the Jacobins' objectives.

Because Russian peasants, in Tkachev's opinion, were hopelessly conservative, and incapable of taking positive action to improve their lives, the professional revolutionaries he considered necessary to take power in Russia would have to hold onto it afterwards, probably for several generations. In Tkachev's case, there was reason to believe that this 'conspiracy in power', like the one that ruled the Soviet Union until its implosion in 1991, would never relinquish power voluntarily.[66] But at least in his own mind, Tkachev's conspiratorial politics had an expiration date, however vague he may have been about the conditions that would have to exist for it to end. Moreover, as a scenario of revolution applied to Russia in the late nineteenth century, Tkachev's penchant for conspiracy conformed to the empirical realities—not just the peasants' inability, for the foreseeable future, to make a revolution on their own, but also the government's prohibition of politics of any kind in Russia, thereby necessitating underground parties organized hierarchically with conspiracy as their modus operandi. For both of these reasons, any party that was attentive to the peasants' needs could come to power only by means of a *coup d'état*. In Tkachev's scenario the peasants would be the beneficiaries but not the instrument of their own emancipation—a scenario Lenin and the Bolsheviks would adhere to in 1917, their only alteration being the substitution of the proletariat for the peasantry.[67]

Notwithstanding this scenario's similarity to what the Bolsheviks would actually do several decades later, Tkachev's claim and that of others in the revolutionary movement in the late nineteenth century that it closely replicated the French Revolution was clearly incorrect. For one thing, revolutionaries like Tkachev believed the Jacobins represented a definable and recognizable class, or subclass, of the French population: they were either bourgeois or petit-bourgeois or a precursor of sorts of the proletariat. But it seems more accurate to define the Jacobins on political grounds, and thus to consider the clubs they established vehicles for bringing together like-minded men (and some women) who sought for France more or less the same thing irrespective of their economic class or

---

[66] 'A conspiracy in power' is precisely how Martin Malia characterized the Soviet system in *The Soviet Tragedy: A History of Socialism in Russia, 1917-1991* (New York, 1994), p. 115.

[67] Hardy's evaluation of Tkachev's views on these issues, in *Petr Tkachev*, is similar to those expressed here. See especially pp. 186–203, 258–77, and 309–14.

social category.[68] For what it says about politics in France, the term 'Jacobin' has genuine utility; as a means of distinguishing social classes in France, it confuses more than it clarifies. This, at least, is what happened in Russia. But Russian revolutionaries misunderstood what Jacobinism was and how the Jacobins functioned prior to their taking power in an even more fundamental way. The conspiracy the Jacobins practised existed only *after* they took power in France. Before then their meetings were usually 'above ground', their organization, such as it was, surprisingly decentralized, and most Jacobins did not feel themselves bound by any particular notion of 'party discipline'.[69] The first Jacobin Clubs were established in 1789 and 1790 so that delegates to the Estates General, and to the National Assembly that succeeded it could mingle openly and exchange ideas and opinions.[70] And once the original club had inspired the creation of others, no single club, either in Paris or anywhere else in the country, dictated tactics and strategy to all the others. The mere fact that by the time the Jacobins lost power there were thousands of clubs dispersed all over France meant that, in the absence of modern means of transportation and communication, the strict centralization of authority Tkachev believed existed both among the Jacobins and in how they ruled France did not exist and in fact was impossible.[71]

To be sure, there were similarities between the terror the Jacobins practised and the terrorism of *Narodnaia Volia*. Both tactics were adopted reluctantly, thereby demonstrating that terror in France and terrorism in Russia were more a product of circumstance than reflective of some preexisting psychological deficiency.[72] In other words, the psychosis and paranoia that are often thought to be conducive to terror and terrorism were more the consequence of these tactics than the reason for them. Vera Zasulich, who won notoriety and acclaim in Europe as well as in Russia for shooting at (but not killing) the governor of St Petersburg in 1878, noted perceptively some years later that, as a weapon of political struggle, terrorism was too divisive, too exhausting, and too convenient an excuse for government repression to be effective in actually bringing the work of government to a standstill. Even worse, in her opinion, was that it would remain an alluring alternative to the tedious and difficult, but in the long run more consequential

---

[68] Isser Woloch, *Jacobin Legacy: The Democratic Movement under the Directory* (Princeton NJ, 1970), pp. 11–14.

[69] Crane Brinton, *The Jacobins: An Essay in the New History* (New York, 1930), pp. 10–45; Palmer, *Age of Democratic Revolution*, vol. II: p. 30; Michael L. Kennedy, 'The Best and the Worst of Times: The Jacobin Clubs from October 1791 to June 2, 1793', *Journal of Modern History* 56, no. 4 (1984): pp. 635–36, p. 663.

[70] Doyle, *History of the French Revolution*, p. 142.

[71] Jonathan Sperber, *The European Revolutions, 1848–1851* (Cambridge, 2013), p. 265.

[72] After denying that the Jacobins were 'born conspirators', Patrice Higonnet goes so far as to claim, in the next sentence, that they were 'confirmed parliamentary democrats, however confusedly they expressed that feeling': Patrice Higonnet, *Goodness Beyond Virtue: Jacobins During the French Revolution* (Cambridge MA, 1998), p. 330.

work of generating revolutionary consciousness among the peasants. Finally, there was also the fact that, practised long enough, terrorism would become a psychological obsession.[73]

But the terror the Jacobins practised was so different from the terrorism of Russian revolutionaries as to render any analogy between them a cause for confusion. The Jacobins, of course, inflicted terror with the full force of the state mobilized on behalf of this objective, and justified it on the grounds, however dubious by the time the Committee of Public Safety was created, that they represented the people of France. For the Jacobins, the principle of popular sovereignty was one they accepted and believed themselves to personify even when they violated it. By contrast the Russian terrorists viewed terrorism as a tactic of last resort, rather than as something intrinsic to Russian national history and culture, after propaganda and agitation among the peasants had produced such paltry results; some peasants even turned in revolutionaries in their midst to the tsarist police.[74] In addition, the Jacobins, unlike the Russian terrorists, were not socialists, and their nationalism had no equivalent, after Pavel Pestel, in the Russian revolutionary movement. Finally, one must bear in mind before imputing similarities between the Jacobins and the Russian terrorists that the Jacobins' objectives were considerably more ambitious, inasmuch as they considered the revolution they came to lead in 1793 nothing less than the first step in the liberation of all people, a process fully legitimized by the vision driving it of a General Will like Rousseau's determining how everyone should live once all the enemies of the Jacobins had been vanquished.[75]

However, Tkachev was not entirely wrong in believing that 'the history of France provide[d] us with extremely edifying lessons'.[76] Taking his own advice, he examined French history after the French Revolution and found in it a much more edifying analogue than Robespierre and the Jacobins, whom he wrongly imagined acted conspiratorially before taking power to achieve objectives he wrongly thought were consistent with his own peasant socialism. This new analogue was Louis-August Blanqui, who shared Tkachev's penchant for conspiracy while suffering for it far more than Tkachev ever did, spending practically his entire adult life in prison. As it happened, Tkachev learned of Blanqui and his

---

[73] Vera Zasulich, 'Kar'era nigilista', *Sotsial-demokrat*, no. 4 (1892), in Vera Zasulich, *Sbornik statei* (St Petersburg, 1907), vol. II, pp. 111–47.

[74] The only success Russian revolutionaries enjoyed in that respect was in 1876 in the Chigirin District near Kiev, when they forged a manifesto ostensibly signed by the tsar calling on peasants to seize nobles' lands. Some peasants followed the manifesto's instruction, but the hoax was finally revealed and peasant agitation ceased. Bergman, *Vera Zasulich*, pp. 24–5.

[75] Stanley Hoffmann stresses Rousseau's paternity in this respect in A Note on 'The French Revolution and the Language of Violence', *Daedalus: Proceedings of the American Academy of Arts and Sciences* 116, no. 2 (Spring 1987): pp. 152–3, as did the Soviet historian, A. Z. Manfred, in 'O prirode iakobinskoi vlasti', *Voprosy istorii*, no. 5 (1969): p. 100.

[76] Tkachev, 'Retsenziia no knigu A. Rokhau', p. 194.

followers from Gaspar Mikhail Turskii, a wealthy Pole who supported Russian revolutionaries financially while occasionally participating in their activities.[77] Although the two men apparently never met, Tkachev nonetheless was among those who eulogized the venerable French revolutionary at his funeral in 1881, calling him 'our inspiration and our guide in the great art of conspiracy'.[78] To an extent, Tkachev's admiration was misplaced. The Blanquists, far more than Blanqui himself, preferred conspiracy to mass action. Not only did Blanqui's serial prison terms obviously preclude political activities of any kind, but on the rare occasions when he had the opportunity to participate in politics, as he did in the Revolution of 1830, Blanqui opted not for conspiracy but to fight on barricades Parisians had erected to defend themselves against government troops. And in 1848, after delivering a fiery speech to Parisian radicals, he marched with them to the National Assembly for the purpose of overthrowing it; only in 1861 was he arrested for conspiracy per se. Ironically it was the Blanquists, not Blanqui himself, who practised the conspiratorial politics with which the latter's name is still inextricably linked.[79]

Tkachev's affinity for the larger phenomenon of Blanquism went well beyond tactics. His objectives and those of Blanqui and the Blanquists were remarkably similar: they all rejected modernity in favour of a pre-industrial, pre-capitalist society, based in Tkachev's case on the peasant commune, the ostensible socialism of which was very different from that of the socialist parties emerging in Western Europe in the late nineteenth century. In fact, one can easily imagine the Russian refusing the invitation extended to Blanqui in 1880 by Paul Lafargue, Marx's son-in-law, to assist in drawing up a programme for the recently established French Workers' Party—an invitation the French revolutionary, by now exhausted and near death from years of incarceration, refused.[80] But there was more to Blanqui's refusal than that. While a clear precursor of Lenin and the Bolsheviks in his preference for conspiracies because the masses lacked the revolutionary consciousness to make a revolution on their own, Blanqui's politics were actually (paraphrasing Patrick Hutton) 'a politics of remembrance', galvanized by a desire not to accelerate the course of history forward, as the Bolsheviks hoped to do, but to reverse it for the purpose of recreating in France the original vision of the French Revolution of a nation of small property owners oblivious to the temptations, and the dangers, of industrial capitalism.[81]

*   *   *

[77] Hardy, *Petr Tkachev*, pp. 249–50.

[78] Quoted in Michael Karpovich, 'A Forerunner of Lenin: P. N. Tkachev', *Review of Politics* 6, no. 3 (July 1944): p. 341.

[79] Patrick H. Hutton, *The Cult of the Revolutionary Tradition: The Blanquists in French Politics, 1864–1893* (Berkeley CA, 1981), pp. 18, 20, 21.

[80] Ibid., p. 10.   [81] Ibid., p. 11.

The Russian revolutionary movement left behind a varied aggregation of opinions on the French Revolution. The only aspect of the revolution on which there was unanimity was, however, an important one, namely that France and eventually all of humanity were better off for it having happened. Everyone agreed that the *ancien régime* of the Bourbons was intolerable. It was brutal and oppressive, capricious and irrational in governance, and utterly antediluvian in the way political power was transferred by dynastic succession. Nothing about it was morally redeeming, and the sooner it was disposed of, the better France and the rest of Europe would be.

Beyond this foundational belief, the opinions of Russian revolutionaries varied considerably—just as they did among conservatives opposed to the French Revolution and among liberals, for whom it was always, at best, a mixed blessing. While there was a general consensus on the left in Russia that the revolutionary governments prior to the Jacobins had much to commend them even though they did not remedy all the injustices for which the Bourbons were responsible, this consensus broke down over the meaning and moral value of the Jacobin dictatorship. That it did so is not surprising. The Jacobins did many things, all of them consequential and all of them subject to varying interpretations even among those who agreed that the revolution before the Jacobins continued it—or betrayed it, as their critics contended—was predominantly or entirely a good thing. The Jacobins were simultaneously administrators of the most populous country in Europe who mobilized much of its manpower and resources to fight its enemies abroad; practical politicians who had to protect their sinecures in a new political environment lacking established rules of procedure; and finally ideologues possessed of a vision encompassing nothing less than the transformation of France and the rest of Europe, and eventually of humanity itself.

But none of the Russian revolutionaries who saw in the French Revolution a source of legitimacy, inspiration, or guidance in how a revolution in Russia should be carried out, found in it a philosophy of history that ensured its inevitability. Indeed, the individuals who, in their multifarious ideologies, made the French Revolution never equated what was desirable with what was inevitable. The revolution occurred, it did what it did, but things could easily have turned out differently; one could even imagine circumstances in which it would never have happened at all, or at a time so far in the future as to be virtually unrecognizable.

Applied to Russia, which in the nineteenth century seemed condemned to monarchy and autocracy in perpetuity, any scenario of revolution, and of history itself, that lacked the component of inevitability seemed little more than a counsel of despair. If the revolution in France had never happened, or if the beneficial changes it brought about had actually been deleterious, then revolutionaries in Russia, once they recognized how formidable was the autocracy's commitment to preserving the status quo, might have eschewed politics entirely and taken up a different profession. Some, in fact, did precisely that. (The *narodovol'tsy* and perhaps Bakunin, in his belief that a peasant conflagration was just a match or two short of ignition, were the proverbial exceptions that proved the rule.) But help was on the way. Russian revolutionaries in the late nineteenth century were the recipients of a *deus ex machina*, in the form of an ideology that considered not just revolution, but history itself, to be governed by laws the universality and infallibility of which essentially enabled its adherents to believe that what they wanted was destined to occur irrespective of how unlikely that might seem at any particular time. The ideology, of course, was Marxism. By rendering the French Revolution inevitable, Marxism seemed to make a Russian Revolution inevitable as well. In fact, Russian revolutionaries might even tweak it sufficiently so that they would not only make a revolution, but also enjoy its benefits, in the form of socialism or something close to it, within their lifetime. If the arguments, impressions, and interpretations that the Russian revolutionary movement collectively offered about the French Revolution provided the context in which the Bolsheviks approached it, the works of Karl Marx and Friedrich Engels were the prism through which they viewed it.

3

The Marxist Inheritance of the French Revolution

For Marx, the French Revolution was the Great French Revolution. The adjective he appended to it was meant to signify that it was more than what Marxist ideology, taken literally, considered it—the means by which the bourgeoisie gained the political power it was entitled to by its rapidly growing prosperity, in contrast to the aristocracy, which previously dominated the bourgeoisie and the classes below the bourgeoisie through the political instrument of the monarchy. The French Revolution, in other words, adjusted the political balance of power in France to align it with new and different economic realities. But the French Revolution was more than that. It did not merely ratify politically the economic dominance of the bourgeoisie, thus enabling the emergence in France of industrial capitalism. It was also, and far more importantly, an avatar of modernity itself, a seminal event in history when man first rationalized his environment through the application of reason, thereby creating the preconditions for the socialism and communism that would follow it. Of course one wonders how Marx could be so sure his analysis of the past and his predictions of the future were correct. The reason—though Marx never stated this explicitly—is that he had inherited the rationalism the French Revolution had itself inherited from the Enlightenment; the result was that in some sense the revolution gave Marx the means for analysing it. But whether Marx's rationalism came from the Enlightenment directly or was mediated through the French Revolution was irrelevant. What mattered was that the analysis Marx produced of the revolution—with the emendations and clarifications Engels provided—was always intentionally grounded in evidence and defensible by reason.

But Marx was also driven by impulses alien to his ostensibly omnipresent rationality to look to France, and in particular to Paris, as the epicentre of the first great political transformation in modern history. Marx might not have shared completely in the confluence of reason and emotion implicit in Engels' estimation of the French capital as 'the head and the heart of the world'.[1] But he was well aware that Paris was where, beginning in 1789, large numbers of people, in Martin Malia's felicitous phrase, 'violated the immemorially inviolable', and in doing so

---

[1] Quoted in Wilson, *To the Finland Station*, p. 203.

began the process, made possible by the endless transmutations of the Marxist dialectic, of bringing a qualitatively different kind of human existence not only to France, but to Europe and, in due course, to the rest of the world.[2] For all of his claims to rationality, for all the pretensions implicit in his calling his doctrine 'scientific socialism' rather than Marxism, Marx was attracted to, and profoundly impressed by, the heroic, the grandiose, and the valiant—by what human beings could accomplish through the application of will, determination, and courage. History in general, and the French Revolution in particular, were propelled not just by impersonal economic forces, but by the best of what humanity was capable of, albeit within the limits these forces imposed. From the storming of the Bastille to the military successes its armies achieved against the major powers of Europe, the French Revolution was defined, as Marx perceived it, as much by the virtues of the individuals who carried it out as by the particular constellation of economic forces that pertained in France when the revolution began.

In short, Marx apotheosized the French Revolution for the same reason Edmund Burke loathed it—because it was the result of human agency that caused an entire country—or at least a significant percentage of its inhabitants—to reject the accumulated experiences, traditions, and patterns of life that had existed for centuries. Although industrial capitalism emerged in England long before it did in France, the English Revolution and the Glorious Revolution of the seventeenth century that followed it forty years later could hardly hold a candle to the French Revolution in their dramatic potential. It was for this reason, more than the scholarship he produced demonstrating that everything about it was predetermined and the result of impersonal economic forces, that caused Marx to proclaim the French Revolution the first revolution in history to look forward to the distant future, rather than backward to an idealized and semi-mythical past. Early in his life the French Revolution captured Marx's imagination, and despite the criticisms his investigation of its actual history produced—of which there were many—he never doubted its centrality in the modern history of humanity. It was not for nothing that Marx usually ended his letters to Engels with the French word *salut*—an obvious short-form for the Jacobin greeting '*Salut et Fraternité*'.[3]

In the 1840s Marx intended to write a history of the Convention.[4] In 1845, enlarging the project to a history of the revolution as a whole, he even promised

---

[2] Malia, *History's Locomotives*, p. 196.

[3] Jonathan Sperber, *Karl Marx: A Nineteenth-Century Life* (New York, 2013), p. 535. Of the approximately 400 books in Marx's library, some 200 concerned France and fifty were histories of the French Revolution and the Revolution of 1830. Maximilien Rubel, 'The French Revolution and the Education of the Young Marx', *Diogenes* (Winter 1989): p. 23. In explaining Marx's affinity for France and the French Revolution, one should also bear in mind that his father, on at least one occasion, sang *La Marseillaise*, the French revolutionary anthem, and favoured retention of Napoleonic law in the Rhineland, where, in the town of Trier, Marx had been born. Sperber, *Karl Marx*, pp. 27–28, 34.

[4] Hunt, *Politics, Culture and Class*, p. 4.

a publisher in Brussels to deliver a manuscript shortly.[5] By that time, two years after arriving in Paris, where he hoped to produce a newspaper congenial to the large community of German radical *émigrés* already living there, he had studied French history intensively. Apparently Guizot's history of the revolution, in which the urban middle class played the dominant role, especially impressed him.[6] But more pressing projects took precedence. In the end, Marx never wrote a single article, much less a book, on the revolution per se. The reason he failed to do so may be because, in contrast to the 1848 Revolutions and the Paris Commune, both of which Marx lived through and believed might be followed soon by a more successful revolution if he could explain their failure convincingly, the French Revolution ended before Marx had even been born, and could thus be analysed without the immediacy that pervades *The Class Struggles in France* (on the 1848 Revolution) and *The Civil War in France* (on the Paris Commune). Nevertheless, Marx wrote enough about the revolution for his readers to infer his opinions of it. Indeed, it seems not at all an exaggeration to say, as many historians have argued irrespective of their political and ideological predilections, that the French Revolution played a significant role, in the words of one Soviet historian, 'in formulating the theory of scientific communism'.[7] François Furet, who was the antithesis of Soviet historians politically, argued essentially the same thing.[8]

Marx's first allusion to the French Revolution was in 1842, in an article on censorship in Prussia in which he condemned, without explanation, 'the laws of terrorism Robespierre proclaimed and enforced'.[9] These apparently so incensed him that he said it was even worse than Peter the Great ordering the Cossacks to shave their beards.[10] Whether Marx meant by this that the revolution as a whole was deficient was not clear, although in another article written in the same year he located in the National Assembly, which of course preceded the Jacobin dictatorship, the principal virtue of the revolution, which he said consisted of 'the liberation of the new spirit from old forms'.[11] In 1843 Engels was equally complimentary, stating simply that the French Revolution marked 'the beginning of democracy in Europe' and that Babeuf's communism, which Engels implied was the prevailing ideology of the revolution as a whole, was worthy of the working class's consideration and respect.[12]

---

[5] Rubel, 'The French Revolution', p. 25.

[6] François Furet, *Marx and the French Revolution* (Chicago IL, 1988), p. 34.

[7] Dzhedzhula, *Rossiia i velikaia frantsuzskaia burzhuaznaia revoliutsiia*, p. 10.

[8] Furet, *Marx and the French Revolution, passim.*

[9] Karl Marx, 'Comments on the Latest Prussian Censorship Instruction', in Karl Marx and Frederick Engels, *Collected Works* (New York, 1975), vol. I, p. 119.

[10] Ibid., p. 120. That Marx, who was a notorious Russophobe, made a comparison in which something Russian was the less repugnant underscored the extent to which, at this point in his life, he found the Jacobin Terror objectionable.

[11] Karl Marx, 'The Philosophical Manifesto of the Historical School of Law', ibid., p. 205.

[12] Quoted in Manfred, *Velikaia frantsuzskaia revoliutsiia*, p. 379.

The next time Marx mentioned the French Revolution, also in 1843, was in a letter to Arnold Ruge.[13] The revolution, he wrote, 'restored man to his estate', but he neglected to explain what he meant by this.[14] All one can reasonably infer is that he considered revolution a positive phenomenon in properly adjusting man's relationship to his economic and social environment. But in his essay on 'The Jewish Question', written in 1844, Marx elaborated on this cryptic comment, arguing that the French Revolution entailed a partial liberation of the individual from private, egoistic concerns, thereby enabling him to become a real citizen, which to Marx meant that he was now a genuine member of his community. The political freedom the revolution promised was not an end in itself, but a means to a kind of universal liberation, which only a revolution could make possible because conditions in France had not advanced sufficiently to allow it.[15] It is not clear whether Marx meant that these circumstances were peculiar to France in the late eighteenth century or instead were the result of external forces that were European or possibly even global in scope. What is clear in the essay is that the beneficial changes Marx believed the revolution would produce were incomplete. True, the revolution enabled the emergence of a 'civil society' independent of politics. But the French people, albeit to a much less extent than before the revolution, remained egoistic.[16] (The role of the Jews in all of this—which explains the essay's title—was to serve as the archetypical egoists whose obsession with self-aggrandizement at the expense of the larger society made them the most obvious and odious personification of capitalism.) Even the Declaration of the Rights of Man, which Marx rightly considered the paradigmatic document of the French Revolution, came in for criticism. But instead of condemning it (and the revolution itself) for subordinating the individual's welfare to that of the nation, Marx argued that its harmful effect consisted precisely in perpetuating the individual's isolation, which robbed him of his humanity.[17] As he emphasized in other writings from the 1840s, the French Revolution conferred liberty on only a small segment of the population, so that, for everyone to enjoy its benefits, there had to be additional changes not just in the material circumstances in which the vast majority of the French people lived, but also in their internal psychological state, which Marx believed reflected 'alienation' just as destructive of the individual personality as material impoverishment and economic exploitation.[18]

But compared to Germany, the ancestral home of both Marx and Engels, France was the avatar of history's progress. Having already experienced one

---

[13] 'Letter, Marx to Arnold Ruge (May 1843)', in Furet, *Marx and the French Revolution*, pp. 103–4.

[14] Ibid., p. 104; Karl Marx, 'Letters from the "Franco-German Yearbooks"', in Karl Marx, *Early Writings* (New York, 1975), p. 201.

[15] Karl Marx, 'On the Jewish Question', ibid., pp. 227–33.   [16] Ibid., p. 229.

[17] Ibid., p. 230.

[18] Karl Marx, 'Critical Notes on the Article "The King of Prussia and Social Reform. By a Prussian"', in Marx, *Early Writings*, p. 418.

revolution, it might soon experience another, more radical one, probably before a revolution like the first one in France occurred in Germany. Marx's contempt for his homeland was real, and deeply felt. In his aforementioned letter to Ruge, Marx wrote that the German states embodied 'the philistine world' in its most complete incarnation, causing it 'to lag behind the French Revolution'.[19] And in his intro-duction to his critique of Hegel's philosophy, written in 1843 and published in 1844, Marx went even further, acknowledging that conditions in the German states were presently much like those in France in 1789—but then rejecting the plausible inference that they were on the verge of a revolution because the German bourgeoisie was an imperfect facsimile of its French equivalent, and therefore constitutionally incapable of initiating a revolution resembling that which had begun in France a half-century earlier.[20] This Franco-German dichotomy Marx first posited in the early 1840s would widen after the failure of revolutions in both France and the German states in 1848, and contribute significantly to his evolving assessment of the revolutionary potential of both the French and the Germans for the remainder of his life. A reflection more of Marx's scepticism about the ability of the German bourgeoisie to make a bourgeois revolution than of his perhaps excessive confidence in the ability of the French proletariat to make a proletarian revolution, the antithesis Marx claimed to see between the two peoples seems inexplicable in terms of Marxist ideology, and for that reason was perhaps a reflection of impulses more visceral than rational in his psyche.

In the 1840s Marx laid out the basic tenets of Marxist ideology, incorporating into the ideological edifice he was constructing the ideas he considered its building blocks. This brought the French Revolution into sharper focus, so that Marx gained a better sense of both its achievements and its failures. In *The Holy Family*, published in 1845 and co-authored with Engels, Marx stressed the assumption implicit in the philosophical materialism he had determined was the foundational principle of all human existence: that ideas are basically a reflection of the material circumstances in which people live and that, standing alone, '[they] cannot carry out anything at all'.[21] The French Revolution was still the political phenomenon Marx had suggested it was in earlier references, but now he unequivocally considered it the result of economic and social factors, rather than of ideas. The latter, he now seemed to be saying, drove history forward only to the extent that

---

[19] 'Marx to Ruge', in Furet, *Marx and the French Revolution*, p. 104.
[20] Karl Marx, Introduction to 'A Contribution to the Critique of Hegel's Philosophy of Right', in Marx, *Early Writings*, pp. 245, 254–6.
[21] Karl Marx and Frederick Engels, *The Holy Family, or Critique of Critical Criticism. Against Bruno Bauer and Company*, in Marx and Engels, *Collected Works*, vol. IV, p. 119. For convenience sake and because Marx dominated Engels personally and intellectually, only Marx will be considered the author in the analysis that follows, and in all subsequent instances in which an article or book to which both men contributed is discussed. The advantage Engels enjoyed over Marx, in terms of expanding their readership, was that the former reduced to simplicity the complexity and opaqueness of the latter's often convoluted prose.

they were consistent with the economic relationships that existed at any particular time. Ideas that in some way strengthened classes that were already economically dominant—such as the aristocracy under feudalism or factory owners under capitalism—were themselves influential; conversely, if the existing order was one in which the dominant class was declining, the most powerful ideas were those that served the interests of the class that was destined to destroy it, such as the bourgeoisie prior to the overthrow of the aristocracy or, at a later stage of history, the proletariat prior to the overthrow of the bourgeoisie.

As it happened, Marx and Engels wrote *The Holy Family* as a rebuttal to the views Bruno Bauer had expressed earlier, in which Bauer cited the French Revolution to prove the autonomy and centrality of ideas in causing significant and lasting changes in the lives of ordinary people. The French Revolution, in Bauer's opinion, failed to achieve all of its objectives because the French people did not fully share the ideas of its leaders.[22] Marx disagreed. By essentially seeking to recreate what they understood to be the morality and the institutions of antiquity, the French revolutionaries who failed to retain power, namely the Jacobins, did so because they acted in ways that the prevailing economic conditions would not permit. The result, which Marx considered inevitable, was the reaction that began on 9 Thermidor.

Marx's conclusion was consistent with what he had written previously. But it also suggested something radically new in Marx's thinking, namely that the French Revolution, while still a bourgeois revolution, was one in which the bourgeoisie, after starting the revolution in 1789, betrayed it four years later, when it falsely concluded that its interests actually coincided with the class it had originally defeated, namely the landed nobility (by which Marx meant the aristocracy). In short, the bourgeoisie began the French Revolution but was unable to finish it. As a result, in 1793, the Jacobins took power from the bourgeoisie and tried to continue what the bourgeoisie had begun. But the Jacobins, after essentially finishing the revolution, tried to extend it beyond the limits history had imposed on it, and for that reason lost power in 1794, little more than a year after acquiring it. In purely personal terms, the Jacobins were far superior to the bourgeoisie as a whole, and to distinguish them from it Marx often called them 'petit-bourgeois', which in his particular lexicon suggested particular personal qualities he admired, such as courage and ruthlessness, as well as impersonal factors such as occupation and income.

As a result, the Jacobins, in Marx's taxonomy of the classes involved in the French Revolution, comprised a segment of the bourgeoisie but differed from it simultaneously. In fact, it was the Jacobins' differences with the bourgeoisie that enabled them, for a brief period in the winter of 1793–4, to act in ways consistent

---

[22] Furet, *Marx and the French Revolution*, p. 134.

with the economic interests of classes and categories of the population below them. Whether these included a genuine proletariat is not clear from a reading of *The Holy Family*. Whatever the case, the Jacobins lost power not long after gaining it, at which point the French Revolution, according to Marx, came to an end. Nevertheless, the revolution, considered as a whole, was not a failure. The Jacobins' successor in 1794 was not the reactionary class in 1789, namely the aristocracy, but rather the reactionary class in 1793, namely the bourgeoisie, whose domination of French politics would continue well into the nineteenth century. In the French Revolution the bourgeoisie—even though it did not deserve to do so—triumphed over 'the pen of Marat, the guillotine of the Terror, and the sword of Napoleon', and in 1830 over 'the crucifix and the blue blood of the Bourbons'.[23] In short, the Jacobins attempted too much too quickly, and paid the price for this politically, and in the case of their leadership, with their lives.

According to Marx, the reason the Jacobins overextended themselves was that they were wrong to think that will and perseverance, by themselves, could eliminate social pathologies such as poverty and pauperism. What they ignored were the immovable limits imposed by the economic realities in France in the late eighteenth century.[24] These forces could not prevent the Jacobins from acquiring power, but they were sufficient to preclude their retaining it. Not even terror could save them. In an article in November 1847, Marx phrased his objections in the form of a warning of what would happen if the proletariat—like the Jacobins in the French Revolution—should somehow take power from the bourgeoisie before the objective conditions necessary for its doing so existed. In that event:

> its victory will be only temporary, only an element in the service of the bourgeois revolution itself, as in the year 1794, as long as in the course of history, in its 'movement', those material conditions have not been created which make necessary the abolition of the bourgeois mode of production and therefore also the definitive overthrow of political bourgeois domination.[25]

In purely personal terms, the Jacobins were hardly likely to inspire confidence in those who shared their political objectives. In the same article, Marx sneeringly dismissed them as 'bloodhounds' and 'monsters'.[26] But what sealed their fate politically was the particular configuration of impersonal economic forces they were powerless to change in any meaningful way.

For all of its world-historical significance as the first bourgeois revolution, the French Revolution, for Marx, was also a cautionary tale about the perils of trying

---

[23] Marx and Engels, *Holy Family*, p. 81.

[24] Marx, 'Critical Notes on the Article', in Marx, *Early Writings*, pp. 409–11.

[25] Karl Marx, 'Moralising Criticism and Critical Morality: A Contribution to German Cultural History Contra Karl Heizen', in Marx and Engels, *Collected Works*, vol. VI, p. 319. Viewed retrospectively, Marx in 1847 was condemning what Lenin and the Bolsheviks would do exactly seventy years later.

[26] Ibid., p. 335.

to accelerate the course of history.[27] But this was not the only lesson Marx drew from the revolution prior to his witnessing (and, to a limited extent, his participating in) the revolutions that began in Western Europe in 1848, barely three months after his derogation of the Jacobins. In these, the earliest years of his life as a revolutionary actor and analyst, Marx found much to admire in the French Revolution, even if he felt himself obliged to write about its failures because he thought his doing so would help future proletarian revolutions to succeed. He never denied the revolution's success in ridding France of feudalism, nor did he ever minimize the significance of this. The year 1789 marked the beginning of a new stage in history, and given Marx's low opinion of his fellow Germans, it seems reasonable to suppose that, when he and Engels wrote the manifesto of the Communist League—which, once published, would be known as *The Communist Manifesto*—he fully expected France to be the site of the next great revolution in history, in which the bourgeoisie, the victor in the first French revolution despite

---

[27] Marx's contention that the French Revolution was a bourgeois revolution has not gone unchallenged by historians of France. See, for example, Alfred Cobban, *The Social Interpretation of the French Revolution* (Cambridge, 1964); and George V. Taylor, 'Non-Capitalist Wealth and the Origins of the French Revolution', *American Historical Review* 72 (1967): pp. 469–96. In their view, the groups that initiated, carried out, and benefitted from the French Revolution had little interest in the kind of entrepreneurial, industrial capitalism that a genuine bourgeoisie would be apt to pursue. By giving land to peasants, jobs to the bureaucracy, and the *biens nationaux* at bargain rates to persons of proprietary wealth, the revolution retarded rather than accelerated industrialization. Other historians have argued, contrary to Marxist orthodoxy, that the revolution enabled the bourgeoisie and the nobility to fuse, creating the order of *notables* from which the French political elite would be drawn for much of the nineteenth century. Doyle, *History of the French Revolution*, p. 405; Colin Lucas, 'Nobles, Bourgeois, and the Origins of the French Revolution', *Past and Present*, no. 60 (August 1973): pp. 84–126; and Simon Schama, *Citizens: A Chronicle of the French Revolution* (New York, 1989), pp. 116–17, 520. In the same work (pp. 184–5, 787) Schama even argues that the French Revolution, far from a catalyst of economic modernization, was actually an impediment to it, while Guy Chaussinand-Nogaret, in *The French Nobility of the Nineteenth Century* (Cambridge, 1984), pp. 84–116, claims that the first real capitalists in France were nobles who not only dominated certain industries, such as textiles and mining, but also were prominent in the development of steam technology and joint-stock companies. Elizabeth Eisenstein, in 'Who Intervened in 1788? A Commentary on *The Coming of the French Revolution*', *American Historical Review* 71 (October 1965): pp. 77–103, criticized the Marxist view of the French Revolution on different grounds, arguing that class lines broke down in the revolution; as a result, regional differences were more significant that those based on class, and the growth of literacy enabled coalitions to form that transcended it. In any event, the whole notion of a bourgeoisie is so elastic and amorphous that Marx's using the term analytically generated more confusion than clarity. Still other historians have argued that much of what is considered the legacy of the French Revolution, such as the centralization and rationalization of government, actually began under the Old Regime and that these and other changes were the result not of impersonal forces but of policies initiated by the last Bourbon kings. Doyle, *History of the French Revolution*, pp. 423–4. Marx's view of the French Revolution as 'bourgeois' would be reaffirmed, albeit with qualifications for which they would be strongly criticized by Soviet historians, by Jean Jaurès in the nineteenth century, and by Albert Mathiez, Georges Lefebvre, and Albert Soboul in the twentieth. Mathiez, for example, was taken to task by N. M. Lukin in 'Al'ber Mat'ez (1874–1932)', *Istorik marksist*, vol. 3 (1932): pp. 60–86, for ostensibly deviating from Marxist orthodoxy even in Mathiez's essay, *Le Bolchevisme et le Jacobinisme* (Paris, 1920), in which the French historian praised the Bolsheviks for what he considered their striking resemblance to the Jacobins. V. G. Revunenkov, in 'Novoe v izuchenii velikoi frantsuzskoi revoliutsii i vzgliad V. I. Lenina', in *V. I. Lenin i istoricheskaia nauka*, edited by N. A. Zakher and V. V. Makarov (Moscow, 1969), p. 125, criticized Soboul for claiming that, because the objectives of the *sans-culottes* were utopian, they contributed little to the destruction of feudalism.

its inaction during the Jacobin interregnum, would be the principal loser in the second one. Industrial capitalism, which Marx believed in 1848 was experiencing its death throes, in reality was still in its infancy. But Marx could hardly be faulted for not knowing this, and he welcomed the advent of 1848 convinced that the proletarian revolutions he believed to be imminent would finish what the French Revolution had started.

*   *   *

The conventional wisdom on Marx's pronouncements on the 1848 Revolution in France is that it caused him to emphasize the 'voluntarist' aspect of his ideology at the expense of its determinism, causing him to revise upward his opinion of the French Revolution as a whole, and of the Jacobins and the Terror in particular. The reason for this is that in a year that initially generated great expectations, only to destroy them, seemingly completely and for the foreseeable future, his emotions prevailed over his rational faculties. If, in 1848, Marx's head told him one thing—that any proletarian revolution that occurred was bound to fail because capitalism had not oppressed the proletariat sufficiently for the latter to possess the revolutionary consciousness necessary for a proletarian revolution to succeed—his heart told him another, namely that seizing power prematurely, as the Jacobins did, need not have precluded their holding on to it. The fact that the Jacobins were unable to do so was *not* inherent in the historical circumstances that pertained in France in the 1790s. Rather, this was because the Jacobins made mistakes.

In this instance, the conventional wisdom is correct. Marx's opinion of the Jacobins improved over the course of the year, as he compared the ongoing revolution to the earlier one. Increasingly clear to him was the simple fact that the 1848 Revolution in France followed a course that was practically the exact opposite of the French Revolution: the 1848 Revolution, over time, became less radical, while the French Revolution, in its evolution, became more radical. In addition, the descending trajectory of the former proceeded far more rapidly than the ascending trajectory of the latter. For this reason, one can trace in Marx's writings in 1848 on the revolution unfolding before him expressions of excitement and anticipation yielding to depression and even occasional despair as the tide turned against it, first as a result of the events culminating in the June Days, when (in Marx's conception of the revolution) the proletariat lost power to the bourgeoisie, and again in December, when Louis Napoleon was elected president of France with the support of classes Marx considered retrograde and reactionary. Remarkably, however, his newfound admiration of the Jacobins remained more or less constant: his optimism during the first half of 1848 caused him to applaud the Jacobins for their activism and fearlessness in taking power and dealing severely with the elements in the population opposing them. In the second half of the year he still lauded the Jacobins, only now for their (supposedly) conspiratorial tactics prior to gaining power, and for the degree to which they centralized the government and ruled dictatorially afterwards. In short, the Jacobins provided Marx with a model both for taking power and using it. Indeed, the proletariat's failure in 1848 was caused precisely by the absence of leaders within its ranks willing and able to take power—or more precisely to retake power after the crushing defeat it suffered in the June Days—and to rule the way the Jacobins did a half-century earlier.

What is often forgotten or ignored in all of this is that Marx's reappraisal of the Jacobins had started even before the 1848 Revolution began. One suspects that that was the case because Marx became an actual participant in revolutionary politics not in 1848, when he established in Cologne a newspaper, the *Neue Rheinische Zeitung* (*New Rhineland News*), for the purpose of inciting a revolution, but in 1847, when he and Engels agreed to write the manifesto of the Communist League, which, located for safety's sake in London, played no role in any of the revolutions on the European continent that began shortly after its creation.[28] In 1846 Engels had written that Robespierre and the Jacobins actually represented the proletariat in France, and for that reason were overthrown by the bourgeoisie.[29] And in November 1847, in the same series of articles in which he criticized the Jacobins for taking power prematurely, Marx also credited them with completing the process of destroying feudalism in France after the bourgeoisie shrank from doing so, thereby creating a political vacuum they filled themselves. In these same articles Marx even justified the terror the Jacobins employed because by taking power prematurely, they confronted enemies so numerous and powerful that only the application of force could neutralize them while the Jacobins finished what the bourgeoisie had begun.[30]

Marx's public comments on the Jacobins changed remarkably little over the course of the year. In an article in *Neue Rheinische Zeitung* written shortly after the June Days, he made clear he did not underestimate the seriousness of the defeat the proletariat had just suffered at the hands of General Cavaignac and the French army, which he ascribed partly to 'pedants [rejecting] the old revolutionary tradition of 1793' as a precedent the proletariat and their leaders should have followed.[31] In fact, elsewhere in the same article he broadened his earlier condemnation of the bourgeoisie, which he now claimed was responsible for Cavaignac's assault, to include its earlier incarnations in 1789 and 1830, when, just as in 1848, it 'retained the class rule, the slavery of the workers, [and] the bourgeois system'.[32] In all three revolutions' the bourgeoisie—which one would think included the Jacobins—co-opted the lower classes, and in that respect acted in ways that would have to be considered reactionary. But in the same month, also in *Neue Rheinische Zeitung*, Marx again

[28] Marx's and Engels' activities and peregrinations in these years are described cogently and in detail in Sperber, *Karl Marx*, pp. 197–236.
[29] Frederick Engels, 'The Festival of Nations in London', in Marx and Engels, *Collected Works*, vol. VI, pp. 4–5.
[30] Marx, 'Moralising Criticism and Critical Morality', ibid., vol. VI, pp. 319, 322–3.
[31] Karl Marx, 'The June Revolution', ibid., vol. VII, p. 147.
[32] Marx, 'The June Revolution', ibid., vol. VII, p. 147.

praised the Jacobins, this time to underscore by comparison the timidity of the Germans in Frankfurt, Prussia, and elsewhere in Germany who were taking steps Marx considered insufficient to achieve political unification and a successful bourgeois revolution simultaneously; Marx considered both objectives prerequisites for a proletarian revolution in all of Germany. The best way to achieve these objectives, according to Marx, was to repeat the events in France from 1792, when under the Jacobins the country essentially declared war on the rest of Europe, thereby unifying it against its external enemies, to 1794, when the highly centralized government the Jacobins had established the year before ensured the long-term success of the original revolution and its foremost achievement of ending feudalism.[33] In fact, Marx expressed the hope that any German republic that was established would be 'one and indivisible', which was precisely the slogan the Jacobins had adopted to defend the republic they had inherited from the Convention in 1793.[34] However dangerous a repetition of the French Revolution might be in France in 1848, in Germany it was precisely the precedent that should be followed. And among the lessons of the revolution German radicals should find relevant was that the radicalization of policy, the expansion of the revolution geographically, and the centralization of political power the Jacobins pursued simultaneously were mutually reinforcing—until other policies they adopted, most egregiously the suppression of the Hébertists and other elements to their left politically, weakened them severely and thereby hastened the Thermidorian reaction.[35]

Provided it was directed against enemies of the revolution more conservative than the Jacobins, terror, as a means of ensuring the successful implementation of policy, was not only morally justified but, in the circumstances that pertained in France in 1793–4, absolutely essential. Commenting in November 1848 on the collapse of the revolution in Austria, Marx counselled that 'there is only one means by which the murderous death agonies of the old society and the bloody birth throes of the new society can be shortened, simplified and concentrated, and that is by revolutionary terror'.[36] One month later, Marx praised the Jacobin Terror, describing it as 'a plebeian means of eliminating the enemies of the bourgeoisie, absolutism, feudalism, and philistinism'.[37] Significantly, by using the word 'plebeian' to describe it, Marx could distinguish it from the terror the bourgeoisie had previously employed while acting as the principal agent of the revolution after it began. But when the bourgeoisie, in 1793, believed, rightly or wrongly, that it had achieved its objectives, and that advancing the revolution further was both impossible and inadvisable, power passed to the Jacobins, who, in their objectives were acting on behalf of the 'plebeians', which for Marx and Engels was an amorphous and elastic social category appropriate in countries like France

---

[33] Sperber, *Karl Marx*, pp. 225–6.   [34] Ibid., p. 225.   [35] Ibid., pp. 225–6.
[36] Karl Marx, 'The Victory of the Counter-Revolution in Vienna', in Marx and Engels, *Collected Works*, vol. VII, p. 506.
[37] Karl Marx, 'The Bourgeoisie and the Counter-Revolution', ibid., vol. VIII, p. 161.

in 1793 where the bourgeoisie has ended feudalism but industrial capitalism has barely begun.

When Marx first used the term, he stated that he meant by it 'the proletariat and the non-bourgeois strata of the middle class'.[38] But these could include all sorts of social categories whose interests, one would think, would rarely coincide, if ever. Artisans and craftsmen, petty merchants and others who might be considered members of a petit-bourgeoisie, workers in the first factories, and even peasants, who by definition had nothing 'urban' about them—these all could be considered 'plebeian'.[39] But according to Marx, despite their obvious sociological differences, they somehow coalesced to play an active and mostly positive role in the French Revolution because the bourgeoisie, in 1793, tired of the obligations imposed on it by history, or simply out of cowardice, yielded political primacy to the Jacobins, who, acting on behalf of the plebeians, extended the revolution to its outermost limits, only to exceed them in 1794 and thereby ensure their own destruction. Indeed, it was because the Jacobins took the revolution more seriously than anyone else in France that they had to employ the guillotine— first against reactionary enemies of the revolution, such as the Girondins (and many Jacobins themselves, most notably Danton) and then against radical ones like the Hébertists and *les enragés* who had once supported the Jacobins but had since come to consider them retrograde and reactionary. In the end, the Jacobins exaggerated their own power and security and lost both on 9 Thermidor.[40] But the Jacobins at least gained power, and thus could finish in France the task of ending feudalism that the bourgeoisie in Germany, by 1848, had not even begun.[41]

Prior to 1848 Marx had written much about the Jacobins, some of which he repeated in 1848. Prior to 1848, he considered the Jacobins' losing power inevitable; in 1848 he believed it avoidable had the Jacobins made different choices. In explaining this change, one must bear in mind that, in 1848, his attention was more on Germany and the German states than on France, so that the principal comparison he drew throughout the year was not between 1789 and 1848 in

---

[38] Marx, 'The Bourgeoisie and the Counter-Revolution', ibid., vol. VIII, p. 161.

[39] Whether the Jacobins themselves were plebeians or rather members of the petit-bourgeoisie who acted as the political instrument of the plebeians was a question that especially bedeviled both the Bolsheviks and Soviet historians, and generated several heated polemics, up to and including the Gorbachev era. Soviet historians also disagreed, though not as often or with the same degree of emotion, on who the plebeians actually were and on how they differed—if they differed at all—from both the Jacobins on the one hand and a genuine proletariat on the other.

[40] Marx's emphasis in 1848 on the legitimacy of revolutionary terror, and on the implication that the Jacobins resorting to it because they possessed the personal qualities necessary to practise it, appealed profoundly to the Bolsheviks and would be implicit in the panegyrics in which Soviet historians praised them. A. V. Manfred, for example, quoted with obvious approval Marx's comment in 1848 that the Jacobins became for him in that year of continental revolution 'the communists of our day'. Manfred, *Velikaia frantsuzskaia revoliutsiia*, p. 388. The constant refrain that the French bourgeoisie (which included the Girondins) were cowards only accentuated, by contrast, the courage and audacity of the Jacobins.

[41] Ibid., p. 162.

France, but between 1789 in France and 1848 in Germany. A typical example was in an article in July in *Neue Rheinische Zeitung*, in which he disparaged the German Revolution of 1848 as a mere 'parody' of the French Revolution of 1789.[42] In essence, Marx was comparing a bourgeois revolution that, within the limits imposed on it by impersonal historical forces, had more or less succeeded— even though its success required the intervention of cadres of professional revolutionaries who did not even represent the class that began the revolution in the first place—to one that did not. For that reason a second revolution was required. From the perspective of 1848, the course the French Revolution took seemed fixed and unchangeable; in Germany the course its (second) revolution might take was multifarious, though not, to be sure, completely unlimited. It therefore made sense, in 1848, for Marx to deem the Jacobins' fall from power contingent on choices they made, rather than the result of impersonal forces beyond their control.

In Marx's exposition of the teleology of the French Revolution—in which the class that began the revolution was unable to finish it, and for that reason relinquished power to a coterie of revolutionaries representing very different categories of the population—much remains unclear. For example, in December 1848, when he could now look back at the events of the year with the benefit of at least a modicum of hindsight, he wrote the following about the original French Revolution, obviously in the hope of finding insights relevant to his current endeavour:

> [T]he bourgeoisie was the class that really headed the movement. The proletariat and the non-bourgeois strata of the middle class had either not yet interests separate from those of the bourgeoisie or they did not yet constitute independent classes or class sub-divisions. Therefore, where they opposed the bourgeoisie, as they did in France in 1793 and 1794, they fought only for the attainment of the aims of the bourgeoisie, even if not in the matter of the bourgeoisie.[43]

But while Marx in this passage explained why the Jacobins and their 'proletarian' supporters lost power, he left unanswered in his article the question of why—as opposed to how—they were able to take power in the first place. To answer it, one had to have more guidance than Marx provided. The most he could muster in that regard was to advance the argument—mostly by implication rather than openly and explicitly—that the Girondins, who were the only members of the bourgeoisie who had any chance of keeping the Jacobins from power, were simply cowards and thus too irresolute to do what they should have done.

---

[42] Karl Marx, 'The Bill Proposing the Abolition of Feudal Obligations', in Marx and Engels, *Collected Works*, vol. VII, p. 294.

[43] Marx, 'The Bourgeoisie and the Counter-Revolution', ibid., vol. VIII, p. 161. For stylistic reasons I have altered the translation slightly.

One is struck, on reading Marx's comments on the French Revolution while France was experiencing another revolution a half-century later, by the contrast he created for his readers between the bourgeoisie in 1848, when it (unfortunately) succeeded, in the June Days, in wresting control of the revolution from the proletariat, and the bourgeoisie in 1793, when it (fortunately) relinquished power to the Jacobins. Could the reason for its action (or lack of it) in the latter instance have really been just cowardice—which was how Marx usually explained the passivity of the German bourgeoisie in 1848? Or was the enormity of the task, given that this was the Great French Revolution, the first genuinely bourgeois revolution in history, just too much for the bourgeoisie as a class, and that only an elite of ruthless revolutionaries—like that which Lenin would create in Russia many years later—could finish the task the bourgeoisie began but could never end? Or was the French bourgeoisie, or maybe France itself, in some inexplicable way still not entirely ready for a bourgeois revolution in 1789—in which case the adjective imputing greatness to the French Revolution that Marx always included when he mentioned it would be unwarranted? Marx did not say.

Moreover, while in 1848 Marx was clear about what the Jacobins did in the French Revolution, he never clarified what they were in terms of the class or social category they belonged to: were they themselves 'plebeian' or were they members of the bourgeoisie who somehow ended up representing a different class entirely? If the latter, should they be designated as 'petit-bourgeois', rather than simply as bourgeois, because they served to perpetuate, if only for a matter of months, the interests of classes and categories of the population that were lower than the bourgeoisie and strongly opposed to it?[44] Finally, what would be the fate of the plebeians once the unusual circumstances in which they appeared in France disappeared? Once again, Marx did not say, and he remained silent on these questions for the remainder of his life, leaving it to Lenin and the Bolsheviks to answer them, as it were, on his behalf. But one can speculate that as the product of a transitional phase in history in which the bourgeoisie has taken power but before industrial capitalism has developed sufficiently to produce a demographically dominant proletariat, the plebeians, in the context of Marx's ideology, would eventually become members either of the bourgeoisie or of the proletariat.

By the summer of 1849, with his hopes for another revolution seemingly shattered, Marx left Germany for Paris, and then, two months later, moved to London, where he and Engels spent the remaining years of their lives. Still, it took time for Marx's earlier optimism to disappear completely. In 1850 he and Engels joined French and German Blanquist émigrés in establishing the Universal League

---

[44] Among the Russian Marxists who answered the question Marx evaded was Georgii Plekhanov, who, while defining the Jacobins as petit-bourgeois and thus a subgroup of the bourgeoisie, claimed that they nonetheless sought to protect the interests of what was then an embryonic proletariat. G. V. Plekhanov, 'Stoletie velikoi revoliutsii (1889)', in G. V. Plekhanov, *Sochineniia*, edited by D. Riazanov, 24 vols (Moscow, 1923–7), vol. IV, pp. 66–7.

of Revolutionary Communists, which agitated for an immediate revolution transferring power, at least in Marx's expectations, to the proletariat.[45] While Marx now understood rationally that the proletariat could not possibly overthrow the bourgeoisie in the foreseeable future, he was simultaneously formulating in his mind a scenario in which it would. With Engels as co-author, he presented it publicly for the first time, in March 1850, in his 'Address to the Central Committee of the Communist League', which was distributed to members of the organization both in London and on the European continent.[46] One month later, as if in confirmation of his belief in its correctness, he and Engels attended in the British capital a celebration of Robespierre's birthday.[47]

In the address, Marx endeavoured to explain why two years earlier the German Revolution had failed. Perhaps because when he co-wrote the address he was also writing *The Class Struggles in France*, a much longer exegesis on what had caused France's revolution, also two years earlier, to fail, he barely mentioned the French Revolution. Understandably more invested emotionally in events in Germany in 1848 than in those in France, Marx put the blame for Germany's failure squarely on its 'liberal bourgeoisie', singling out for special condemnation its perfidy and cowardice. To be sure, Marx mentioned the objective conditions that then prevailed, but then continued his *ad hominem* recriminations.[48] For any future German revolution to succeed, both its supporters and its enemies would have to be different. The segment of the population currently most strongly opposed to a bourgeois revolution and also most likely to oppose any future one was, paradoxically, a segment of the bourgeoisie itself, namely 'the democratic petit bourgeoisie', which Marx had never mentioned or identified as such in any earlier writings, but now defined as an amalgam of the aforementioned liberal bourgeoisie and other elements drawn from the petit bourgeoisie.[49] To prevent these nefarious enemies of progress from stifling any future revolution, whoever carried it out had to include among its objectives not just the overthrow of the feudal order that still prevailed in Germany (but not in France after the French Revolution), but also the destruction of whatever species of bourgeois or petit bourgeois regime that Marx expected to succeed it. In this second endeavour—which Marx considered for all intents and purposes a second revolution—the proletariat would be both its principal agent and its principal beneficiary. Moreover, this second revolution would follow so closely upon the first that together they could be considered a single revolution—a construction remarkably similar to Trotsky's formulation concerning Russia at

---

[45] James Billington, *Fire in the Minds of Men: Origins of the Revolutionary Faith* (New York, 1980), p. 283.

[46] Furet, *Marx and the French Revolution*, p. 201; Karl Marx and Frederick Engels, 'Address of the Central Authority to the League', in Marx and Engels, *Collected Works*, vol. X, pp. 277–87.

[47] Furet, *Marx and the French Revolution*, p. 193.

[48] Marx and Engels, 'Address of the Central Authority to the League', pp. 278–9.

[49] Ibid., pp. 279, 287.

the beginning of the twentieth century and that which Lenin would adopt to justify the Bolshevik seizure of power in 1917. In fact, Marx concluded his address with a stirring call, using the same terminology Trotsky would adopt to elucidate the correlation of forces and classes he believed would enable a country like Russia that was just beginning to industrialize to experience a bourgeois revolution that would morph seamlessly into a proletarian one:

> If the German workers are not able to attain power and achieve their own class interests without completely going through a lengthy revolutionary development, they can at least know for a certainty this time that the first act of the approaching revolutionary drama will coincide with the direct victory of their own class in France and will be very much accelerated by it.
>
> But they themselves must do the utmost to their final victory by making it clear to themselves what their class interests are, by taking up their position as an independent party as soon as possible and by not allowing themselves to be misled for a single moment by the hypocritical phrases of the democratic petty bourgeoisie into refraining from the independent organization of the party of the proletariat. Their battle-cry must be: The Revolution in Permanence.[50]

Especially significant in this scenario Marx envisioned was the role he believed a future proletarian revolution in France would play in accelerating a bourgeois revolution in Germany, and thus, indirectly, a proletarian revolution in Germany. It is, in fact, nothing short of astonishing that, in both Marx's vision and Trotsky's, a bourgeois revolution occurring in one country required a proletarian revolution in another country (or in Trotsky's case, in several countries) to succeed. To the extent that that was the case, neither the bourgeois revolution that came first, nor the proletarian revolution that would follow it, was self-sufficient. The latter, to succeed, required the former. But what made what Marx and later Trotsky proposed even more remarkable in the context of orthodox Marxist ideology was that the two men envisioned both revolutions, the second just as much as the first, occurring in countries (Germany for Marx, Russia for Trotsky) where the prerequisites for the first revolution—not to mention those for the second revolution—were either absent or just beginning to appear. By the parameters of Marxist ideology, this could never happen. Revolutions appropriate to economically advanced countries could not occur, or at least not succeed, in less advanced ones. But the history of European socialism and communism is filled with instances of hopes and expectations trumping ideologies conceived rationally. This was certainly one of them.

Since his own ideology could not justify what he was advocating in his address, Marx, once again, looked to the French Revolution for guidance. But since what he was advocating for Germany was a revolution in which the ultimate beneficiary was the proletariat, rather than the bourgeoisie, which was the principal

---

[50] Ibid., pp. 286–7.

beneficiary of the French Revolution, he had to revise a good deal of what both he and Engels had previously written about it. In the address to the Communist League in 1850 on which the two men collaborated, the Jacobins still received credit for continuing the endeavour the bourgeoisie had begun of destroying feudalism and the Bourbon monarchy.[51] But once having done that, the Jacobins stopped. Having completed, or at least having come reasonably close to completing a bourgeois revolution, the Jacobins could not commence, much less carry to fruition, a proletarian revolution or even a plebeian one. As a result of his focusing on this particular aspect of the French Revolution, Marx's earlier admiration for the Jacobins for centralizing political power in France diminished, vitiated as it was by the importance he now placed on the Jacobins' inability, through no fault of their own, to use the power they possessed to radicalize the French Revolution beyond the degree to which they had already radicalized it.

Marx was surely aware when he co-wrote the address that France, in 1793, was not ready for a proletarian revolution. In fact, in those of his writings after 1848 that did more than merely mention the French Revolution, one sees a recognition that, for all the changes the revolution brought about both in France and in the rest of Europe, it was unable to bring history to an end. Only the proletariat, by means of socializing the means of the production, could do that. The Jacobins, by contrast, were actually prisoners of the time in which they lived, their choices limited by the existing configuration of classes. As Marx makes clear in the 1850 Address, the Jacobins were not plebeians, and they certainly were not proletarians. Rather, they were petit-bourgeois—which explains why they wanted those receiving large plots of land in the property settlement of the revolution to become a conservative force politically, supportive of the status quo and impervious to the continued poverty of those receiving smaller plots of land. One could even infer from the address that Marx considered the Jacobins personally culpable for the terror they inflicted, and that the killings he most strongly objected to were those that took the lives of persons who had suffered most from the Jacobins' new-found conservatism.[52]

---

[51] Nowhere in the address are the Jacobins cited explicitly. But the authors' reference to policies pursued in France in 1793 makes clear that they consider the Jacobins responsible for them. Marx and Engels, 'Address of the Central Authority to the League', p. 285. In notes to a German edition of the address published in 1885, Engels 'walked back' his and Marx's earlier statements lauding the Jacobins for centralizing political power by arguing that, while the Convention existed (which is to say, during the entire period the Jacobins were in power) France was far more decentralized than was generally imagined. In fact, it bore a strong resemblance to the United States, with its federalism and tradition of states' rights. Engels did not use these terms explicitly, but it is clear from the context in which he mentioned the two countries that the decentralization of power the terms implied was what he had in mind. Frederick Engels, 'On the History of the Communist League', in Karl Marx and Frederick Engels, *Selected Works* (Moscow, 1968), vol. III, pp. 173–90.

[52] Marx and Engels, 'Address of the Central Authority to the League', pp. 284–5. Although Marx never specifically cited the Jacobins in the address, he was obviously referring to them when praising 'the petit bourgeois in the French Revolution [who gave] the feudal lands to the peasants as free

In *The Class Struggles in France*, Marx's valedictory to the failed revolution in that country in 1848, the French Revolution is notable for its virtual absence. The failure of the 1848 Revolution seemed to tarnish the reputation, and to reduce the significance, of its supposedly illustrious predecessor. Marx mentioned the earlier revolution only to demonstrate that even its most enduring achievements could not prevent its beneficiaries from experiencing degradation and increasing poverty during the half-century that followed it. Far from ensuring the peasants' well-being, it actually had the opposite effect: 'Whereas the Revolution of 1789 began by shaking the feudal burdens off the peasants', it was powerless to prevent prospectively 'the 1848 Revolution announcing itself with a new tax on the rural population, in order not to endanger capital and to keep its state machine going'.[53] The best thing the French could do, now that the 1848 Revolution had failed so ignominiously, was not to look backward to 1789, as so many in 1848 had done with so little to show for it, but to look forward while there was still a chance the revolution that just ended might resume.

The way Marx phrased his criticism could even be taken as proof that he now believed drawing historical analogies of any kind harmed the heroic undertaking he had assumed of showing humanity how to extricate itself from the ethical morass that was industrial capitalism and guiding it first to socialism and then to communism. In fact, that was precisely the point he soon made explicit in his next major work, *The Eighteenth Brumaire of Louis Bonaparte*, written two years later. 'The social revolution of the nineteenth century', he wrote, 'cannot draw its poetry from the past, but only from the future. It cannot begin...before it has stripped off all superstition in regard to the past.'[54] To be sure, Marx then proceeded to invoke a historical analogy in explaining Louis Napoleon's political dominance of France, namely by comparing him to his uncle, Napoleon Bonaparte. Analogizing the two Bonapartes came naturally to anyone in France in the mid-nineteenth century with even only a rudimentary knowledge of its history, and Louis Napoleon shrewdly used to considerable advantage the implication in the analogy that the nephew was the equal, or near-equal of his illustrious uncle, who by 1848 had become a symbol of France itself. But after invoking the analogy, Marx quickly rejected it. Louis Napoleon, he stressed, was not an analogue of Napoleon Bonaparte. Rather, he was a pathetic parody of the revolutionary emperor and conqueror he was trying so hard to emulate. For all his success in gaining power in France, Louis was nothing more than a mediocrity lacking the qualities of leadership necessary to rule a country successfully. Although his lineage had

---

property'. Ibid., p. 284. While it is true that peasants received land in the revolution before the Jacobins took power, Marx considered the haute-bourgeoisie, not the petit-bourgeoisie, responsible for this.

[53]   Karl Marx, *The Class Struggles in France 1848 to 1850* (New York, 1964), p. 49.
[54]   Karl Marx, *The Eighteenth Brumaire of Louis Bonaparte* (New York, 1968), p. 18.

enabled him to gain power, it could not prevent his losing it, at which point the inexorable march of history towards proletarian revolution and socialism would resume. One must bear in mind that for Marx, the phenomenon that was Louis Napoleon was not supposed to happen in France in the mid-nineteenth century. Quite apart from his abysmal lack of *gravitas* in purely personal terms, Louis came to power not by representing a particular class, but by transcending all classes, and as Marx himself reluctantly acknowledged in *The Eighteenth Brumaire*, using the state he dominated to keep them quiet.[55] For that reason Marx had to invent a new term to describe Louis's unique form of leadership, and the term he came up with was 'Bonapartism'.

Still, Marx was too much the student of history, still wedded to the notion that early events prefigured later ones, to forswear historical analogies entirely. Even if the analogy between the two Napoleons was non-existent (except in the negative sense that the later Napoleon was a pale imitation of the earlier one), other analogies, if they were drawn carefully and correctly, had the potential to educate, enlighten, and even, in certain instances, inspire. Marx seemed to recognize intuitively that to revolutionaries seeking the moral and material improvement of humanity through the creation of a radically new society, historical analogies, however strained they might be, could nonetheless be helpful. One could learn from the past irrespective of how little the future will resemble it. Historical analogies, in short, could be instructive. Even when incorrect, revolutionaries could learn from them; false analogies could tell them what not to do. But that did not exhaust their utility. Historical analogies, Marx wrote, could simultaneously inspire and legitimize. In short, they could provide revolutionaries with the raw material needed to construct a credible and compelling mythology that, by explaining their actions simply and clearly, could legitimize the revolutionary transformation they intended in the eyes of the masses whose support they needed:

> Just when men seem engaged in revolutionising themselves and things, in creating something that has never yet existed, precisely in such periods of revolutionary crisis they anxiously conjure up the spirits of the past to their service and borrow from them names, battle cries, and costumes in order to present the new scene of world history in this time-honoured disguise and this borrowed language.[56]

---

[55] Marx, *Eighteenth Brumaire*, p. 123. To be precise, in the same page Marx claimed that Louis, far from transcending class, in reality represented 'small-holding peasants'. Elsewhere in the essay he identified his supporters in towns and cities as 'lumpenproletarians', by whom he meant workers without the political consciousness he expected of an actual proletariat. Ibid., p. 75.

[56] Ibid., p. 15. Engels reaffirmed his good opinion of history's relevance to revolutionaries in less grandiose language in 1852. 'A well-contested defeat', he stated in obvious reference to 1848, 'is a fact of as much revolutionary importance as an easily-won victory'. Friedrich Engels, *Revolution and Counter-Revolution in Germany in 1848* (London, 1896), p. 96.

Not surprisingly, Marx went on, in *The Eighteenth Brumaire*, to draw analogies of his own. Resurrecting the teleologies he had previously invoked in explaining events in 1848, Marx argued, once again, that while in the French Revolution power passed from moderates to radicals, in 1848 this sequence was reversed. In that year power passed in France from the proletariat to the bourgeoisie, and ultimately to someone who was a parody of the bourgeoisie, after the army, led by General Cavaignac and serving as the instrument of the bourgeoisie, had already stripped the proletariat of its power.[57] Also revived was the ethical gloss Marx had placed on the two teleologies: like history itself, the first one (that which traced the course of the French Revolution) was progressive and thus beneficial for the people of France, while the second one (which characterized the 1848 Revolution in France) was regressive, in the sense of history running backwards, which of course was harmful to the people of France. What distinguished Marx's formulation in *The Eighteenth Brumaire* from that which he had posited in 1848 was that he was now extending the temporal limits of the two revolutions to include the Napoleonic era in the case of the French Revolution, and Louis Napoleon's rise to power in the case of the revolution in 1848. But by extending the two revolutions' chronologies, Marx reduced the dissimilarities between them: both Napoleons, he remarked in *The Eighteenth Brumaire*, were 'statists' of a sort, intent on increasing the already considerable distance between the individual and the state that already existed when each one took power. In fact, the original Napoleon ably continued the work of the French Revolution, and by increasing the power of the state, brought it to a point of near completion:

> The first French Revolution, with its task of breaking up all separate local, territorial, urban and provincial powers in order to create the civil unity of the nation, was bound to develop what the absolute monarchy had begun: centralization, but at the same time the extent, the attributes and the agents of government power. Napoleon perfected this state machinery.[58]

Although Marx did not use the term in *The Eighteenth Brumaire*, this, in essence, was what in other writings he called 'Bonapartism'. In this context the term was clearly not a synonym for a military dictatorship. Louis Napoleon, unlike his uncle, was a civilian. Nor, at least in the case of Napoleon Bonaparte, was the term applied pejoratively. Marx always considered the latter's legacy morally and politically ambiguous, which of course was how he considered the bourgeoisie as a class: progressive in comparison to the aristocracy under feudalism, but reactionary in comparison to the proletariat under capitalism.[59]

---

[57] Marx, *Eighteenth Brumaire*, pp. 42–3.   [58] Ibid., p. 122.

[59] The Soviets would use the term as an unalloyed epithet, and after the Stalin era, in contrast to Marx's application of the term, mostly military personnel—rather than civilians—were accused of it. The evolution of Bonapartism and the role it played in the history of the Soviet Union will be described and analysed in a later chapter devoted entirely to it.

If one takes at face value what Marx now seemed to be suggesting, namely that the French Revolution ended not on 9 Thermidor or even on 18 Brumaire, but with the end of the Napoleonic Era in 1815, then the Jacobins' role in the revolution is necessarily diminished. Marx rarely mentioned the Jacobins after 1852, and in the 1860s, as his concerns turned from France to events in Ireland and the German states, his sense of their uniqueness in the revolution—that they acted on behalf of a class they did not belong to (the plebeians) to continue a revolution when the class that began the revolution (the bourgeoisie) refused to do so—diminished as well. In one of his few references to the Jacobins, in a letter to Engels in 1865 expressing opposition to Prussia's recent Anti-Combination Law prohibiting workers from forming unions, he stated that the Jacobins did little or nothing that was contrary to the interests and the wishes of the bourgeoisie; he also singled out Robespierre in this regard for having approved the *Loi le Chapelier*, passed by the National Assembly in 1791, which by forbidding artisans and craftsmen from forming guilds, effectively prohibited them from staging strikes.[60]

Still, the French Revolution proved a bountiful source of analogies whenever Marx needed one to make a point or to clinch an argument. The same was true for Engels. In September 1870 he described the Jacobins cuttingly as 'little philistines who wetted their pants [and] practiced terrorism out of fear'.[61] The context in which Engels offered his pejorative opinion was significant. By the time Engels was writing, Prussia had soundly defeated France in the Franco-Prussian War, and the political vacuum created by the collapse of the Second Empire opened a window of opportunity for the working class in the French capital. Louis Napoleon, who had taken personal command of French forces, surrendered at Sedan on 2 September, and was deposed as emperor immediately afterwards. The Third Republic—with Paris still in the hands of the Prussians—was proclaimed on 4 September. But Marx counselled caution. Because the 1848 Revolution had ended disastrously, the enthusiasm he had mustered when it began was now nowhere in evidence. In an address to the General Council of the International on 9 September, he advised French workers 'not to be swayed by the national *souvenirs* of 1792' and commence an insurrection in Paris that could not possibly succeed.[62] In a letter to Marx, Engels was even more emphatic in warning Parisians not to take up arms, much less do anything resembling what the Jacobins had done nearly a century earlier. Moreover, practising terror would be especially counterproductive. The only exculpatory argument Engels mustered to temper the severity of his and Marx's criticisms of the Jacobins was that the terror they practised was the result not just of their personal deficiencies, which were admittedly considerable,

---

[60] Manfred, *Velikaia frantsuzskaia revoliutsiia*, p. 380.

[61] Quoted in Bruno Naarden, *Socialist Europe and Revolutionary Russia: Perception and Prejudice, 1848–1923* (New York, 2002), p. 69.

[62] Karl Marx, 'Second Address of the General Council of the International Working Men's Association on the Franco-Prussian War', in Marx and Engels, *Collected Works*, vol. XXII, p. 269.

but also of the exigencies arising from having to fight for France's survival.[63] In other words, the Jacobins could not have done anything other than what they actually did.

* * *

The establishment of the Paris Commune in 1871, followed less than three months later by its destruction, produced in Marx the same extremes of emotion he had experienced in 1848. Exhilaration and enthusiasm yielded to disillusionment and even despair. But just a few years later, his pessimism dissipated. The exploits of Russian revolutionaries caused Marx to believe they would soon instigate a peasant revolution leading to socialism in Russia without the capitalist stage of history preceding it. The reason Russia could follow a path *sui generis* among the countries of Europe was because the peasants' commune, or *obshchina*, that regulated various aspects of peasant life reflected their instinctive collectivism and disdain for private property. That many of these revolutionaries would form organizations resembling the Jacobins in their centralized structure and willingness to practise terrorism for the purpose of inciting a peasant revolution required Marx and Engels to revise upward their recent denigration of the Jacobins.

Often forgotten in descriptions of this transformation is that it caused Marx to soften his earlier Russophobia, which had become especially vitriolic after Nicholas II sent troops to suppress a revolution in Hungary in 1849. Russia's suppression of the Polish Revolt in 1863 only confirmed his belief in its irredeemable iniquity. For years both Marx and Engels had been hostile to Russian revolutionaries. They considered Herzen frivolous because of his infatuation after 1848 with the same peasant commune they would extol in the late 1870s and 1880s, and Marx's hatred of Bakunin, which reflected the latter's national identity as well as his anarchism, is well known. By the late 1860s Marx's hatred of all things Russian had become so deep and unforgiving, so central a component of his personality and politics, that he recognized the irony in the fact that Russian revolutionaries were the first ones to translate *Capital* into their native language.[64] But instead of softening his animosity, this seemed to harden it. In the same letter in which he confessed his amazement at what these Russian revolutionaries were doing, he castigated Russian nobles working for the government as 'scoundrels'.[65]

One result of Marx's Russophobia after 1848 was a new-found interest in the original Napoleon; while not defeating Russia in 1812, he should not be condemned too harshly for attacking it. Moreover, Napoleon's grandeur as the overseer of Europe for nearly a decade only confirmed his and Engels' opinion of his nephew as 'the stupid Napoleon'.[66] To be sure, Marx and Engels continued to consider Bonaparte the 'gravedigger' of the French Revolution, who after

[63] 'Letter, Engels to Marx (4 September 1870)', ibid., vol. XLIV, p. 63.
[64] 'Letter, Marx to Ludwig Kugelmann (12 October 1868)', ibid., vol. XLIII, p. 130.
[65] 'Letter, Marx to Ludwig Kugelmann (12 October 1868)', ibid., vol. XLIII, p. 131.
[66] 'Letter, Engels to Marx (3 December 1851)', ibid., vol. XXXVIII, p. 504.

completing it by establishing the Code Napoleon and making other reforms in the organization and administration of the state, betrayed it by concentrating so much power in his own hands that the historical forces simultaneously driving the bourgeoisie to practise industrial capitalism, and the emerging proletariat to oppose it, were temporarily weakened.[67] When Marx, in a letter to Lassalle in 1859, described Louis Napoleon's regime as a form of Bonapartism, he could surely have applied the same sobriquet to Napoleon Bonaparte's.[68]

But what is especially notable about Marx's and Engels' comments on the original Napoleon is that so many of them concerned his inadequacies as a military strategist. In explaining his ultimate demise at Waterloo, Engels stressed Bonaparte's ignorance of the potentialities of naval power.[69] But given his and Marx's Russophobia, one cannot help but conjecture that what concerned them most were the mistakes Bonaparte had made commanding forces on land, particularly in 1812, when he sent the *Grand Armée* into to Russia to force Alexander I to comply with his Continental System, which the tsar was violating by exporting timber and grain to Great Britain. The failure of Napoleon's Russian campaign must have gnawed at Marx and Engels. Had it been successful, Russia could not have played the outsized role it assumed later in the century as the Gendarme of Europe, suppressing radical revolutions and supporting reactionary regimes.

But none of this prevented Marx and Engels, after the debacle in Paris in 1871, which was followed by the final collapse of the International in 1876, from welcoming the emergence in Russia towards the end of the decade of revolutionary organizations they could easily convince themselves were on the verge of overthrowing the Russian autocracy, which they hated nearly as much as Russian revolutionaries did. Despite their Russophobia, Marx and Engels were surely gratified in 1869, when *The Communist Manifesto* was translated into Russian, and again in 1872, when Nikolai Danielson's translation of the first volume of *Capital* marked the first time it appeared in a language other than German and English.[70] Indeed, their interest in the country they had previously vilified increased in the 1870s to the point where in 1879 Marx, even more effusively than Engels, praised the first dissertation in Russia on the French Revolution, N. I. Kareev's, on the role of the peasantry.[71]

---

[67] 'Letter, Marx to François Lafargue (12 November 1866)', ibid., vol. XLII, p. 334.

[68] 'Letter, Marx to Ferdinand Lassalle (4 February 1859)', ibid., vol. XL, pp. 380–3.

[69] 'Letter, Engels to Marx (17 November 1856)', ibid., vol. XL, p. 84.

[70] Sperber, *Karl Marx*, p. 532. Franco Venturi, *Roots of Revolution: A History of the Populist and Socialist Movements in Nineteenth Century Russia* ((New York, 1966), p. 384, names Bakunin as the translator of the *Manifesto*. Woodford McClellan, in *Revolutionary Exiles: The Russians in the First International and the Paris Commune* (Totowa, NJ, 1979), p. 41, argues that Bakunin and Sergei Nechaev shared the task, with the latter doing most of the work.

[71] Manfred, *Velikaia frantsuzskaia revoliutsiia*, pp. 157–8.

But it was the creation of *Narodnaia Volia* in 1879, even more than that of its parent organization, *Zemlia i Volia* in 1876, that opened Marx's and Engels' eyes to what seemed to them the very real possibility of a revolution in Russia destroying the autocracy and replacing it with a more humane way of life organized around the peasant commune and informed by its ethical purity.[72] The impunity with which the terrorists in charge of the organization murdered government officials was a testament to the inefficiency of the government's efforts to apprehend them. However, these murders failed to bring down the government, and the *narodovol'tsy* determined that only regicide—the assassination of Tsar Alexander II—would do so. They put their minds to this objective with singular determination and ingenuity. One member detonated a bomb in the Winter Palace; others dug a tunnel under a St Petersburg street for the purpose of blowing up the Imperial Carriage as it passed above. In both instances the tsar escaped with his life. In the former he was too far away from the explosion; in the latter his carriage did not appear at the expected time.[73] Nonetheless, it seemed likely the terrorists would eventually succeed, and in doing so inspire the peasants to rise up in yet another of the anarchic but profoundly powerful revolts that had occurred periodically in Russia for several centuries.

The effect of all this on the two now elderly revolutionaries in London was electric. Marx, in a letter to a Russian revolutionary newspaper in 1877, expressed his conviction, which he said was the result of learning the Russian language and studying its economic development, that 'if Russia continues along the road she has followed since 1861, she will forego the finest opportunity history has ever placed before a nation, and will undergo all of the fateful misfortunes of capitalist development'.[74] In 1880, in a letter to F. A. Sorge, he attacked *Chernyi Peredel*, an organization of Russian revolutionaries opposed to *Narodnaia Volia* because it considered bombings and assassinations unlikely to radicalize the peasants absent mass propaganda; ironically, a number of the *chernoperedel'tsy*, whom Marx castigated for their 'tedious doctrinairism' and their unwillingness to return to Russia from abroad and fight alongside the terrorists against the autocracy, later became Marxists.[75] Responding in 1881 to a request from one of the *chernoperedel'tsy*, Vera Zasulich, for clarification of his views on the peasant commune, Marx wrote that the general laws of economic development need not apply to

---

[72] The name of the organization, which in English means 'The People's Will', was deliberately misleading. At no time during its existence did it include more than 500 members. Its executive committee never numbered more than thirty. Walter Laqueur, *The Age of Terrorism* (Boston, 1987), p. 94; Adam B. Ulam, *In the Name of the People: Prophets and Conspirators in Prerevolutionary Russia* (New York, 1977), p. 327.

[73] Ulam, *In the Name of the People*, pp. 340–1, 351.

[74] 'Marks v redaktsiiu 'Otechestvennykh Zapisok (November 1877)', K. Marx and F. Engels, *Izbrannye pis'ma* (Moscow, 1947), p. 314.

[75] 'K. Marks k F. A. Sorge (5 November 1880)', ibid., pp. 338–40.

Russia, and that institutions peculiar to Russian society like the commune could lead it in a direction different from that of every other nation.[76]

As it happened, the terrorists succeeded in killing Alexander II. But despite the absence of any subsequent peasant revolution, Marx was undeterred. In 1882, in an introduction to a new Russian edition of the *Manifesto*, he and Engels posed the question of whether the peasant commune could serve as the basis for socialism in Russia, thereby making unnecessary industrial capitalism and the oppression of the proletariat they had previously considered prerequisites for socialism. They then answered their own question as follows:

> If the Russian revolution is a signal for proletarian revolution in the West, so that the two can supplement each other, then modern Russian communal ownership can serve as a point of departure for communist development.[77]

In their answer Marx and Engels effectively contradicted much of the edifice of the ideology Marx in particular had spent countless hours carefully constructing for nearly the entirety of their adult lives. Remarkably, there is evidence that Marx was cognizant of this. He made a point of asking Zasulich not to make public his earlier response to her question about the commune, with the result that it was known only to a few until it was published in the Soviet Union in 1924.[78] Also noteworthy about his response, and about everything he wrote, either singly or with Engels, on the possibility of the peasant commune serving as the basis for socialism in Russia is that it was precisely that, a possibility but not a certainty. Marx, in other words, was giving himself grounds for exoneration should his prediction prove incorrect.

No such concerns inhibited Engels. In the late 1870s and early 1880s, he repeatedly lauded the Russian terrorists for their audacity, and expressed his certainty that their exploits would soon trigger a peasant revolution. Cognizant of the absence of revolutions everywhere in Western Europe after the destruction of the Paris Commune, the aged revolutionary understandably latched onto a peasant revolution in Russia as a *deus ex machina* that would revive his spirits and lend meaning to his life, and to Marx's, as their deaths seemed increasingly imminent. To analogize Russia to France in 1789 was a temptation Engels could not forego. In 1880, writing to the *narodovolets*, German Lopatin, he proclaimed that 'Russia is the France of this century' and therefore 'on the verge of a new

[76] 'Pis'mo K. Marksa k Vere Ivanovne Zasulich (8 March 1881)', in Lev Deich, ed., *Gruppa 'Osvobozhdenie Truda': Iz arkhivov G. V. Plekhanova, V. I. Zasulich i L. G. Deicha* (Moscow/Leningrad, 1923–8), vol. II, pp. 223–4.
[77] Quoted in Solomon M. Schwarz, 'Populism and Early Russian Marxism on Ways of Historical Development in Russia', *Continuity and Change in Russian and Soviet Thought*, edited by Ernest J. Simmons (Cambridge MA, 1955), p. 51.
[78] Bergman, *Vera Zasulich*, p. 76.

social transformation'.[79] And in 1885, in a letter to Marx's onetime interlocutor, Vera Zasulich, Engels wrote the following:

> What I know or believe about the situation in Russia impels me to the opinion that the Russians are approaching their 1789. The revolution must break out there in a given time; it may break out there any day.... This is one of the exceptional cases where it is possible for a handful a people to *make* a revolution, i.e. with one small push to cause a whole system, which ... is in more than labile equilibrium, to come crashing down, and thus by one action, in itself insignificant, to release uncontrollable explosive forces.... When 1789 has once been launched, 1793 will not be long in following.[80]

One would think that in analogizing Russia to France in 1789, Engels would single out either the Parisian lower classes or the Jacobins or both as exemplars of the values their Russian counterparts should hold dear. But in his letter to Zasulich Engels cited instead the Blanquists, of whom both he and Marx had been critical, but whose 'fantasy of overcoming an entire society through the action of a small conspiracy' he evidently thought had some salience in the circumstances then prevailing in Russia.[81] One wonders if Engels substituted the Blanquists for the Jacobins as the relevant analogue because he recognized the preference of the Russian terrorists for the strategy the Blanquists had pioneered in France, after rejecting the more tedious and time-consuming strategy of inculcating revolutionary consciousness among the masses, of taking power in an insurrection resembling a classic *coup d'état*. Engels was so smitten by this particular strategy that he thought it might also work in Western Europe, bringing socialists there the success that had long eluded them. Both he and Marx may also, in the last years of their lives, have come to admire Blanqui and his followers for their courage and stubborn adherence to principle during the years they spent in prison and had no influence on politics in France. Never exercising power, they never tainted their reputations, as the Jacobins did by killing thousands of innocents in addition to the much smaller number of Frenchmen who actually threatened them politically.

In the last years of his life, Engels was no more able to make up his mind about the Jacobins than he was in earlier phases of his career as a revolutionary actor and theorist; the same, of course, had been true of Marx. In a letter in 1889 to the Austrian socialist Victor Adler, Engels justified the Jacobins' guillotining the Hébertists—which neither he nor Marx had ever done before.[82] But even then, he felt compelled to condemn the Jacobins for intensifying the terror they

---

[79] Quoted in 'G. A. Lopatin—M. N. Oshaninoï', *Russkie sovremenniki o K. Markse i F. Engel'se* (Moscow, 1969), p. 201.
[80] 'Letter, Engels to Vera Zasulich (23 April 1885)', in Karl Marx and Frederick Engels, *Selected Correspondence 1846–1895* (Westport CT, 1942), pp. 437–8.
[81] Ibid.
[82] 'Letter, Engels to Victor Adler (4 December 1889)', in Marx and Engels, *Selected Correspondence*, p. 457.

began 'to a pitch of insanity', which left them defenceless against the counter-revolutionaries in the Directory who succeeded them.[83]

*   *   *

Considering their work in its totality, it is clear that Marx and Engels left Russian revolutionaries a diverse menu to choose from when it behooved them to invoke the French Revolution. The options these revolutionaries could select—concerning the tactics they should use, the organizations they should create, and the objectives they should emphasize—can best be understood by assigning them to one of two camps, each the opposite of the other. Taken together, they demonstrate the ambivalence with which Marx and Engels viewed the revolution, which future revolutionaries better situated than they were in Victorian England might finally resolve. One of these camps was characterized by a rigid determinism that viewed history as subject to impersonal laws largely impervious to alteration. There was certainly a time for revolution, but there were also circumstances when revolutionaries should do nothing at all. Attempting a revolution before the preconditions for it existed was a recipe for failure. The other camp reflected a belief in the primacy of human agency. While not denying the existence of impersonal historical laws, like the dialectic, that determined the ultimate course of human events, it considered these laws sufficiently malleable to allow their acceleration, so that premature revolutions might nonetheless succeed. One might even draw from this the conclusion that a revolution that succeeded could not, by definition, be considered premature. At different times in his life, Marx inhabited one or other of these camps, stressing a form of 'voluntarism' in 1848 when it seemed that a premature revolution might nonetheless succeed, only to retreat to a kind of quietism and watchful waiting on history after it failed. For Marx, this oscillation from one camp to the other was not just the result of a rational choice, of his revising upward or downward the prospects of a revolution's success after a dispassionate re-evaluation of the tactical and strategic possibilities that pertained at any particular time. It also reflected Marx's personality and temperament.

Remarkably, Marx seemed to encompass within himself the traits appropriate to both of these dichotomous positions concerning when exactly revolutionaries should attempt a revolution. Among Russian revolutionaries, this kind of ambivalence was rare, in large part because they tended to radicalize, and to defend as the reflection of an absolute moral principle, virtually every political choice they made; for many this characterized their actions in non-political circumstances as well. Whether this particular trait or characteristic generated a certain kind of personality or was a reflection of it is impossible to answer. But what one can assert with a reasonable degree of confidence is that this moral and political absolutism made for an atmosphere within the Russian revolutionary movement

---

[83] Ibid. p. 458.

conducive to conflict and strenuous disagreement rather than to compromise and reconciliation. In this regard, one must also bear in mind that prior to 1917 the Russian revolutionary movement was a failure—which had the effect of generating fratricidal recriminations over what went wrong, which only further reduced what little chance existed of success. In such an atmosphere, political opinions and moral judgements that were already polarized because there was no way to evaluate their validity empirically became even more extreme, in the case of politics, and even more absolute, in the case of personal morality.

As a result, what revolutionaries of the late nineteenth century wrote and said about the French Revolution—and about practically everything else as well—was a substitute for the actions they were as yet unable to undertake in pursuance of their own objectives in Russia. Indeed, the French Revolution assumed special significance because its success as a bourgeois revolution contrasted so sharply with the dismal prospects in Russia for a proletarian revolution—or really for any kind of a revolution. As a result, questions about whether one's politics were Jacobin or Girondin spoke directly to whether one could be relied on to make the right kind of revolution rather than the wrong kind of revolution, or no revolution at all. After 1903, when Lenin split the nascent Russian Social Democratic Workers' Party (RSDLP) and for the first time applied the word 'Bolshevik' to his supporters, with its connotations of strength in numbers, ferocious debates commenced within the ranks of this new party over whether Bolshevism was a contemporary embodiment or expression of Jacobinism, a complete negation of it, or something in between.

For that reason, it is to the Bolsheviks and their views on the French Revolution to which we now turn.

4

Lenin

The Russian Robespierre

Consideration of how the Bolsheviks viewed the French Revolution begins with Lenin. Before 1917 the French Revolution was of inestimable value in helping him formulate a plan for taking power in Russia. This was also true, after 1917, in establishing the Soviet state. Both of these endeavours required Lenin to exceed the limits of Marxist ideology, and fashion policies consistent with the realities he faced in a country that had barely begun to industrialize, much less develop a proletariat sufficiently large and politically conscious to carry out a proletarian revolution. Lenin was by far the most flexible Bolshevik ideologically, and his willingness to extract from the French Revolution insights directly relevant to the organization and tactics of a revolutionary party amply demonstrates this. In addition, the French Revolution provided a vocabulary of politics Lenin was able to utilize as a polemical weapon in the internecine rhetorical wars Russian socialists waged among themselves prior to the October Revolution; these were especially vitriolic and *ad hominem* because, with so many of them in prison, Siberian exile, or in emigration in Western Europe, these socialists were powerless to affect the course of events in their own country. And because they could not test their ideas empirically, those they conjured often had an abstract, almost other-worldly quality, causing them, at times, to seem more real than the realities to which they were meant to apply.

Lenin was not the first Russian socialist to canvass the French Revolution for concepts and terminology that might prove useful. In fact, it was mostly in response to others invoking the revolution to attack him and to undermine his authority as the leader of the Bolsheviks that he first looked to it for assistance in defending himself. To be sure, his opinion of Paris, at least, was always a positive one. In a letter to his mother in 1895, shortly after arriving for the first time in the City of Light, he described it as having 'broad, light streets, many boulevards, and lots of greenery'.[1] As a child he had studied French along with German, Latin, and Greek, and as an adolescent read histories of the revolution; in the library in his quarters in the Kremlin years later could be counted eighty-seven books on French

---

[1] 'Letter, V. I. Lenin to M. A. Ulianova (8 June 1895)', in V. I. Lenin, *Collected Works* (Moscow, 1977), vol. XXXVII, p. 74.

history, many of which concerned the French Revolution.[2] While living in London in the early 1900s, he and Lev Deich, whose politics he would soon condemn as muddleheaded and insufficiently Marxist, in lighter moments playfully referred to one another by the Russian word for citizen, *grazhdanin*, because the French equivalent, *citoyen*, was the preferred salutation during the French Revolution.[3]

More significant, in terms of Lenin's growing proximity to the French Revolution, were contacts he established in the early 1890s, during his conversion to Marxism from the populism he had earlier embraced, largely out of filial loyalty to his older brother Alexander, a *narodovolets* who was executed in 1889 for participating in an unsuccessful attempt to kill the tsar. In 1891 he conversed at length with the Tkachevite, M. I. Iaseneva, in which they discussed, inter alia, the seizure of power in Russia by a revolutionary elite.[4] Between 1887 and 1893 he also befriended *narodovol'tsy* and one-time supporters of both Zaichnevskii and Nechaev.[5] It is quite likely that at least some of these revolutionaries impressed upon the young Lenin the virtues of the personal qualities the original Jacobins embodied, along with their ostensible emphasis on conspiracy and the centralization of political power.[6] But for all of the evidence indicating Lenin's early receptivity to the lessons older revolutionaries had drawn from the French Revolution, one must also bear in mind his cautionary admonition in 1899 that France and Russia were very different. In his words, 'we should never consign Russia's distinctiveness to oblivion'.[7]

In ideological terms, Lenin's first comments on the French Revolution were predictable. In 1895 he described it as a revolution of the bourgeoisie that ended in 1793. He also stated that Babeuf had no chance of taking power under the Directory because the revolution could never embrace, much less impose on an unwilling populace, his more radical objectives.[8] In 1897 he explicitly rejected the conspiratorial tactics practised by both by the Blanquists in France and the *narodovol'tsy* in

---

[2] George Jackson, 'The Influence of the French Revolution on Lenin's Conception of the Russian Revolution', in *The French Revolution of 1789 and its Impact*, edited by G. M. Schwab and John R. Jeanneney (Westport CT, 1995), p. 275; *Biblioteka V. I. Lenina v Kremle* (Moscow, 1961), pp. 242–5.

[3] B. I. Gorev, *Iz partiinogo proshlogo: vospominaniia 1895–1905* (Leningrad, 1924), p. 59.

[4] J. L. H. Keep, *The Rise of Social Democracy in Russia* (London, 1963), p. 34.

[5] Richard Pipes, 'The Origins of Bolshevism: The Intellectual Evolution of Young Lenin', in *Revolutionary Russia: A Symposium*, edited by Richard Pipes (New York, 1969), pp. 36, 42. Pipes calls these associations 'Jacobin'.

[6] It is true, as Robert Mayer asserts in 'Lenin and the Jacobin Identity in Russia', *Studies in Eastern European Thought*, 51 (1999): p. 141, that there is no evidence proving that Lenin was influenced by 'Russian Jacobins' such as Tkachev and his followers. But Lenin's contacts with these individuals is surely proof that he may have been influenced by them. While Lenin's 'Jacobinism', in the sense of his favouring conspiracy and the strict centralization of power in the parties and organizations he was involved in, would not yet manifest itself until the 1900s, there is good reason to believe such ideas were germinating in his mind in the 1890s.

[7] V. I. Lenin, 'Proekt programmy nashei partii (1899)', in V. I. Lenin, *Polnoe sobranie sochinenii* [hereafter rendered as *PSS*], 5th edn, 55 vols (Moscow, 1958–65), vol. V, p. 220.

[8] V. I. Lenin, 'Conspectus of the Book, *The Holy Family* by Marx and Engels', in V. I. Lenin, *Collected Works* (Moscow, 1977), vol. XXXVIII, pp. 23–4.

Russia. Both failed because they lacked popular support.[9] But for the next four years, while commenting occasionally on the role of the proletariat in the 1848 Revolution (he deemed it considerable but insufficient to prevent the revolution's failure) and the French peasantry under Louis Napoleon (it was, predictably, conservative) Lenin wrote nothing and said nothing about the French Revolution itself.[10] Finally, in 1901, he did, but the reason was not to offer an idea or to propose an explanation that had occurred to him spontaneously, but in response to an article Plekhanov had written recently, with which he disagreed especially strongly because he believed it was directed partly at him.

To understand Lenin's rebuttal, one must know something of Plekhanov's views on the French Revolution. It was obvious the latter had thought deeply about it, and considered it relevant to Russia despite a full century having passed since its conclusion. The same was true, albeit to a lesser extent, for Pavel Axelrod, who, with Zasulich and Alexander Potresov, had joined with Plekhanov in 1883 to form the first Marxist organization in Russia, the *Gruppa Osvobozhednie Truda* (Group for the Emancipation of Labour). Lenin and Iulii Martov, both of them a full generation younger, joined the group in the 1890s. In relation to his colleagues, Plekhanov was always *primus inter pares*, and for that reason his opinions on the French Revolution—and on most other matters—the other members usually found persuasive. At the very least, his views were always accorded serious consideration. Complete agreement, however, proved difficult because Plekhanov's views on the French Revolution, and on the Jacobins in particular, changed considerably with the passage of time. At times he attacked the Jacobins. At others he defended them. There were even occasions when he attacked them and defended them simultaneously. Obviously these changes were not inconsequential. What Plekhanov thought at any particular time about the French Revolution played a significant role in determining what he thought about the Russian Revolution.

At times Plekhanov gravitated towards an extreme form of what he and other Marxist revolutionaries—not only Russian ones—called 'Jacobinism', by which was meant a political party organized as a conspiracy, with political authority concentrated in a 'centre' of professional revolutionaries ready to take power when opportunities arose irrespective of the Marxist axiom that the objective conditions that pertained at any particular time imposed limits on what was possible politically. At other times, however, Plekhanov—like Marx before him—argued the opposite: that a socialist party should always seek mass support, but because Russia was an autocracy in which politics of any kind was forbidden, this would

---

[9] V. I. Lenin, 'Zadachi russkikh sotsial-demokratov', in Lenin, *PSS*, vol. II. p. 459.

[10] V. I. Lenin, 'Protest rossiiskikh sotsial demokratov (1899)', *PSS*, vol. IV, p. 169; Lenin, 'Proekt programmy', p. 231.

be very difficult. In addition, the party should welcome differences of opinion, and ensure that while authority was exercised, as it were, from the top down, it should also be informed by the opinions directed from the bottom up. Finally, and perhaps most critically, Plekhanov argued that Russian socialists should not take power prematurely, as he believed the Jacobins had; if they did so, like the Jacobins they would lose power shortly afterwards. After years of oscillating between these two positions—which he and other Russian Marxists habitually termed 'Jacobin' and 'anti-Jacobin' respectively—Plekhanov finally resolved his ambivalence in the aftermath of the 1905 Revolution. For the remainder of his life he never deviated from the opinion that under no circumstances should Russian socialists emulate the Jacobins, and that any socialist party that did so was not really socialist and therefore destined to fail. The circumstances under which the Bolsheviks came to power in 1917 seemed to him tangible confirmation of his conclusion.

But Plekhanov's earlier ambivalence on the whole matter of Jacobinism was characteristic of Russian Marxism as a whole. In explaining this, one might suggest that it reflected the same conflict evident in Marx between the heart and the mind: between wanting desperately, on the one hand, that a proletarian revolution occurred soon enough to enjoy the benefits it would confer—and recognizing on the other hand, in what one imagines were more contemplative moments, that, if Marxism meant anything at all, revolutionaries in Russia who espoused it would be dead long before any such revolution could occur. When Russian Marxism was in its infancy, Russia had not yet experienced a bourgeois revolution, and the industrial capitalism the triumphant bourgeoisie would legitimize could not be avoided or truncated temporally if the proletarian revolution that followed it was to succeed. In short, there were many Russian Marxists, Plekhanov among them, who at times thought the requirements of Marxist ideology could be safely ignored, while on other occasions recognizing that the limits Marxism imposed on what was politically feasible should be adhered to both in the interest of ideological consistency and as a matter of simple prudence and collective self-protection. In short, Russia, in 1900, was hardly ready for a proletarian revolution, a bourgeois revolution, or really any revolution at all.

Plekhanov personified these dichotomous positions perfectly. His activist impulses, when they were triggered for one reason or another, would cause him to praise the Jacobins lavishly. But on other occasions, when for whatever reason he was calmer, he would condemn them for their excessive activism and volun- tarism, for their unfortunate penchant for getting ahead of themselves ideologic- ally and politically. At times, he even appended to strong criticisms of the Jacobins an acknowledgement that on an emotional level he knew what it was like to have been one. Scattered throughout Plekhanov's voluminous writings are examples of this. In 1885 he wrote that while admiring the Jacobins for their personal qualities, he also equated their 'theory of government' with 'a revolutionary dictatorship of the minority'.[11] To be sure, the Blanquists, for all of their courage and heroism, were even worse. Absent mass support, their conspiratorial methods, applied in Russia, would not yield anything beneficial to the Russian proletariat.[12] But worst of all, in Plekhanov's estimation, was how 'the traditions of French Jacobinism' had been transmuted by Tkachev (and *narodovol'tsy* such as Lev Tikhomirov) into a strategy for taking power that, in contrast to that which the original Jacobins had pursued successfully, would lead in Russia to disaster.[13] The problem, as Plekhanov defined it, was that France in 1789 bore little relation to Russia in the late nineteenth century; the latter was far more backward because a much larger percentage of its population consisted of peasants. Moreover, instead of acknowledging this, and fastening on the proletariat as the proper instrument for the achievement of the social justice they claimed to favour, Russian populists and terrorists like the two he singled out for opprobrium had shown recently an exceedingly destructive aversion to political activity of any kind. For that, Plekhanov concluded, the Jacobins deserved at least some of the blame. Indeed, by the time Plekhanov was writing his essay, Russia, in his opinion, was so different from France when the Jacobins controlled it that infantile and shamefully ignorant Russian revolutionaries, by ripping the Jacobins' methods out of their original historical context and misapplying them in ways unimaginable when the Jacobins were alive, were diminishing the Russian revolutionary movement to the point of oblivion.[14] So corrupted by this misuse of history were the likes of Tkachev and Tikhomirov that Plekhanov considered them contemptible both as revolutionaries and as human beings.

In 1888, Plekhanov praised and criticized the Jacobins simultaneously, this time self-referentially, in a letter to Axelrod in which he admitted sheepishly to being something of a Jacobin himself. But since he preferred that that not continue, he told his fellow Marxist that 'it is necessary that you restrain me'.[15] One year later, he expressed his ambivalence in the form of a coherent argument in an essay commemorating the centenary of the French Revolution. He began the essay by acknowledging that while the Jacobin dictatorship was politically necessary and the terror it inflicted morally just, simply repeating in Russia the Jacobin phrase of the French Revolution would be a terrible mistake. The Jacobins, he took pains to emphasize, were hardly exemplary revolutionaries. The tactics they adopted were repugnant, and what to Plekhanov was just as bad, counterproductive of their political and ideological objectives. But he also stressed that, for all of their faults, the Jacobins were neither reactionaries nor counter-revolutionaries. In fact, the

---

[11] G. V. Plekhanov, *Nashi raznoglasiia*, in Plekhanov, *Sochineniia*, vol. II, pp. 294, 330–1.

[12] Ibid., p. 331.   [13] Ibid., p. 158.   [14] Ibid., pp. 329–31.

[15] 'Letter Plekhanov to Axelrod (May 1888)', *Perepiska G. V. Plekhanova i P. B. Aksel'roda*, edited by B. I. Nikolaevskii, P. A. Berlin, and V. S. Voitinskii (Moscow, 1925), vol. I, p. 44. In February 1900 he admitted more or less the same thing, this time describing his Jacobinism as something to which 'I was beginning to incline'. 'Letter, Plekhanov to Axelrod (24 February 1900)', ibid., p. 118.

differences between the Jacobins and their principal rivals, the Girondins, were not reducible to a simple dichotomy of good versus evil. The Girondins, for all their failings, desired freedom and republicanism for France just as much as the Jacobins did, while the Jacobins, for all their professions of moral virtue, established a regime based on force and coercion that led inexorably to despotism. Nevertheless, the Jacobins did what they did not out of any inherent propensity for evil. Under the circumstances, any government run by rational people would probably have done the same. Terror was the only means of defeating the very real foreign enemies the Jacobins faced, and they should not be criticized on moral grounds for employing it.[16]

One might think, after reading the first half of the article, that Plekhanov was calling on Russian socialists to emulate the Jacobins only selectively, adopting all that was virtuous in their personal character, while eschewing all that was counterproductive. But that was not his intention. Following his qualified embrace of Jacobinism as a guide to revolutionary action generically, Plekhanov admonished his readers that Russia in 1889 was vastly different from France a century earlier, and that the Russian proletariat bore obligations that by virtue of its temporal location in the Marxist scenario of history were very different from those that history had imposed on the Jacobins.[17] The working class, he wrote confusingly, must condemn 'the bourgeois spirit of the Great French Revolution', while remaining faithful to the revolutionary spirit he was certain would carry the proletariat well beyond the French Revolution.[18]

The same equivocation was evident in Plekhanov's other early writings on the French Revolution. In one essay, he claimed that Robespierre and Saint-Just failed as revolutionaries because they tried to accelerate the course of history beyond what was then feasible according to the inviolable tenets of Marxist ideology.[19] But he also wrote, a few years after that, that in fighting despotism in Russia—by which Plekhanov clearly meant the regime of Tsar Nicholas II—'dynamite is not a bad weapon, but the guillotine is even better'.[20] To achieve maximum publicity, a facsimile of the French original should be set up in Kazan Square, in the heart of St Petersburg; to achieve maximum effect its victims should include not just the tsar but also his retainers. In sum, 'every Social Democrat ha[s] to be a terrorist like Robespierre'.[21] In more reflective philosophical writings, however, such as his rumination on the role of the individual in history written in 1898, Plekhanov was able to detach himself emotionally from the French Revolution to the point where

---

[16] Plekhanov, 'Stoletie velikoi revoliutsii (1889)', *Sochineniia*, vol. IV, pp. 55–61.

[17] Ibid., pp. 62–7. Pavel Axelrod stuck even more closely and consistently to the Marxist script, stating often, as he did in 1901, that Russia presently was not like France in 1789.

[18] Ibid., p. 65.

[19] G. V. Plekhanov, 'N. G. Chernyshevskii', in Plekhanov, *Sochineniia*, vol. V, p. 57.

[20] Quoted in V. Rumii, 'Plekhanov i terror', *Pod znamenem Marksizma*, no. 6–7 (June–July 1923): p. 24.

[21] Quoted in ibid., p. 32.

he could use it in illustrating his conclusion, which was a synthesis of sorts of the two aspects of his political *persona*, that individuals can affect the timing of events, but not their outcome.[22]

But the synthesis Plekhanov had finally arrived at in 1898 did not last long. Lenin's emergence as a political figure of some significance in the small and incestuous world of Russian socialism forced the Father of Russian Marxism to choose one of the two dichotomous tendencies—the Jacobin and the anti-Jacobin—he seemed to have successfully synthesized. From 1898 to 1903, Plekhanov surrendered to his own Jacobin impulses, and in 1903 supported Lenin's throughout the Second Congress of the RSDLP. Several months later, however, Plekhanov reversed himself, and began excoriating his younger colleague with the same rhetorical abandon with which he had previously defended him. Lenin, whose penchant for venomous rhetoric was unmatched among Russian socialists, responded in kind.

What prompted Lenin to formulate his own views on the French Revolution was Plekhanov's article in 1901 in *Iskra*, the newspaper established the year before of which both men, with four others, were the editors. Plekhanov argued that the conflict in the revolution between the Mountain (by which Plekhanov meant the Jacobins) and the Girondins was analogous to the current division in European and Russian socialism between socialists such as himself, who were faithful to Marxism and thereby furthering the interests of the working class, and socialists in Russia and Europe who in his opinion were betraying Marxism in one way or in multiple ways. Among the latter were the so-called Economists, who believed that addressing the economic needs of workers took precedence over indoctrinating them ideologically, and also the followers of Eduard Bernstein in Germany, who believed socialists could take power peacefully and democratically and should revise their tactics accordingly. Their common betrayal, while substantively different, of what Plekhanov believed to be orthodox Marxist ideology was so obvious that he considered it reason enough to exclude them from the ranks of true socialists.[23]

---

[22] Plekhanov also argued that if Robespierre had been hit on the head by a brick and died, or if Napoleon had been deposed before he completed his plan to dominate Europe, other persons would have emerged to replace them, with the result that while not everything the two men desired would be achieved, much of what they desired would have been achieved, though not nearly as quickly. The same would be true for their demise. Even if both men had retained power longer—Robespierre after 1794, Bonaparte after 1815—eventually each of them would have lost it. G. V. Plekhanov, 'K voprosu roli lichnosti v istorii (1898)', in G. V. Plekhanov, *Izbrannye filosofskie proizvedeniia* (Moscow, 1956), vol. II, pp. 317–26.

[23] G. V. Plekhanov, 'Na poroge dvatsatago veka', *Iskra*, no. 2 (February 1901): p. 1. In a note Lenin appended to a new edition of *What is to be Done?* in 1907, in which he criticized the Mensheviks for their excessive zeal to drawing analogies between 'Jacobinism' and 'Russian Social Democracy', he cited Plekhanov's article as a useful corrective, implying that Plekhanov, unlike the Mensheviks, drew analogies only when they were historically accurate. The one Plekhanov drew in the article appealed to Lenin because it judiciously distinguished genuine revolutionaries (like himself) from 'the opportunists' (by whom he meant the Mensheviks and others occupying 'the right-wing of Social Democracy').

In a speech delivered several months after Plekhanov's article appeared, Lenin did not disagree. What made his speech distinctive, in comparison to his earlier writings, was his invocation of the French Revolution to illustrate and corroborate his own arguments. He began by claiming that the socialists who published the newspaper *Rabochee delo*—by whom he meant socialists sympathetic to the heresies Plekhanov had attacked—were the equivalent of the Girondins, while the editors of *Iskra*—who included Plekhanov and Lenin—were comparable to the Montagnards (by whom Lenin, like Plekhanov, meant the Jacobins). But Lenin now included among the Marxist heretics Plekhanov had earlier attacked the supporters of Alexandre Millerand in France, who in 1899 became the first European socialist to accept a ministerial portfolio in a socialist government. In fact, Lenin seemed as interested in denouncing the ideological crimes of Millerand, Eduard Bernstein, and the Economists as he was in analogizing their transgressions to those of which the Girondins, in the French Revolution, were guilty.[24] Lenin returned to the Jacobin–Girondin dichotomy in April 1902, this time in the course of criticizing Plekhanov for not making clear the sharp distinction Lenin claimed to exist between the 'small producers' in Russia and a genuine proletariat: while both were exploited, the degree and manner of their exploitation were different. Indeed, the same was true for the revolutionaries who claimed to represent them politically. Those representing small producers, who in comparison to the proletariat were a retrograde class, were themselves not really socialists—and thus analogous to the Girondins. Those representing the proletariat, which in comparison to other classes was always the most progressive one, were of course Lenin and his followers, who by analogy were comparable to the Montagnards; increasing the iniquity of these ersatz socialists, Lenin continued, was that, like the original Girondins, they not only represented a retrograde class, but also claimed falsely to represent a progressive class. In short, Lenin's adversaries were both wrong and disingenuous.[25]

To Lenin it was essential that the distinction between genuine socialists and false ones remained clear. Only if that were the case could the latter be prevented from corrupting the proletariat; if in some unfortunate turn of events, they were able to do so, their entire revolutionary endeavour would collapse. The proletariat would never learn to make a revolution which required them to follow professional revolutionaries like Lenin, who knew that the 'trade union consciousness' workers possessed would leave them no better off than if they had no consciousness of

V. I. Lenin, *What is to be Done? Burning Questions of our Movement*, in V. I. Lenin, *Selected Works* (New York, n.d.), vol. II, p. 34.

[24] V. I. Lenin, 'Rech' sentiabria 4: Ob"edinitel'nyi s"ezd zagranichnykh organizatsii RSDRP 21–2 sentiabria (4–5 octiabria) 1901 g.', in Lenin, *PSS*, vol. V, pp. 271–6.
[25] V. I. Lenin, 'Otzyv o vtorom proekte programmy Plekhanova', in Lenin, *PSS*, vol. VI, pp. 237–8.

the world around them whatsoever. Strikes and unions—in which workers with trade-union consciousness invested their hope for a better life—could never help them. Only a political revolution eliminating the capitalism that was the ultimate cause of their exploitation could do that. But Lenin could not instill among Russian workers the revolutionary consciousness they needed to understand this as long as 'neo-Girondins' in Russia and Western Europe could still delude them with counterproductive, non-Marxist notions about evolving into socialism peacefully and democratically.

For this reason it was essential that these modern-day Girondins be unmasked. By claiming to be socialists when they clearly were not, Millerand and Bernstein threatened the entire socialist movement far more than political figures who had never been socialist and had never claimed falsely that they were. Lenin's writings early in the twentieth century fairly brim with denunciations of contemporary socialists who, in his jaundiced opinion, betrayed it. So intent on defaming his political enemies that he ignored simple logic in doing so—Millerand and Bernstein could not have betrayed socialism if they themselves had never been socialists—Lenin found in the Jacobin–Girondin polarity the perfect analogy to illustrate the depths and the historical provenance of his enemies' depravity. To act in the tradition the Girondins began was to reveal a degree of apostasy that Lenin might have inveighed against with such vehemence not in spite his own ideological heresies, which he would express publicly in 1902 in *What is to be Done?*, but rather because of them. Lenin's own betrayal of Marxism would be obscured by focusing on the far greater betrayal of his enemies. This, at any rate, was the strategy Lenin adopted.

And so Lenin, in 1900, began analogizing various Russian and European socialists he disliked and feared—not just Millerand and Bernstein and the Russian economists—to the Girondins. He did so, quite clearly, to underscore their mendacity while simultaneously shielding his own, rather than to suggest any larger analogy between the French Revolution and the revolution he anticipated in Russia. But charges after the split occurred in the RSDLP that he was a putative Robespierre, waiting in the wings until he could drown Russian socialism in a sea of blood, forced him to immerse himself much further than he ever had before in the events in France after 1789, and then to use them rhetorically in defending himself.

*   *   *

The Second Congress of the RSDLP crystallized and confirmed for many Russian socialists the suspicion they had harboured since Lenin first involved himself in revolutionary politics that he was, in the vocabulary of the French Revolution, a Jacobin: that he shared the Jacobins' supposed penchant for conspiracy and secrecy, their intolerance of dissent and disagreement, and their limitless lust for power. At times, Lenin's conduct at the congress seemed to suggest—as was the case for the Jacobins—that the very purity of his objectives imposed no ethical limits on the means he might use to achieve them. Not even violence or coercion or mass terror should be excluded a priori.[26] As it happened, the purpose of the congress—which reconvened in London after the Belgian government, under pressure from the Russian government, was about to arrest its participants, who had originally gathered in Brussels—was to create a unified socialist party; groups sending representatives were as diverse in their objectives and ethnic identity as the economist-minded newspaper *Rabochee delo*, the Jewish Bund, and Latvian and Polish socialists. But the result was the opposite: the socialist party that emerged did not include the Bundists, among others, and it was immediately riven by bitter disagreements impervious to compromise.

Lenin and Plekhanov bore much of the responsibility for this. Lenin, as one of the six editors of *Iskra*, which everyone agreed would be the new party's public face, had succeeded in packing the congress with supporters who shared his preference for hard-nosed tactics; no less important was the agreement of all the editors that the gradualism Bernstein was advocating in Germany posed a grave danger to the whole endeavour of overthrowing the monarchy in a bourgeois revolution and then, at some point in the future, overthrowing the bourgeoisie in a proletarian revolution. At first, Lenin failed to convince the delegates to approve a definition of party membership slightly more 'Jacobin'—in the sense of limiting membership to 'participants' in the party's business—than Iulii Martov's defin-ition, which would ensure a somewhat larger party, and one less easily controlled from the centre, by providing membership to 'supporters' of the party. But after Jewish Bundists and two delegates representing *Rabochee delo* left the congress for reasons of their own, Lenin found himself with a working majority that approved his proposal to reduce membership on the newly created Central Organ, which would run the party, from six to three. Since it was assumed that the six-person editorial board of *Iskra* would constitute this central organ, its reduction by half required the same of the editorial board. The result was that Plekhanov, Martov, and Lenin were designated to run both institutions. With Plekhanov in one of his 'Jacobin' phases, when his views were generally in alignment with Lenin's, the latter did not need Martov's support to secure a majority in either of them. To all intents and purposes, Lenin was now, if not the leader of the RSDLP, then certainly *primus inter pares*. Fully cognizant of his new status, Lenin dubbed his followers at the congress 'Bolsheviks', or people of the majority, to distinguish them from his detractors, whom he shrewdly dubbed 'Mensheviks', or people in the minority. Foolishly, those so derogated accepted the descriptive, and to their detriment both descriptives proved to be permanent.

---

[26] It is true that in 1902 in *What is to be Done?*, Lenin had translated the authoritarianism others sensed in his temperament into a conception of how a revolutionary party should be organized that stressed the necessity of hierarchy and strict obedience once its policies had been determined. But the negative reaction among many Russian socialists paled in comparison to what it would be to Lenin's actions at the Second Congress one year later.

While powerless to stop Lenin from splitting the party, his numerous antagonists wasted little time in denouncing him for doing so. In their diatribes, allusions to the French Revolution were common. The Economist Vladimir Akimov declared that the authoritarianism Lenin (and Plekhanov) had revealed at the congress smacked of Jacobinism, and that, if unchecked, could lead to the application of terror. In contrast to Lenin, who considered the Jacobins and the Blanquists polar opposites, by claiming that both of these terms were descriptive of Lenin Akimov made clear that, as far as he was concerned, there was little difference between them; both the Jacobins and the Blanquists were either openly or surreptitiously authoritarian.[27] But to Akimov, this was hardly cause for despondency. His derogation of Lenin was a warning, not a prediction. Russian socialism was strong enough to ensure Lenin's eventual demise, after which he would be as powerless as Blanqui and the Blanquists had been through much of the nineteenth century. For Akimov, French history demonstrated how a revolutionary movement could turn bad, but it also showed that it could remain strong as long as unscrupulous individuals intent on betraying it did not take power (as was true of the Blanquists), or if they did, be forced to relinquish it (which was true of the Jacobins and would the case for Lenin).[28]

Akimov was a minor figure in Russian socialism. Far more influential was Iulii Martov, whose criticisms of Lenin following the congress were taken especially seriously because of the longstanding friendship between the two men, which was now severely tested, and in fact would never be repaired.[29] Martov had been interested in the French Revolution and in the revolutions in France that followed it even before his conversion to Marxism. As a youth he read Herzen and Victor Hugo, and in his memoirs mentioned his infatuation with Mirabeau, the Girondins, Danton, and Robespierre; he also found the speeches of Desmoulins, Hébert, and Babeuf inspirational.[30] As a university student in St Petersburg, he mostly ignored debates over whether Russia had to experience industrial capitalism before advancing to socialism. To establish one's credentials as a revolutionary, it was enough simply to commit oneself to socialism, and to recognize that only through 'a Jacobin revolution' could socialism be achieved. This, at any rate, was

---

[27] V. P. Makhnovets [V. Akimov], *K voprosu o rabotakh II-go s"ezda* (Geneva, 1904), pp. 41–2; V. P. Makhnovets', *Ocherk razvitiia sotsialdemokratii* (St Petersburg, 1905), p. 141.

[28] Makhnovets, *K voprosu o rabotakh*, p. 42.

[29] When Martov was mortally ill in the early 1920s, Lenin, perhaps recalling their friendship in the 1890s, ordered for him the finest medical treatment despite his strenuous criticism—which included charges of Jacobinism—of Lenin's new regime. The Soviet government, moreover, only subjected Martov to house arrest, rather than imprisonment, or worse. But Lenin's agreeing to Martov's subsequent request to leave the Soviet Union permanently was hardly motivated by fond memories. Rather, Lenin calculated that whatever influence Martov still exerted would be minimal if he were abroad. Israel Getzler, *Martov: A Political Biography of a Russian Social Democrat* (London and New York, 1967), pp. 207–8.

[30] Ibid., pp. 6–7; Iu. O. Martov, *Zapiski sotsial-demokrata* (Berlin, 1922), p. 48.

how he explained his political maturation in his memoirs.[31] What Martov evidently meant by a Jacobin revolution was a *coup d'état* by professional revolutionaries following an orchestrated campaign of terrorism designed to reduce the capacity of the government to defend itself.

By 1900 Martov had changed his mind. He now rejected as a recipe for authoritarianism and dictatorship the Jacobinism he had previously praised. And by 1904, he was condemning Lenin as its most obvious personification in Russian Social Democracy. While in November 1903, in a letter to Axelrod describing Lenin's losing control of *Iskra*, Martov had referred to Plekhanov's calling Lenin 'Robespierre' without either endorsing or rejecting this appellation, in 1904 he made clear that his opinion was now identical to Plekhanov's. Everyone in the newly created RSDLP who believed it functioned best in a state of siege, with political authority strictly centralized, Martov attacked bitterly as *Robesp'erchiki* ('adherents of Robespierre'); that his actual target was Lenin was unmistakable.[32] In a letter to Axelrod in October 1905 expressing concern about a seizure of power in St Petersburg, where the government had been rendered virtually powerless by the general strike that had paralysed the city, Martov stated flatly that the worst possible outcome for Russia would be a Jacobin dictatorship.[33]

Yet another socialist who invoked the French Revolution to condemn Lenin for his authoritarianism was Leon Trotsky. It took time for Trotsky, as it did for Martov, to acknowledge this, and then to attack Lenin publicly. At the Second Congress, in defending the *Iskra* editorial board against Akimov's accusation, repeated by Alexander Martynov, that its actions resembled those of the Jacobins, Trotsky, in effect, turned their accusation into praise by expressing his approval of the Jacobinism Akimov and Martynov had condemned.[34] And to Akimov's description of the proletarian dictatorship he feared Lenin wanted to establish as 'an act of Jacobinism', Trotsky responded that Russian socialists had nothing to worry about.[35] A proletarian dictatorship, he wrote, would not be the consequence of any 'conspiratorial seizure of power', but rather 'the political rule of the organised working class, which will then constitute the majority of the nation'.[36] But once Trotsky considered seriously the implications of Lenin's actions at the congress, he denounced them. In a summary of the proceedings he prepared for the organization from Siberia he had represented at the congress, Trotsky

[31] Martov, *Zapiski*, pp. 94, 98.
[32] 'Pis'mo Iu. Martova k P. B. Aksel'rodu (4 November 1903)', *Pis'ma P. B. Aksel'roda i Iu. O. Martova, 1901–1916*, edited by F. Dan, B. Nikolaevskii, and L. Tsederbaum-Dan (The Hague, 1967), p. 97; Iu. O. Martov, *Bor'ba s 'osadnym' polozheniem' v Rossiiskoi sotsial'demokratovskoi rabochei partii: otvet na pis'mo n. Lenina* (Geneva, 1904), p. 10.
[33] 'Pis'mo Iu. O. Martova k P. B. Aksel'rodu', *Pis'ma P. B. Aksel'roda i Iu. O. Martov*, p. 146.
[34] Isaac Deutscher, *The Prophet Armed: Trotsky. 1879–1921* (New York, 1954), p. 76.
[35] Quoted in Jonathan Frankel, ed., *Vladimir Akimov on the Dilemma of Russian Marxism 1895–1903* (Cambridge, 1969), p. 94.
[36] Ibid.

castigated Lenin as 'a Robespierre [who] transformed the modest [Party] Council into an all-powerful Committee of Public Safety'.[37] Just like the leader of the Jacobins, Lenin was leading his followers, and the newly established party as a whole, to disaster. By so thoroughly centralizing political authority, Lenin was making divisions within it more likely. Even worse, the authoritarian temperament Lenin shared with Robespierre explained why each of them was capable of using violence to achieve his objectives. Robespierre, of course, had already done so, while Lenin's killings were still hypothetical. But that did not diminish the danger Lenin's centralism posed to the party, which in Trotsky's opinion could easily degenerate into an actual dictatorship should the party lead the proletariat in a successful revolution and then take power itself, rather than relinquish leadership to the proletariat. This of course could not be permitted under any circumstances.

But this particular scenario could not occur for quite some time, and in any event Trotsky's references to Robespierre and the Jacobins were intended to illustrate that Lenin's centralism was dangerous, rather than that it actually replicated that of the Jacobins. Unlike Lenin in 1903, the Jacobins controlled a country and exercised real power. At some point in the future, Lenin might be in the same position and do the terrible things the Jacobins had done. Then again, he might not. For that reason Trotsky carefully refrained from asserting any analogy or similarity between the French and the Russian situations, while claiming simultaneously that Lenin resembled Robespierre only in caricature. Paraphrasing Marx's famous remark about Louis Napoleon, Trotsky concluded that Lenin differed from Robespierre roughly 'as a vulgar farce differs from a historical tragedy'.[38]

In 1904, Trotsky composed a pamphlet entitled, in English translation, *Our Political Tasks*, in which he responded to Lenin's recent comments praising the Jacobins and Jacobinism by fleshing out his earlier explanation why French Jacobinism and Russian Social Democracy were mutually exclusive. These two

---

[37] L. Trotsky, *Vtoroi s''ezd RSDRP (Otchet Simbirskii delegatsii)* (Geneva, 1903), p. 29.

[38] Ibid., p. 33. Trotsky, who prior to the summer of 1917 ostentatiously refused to become a Bolshevik—or to join any other organization or party within the larger rubric of Russian socialism—understandably had good reason to pretend, after finally becoming a Bolshevik, that his differences with Lenin were minimal, and in any case had been misunderstood and exaggerated. In his biographical sketch written three months after Lenin's death in 1924 which Trotsky intended as a general introduction to a full-scale biography of the Soviet leader, which he never completed, Trotsky repeated Plekhanov's condemnation of Lenin—that he possessed 'the stuff of which Robespierres are made'—but offered none of his own. Leon Trotsky, *Lenin: Notes for a Biographer* (New York, 1971), pp. 8–9, 69. In 1927, in an article entitled 'Thermidor' explaining its relationship to the French Revolution itself, Trotsky chose to deal with the matter of his differences with Lenin more directly, now acknowledging that the latter had been right all along in claiming 'continuity' between the Jacobins and the Bolsheviks. The article is reprinted in Leon Trotsky, *The Challenge of the Left Opposition* [hereafter rendered as *CLO* followed by the year or years] *1926–27* (New York, 1980), p. 263.

historical phenomena, he maintained, were, in fact, so radically different that any useful comparison between them was impossible. In Trotsky's words:

> Jacobinism is not a supra-social 'revolutionary' category but a historical product. Jacobinism is the highest moment reached by the tension of revolutionary energy during the period of the self-emancipation of bourgeois society. It is the maximum radicalism which can be produced by bourgeois society—not by the development of its internal contradictions but by the suppression and stifling of these: in theory, by appealing to the rights of the abstract man and the abstract citizen, in practice, with the help of the guillotine.[39]

Trotsky went on to explain in more detail why the Jacobins had failed. Because they proclaimed the universality of their political principles, the Jacobins, through their rhetoric—which masked their indebtedness to the particular class from which they originated and to which they still belonged—energized nearly everyone who opposed them, with the result that they were forced to rule by terror, which turned out to be the most proximate reason for their subsequent demise. Of course the Jacobins were not the only actors in the French Revolution who failed. So, too, did the Abbé de Sieyès, whose conviction, which resembled Lenin's, that power in any political institution should 'come from above' caused him to lose power in 1799 to Napoleon.[40] But none of this, in what it might portend for Russian Social Democracy, should be worrisome. Because Russian socialists would likely keep their goals in consonance with what was politically possible, the application of terror would be unnecessary:

> [The Jacobins] were utopians; we aspire to express objective tendencies. They were idealists from foot to head; we are materialists from head to foot. They were rationalists; we are dialecticians. They believed in the saving force of a supra-class truth before which everyone should kneel. We believe only in the class force of the revolutionary proletariat.... Their method was to guillotine the slightest deviations; ours is to overcome differences ideologically and politically. They cut off heads; we enlighten them with class consciousness.[41]

To be sure, Trotsky freely acknowledged in his pamphlet that the Jacobins and Russian socialists were similar. Both fought resolutely against the heresies of reformism and opportunism. And while Russian socialists would never inflict indiscriminate terror on an entire population, as the Jacobins had done, Trotsky could not promise that Lenin would not follow the Jacobins' example. Robespierre's aphorism that there are only two kinds of citizens in a body politics, virtuous

---

[39] L. Trotsky, *Nashi politicheskie zadachi* (Geneva, 1904); *L. D. Trotsky o partii v 1904 g.* (Moscow/Leningrad, 1928), p. 183.

[40] Trotsky did not cite Napoleon's coup as the specific cause for the failure for which he held Sieyès' centralism responsible, but this is almost certainly what he had in mind.

[41] Ibid., p. 184.

ones and evil ones, was 'engraved on the heart of "Maximilien Lenin"', whose temperamental affinity for the tactics the Jacobins had employed could only lead the RSDLP to disaster.[42] But the two phenomena themselves, Jacobinism and Russian Social Democracy, because they emerged at different times in history, were fundamentally and irreconcilably different. To claim otherwise was not only false but a perversion of language. In fact, if Jacobinism should come to pervade Russian Social Democracy in its entirety, a different term would be needed to describe it.

It was certainly possible, according to Trotsky, that individuals plausibly claiming to be socialists and orthodox Marxists could manifest personal qualities consistent with those of the original Jacobins. Lenin, of course, was the perfect example of such a person, and it was obviously with Lenin in mind that Trotsky spoke passionately, though also only hypothetically, about the party organization substituting itself for the party, the Central Committee substituting itself for the organization, and finally a dictator, presumably Lenin, substituting himself for the Central Committee.[43] But Trotsky's celebrated strictures on the dangers of centralism (or Jacobinism) were intended more as warnings than as predictions. Because they were Marxists, Russian Social Democrats were not like the Jacobins, as a result of which '[their] attitude towards elemental social forces, and therefore towards the future, is one of revolutionary confidence'.[44] At most, Jacobinism would remain a political tendency in Russian socialism, but one that had little chance of perverting or preventing a proletarian revolution. As on so many other occasions throughout his career, Trotsky's powerful intellect and historical consciousness enabled him, in 1903 and 1904, to sense danger in the course the Bolsheviks were following, only to dismiss the danger as illusory out of an unshakable optimism about the objective laws of history—and an equally unshakeable confidence in the veracity and persuasive power of his own views. Having raised the disturbing precedent of the Jacobins, Trotsky ended up rejecting it.

The next time Trotsky addressed the whole issue of Jacobinism was in 1906, not long after the 1905 Revolution had ended in failure. For Trotsky, however, the revolution was not without its benefits. As chairman of the St Petersburg Soviet of Workers' Deputies, Trotsky had the opportunity to demonstrate his oratorical ability. What is more, the revolution prompted Trotsky to conjure a scenario of revolutions so close to one another temporally as to constitute a single, continuous revolution. In the sequence of events Marx and Engels had proposed and that their followers, with few exceptions, considered inescapable, the bourgeois revolution that ended feudalism would produce an ersatz democracy, controlled by the bourgeoisie, that would delude the proletariat (and the lower strata of the peasantry)

[42] Ibid. p. 190.   [43] Ibid., p. 127.   [44] Ibid., p. 187.

into believing that the bourgeoisie was attentive to their interests and committed to their material and spiritual improvement. Moreover, it would take decades, even centuries perhaps, for the proletariat, as its economic condition worsened, to realize that this democracy was just a ruse intended to perpetuate the economic supremacy of the bourgeoisie. Finally, it would do so, and at that point the bourgeoisie's destruction in a proletarian revolution would be imminent.

Because Marx and Engels considered history impervious to anything that might cause it to deviate from its predetermined path, it followed logically that history could not be rushed. But Trotsky, in 1905, was a revolutionary in a hurry, and the speed at which he wanted history to proceed got the better of his Marxist determinism. What he did, in stating the course he believed history could follow in Russia, was to merge the bourgeois and proletarian revolutions into one continuous revolution, in which the proletariat would take from the bourgeoisie the political power it had just wrested from the aristocracy, and together the proletariat and the most progressive elements of the peasantry—led, of course, by professional revolutionaries like Trotsky himself—would establish socialism in Russia. The only caveat Trotsky included in his extraordinarily optimistic—and ideologically heterodox—scenario was that there be simultaneous proletarian revolutions in Western Europe enabling the proletariat there to assist its Russian equivalent should its assistance be necessary. In this way, the entire period in Russia's history during which the bourgeoisie held power would be compressed into a matter of weeks, days, or even hours. In fact, Trotsky even allowed, if only by implication, for the possibility that the bourgeoisie, by conferring on the proletariat and the peasantry the responsibility of carrying out the bourgeois revolution, would never exercise power at all. In other words, the proletariat and the peasantry, instead of participating alongside the bourgeoisie in the bourgeois revolution, would carry out the revolution without it.

It seemed to follow from Trotsky's scenario that analogies with the French Revolution were entirely invalid. In *Itogii i perspektivy* (*Results and Prospects*), written in 1906, he made clear that this was precisely what he wanted his followers to believe. 'History', he said, 'does not repeat itself. However much the Russian Revolution can be compared with the Great French Revolution, the former can never be transformed into a repetition of the latter.'[45] Indeed, the differences between the French Revolution, as all Marxists considered it, and Trotsky's theory of Permanent Revolution—as it came to be known—were obvious. While in the French Revolution, it was the bourgeoisie that ended feudalism, in Trotsky's vision of the future Russian Revolution the proletariat and the peasantry would either join with the bourgeoisie in ending feudalism, or achieve the same objective on their own. And while in the French Revolution the Jacobins' attempt to radicalize

---

[45] L. Trotsky, *Itogi i perspektivy* (Moscow, 1919), p. 25.

it ended in failure, in the Russian Revolution, in Trotsky's prognostication, the proletariat's attempt to radicalize it would succeed.

What this implies about the possibility of Jacobinism in the Russian Revolution is rather subtle. To the extent that the Jacobins in France were unable to remain in power after wresting it from the bourgeoisie, Russian socialists would be well advised not to imitate them. But to the extent that the Jacobins succeeded in taking power from the bourgeoisie, and then attempted to make the French Revolution something more than what it was, Russian socialists, while avoiding the Jacobins' mistakes, should nevertheless honor their noble intentions, apply to their own situation the insights the Jacobins had gained from their experience, and find psychological sustenance in the epic saga of their rise and fall. That the Jacobins' failure, no less than their success, was inevitable hardly detracted from the precedent of heroism and martyrdom they left behind. The legerdemain with which Trotsky, in 1906, defended the Jacobins against accusations that he, among others, had expressed just a few years earlier, is clear in the following passage from *Results and Prospects*:

> Jacobinism is now a term of reproach on the lips of all liberal wiseacres. Bourgeois hatred of revolution, its hatred of the masses and of the force and grandeur of the history that is made in the streets, is concentrated in one cry of indignation and fear—Jacobinism! We, the world army of Communism, long ago made our historical reckoning with Jacobinism.... We subjected its theories to criticism, we exposed its historical limitations, we unmasked its social contradictions, its utopianism, and its phraseology, and we broke with its traditions, which for decades had been regarded as the sacred heritage of the revolution.
>
> But we come to the defence of Jacobinism against the attacks, the slander, and the mindless vituperation of anemic, phlegmatic liberalism. The bourgeoisie has shamefully betrayed all the traditions of its historical youth, and its current lackeys dishonour the graves of its ancestors and scoff at the ashes of their ideals.... However radically the proletariat may have broken in practice with the revolutionary traditions of the bourgeoisie, it nevertheless preserves them as a heritage of great passion, heroism, and initiative, and in its heart beats sympathetically with the speeches and the acts of the Jacobin Convention.[46]

Without saying so explicitly, Trotsky has now qualified significantly his earlier strictures both on emulating the Jacobins and on drawing analogies with the French Revolution. Perhaps a Russian Robespierre—irrespective of whether Lenin would assume that particular role—would be a good thing for Russian Social Democracy.

Other Russian socialists, however, had no second thoughts about Lenin's authoritarianism and the harm it might inflict on Russian Social Democracy.

---

[46] Ibid., pp. 26–7.

Some, like Vera Zasulich, condemned what they saw as Lenin's dictatorial proclivities without referring to the Jacobins or the French Revolution.[47] Conversely, socialists who were not Russian sometimes cited the revolution in doing so. The most prominent was Rosa Luxemburg, who, in the course of her career, which ended prematurely with her assassination in Germany in 1919, involved herself in varying degrees in German, Polish, and Russian socialism. Although she did not attend the Second Congress, she knew enough about Lenin from his writings to recognize that they were entirely consistent with what she had learned from others about his actions at the Congress. A year later, she summarized her objections in an article published both in *Neue Zeit*, the official organ of the German Social Democratic Party, and in *Iskra*, on the editorial board of which Lenin was still a member, though regularly outvoted now because of Plekhanov's recent repudiation of the hard line he had followed at the congress in favour of a softer one.[48] In the article, Luxemburg argued that any parties and organizations Social Democrats created should be different from those of the Jacobins and the Blanquists. This was because the Jacobins and, to an even greater extent, the Blanquists separated themselves politically from the classes and categories of the population they claimed to represent; the result, in the case of the Jacobins, was a revolutionary elite that claimed to rule in ways that helped the people while actually harming them. The Blanquists, of course, never gained power, but the implication of what Luxemburg wrote about them was that, if they had taken power, they, too, would soon have ignored the interests of whichever segment of the population supported them.

In Luxemburg's opinion, Lenin was no different. Both his personality and his actions bespoke a genuine authoritarianism, and one can consider her more extensive, more impassioned, and ultimately more prophetic denunciation in 1918 of the Soviet state of a piece with what she had written in 1904.[49] Luxemburg and Pavel Axelrod were the first socialists to sense Lenin's authoritarianism, the first to recognize that he might never honour the promises he made to transfer political authority to the workers once they had acquired the political consciousness sufficient to carry out a socialist revolution. But one must be careful in stating precisely what it was about Lenin that Luxemburg, both in 1904 and in 1918, was rejecting. It was not a centralized party per se. Nor was it the notion of the party as

[47] She did, however, compare Lenin to Louis XIV, analogizing the latter's identification of himself with the state ('*L'état c'est moi*') with what she considered the former's proprietary designs on the newly created RSDLP. Vera Zasulich, 'Organizatsiia, partiia, dvizhenie', *Iskra*, no. 70 (25 July 1904): pp. 4–6. See also Vera Zasulich, 'K istorii vtorogo s"ezda (5 November 1904)', *Katorga i ssylka*, no. 7–8 (1926): pp. 128–30.
[48] R. Luxemburg, 'Organizatsionnye voprosy russkoi sotsial demokratii', *Iskra*, no. 69 (10 July 1904): pp. 2–7. The essay has been published in English translation as 'Leninism vs. Marxism', in Rosa Luxemburg, *The Russian Revolution and Leninism or Marxism?* (Ann Arbor MI, 1972), pp. 81–108.
[49] Luxemburg, *Russian Revolution*, pp. 25–80.

the 'vanguard' of the proletariat. When the RSDLP was established, Luxemburg, no less than Lenin, recognized that the workers lacked political consciousness and were thus susceptible to the two deviations from Marxism orthodoxy, Economism and Bernstein's evolutionary socialism, that Lenin and Plekhanov had denounced. However, Lenin's deviation from Marxist orthodoxy, as Luxemburg saw it, was entirely different, and in terms of the future of the party, even more dangerous: instead of perpetuating the unequal relationship between the workers and the professional revolutionaries until it could be reversed once the former had gained from the latter the knowledge of Marxist ideology they needed to make a successful revolution, the future Soviet leader was acting in ways that might soon sever this relationship entirely. As a result, the revolution Luxemburg believed in 1904 would occur in the distant future would not be a revolution at all. Instead, it would be what it was in 1917, namely a *coup d'état* masquerading as an urban insurrection, claiming falsely not just to represent the proletariat, but actually, in some fashion, to embody it.

Although it took some time, in Plekhanov's case, for Lenin's behaviour at the Second Congress to have a similar effect, once he reversed his opinion, he attacked Lenin loudly and repeatedly. In the immediate aftermath of the Second Congress, Lenin still had no reason to doubt Plekhanov's loyalty, or his continued belief in the efficacy of the Jacobinism many of his colleagues had already condemned. In an article in *Iskra* in September 1903, Plekhanov argued that the Terror in the French Revolution, which he now construed to include the storming of the Bastille in 1789, had mass support.[50] Terror on behalf of the masses, he argued, was often inspirational, and thus could reinvigorate a revolution showing signs of slowing down. For that reason, Russian revolutionaries would be wise to study carefully the terror the plebeians of Paris employed in 1789, because by doing so they would be better able 'to storm our own, our all-Russian Bastille'.[51] But two months later, he came to question the Jacobinism he had previously praised— which in turn caused his good opinion of Lenin to disappear. Whether Plekhanov's less favourable opinion of the Jacobins caused the change in how he viewed Lenin, or whether his less favourable opinion of Lenin caused the change in how he viewed the Jacobins, is unclear. But the result was undeniable. When Lenin lost control of *Iskra* in November 1903, Plekhanov analogized his defeat to Robespierre's, and not even the implication in his analogy that losing control of a newspaper was somehow comparable to arrest and execution seemed to bother him or to cause him to question the analogy after proposing it.[52] In reality, Plekhanov's oscillations in the matter of the Jacobins continued. In 1906 he argued that 'Jacobins without popular support are pitiable', and that Russian

---

[50] G. V. Plekhanov, 'Belyi terror', in Plekhanov, *Sochineniia*, vol. XII, pp. 449–50.
[51] Ibid., p. 450.   [52] Mayer, 'Lenin and the Jacobin Identity', p. 143.

socialists would do better preparing the latter for a popular revolution.[53] But he also saw no need to revise his earlier view, in his article on the centenary of the French Revolution, that only the Jacobins could have saved it from destruction in 1793, prior to the article's reissue, also in 1906, in St Petersburg.[54]

Implicit in Plekhanov's argument was that the Jacobins were not only revolutionaries but also French patriots espousing a kind of revolutionary nationalism similar to that which would cause him, in 1914, to favour Russia's participation in the First World War. In fact, in November 1917, barely a month after the October Revolution, in a letter his wife wrote that one of his biographers claims to reflect accurately Plekhanov's views when she wrote it, Lenin was condemned for allowing Russia 'to be torn to pieces' by foreign enemies, unlike the Jacobins in the Convention, who to their credit had prevented the same thing from happening to France.[55] But after 1906 other issues, such as how socialists should respond to the outbreak of war in 1914, assumed greater significance, and Plekhanov's comments on the Jacobins and the French Revolution diminished accordingly.

Plekhanov's apostasy in the fall of 1903 infuriated Lenin. But it was actually Pavel Axelrod who prompted the Bolshevik leader finally to address the accusation of authoritarianism publicly. In 1904, in an article in *Iskra* that because of its length appeared serially in two issues of the newspaper, Axelrod, without mentioning Robespierre or the Jacobins, described Lenin pejoratively in terms many Russian socialists would understand.[56] Axelrod stated his objections to Lenin clearly and emphatically. If allowed to accumulate even greater power than he already had, Lenin would destroy everything that made socialism virtuous. And the reason for this was that Lenin made a 'fetish' of his centralism.[57] According to Axelrod, centralizing political authority within the party was not necessarily a bad thing. In 1905, when Russia was actually experiencing a revolution, he advocated the creation of 'central clubs' modelled on the Jacobins' that would 'rally the proletariat and form a strong revolutionary atmosphere'.[58] But until a revolution occurred, Russian socialists had to recognize and accept the harsh reality that with

[53] G. V. Plekhanov, 'Pis'ma o taktike i bestaktnosti (June 1906)', in Plekhanov, *Sochineniia*, vol. XV, p. 110.
[54] G. V. Plekhanov, *Stoletie velikoi revoliutsii* (St Petersburg, 1906).
[55] Samuel H. Baron, *Plekhanov: The Father of Russian Marxism* (Stanford CA, 1963), p. 358.
[56] P. B. Axelrod, 'Ob"edinenie rossiiskoi sotsialdemokratii i eia zadachi', *Iskra*, no. 55 (15 December 1903): pp. 1–4 and no. 57 (15 January 1904): pp. 2–4. In 1921 Axelrod repeated these arguments, and acknowledged that they were identical to those he first made in 1903 and 1904. In 1921, however, he dressed them explicitly in the language of the French Revolution, arguing that 'the Jacobinism of the Bolsheviks [was] a tragic parody of its original'. 'Tov. P. B. Aksel'rod o bol'shevisme i bor'be s nim!' *Sotsialisticheskii vestnik*, no. 6 (20 April 1921): pp. 3–7, and no. 7 (4 May 1921): pp. 4–5. Two years earlier he had added to his original indictment that Lenin split the RSDLP in 1903 not over anything substantive but only to accumulate power, the additional derogation that this was the result of Lenin's 'Bonapartism'. After the October Revolution he also termed the new Bolshevik regime as a whole to be 'tsarist-Bonapartist'. Naarden, *Socialist Europe and Revolutionary Russia*, p. 302.
[57] Axelrod, 'Ob"edinenie rossiiskoi sotsialdemokratii i eia zadachi' (1904), p. 4.
[58] P. B. Axelrod, *Narodnaia duma i rabochii s"ezd* (Geneva, 1905), p. 8.

their leaders almost entirely in emigration and their influence in Russia practically nil, a measure of centralism in how party cells inside Russia were organized was still essential. But in this sense there could be too much of a good thing—and it was Lenin, more than anyone else in the party, who could ensure that that would happen. His authoritarian temperament, combined with an iron will and an intolerance of opposing points of view, was a real and present danger to all that was best in socialism. In fact, should a party led by Lenin take power in Russia, it would quickly degenerate into a ruthless and brutal dictatorship.[59]

Barely four months after his denunciation of Lenin in *Iskra*, Axelrod amplified his earlier criticisms in another article, also in *Iskra*, which he felt compelled to write after receiving a letter from Karl Kautsky in which the German socialist showed what Axelrod considered a woeful lack of understanding of what distinguished Mensheviks from Bolsheviks.[60] In the article Axelrod remarked that Lenin's emphasis on discipline and centralism reminded him of Blanquism and Jacobinism.[61] But not even the authoritarianism these terms implied could fully capture the danger Lenin posed to the moral fibre of Russian Social Democracy; the only analogy Axelrod could conjure was that the Bolshevik leader, both in his views and in his temperament, resembled 'the bureaucratic-autocratic system of the (tsarist) Ministry of the Interior'.[62] Although the emphasis in the article was obviously on Lenin's dictatorial proclivities, there is also evident the rudiments of the argument that not everything that happened in the French Revolution was salubrious, and that the Jacobins' penchant for repression and hostility to any free expression of opinion were as abhorrent as the worst excrescences of tsarist autocracy.

By the time Axelrod had written this, Lenin had preemptively unleashed his rhetorical fusillades in an essay entitled, in English translation, *One Step Forward, Two Steps Back (The Crisis in our Party)*, which was published as a book in Geneva in May 1904.[63] It was more a polemic than a calm and carefully considered exegesis. Its intent was to defame rather than to illuminate. But it nonetheless

---

[59] In 1925 the Menshevik P. A. Garvi credited Axelrod with identifying and calling attention to what Garvi called Lenin's 'Bonapartist habits', and praised the striking similarities Alexrod had seen between Lenin's conception of a socialist party and the Jacobin clubs, with their conspiratorial methods and centralized organization. P. A. Garvi, 'P. B. Aksel'rod i Men'shevizm', *Sotsialisticheskii vestnik*, no. 109–10 (1925): pp. 11–12. Garvi's low opinion of both Napoleon and the Jacobins, however, did not vitiate his longstanding admiration for the original French Revolution. While living in Paris in emigration after the October Revolution he made a point of visiting the site of the Bastille on Bastille Day because the holiday was 'an echo of a heroic past and a living, breathing expression of freedom'. P. A. Garvi, *Vospominaniia Sotsialdemokrata: stat'i o zhizni i deiatel'nosti* (New York, 1946), p. 400.

[60] P. Axelrod, 'K voprosu ob istochnike i znachenii nashikh organizatsionnykh rasnoglasii', *Iskra*, no. 68 (25 June 1904): p. 2.

[61] Ibid.

[62] Ibid. For the sequence of events that prompted Axelrod to write the article, see Ascher, *Pavel Axelrod*, pp. 210–11.

[63] V. I. Lenin, *Shag vpered, dva shaga nazad (Krizis v nashei partii)*, in Lenin, *PSS*, vol. VIII, pp. 185–414.

contained a serious argument. Since the publication of *What is to be Done?*, Lenin had maintained in his mind a vision of how a revolutionary party in Russia should be organized and administered in order to survive under a repressive autocracy. At this point in life, the future founder of the Soviet state did not think much beyond the party's survival. The tsarist autocracy was too strong, and the Russian proletariat too weak and politically illiterate for him to conceive of scenarios in which the RSDLP might somehow seize power in an urban insurrection. But Lenin was certain that only revolutionaries possessing certain personal qualities could create the revolutionary party he desired. These revolutionaries, like Rakhmetov in Chernyshevskii's novel, had to be tough, totally committed to the cause, and ruthless enough to exclude from it anyone showing the slightest sentimentality. To Lenin, not only Axelrod, but also Martov, Akimov, and Zasulich were the embodiment of all the qualities Russian revolutionaries should eschew. These individuals in particular were the antithesis of the revolutionary he imagined himself to be, and their specific recommendations on tactics and ideology could not be anything other than ill-conceived and counterproductive. Because of their personal traits, they were destined to fail.

In *One Step Forward*, Lenin did not have to invoke the French Revolution to make his argument. But he did so anyway. Alluding to it made his arguments more persuasive—or so Lenin believed—and also to heighten the embarrassment he wanted their targets to experience. The way he did this was by employing a rhetorical sleight of hand that he would use no less effectively in the future. Instead of denying the charge that he was a Jacobin and the Russian Robespierre, he welcomed it, thereby turning what was intended as an epithet and a pejorative into a virtue. Dredging up the debate at the Second Congress on the importance of how best to ensure that the party they were creating would remain a proletarian one, Lenin drew a sharp distinction between himself and those who opposed him, and drove home the moral and political dichotomy he was suggesting in the form of a series of questions:

> Who defends the proletarian trend in our movement? Who insists that the worker is not afraid of organization, that the proletarian has no sympathy for anarchy, that he values any incentive to organize? Who warns us against the bourgeois intelligentsia, which is permeated thoroughly with opportunism? The Jacobins of Social Democracy. And who tries to smuggle radical intellectuals into the party? Who is concerned about professors, high-school students, free-lancers, and radical youth? The Girondin Axelrod together with the Girondin Lieber.[64]

After excoriating Axelrod for adopting 'the hackneyed Bernsteinian refrain about Jacobinism and Blanquism', which only confirmed his own 'opportunism', Lenin

---

[64] Ibid., p. 370. Mikhail Lieber was of course another Menshevik.

proclaimed—in the most revealing and politically consequential statement of his on the French Revolution prior to the October Revolution—that Jacobinism was not a deviation from Social Democracy but its best expression and its highest embodiment: 'A Jacobin who wholly identifies with the organization of the proletariat—a proletariat that is conscious of its class interests—is a revolutionary Social Democrat.'[65] Lenin then analogized to the Girondins a mentality he saw far too often among the Social Democrats whose words and writings he was finding increasingly abhorrent'. Excoriating the 'phrase-mongering' typical of these Russian Girondins, who rejected the centralized party he considered essential to its eventual success, Lenin castigated the tactics they preferred to his as little more than 'autonomism, aristocratic and overly-intellectualised anarchism, and tailism' dressed up as Marxism and Social Democracy.[66] In fact, the fear these Russian Girondins had of actually establishing a proletarian dictatorship was the most obvious expression of the cold but undeniable fact that they were not really revolutionaries at all.

Invoking the Jacobins was surely, for Lenin, a matter of sober calculation. Adopting the terminology his opponents had directed against him while reversing the moral value they placed on it showed the degree to which, by 1904, he had become a cunning, resourceful, and ruthless politician. In addition, because Russian socialists had effectively divorced the whole notion of Jacobinism from its actual origins in the French Revolution, the term was sufficiently amorphous, and its boundaries sufficiently elastic, so that it could include or exclude practically anything; in the early 1900s in Russia, it could be used, and was used, to justify, or to condemn, virtually any political party Russian socialists created. Indeed, the very uncertainty about what the term actually meant enabled Lenin to obscure the distinction between the class the Jacobins belonged to (the bourgeoisie or some subset of the bourgeoisie) and the social classes and categories the Jacobins had represented politically (mainly impoverished peasants and an urban 'proto-proletariat'). This conception of the Jacobins was particularly felicitous in substantiating Lenin's sense of himself as Marx's successor because it applied equally well to Marx and Lenin. Both men belonged to the bourgeoisie but claimed to know what the proletariat and other oppressed classes wanted and needed— even though in doing so they were reversing Marx's axiom, without which Marxism is no longer Marxism, that being determined consciousness.

But calling himself a Jacobin—which is exactly what he did in his article without doing so explicitly—was more than a manifestation of tactical acumen and a subtle way of squaring an ideological circle. There was, in addition, a personal element to Lenin's identification with the Jacobins. In his mind they were, clearly and undeniably, the figures of the French Revolution who most

---

[65] Ibid., p. 370.   [66] Ibid., pp. 385, 394.

resembled him. To say that when Lenin looked at Robespierre and Saint-Just he saw himself is more than a rhetorical flourish. By focusing his praise on their personal qualities rather than on what they actually accomplished, Lenin was extricating the Jacobins from the milieu in which they lived, and indeed from history itself. In the way Lenin understood the term, 'Jacobinism' was part of a universal revolutionary lexicon suggesting certain qualities of firmness, determination, and will that were as desirable in Russia in the twentieth century as they were in France at the end of the eighteenth.

It is certainly true that Lenin first concerned himself with the French Revolution only reluctantly, when opponents invoking it to condemn him forced him to do the same in response. But once immersed in the revolution, he found in the Jacobins a kindred spirit. While never, in his own mind, a Jacobin per se, Lenin seems to have cultivated in himself the very qualities he found admirable in the Jacobins. Being called a Jacobin, in other words, was for Lenin a compliment, however much his opponents would have recoiled in horror—and probably avoided references to the Jacobins entirely in their diatribes against him—had they realized how much Lenin welcomed the analogy. In purely ideological terms, Lenin actually had more in common with Babeuf, a genuine communist, than with the Jacobins, whom Lenin always remembered, albeit reluctantly and with genuine regret, were not themselves proletarian and never intended a proletarian revolution. In addition, Babeuf's penchant for conspiracy was more in keeping with Lenin's conception of how a socialist party should be organized than were the Jacobin Clubs, which even before the Jacobins took power were decentralized and had no need to adopt conspiratorial tactics. But Babeuf and his followers, in contrast to the Jacobins, never took power, and the reason for this, at least as far as Lenin was concerned, was not just because capitalism in France had not existed long enough for communism to replace it. Lenin never expressed any particular admiration for the personal qualities the Babouvists possessed other than a foolish courage, not dissimilar from that of the *narodovol'tsy* decades later, that made their martyrdom especially poignant because it was so politically useless. The Jacobins, however, were different. In Robespierre and Saint-Just Lenin found actual figures in history to complement Rakhmetov, who of course existed only in Chernyshevskii's imagination, and in Lenin's, and Lenin admired all three of them for choosing, as he did, a profession consistent with their personality. Indeed, by virtue of living in an age when a proletariat actually existed, Lenin could utilize the character traits he shared with the Jacobins in changing history to an extent of which the Jacobins, by living in an earlier stage of history, were incapable.[67]

---

[67] In this context one is reminded of Plekhanov's comment to Lenin that he is 'baked of the same dough as Robespierre', and of Lenin's reply, after agreeing with Plekhanov's description, that 'a Jacobin joined with the working class is the only true revolutionary'. Quoted in Simon Liberman, *Building*

The Mensheviks, unsurprisingly, were not convinced of any of this. If anything, Lenin's identification with Jacobinism only deepened their suspicions that any party he ran would be an authoritarian one, and thus contrary to all that was best in socialism and Marxism. Of all their responses to *One Step Forward*, Alexander Martynov's, published in January 1905 and titled *Two Dictators*, was the one Lenin disliked the most.[68] Martynov was a fairly decent polemicist, and his rhetorical attacks clearly irritated the future founder of the Soviet state. Lenin would seldom miss an opportunity over the next few years to respond in kind, and while Axelrod may have been the most perspicacious of the Mensheviks in intuiting the kind of regime Lenin intended, Martynov wielded his pen as a rapier more adeptly. Indeed, his allusions to the French Revolution were one of the reasons for his rhetorical success.

According to Martynov, nothing good could come from any party Lenin led, any revolution he ordered, or any regime in which he exercised power. Martynov rejected emphatically the positive gloss Lenin placed on the Jacobins and Jacobinism. Lenin, in his opinion, was a Russian Jacobin, and as such favoured conspiratorial tactics that could bring about a revolution in Russia only 'by means of an aristocratic *coup d'état*'.[69] Social Democracy and Jacobinism were incompatible, he argued, because the latter entailed 'the hegemony of an organization of professional revolutionaries over all opposition movements'.[70] Even worse, it carried with it tacit permission for Russian socialists to seize power prematurely. But Russia was not ready for socialism in 1905, and when it would be, Jacobin tactics would not be needed because the working class would be large enough and politically conscious enough to stage a revolution on its own, with only minimal assistance from professional revolutionaries. In effect, Martynov argued, Lenin was trying to fuse Marxism and Jacobinism into an ideological and tactical hybrid in which the latter was a means of achieving the objectives of the former. But while the Jacobins replaced the bourgeoisie in 1793 and then extended the revolution beyond what the bourgeoisie intended, the fact that they lost power soon afterwards showed that 'neither the God that was Jean Jacques Rousseau, nor the heroic forces of the Mountain, could defy the laws of historical necessity'.[71] In fact, in Martynov's rendition of the French Revolution, the petit-bourgeois dictatorship the Jacobinism established caused the Girondins, in reaction, to embrace federalism and eventually a form of royalism, while the Jacobins came

---

Lenin's Russia (Chicago IL, 1945), p. 16. According to Nikolai Valentinov, who was a supporter of Lenin when Plekhanov made his remark but eventually rejected Bolshevism and became a Menshevik, Plekhanov thought less of the Jacobins after Lenin made clear he thought highly of them. Nikolai Valentinov, *Encounters with Lenin* (New York, 1968), p. 128.

---

[68] Alexander Martynov, *Dve diktatury* (Geneva, 1905).   [69] Ibid., p. 10.
[70] Ibid., p. 11.   [71] Ibid., p. 35.

to practise imperialism abroad and inflict mass terror at home. As 'revolutionary ideologues of the petit-bourgeoisie', the Jacobins were bound at some point to turn on the *sans-culottes*, whose support the Jacobins had wrongly taken as evidence that their dictatorship transcended class, and thus was destined to endure.[72] But even with the *sans-culottes* terrorized into a passive neutrality, the Jacobins could not rule by coercion alone. In the end, 'their most exalted argument was the guillotine', and it was clearly not enough to save them.[73] In Martynov's analysis of the French Revolution, 9 Thermidor became inevitable at the very moment when the Jacobins, a year earlier, had seized power prematurely.

But instead of learning from the French Revolution, Lenin, in Martynov's jaundiced opinion, was bent on repeating its mistakes, most egregiously the Jacobins' miscalculation of their chances of retaining power after seizing it. Lenin, in fact, was no different from the Jacobins, and therefore the same 'adventurism' that was the Jacobins' principal legacy would lead any party Lenin headed to ruination. In other words, Martynov, in his essay, was questioning not only the wisdom of Lenin's tactical choices and temperamental tendencies, but his credentials as a socialist and revolutionary.

Lenin's loathing of Martynov and of the Mensheviks who shared his views was understandable.[74] Not even the outbreak of revolution in Russia in January 1905, which one would think would lessen the antagonisms that had developed among Russian socialists as a consequence of their isolation and political impotence, diminished his hostility. Instead, it increased. The very real possibility, at least in Lenin's mind, that events in Russia would culminate in the downfall of the monarchy, and then somehow precipitate a workers' revolution, only underscored the costs of adopting policies he believed might have doomed this revolution before it even began. On 8 February, Lenin called for Russian socialists to shelve their internecine rhetorical warfare and instead work to instill in the masses awareness that 'attacking the autocracy is a burning necessity'.[75] Doing so, he stated, 'is the constant common duty of Social Democrats always and everywhere'.[76] But Lenin, at this point in his article, could no longer restrain himself. He filled the rest of his article with his customary invective. Martynov and the other 'incorrigible Girondins of socialism' were nothing more than 'tailists', whose acquiescence in their own cowardice and weakness, conducive to tactically retrograde prescriptions, Martynov dressed up in the clothing of a supposedly respectable philosophy.[77]

---

[72] Ibid., p. 52.   [73] Ibid., p. 53.

[74] Soviet historians, not surprisingly, shared Lenin's low opinion of Martynov. B. G. Veber, for example, denigrated him as the leader of 'the Social Democratic "Gironde"'—a failing Veber ascribed to Martynov's reading Aulard, Michelet, and Jaurès on the French Revolution instead of Marx and Engels. B. G. Veber, 'V. I Lenin i istoricheskoe nasledie iakobintsev', *Frantsuzskii ezhegodnik: stat'i i materialy po istorii Frantsii 1970* (Moscow, 1972), pp. 23, 24.

[75] V. I. Lenin, 'Dolzhy li my organizovat'revoliutsiiu', in Lenin, *PSS*, vol. IX, p. 269.

[76] Ibid., p. 269.   [77] Ibid., p. 271.

Two weeks later Lenin resumed his rhetorical assault in not one but two articles that appeared on the same day in the same venue. In one of these, he wrote that Social Democrats who claimed to be ardent revolutionaries were only pretending. Like Madame Roland in 1793, when she wrote that France had no men, only dwarfs, and for that reason knew that the revolution could advance no further, these ersatz revolutionaries in Russia 'should retire and leave the field clear for younger forces who make up in enthusiasm what they lack in experience'.[78] Lenin reserved his attack on Martynov for the other article, which began by stating condescendingly that by now it was unnecessary to condemn him: he had been unmasked as a Russian Girondin in the liberal newspaper, *Osvobozhdenie*, which by deeming *Two Dictators* consistent with socialism, only confirmed its fraudulence.[79] Reading Lenin's attack, one expects him at various points to banish Martynov and his ilk from the ranks of Russian Social Democracy. Lenin even asked rhetorically whether the Girondins—who here and elsewhere in Lenin's writings were obviously stand-ins for the Martynovites—were 'traitors to the cause of the Great French Revolution'.[80] But in a rare moment of magnanimity he then conceded that Martynov and his acolytes had never betrayed the cause of socialism. But to the extent that they were 'inconsistent, indecisive, and opportunist champions of the cause', they were identical to the Girondins, whom he condemned in the article for more or less the same transgressions and in similar language.[81] In fact, it was the Girondins' inconsistency and opportunism that caused the Jacobins to oppose them. In contrast to the Girondins, the Jacobins 'upheld the interests of the advanced class of the eighteenth century as consistently as the revolutionary Social-Democrats—by whom Lenin of course meant the Bolsheviks—upheld the interests of the advanced class of the twentieth'.[82] In both articles—in one implicitly, in the other explicitly—Lenin dichotomized the Girondins and the Jacobins morally and politically, with the result that at the end of each article it seems that the French and the Russians have merged in his mind: while 'the most honourable Girondin Martynov' and his new *Iskrist* allies might not be traitors by intention, the fact that they were supported by actual traitors was good reason to question their bona fides as socialists and revolutionaries.[83]

Not even the anarchy prevalent in Russia in the spring and early summer of 1905—which made easier an urban insurrection by Leninist cadres of professional revolutionaries—could distract the Bolshevik leader from his self-imposed task of splitting Russian socialism by anathematizing everyone who disagreed with him;

---

[78] V. I. Lenin, 'Novye zadachi i novye sily (23 February 1905)', ibid., p. 306.
[79] V. I. Lenin, 'Osvobozhdentsy, neoiskrovtsy, monarkhisty, i zhirondisty (23 February 1905)', ibid., pp. 307–8.
[80] Ibid., p. 308.   [81] Ibid., p. 308.   [82] Ibid., p. 308.
[83] Among the 'traitors' Lenin was referring to were Pëtr Struve, the editor of *Osvobozhdenie*, who had been a Marxist and Social Democrat before becoming a liberal, and his liberal supporters.

whether they were Mensheviks, Bundists, or Martynovites did not matter. After the revolution ended in December in failure, Lenin would do the same thing in response both to the 'God-Builders' within the RSDLP, who tried to synthesize Marxism and religion, and to other, equally errant Bolsheviks seeking to reconcile Marxism and an abstruse theory of knowledge called 'empiriocriticsm'.[84] This kind of 'splitting', which for Lenin was as much a psychological necessity as a political one, seemed to solidify his identification with the Jacobins, who certainly did some splitting of their own, destroying sequentially those they claimed had betrayed the revolution—first the Girondins, then Danton and the Dantonists, and finally Hébert and the Hébertists. But Lenin's identification with the Jacobins was not mindless. Nor was his admiration boundless or driven entirely by his own emotions. He was well aware that the splitting they engaged in narrowed their political base sufficiently to make them vulnerable to the conspiracy that brought them down and destroyed them physically as well as politically. In that respect, the last thing Lenin wanted was for the French Revolution to repeat itself in Russia.

All of this found expression in July 1905, when it seemed increasingly likely that the anarchy that had been unleashed in Russia in January, in the aftermath of 'Bloody Sunday', when tsarist troops killed unarmed demonstrators in Palace Square in St Petersburg, would lead to the collapse of the monarchy itself. In a pamphlet entitled *Two Tactics of Social Democracy in the Democratic Revolution*, Lenin attacked his enemies with rhetoric no less vituperative than that he had used before—and with the same terminology he had previously borrowed from the French Revolution.[85] Five months earlier Lenin had excoriated 'the opportunists of the new *Iskra* ... for crying hysterically about a sinister "Jacobin plan"'.[86] The plan the new *Iskra* editors had in mind was of course Lenin's, and one suspects that that was what prompted him to respond with a degree of vehemence unusual even for him. It may also have increased the likelihood of his drawing upon the French Revolution for empirical support. In any event, Lenin went further in *Two Tactics* than he ever had before in defending his belief that only a party that centralized authority and practised conspiracy could survive the harsh repression of the tsars while simultaneously instilling political consciousness in the vast majority of the Russian proletariat that still lacked it. The way he did so was by proclaiming, yet again, that the Jacobinism for which his enemies attacked him was a virtue, and for that reason he was effectively a Jacobin himself. And to the charge that Jacobinism was proof not just of some personal and political deficiency or defect that disqualified anyone possessing it from participation in the glorious enterprise of building socialism and communism, Lenin proclaimed

[84] Ulam, *The Bolsheviks*, pp. 270–6.
[85] V. I. Lenin, *Dve taktiki sotsialdemokratii v demokraticheskoi revoliutsii*, in Lenin, *PSS*, vol. XI, pp. 1–131.
[86] V. I. Lenin, 'Dve taktiki (1 February 1905)', ibid., p. 259.

simply that 'the Bolsheviks are the Jacobins of contemporary Social Democracy'.[87]
In keeping with the tactics the Jacobins adopted after defeating the Girondins and
consigning them to political oblivion, he and the other Bolsheviks were now
'attempting by their slogans to raise the revolutionary and the republican petit-
bourgeoisie, and particularly the peasantry, to the level of the consistent democ-
ratism of the proletariat, which retains its complete individuality as a class'.[88] At
this point in his polemic, Lenin suddenly adopted a different tone entirely,
imploring his readers not to read too much into the kind words he had for the
Jacobins, even with his personal identification with them taken fully into account.
None of what he wrote about them was meant to suggest

> that we intend to imitate the Jacobins of 1793, to adopt their views, programmes,
> slogans, and methods of action. Nothing of the kind. Our programme is not an
> old one, it is a new one—the minimum programme of the Russian Social-
> Democratic Workers Party. We have a new slogan: the revolutionary-democratic
> dictatorship of the proletariat and the peasantry.[89]

*   *   *

With these words, Lenin made clear that, as far as the French Revolution was
concerned, its utility in the future would be different from what it had been before
the anarchy triggered by the outbreak of revolution in 1905 caused him to
contemplate the possibility of the proletariat and the peasantry making a revolution after the bourgeoisie had refused to do so. This revolution, he insisted, would
be a bourgeois revolution programmatically. Foremost among its objectives would
be the elimination of the monarchy, followed by measures ending feudalism
and the domination of the nobles in the countryside. One might think that once
these objectives had been accomplished, Lenin would order the Bolsheviks and
the classes they led politically to desist, stand down, and wait for capitalism to
progress—or more precisely to degenerate—sufficiently for the proletariat, now in
charge of the party Lenin had helped to create many years earlier, to take power
and then began the task of establishing socialism. But that would not be the case.
In the twelve years separating the two revolutions in Russia in the early twentieth
century, even bigger things begin to germinate in Lenin's mind, namely a scenario
of revolution—remarkably similar to Trotsky's—in which the Russian proletariat
and the most impoverished elements of the peasantry, after making a bourgeois
revolution (because the bourgeoisie was either unable or unwilling to do so
itself), would then make a proletarian revolution even though that would clearly
exceed what was possible politically in light of economic realities—specifically
Russia's relative backwardness as a country just beginning to industrialize—that

---

[87] Lenin, *Dve taktiki sotsialdemokratii*, Lenin, *PSS*, vol. XI, p. 47.
[88] Ibid.   [89] Ibid., p. 48.

would not change in any fundamental way for decades or even for centuries. But Lenin, nearly as much as Trotsky, was also a revolutionary in a hurry. Perhaps unconsciously, he wanted to experience a proletarian revolution and to enjoy its salubrious results within his own lifetime.

To be sure, it took some time for Lenin to formulate this scenario in his mind, and he would not infer from it a concrete strategy until he was actually executing it in 1917. In that year, after years of isolation, immobility, and failure, Lenin found himself improvising madly and making day-to-day decisions on the basis of his political instincts—which in 1917 proved to be impeccable—rather than on the basis of a plan conceived calmly and deliberately prior to its implementation. But until then, Russian socialists confined to Western Europe could do little more than daydream about victories in the future that seemed, with every year that passed, increasingly unlikely. But Lenin, while certainly prone to idle rumination—before the October Revolution much of his political thought amply qualified as such— was able also to ponder the limits of what was politically and ideologically possible, which was certainly a more fruitful use of his time and energy than pointless contemplation of how Marxism and religion, or Marxism and obscure philosophies such as 'Machism', might be reconciled and find expression in a new, synthetic ideology.[90] These heresies Lenin denounced, quite correctly, as incompatible with Marxist ideology. After the 1905 Revolution ended with the monarchy still in power, and Russian socialism once again consigned to the extreme periphery of Russian politics, its members consumed by the feuding and recriminations failure invariably generates, Lenin almost never lost his self-confidence and his belief that at some point in the future—of course he preferred it would be sooner rather than later—his peregrinations in the political wilderness just as much as his Marxist ideology would be vindicated.

In the meantime, Lenin and, to a lesser extent, the other Bolsheviks, continued their exploration of the French Revolution in terms of its relevance and utility to Russian revolutionaries living well over a century after it ended. Before 1906 the revolution provided insights into a how a revolutionary party in Russia should be organized. From 1906 to 1917, however, Lenin mined it for a different kind of ore. In these years he focused on the relationship of the Jacobins to French society. In particular he was concerned with ascertaining if this relationship constrained the Jacobins or made them more flexible in the tactical and programmatic decisions they had to make during the brief time they wielded power. Whether the Jacobins did what they did because of the class they belonged to, or in response to the class or classes they represented politically, might seem a question too arcane even for Russian socialists whiling away their time idly chatting in cafes in Geneva, Munich, Paris, and London—to consider. But that proved not to be the case.

---

[90] Bertram D. Wolfe, *Three Who Made a Revolution: A Biographical History* (New York, 1964), pp. 496–517.

And as far as Lenin was concerned, this particular question concerned him precisely because he recognized its relevance and importance for any socialist— or really for anyone seeking power and expecting to exercise it.

In the whole matter of what Jacobinism consisted of, and whether it was something the Bolsheviks should inculcate among themselves, Lenin was a relative latecomer; he addressed the issue only after others had begun using it to demean him and to derogate his credentials as a revolutionary. But on the issue of the coalition the Jacobins headed while in power, Lenin was the first Bolshevik to address it, and the only Bolshevik to do so repeatedly and voluntarily between 1906 and 1917.

For that reason, his views on the matter require serious consideration.

5

Bolsheviks and Mensheviks on the Jacobins and the Girondins

The revolution in Russia in 1905 caused many Russians, not all of them revolutionaries, to consider it analogous to the French Revolution. On this there was, of course, no unanimity. Some Russians accepted the analogy; others rejected it. But proponents of each of these dichotomous positions believed that drawing the analogy was a useful endeavour, if for no other reason than to confirm the clarity and veracity of opinions already conceived. Naturally one wonders whether any of those who drew the analogy did so because of what revolutionaries like Lenin had previously written about it, indeed, whether these revolutionaries had any role in simply acquainting Russians with the French Revolution. In both respects the answer is no: the acquaintance ordinary Russians had with the revolution reflected a popular culture that had evolved independently of revolutionaries confined in jail, Siberia, or European emigration—and thereby far removed from the urban centres of Russian culture, principally Moscow and St Petersburg. Russian revolutionaries tended to create their own insular and self-contained subculture wherever they were.[1] When separated from Russia geographically, they deliberately remained aloof from the native, national culture, be it French, German, or English, that surrounded them; that it was French, German, or English made no difference. In that way, Russian revolutionaries were cut off from two cultures, not just one.

For this reason the fact that both Russian revolutionaries and ordinary people in Russia found the French Revolution relevant in 1905—or, for that matter, at any other time in Russia's history—does not imply any causal relationship one way or the other. Nor does it mean that any proprietary claim revolutionaries made on the revolution was more valid than those whose politics were more conventional. In fact, the French Revolution was such a multicoloured tapestry of events, personalities, political parties, coalitions, and cliques that observers in

---

[1] Miller, *Russian Revolutionary Emigres*, pp. 3–10. Moreover, many biographers of individual Bolsheviks, such as Lenin and Stalin, make a point of showing how uninterested they were in their surroundings either in exile domestically or as *émigrés* in Western Europe. Trotsky seems to have been exceptional in that regard. Marc Raeff, in *Russia Abroad*, pp. 3–15, shows that the same dynamic characterized the emigration after the October Revolution, which of course included non-revolutionaries, counter-revolutionaries, and many who were apolitical.

Russia and elsewhere could make use of it in much the way one eats in a cafeteria—by seeing what every item looks like, and then selecting some, but not others, in accordance with one's particular preferences. In the case of the cafeteria customer, these could be based on taste, aesthetic appreciation, or medical necessity; in the case of Russians during the 1905 Revolution, politics and ideology were usually decisive.

By 1900 Russians were learning about the French Revolution in many ways. The orations of many of its principal figures were well-known to many of the educated elite; some were considered models of rhetorical eloquence.[2] Nikolai Bukharin recalled that at the age of seventeen he was greatly impressed by a lecture on the revolution delivered by the well-known historian M. N. Pokrovskii, in which he extolled the virtues of 'proletarian Jacobinism'.[3] The word *burzhuaziia'* had entered the Russian language around the turn of the century, and by 1905 the works of the major French historians of the revolution had been published in Russian translation.[4] Of these historians the most read were Thiers, Aulard, Sorel, Taine, and Jaurès.[5] How precisely these historians affected the course of events in Russia is difficult to determine. But there is no doubt that in educating Russians about the revolution, so that those who admired it could consider it, in 1905, a noble precedent of the revolution they themselves were experiencing, these historians played a significant role. A typical comment about the 1905 Revolution, even after it failed, was that by finally 'freeing people from the chains of unbearable slavery', it made 'the image of the great French emancipatory struggle especially dear and near to us'.[6] Sentiments such as these were expressed frequently in 1905, and another of the reasons for their prevalence was the publication and performance of a cycle of plays by Romain Rolland, entitled *Théâtre de la Révolution*, that glorified the French Revolution in ways that made its uplifting message of universal freedom accessible to people disinclined to read books.[7]

In Russia the most obvious symbol of the French Revolution was its iconic anthem, the *Marseillaise*. Though singing it was a crime, many were acquainted with it from its inclusion in Tchaikovsky's *1812 Overture*, which was written in 1880 and first performed, at the government's request, at the Moscow Arts and Industry Exhibition in 1882.[8] For some, the anthem symbolized allegiance to one's

    [2] M. Vinaver, *Nedavnee: vospominaniia i kharakteristiki, 1907* (Paris, 1926), p. 165.
    [3] N. Bukharin, 'Professor s pikoi', *Pravda*, no. 249 (4081), (25 October 1928): p. 3; Stephen F. Cohen, *Bukharin and the Bolshevik Revolution: A Political Biography, 1888–1938* (New York, 1973), p. 9.
    [4] Keep, 'Tyranny of Paris over Petrograd', p. 25.   [5] Ibid.
    [6] Quoted in P. Zaborov, 'Velikaia frantsuzskaia revoliutsiia v russkoi pechati 1905–1907 gg. (Bibliograficheskii materialy)', *Revue des Études Slaves*, 61 (1989): p. 144.
    [7] G. I. Il'ina, 'Obraz evropeiskikh revoliutsii i russkaia kul'tura', in *Anatomiia revoliutsii 1917 goda v Rossii: massy, partii, vlast'*, edited by V. Iu. Cherniaev (St Petersburg, 1994), p. 384.
    [8] Margaret MacMillan, *The War That Ended Peace: The Road to 1914* (New York, 2014), p. 159; Anthony Holden, *Tchaikovsky: A Biography* (New York, 1995), pp. 203–4. The strains of the *Marseillaise* one hears in the first half or so of the overture are meant to symbolize Napoleon's incursion into Russia.

own country; for others it implied rejection. In 1905 it was sometimes sung spontaneously. In October of that year, when striking workers in the railway industry sparked a general strike in St Petersburg that brought the Russian capital to a standstill, ordinary people supportive of the strike demonstrated their sympathies by singing it.[9] And even after the revolution had ended in defeat, the anthem remained a symbol of hope and defiance. In April 1906, in the provincial city of Saratov, a crowd of ten thousand at the railway station sang the anthem as the delegates who would represent them in the First Duma left for St Petersburg.[10] On May Day 1906, meetings of workers in the Russian capital and elsewhere did the same thing to mark the end of their deliberations. One month later, inebriated Cossacks preparing a demonstration of their own—its objectives no doubt more and more obscured as the consumption of alcohol increased—sang the anthem as a way of showing solidarity with everyone who shared their vaguely libertarian ethos. But perhaps the most poignant renditions of the anthem occurred when hopes for a better future seemed unwarranted. When the First Duma was prorogued by the tsar in 1906, not long after its convocation, the fact that what he did was perfectly legal did not preclude the anthem being sung at demonstrations protesting the tsar's decision.[11]

Another symbol of the French Revolution that had real salience for Russians in 1905 was the red flag, the first use of which in a political context was by the Jacobins in 1792; in the nineteenth century it symbolized socialism not only in Western Europe but also in Russia.[12] Although many of the Russians who carried red flags in 1905 were unaware of their provenance, the fact that the Russian word for red (*krasnyi*) was the root of the words *prekrasnyi*, which means 'splendid' or 'fine', and *krasivyi*, which means 'beautiful' or 'handsome', may have been another reason they became a means of expressing one's politics symbolically.[13] Many of the demonstrators in St Petersburg in 1905 who sang the *Marseillaise* also unfurled red flags as a way of symbolizing their defiance visually as well as aurally.[14] That this occurred as frequently as it did suggests that the crowds observing such events found these particular symbols of the French Revolution inspirational.

In 1905 the revolution provided guidance as well as inspiration. A. I. Gukovskii, a well-known jurist and professor, proclaimed while the outcome of the revolution in Russia was still uncertain that the country needed another 'Declaration of the

---

[9] 'Biulleten' no. 12 moskovskogo komiteta RSDRP o sobytiiakh v Moskve 17–19 Oktiabria', in *Listovki moskovskikh Bol'shevikov v period pervoi russkoi revoliutsii* (Moscow, 1955), p. 319.

[10] Abraham Ascher, *The Revolution of 1905: Authority Restored* (Stanford CA, 1992), p. 54.

[11] Ibid., pp. 133, 158, 209.

[12] Victoria Bonnell, *Iconography of Power: Soviet Political Posters under Lenin and Stalin* (Berkeley CA, 1998), p. 13.

[13] Orlando Figes and Boris Kolonitskii, *Interpreting the Russian Revolution: The Language and Symbols of 1917* (New Haven CT, 1999), p. 32.

[14] 'Biulleten' no. 12 moskovskogo komiteta RSDRP o sobytiiakh v Moskve 17–19 Oktiabria', p. 319.

Rights of Man'. Its purpose, he believed, was not to supersede the French original but to complement it by including provisos relevant to Russia of which revolutionaries more than a century earlier could not possibly have been aware.[15] But one did not have to be a white-collar professional like Gukovskii to find in the French Revolution insights relevant to the ongoing revolution in Russia. In October 1905, as the revolution was approaching its apogee, a student organization in St Petersburg called on the RSDLP's newly formed committee in the Russian capital to acknowledge that the revolution Russia was experiencing was a bourgeois revolution like that which had occurred in France. By including in their statement their regret that the revolution in the German states in 1848 had failed so miserably, they made clear their belief that to learn what they should do, Russians should look to France rather than to Germany.[16]

*   *   *

Lenin was not in Russia when the 1905 Revolution began. But word of it seemed to stimulate the 'voluntarist' element of his temperament and political personality. As early as the third week in February he proclaimed confidently that the oppression workers had had to endure for many years made them eager to lash out at those responsible for their predicament. Indeed, all that was needed to trigger an actual revolution was for revolutionaries cognizant of Marxist ideology to convince the workers that the government was ultimately responsible for all the evils from which they suffered, and should therefore be overthrown immediately. Lenin phrased his hopes and expectations as follows:

> Never has revolutionary Russia had such a multitude of people as it has now. Never has a revolutionary class been as fortunate in the relationships that exist among temporary allies, self-avowed friends, and unconscious supporters as the Russian proletariat is today. These are masses of people; all we need to do is get rid of tailist ideas and concepts, give free rein to initiative and enterprise, to 'plans' and 'undertakings', and then we will show ourselves to be worthy representatives of the great revolutionary class. Then the proletariat of Russia will carry out the great Russian revolution in its entirety as heroically as it has begun it.[17]

In Lenin's opinion, Russia in 1905 was like France in 1793. In both countries there were persons susceptible to calls for revolution and also, no less important, professional revolutionaries eager to issue them. In France the Jacobins—and only the Jacobins—were capable of mobilizing mass discontent; in Russia the same was true for the Bolsheviks. But before they could act, they had to eliminate

[15] Viktor Chernov, *Pered burei: vospominaniia* (New York, n.d.), pp. 263–4.
[16] 'Listovki ob"edinennoi studencheskoi organizatsii pri Peterburgskom Komitete RSDRP s prizyvami k vooruzhdennomu vosstaniiu', *Listovki Peterburgskikh Bol'shevikov 1902–1917* (Moscow, 1939–57), vol. I, p. 263.
[17] Lenin, 'Novye zadachi i novye sily', in Lenin, *PSS*, vol. IX, p. 306.

from the RSDLP the detritus of all the retrograde and ersatz ideologies—
Menshevism, Economism, and evolutionary socialism—that if put into practice
on a national scale would preclude a genuine revolution rather than facilitate it.
That was why, two weeks earlier, he had condemned as 'incorrigible Girondins of
socialism', the editors of *Iskra*, who by that time seemed to him the personification
of everything he found distasteful in revolutionaries lacking the courage to make a
revolution and the tactical flexibility to ensure its success.[18]

But while Lenin in 1905 condemned the Girondins and praised the Jacobins
just as fervently as he had on previous occasions when the prospects for revolution
in Russia seemed nil, the circumstances that now pertained were radically different. When revolution in Russia seemed inconceivable, arguments about the
French Revolution broke out partly because Russian socialists had good reason
to believe that the cause to which they were dedicating their lives might prove
illusory. The possibility that a revolution of any kind in Russia would not occur
within their lifetime seemed very real, and for that reason the invective with which
the participants in these arguments phrased their opinions was very sharp. In 1905
the same thing was true, but this time it was a reflection of the belief that, with the
outbreak of revolution in Russia, Russian socialists might actually succeed; the
only disagreement, albeit one of critical significance, was whether the bourgeois
revolution that erupted in January should be followed shortly by a proletarian one.
While for those remaining faithful to Marxist orthodoxy decades, even centuries,
had to pass before conditions were finally conducive to this second revolution, the
fact that the first revolution was occurring was undeniable. In the spring and
summer of 1905 it was success, not failure, that kept the conversation among
Russian socialists over tactics and ideology just as vituperative and *ad hominem* as
it had been before. At the end of March Lenin attacked unnamed socialists whose
'schoolboy's understanding of history' caused them to imagine history 'as something in the shape of a straight line moving slowly but steadily upwards'.[19] For more
than a century or so, 'as was the case in France from 1789 to 1905', this view of
history was correct.[20] But only 'a virtuoso of philistinism', Lenin concluded, 'would
consider this relevant to a plan of action in [the current] revolutionary epoch'.[21]

For this reason Lenin's references to the French Revolution after the 1905
Revolution began concerned matters of tactics and strategy rather than with
determining which of its participants were similar to the Bolsheviks, and which
were not. At the Third Congress of the RSDLP in April 1905, Lenin quoted Marx
approvingly on the admissibility of terror in the context of a progressive revolution like the French. Even if the Bolsheviks somehow took over St Petersburg and

---

[18] Lenin, 'Dolzhny li my organizovat'revoliutsiiu', ibid., p. 271.
[19] V. I. Lenin, 'Revoliutsionnaia demokraticheskaia diktatura proletariata i krest'ianstva (30 March
1905)', in Lenin, *PSS*, vol. X, p. 26.
[20] Ibid.   [21] Ibid.

guillotined Nicholas II, he noted, there would still be *Vendées*—by which Lenin meant counter-revolutionary elements in Russia—that would have to be dealt with severely.[22] Jacobin terror, he stated, was simply the way 'plebeians settled accounts with counterrevolution and absolutism', and for that reason the Bolsheviks would do well to follow the Jacobins' example, leaving 'Girondin methods' to *Iskra*.[23] At the beginning of May, Lenin amplified his praise for the Jacobins, defending them as 'the most consistent of all bourgeois democrats', while claiming that charging genuine revolutionaries like the Bolsheviks with Jacobinism was just a means 'hopeless reactionaries and philistines' had adopted to defame them.[24] But their efforts, he remained certain, would come to naught.

Lenin's description of the Jacobins as 'bourgeois' was significant. Because by the spring of 1905 he was considering the possibility of the bourgeois revolution that had begun in January evolving organically into a proletarian revolution, it would seem he could no longer consider the French Revolution a useful analogue: fully three years elapsed in the French Revolution between the original bourgeois revolution in 1789 and its radicalization in 1792 into what Lenin considered the first precursor of a proletarian revolution. But what required three years to occur in France in the late eighteenth century could be virtually complete in Russia in the early twentieth century in a matter of weeks or, at most, a few months if Lenin's powers of prognostication were real.

That said, the Bolshevik leader was unwilling to downgrade the French Revolution as a precedent, much less acknowledge that his self-identification with the Jacobins had been a mistake. Rather, he seemed unable to make up his mind on the whole matter. His indecision is evident in what he wrote about the Jacobins in the summer of 1905. On 16 August, in an article in the newspaper *Proletarii*, he stated that Russia had a reached a point where it was nearly analogous to France on 10 August 1792, when demonstrators led by the Jacobins overthrew the Legislative Assembly and shortly afterwards proclaimed the Bourbon monarchy abolished and France a republic.[25] But on 23 August he reversed position, stating in another article, also in *Proletarii*, that Russia had not yet attained the point at which, in the French Revolution, the Bastille was stormed, thereby demonstrating that the lower classes in Paris were now active participants in the ongoing revolution. The Russian Bastille, by contrast, had yet to be stormed.[26]

One might think that this second article, so definitive in the conclusion it expressed about the French Revolution, showed that Lenin had finally achieved

[22] V. I. Lenin, 'Doklad ob uchastii sotsial-demokratii vo vremennom revoliutsionnom pravitel'stve (18 April 1905)', in Lenin, *PSS*, vol. X, p. 138.

[23] Ibid.

[24] V. I. Lenin, 'Politicheskie sofizmy (5 May 1905)', in Lenin, *PSS*, vol. X, p. 203; V. I. Lenin, 'Sovety konservativnoi burzhuazii (21 May 1905)', ibid., p. 226.

[25] V. I. Lenin, 'Edinenie tsariia s narodom i naroda s tsarem', in Lenin, *PSS*, vol. XI, p. 188.

[26] V. I. Lenin, 'V khvoste u monarkhicheskoi burzhuazii ili vo glave revoliutsionnogo proletariata i krest'ianstva?', ibid., pp. 205–6.

some clarity on its relevance to the revolution that was still unfolding in Russia. But that was not the case. If anything, he was more confused than ever. On 23 August there appeared in *Proletarii*, in addition to the aforementioned article, a 'note' by Lenin on a recently published book, in which he directly contradicted what appeared under his own name in the same issue. 'The parallel between the Russia of 1905 and the France of Louis XVI', Lenin wrote in the note, was 'amazing'.[27] In explaining Lenin's indecision, specifically his unwillingness or inability to make clear what exactly was the relationship—assuming any existed—between the two revolutions, one might propose, in Lenin's defence, that the 1905 Revolution, when it began, came as a surprise, perhaps even as a shock, and that the anarchy and the breakdown of political authority that ensued after Bloody Sunday created opportunities that previously had been nonexistent. As a result, the proletarian revolution he previously believed would be so far in the future as to be virtually an abstraction was now, suddenly, a real possibility. All that remained for Lenin to do in order for the Bolsheviks to participate in the radicalization of the revolution he now fully expected was to come up with a slogan descriptive of the scenario he was conjuring that his readers, and possibly also the Russian workers engaged in actions disruptive of the status quo, could easily understand. The one he soon decided on—to which he was indebted deeply to Trotsky—was 'the democratic-dictatorship of the proletariat and the peasantry'.

Fortunately for Lenin, Trotsky never wavered in his belief that the weakness of the bourgeoisie in Russia did not preclude a proletarian revolution provided that the proletariat and peasantry assumed the role Marx had usually thought the bourgeoisie would play of overthrowing the monarchy and ending feudalism. In August 1905 he wrote an 'open letter' to Pavel Miliukov, the de facto leader of Russian liberals who had just praised the tsar's proposal to establish a consultative duma, which Trotsky of course considered a ruse to regain the allegiance of moderates weakly supportive of the revolution.[28] In the letter Trotsky contrasted what he considered Miliukov's cowardice with the courage of the revolutionaries in France who had established a republic in 1792 not because the king, in a spirit of paternalistic solicitude, had agreed to it, but because the people of France demanded it; only through struggle, which in the French Revolution involved the masses arming themselves and defending their rights through the stringent application of force and violence, could people gain what was rightfully theirs.[29] And even after the revolution in Russia was finally crushed in December, when the government suppressed an attempted insurrection in Moscow, Trotsky never lost hope. The government's survival was always for him a close-run thing. Had the

---

[27] V. I. Lenin, 'Primechanie k stat'e "Finansy Rossii i revoliutsiia"', ibid., p. 214.

[28] L. Trotsky, 'Otkrytoe pis'mo professoru P. N. Miliukovu', in L. Trotsky, *Sochineniia*, 23 vols (Moscow/Leningrad, 1924–7), vol. II, pp. 196–205.

[29] Ibid., p. 198.

correlation of political power in Russia in 1905 shifted even only slightly in favour of the revolutionaries, their efforts would have achieved the desired results.

For this reason, from the end of the 1905 Revolution to the outbreak of the First World War in 1914, Trotsky saw no reason to modify the scenario of permanent revolution he had conjured earlier. Not only was a bourgeois revolution still possible even without the participation of the bourgeoisie; in addition, this bourgeois revolution would lead directly to a proletarian revolution that, by its very audacity, would inspire the proletariat in more advanced countries in Europe, such as France, Germany, and England, to take power. Once that was done, it could render whatever assistance the new proletarian regime in Russia required to survive. As far as Trotsky was concerned, the mental universe he inhabited he filled with visions of humanity everywhere redeeming itself through the elimination of private property and the establishment of socialism and communism. But these visions—one might fairly consider them, under the circumstances, to be hallucinations—became more real to him than the harsh realities Russian socialists were understandably afraid to confront from 1906 to 1914, when it seemed possible that Russia might evolve peacefully into a constitutional monarchy that satisfied the material needs of the lower classes. Images of courageous workers and urban artisans storming the Bastille had an intoxicating effect even on revolutionaries like Trotsky who wrongly prided themselves on their rationalism and dispassionate comprehension of the impersonal laws of history.

Trotsky's optimism is obvious even in the book he intended as a post-mortem on the 1905 Revolution.[30] His task in the book, as he saw it, was not just to explain the circumstances requiring the proletariat and peasantry to replace the bourgeois in a bourgeoisie revolution. It was also to explain why the proletariat and peasantry would succeed in this endeavour. In fulfilling this second obligation, he revisited the French Revolution, asking rhetorically if St Petersburg or Moscow at the present time was analogous to Paris in 1789; the cities were obviously stand-ins for Russia and France respectively. His answer was that they were not: Russia presently lacked even 'a trace of that sturdy middle class which . . . hand in hand with a young, as yet unformed proletariat, stormed the Bastilles of feudalism'.[31] This would seem to suggest that a bourgeoisie revolution, and *a fortiori* a proletarian revolution, could not occur for decades, perhaps even centuries. But the French Revolution, when it began, was more or less localised 'within the walls of Paris'.[32] In a pre-industrial age, considerable time had to pass before an urban insurrection in the capital or in the largest city in a country could become a genuinely national revolution. In Russia, however, circumstances were different. Capitalism and modern technology, most notably railroads and the telegraph,

---

[30] The book, when it appeared in 1907, was entitled *Nasha revoliutsiia*. It acquired the title *1905*, by which it is known today, in 1922, when it was published in the Soviet Union.
[31] Leon Trotsky, *1905* (New York, 1971), p. 41.   [32] Ibid., p. 103.

ensured that news of any insurrection in St Petersburg would spread quickly, and because both the proletariat and the peasantry by the beginning of the twentieth century were sufficiently aggrieved by the oppression they experienced to possess the requisite political consciousness, they would be inspired by events in the Russian capital to replicate them everywhere.

What Trotsky did in 1905 was to turn France's revolution, which Marx and orthodox Marxists considered a success, into a failure, while virtually guaranteeing that the revolution in Russia he anticipated would succeed. France's revolution, because it occurred when industrial capitalism was just emerging, could not exceed the limits history had placed on it. While successful in purging France of feudalism and the Bourbons (if only until their restoration in 1815), the French Revolution could not transcend itself. It could not morph seamlessly from a bourgeois revolution to a proletarian or proto-proletarian revolution, and the Hébertists and the Babouvists who tried to achieve this had failed miserably, and in many cases paid for their failure with their lives. By contrast, because it was a consequence of industrial capitalism rather than the impetus to it, as was the French Revolution in Marx's interpretation of its history, any future revolution in Russia had an excellent chance of success. In mathematical terms, Trotsky's scenario boiled down to a simple equation: industrial capitalism plus a recalcitrant bourgeoisie equals a bourgeois revolution that becomes a proletarian revolution.

Trotsky essentially conceded in 1905 that, as a general rule, for revolutions to be radicalized, the individuals who begin the revolution have to be replaced before this radicalization—which, for all intents and purposes, can also be called a second revolution—can occur. This was how the French Revolution had progressed: the class that made the original revolution in 1789 had to be replaced in 1792 by a different class—or more precisely a coalition of urban craftsmen and merchants who collectively comprised the *sans-culottes*—before it could start making policies, in 1793, of which the bourgeoisie was incapable. But Russia, compared to other countries that had experienced a bourgeois revolution, was *sui generis*. In Russia the replacement of one coterie or class of revolutionary actors by another was not a necessary prerequisite for a revolution there to be radicalized. Nor was it a necessary prerequisite for that second, more radicalized revolution to succeed. Trotsky summarized the difference between the circumstances that pertained in France in 1789 and those existing presently in Russia in the following way:

> In the French Revolution the conditions for the hegemony of a capitalist bourgeoisie were prepared by the terrorist dictatorship of the victorious *sans-culottes*. This happened at a time when the main mass of the urban population was composed of a petty bourgeoisie of craftsmen and shopkeepers. This mass was led by the Jacobins.
>
> In Russia today the main mass of the urban population is composed of the industrial proletariat. Is this analogy enough to suggest that a potential historical

situation in which the victory of a 'bourgeois' revolution is rendered possible only by the proletariat gaining revolutionary power? Or does the revolution therefore stop being a bourgeois one. Yes and no.... If the proletariat is overthrown by a coalition of bourgeois classes, including the peasantry, whom the proletariat itself has liberated, then the revolution will retain its limited bourgeois character. But if the proletariat succeeds in using all means to achieve its own political hegemony and thereby breaks out of the national confines of the Russian revolution, then that revolution could become the prologue to a world socialist revolution.[33]

In *1905* Trotsky made clear that, for revolutionaries like himself, the French Revolution had become more an anachronism than an analogue. The Russian revolution he anticipated and expected would be radically different, and invoking the earlier revolution for insights into the course the later one would take would be a waste of time. But throughout the book, Trotsky always showed the French Revolution genuine respect. It was a milestone in human history no less trans-formative because Russia would likely go well beyond its foundational teleology. But when it came to particular figures in the revolution of whose actions he disapproved, Trotsky, a few years later, could not restrain himself. In 1908 he directed at Lafayette and Anacharsis Cloots the derisive and opprobrious rhetoric he usually reserved not for counter-revolutionaries and reactionaries permanently hostile to historical progress, but for pseudo-revolutionaries who either skilfully masked their fundamentally malevolent intentions behind a smokescreen of progressive rhetoric, as Lafayette did, or showed incredible naiveté, of which Cloots was undeniably guilty, in promoting policies that were completely unrealistic and unattainable.[34] But why Trotsky chose these two, very dissimilar person-ages in the French Revolution to excoriate is not clear. He could just as easily have denounced Mirabeau instead of Lafayette, and the Girondins instead of Cloots. All the two men had in common, as far as Trotsky was concerned, was that they both belonged to classes that obviated any possibility of their understanding socialism. Lafayette was a typical aristocrat, who betrayed the revolution when he realized it would harm his own class. Cloots, by contrast, was a revolutionary dreamer labouring under the illusion that a bourgeois revolution like the French could emancipate humanity as a whole.[35] Trotsky disagreed. Only a socialist revolution led by the proletariat could do that.

Trotsky was not the only Russian socialist intoxicated by the 1905 Revolution to the point where Marxist assumptions about what kind of revolution it was were forgotten. Pavel Axelrod, whose strictures on the dangers of Jacobin dictatorship predated his recognition that Lenin aspired to something akin to it, nevertheless

[33] Ibid., pp. 240–1.
[34] L. Trotsky, 'Nashe otchestvo vo vremeni (12 April 1908)', in Trotsky, *Sochineniia*, vol. XX, p. 267.
[35] In his jeremiad, Trotsky mocked Cloots for supposedly considering himself the embodiment of all of humanity. Ibid.

wrote in 1905 that 'a central club' should be created 'to rally the local proletariat and to form a strong revolutionary atmosphere modelled on the Jacobin clubs in France'.[36] But most of the Mensheviks resisted the temptation to which Axelrod succumbed. Even as the revolution approached its climax in October, Martov remained convinced that any facsimile of the Jacobins controlling it was a recipe for disaster; not even the benefits a bourgeois revolution would normally confer could come about in Russia, and with a proletarian revolution precluded by Russia's backwardness, the country would find itself in a cul-de-sac from which its extrication would be exceedingly difficult.[37] As for Plekhanov, the lesson he drew from 1905 was that it failed because Russia was not ready for it. Despite achieving the highest industrial growth rates in history in the 1890s, the country still lacked the essential prerequisites of a bourgeois revolution. For that reason he considered Lenin's and Trotsky's seductive notion of combining the two revolutions into one the most odious form of ideological apostasy. To underscore his disgust, in both 1905 and1906 he analogized what they intended to the elitism of *Narodnaia Volia*, which in turn reminded him of everything he disliked about the Jacobins. The *narodovol'tsy*, in his scathing derogation of them, were just 'our homegrown Jacobins'.[38] Any revolution led by Lenin—who by this time was for Plekhanov no more a Marxist than the Russian terrorists he had excoriated well over a quarter-century earlier—would lead inevitably to a reaction strongly resembling Thermidor. To be sure, this would not be an unmitigated disaster. In fact, in Russia it would be a significant improvement over a stagnant form of feudalism that only grudgingly allowed the emergence of bourgeois class relations. But any Leninist insurrection would delay their appearance unnecessarily, and would constitute for the proletariat a dead end yielding no discernible advantage.[39]

Lenin and Trotsky were well aware of Plekhanov's scepticism about their ruminations on accelerating the course of history. It must therefore have come as a pleasant surprise for them that their scenarios, which differed only in the greater role Trotsky's assigned to the proletariat in countries more advanced than Russia, were considered well within the realm of possibility by Karl Kautsky, one of the leaders of the German Social Democratic Party, which before its supposed betrayal of socialism in 1914, when it supported Germany's decision to go to war, both Lenin and Trotsky held in the highest esteem. In a pamphlet prompted by several of Plekhanov's in 1906 and 1907 advising against an armed uprising in Russia, Kautsky agreed with Plekhanov's contention that the Russian bourgeoisie

[36] P. B. Axelrod, *Narodnaia duma i rabochii s"ezd* (Geneva, 1905), p. 8.
[37] 'Pis'mo Iu. O. Martova k P. B. Aksel'rodu', pp. 145–7.
[38] Veber, 'Lenin i istoricheskoe nasledie iakobintsev', p. 22.
[39] G. V. Plekhanov, 'K agrarnomu voprosu v Rossii (March 1906)', in Plekhanov, *Sochineniia*, vol. XV, pp. 28–9.

was too weak to make a bourgeois revolution on its own.[40] After its creation in 1906, the sorry record of Russia's liberal party in addressing and solving Russia's problems was proof of the lassitude and lack of political will of the urban middle class.[41] To the extent that that was true, the French Revolution, which when it began was a purely bourgeois revolution, was not an example Russian socialists should emulate. But Kautsky did not believe this to be a cause for despair. According to the German socialist, the Russian proletariat, while not strong enough to make a bourgeois revolution by itself, could do so if advanced elements of the Russian peasantry assisted it. In that way, the Russian monarchy and the feudalism it perpetuated could be destroyed. To be sure, in recommending this course of action Kautsky did not jettison every aspect of the Marxism he professed. Although the coalition Lenin envisioned of the proletariat and the peasantry might succeed in making a bourgeois revolution, Kautsky did not think it strong enough, at least not for the foreseeable future, to radicalize the revolution to the point where the preconditions for socialism existed. The most likely result, in his view, would be:

> an entirely original process, occurring on the boundary between bourgeois and socialist society, facilitating the liquidation of the first, then preparing the conditions for the establishment of the second, and in any case giving powerful impetus to the progressive development of the countries where capitalist civilization existed.[42]

Even though Kautsky's endorsement of the scenario Lenin was considering was hardly a full-throated one, his article, which Lenin translated into Russian and for the publication of which produced a laudatory introduction, was certainly, from Lenin's perspective, a welcome development. Although his description of Kautsky's article as 'the most brilliant confirmation' of the Bolsheviks' tactics was unabashed hyperbole, Lenin was pleased to receive support from any quarter, and the fact that it came from one of the leading lights of German socialism was especially welcome.[43]

---

[40] K. Kautsky, *Dvizhushchie sily i perspektivy russkoi revoliutsii* (Moscow/Leningrad, 1926), pp. 15–17.

[41] Ibid., pp. 22–6.   [42] Ibid., p. 29.

[43] Ibid., p. 6. Of course when he wrote these words Lenin had no way of knowing that in 1914 Kautsky would change his mind, and exclude the peasants from any revolutionary coalition based on the proletariat. Nor, more significantly, could Lenin know in 1907 that in 1914 he would denounce Kautsky for his pro-war position—which caused Lenin thereafter to disparage him invariably as 'the Renegade Kautsky'. Nor could he possibly know in 1907 that in 1920 he and Trotsky would train on the German socialist a withering barrage of insults for the heresy of openly opposing the new Soviet state. Kautsky of course was not the only socialist in Europe who became a patriot in August 1914. Jules Guesde of France, for example, stated at the time that his own country 'will have no more ardent defenders than socialists'. Robert Tombs, *France 1814–1914* (New York and London, 1996), p. 320. But Alexandre Millerand's decision to join a bourgeois government in France in 1899 disgusted Lenin and lowered his opinion of French socialism generally to such an extent—his writings in the years that followed are filled with denunciations of Millerand himself and of the party he belonged to—that one suspects he was less surprised and angered by Guesde's heresy in 1914 than by Kautsky's.

To be sure, it took some time, in the aftermath of the 1905 Revolution, for Lenin to conceptualize the scenario conjured by Trotsky in 1906 and reaffirmed by Kautsky in 1907. The confusion in Lenin's writings while the revolution was still in progress was resolved after it failed—but not before his experiencing genuine despondency. In an article he wrote for *Novaia zhizn'* (*New Times*) that appeared in two installments in the late fall of 1905, Lenin maintained that Russian capitalism was now more developed than it was in France in 1789. But he then conceded that the oppression it made necessary was not yet sufficient for a proletarian revolution to occur.[44] The Russian proletariat, he admitted, presently sought a 'cleansing' of capitalism rather than its overthrow.[45] By May 1906, however, his mood had brightened. In a report on the so-called Unity Congress of the RSDLP, Lenin invoked the French Revolution yet again, in this instance citing the weakness of the backward and 'semi-feudal' countries surrounding France when the revolution began.[46] In fact, with every year they got weaker, which enabled the revolution to survive their efforts, through the application of military force, to restore the *ancien régime*. At this point in Lenin's argument, any comparison with the revolution would seem to reinforce the pessimism that pervaded the aforementioned article in *Novaia zhizn'*. The capitalist countries of Western Europe were undeniably stronger in 1906 than the feudal states and principalities bordering France in 1789. But their strength, paradoxically, was actually, according to Lenin, a sign of weakness: the more advanced a capitalist country was, the more radical and potentially subversive was the proletariat it oppressed. In Lenin's phraseology, the proletariat at the beginning of the twentieth century was 'a social force capable of becoming the reserve of the revolution'.[47]

Left unsaid in Lenin's argument was the assumption that the proletariat in Germany, France, or Great Britain, on taking power, would be willing and able to assist the proletariat in Russia, a thousand miles to the east, in whatever revolution—in his report Lenin did not indicate whether it would be bourgeois or socialist—it might choose to undertake. One month later, in an article ridiculing the proposal that Russian socialists should collaborate with the Kadets because they were equally committed to overthrowing the monarchy in a bourgeois revolution, Lenin forthrightly excluded the bourgeoisie from participation in this endeavour. Even more daringly, he claimed that this exclusion should be enforced before the proletariat and the peasantry, after replacing the bourgeoisie at the forefront of those clamouring for a bourgeois revolution, were strong enough to ensure that any revolution the two classes began would succeed. In this instance, as in many others

---

[44] V. I. Lenin, 'Sotsialisticheskaia partiia i bespartiinaia revoliutsionnost', in Lenin, *PSS*, vol. XII, p. 134.
[45] Ibid., p. 135.
[46] V. I. Lenin, 'Doklad ob Ob"edinitel'nom s"ezde RSDRP (Pis'mo k Peterburgskim rabochim)', in Lenin, *PSS*, vol. XIII, p. 17.
[47] Ibid., p. 18.

in Lenin's career, his enormous self-confidence, now fully restored, enabled him to banish any doubts he might still have had about the imminence and viability of a proletarian revolution in Russia. That Lenin included in his article the following reference to the French Revolution shows the role it played in enabling him to claim to know what the future would bring:

> Our Russian opportunists [by whom Lenin meant Social Democrats seeking an alliance with the Kadets] are like all opportunists: they demean the teachings of revolutionary Marxism and the role of the proletariat as the vanguard. They labour under the illusion that the liberal bourgeoisie must inevitably be the 'boss' in any bourgeois revolution. They fail totally to understand the historical role played, for example, by the Convention in the great French Revolution as the dictatorship of the lower strata of society, specifically of the proletariat and the petit-bourgeoisie. They fail totally to understand the idea of the dictatorship of the proletariat and peasantry as the only possible social bulwark of a fully victorious bourgeois revolution in Russia.[48]

Underlying Lenin's reference to the French Revolution was the assumption in Marxist ideology that knowing the past enabled one to predict the future.

As the notion of the proletariat allying with the peasantry was germinating in Lenin's mind, he had to respond to attacks from Plekhanov and other socialists for whom the schemata of revolution inherited from Marx and Engels since their deaths had acquired the patina of holy writ. This was especially the case now that several of them, notably Lenin and Bernstein, were exploring different ways of achieving the same objective, thereby making them vulnerable to the charge, however unfair, that by substituting their own tactics for Marx's, they were somehow repudiating Marx's objectives, which were socialism and communism. In several articles that were written in 1906, Lenin took up the cudgel he had earlier wielded against critics claiming that, in exceeding the limits of what was tactically permissible, he was really a Blanquist—a term which in the circles Lenin inhabited could only be a pejorative. Blanquists were generally believed to have been conspirators without even a smidgen of popular support; for that reason their efforts to create socialism were doomed to fail. Lenin was very sensitive to the charge of Blanquism in part because the charge was accurate. In May 1906 he wrote the following about the tactical heresy with which he was charged:

> Blanquism is a theory that rejects class struggle. Blanquism expects that mankind will be emancipated from wage slavery, not by proletarian class struggle, but by means of a conspiracy hatched of a small minority of intellectuals. . . . By using the ruse of 'Blanquism', the bourgeoisie wants to belittle, discredit, and slander the people's struggle for power. . . . The right-wing Social Democrats use the word

---

[48] V. I. Lenin, 'Kto za soiuzy s kadetami', in Lenin, *PSS*, vol. XIII, pp. 244–5.

'Blanquism' merely as a rhetorical device in their polemics—while the bourgeoisie meanwhile converts the word into a weapon against the proletariat.[49]

Like many others within the self-contained little universe of Russian socialists prior to the October Revolution, the debate over Lenin's Blanquism continued until 1917, when arcane disputes like this one finally yielded to matters of practical significance. One reason for this was that, in reality, there was little else to do. Plekhanov and the Menshevik Iurii Larin both claimed that this particular deviation from Marxist orthodoxy called into question Lenin's commitment to socialism itself—to which Lenin replied in *Proletarii* that by levelling the charge, Plekhanov, at least, was merely 'venting his spleen'.[50] Perhaps surprisingly, in light of what she had written about Lenin in 1904 and would write in 1918, after the new Bolshevik government in Petrograd convinced her, by its actions, that it was a ruthless dictatorship and would never relinquish power voluntarily, Rosa Luxemburg came to Lenin's defence. In an article written in Polish that was published in June 1906, she exonerated the leader of the Bolsheviks of the ideological crime of which Plekhanov, Larin, and others had judged him guilty:

> If today the Bolshevik comrades speak of the dictatorship of the proletariat, they have never given it the old Blanquist meaning, nor have they ever fallen into the mistake of *Narodnaia Volia*, which dreamt of 'taking power for itself'. On the contrary, they have affirmed that the present revolution will succeed when the proletariat—all the revolutionary class—takes possession of the state machine. The proletariat, as the most revolutionary element, will perhaps assume the role of liquidator of the old regime by 'taking power for itself' in order to defeat counter-revolution and prevent the revolution being led astray by a bourgeoisie that is reactionary in its very nature. No revolution can succeed other than by the dictatorship of one class, and all the signs are that the proletariat can become this liquidator at the present time.[51]

The debate over Lenin's ostensible Blanquism continued with the same intensity until 1912, when Lenin declared the Bolshevik faction of the RSDLP an independent entity, thereby obviating the necessity of responding to every Menshevik attack or insinuation. In 1907 he responded to Plekhanov's charge that he and his supporters were Blanquists by noting that Marx in 1871 had refused to condemn the Blanquists and Proudhonists supporting the Paris Commune because its survival was more important than the ideological deviations of

---

[49] V. I. Lenin, 'V itogam s"ezda', ibid., pp. 76–7.

[50] V. I. Lenin, 'Predislovie k russkomu perevodu broshiury V. Libknekhta "Nikakikh kompromissov, nikakikh izbiratel'nykh soglashenii" (December 1906)', in Lenin, *PSS*, vol. XIV, p. 220. To be precise, Larin accused not just Lenin, but the Bolsheviks as a whole, of 'anarcho-blanquism'. V. I. Lenin, 'Krizis Men'shevizma (7 December 1906)', ibid., p. 154.

[51] Rosa Luxemburg, 'Blankizm i Socjałdemokracia', *Czerwony Sztandar*, no. 86 (June 1906), https://www.marxists.org/archive/luxemburg/1906/06/blanquism.html.

which they were both guilty.[52] But in 1911 Lenin was the attacker, in this instance accusing Martov, and by implication the Mensheviks collectively, of precisely that which they had ascribed to him several years earlier. When Lenin was writing, he was disturbed by what was called, in the pejorative, 'liquidationism'. By this was meant the notion, which Lenin abhorred, that much, if not all, of the conspiratorial apparatus with which Russian socialists had protected their party against the tsarist police could be eliminated because repression in Russia by now had diminished significantly. But to Lenin—if one considers his public statements a reflection of what he actually believed—the Mensheviks (especially Martov) were advocating this course of action because their objectives and those of the Kadets (the Russian liberals) made a separate and distinct socialist party, operating underground beneath the increasingly hospitable environs of parliamentary politics, unnecessary and even a handicap. To the Mensheviks, its liquidation would make a bourgeois revolution, led by the Kadets with the Mensheviks in a subordinate position, much easier. Lenin, of course, strongly disagreed. In fact, he turned the charge of Blanquism against the Mensheviks, who he said deserved the appellation because they now considered a revolutionary party unnecessary.[53] That they did so for a reason no true Blanquist could ever accept was of course a caveat Lenin omitted from his polemic.

It should be borne in mind that Lenin, while *sui generis* in his tactical improvisations to compensate for Russia's unreadiness for a socialist revolution, did not fight Martynov and the Mensheviks alone. He had allies. One was Anatolii Lunacharskii, the future Commissar of Education in the Soviet Union. Lunacharskii was well-positioned to assist Lenin. As one of the editors of *Vpered*— M. S. Ol'minskii and V. V. Vorovskii were the others—from December 1904 to May 1905, he had easy access to a forum from which to disseminate his views. That the journal was published openly in Geneva made them accessible to the exile community not just in Switzerland but in all of Western Europe. For many years, Lunacharskii remained mute as the debate over Jacobinism became more and more acrimonious. But the polemics it produced intensified in 1904, and in January 1905, barely more than a week before the outbreak of revolution, Lunacharskii finally addressed the larger issue it concealed, namely whether the bourgeoisie could be trusted to bring any revolution in Russia to fruition and, in that event, whether a more advanced, proletarian revolution might closely follow it. The arguments he mustered, like Lenin's, relied heavily on the French Revolution for clarification and corroboration.[54]

---

[52] V. I. Lenin, 'Predislovie k russkomu perevodu pisem K. Marksa k Kugel'manu', in Lenin, *PSS*, vol. XIV, p. 376.

[53] V. I. Lenin, 'O sotsial'noi structure vlasti, perspektivakh i likvidatorstve', ibid., vol. XX, p. 201.

[54] A. Lunacharskii, 'Ocherki po istorii revoliutsionnoi bor'by evropeiskogo proletariata', *Vpered*, no. 2 (1 January 1905): pp. 2–3.

In Lunacharskii's opinion, the Russian proletariat, in 1905, could draw both inspiration and guidance from the events in France beginning in 1789. The French proletariat—by which Lunacharskii always meant the *sans-culottes* in Paris—was too immature politically to act on its own after the revolution began; understandably it saw the bourgeoisie as an ally whose strength was reason enough to support it. Moreover, until feudalism was destroyed, the interests of the bourgeoisie and the proletariat in France coincided. But the mistake the French proletariat made was in thinking that the bourgeoisie's solicitude for its welfare was genuine, rather than the result of political calculation. As it happened, once feudalism ended, the bourgeoisie turned on the proletariat and neutered it politically. But the Russian proletariat, in Lunacharskii's effusively optimistic estimation, was not susceptible to such naiveté. Because its political consciousness greatly exceeded that of even the most radical of the *sans-culottes* in the French Revolution, it would not only not align with the bourgeoisie, the upper echelons of which would almost certainly not participate in any bourgeoisie revolution, but it would also repudiate elements of the petit-bourgeoisie that might want to assist it after the bourgeois revolution had succeeded. The Russian proletariat, in other words, was now strong enough to make a socialist revolution by itself.

Lenin edited at least one of the essays Lunacharskii wrote and published in *Vpered* in 1905; he may even have tried to accelerate their publication.[55] Obviously he recognized how closely Lunacharskii's vision of the socialist revolution emerging organically from the bourgeois revolution, with the proletariat as the driving force in both of them, resembled his own. But Lunacharskii, while describing his prediction of events in Russia dispassionately, seemed to be more invested emotionally in the French Revolution than Lenin was. For Lunacharskii, the revolution was not the asseveration of a cold rationality traceable to the Enlightenment, but of emotions that were grounded in a visceral demand for justice. For Lunacharskii, the most iconic event of the revolution was the storming of the Bastille, which he described in language even more florid than that to which he was normally inclined. In his description, revolutionaries 'raising their banners for all the oppressed…possessed intangible advantages that made the fortress, which seemed impregnable, an easy target, for in the end, as a symbol of the status quo, it was weak in an ethical sense: the *ancien régime* it represented had lost its legitimacy and stood for little more than its own perpetuation and the continued oppression of the lower classes.[56] In fact the French Revolution, in Lunacharskii's estimation, was as much a culturally transformative event as it was the political prerequisite of industrial capitalism. In his mind, the revolution improved the

[55] 'Spisok izdanii redaktirovannykh V. I. Leninom', in Lenin, *PSS*, vol. XI, p. 437; *V. I. Lenin i A. V. Lunacharskii. Perepiska, doklady, dokumenty—Literaturnoe nasledstvo* (Moscow, 1971), vol. LXXX, pp. 527–33.

[56] A. Lunacharskii, 'Ocherki po istorii revoliutsionnoi bor'by evropeiskogo proletariata', *Vpered*, no. 9 (23 February 1905)': pp. 2–3.

moral calibre of nearly all of its participants, and in doing so prepared the stage, so to speak, for the next act in the ongoing Marxist revolutionary drama. Lunacharskii's comments on the French Revolution, considered in their totality, were reason enough for his selection, after the October Revolution, to head the Commissariat of Education. More than most Russian socialists, excepting only Trotsky and Lenin, Lunacharskii was sensitive to the propagandistic possibilities in revolutions and revolutionary mythologies, and it was hardly a coincidence that after the October Revolution much of the pageantry Lunacharsjkii mobilized to legitimize it included innumerable references—in music, theatre, literature, and the visual arts—to its French analogue and antecedent.

A very different ally in Lenin's rhetorical wars was the young Joseph Stalin. It is not known if Lenin was aware of Stalin's writings in the months when he was battling his enemies within the ranks of Russian socialism and beyond them. Nor can one be sure that the reverse was true prior to Lenin elevating the Georgian to the central committee of the newly proclaimed Bolshevik party in 1912. But the resemblance between what the two men wrote during the 1905 Revolution and in its immediate aftermath is striking. Indeed, this similarity pervaded what each believed about the French Revolution.

Stalin, while an autodidact, was not the ignoramus many of his future rivals—and future allies—considered him. A voracious reader at an early age, by adulthood he had familiarized himself with many of the classics in European and Georgian literature.[57] One of the many books he read while a student in the theological seminary he attended before becoming a revolutionary was Victor Hugo's last novel, *Ninety-Three*, which brought to life the disparate personalities of that critical year in a way few works of history, no matter how well-written, could match.[58] The result was that when Stalin first wrote about the French Revolution, he knew a great deal about it, certainly far more than one would expect from someone growing up in a milieu so far removed, culturally no less than geographically, from Western Europe.[59] Although he wrote nothing about the debate within the RSDLP over the Jacobins, the outbreak of revolution in 1905 prompted Stalin to put his more general thoughts about the French Revolution on paper.

In August 1905 Stalin drew an analogy between the two revolutions, the French and ongoing one in Russia, but only for the purpose of rejecting it.[60] The French

---

[57] Stephen Kotkin, *Stalin: Paradoxes of Power, 1878–1928* (New York, 2014), pp. 32, 36.

[58] Ian Grey, *Stalin: Man of History* (Garden City NY, 1979), p. 21; Robert C. Tucker, *Stalin as Revolutionary 1879–1929* (New York, 1974), p. 86.

[59] Stalin also read about the French Revolution when he was exiled to Siberia several times before the October Revolution. According to one of his biographers, he found especially impressive Robespierre's decisiveness in dealing with enemies of the revolution. Dmitrii Volkogonov, *Stalin, Triumph and Tragedy* (New York, 1996), p. 279.

[60] J. V. Stalin, 'Vremennoe revoliutsionnoe pravitel'stvo i sotsial-demokratiia', in J. V. Stalin, *Sochineniia*, 13 vols (Moscow, 1946–51), vol. I, pp. 149–51.

Revolution, he wrote, was a bourgeois revolution, while the Russian one, at least in its leadership, was proletarian. In the short, declarative sentences that would characterize his prose for the rest of his life, Stalin starkly dichotomized the two revolutions:

> In France the bourgeoisie was at the head of the revolution; in Russia it is the proletariat. There, the bourgeoisie determined the fate of the revolution; in Russia the proletariat will do so. And is it not clear that with such a realignment of the leading revolutionary forces the results for the respective classes cannot be identical? If, in France, the bourgeoisie, being at the head of the revolution, reaped its rewards, must it also reap them in Russia, notwithstanding the fact that the proletariat here stands at the head of the revolution? Yes, say our Mensheviks; what happened there, in France, must also happen here, in Russia. These gentlemen, like undertakers, take the measure of something long dead—but then apply its lessons to the living.[61]

Because the Mensheviks were 'capable of learning historical facts only by rote', Stalin continued, they could not possibly comprehend the difference between the conditions in France in 1789 and those in Russia in 1905.[62]

In two statements he made in 1906 and 1907 respectively, Stalin explained further why he considered the two revolutions dichotomous.[63] In the course of reiterating Lenin's scenario of the proletariat in Russia leading a bourgeois revolution and then going well beyond it to a socialist revolution, Stalin made clear that the failure of the 1905 Revolution was not cause for discouragement, because the proletariat still had a political party, the RSDLP, representing it. The party had already instilled in the proletariat the cognizance of its own objectives that it needed to act politically, so that when the time came to advance its own interests, rather than those of another, retrograde class—in this instance the bourgeoisie—it would do so. Moreover, in the proletariat's independence, the contrast to what the French proletariat had done in the French Revolution would be unmistakable. In that particular instance, the workers did the difficult and dangerous work of confronting the revolution's enemies, while the bourgeoisie took power and reaped its rewards. But in Russia the proletariat would not be content with 'dragging the tail' of the bourgeoisie, and for that reason 'our revolution [will have] an advantage over the Great French Revolution in that it will culminate with the people gaining total sovereignty'.[64] In fact, the proletariat, as Stalin described it, would likely resist all efforts by the bourgeoisie, and by treacherous pseudo-socialists only pretending to have its interests at heart, to

[61]   Ibid., p. 150.   [62]   Ibid., p. 155.

[63]   J. V. Stalin, 'Sovremennyi moment i ob"edinitel'nyi s"ezd rabochei partii (1906)', in Stalin, *Sochineniia*, vol. 1, pp. 254–8; J. V. Stalin, 'Londonskii s"ezd rossiiskoi sotsial-demokraticheskoi rabochei partii (Zapiski delegata) (20 June and 10 July 1907)', ibid., vol. II, pp. 60–2.

[64]   Stalin, 'Sovremennyi moment', in Stalin, *Sochineniia*, vol. 1, pp. 255–6.

sabotage it in its ongoing effort to improve its material condition. In short, because the bourgeoisie was so inherently perfidious and malevolent, the proletariat should never allow itself 'to pull its chestnuts out of the fire'—by which Stalin meant that the proletariat should never act as a surrogate of the bourgeoisie, or of any other class; more broadly, he meant that one should always act, and only act, in the service of one's own interests, not those of anyone else.[65] In this respect, Stalin identified Martynov as the worst offender among the Mensheviks in their efforts to prevent the Russian proletariat from acting on the basis of its own interests and to serve those of the bourgeoisie instead. Like Lenin, Stalin, moreover, personalized political disagreements—in the 1930s he would do so to the point where they were *ipso facto* evidence of treason—and for that reason his criticisms of political opponents, in this case Martynov, were no less caustic and *ad hominem* than Lenin's.

In 1907 Stalin also wrote a preface, in some ways similar to Lenin's of the same year, to Kautsky's aforementioned pamphlet, in which he expressed agreement with the latter's scenario of the proletariat and peasantry replacing the bourgeoisie in a bourgeois revolution. Once again, Stalin implied that what distinguished the French Revolution from any bourgeois revolution that might occur in Russia was more significant than any similarities between them. The principal difference, according to Stalin, was that in the French Revolution, which both he and Kautsky considered a bourgeois revolution, the 'liberal bourgeoisie' played the dominant role, partly because this was the role Marx intended for it, but also because the proletariat was too weak to do anything but provide incidental or mostly ineffectual assistance.[66] But in Russia in 1907, circumstances were different. The liberal bourgeoisie was no longer revolutionary; indeed, the Kadets, who served as its political instrument in Russia, now 'seek protection under the wing of reaction' even before a bourgeois revolution has occurred.[67] But the proletariat, according to Stalin, was ready for action, and it was only a matter of time before it would rise up against the existing order and destroy it.

If only by implication, Stalin adopted Lenin's whole scenario of revolution in the aftermath of the 1905 Revolution, and in doing so utilized the example—or more precisely the counter-example—of the French Revolution in distinguishing what he believed would happen in Russia from what unfortunately happened in

---

[65] Ibid., p. 256. This was the same phrase Stalin used in his speech to the Eighteenth Party Congress in March 1939 to indicate subtly to Hitler that he would likely not sign any agreement with Great Britain and France directed at Nazi Germany. Hitler rightly interpreted Stalin's comment as indicating a readiness to explore the possibility of a *rapprochement* between the two dictatorships, which was achieved with the signing of a non-aggression pact in August 1939, thereby enabling Nazi Germany to invade Poland ten days later, convinced that not only the Soviet Union, but also the Western Democracies would not attack it.

[66] J. V. Stalin, 'Predislovie k gruzinskomu izdaniiu broshiury K. Kautskogo "Dvizhushchie sily i perspektivy russkoi revoliutsii"', in Stalin, *Sochineniia*, vol. II, p. 4.

[67] Ibid.

the past when the proletariat foolishly aligned itself with the bourgeoisie in the entirely mistaken belief that the latter was its ally. Henceforth Stalin would not deviate from this particular aspect of Leninist orthodoxy, and would expound it with the same single-minded obstinacy with which he expressed political opinions generally. Like Lenin, Stalin much preferred a sledgehammer to a stiletto in eviscerating his political opponents rhetorically.

To be sure, there were differences, some of them subtle, between what Lenin and Stalin each wrote about the French Revolution. While Stalin agreed with Lenin that Jacobinism was a virtue that anyone engaged in making a full-scale revolution would do well to adopt, he disagreed with him on Blanquism. In contrast to Lenin, for whom the term was always one of opprobrium and its application to him a grave injustice, Stalin, like Lenin after being accused of Jacobinism, welcomed the charge, thereby turning an expletive into a compliment. At least in what he wrote publicly about it, Blanquism was just a short-form for the scenario he envisioned of professional revolutionaries like himself and Lenin one day leading the masses in creating the more equitable society the proletariat deserved. According to Stalin, Bolshevism and Blanquism were synonymous: they both prescribed 'the introduction of consciousness and organization into [any] sporadic insurrection that has broken out spontaneously'.[68] To Stalin it seemed not to matter that the Bolsheviks—like the Blanquists—had few followers. The important point was that they would acquire them in the future—but well before the proletarian revolution both Stalin and the other Bolsheviks predicted. Although there exists no empirical evidence to prove it conclusively, it seems reasonable to suggest that Stalin thought the Blanquists wise not to disavow the conspiratorial tactics they practised not just because they lacked mass support, but also because he thought such tactics absolutely essential once the Bolsheviks took power. In other words, the hegemony professional revolutionaries exercised over the workers that Russian socialists without exception considered a regrettable, but temporary, necessity—Lenin always claimed that he shared in this consensus, but many who knew him did not believe him when he said it—Stalin considered this imbalance of power a virtue and believed it should continue at least until socialism existed, and possibly even under communism itself—even though the whole notion of communism would be rendered meaningless as a result.

Another difference between the two men in how they viewed the two revolutions, the French and the Russian, was that Stalin was more ready than Lenin to distinguish them both morally and ideologically. In Lenin's explication of the French Revolution, he always considered it morally equivalent—though not ideologically equivalent—to any proletarian revolution that might occur in the future. Both were inherently progressive, and one could hardly blame the French

---

[68] J. V. Stalin, 'Marks i Engel's o vosstanii (13 July 1906)', in Stalin, *Sochineniia*, vol. II, p. 243.

in 1789 for not making a revolution more radical than what the existing objective conditions in France permitted. Undoubtedly Lenin, at a visceral level, admired revolutionaries like Babeuf and the Hébertists for wanting to go further. But his cold rationalism prevented his admiration from overpowering his judgement. Even the language Lenin normally used in describing and explaining the French Revolution only rarely descended into the *ad hominem* recriminations he regularly directed at contemporaries who for one reason or another displeased him. In the final analysis, the French Revolution was revealed to Lenin through the application of reason. But with Stalin, the revolution suffered from a failing that for Stalin originated more in his own psyche than out of any rational application of Marxist ideology. In practically everything Stalin wrote and said about the French Revolution there was implicit a genuine preference, more inchoate and unformed than carefully arrived at, for Russian revolutions because they would occur in Russia. The same was true, in reverse, for the French Revolution. Stalin wrote about it coldly, even dismissively, not just because it was a bourgeois revolution, but also because it occurred it France, rather than in Russia. The Russian nationalism that lurked beneath the surface of Soviet Communism that Stalin shared and employed adroitly in mobilizing the Soviet population against the Nazis decades later is evident, albeit in embryo, in his early writings on the French Revolution.

*   *   *

In making sense of Lenin's references to the French Revolution from 1905 to 1914, one must bear in mind that the revolution served during those years as a comforting counterpart to the powerlessness and isolation that, while not created by the failure of the 1905 Revolution, was certainly aggravated by it. Indeed, it seems that the French Revolution created for Lenin practically a parallel universe, in which moral virtue, at least in the beginning, was triumphant, power was exercised effectively, and any defeats that occurred were avenged in the future. That was certainly true in November 1907, when Lenin praised the National Assembly for emancipating the peasantry in France in 'one night in the summer of 1789'.[69] What made his paean to the assembly unusual, in addition to his praising an institution he had previously denigrated for its hostility to the lower classes, was that he now considered it the antithesis, morally and politically, of the Third Duma in Russia, the delegates to which had recently been elected in accordance with laws giving disproportional weight to the votes of nobles and affluent townspeople. By conjuring the National Assembly in his mind, he could create for himself a reality that, however idealized it might have been in comparison to actual events in Russia, remained a source of comfort and reassurance.

---

[69] V. I. Lenin, 'Prigotovlenie "otvratitel'noi orgii"', in Lenin, *PSS*, vol. XVI, p. 152.

The same dynamic helps to explain comments Lenin made at the Fifth Congress of the RSDLP, held in London in the spring of 1907, and immediately following it. Responding to a liberal who had characterized as unfortunate 'the road taken [in France] by the revolution of 1789–1793', Lenin, once again, effectively rehabilitated the first phase of the French Revolution, thereby contradicting previous iterations of its evolution, according to which the haute-bourgeoisie kept the radicals on a tight leash until the Jacobins came to power and radicalized the revolution beyond anything the bourgeoisie intended.[70] The Jacobin Terror, he wrote in February 1908, in response to the recent assassination of the King of Portugal, was 'genuine', 'popular', and 'truly regenerative', in contrast to the terror exemplified by the assassination, which he was certain would have no effect.[71] Two months later, Lenin decided that the events of the French Revolution, because they included peasant uprisings, were grounds for upgrading the 1905 Revolution to something that nearly succeeded; in fact these peasant uprisings showed that in any future revolution in Russia, the proletariat would guide the peasantry in a second revolution after both had replaced the bourgeoisie in the first one.[72] In 1911 Lenin once again spun the Janus-like sides of the French bourgeoisie; this time the side facing forward depicted the bourgeoisie, in 1789, as a genuinely progressive force, not making 'sour faces' when its 'younger brother'—the lower classes—spoke with conviction and eloquence about a future superior to anything that existed at the time.[73] But by the end of the year, the opposite side of the revolution, when the French bourgeoisie turned reactionary, appeared in yet another of Lenin's articles both advocating and predicting an alliance of the proletariat and the peasantry. Contrary to what he said was Martov's good opinion of it, the French bourgeoisie was cowardly and reactionary to the core. It carried out a bourgeois revolution only under pressure from the proletariat from 1789 to 1793, at which time it retired from politics, only to re-emerge in 1848 to betray the proletariat again. But fortunately the proletariat and the classes and categories of the population that supported it completed the bourgeois revolution the bourgeoisie began, thereby establishing the political system in France that exists today.[74] In fact, by 1913, Lenin was applying the lessons of the French Revolution to the whole issue of minority nationalism in the Russian Empire. In a letter to the Georgian Bolshevik, Stepan Shaumian, he contrasted the democratic centralism the Jacobins favoured to the federalism preferred by the Girondins. But after expressing agreement with the Jacobins, as he had done countless times before, in this instance Lenin went beyond his customary Jacobin–Girondin

[70] V. I. Lenin, 'Rech' ob otnoshenii k burzhuaznym partiiam (12 May 1907)', ibid., vol. XV, p. 336.
[71] V. I. Lenin, 'O proisshestvii s Korolem Portugal'skim', ibid., vol. XVI, p. 441.
[72] V. I. Lenin, 'K otsenke russkoi revoliutsii', ibid., vol. XVII, pp. 46–7.
[73] V. I. Lenin, 'O starykh, no vechno novykh istinakh (11 June 1911)', ibid., vol. XX, p. 281.
[74] V. I. Lenin, 'Printsipal'nye voprosy izbiratel'noi kompanii (December 1911 and January 1912)', ibid., vol. XXI, pp. 83–4.

dichotomy and declared the relevance to Russia of what he called 'autonomy', by which he seemed to mean something in between the centralism the Jacobins favoured, and the federalism the Girondins preferred.[75]

What was significant about Lenin's preference for a compromise between a centralized polity and a federative one was not just that he considered it an amalgam of what the Jacobins and the Girondins had each preferred. Even more important was that it predated by several years what he recommended for what remained of the Russian Empire after the Bolsheviks had taken power in 1917, namely a middle course between two extreme positions that would give the national minorities the illusion they enjoyed autonomy while actually binding them to the Centre in perpetuity. Independence could be promised in the Soviet Constitution of 1922 because Lenin believed conditions in the Soviet Union would be so wonderful that no Soviet citizen in his right mind would want to leave it.

The outbreak of the First World War in August 1914 created new realities Lenin had to comprehend and comment on if his views were not to sink into irrelevance. Once again he called upon the French Revolution for assistance. In this instance, however, he situated the revolution historically within the larger rubric of the tradition of revolutions in France, which he defined temporally as encompassing the eighty-two years between the outbreak of the French Revolution in 1789 and the emergence and suppression of the Paris Commune in 1871.[76] What distinguished this period both from what preceded it and what followed it was the triumph and continued dominance of the bourgeoisie first in France and then, somewhat later, elsewhere in Western Europe, and finally in Central Europe. In some countries, including France, its victory was rapid and fairly easy, while in others, such as Germany, it was difficult and took some time. But in every instance it achieved 'the breakdown of the obsolete feudal-absolutist institutions'.[77]

The Marxist dialectic, however, drove history beyond what the bourgeoisie desired. Beneath the surface of its seemingly incontestable victory over feudalism were buried the seeds of its eventual demise. In Europe its decline began in 1871. In every year that followed, the bourgeoisie could not help but transform itself from its 'original progressive character towards reactionary and even

---

[75] V. I. Lenin, 'Letter to S. G. Shaumian (6 December 1913)', Lenin, *Collected Works*, vol. XIX, p. 500.

[76] V. I. Lenin, 'Pod chuzhim flagom (no earlier than February 1915)', ibid., vol. XXVI, p. 143. Lenin, to be sure, never wrote or spoke explicitly about a French revolutionary tradition or explained the reason for his particular choice of dates. But those he chose (1789 and 1871) make clear that he believed such a tradition existed and that it defined a discrete period within the larger capitalist phase of history Marx had earlier claimed to discern. Between the outbreak of the First World War and the February Revolution in Russia, Lenin wrote often about what made 1789–1871 distinctive not only in the history of France but also in the history of Europe. See, as examples, 'Sotsializm i voina (otnoshenie RSDRP k voine) (July–August 1915)', ibid., vol. XXVI, pp. 312–13 (co-authored with Zinoviev); 'Opportunizm i krakh II Internatsionala,(end of 1915)', ibid., vol. XXVII, pp. 100–1, 116–17; and 'O karikature na marksizma (August–October 1916)', Lenin, *PSS*, vol. XXX, pp. 80–1, among others.

[77] Lenin, 'Pod chuzhim flagom', ibid., vol. XXVI, p. 143.

ultra-reactionary finance capital'.[78] In an adumbration of what he would argue at greater length in his 1916 exegesis on imperialism, Lenin claimed that this period of bourgeois decay reached its apogee in 1914, when the internal contradictions of capitalism had weakened the class sufficiently so that not even imperialism—which provided capitalists with markets to compensate for the inability of impoverished workers to purchase all of the industrial goods the capitalists produced—could prevent its collapse.

What Lenin concluded from all of this was that it made no sense for the Russian proletariat to participate in Russia's defence against its more advanced capitalist enemy, namely Germany. In fact, Lenin explicitly rejected the argument of Martov and several Mensheviks—who had agreed with him in 1914 that Russian socialists should not support Russia's involvement in the war—that should 'the autocratic and feudal militarised imperialism' that caused the war be 'swept away' and replaced by 'bourgeois-democratic revolutions and republic', the proletariat should then support the countries where such a transfer of power within the bourgeoisie had occurred.[79] To Lenin such a course of action would be foolish. A different faction of the bourgeoisie might come to power, one less inclined to the bourgeois democracy Martov preferred to any bourgeois dictatorship, but the nature and objectives of the war would remain the same. The only circumstance under which Russian socialists should support the war, according to Lenin, would be if the proletariat somehow came to power in the course of it. But of course once the proletariat came to power in one of the countries waging war, it was highly likely—at this point Lenin was still reluctant to consider it inevitable— that *all* the combatants would soon stop fighting because the proletariat—which in the classic formulation of the Second International 'had no country'—would come to power nearly everywhere in Europe and render the original causes of the war an anachronism. In Lenin's tripartite division of modern history since 1789, the wars fought between 1871 and 1914 were imperialist wars, but now that imperialism, at least in Europe, could no longer save capitalism from destruction, the First World War was losing its *raison d'être*. To clarify his argument and to make it more convincing, Lenin yet again invoked the example of the French Revolution:

> [I]n 1793 the foremost class in the bourgeois revolution in France fought against European pre-revolutionary monarchies, whereas the Russia of 1915 is fighting not the more backward countries, but the more advanced ones, which are on the eve of a socialist revolution. For that reason, in the war of 1914–15 only a proletariat that is carrying out a victorious socialist revolution can play the part of the Jacobins of 1793. Consequently, in the present war, the Russian proletariat

---

[78] Lenin, 'Pod chuzhim flagom', ibid., vol. XXVI, p. 143.

[79] V. I. Lenin, 'Prikrytie sotsial-shovinistskoi politiki internatsionalistskimi frazami (21 December 1915)', ibid., vol. XXVII, p. 90.

could 'defend the fatherland', and consider 'the character of the war changed fundamentally', if, and only if, the revolution installed the party of the proletariat in power, and allowed only that party to direct the full force of a revolutionary upheaval and the machinery of the state towards an instant and direct conclusion of an alliance with the socialist proletariat of Germany and Europe.[80]

What is especially noteworthy about Lenin's whole scenario is that while he still considered a proletarian revolution in Russia by no means inevitable, or even likely, he seemed certain that, were such a revolution to occur in the context of proletarian revolutions in more economically advanced countries in Europe—it mattered not that it be Germany, which was fighting Russia, or Great Britain and France, which were its allies—the new proletarian regime in Russia would consider it essential to end the war as quickly as possible. In contrast to the French Revolution, which for all of its virtues could never eliminate opposition from 'feudal' elements opposed to it both at home and abroad, the countries fighting in the First World War would find the issues that caused them to go to war irrelevant once they jettisoned their bourgeois leadership and replaced it with proletarian regimes intent on establishing socialism and communism. Whereas wars fought between 1789 and 1871, and between 1871 and 1914, were incapable of changing the underlying economic rivalries and inequalities that caused them to erupt in the first place, the First World War, from Lenin's perspective, always had the potential to transform the existing constellation of forces in Europe, and to usher in an entirely new epoch in its history.

For Lenin this required a diminution in the relevance and importance of the French Revolution. In an article composed in the late summer and early autumn of 1916, he lumped France with Germany and England under the rubric of advanced capitalist countries that were once in the forefront of humanity, especially in 1789–1871, in forming national states, but which were now just the detritus of an era that was irretrievably lost.[81] In fact, these three countries had morphed into their antithesis: 'liberated nations have become oppressor nations, nations of imperialist rapine, nations approaching the eve of capitalism's collapse'.[82] In December 1916, barely a few weeks before the strikes and demonstrations that resulted in the collapse of the monarchy in Russia, Lenin reiterated his earlier tripartite division of Europe's modern history: 1789–1871, 1871–1914, 1914 to whenever proletarian revolutions erupt in Russia and Western Europe. This time, however, it came with the corollary that whatever moral capital France had acquired from its original revolution and the wars it fought to defend it it managed to squander later on, not only by suppressing revolutions in 1848 and in

---

[80] Ibid., vol. XXVII, p. 90.
[81] V. I. Lenin, 'O karikature na Marksizma i ob "imperialisticheskom ekonomizme"', ibid., vol. XXX, p. 88.
[82] Ibid., vol. XXX, p. 88.

1871 but also by participating in the First World War from its inception.[83] In Lenin's mind, the dichotomy between the virtuous France of 1789 and the iniquitous France of 1914 was obvious:

> It is not true that France is waging this war in 1914–1917 for freedom, national independence, democracy, and so on. She is fighting to retain her colonies, and for England to retain hers, colonies to which Germany would have had a much greater right—of course from the standpoint of bourgeois law.... Consequently this war is being waged not by democratic and revolutionary France, not by the France of 1792 or of 1848, nor by the France of the Commune. It is being waged by bourgeois France, reactionary France, that ally and friend of tsarism, 'the universal userer', who is defending his booty, his 'sacred right' to colonies, his 'freedom' to exploit the entire world with the help of the millions loaned to weaker or poorer nations.[84]

In earlier writings, going back even before the establishment of the RSDLP and the emergence of Bolshevism, Lenin had excoriated contemporary French socialists such as Millerand, Guesde, and Jaurès mercilessly as traitors to socialism. But only during the First World War did he make clear the depths of the moral abyss into which France had fallen in the nineteenth century. What made these ersatz socialists especially abhorrent, as far as Lenin was concerned, was that in betraying socialism they were also betraying the French Revolution, and indeed the entire tradition of revolution in France that ended with the suppression of the Paris Commune in 1871.

In sum, the outbreak of a European war in 1914 enlarged the French Revolution for Lenin to the point where it was no longer a revolution notable only in its own right, for what it had accomplished (and did not accomplish) in France beginning in 1789. What it now became—and what it would remain for him for the remainder of his life—was the first manifestation of a longer and larger revolutionary tradition in France, the full implications of which were truly European. What this seemed to suggest to Lenin, however obliquely, about what might happen in Russia specifically was that a revolution there, like the French original, would transform events elsewhere in Europe—only this time, unlike the bourgeois revolutions the French Revolution had inspired outside France that eventually

---

[83] V. I. Lenin, 'Otkrytoe pis'mo Borisu Suvarinu', ibid., vol. XXX, pp. 262–3. In the same article, Lenin seemed to waver on whether what happened in France in 1792 constituted a more radical phase of the original French Revolution or instead was a separate revolution entirely. He also variously dated this distinction, while sometimes defining it differently, to 1792 and 1793.

[84] Ibid., vol. XXX, pp. 263–4. Lenin resurrected the analogy in the paragraphs that follow this one, where he stated that the class in France that was prepared to make a revolution in 1780 was just as insignificant politically and numerically as the proletariat was in Russia in 1900. But he then went on to write about the proletariat as already having 'led the masses'—which suggests that he was referring to the 1905 Revolution. Ibid., vol. XXX, pp. 266–7. Because the letter was not published until January 1918, it is possible, though unlikely, that Lenin wrote this section of his letter after the Bolsheviks, in October 1917, had already seized power.

collapsed, the proletarian revolutions a Russian revolution would inspire outside Russia would endure, and even be able to offer the revolutionaries in Russia now in power valuable, indeed indispensable assistance. Where the French Revolution had failed, namely in universalizing itself in such a way as to assure its own survival, the Russian Revolution Lenin anticipated would succeed.

But from none of this, while it was germinating in Lenin's mind prior to 1917, should one infer that when the monarchy collapsed in Russia in that year, and thereby opened up possibilities Lenin previously had not considered either likely or imminent, the French Revolution lost its salience. Rather, its value and utility changed. From providing a model of organization and tactics relevant to a party and a movement with little chance in the immediate future of influencing events, it now offered a menu of strategies that might prove useful should taking power become a real possibility. And once this seemingly improbable undertaking was achieved, the French Revolution provided a useful template for what the Bolsheviks should do to remain in power, albeit one more negative than positive in its helping the Bolsheviks distinguish strategies they should avoid from those they should pursue. For Lenin and the Bolsheviks, the French Revolution was not completed by Napoleon after 1799, as many Western historians have argued, but rather stopped in 1794 with the demise of the Jacobins and the onset of Thermidor, in which a number of the achievements of the original revolution were reversed, albeit temporarily.[85] For that reason, the Bolsheviks could take power in 1917 and consolidate it successfully in the years that followed with the Jacobins—and the Terror the Jacobins inflicted on the people of France—once again uppermost in their minds. It concerned the Bolsheviks greatly after 1917 whether the Jacobins calibrated the amount of terror they inflicted or simply killed people indiscriminately—or did both of these things sequentially, as a rational pre-emptive strike against real and potential enemies degenerated into something larger that was indefensible both morally and politically. After 1917 the Bolsheviks were no longer exiles and *émigrés* for whom revolution and the construction of a new government and society was an intellectual exercise. They were now the

---

[85] See, for example, Crane Brinton, *A Decade of Revolution 1789–1799* (New York, 1934), and Jonathan Israel, *Revolutionary Ideas: An Intellectual History of the French Revolution from* The Rights of Man *to Robespierre* (Princeton NJ, 2014), especially pp. 12–13. One of the few Western historians to share Lenin's opinion on when the French Revolution ended is Simon Schama, who in *Citizens* ends his narrative with Robespierre's arrest and execution, and claims that 'violence' was the common factor that distinguished the French Revolution and drove it forward (pp. 847, 859). Of course Schama reverses the moral gloss Lenin placed on the French Revolution, condemning what Lenin and most of the other Bolsheviks applauded. One of the few Soviet historians who rejected Lenin's claim that the revolution ended in 1794—thereby agreeing with many Western historians who were neither Marxists nor sympathetic to the Soviet Union—was V. G. Revunenkov, in *Ocherki po istorii Velikoi frantsuzskoi revoliutsii. Iakobinskaia respublika i ee krushenie* (Leningrad, 1983), whose apostasy was noted calmly during the Gorbachev era, when opinions contrary to the preexisting Soviet orthodoxy were readily expressed, for example, by L. A. Pimenova, 'O sovetskoi istoriografii Velikoi frantsuzskoi revoliutsii (1979–1986 gg.)', *Frantsuzskii ezhegodnik* (1989), p. 123.

custodians of a country that their ideology compelled them to transform into a political entity different in every way from all those that had preceded it in history—while simultaneously inciting revolutions rooted in that very same ideology in other parts of Europe, and indeed in other parts of the world.

But in order to understand what the Bolsheviks actually did in this respect, and how the French Revolution affected the choices they made and the decisions they reached, one must know something of the role the revolution played in shaping the culture of Russia itself both in 1917 and thereafter. The French Revolution was no less a factor in the calculations of the Bolsheviks' opponents than it was in those of the Bolsheviks themselves, and it is to these wider manifestations of the influence of the French Revolution to which we now turn.

6
1917—Russian Jacobins Come to Power

By 1917 the French Revolution had become part of the collective memory of educated Russians. As a result, its images and symbols would be invoked both to comprehend the events of that tumultuous year and to pass moral judgement on them. Russians of all political persuasions—though especially those at the opposite ends of the political spectrum—found in the books and articles that were written about the revolution ample corroboration of their own opinions and beliefs. For every work that condemned the revolution, such as Anatole France's *The Gods are Athirst*, which after its translation into Russian in 1912 served for supporters of the monarchy as an object lesson in the horrors that would ensure upon its overthrow, there were others, such as Alphonse Aulard's, that praised the French Revolution, or certain aspects of it, effusively.[1] Histories of the revolution published in 1917 often were bound deliberately in red, to indicate that they had something to do with socialism, or at least with revolution.[2] Politicians intent on applying to their own careers any lessons the revolution might provide were prominent among those who purchased them. In addition, imperfect reproductions of paintings by Jacques-Louis David, the acknowledged iconographer of the French Revolution, appeared on the covers of Russian newspapers and journals, and it was not uncommon to see plastered on their first page Danton's celebrated injunction on the need for 'audacity' in order for a revolution to succeed.[3] Histories of the French Revolution sold well in the spring and summer of 1917.[4] Those by Michelet and Louis Blanc were especially popular.[5]

[1] Shlapentokh, *French Revolution and the Russian Anti-Democratic Tradition*, pp. 93, 133. In 1917 Aulard reciprocated the interest shown in his work in Russia by writing a public letter urging the Provisional Government not to renounce its obligations to France and to remain a combatant in the First World War. *La Révolution française et la Révolution russe: letter aux citoyens de la libre Russie* (Paris, 1917), in *La Révolution française* 70 (1917): pp. 193–204. Aulard's original, very favourable view of the Russian Revolution was shared by many Frenchmen. In February 1917, the Society for the Study of the French Revolution in Paris sent a telegram to the Duma analogizing it to the Convention. In April the League of the Rights of Man and of the Citizen held a meeting in Paris, the only one it convened during the First World War, to honour the Russian Revolution. A. A. Aulard, 'Dve revoliutsii (1789–1917)', *Volia Rossii*, no. 20 (1923): p. 14.

[2] Philip M. Price, *My Reminiscences of the Russian Revolution* (London, 1921), p. 16.

[3] Il'ina, 'Obraz evropeiskikh revoliutsii i russkaia kul'tura', pp. 385–6. In the original French, Danton's exhortation, in full, is as follows: 'De l'audaçe, encore l'audaçe, toujours de l'audaçe'.

[4] Pitirim Sorokin, *Leaves from a Russian Diary—and Thirty Years After* (Boston MA, 1950), p. 39.

[5] Il'ina, 'Obraz evropeiskikh revoliutsii i russkaia kul'tura', p. 386.

In 1917 opinions on the revolution varied widely. Some who believed it had predictive value thought Russians should replicate its principles not only in politics but in everyday life.[6] One foreigner visiting Siberia wrote of his amazement on witnessing a child invoking the revolution in explaining her vow to dedicate her life, as a physician, not only to the physical improvement of the Russian people, but also to their moral improvement.[7] According to another eyewitness to the events of the year, many Russians sympathetic to the revolution even imitated in their speech and mannerisms how they imagined the *sans-culottes* spoke and behaved.[8] No doubt many of those who did so were among the much larger number of Russians who referred to one another in 1917 as *grazhdanin* and *grazhdanka*, the masculine and feminine equivalent in Russian of *citoyen* and *citoyenne* respectively, which during the French Revolution were used by its supporters in conversation to demonstrate their rejection of elitism and privilege.[9] On some of the signs advertising the 'freedom icons' the Provisional Government distributed to generate political support were written, in Russian translation, the iconic triad of the French Revolution: *liberté, égalité, fraternité*.[10] According to one Russian historian of the revolution's effects on Russia, Tamara Kondratieva, in 1917 it was hard to find a Russian revolutionary without Robespierre, Danton, or the *Vendée* on his mind.[11] In *Krasnoe Koleso* (*The Red Wheel*), his *summa* on the collapse of the monarchy and the advent of the Bolshevik dictatorship, Alexander Solzhenitsyn, who loathed the Soviet Union for rejecting Russian Orthodoxy in favour of the secularism and rationalism of Marxism–Leninism, said much the same thing, but enlarged the applicability of Kondratieva's comment to encompass the entire population of Petrograd: 'soaring parallels to the Great French Revolution hung in the Petrograd air [and] were on everyone's lips'.[12] Even Russian officers serving on the Western Front in France were said to have learned much from Lazare Carnot and Napoleon, both of whom enhanced the effectiveness of the French army sufficiently for it to secure numerous victories and to delay to 1815 the restoration of the Bourbon monarchy.[13] Also in 1917, many political figures, in their oratory, tried to emulate the extravagant rhetoric of

[6] N. I. Kareev, *Prozhitoe i perezhitoe* (Leningrad, 1990), p. 292.

[7] Ernest Poole, *The Village: Russian Impressions* (New York, 1918), pp. 146–48.

[8] Sorokin, *Leaves from a Russian Diary*, p. 39.

[9] Figes and Kolonitskii, *Interpreting the Russian Revolution*, p. 31.

[10] E. P. Stebling, *From Czar to Bolshevik* (London, 1918), p. 50–51. Richard Stites correctly notes that, for all the visual imagery intended to underscore analogies, or even identities, between the French Revolution and the revolutions in Russia in 1917, there was no equivalent in the latter, or in the early years of the Bolshevik regime, to Jacques-Louis David, whom Stites, in *Revolutionary Dreams*, p. 84, aptly terms 'the pageant-master of the French Revolution'.

[11] Quoted in Frederick C. Corney, *Telling October: Memory and the Making of the Bolshevik Revolution* (Ithaca NY, 2004), p. 6.

[12] Alexander Solzhenitsyn, *Krasnoe koleso* (Paris, 1988), knot III, p. 475.

[13] Shlapentokh, *Counter-Revolution in Revolution*, p. 56.

Camille Desmoulins.[14] And to enemies of the Russian Revolution charging in 1917 that there was nothing romantic, unselfish, or self-sacrificial in the French Revolution, and that it was energized only by greed and parochial self-interest, Maxim Gorky proclaimed that the French Revolution should be judged on its own terms. But of one thing about the revolution he was certain—that the replication in Russia of its most iconic events, such as the storming of the Bastille, required persons possessing the courage and heroism of its principal actors.[15]

Russians like Gorky who admired the French Revolution while believing its Russian successor would do even more to alleviate poverty and material deprivation tried to translate their admiration into action. For some, that meant trying to prevent the repetition in Russia of the most egregious excesses of the revolution, most notably the Jacobin Terror. Leading Mensheviks and Socialist Revolutionaries promised that no matter what course the revolution in Russia followed, Nicholas II would not suffer the fate of Louis XVI.[16] But there were others who thought the legacy of the French Revolution was indivisible and should be applied to Russia in its entirety. In Siberia, after taking power in several localities, ordinary citizens deliberately called the governing agencies they established Committees of Public Safety, on which police powers were swiftly conferred, in one case without any concern about their practising terror because the democratic procedures that created them would presumably prevent it.[17] Along these same lines, an anonymous article in *Izvestiia* in July praised the French and the ongoing revolution in Russia in equal measure because both, in the opinion of the author, were infused with the idea of democracy. The Constituent Assembly, once it convened, would retroactively vindicate the Russian Revolution the way the Estates-General prospectively vindicated the French Revolution in the spring of 1789; in the moral virtue of the two institutions there was little to distinguish them.[18] Of course not everyone assumed that everything Russians did in 1917 would exceed, or even equal the achievements of the French. In July an article in *Obozrenie teatrov* (*Survey of Theatres*) noted plaintively that the ongoing revolution in Russia had yet to generate poetry comparable to that which appeared in France after the revolution began there.[19]

[14] Iu. A. Limonov, 'Prazdnestva Velikoi frantsuzskoi revoliutsii v 1789–93 gg. i massovye prazdniki Sovetskoi Rossii v 1917–1920 gg.', *Frantsuzskii ezhegodnik: stat'i i materialy po istorii Frantsii 1989* (Moscow, 1989), p. 401. That Desmoulins was guillotined—on the same day Danton suffered the identical fate—proved to be no deterrent in that respect.

[15] Maxim Gorky, *Untimely Thoughts: Essays on Revolution, Culture and the Bolsheviks* (New York, 1968), p. 32.

[16] Kerensky, for example, vowed on 7 March that he would never execute the Provisional Government's enemies, and predicted optimistically that the tsar would soon find safety in England. Meriel Buchanan, *Petrograd: The City of Trouble, 1914–1918* (London, 1918), p. 109.

[17] Doreen Stanford, *Siberian Odyssey* (New York, 1964), pp. 50, 55.

[18] 'Nakanune Uchreditel'nago Sobraniia vo Frantsii i v Rossii', *Izvestiia*, no. 130 (29 July 1917): p. 2.

[19] Nils Ake Nilsson, 'Spring 1918. The Arts and the Commissar', in Nilsson, ed., *Art, Society, Revolution: Russia, 1917–1921* (Stockholm, 1979), p. 12.

Not surprisingly, many Russians who considered the French Revolution worth emulating disagreed on precisely what aspects of it they should replicate. Because its most prominent figures were so outsized and distinctive personally as well as politically, it was inevitable that Russians should have identified variously with the Girondins, the Jacobins, and several of the other factional configurations in the revolution, and even more so with their respective leaders, such as Danton, Robespierre, Saint-Just, Mirabeau, Brissot, and Madame Roland. At the same time, Russians less favourably disposed to the revolution considered some or all of these figures the personification of evil itself.

Support for the revolution in Russia was not monolithic. Very quickly after the monarchy fell in February a distinct fissure emerged between those who believed that its agenda was sufficient to achieve their own objectives, and those who, while admiring the revolution, thought the ongoing revolution in Russia should supersede it and make real an ideology—specifically some variant of socialism—to which nearly all the principal actors in the earlier revolution had been oblivious or openly hostile. This is evident in the evolution of the *Marseillaise* in 1917 from a unitary symbol admired by practically everyone in Russia into something more complex, with multiple meanings that varied depending on one's particular political convictions.

When the monarchy collapsed in February, the French national anthem became de facto the national anthem of Russia. An Englishman in Petrograd at the time commented that 'the *Marseillaise* was on every tongue'.[20] This was partly because the anthem was a paean to revolution and patriotism simultaneously. Its lyrics spoke to revolutionaries, patriots, and patriotic revolutionaries in equal measure. In Russia in 1917 it was sung to assuage the sentiments of all three of these subdivisions of the population. This was particularly true of the army. Some of the soldiers who sang it—often after their oath of allegiance to the Provisional Government—hoped that the new government might prosecute the ongoing war more effectively than the monarchy had been able to do. But for others, the revolutionary message it implied was the motivating factor.[21] Troops ordered to Petrograd in March to break up workers' strikes sometimes sang the anthem as they disobeyed their orders and fraternized with the strikers instead.[22] The same thing had occurred during a march on the Duma, just prior to its dissolution the month before, to pressure its deputies not to accept any kind of regency enabling the monarchy and the Romanov dynasty to continue.[23] Even rioters breaking into bakeries in search of bread sang the anthem while doing so because they believed it

---

[20] Isaac Frederick Marcosson, *The Rebirth of Russia* (New York, 1917), p. 51.
[21] Figes and Kolonitskii, *Interpreting the Russian Revolution*, p. 45.
[22] R. H. Bruce Lockhart, *The Two Revolutions: An Eyewitness Study of Russia, 1917* (Chester Springs PA, 1967), p. 71.
[23] James L. Houghteling, *A Diary of the Russian Revolution* (New York, 1918), p. 137.

conferred a kind of moral legitimacy—though one wonders how they could articulate the lyrics while cramming bread into their mouths.[24] Very quickly after the fall of the monarchy, it seemed that the anthem was nearly ubiquitous in Petrograd, sung or performed by bands not merely on political occasions, such as when a regiment in the Tauride Square in full formation demanded that a band be found to play it, but also to sacralize mass funerals on the Champs de Mars in Petrograd—a large open space that by its name alone was redolent of the French Revolution—of fallen heroes of the Russian Revolution.[25] During at least one of these, Chopin's *Funeral March* was played along with the *Marseillaise*.[26]

In Petrograd in particular the anthem informed aspects of daily life. High school students sang it as part of their normal school day.[27] By March it was played at the beginning of most concerts and recitals, largely as a way of affirming collectively one's personal identification with both revolutions, the Russian as much as the French. Failure to honour the new custom sometimes generated vocal disapproval. When, in April, the orchestra at an opera house in Petrograd on one occasion did not began its performance with the *Marseillaise*, as had become customary in the major cities of Russia, the audience began yelling for it. But its protests were in vain. The orchestra refused to play it. The same thing occurred before the second act, and yet again before the third act—but at that point the orchestra finally relented and did what the audience demanded.[28]

By the time the Bolsheviks seized power in October, the anthem had become so much a part of the common culture in Russia that it was no longer just a call to oppressed people casting off the chains that metaphorically enslaved them, and finally enjoying the blessings of liberty. Nor was it merely a means of expressing patriotism and one's willingness to fight for one's country, as the French had done in the 1790s. For many, singing it was now a ritual sanctifying the comity that ensued when everyday disputes ended happily. Shortly after the October insurrection, John Reed, the proletarian bard of the Bolsheviks, whose account of their seizure of power Lenin praised lavishly, visited the Police Prefect in Petrograd for the purpose of finding an apartment. The individual holding the position agreed

---

[24] Irina Skariatina, *A World Can End: A Diary of the Russian Revolution* (New York, 1931), p. 96.
[25] Nikolai Nikolaevich Sukhanov, *The Russian Revolution, 1917: A Personal Record* (New York, 1955), vol. I, pp. 218–19. The original Champs de Mars in Paris was where, in 1790, crowds celebrated the first anniversary of the storming of the Bastille; in 1794, also on the Champs de Mars, Robespierre, on behalf of the Jacobins and the Committee of Public Safety, inaugurated the Cult of the Supreme Being, the deistic alternative to the Christian God he believed would bind the French nation as it ascended to higher and higher plateaus of moral virtue and social justice. To symbolize the upward trajectory of the French Revolution, Jacques-Louis David oversaw the construction on the field of a small mountain, from which Robespierre, like Moses at Mount Sinai, dramatically descended at a critical moment in the proceedings. Schama, *Citizens*, pp. 834–6; Martin Warnke, *Political Landscape: The Art History of Nature* (London, 1994), p. 98.
[26] Edward T. Heald, *Witness to Revolution: Letters from Russia 1916–1919* (Kent OH, 1972), p. 77.
[27] Arthur Ransome, *Russia in 1919* (New York, 1919), p. 187.
[28] Heald, *Witness to Revolution*, pp. 89–90.

to help, but advised that before the two men got down to business, they should sing the French national anthem.[29]

Over the course of this extraordinarily consequential year in Russia's history, the *Marseillaise*, depending upon the needs of those for whom it was sung or played instrumentally, acquired multiple meanings. By the end of the year there were no less than four separate versions, the original and three new ones, each intended for a different social class or category, specifically peasants, soldiers, and workers. One suspects that the version most suitable for workers was favoured by the Bolsheviks after Lenin's April Theses conferred on them the task of carrying out their own, more radical revolution that would supersede the ongoing bourgeois revolution.[30] The new versions had their own lyrics, rhythm, and melodic variations, and none bore more than a vague resemblance to the original, which was played, when it was played at all, mostly by orchestras.[31] The 'Workers' *Marseillaise*'—as the version for workers was dubbed—was actually the creation of the pre-revolutionary popu-list, Pëtr Lavrov, who in 1875 had substituted lyrics, rendered in Russian, that transformed the anthem into a direct exhortation to class warfare:

> To the parasites, to the dogs, to the rich!
> Yes and to the evil vampire-tsar!
> Kill and destroy them, the villainous swine!
> Light up the dawn of a new and better life![32]

It is difficult to know, absent direct evidence, which version was played on ceremonial and symbolic occasions, such as Lenin's arrival at the Finland Station in Petrograd in April 1917. Someone in the crowd that had assembled there started singing the *Marseillaise*, and all those who knew the words and the melody joined in. But none of the chroniclers of the event indicated which version was sung.[33] The same uncertainty was true of the demonstrations outside the Tauride Palace during the July Days. The military band that apparently was playing the anthem as military units suppressed the demonstrations might plausibly have opted for the French original, for one of the variations, or perhaps even for multiple variants played sequentially, depending on whether the musicians' senti-ments were patriotic, which was entirely possible, or driven by loyalty to the Provisional Government, soon-to-be headed by Alexander Kerensky, that had

---

[29] Albert Rhys Williams, *Through the Russian Revolution* (New York, 1967), p. 182. Williams' admiration for the French Revolution was boundless. He considered it the first step in the conquest of outer space, an endeavour he said would include trips to the moon, the planets, and the sun. Joshua Kunitz, 'A Biographical Sketch of Albert Rhys Williams' in Albert Rhys Williams, *Through the Russian Revolution* (New York, 1967), p. cxxii.

[30] Unaniants, N. T. 'Velikaia frantsuzskaia revoliutsiia v sovetskoi muzykal'noi zhizni. 1917–1940 gg.', in *Frantsuzskii ezhegodnik* (1989), p. 441; Orlando Figes, *A People's Tragedy: The Russian Revolution 1891–1924* (New York, 1988), p. 357.

[31] Figes and Kolotnitskii, *Interpreting the Russian Revolution*, p. 40.   [32] Ibid.

[33] For example, E. Stasova, *Vospominaniia* (Moscow, 1969), p. 135.

ordered the suppression, or for some other, unspecified reason.[34] It is also, for much the same reason, unclear which version the Socialist Revolutionaries (SRs) sang—either a version of the anthem (probably the one for peasants) or the original—as they walked out of the Second Congress of Soviets in December 1917 in protest over the Bolshevik seizure of power in October.[35] Because the SRs (excluding the so-called Left SRs, who supported the Bolshevik insurrection) were simultaneously patriotic and politically radical—they supported Russia's involvement in the First World War while advocating a form of socialism based on the peasant commune—they could have opted just as easily for the patriotic version as for the politically radical one. The same uncertainty exists regarding the version that was played on 6 January 1918, at the request of some of the supporters of the Constituent Assembly, which they had presumed would succeed the Provisional Government, to protest the Bolsheviks' disbanding it after only its first day of deliberations.[36]

Many in the Bolshevik rank and file found the *Marseillaise* inspiring, and on ceremonial occasions, such as the inauguration of the Third Congress of Soviets in January 1918, demanded that it be played—which version they wanted for this particular event is not known.[37] It was also played, by request, for the Red Guards in Moscow, shortly after the October Revolution, to welcome home those of their colleagues who had participated in the dramatic events in Petrograd.[38] But Lenin and most of the other Bolshevik leaders either disliked the *Marseillaise* or had decidedly mixed feelings about it, despite its recently acquiring a version with lyrics appropriate for the proletariat. To them, the anthem, in France, was originally a means of legitimizing and engendering popular support for a revolution that, for all of its virtues, was, at bottom, a bourgeois revolution. In Russia its symbolism might still be useful depending on the political requirements of any particular occasion. But it should not be played mindlessly or so frequently that audiences lost sight of the Bolsheviks' objectives, which of course were well beyond the comprehension of most Frenchmen in the late eighteenth century.[39] For that reason Lenin much preferred the *Internationale*, the official anthem of the Second International, despite the great betrayal of which he considered most of its leaders guilty in August 1914; he even requested that it be sung upon his arrival in

---

[34] Alexander Rabinowitch, *Prelude to Revolution: The Petrograd Bolsheviks and the July 1917 Uprising* (Bloomington IN, 1991), p. 199.

[35] Oliver Radkey, *The Sickle under the Hammer: The Russian Socialist Revolutionaries in the Early Months of Soviet Rule* (New York, 1963), p. 243.

[36] Figes and Kolotnitskii, *Interpreting the Russian Revolution*, pp. 66–7.

[37] Ia. M. Sverdlov, 'Vystuplenie pri otkrytii s"ezda (10 January 1918)', in Ia. M. Sverdlov, *Izbrannye proizvedeniia* (Moscow, 1959), vol. II, p. 99.

[38] John Reed, *Ten Days That Shook the World* (New York, 1960), p. 325.

[39] The Mensheviks never really warmed to the *Marseillaise* for the same reason, though of course without sharing Lenin's enthusiasm for an imminent proletarian revolution in Russia. V. L. L'vov-Rogachevskii, ed., 'Predislovie', *Sotsialisty o tekushchem momente: materialy velikoi revoliutsii 1917 g.* (Moscow, 1917), p. 2.

Petrograd in April 1917, after the crowd of admirers gathered at the Finland Station to welcome him had finished singing the *Marseillaise*.[40] In fact, beginning a few years after the October Revolution the two anthems were at times rendered sequentially.[41] The *Marseillaise* was usually played or sung first, and the *Internationale* second, so as to symbolize the October Revolution superseding the French Revolution. But this arrangement proved politically and ideologically confusing to many audiences—this, at any rate, was what the Soviet leadership concluded in the early 1920s, and the *Internationale* replaced the *Marseillaise* as the de facto anthem of the Soviet Union—only to be replaced itself by a more intrinsically Russian one, with lyrics supportive of the Soviet Union's struggle against Nazi Germany, in 1944.

* * *

Given their ideology, the Bolsheviks' ambivalence about the *Marseillaise* is understandable. Others, situated elsewhere on the political spectrum in Russia in 1917, were not similarly constrained in their enthusiasm. The Russian liberals and non-Bolshevik socialists who established the Provisional Government positively revelled in the French Revolution, channelling the interest the revolution had already evoked in ways they thought would be politically helpful. In this respect there was, in 1917, a felicitous convergence of the spontaneous and the coldly preconceived. This was particularly true of the celebrations and commemorations of the fallen heroes of the February Revolution the Provisional Government had previously determined should be held on the Champ de Mars in Petrograd. Because it had never been elected democratically, the Provisional Government believed it lacked the legitimacy to rule Russia permanently. For that reason it never shared the transformational objectives of the Jacobins, and the public gatherings it sponsored never approached in size or solemnity the *fêtes* the Jacobins staged to launch the so-called Cult of the Supreme Being in 1794.

Nonetheless, the gatherings on the Champ de Mars made clear the legitimizing function the French Revolution served for the Russian Revolution. In the words of two historians who have written extensively on how the Provisional Government tried to legitimize itself through language and visual symbolism, the field served in the months between the February and the October Revolutions as 'the main public space of commemoration' in Petrograd, possibly even in the country as a whole.[42] But there were other sites in the city the Provisional Government hoped to utilize for the same purpose. That they were all outdoors reflected the conviction of Kerensky and the other ministers that class distinctions would be less obvious

---

[40] Stasova, *Vospominaniia*, p. 135.
[41] This is what happened at the Third Congress of Soviets. Figes and Kolotnitskii, *Interpreting the Russian Revolution*, p. 67.
[42] Ibid., p. 31.

than they would be in indoor facilities originally constructed under the monarchy and frequented primarily by the upper classes.[43] In August the government made plans for a mass celebration—part carnival, part spectacle—in the so-called Summer Garden in the Russian capital. The site, to which on Sundays residents of the city often repaired for relaxation, would be transformed to resemble Paris, so that the most consequential and inspiring events of the French Revolution could be re-enacted properly; the reason for doing so was to demonstrate concern for Russian POWs in Germany and Austria. There is no evidence, in fact, that this particular festival, obviously intended to replicate, on a much smaller scale, the elaborate *fêtes* of the French Revolution, ever occurred.[44] But its purpose was understandable nonetheless, namely to generate political support for the Provisional Government, in this particular instance by suggesting symbolically that the government stood on the same moral high ground once occupied by the heroes who had carried out the French Revolution. Like the even more monumental spectacles the Bolsheviks would subsequently sponsor, those the Provisional Government was responsible for in 1917 were intended, in Richard Wortman's apt expression, which he applied to tsarist celebrations that had similar objectives, as 'presentations of power'.[45]

The same was true for yet another public event that, had it actually occurred, would have symbolized for large numbers of Russians the triumph of moral virtue over evil, and of the powerless over the powerful, that many saw as the essence of the February Revolution in 1917. This was the destruction of the Lithuanian Castle in Petrograd, where political prisoners under the tsars had been incarcerated. The Provisional Government hoped the event would be cause for celebration, and did nothing to vitiate the obvious parallel between the castle and the Bastille in Paris; the destruction of the former could obviously be viewed as analogous to the storming of the latter.[46] But again the intended event never went beyond the planning stage, and devotees of this particular analogy could console themselves by analogizing the Bastille to the Schlusselburg Fortress in Petrograd, which in 1917 acquired the sobriquet 'the Russian Bastille', and to the Peter-Paul Fortress, also in Petrograd, which became known as 'the Petrograd Bastille'.[47] Both structures had housed political prisoners for decades prior to the February Revolution, and for Russian revolutionaries had long served as symbols of tsarist repression.

It was thus virtually inevitable, given a public already marinated in the mythology of the French Revolution, that in 1917 prisons in particular would evoke

---

[43] James Von Geldern, *Bolshevik Festivals, 1917–1920* (Berkeley CA, 1993), p. 51.
[44] Ibid., pp. 23, 154.
[45] Richard Wortman, *Scenarios of Power: Myth and Ceremony in Russian Monarchy from Peter the Great to the Abdication of Nicholas II* (Princeton NJ, 2006), p. 13 and *passim*.
[46] Anatolii Strigalev, 'Sviaz' vremen'. *Dekorativnoe iskusstvo SSSR*, no. 4 (1978): p. 1.
[47] Stites, *Revolutionary Dreams*, p. 67; Sorokin, *Leaves from a Russian Diary*, p. 118.

comparisons with the Bastille, and cause the Provisional Government to consider their destruction as latter-day re-enactments of the events in Paris on 14 July 1789. But one must bear in mind the distinction between the original festivals of the French Revolution and the way they were replicated in Russia. As Mona Ozouf has pointed out perceptively, the *fêtes* and festivals of the French Revolution were intended to rearrange time and space, and in that way sacralize values considered inherently virtuous—the family, the nation, and a deity like the Divine Providence as conceptualized by the *philosophes* of the Enlightenment.[48] These, in turn, would provide the moral underpinnings of a new, largely secular society, its government and economy organized on the basis of reason. While the rhetoric of the revolution implied that it was merely the initial step in the emancipation of humanity, the first of perhaps an endless progression of uprisings that would spread to all the continents of the world, many of its supporters considered its accomplishments neither insufficient nor excessive. Rather, they were exactly what they should be, and the revolutions that followed would ideally have the same objectives.

Russian socialists, irrespective of whether they were Bolshevik, Menshevik, anarcho-syndicalist, or Socialist Revolutionary, disagreed. For them, the French Revolution marked just the beginning of a long journey humanity was engaged in that would lead eventually to a utopia in which private property, which was considered the principal source of oppression and injustice, had not merely been redistributed equitably, as the revolutionaries in France intended, but abolished entirely. For that reason, the celebrations of the February Revolution in Russia in 1917, and those that followed after the Bolsheviks took power in October 1917, were generated by a different dynamic, one based on the assumption that history was both linear and progressive, and that since socialism—and for the Bolsheviks, communism—had not yet been achieved, a good deal of history would have to pass before it emerged; exactly how much was the issue that most clearly separated the Bolsheviks from the Mensheviks. For that reason, the principal actors in the Russian Revolution of 1917 chose to sacralize what they were doing not by rearranging space and time as if the end of history had already come about, as Ozouf shows was true of the French Revolution, but by demonstrating that space and time were both evolving in a linear fashion towards a future utopia. Since February much had been accomplished in that regard, but a great deal more remained to be done.

To be sure, the symbolism and mythology of the French Revolution were often mobilized in Russia in 1917 for less exalted purposes; in some instances these were nakedly political. This was certainly true for Alexander Kerensky, who, while affecting aspects of the revolution in his policies, rhetoric, and even personal appearance, for purely political reasons wanted the flexibility to repudiate it or to

---

[48] Mona Ozouf, *Festivals and the French Revolution* (Cambridge MA, 1988), pp. 126–96.

proclaim it irrelevant should he believe this to be in his own interest. There was nothing uniquely untoward or objectionable in this. Politicians often adopt symbols and perpetuate myths in their pursuit of power. In Kerensky's case, his inclusions and exclusions reflected his tendency to dichotomize the French Revolution, approving most aspects of it prior to the Jacobins gaining power, but rejecting most everything that ensued. The only exception was his calling 'the Directory' the secret group he organized in August with Mikhail Tereshchenko and Nikolai Nekrasov in a last-ditch effort to save the Provisional Government.[49] But that still left much from which he could pick and choose as circumstances warranted. In May, he proclaimed grandly that 'it is our fate to repeat the tale of the great French Revolution'.[50] Shortly afterwards he explained that this required Russia to strive for universal peace while maintaining its faith 'in the well-being and the grandeur of the [Russian] people'.[51] In June, he stated emphatically that 'the watchwords' of the Provisional Government were *liberté*, *égalité*, and *fraternité*.[52] With that in mind, he recommended that the Provisional Government formally call those it sent to oversee the Russian army 'commissars', which was the same term used in the French Revolution for those performing the identical role.[53] Finally, it bears mention that Kerensky argued for a military offensive in the summer of 1917 because he believed Russia should capitalize on a strategic opportunity similar to that which France enjoyed in 1792, when it essentially declared war on the rest of the Europe, and despite severe deficiencies in its economy, managed to defeat the Old Regimes of Europe and thereafter annex territory in western Germany, parts of Italy, and what would soon become Belgium. What Kerensky ignored, however, was that while French peasants went to war in 1792 to protect land they had already taken or received in the revolution, and therefore fought willingly to defend it, their Russian counterparts deserted from the Russian army in 1917 to take land they considered rightly theirs.[54] But that did not prevent the prime minister, in keeping with his sense of himself as a leader of a country at war, from adopting military dress—knee-high boots, officer's breeches, and a khaki jacket—while inspecting troops and sometimes inspiring them with flights of grandiloquent rhetoric about the patriotic mission it was theirs to undertake.[55] That his right arm was often in a sling—the real reason for which may have been bursitis or the result of excessive hand-shaking—contributed to the impression he clearly wanted to cultivate that he himself

[49] Viktor Chernov, *Rozhdenie revoliutsionnoi Rossii* (Paris, 1934), p. 403.
[50] Ibid., p. 402.
[51] Quoted in Pavel N. Miliukov, *The Russian Revolution* (Gulf Breeze TX, 1978), vol. I, p. 97.
[52] Quoted in Shlapentokh, *Counter-Revolution in Revolution*, p. 41.
[53] Andrei Lobanov-Rostovsky, *The Grinding Mill: Reminiscences of War and Revolution* (New York, 1935), p. 211.
[54] Lewis Namier, *Avenues of History* (London, 1952), pp. 6–7.
[55] Figes, *A People's Tragedy*, p. 411.

was a victim of the foreign enemies intent on harming Russia by ending its revolution and restoring its *ancien régime*.[56]

Many in Petrograd and elsewhere in Russia had cause to compare Kerensky, first as Minister of Justice in the Provisional Government and then as its prime minister, to several of the major figures of the French Revolution. Mirabeau was one, Saint-Just, less approvingly by the French Ambassador, was another. Napoleon Bonaparte, though not, strictly speaking, a figure of the revolution because his career extended well beyond its expiration, was yet another.[57] There is considerable debate over whether Kerensky welcomed or rejected comparisons with the French *général* and *imperator*.[58] But of all the comparisons that came to mind when the prime minister was concerned, he might have liked most of all Viktor Chernov's analogizing him to Lazare Carnot, who was largely responsible for organizing and training the army of the First French Republic, which fought so capably against the its enemies.[59] That the army scored significant victories under the Directory as well as under the Jacobins might have been the reason Kerensky, while claiming to reject the Directory's serial manipulations of existing electoral laws, nevertheless used the word itself as a short-form for one of the coalitions he formed as prime minister of the Provisional Government.[60]

To be sure, Kerensky usually maintained the distinction he drew between the first phase of the French Revolution, which he praised, often lavishly, and the second phase, beginning in 1792, which he frequently, and often vehemently, deplored. Almost immediately after the fall of the monarchy and the establishment of the Provisional Government, he was warning Russians of the dangers

---

[56] Ibid.; Louise Erwin Heenan, *Russian Democracy's Fatal Blunder: The Summer Offensive of 1917* (New York, 1987), p. 103. One should avoid the facile conclusion that Kerensky dressed as he did in imitation of Napoleon, much less that he intended a dictatorship like that which the latter established in France. The most plausible explanation, in light of Kerensky's belief that the military offensive he ordered would not only save the revolution but ensure its expansion, is the one offered here, namely that his attire would cause soldiers to believe he was a soldier himself, and therefore fight harder and more effectively. Partly because Kerensky's 'Bonapartism' in 1917 was, in fact, a misperception by others rather than something to which he truly aspired, the way the term was applied to him will be considered in a later chapter, after Marx's paternity for the term in the aftermath of the Revolution of 1848 has been established.

[57] Figes and Kolotnitskii, *Interpreting the Russian Revolution*, p. 30; Richard Abraham, *Alexander Kerensky: The First Love of the Revolution* (London, 1987), p. 151.

[58] Orlando Figes, in *A People's Tragedy*, p. 411, states that Kerensky kept a bust of Napoleon on his desk in Petrograd. But even if Kerensky not only admired the French Emperor but also sought to replicate his achievements, one has to wonder how he could have considered their replication possible in Russia after the Russian army's defeat and virtual disintegration in the early autumn of 1917. If Kerensky actually harboured 'Bonapartist' aspirations, the likelihood of his achieving them was nil. In that respect, his predicament was different from Trotsky's, who was first accused of Bonapartism not long after the Bolsheviks' victory in the Civil War in 1921, for which Trotsky, who had commanded the Red Army during the war, could legitimately claim partial credit. Stephen Kotkin, in *Stalin*, p. 185, claims that Kerensky's role model was actually Mirabeau.

[59] Chernov, *Rozhdenie revoliutsionnoi Rossii*, p. 402.   [60] Ibid., p. 403.

of mindlessly re-enacting events and episodes in the French Revolution he considered immoral and inhumane. Foremost among them was the execution of Louis XVI; to inflict the same punishment on Nicholas II, he argued in an address to the Moscow Soviet on 7 March, would be even more harmful than simply incarcerating him. Only those wanting 'to re-enact the drama of the French Revolution', he said, would endorse something so profoundly immoral.[61] To indicate that the whole issue of terror had a moral dimension above and beyond its practical ramifications, Kerensky, after a brief flirtation with Marat, during which he aspired to be the French Jacobin's equivalent, stated flatly that he would never 'make the guillotine part of the arsenal of the machinery of our state' and that he would never be 'the Marat of the Russian Revolution'.[62] While never identifying with the Girondins at any point in 1917, on at least one occasion he expressed contempt for those who considered him 'the Russian Robespierre'.[63]

According to Louise Bryant, whose reportage from Russia was highly sympathetic to the Bolsheviks after they took power in October 1917, Kerensky always saw the French Revolution as primarily a political revolution, in sharp contrast to the February Revolution, which in its aspirations and agenda for reform he considered predominantly an economic revolution.[64] What this meant in practical terms for the prime minister was that he was acutely aware of the French Revolution in dealing with the very real threats he faced, primarily, but not exclusively, from the Bolsheviks. While fears of a military coup like Napoleon's caused Kerensky to exaggerate the threat he believed General Kornilov's army posed to his own fortunes and those of the Provisional Government in the late summer of 1917, there is little doubt that the whole issue of how he should respond to Lenin's public threats to destroy his government plagued the prime minister virtually from Lenin's return from exile in April. On 17 June, at a session of the First Congress of Soviets in Petrograd, he responded to Lenin's claim that the ongoing revolution in Russia needed to continue, rather than to stop, because 'in times of revolution it is impossible to remain in one place'.[65] According to Kerensky, the French Revolution showed how seductive repressive measures can be to governments created in the aftermath of a successful revolution that are nonetheless confronted by implacable enemies who will not be satisfied until the revolutions that brought these governments to power are reversed, whether as a

[61] Alexander Kerensky, *Russia and History's Turning Point* (New York, 1965), p. 238.

[62] Quoted in M. S. Frenkin, *Russkaia armiia i revoliutsiia 1917–1918* (Munich, 1978), p. 265; and in Buchanan, *Petrograd: The City of Trouble*, p. 102. On Kerensky's brief identification with Marat, see F. I. Rodichev, *Vospominaniia i ocherki o russkom liberalizme* (Newtownville MA, 1983), p. 126.

[63] Chernov, *Rozhdenie revoliutsionnoi Rossii*, p. 503; Jacques Sadoul, *Notes sur la Révolution Bolchevique, Octobre 1917* (Paris, 1920), p. 47.

[64] Louise Bryant, *Six Red Months in Russia* (New York, 1970), p. 120.

[65] Lockhart, *The Two Revolutions*, p. 90.

result of foreign conquest or by the application of terror domestically. He explained the predicament Russia faced in the following way:

> The problem of the Russian Socialist parties and of Russian democracy is to prevent such an end as there was in France—to hold onto the revolutionary conquests already made, to see to it that our comrades who have been released from prison do not return there; that Comrade Lenin, who has been abroad, may have the opportunity to speak here again, and not be obliged to flee back to Switzerland.[66]

Then, addressing Lenin directly, Kerensky warned him that should his party take power with the assistance of 'reactionaries', the result would be 'a dictatorship like the Jacobins', that did not flinch at the prospect of inflicting mass terror.[67]

Kerensky had many detractors in the SR Party, to which he belonged. A considerable minority, the so-called Left SRs, supported the Bolshevik regime after the October Revolution, only to turn on it when, at Lenin's urging, it signed a humiliating treaty with Germany that offended the Left SRs' patriotic sensibilities. But whatever their internal differences, the SRs, like most other socialists in Russia, were genuinely 'hypnotised' by the French Revolution both in 1917 and thereafter.[68] According to the Belgian socialist, Hendrik de Man, this was because they were 'obsessed by the idea that the Russian Revolution, in all its phases, had to replicate the Great French Revolution.... Some wanted to be Girondins, others Jacobins; still others dreamed of an 18 Brumaire.'[69] According to the foremost historian of the SRs, this was to a large degree the result of their predilection for French culture, which caused them, even before the events of 1917 invested analogies with the French Revolution with special significance, to view the revolution favourably.[70]

The SRs manifested their good opinion in several ways, some of which, in practical terms, were incompatible. The aspects of the revolution the SRs variously considered applicable foreshadowed the split in the party after the Bolsheviks seized power in Petrograd—from which the party never recovered and may have contributed to the fateful decision of the party's leader, Viktor Chernov, not to resist forcibly the Bolsheviks' refusal, in January 1918, to allow the Constituent Assembly, in which the SRs enjoyed a plurality, to reconvene. Mark Natanson, who as a Left SR supported the Bolsheviks, hoped that the government they created would be modelled on the Convention.[71] Maria Spiridonova, like Natanson, a strong, even fanatical advocate of violence directed at anyone opposed to her objectives, in 1917 expressed agreement with others in the party advocating mass killings like those of the Jacobins; the Kadets, whom she considered hardly

---

[66] Ibid.   [67] Ibid.   [68] Chernov, *Rozhdenie revoliutsionnoi Rossii*, p. 401.
[69] Ibid.   [70] Radkey, *Sickle under the Hammer*, p. 479.   [71] Trotsky, *Lenin*, p. 112.

better than the Black Hundreds, should be prominent among the victims.[72] Yet another SR, Evgeniia Ratner, evoked the 'honest bourgeoisie' of the French Revolution in advancing the argument that under no circumstances should Russia repudiate her alliance with Great Britain and France, while Pitirim Sorokin commented in his memoirs that one member of the Petrograd Soviet in the spring of 1917 reminded him of Robespierre because, in apparent imitation, a red rose was affixed to his jacket.[73] In Tambov in 1921 during the peasant uprising that required considerable force to suppress it, Sorokin imagined himself at the epi-centre of 'a Russian *Vendée*'.[74]

Under Chernov's leadership, the SRs did not allow their personal and ideological distaste for the Bolsheviks, whom they often analogized to the Jacobins, to vitiate their admiration of the French Revolution itself. Not long after the October Revolution, the party requested that the new Bolshevik government issue a degree formally designating every person in Russia, irrespective of class or political predilection, 'a citizen of the Russian Republic' because the terminology was redolent of the French Revolution.[75] For Chernov himself, the revolution provided a rich menu of choices in making sense of the kaleidoscopic cauldron of events that simultaneously intrigued and bewildered Russian revolutionaries in 1917 because the collapse of the monarchy that produced it had been so rapid. Mikhail Rodzianko, the chairman of the now-defunct State Duma and one of the architects of the February Revolution, seemed to the SR leader 'a living Russian parody of Mirabeau' in his efforts to save the monarchy.[76] Unalterably convinced that the innate benevolence of the peasantry somehow guaranteed their eventual emancipation and salvation, Chernov took pains in his history of the Russian Revolution—which he considered a failure because it culminated in Bolshevism—to ascertain what had enabled the French Revolution, by contrast, to achieve objectives that were morally virtuous. The principal reason, he concluded, was that it was, at once, anti-monarchical, anti-feudal, pro-peasant, and, in Babeuf's Conspiracy of Equals, proto-proletarian. The French Revolution, in other words, was the result of a tacit alliance of distinct constituencies with incompatible objectives that were nonetheless capable of working together because they all loathed the Bourbons and the *ancien régime*. To Chernov, the Russian who did more than anyone else to prevent the formation of a similar coalition, in this case of

---

[72] Shlapentokh, 'Images of the French Revolution in the February and Bolshevik Revolutions', pp. 38–9. The Black Hundreds were extreme supporters of tsarist autocracy who even murdered Kadet delegates serving alongside their own delegates in the duma, or legislature, Nicholas reluctantly agreed to in October 1905. The first one convened in May 1906.

[73] Radkey, *Sickle under the Hammer*, p. 478; Sorokin, *Leaves from a Russian Diary*, p. 35.

[74] Sorokin, *Leaves from a Russian Diary*, p. 256.

[75] John L. Keep, *The Debate on Soviet Power: Minutes of the All-Russian Central Executive Committee of Soviets: Second Convocation, October 1917–January 1918* (Oxford, 1979), pp. 107–8. Perhaps in the interest of brevity, the Bolsheviks opted instead for 'comrade'.

[76] Chernov, *Rozhdenie revoliutsionnoi Rossii*, p. 403.

everyone in Russia seeking socialism, was Vladimir Lenin. 'Cold, Spartan, and severe' in his manner, Lenin, in Chernov's estimation, eschewed even the most minimal forms of cooperation in favour of a dictatorship that, while not, strictly speaking, based on any precedent in the French Revolution, nevertheless resembled Robespierre's, presumably because in personal terms the two men were so similar.[77] Far preferable to Lenin's dictatorship would have been a government headed by someone like Danton, whose failure to defeat his principal rival may have reminded Chernov and the other SRs who admired the great orator of the French Revolution of their own inability to prevent a Bolshevik dictatorship.[78]

No less obsessed with the French Revolution were many Mensheviks, for whom it provided a convenient means of sharpening arguments that might otherwise have been expressed less effectively or not at all. This was especially true for Nikolai Sukhanov, who, in his eyewitness account of the Russian Revolution, revealed the degree to which the French Revolution informed his recollections of the events he witnessed. One example was his calling a worker in the Tauride Palace a *sans-culotte* because the blue blouse he was wearing reminded him of how he thought the Parisian lower classes dressed in the late eighteenth century. Similarly, the cap on the worker's head may have reminded Sukhanov of the Phrygian caps and bonnets worn during the French Revolution to express support for it.[79] Another example was Sukhanov's disdain for Nicholas Chkheidze and Matvei Skobolev, fellow Mensheviks he considered irresolute and indecisive, and for that reason reminded him of the delegates to the Convention in the French Revolution who, by sitting in the 'swamp' between the Jacobins and the Girondins, ostensibly demonstrated their political independence. To Sukhanov this smacked of a particularly dysfunctional form of cowardice—a refusal to make the hard decisions often required of revolutionaries if their objectives are to be achieved.[80] In June 1917, at a meeting of the Petrograd Soviet, Sukhanov called Irakli Tsereteli 'Danton' in the context of condemning him after the Georgian had proposed disarming the Bolsheviks.[81] Unlike Chernov, Sukhanov considered Robespierre's celebrated rival, rather than Robespierre himself, the most obvious embodiment in the French Revolution of the qualities conducive to political dictatorships, and one suspects that in the heat of the moment—Sukhanov's description of the incident makes clear it occurred when emotions were running high—an example from the French Revolution came to mind because it was so frequently on Sukhanov's mind throughout the year. The same dynamic might explain Plekhanov's comparing himself to Danton after Trotsky, at the First Congress of Soviets in June, had publicly mocked Plekhanov's continued support of Russia's involvement in the First World War.[82] In his response, the older Marxist praised

---

[77] Ibid., p. 404.   [78] Ibid., p. 404.   [79] Sukhanov, *Russian Revolution*, vol. I, p. 450.
[80] Ibid., p. 245.
[81] Keep, 'Tyranny of Paris over Petrograd', p. 30.
[82] Deutscher, *Prophet Armed*, p. 267.

the army the Jacobins had raised to fight their enemies in Europe, and expressed the hope that their Russian equivalent would drink from 'the [same] sap of revolution', and defend Russia as capably as the French revolutionary armies had defended France.[83]

But the French Revolution served a more serious and substantive purpose for the Mensheviks. Curiously, it comforted them and concerned them simultaneously. Mensheviks like Martov and Plekhanov, who had long ago repudiated his infatuation with the Jacobins, could plausibly find in the revolution confirmation of their conviction that exceeding the limits of the February Revolution in Russia would only embolden reactionaries and increase the likelihood of a military dictatorship. Like practically everyone else on the non-Bolshevik Left in 1917, they thought the principal danger to the February Revolution came from the Right, in the form of a military dictatorship, rather than from the Bolsheviks, who they thought would either fail to take power or be unable to hold onto it in the unlikely event that they succeeded. For that reason, the Mensheviks really had little to worry about from the Bolsheviks. Instead they should devote their efforts to preventing a military dictatorship, which their knowledge of French history told them might be personified in a facsimile of the original Bonaparte. But Plekhanov and Martov were also well aware of Lenin's authoritarian inclinations and the degree to which it mirrored the Jacobins'; that the latter held power long enough to practise terror could hardly have reassured them that the same thing would not happen in Russia. In 1917 Plekhanov took pains to make known his belief, which he claimed was also Marx's, that revolutions in any one country required time between them to be successful. Moreover, the leaders of revolutions who by some quirk of history took power prematurely would have no choice but to practise terror, and while doing so invoke the Jacobins—or some other historical precedent—in seeking legitimacy for a policy even less acceptable in the twentieth century in Russia than it was in the eighteenth century in France.[84] But this was precisely what Plekhanov believed the Bolsheviks would do should they take power.

For Plekhanov, the Jacobins were eighteenth-century Bolsheviks just as much as the Bolsheviks were twentieth-century Jacobins; the only difference between them—which for Plekhanov was a considerable one—was their objective: industrial capitalism in the case of the Jacobins, ersatz socialism in the case of the Bolsheviks. In their temperament, and indeed in their whole revolutionary persona, however, the Jacobins and the Bolsheviks were remarkably similar and even, in some ways, identical. As for Martov, he considered the Jacobin dictatorship and any regime the Bolsheviks might establish potentially analogous because the latter could conceal its authoritarianism by claiming that the proletariat, as a class, supported it. In fact, the Jacobins had perpetrated a similar canard concerning their relationship with the lower classes in France. But even after the Bolsheviks

---

[83] Quoted in ibid.   [84] Baron, *Plekhanov*, p. 358.

seized power in October, Martov was convinced the analogy with the Jacobins was valid, and for that reason that the Bolshevik state would be no more stable than the Jacobins', and soon suffer its fate.[85] Other Mensheviks, however, were not so sanguine. Ivan Kubikov, who shared Martov's disdain for Lenin and the Bolsheviks, expressed in *Rabochaia mysl'* (*The Worker's Thought*), his foreboding that while the Bolsheviks piously condemned capital punishment, they nonetheless 'preached the guillotine', and undoubtedly would resort to it should they come to power.[86] But unlike Martov, Kubikov did not sugarcoat his prediction with soothing words about how vulnerable any Bolshevik regime that came to power undemocratically would be.

Russian liberals, like the Mensheviks, believed a Bolshevik *coup d'état* would be a catastrophe for Russia. However, their belief was driven by a concern for individual rights and how these might be violated, or even prohibited in perpetuity, under a Bolshevik dictatorship, rather than from any concern that such a dictatorship would preclude the economic equity and fairness the Mensheviks believed would exist under socialism. But however much Russian liberals feared the concentration of power in the state that socialism necessarily required, they feared a military dictatorship even more. For that reason, comparisons with the French Revolution—in contrast to warnings of Bonapartism—were few; many liberals, in fact, considered such comparisons misleading and profoundly unhelpful. An example was an unsigned and untitled editorial in the liberal newspaper *Rech'*, on 11 March, possibly authored by Miliukov, that denied entirely any analogy between the French Revolution and the ongoing revolution in Russia.[87] The *idée fixe* many liberals applied to virtually all political issues in 1917 was that the French Revolution was threatened far more by its enemies on the Right than by those on the Left. Miliukov, for example, seemed not to mind when a speech of his was interrupted by the *Marseillaise*.[88] He may even have considered the juxtaposition complimentary of both. But he also reproached Kerensky for invoking the revolution in speeches the latter made to soldiers, whose support for Russia's continued involvement in the First World War Miliukov believed essential if the Provisional Government was to endure until a democratically elected legislature could replace it. By invoking the French Revolution without enumerating, or even merely acknowledging its less salubrious aspects, Kerensky, in

---

[85] Iu. O. Martov, *Mirovoi bol'shevizm* (Berlin, 1923), p. 40.

[86] Shlapentokh, *Counter-Revolution in Revolution*, p. 81.

[87] Shlapentokh, *French Revolution and the Russian Anti-Democratic Tradition*, p. 224. This did not mean that Russian liberals had lost their longstanding admiration for French culture, language, and customs. Shortly after the collapse of the monarchy in February 1917, Georgii L'vov, the first (and largely ineffectual) prime minister in the Provisional Government, had his personal calling card replicated in French. Figes, *A People's Tragedy*, pp. 357–8. Militating against Miliukov's authorship of the editorial is that 11 March was the day he resigned as foreign minister in the Provisional Government, and for that reason may have been too busy to write it.

[88] A. Tarasov-Rodionov, *February 1917: A Chronicle of the Russian Revolution* (Westport CT, 1931), p. 111.

Miliukov's jaundiced opinion, was effectively dispensing 'a fairy tale'.[89] Although Miliukov failed to indicate precisely what it was he thought Kerensky was ignoring, one can be reasonably sure that, as a liberal, Miliukov had in mind the Jacobin Terror, which, in addition to costing lives, robbed the French people of their inalienable rights.

*   *   *

In 1917 the Bolsheviks were busy. Organizing themselves into a viable political force in a country from which most of them had been absent for many years was a formidable task, exceeded only by that of actually taking power in an urban insurrection that only Lenin and a few others believed could succeed. For that reason they no longer had the leisure to ruminate endlessly on analogies with earlier revolutions. But Lenin and Trotsky in particular were aware of how their rivals on the left invoked the French Revolution in 1917 not just to explain events in Russia in 1917, but also to attack the Bolsheviks. However wrenching their break with European socialism in 1914, Lenin and Trotsky still felt the need to respond to attacks from its leading lights in Western Europe, which in their mind called their credentials as revolutionaries into question.

Lenin was unsurpassed among the Bolsheviks in defaming anyone who criticized them for any ostensible deviation from orthodox Marxism; only Trotsky (who became a Bolshevik in the summer of 1917) came close to matching his abilities in that regard. In 1917, however, Lenin took umbrage even more quickly than in earlier years despite the enormous responsibilities he assumed and had to carry out in that tumultuous year. As he groped for justifications for seizing power in a country that by Marxist standards would not be ready for socialism for years, or even decades, lambasting his rivals for their supposed mistakes became a means of confirming his own ideological rectitude, a way of convincing himself, perhaps even more than others, that what he was attempting would succeed, and thereby validate retroactively the deviations from Marxist orthodoxy he believed to be necessary politically. In this endeavour the French Revolution played a significant role.

Upon his arrival in Petrograd in April, Lenin quickly confronted the political dilemma he faced: whether taking power in what would be in all but name a *coup d'état* could be compatible ideologically and in practical terms with the establishment of a proletarian state that guaranteed the Russian people freedom. The problem was that the means he chose for achieving such a state, instead of increasing the amount of freedom in Russia, would almost certainly diminish it. Seizures of power by a small minority of professional revolutionaries by definition could not be anything other than authoritarian, and governments created in an authoritarian fashion were likely to function in an authoritarian fashion.

---

[89] P. N. Miliukov, *History of Russia: Reforms, Reaction, Revolutions (1855–1922)* (New York, 1969), vol. III, p. 343.

But Lenin possessed enormous self-confidence, and with the assistance of comparisons with the French Revolution easily conjured a scenario he was certain would not result in a dictatorial regime. In April 1917, responding in print to accusations of Blanquism, Lenin condemned, yet again, any insurrection or seizure of power by a small minority that lacked mass support, and proclaimed that that, in fact, was the furthest thing from his mind. The regime he envisioned would not be based on force or coercion, but rather derive legitimacy from the support of the soviets, the councils of peasants, workers, and soldiers that had emerged following the collapse of the monarchy independently of any political party or faction.[90] For Lenin, *coups d'état* should be judged by the degree to which they were supported tacitly by the people. Coups that lacked such support were 'Blanquist', and thus to be avoided, while those that enjoyed it were perfectly legitimate because the political system that would follow would automatically vest popular sovereignty in the masses. For proof, Lenin cited Engels on the French Revolution, specifically his comments on the seizure of power by the Jacobins in 1793, which ensured that for some time thereafter six years 'France...was governed by locally elected bodies without any supervision from above'.[91] These bodies, in Lenin's description, 'did not "fall apart" or "disintegrate"'. On the contrary, '[they] gained strength and became organised democratically'.[92] Any government the Bolsheviks established would be accountable to the soviets, and thus be politically and ideologically legitimate. To claim otherwise was to claim, in effect, that the Bolsheviks were Blanquists, and to do that was to smear the Bolsheviks unconscionably.[93]

What Lenin contemptuously dismissed as Blanquism was not the only deviation from Marxist orthodoxy he believed his enemies would invoke in attacking him. 'Anarchism' was no less an ideological epithet, and this was the case not only because Plekhanov had included it among the charges he levelled against the Bolsheviks in the spring of 1917. Lenin always maintained that socialism and anarchism were incompatible, indeed that they were polar opposites. For that reason, his tactical and ideological peregrinations over the course of the year can be explained as an effort to chart a course for the Bolsheviks that avoided the Scylla of Blanquism on the one hand, and the Charybdis of anarchism on the other—with the Jacobins sometimes viewed as having completed a comparable journey successfully, but at other times seen as having failed to do so because their manic obsession with physically destroying their enemies to their left made possible a partial restoration, on 9 Thermidor, of their enemies to their right.

---

[90] V. I. Lenin, 'K chemu vedut kontrrevoliutsionnye shagi Vremennogo Pravitel'stva', in Lenin, *PSS*, vol. XXXI, p. 464.

[91] Ibid., vol. XXXI, p. 464.   [92] Ibid., vol. XXXI, p. 464.

[93] V. I. Lenin, 'Pis'ma o taktike (April 1917)', ibid., vol. XXXI, p. 138. Lenin was particularly perturbed when the ascription of Blanquism (and also anarchism) to the Bolsheviks. Ibid., vol. XXXI, p. 138.

One can trace Lenin's vacillations on the Jacobins virtually from month to month, even, at times, from week to week. In the article in April extolling the Jacobins for seizing power with popular support, he nonetheless said nothing about the terror that followed it, perhaps because mentioning it would suggest that the democracy Lenin claimed the Jacobins practised was in fact fraudulent— that the Jacobins ruled not as a result of their somehow being vested with a kind of sovereignty originating in the French people as a whole, but rather by force and coercion. At the end of May, in an article in *Pravda* subtitled 'Jacobinism without the People', Lenin repeated his earlier claim that the Jacobins enjoyed popular support. But this time he stated explicitly his approval of the Jacobin Terror by citing this support as one reason they were acting ethically as well as efficaciously in exterminating the forces inside France that opposed them. The other reason, of course, was that these forces were genuinely retrograde and reactionary; objectively speaking, there was no particular reason why they should not be eliminated.[94] There were, Lenin acknowledged, true Jacobins and false Jacobins, virtuous Jacobins and iniquitous ones. The former were the actual Jacobins of the French Revolution, the latter were enemies of the Jacobins pretending to be real Jacobins; in Russia their ranks, not surprisingly, included many of Lenin's own enemies. Among them were Plekhanov and Miliukov, whose notion of what Jacobinism required in practical terms excluded precisely the firmness of purpose and the willingness to take decisive action, even to the point of practising terror, that Lenin believed were what made the original Jacobins in France so admirable.[95] As long as the Jacobins represented a majority of Frenchmen, or at least a majority of those who were politically progressive, any tactic they deemed necessary was morally justified. Lenin articulated his argument in the following fashion:

> The historical greatness of the actual Jacobins, the Jacobins of 1793, stems from the fact that they were 'Jacobins with the people', with the revolutionary majority of the people, with the revolutionary advanced classes of their time.

The 'Jacobins without the people' are ridiculous and pitiful. They merely pose as Jacobins, but are afraid to declare clearly, openly, and for all to hear that the exploiters, the oppressors of the people, the servants of monarchy in all countries, and the defenders of the landowners in all countries are enemies of the people.[96] None of what Lenin wrote about the Jacobins should be construed to mean that he considered the Bolsheviks identical to the Jacobins or that the circumstances that pertained in 1917 resembled those in France in the 1790s. For one thing, the wars France and Russia fought were different. In a lecture delivered in May, Lenin rejected what he said were 'attempts, especially on the part of the capitalist press,

---

[94] V. I. Lenin, 'Perekhod kontrrevoliutsii v nastuplenie (Iakobintsy bez naroda)', ibid., vol. XXXII, p. 216.

[95] Ibid., vol. XXXII, p. 217.   [96] Ibid., vol. XXXII, pp. 216–17.

whether monarchist or republican, to read into the present war a historical meaning it does not possess'.[97] The current war, he argued, involved countries that were exclusively capitalist, and was therefore indefensible. The wars of the French Revolution, by contrast, were fought between countries with different political and economic systems, and since the Jacobins ruled the most progressive of them, any military operations they engaged in were morally justifiable; whether these were defensive, in the sense of protecting France and the revolution from destruction at the hands of external enemies, or intended to spread the revolution to other parts of Europe, was irrelevant.[98] In June, in articles in *Pravda*, Lenin added to his earlier indictment of the current war the implication that the Jacobins, if they somehow could be brought back to life, would be able to distinguish their own wars, which Lenin again claimed were morally virtuous, from the current war, which he was certain they would condemn.[99]

In effect, Lenin was now not just embracing, but enlarging the boundaries of an equivalence he had previously rejected. In this new installment of his peripatetic ruminations on the French Revolution, not just the Bolsheviks, but 'the workers and the semi-proletarians' in Russia in 1917 were like the Jacobins. But Lenin quickly amended what he said so that these two entities, separated by over a thousand miles and a century of history, were not just similar to one another, but as close to being identical as was humanly possible given the obvious differences in the external circumstances in which they each existed.[100] What this, in turn, seemed to suggest was that Lenin, in the summer of 1917, had come to consider the Bolshevik party a universal revolutionary party that embodied all that was best in both Jacobinism and Bolshevism and knew exactly what to do in every conceivable situation. In tactics, organization, and temperament, the Bolsheviks were truly latter-day Jacobins. Together they personified a veritable Platonic ideal of Revolutionary Virtue that existed outside the limits Marxism imposed on what people could achieve by virtue of the temporal and geographical particularities that surrounded them.

But perhaps because what he was implying was so audacious and so contrary to Marxist ideology, Lenin felt constrained to caution that on many issues the Bolsheviks and the Jacobins differed significantly. In the same article in *Pravda*, Lenin acknowledged that, on the issue of terror, the Bolsheviks would never resort to it because their enemies, in contrast to those of the Jacobins, who were implacable in their opposition to the French Revolution, could be easily neutralized by

[97] V. I. Lenin, 'Voina i revoliutsiia', ibid., vol. XXXII, p. 81.
[98] Ibid., vol. XXXII, pp. 77–81.
[99] V. I. Lenin, 'O vragakh naroda', ibid., vol. XXXII, pp. 306–7; V. I. Lenin, 'Vneshnaia politika russkoi revoliutsii', ibid., vol. XXXII, pp. 335–7.
[100] Lenin, 'O vragakh naroda', ibid., vol. XXXII, pp. 307. That Lenin inserted quotation marks around the word Jacobin when he described workers and others as 'the Jacobins of the twentieth century' merely qualifies this equivalence, rather than vitiating it entirely. Ibid.

simply arresting them. 'The "Jacobins" of the twentieth century would not guillotine the capitalists', Lenin promised, and then added the clarification that following the good example of the Jacobins did not require copying them mindlessly; there were matters in which the Bolsheviks should take pains to avoid what the Jacobins did, not because the latter were intrinsically immoral or lacked the personal qualities Lenin considered essential to the success of any revolutionary enterprise, but because France in the eighteenth century was significantly different from Russia over a century later.[101]

Phrased in this fashion, Lenin's strictures on drawing analogies with the French Revolution had the virtue of ideological and tactical flexibility. Policies the Jacobins pursued that he deemed inimical to the Bolsheviks could be rejected without undermining the larger similarities—indeed at times the exact identity—he claimed to see between the French and the Russian Revolutions. At a meeting of the Kronstadt Soviet in June—when he was otherwise disavowing any intention of destroying his enemies physically should he have the power to do so—Lenin evoked 'a government of the proletariat which had its historical parallel in 1792 in France' as the kind of regime Mensheviks like Tsereteli—who was present and to whom Lenin was directing his comment—claimed to favour but were too cowardly to establish.[102] The obvious implication of Lenin's accusation was that, unlike the Mensheviks, he and the other Bolsheviks possessed the necessary intestinal fortitude to create a regime like the Jacobins' once the Provisional Government, which most of the Mensheviks still supported, had been overthrown. Unlike the Mensheviks, the Bolsheviks, according to Lenin, possessed the audacity Danton had said was essential to the success of any revolutionary undertaking; shorn of the terror the Jacobins had no choice but to inflict on their enemies, the regime they established should be considered a precedent not just by the Bolsheviks, but by all revolutionary parties committed to achieving socialism and communism.

Mined selectively on the basis of its relevance to Russia, the legacy the Jacobins left behind, according to Lenin, offered not just inspiration and legitimacy, but a record of accomplishment reflective of the strength of character the Jacobins possessed. In terms of the policies they pursued, the Jacobins, according to Lenin, were the proverbial mixed bag. Some things they did should be avoided; other things they did should be copied. But the personal qualities they manifested were always beyond reproach. Very much the product of 'feudalism' in what they did, the Jacobins transcended their times in what they were, and for that reason were the closest embodiment Lenin could conjure—excepting fictional characters such as Chernyshevskii's Rakhmetov—of a Universal Revolutionary Type, capable of performing any task for which history selected him.

[101] Lenin, 'O vragakh naroda', ibid., vol. XXXII, p. 307.
[102] Quoted in Price, *Reminiscences of the Russian Revolution*, p. 45.

The centrality of the French Revolution in Lenin's thinking in 1917 is perhaps most apparent in his lengthy essay, *State and Revolution*, which he wrote in Finland in August and September after the failure during the July Days to overthrow the Provisional Government. Very briefly, Lenin had the leisure to contemplate what a Bolshevik state would look like should circumstances change and increase the chances of any future insurrection succeeding. In the second chapter Lenin, quoting Engels, made clear that while the French Revolution was in many ways *sui generis*, the lessons it taught transcended the historical circumstances in which it occurred:

> France ... is the country where, more than anywhere else, historical class struggles have been always fought through to a decisive conclusion, and therefore also where the changing political forms within which the struggle developed, and in which their results were summed up, were stamped in sharpest outline. The centre of feudalism in the Middle Ages, the model country (since the Renaissance) of a rigidly unified monarchy, in the great revolution France shattered feudalism and established the unadulterated rule of the bourgeoisie in a more classical form than [in] any other European land. And here also the struggle of the rising proletariat against the ruling bourgeoisie appeared in an acute form such as was unknown elsewhere.[103]

For this reason the Bolsheviks could find in the French Revolution a solution to the problem Lenin believed would be paramount should the Bolsheviks seize power, namely whether a regime that is centralized politically can allow the people it rules a meaningful measure of personal freedom. In retrospect it is easy to see that the Bolsheviks, once in power, could not help but centralize political authority to such an extent that the regime they established would be, for all intents and purposes, a dictatorship. Having come to power—as the elections to the Constituent Assembly would demonstrate conclusively—with the support of no more than roughly a quarter of the population, the Bolsheviks perhaps could hardly have been expected to do otherwise. Revolutionaries rarely relinquish power or stop seeking it just because their popular support has diminished or was never sufficient to begin with. But when Lenin was writing in the summer of 1917, no one knew what the elections to the assembly would demonstrate, and he could still argue plausibly that personal freedom and the centralization of political power were not inherently incompatible.

The principal argument Lenin mustered on behalf of this proposition, which he seemed to recognize as counterintuitive and thus requiring empirical corroboration, was that the republic that was established during the French Revolution had achieved the seemingly unachievable, namely a genuine equilibrium in which personal freedom and centralized political power co-existed. In fact, the freedom

---

[103] V. I. Lenin, *State and Revolution* (New York, 1969), p. 28.

the French people enjoyed under the republic was actually greater than what would have been allowed in a political system in which power had devolved onto regional or local institutions. As if to emphasize how much this contradicted what an orthodox Marxist would have expected of a bourgeois revolution, which of course required a subsequent proletarian revolution to provide people the personal freedom a bourgeois revolution could only promise, Lenin cited Engels approvingly in *State and Revolution* to underscore his conviction that the French Revolution was an achievement unequalled in history; only under socialism and communism, one was meant to surmise, would it finally be surpassed.[104]

The implications of this for the Bolsheviks were encouraging. Once in control of the government, they could centralize it to whatever extent they considered necessary to defend it, while simultaneously receiving support from classes understandably grateful for the freedom they now enjoyed. As long as this equilibrium continued, the Bolsheviks could do the other things Lenin recommended in *State and Revolution*, such as substituting a people's militia for a regular army, and removing from the police the task it had performed under the tsars of suppressing political opposition. Evidently the benefits of life under socialism rendered criticism and political opposition unnecessary, and if it nonetheless persisted it was simply an expression of ingratitude.

In Lenin's phraseology, the French Revolution had shown that 'the greatest amount of local, provincial, and other freedom known in history was granted by a centralised republic, not a federal republic'.[105] Armed with this knowledge, Lenin proceeded, in early autumn, to the more prosaic, but no less pressing task of actually making a revolution now that circumstances in Russia suggested it might succeed. In September 1917, Lenin grasped the political reality that the Provisional Government had lost practically all of its political legitimacy. Its decision to continue Russia's involvement in the First World War, while understandable given the need to prevent Germany's domination of the European continent, had caused it to lose what little support it still enjoyed among the peasantry. Moreover, Kerensky's obsessive fear of a military dictatorship caused him in August, in a moment of supreme weakness, to allow the Bolsheviks, who had been in hiding since the July Days, to re-emerge, and in Petrograd to form armed regiments, the notorious Red Guards, ostensibly to defend the Provisional Government against its enemies; in reality they would carry out the October Revolution.

Once again, France's history proved useful. While in the autumn of 1917 Lenin mentioned the Jacobins only rarely, he now thought it necessary to dredge up the Blanquists, who in Lenin's hierarchy of revolutionary virtue, were at the bottom and were thus the Jacobins' antithesis. In an article for *Rabochii put'* in early

---

[104] Ibid., p. 28.   [105] Ibid., p. 62.

September, he castigated the Blanquists for their lack of pragmatism and tactical flexibility.[106] In a letter to the Central Committee of the Bolshevik Party, written in the middle of the same month, Lenin phrased his objections in the form of a syllogism: the Blanquists favoured insurrection even in the absence of popular support; the Bolsheviks were not Blanquists; therefore any insurrection the Bolsheviks attempted would have popular support.[107] And at the end of the month, in another article in *Rabochii Put'*, Lenin minimized the threat recalcitrant peasants might pose to a Bolshevik insurrection by citing the *Vendée* as a counter-example. The closest equivalent in Russia to the French peasants, whose guerilla warfare and anarchic violence required four years of counter-insurgency to quell, were not the peasantry but rather the Cossacks, who inhabited regions of the country distant from Petrograd and Moscow.[108] From the countryside the Bolsheviks, for that reason, had nothing to fear. The French Revolution, once again, inspired confidence in Lenin, though in this instance it was because circumstances in France and Russia during their respective revolutions were different rather than similar.

Finally, as October arrived and the fear that the other Bolsheviks would not authorize an insurrection even as the chances of its succeeding were increasing, Lenin fell back on the Dantonesque imperative ('*De l'audaçe, encore l'audaçe, toujours de l'audaçe*') in impressing upon his colleagues the need for immediate action.[109] In his opinion there now existed a genuine window of opportunity that, if not utilized, might soon disappear. But other Bolsheviks disagreed, and hours of arguments and plaintive pleas were required to convince a majority to support a resolution calling for a revolution—though without setting a specific date for its commencement. However, rumours that the Provisional Government—or what remained of it—was about to arrest them caused the Bolsheviks to act, with the result that by 2 November, the Bolsheviks found themselves, while not the masters of Russia, nonetheless in command of its three largest cities (Moscow, Petrograd, and Kiev) and of the territory that was enclosed by them. In his Decree on Peace, the contents of which Lenin revealed' in his speech on 26 October to the Congress of Soviets, whose ratification of the still ongoing insurrection enhanced its legitimacy, the new leader of Russia included 'a series of revolutions of world-historical significance carried out by the French proletariat' among the noble precursors of

---

[106] V. I. Lenin, 'O kompromissakh', in Lenin, *PSS*, vol. XXXIV, p. 133.
[107] V. I. Lenin, 'Marksizm i vosstanie (Pis'mo k tsentral'nomu komitete RSDRP[b])', ibid., pp. 242–3.
[108] V. I. Lenin, 'Russkaia revoliutsiia i grazhdanskaia voina. Pugaiut grazhdanskoi voinoi', ibid., pp. 219–20.
[109] V. I. Lenin, 'Sovet postoronnego (August 1917)', ibid., p. 383. Despite his instinctual disdain for history's losers, Lenin admired Danton profoundly. Soviet historians, however, viewed him less favourably. For example, in *Danton* (Moscow, 1965), p. 235, Ts. Fridland airily dismissed the great orator of the French Revolution as, an 'opportunist to the marrow of his bones', who also 'distrusted and feared the masses'.

what the Bolsheviks, on behalf of workers and peasants everywhere, were in the process of achieving in Russia.[110] Although he did not name these revolutions individually, the fact that he referred to them in concert shows that he now considered the French Revolution part of a larger revolutionary tradition that included the Revolutions of 1830 and 1848, and the Paris Commune in 1871. And by describing all of them as 'proletarian', Lenin was effectively blurring the distinction Marx and Engels had maintained for most of their lives between bourgeois and proletarian revolutions. Although Lenin never indicated why he did this, one can speculate that, by instigating a revolution he said was proletarian only eight months after a revolution he always considered bourgeois had begun, he needed some way of synthesizing all of the revolutions in France and Russia into two revolutionary traditions, a French and a Russian, and then combining them into a larger, transcendent, and seemingly universal revolutionary tradition, unbounded by time and space. In his mind, there now existed not only a French Revolutionary Tradition, but also a Russian Revolutionary Tradition, which included the 1905 Revolution, the February Revolution, and now the October Revolution, which was both a continuation and climax of its two illustrious predecessors. For Lenin, ideological distinctions were fine in the abstract, and his belief in their reality was genuine. But tactical modifications in the service of Marxist ideology were no less legitimate, and if these modifications required changing French revolutions from bourgeois revolutions to proletarian or proto-proletarian ones, then that was a historical fiction Lenin could easily live with.

Trotsky's interest in the French Revolution was even greater than Lenin's. His personal identification with several of its luminaries, irrespective of his early condemnations of Robespierre and Jacobinism, reflected his outsized self-image as a historical actor of the first order whose mission in life, which he accepted eagerly, was imposed on him by the requirements of the Marxist dialectic. In 1917 Trotsky, in his own estimation, was in exactly the right place at the right time. Destined to personify the revolutionary vanguard that would put Russia and eventually the world on a path to universal justice, Trotsky could not help but consider himself the latter-day personification of all that was heroic and histor-ically consequential in the French Revolution.

Many of Trotsky's contemporaries agreed, though not all of them thought that analogies with the French Revolution flattered him. Viktor Chernov claimed in his memoirs that Trotsky's 'greatest ambition [was to be] the Russian Marat'.[111] So did Louise Bryant.[112] Others variously compared him to Danton, Carnot, Saint-Just, and of course Robespierre.[113] Indeed, Trotsky's vow in 1917 that 'the

---

[110] V. I. Lenin, 'Doklad o mire', in Lenin, *PSS*, vol. XXXV, p. 16.
[111] Shlapentokh, *French Revolution and the Russian Anti-Democratic Tradition*, p. 254.
[112] Bryant, *Six Red Months in Russia*, p. 67.
[113] Shlapentokh, *French Revolution and the Russian Anti-Democratic Tradition*, p. 254.

quadrangle of the guillotine' would separate the Bolsheviks from their political rivals only confirmed their fears that Trotsky would not shrink from meting out the ultimate punishment, and would likely justify it on the grounds cited by Bertrand Barère, a Jacobin who served on the Committee of Public Safety, that 'only the dead never come back'.[114] By this time Trotsky had reversed completely his earlier position on the Jacobins, viewing them now as the personification of revolutionary virtue; the Girondins, by comparison, were 'pitiful' and 'ludicrous'.[115]

Implicit in Trotsky's identification with the Jacobins was the notion that the Bolsheviks in Russia were completing, or at least continuing, a process embedded in history that was leading humanity to a better future that the French Revolution had anticipated over a century earlier. The reader will recall that in 1906, in *Results and Prospects*, Trotsky had written that 'history does not repeat itself', and that 'however much one may compare the Russian revolution with the Great French Revolution, the former can never be transformed into a repetition of the latter'.[116] But he also would write, in 1929, that 'rejecting historical analogies would mean rejecting the use of historical experience in general'.[117] It is hard to take the first of these two statements seriously. Trotsky always considered historical analogies useful even when he raised them for the purpose of rejecting them. In particular, Trotsky always claimed a genuine affinity between the two revolutions; and that was especially true after the Bolsheviks took power in October 1917, when, as one of the architects of the new regime, he looked to the French Revolution for guidance. Not even the proletarian revolutions in Western Europe Trotsky believed would follow a Bolshevik seizure of power in Russia would make the prosaic, but nonetheless essential task of formulating specific policies any easier. The French Revolution, while not a panacea, would render assistance.

However much the French Revolution intrigued them, only a few of the Bolsheviks, other than Lenin and Trotsky, had the inclination (or the time) in 1917 to write about it for purposes other than the purely polemical. One who did was Lev Kamenev. Understandably shocked by Lenin's April Theses, which flatly rejected Marxist orthodoxy on the impropriety of making a proletarian revolution prematurely, Kamenev invoked the French Revolution to substantiate his view that any revolution the Bolsheviks attempted should be a mass revolution; since the proletariat in Russia still lacked the political consciousness to support a revolution in numbers sufficient to ensure its success, to call for one, as Lenin did, was

---

[114] Quoted in ibid., p. 237; quoted in Otto J. Scott, *Robespierre: The Voice of Virtue* (New Brunswick NJ and London, 2011), p. 254.

[115] Leon Trotsky, *The Russian Revolution: The Overthrow of Tzarism and the Triumph of the Soviets*, abridged edition (New York, 1959), p. 250.

[116] Trotsky, *Itogi i perspektivy*, p. 25.

[117] Leon Trotsky, 'Questions for the Leninbund' in George Breitman et al., eds, *Leon Trotsky: Collected Writings (1929-1940)*, 14 vols (1929) [hereafter rendered as *LTCW* and followed by the year or years of the writings that are included in the volume] (New York, 1975), p. 314. Isaac Deutscher, in *The Prophet Unarmed Trotsky: 1921-1929* (London, 1963), p. 315, describes Trotsky accurately as having an imagination that was 'overfed with history'.

politically suicidal.[118] Another Bolshevik, Grigorii Zinoviev, limited his references to the revolution to the observation that war and revolution were mutually reinforcing, and that '1793' was a prime example of this. However, Zinoviev also cautioned that there were circumstances in which this maxim did not apply, such as those that pertained in France in 1917, when 'social chauvinists'—the expletive the Bolsheviks applied to European socialists who in 1914 had supported their own country's involvement in the First World War—supported war while opposing revolution. In the essay in which he expressed this opinion, Zinoviev offered the contrary example of the German proletariat, which he believed would shortly follow the example of the Jacobins and make a revolution in wartime, even though Zinoviev believed that the German proletariat, on taking power, would withdraw their country from war rather than have it fight it more effectively, as the Jacobins had done against their own foreign enemies.[119]

As for Nikolai Bukharin, one sees in his single reference to the French Revolution the idea that would animate his policy prescriptions immediately after the October Revolution, when the requirements of international communism, in his view, took precedence over those of the nascent Soviet state. The most obvious example of this was his vehement opposition to Russia withdrawing from the First World War in March 1918 because he believed this would enable Germany to win the war and thereby make proletarian revolutions in Europe impossible. In an article in the spring of 1917, Bukharin praised the French Revolution for igniting what he called 'the torch of revolution' on virtually the entire European continent.[120] But if, in 1789, the bourgeoisie was a progressive force, by the late nineteenth century it had become 'the citadel of reaction', so that by 1917 it was 'standing at its grave', nearly powerless to prevent the proletariat from ending its dominance once and for all.[121] To be sure, there was nothing in Bukharin's teleology to which a Marxist could object. The Russian Revolution, led by the proletariat, would continue the inexorable march of progress to which the French Revolution, driven forward by the bourgeoisie, had long ago contributed, and thereby fulfilled its historical obligation. But Bukharin's obvious preference for viewing this quasi-apostolic succession of revolutions in a purely European context, seemingly with only minimal concern for the fate of Russia, surely followed logically from the opinion he would hold until the 1920s that events in Russia were significant mostly for the effect they had on Western and Central Europe.

---

[118] Cited in Lenin, 'Pis'ma o taktike', *PSS*, vol. XXXI, pp. 139, 143–4; John Keep, *Contemporary History in the Soviet Mirror* (New York, 1964), 204. Bolsheviks like Kamenev were not the only ones confounded by the April Theses. Plekhanov wrote a short essay in 1917 attacking them that bore the title, in English translation, *On the Delirium of Lenin, or Why Delirium is Sometimes Interesting.*

[119] G. Zinoviev, *Vtoroi international i problema voiny ot nazyvaemsia my ot nasledstva?* (Petrograd, 1917) p. 9.

[120] N. Bukharin, 'The Russian Revolution and its Significance', *The Class Struggle*, no. 1 (1917), https://www.marxists.org/archive/bukharin/works/1917/rev.htm.

[121] Ibid.

Very different from Bukharin's were the statements referencing the French Revolution that Stalin expressed in 1917. Whereas Bukharin esteemed it for its internationalism and universalist aspirations, Stalin saw it as an expression, in Erik Van Ree's words, of a primitive form of 'revolutionary patriotism'.[122] In March, Stalin stated unambiguously that the wars the Jacobins fought against their enemies in Europe in the 1790s were morally and politically legitimate.[123] But in Russia in 1917, the war the country was fighting was an imperialist war, in which neither side enjoyed a monopoly of virtue. In fact, they were both engaged in hostilities for the most dubious of motives, namely 'the seizure of foreign, chiefly agrarian territories' the possession of which would increase their own capitalists' profits.[124] The First World War, in other words, was the result of the machinations of the bourgeoisie. But the inference Stalin wanted his readers to draw from all of this, one suspects, was that should Russia fall into the hands of the proletariat, any war it waged in its own defence would be no less legitimate than the wars the Jacobins had fought in defence of their own revolution.

Also in March, Stalin attacked the Provisional Government because, in contrast to the governments that emerged in prior revolutions in France—Stalin failed to specify which revolutions and governments he had in mind—Russia's arose 'not on the barricades, but near them', and was therefore 'being dragged along by the revolution with its tail between its legs'.[125] Finally, in two articles in *Rabochii put'* in early September, Stalin called the coalition Kerensky had recently cobbled together a Directory not just because with five members it resembled the institution of the French Revolution, but also, and more importantly, because he considered it the instrument of the Kadets, who, like most of the Directors, were bourgeois.[126] At the end of the second of these two articles, Stalin opined that 'it [was] the duty of the advanced workers [in Russia] to tear the mask from these non-Kadet governments and expose their real Kadet nature to the masses'.[127] Even though the Directory did not disavow the territorial gains the Jacobins had made in the wars they waged against their enemies, Stalin considered the institution ideologically and politically retrograde, relative to the Jacobin regime that preceded it, and for that reason chose to consider it lacking any virtues whatsoever. Of all the governments of the French Revolution, the one that most clearly practised a revolutionary patriotism akin to that which Stalin argued for in 1917, until Lenin returned to Russia and promptly contradicted him in that regard, was that of the Jacobins.

*   *   *

[122] Erik Van Ree, *The Political Thought of Joseph Stalin: A Study in Twentieth Century Revolutionary Patriotism* (London, 2002), pp. 230–54.
[123] J. V. Stalin, 'O voine', in Stalin, *Sochineniia*, vol. III, pp. 4–5.   [124] Ibid., p. 5.
[125] J. V. Stalin, 'Ob usloviiakh pobedy russkoi revoliutsii', in Stalin, *Sochineniia*, vol. III, p. 14.
[126] J. V. Stalin, 'Krizis i direktoriia', ibid., p. 269; J. V. Stalin, 'O razryve s kadetami', ibid., p. 278.
[127] Stalin, 'O razryve o kadetami', ibid., p. 278.

Not long before his death, Lenin admitted that in 1917 he had found useful Napoleon's celebrated injunction 'On s'engage et puis... on voit', which captures the degree to which Lenin's tactical decisions from the April Theses to the October Revolution were reactions to unexpected events over which he had no real control. It also implied that these decisions were partly or entirely improvised. But Lenin's admission should not obscure the fact that there was something in history that offered the guidance the Bolsheviks needed, and that the French Revolution provided it. In particular it was the example of the Jacobins that strengthened his belief that the Bolsheviks could seize power as the so-called vanguard of a class, the proletariat, that despite Russia's impressive industrial growth beginning in the 1890s, constituted only a small percentage of the country's still mostly agrarian population. Although the Jacobins ruled France for only a matter of months, the analogy the Bolsheviks drew with them was flexible enough so that it would exclude this potentially discouraging piece of information. The result was that the Bolsheviks could reference the analogy whenever necessary, while continuing to believe that the only temporal limit on any government they established was that inherent in the establishment of socialism and the abolition of classes. With the proletariat, once socialism was established, the only class in Russia, there would be, in actuality, no classes in Russia, and for that reason whatever remained of the Bolshevik regime that had been established in 1917 would soon disappear. Whereas the end of the Jacobins' regime signified failure, that of the Bolsheviks would signify success.

Still, it was easy to underestimate the Bolsheviks in 1917, just as it was easy to underestimate the Jacobins in 1792. One suspects that Lenin was well aware of this, and knew how advantageous that perception could be in making a revolution with far less than a majority of the Russian people supporting it, and when the ideology to which he remained genuinely committed practically cried out to him that doing so would be a catastrophic mistake. But one must bear in mind how easily Lenin could conclude from what he knew—or thought he knew—about the Jacobins that such considerations, while worth considering, should not deter him from acting as his political instincts dictated. In fact, it was Lenin's (mostly inaccurate) vision of the Jacobin Clubs as a prototype for the revolutionary party he first described in 1902 in *What is to be Done?*, with its intimations of conspiracies and the strict centralization of authority, that enabled him in 1917 to carry out a successful *coup d'état*. In October 1917 Lenin truly believed that the Bolsheviks were doing what the Jacobins had done in France, and that that was what enabled both sets of revolutionaries to succeed. In light of what it led to, it is hard to imagine an analogy more powerful in its effect on the course of history than that which Lenin conjured in 1917 between the French Revolution and the October Revolution.

7

Mythologizing the New Soviet Regime

One might think that after the Bolsheviks took power they would be less inclined to look to the French Revolution, and to history generally, for guidance, inspiration, and legitimacy. That they were on the verge of building socialism and thereby creating the preconditions for communism, when history ended and social justice prevailed universally, would seem to fill these needs sufficiently so that historical analogies of any kind would no longer be necessary.

But that was not the case. The French Revolution remained relevant. Until the end of the Civil War in 1921, when the Bolsheviks finally consolidated the power they had acquired in 1917, the whole issue of the efficacy and morality of terror caused them to cite, yet again, the Jacobins in responding to charges that the application of terror for any purpose was immoral, and thus destructive of the patina of legitimacy the Bolsheviks enjoyed by having carried out a successful revolution. Moreover, it was during the era of the New Economic Policy (NEP), which mostly coincided with the struggle for power that accelerated after Lenin's death in 1924 and finally ended in 1929 with Stalin triumphant, that the Bolsheviks for the first time had to react to charges—from abroad, from other Russians, and even from critics within their own party—that their revolution was going seriously wrong and that momentum was building inside the Soviet Union for either a reaction that would delay the construction of socialism and communism, or an actual counter-revolution that would bring the Bolshevik regime and the entire revolutionary enterprise to which it was committed to an end. In the debate that ensued, the French Revolution played a significant role, as it had before.

In this instance, however, it was Thermidor, by which was meant the phase of the revolution from 1794 to 1799, rather than the earlier Jacobin one, that assumed special significance. It is no exaggeration to say that, beginning in the 1920s, mere mention of the word evoked fear and foreboding, even of panic, among the Bolsheviks because of what it implied about their taking power before the objective preconditions for their doing so existed; these emotions were also what made any intimation of a Soviet Thermidor analogous to the French as useful for polemical purposes in intra-party politics as it was for its interpretive and predictive implications. In short, the fate of the October Revolution seemed to depend on whether the Soviet Union had succumbed or would soon succumb to Thermidorian reaction or counter-revolution; it mattered greatly, in terms of the chances of reversing any descent into Thermidor, whether it marked merely a reactionary phase that the workings of the dialectic would easily rectify, or a reversion to an earlier stage in history that would set back its progress towards socialism and communism significantly. In contrast to 1917, when the Bolsheviks evoked the Jacobins voluntarily, because they considered them, in purely personal terms, the very model of revolutionary rectitude, when they pondered the unwelcome possibilities of a Soviet Thermidor in the 1920s, they were responding reluctantly to enemies of theirs who had retrieved from the French Revolution the images of a phase in its history that could be wielded against the Bolsheviks as a weapon. That the Bolsheviks in 1921 had instituted a new economic policy that, in its partial allowance of capitalism and market relations resembled an old one, made the charge that they had betrayed their own objectives more plausible. And the fact that some of their critics thought a Soviet Thermidor a good thing, to be welcomed instead of condemned, only underscored the danger it posed to the entire undertaking to which the Bolsheviks had devoted their lives.

*   *   *

In the immediate aftermath of the October Revolution it was the Jacobins' terror, rather than any consideration of Thermidor, that monopolized the Bolsheviks' time and attention. By this time the slightest intimation that the Bolsheviks were about to replicate the killings for which the Jacobins had been responsible in the French Revolution was enough for Lenin or an appropriate surrogate to take up the whole issue, sometimes to distinguish any terror the Bolsheviks might inflict from that of the Jacobins, sometimes to claim, as justification, that the two forms of terror would be very similar, and sometimes to claim that terror, for practical reasons, if not for ethical ones, was not then, and would never be, under consideration. Even before the October Revolution, Lenin's ambivalence and indecision were palpable. In an article in *Pravda* four months earlier, he declared boldly that the workers in Russia were 'the Jacobins of the twentieth century', but then seemed to qualify the identification by stating that while guillotining enemies of the revolution was a perfectly good example to follow, that did not mean it was a policy the workers— and by implication the Bolsheviks—should copy.[1] Moreover, one cannot ascertain from the article whether Lenin's aversion to terror was based on moral principle or on the exigencies of politics.[2] On 1 November, at a meeting of the Central Committee, less than a week after the Bolsheviks had seized power, Lenin plaintively bemoaned his inability, as the head of the new government, to do more than

---

[1] V. I. Lenin, 'O vragakh naroda', in Lenin, *PSS*, vol. XXXII, pp. 306–7.

[2] Even within the Cheka, the police force established on 20 December, support for terror was far from unanimous; some officials (if what they said was not disingenuous) even opposed its application. In the winter of 1917–18, one of its functionaries, Iakov Peters, when asked about the veracity of rumours of a reign of terror, which the questioner analogized to the guillotine, responded that 'it has been over a hundred years since the French Revolution, and I would like to think the world [has] moved [on] since then'. Bessie Beatty, *The Red Heart of Russia* (New York, 1918), p. 307.

take food away from persons doing the same to others. Far better would be simply sending the miscreants to the guillotine.[3] But, as was the case earlier in the year, he did not indicate what prevented him from doing so. In a speech on 4 November to a session of the Petrograd Soviet, the new Soviet leader, after amplifying his objections to terror, made clear these were more practical than ethical:

> We are accused of resorting to terror. But we have not done so—unlike the French revolutionaries, who guillotined unarmed men—and I hope we will not do so in the future, because we have strength on our side.[4]

On 1 December, Lenin argued that the enemies of the revolution were engaging in opposition for the purpose of actually overthrowing the new regime.[5] The Kadets, he said, were in the forefront of these efforts, and strong measures were necessary to stop them. But the remedy was not terror. Instead, Lenin prescribed imprisonment, and to support his preference he cited the Jacobins, who in similar circumstances had simply 'declared bourgeois parties outside the law'.[6]

However, at a meeting of the *Sovnarkom* (the acronym of the Council of People's Commissars, which Lenin headed) five days later, Lenin informed its other members that 'we cannot fail in finding our own Fouquier-Tinville', who during the Jacobin terror had prosecuted many of its victims.[7] By invoking Fouquier-Tinville, whom Lenin's secretary, Vladimir Bonch-Bruevich once called 'one of the unsurpassable fighters for the French Revolution', the Soviet leader was insisting, in effect, that the Bolsheviks had no choice but to destroy their real or potential enemies physically, and that to do so properly 'a staunch proletarian Jacobin' like Fouquier-Tinville was needed.[8] Fortunately for the Bolsheviks, there was already such an individual among them, Felix Dzerzhinskii, the first head of the Soviet political police, who after his premature death in 1926 would be remembered fondly as 'Iron Felix' for showing no mercy towards those whose executions he ordered.[9]

---

[3] 'The Lost Document (1 November 1917)', in Leon Trotsky, *The Stalin School of Falsification* (New York, 1972), p. 110.

[4] V. I. Lenin, 'Rech' na zasedanii Petrogradskogo Soveta 4(17) noiabria', in Lenin, *PSS*, vol. XXXV, p. 63.

[5] Keep, *Debate on Soviet Power*, p. 175.

[6] Ibid. Among those who executed policy (and later people as well), N. V. Krylenko believed from the very beginning of the Bolshevik regime that terror was a legitimate tactic and that 'the French Revolution provided an example of how to fight the bourgeoisie'. The Bolsheviks, he said, were 'its worthy students'. Quoted in V. Smirnov, 'Velikaia frantsuzskaia revoliutsiia i sovremennost', *Mirovaia ekonomika i mezhdunarodnye otnosheniia*, no. 7 (1989): p. 65.

[7] Quoted in V. D. Bonch-Bruevich, *Na boevykh postakh fevralskoi i oktiabrskoi revoliutsii* (Moscow, 1930), p. 197; George Leggett, *The Cheka: Lenin's Political Police: The All-Russian Extraordinary Commission for Combating Counter-Revolution and Sabotage, December 1917 to February 1922* (Oxford, 1981), p. 22.

[8] Bonch-Bruevich, *Izbrannye sochineniia*, vol. III, p. 114; Bonch-Bruevich, *Na boevykh*, p. 197.

[9] In *Izbranneniia*, vol. III, p. 366, Bonch-Bruevich calls Dzerzhinskii 'the Fouquier-Tinville of the Russian proletariat'.

By 1918 Lenin had not reached the point where he had become, in Maxim Gorky's phrase, 'a thinking guillotine', a description the Russian writer considered applicable.[10] But the Soviet leader did not have far to go for the description to fit. On 6 January, he made clear in *Pravda* that like all revolutions the French Revolution had generated implacable enemies; foremost among them were analogues of Chernov and Tsereteli.[11] Enemies like these had to be defeated because if they were not, the Bolsheviks might as well relinquish power and give up the revolution. Wolves, he said, could never become lambs.[12] At the end of the month, and also in the beginning of February, Lenin used the same argument to reach the identical conclusion. But this time, in articles in *Pravda*, he cited the unsuccessful revolutions of 1848 and 1871 in France as evidence of what would be the Bolsheviks' fate if they did not deal with their enemies with the firmness he recommended: 'The whole history of socialism, particularly of French socialism', showed how deleterious would be the consequences of the Bolsheviks treating their enemies leniently.[13]

Not surprisingly, Lenin never relented in his attacks on French socialism, which he maintained until his death was informed by the cowardly revisionism of its leaders, who like their Russian counterparts were not really socialists at all. The apostasy of which, with the exception of Jean Jaurês they were guilty in 1914 became, with the passage of time, even more a cause for rage. But Lenin usually evaluated the French Revolution calmly; the exception, of course, was shortly after the Second Congress in 1903, at which he was attacked as a Jacobin and a Russian Robespierre. This was even the case in the winter of 1918, when Germany threatened a resumption of military operations unless Russia surrendered and signed a treaty Lenin rightly feared would be draconian. In an article in *Pravda* in the beginning of February he made clear that while some analogies with the French Revolution were valid, others were misplaced.[14] Among the latter was that which considered Russian peasants, in their patriotism, like French peasants in 1792. Lenin, however, disagreed, and in doing so made clear that he believed anti-war sentiment among the peasants was as strong now, in 1918, as it had been

---

[10] Maxim Gorky, *Vladimir Il'ich Lenin* (Leningrad, 1924), p. 10. There was in Lenin's mind a significant difference between shooting specific individuals for some particular misdeed that merely harmed the regime, and doing so to those who threatened its survival. Execution on the spot was his preferred remedy for the former; for the latter only mass terror sufficed. Lenin often cited the Jacobins in justifying each of these remedies. But whereas it took some time for him to warm to mass terror, he always seemed receptive to the more individualized ad hoc punishment he instructed Trotsky to inflict in September 1918 on insubordinate or unsuccessful Red Army officers. In his instruction in this particular instance, he specifically cited 'the precedent on the French Revolution'. V. I. Lenin, *Neizvestnye dokumenty: 1891–1922* (Moscow, 1999), p. 250.

[11] V. I. Lenin, 'Liudi so togo sveta', in Lenin, *PSS*, vol. XXXV, p. 230.

[12] Ibid.

[13] V. I. Lenin, 'Doklad o deiatel'nosti soveta narodnykh komissarov 11(24) ianvaria', in Lenin, *PSS*, vol. XXXV, p. 266.

[14] V. I. Lenin, 'O revoliutsionnoi fraze', ibid., pp. 345–6.

in 1917. For that reason, a humiliating peace with Germany was the least harmful of the choices Russia could make: 'Any reminiscing over 1792 [when French peasants willingly went to war to protect the land the Revolution had given them] amounts to mere revolutionary phrase-mongering', and those in Russia inside and outside the party who 'repeat such slogans, words, and war cries are afraid to analyse objective reality'.[15]

But two weeks later, Lenin analogized Russia's current relationship to Germany to that of Prussia to France when the latter, under Napoleon, was militarily and politically stronger. Just as the balance of power between France and Prussia would eventually change in favour of Prussia, so too, he said, would it change to the benefit of Russia in the case of its relationship to Germany.[16] And at the end of the month, he returned to the French Revolution to support his earlier argument that capitulating to the Germans, while humiliating and a tangible setback, should not be cause for despondency:

> The Frenchmen of 1793 would never have said that their gains—the republic and democracy—were becoming purely formal and that they would have to accept the possibility of losing the republic. They were not filled with despair, but with faith in victory. To call for a revolutionary war, and at the same time to talk in an official resolution of 'accepting the possibility of losing Soviet power' [as opponents of his within the party he believed to have done] is to expose oneself completely.[17]

After the Bolsheviks, on 3 March, signed a treaty with the Germans at the Polish town of Brest-Litovsk, which many Bolsheviks considered an unconscionable betrayal of their very identity as Marxist revolutionaries, Lenin was more frantic than ever in drumming up support. In an article in *Pravda* in the middle of March he argued at considerable length that peace with Germany was a regrettable necessity until the German proletariat rose up and destroyed the existing bourgeois government. Among the arguments he mustered was that, in much the way the agreement Alexander I signed with Napoleon at Tilsit in 1809 gave Russia time to prepare for the French attack the tsar considered inevitable, the Treaty of Brest-Litovsk enabled the Bolshevik regime to survive until the German proletariat could do what Lenin was still convinced it would do.[18]

In an article in *Pravda* in April 1918, Lenin summed up what the Bolsheviks had accomplished since the October Revolution by claiming that the Soviet state was now 'approximately at the level [France] had reached in 1793 and 1871'.[19] In fact, the Soviet state had already achieved more than what its French precursors could legitimately take credit for by introducing throughout Russia 'the highest

---

[15] Ibid., p. 346.   [16] V. I. Lenin, 'Neschastnyi mir', ibid., pp. 382–3.
[17] V. I. Lenin, 'Strannoe i chudovishchnoe', ibid., pp. 404–5.
[18] V. I. Lenin, 'IV chrezvychainyi vserossiiskii s"ezd sovetov', in Lenin, *PSS*, vol. XXXVI, pp. 107–9.
[19] V. I. Lenin, 'Ocherednye zadachi sovetskoi vlasti', ibid., p. 175.

type of state—Soviet power'.[20] The next day, in a speech delivered to a session of the Central Executive Committee of the Soviet government, Lenin went further, claiming not only that the Bolsheviks had exceeded the accomplishments of the Jacobins, but that, by remaining in power despite the relentless hostility of their enemies, they had succeeded where the Jacobins had failed. Notwithstanding the praise he had previously lavished on the Jacobins—not to mention his calling himself a Jacobin in the early 1900s—Lenin now wrote, uncharacteristically, that the Jacobins had shown themselves to lack the necessary ruthlessness: instead of destroying their enemies, they merely co-opted them, with the result that the haute-bourgeoisie thereafter exacted its revenge and removed them from power.[21] In 1917 the Bolsheviks did not made the same mistake: '[we] suppressed the Alexeevs, the Kornilovs, and the Kerenskys'.[22] All that remained to be done was 'to put all the saboteurs to work under our control, under the control of Soviet power, to put in place government organs so that there will be strict account-ability and control'.[23]

Lenin's evaluation of the Jacobins closely tracked his sense of the security of the Soviet state, which until the end of the Civil War in 1921 boiled down to whether he thought it could survive until the proletarian revolutions he expected elsewhere in Europe had occurred. When he was optimistic in that regard, or at least not despondent, he either praised the Jacobins or made excuses for their failings. When he was less sanguine, he found them lacking the qualities needed to defend themselves successfully. Lenin was most critical of the Jacobins in 1918, largely because in the first three months of the year the Germans could easily have overthrown the Soviet regime, and in the last six it had to fight a civil war the outcome of which remained very much in doubt. But by 1919, especially after the tide of battle had turned and a Bolshevik victory seemed inevitable, Lenin could be more charitable. For him that meant praising the Jacobins for dealing with their enemies decisively, harshly, and, most important of all, comprehensively—while simultaneously stressing the differences he saw between the Jacobins, who ultimately lost power, and the Bolsheviks, whom he now thought unlikely to suffer the same fate.[24]

As early as 20 January, in a speech to the All-Russian Trade Union Congress in Moscow, Lenin considered the Soviet regime strong enough for him to acknowledge 'that we been more fortunate than the men who made the French

---

[20] Ibid., p.175.
[21] V. I. Lenin, 'Doklad ob ocherednykh zadachakh sovetskoi vlasti', ibid., pp. 256, 266.
[22] Ibid., p. 266.   [23] Ibid., p. 266.
[24] It is certainly possible that Lenin's confidence was purely rhetorical, and that his words were a form of bravado concealing fear and uncertainty. But it seems that anyone who could continue to believe until 1921 that proletarian revolutions would shortly erupt in other parts of Europe; that these revolutions would be successful; and that the proletariat in the countries where this happened would have the time, the energy, and the resources to assist the Bolsheviks, had to have enormous self-confidence.

Revolution, which was defeated by an alliance of monarchical and backward countries'.[25] In March 1919, in a speech delivered to the Eighth Party Congress in Moscow, Lenin pronounced the Bolsheviks more competent than the Convention in satisfying the demands of their respective peasantries.[26] This suggested that any analogy with the French Revolution was now invalid because the Bolshevik Revolution, in certain empirically verifiable ways, had exceeded it. But this did not mean that the analogy had lost its utility. At the First Congress of the Communist International, which also met in March, Lenin told the assembled delegates that the denial of rights for which the Bolsheviks were already responsible was justified because when the bourgeoisie was still 'revolutionary', it acted out of the same need for self-preservation and did the same thing: 'Neither in England in 1649 nor in France in 1793 did it allow "freedom of assembly" to monarchists and nobles, who had summoned foreign troops and "assembled" to organise attempts at restoration.'[27] Since then, Lenin continued, the bourgeoisie had become a reactionary class intent, in Russia, on thwarting the Bolsheviks' efforts to advance the course of history, and for that reason no tactic should be excluded in stopping it. In the meantime, the workers, who thanks to the Bolsheviks now knew what the bourgeoisie intended, 'will only laugh at its hypocrisy'.[28]

In a pamphlet published a few weeks later, Lenin made explicit what had been merely implicit in earlier statements of his on the use of terror, namely that the French Revolution had established a standard of excellence in that regard that few, if any, subsequent revolutions, including the Bolshevik, could ever exceed. Nevertheless, the Bolsheviks should try their best to equal it. Lenin phrased his encomium as follows:

> The French Revolution, against which, at the beginning of the nineteenth century, the old powers hurled themselves in order to crush it, we call great precisely because it was able to rouse to its defence vast masses of people who resisted the entire world; this was one of its greatest merits.[29]

With the outcome of the Civil War still in doubt, Lenin, for all his bravado, admitted his uncertainty about the long-term survival of the Soviet state. This was because the Bolsheviks had captured power in a backward country, before 'others had succeeded in establishing the Soviet form of government'.[30] But the French

---

[25] V. I. Lenin, 'Doklad na II vserossiiskom s"ezde professional'nykh soiuzov 20 ianvaria', in Lenin, *PSS*, vol. XXXVII, p. 447.

[26] V. I. Lenin, 'Doklad o rabote v derevne 23 marta', in Lenin, *PSS*, vol. XXXVIII, p. 195.

[27] V. I. Lenin, 'Tezisy i doklad o burzhuaznoi demokratii i diktature proletariat', in Lenin, *PSS*, vol. XXXVII, p. 494.

[28] Ibid., p. 494.

[29] V. I. Lenin, 'Uspekhi i trudnosti sovetskoi vlasti', ibid., p. 52.

[30] Ibid., p. 52. This was one of the few times Lenin even hinted that what the Bolsheviks had done in 1917 was in any way unorthodox ideologically.

Revolution had established a template for revolutionary regimes that wished to remain in power under difficult circumstances, and Lenin's pamphlet makes clear he believed it was the terror the Jacobins inflicted on their enemies that was the key to their success, however short-lived it turned out to be.

In May Lenin was, if anything, even more effusive in his praise of the revolution for the absence of scruples its leaders demonstrated when reactionaries and counter-revolutionaries had a reasonable chance of destroying it. In a speech delivered to the first All-Russia Congress on Adult Education, Lenin again lumped together the English and the French Revolutions in justifying the denial of rights he had recently ordered. He phrased the analogy as follows:

> When the great bourgeois revolutionaries in England in 1649 and in France in 1792–93 made their revolutions, they did not grant freedom of assembly to monarchists. The French Revolution is called great because it did not suffer from the flabbiness, half-heartedness, and phrase-mongering common among many of the revolutionaries of 1848. It was an effective revolution which, after overthrowing the royalists, crushed them completely. And we shall do the same with the capitalist gentlemen because we know that in order to free the working people from the oppression of capitalism we must deprive the capitalists of their right to assemble freely.[31]

It is noteworthy that when Lenin found it necessary to cite the year when the French Revolution began, he was not consistent. Before 1917 he only occasion-ally cited 1792 or 1793, which was an economical way of indicating that it was only when the Convention was established (in 1792) or when the Jacobins established the Committee of Public Safety (in 1793) that the French Revolution actually began. But beginning in 1917 these dates appear more often in his speeches and writings than the traditional one of 1789, which he used in most of his earlier references. One cannot know for certain why Lenin did this. But one can conjecture that by citing 1792 or 1793 as the year when the French Revolution really began (or when it began a new phase so much more advanced than the first one that it deserved to be called something else), he was now suggesting 'an analogy within an analogy': just as the Bolshevik Revolution was analogous to the French Revolution, so, too, was the relationship of the Jacobins to the National and Legislative Assemblies that preceded them analogous to that between the Bolsheviks and the Provisional Government. In other words, both the French and the Russian Revolutions were really two revolutions: the first ones, in 1789 and February 1917 respectively, were bourgeois; the second ones, in 1792–3 and October 1917 respectively, were more radical.

---

[31] V. I. Lenin, 'Rech' ob obmane naroda lozungami svobody i ravenstva', in Lenin, *PSS*, vol. XXXVIII, p. 349.

But to extend these analogies further was unwarranted. The revolutions of 1789 and February 1917, and the more radical revolutions of 1792–3 and October 1917 that followed them, were different in several ways. The most obvious of these was that while the Bolsheviks (in Lenin's estimation) would surely succeed in replacing capitalism with socialism and communism, the Jacobins did not remain in power long enough to make the capitalism that was just emerging in France less rapacious, much less replace it with a different system of class relations entirely. Left unsaid, or at least unresolved, in Lenin's evaluation of the Jacobins was the apparent contradiction between their class identity—in his descriptions they were either from the petit-bourgeoisie or the bourgeoisie as a whole—and their supporters, some of whom were from classes or categories of the French population 'lower' than the bourgeoisie and thus intent on forcing the Jacobins to posit a vision of society contrary to that which was dominant in the class to which they belonged. This, in turn, created a 'contradiction' that the Jacobins resolved in the spring of 1794, when they guillotined the Hébertists and other progressive elements. But that left them vulnerable to the haute-bourgeoisie on the right, who dispatched the Jacobins fairly easily a few months later.

But even if, as Lenin suggested, the Jacobins could not make permanent the 'supra-capitalist' objectives of its left-wing supporters, the mere fact that they tried to do so, albeit at times unwillingly and only as a result of external pressure, made the French Revolution, in its aspirations even more than in its actual achievements, a Great Revolution. After the Jacobins completed the revolution's original objectives of abolishing feudalism, eliminating the monarchy, and proclaiming France a republic, because of the Jacobins and their more radical supporters it went beyond these objectives and groped half-blindly and hesitatingly, but with great audacity and courage, towards the proletarian revolution that, while premature in the late eighteenth century in France, would be more appropriate (though still premature, but to a much lesser degree) in the early twentieth century in Russia. In Lenin's estimation, the French Revolution was a Great Revolution both because of the capitalism it facilitated and helped to legitimize politically, and because of the socialism and communism of which its Jacobin phase was a dim and distant precursor.

When Lenin invoked the French Revolution, he usually had both its bourgeois achievements and its neo-bourgeois and proto-proletarian aspirations in mind. One can therefore take with the proverbial grain of salt his occasional insistence that it began in 1792–3 with the Jacobins, rather than in 1789 with the Estates-General and the Bastille. A good example was the speech in May 1918 in which he invoked the revolution to justify Bolshevik terror. In making his argument, Lenin seemed to limit the French Revolution to its Jacobin phase. But he also reaffirmed the revolution's centrality in history as the bourgeois revolution par excellence, a force mostly for good that 'left its imprint on the entire nineteenth century, the century which gave civilization and culture to all of humanity', and in so doing marked the beginning of modernity itself.[32] While the revolution did not make real its neo-bourgeois aspirations, much less make its bourgeois achievements invulnerable to their partial retraction after 1815 during the Bourbon Restoration, it nevertheless left behind a legacy of progressive change that the Bolsheviks would eventually improve on, and in a succession no less apostolic than that in the early Christian Church, finally put in place what the most farsighted of all the French revolutionaries had envisioned. In explaining this succession, in which the still ongoing Bolshevik Revolution was now superseding the French Revolution and all the other revolutions, both in France and elsewhere in Europe that preceded it, Lenin encapsulated the relationship between the French and the Russian Revolutions in the most triumphalist rhetoric imaginable:

> Over the past eighteen months our revolution has done immeasurably more for the proletariat, the class we serve, and for the goal we are striving for, namely the overthrow of the rule of capital, than the French Revolution did for the class it served. And that is why we say that even if we take hypothetically the worst possible outcome, even if tomorrow some lucky Kolchak were to exterminate all the Bolsheviks, the revolution would still be invincible.[33]

Unlike the 'bourgeois revolutionaries' who ruled France during its revolution, and confronted hostility from countries that were still feudal, and also from England, which was economically more advanced than France, the Bolsheviks, in Lenin's description, had already succeeded, in the mere months since the October Revolution, 'in making the new state organization they created...comprehensible, familiar, and popular to the workers all over the world, so that they now regard it as their own'.[34] Where the French had failed, the Russians, according to Lenin, would succeed. Socialism was morally superior to even the most humane incarnation of industrial capitalism, and for that reason the French Revolution, for all its greatness, would henceforth remain in the shadow of the October Revolution.

Flowery rhetoric, of course, was no substitute for harsh repression, and it is worth noting that the Bolsheviks had established a political police fully six months before the Civil War began. By 1920 it had arrested and executed Russians in numbers far exceeding the death toll for which the Jacobins had been responsible in France. In both reigns of terror the principal objective was less to eliminate actual opposition than to preclude future opposition by frightening everyone still living into political passivity. In other words, both reigns of terror were meant to have a prophylactic effect. Potential opponents were deemed more dangerous than present ones. Accordingly, in both France and Russia the state mobilized

---

[32] Ibid., p. 367.   [33] Ibid., pp. 367–8.

[34] Ibid., p. 368. Lenin seemed not to notice the anomaly, from his Marxist perspective, of the first bourgeois revolution in history occurring not in England, which in 1789 possessed the most advanced economy in Europe, but somewhere else. If he did, he wisely kept this uncomfortable and unaccountable fact to himself.

much of its resources and established new institutions to ensure that this objective was achieved. But the most significant difference between the two instances of mass terror, even more than in the number of victims, was that while the Jacobins used revolutionary tribunals to pronounce legal judgement, followed by the guillotine to carry it out, under Lenin the Cheka performed both functions. By their utilizing the technological advances in mass killing that were achieved from the eighteenth century to the twentieth, the institutionalized terror the Bolsheviks practised was more effective than the arrangements the Jacobins had devised. And while Lenin's terror paled in comparison to Stalin's, which permeated practically every institution and every aspect of personal and social life in the Soviet Union, it represented nonetheless a great improvement in the impersonal annihilation of people characteristic of modern history since the French Revolution.

Lenin, of course, was too intelligent not to realize how much Russia, in its ability to kill people, exceeded that of France during its original revolution. But the analogy with the Jacobin Terror, while still useful politically, continued to haunt him even after the tide had turned in the Civil War in 1919, and it became especially relevant after the Kronstadt Revolt and the simultaneous inauguration of the NEP, which restored a measure of capitalism and market relations to the Russian economy, showed the Bolsheviks vulnerable to the charge from the left that since 1917 they had betrayed their own objectives and were now, to all intents and purposes, ersatz socialists and revolutionaries.

That the Bolsheviks were cognizant of how dangerous this charge could be was evident at the Ninth Party Congress in the early spring of 1920. One of the criticisms of Lenin's government was that it was not radical enough—which is to say that it was insufficiently committed to socialism. The criticism was often expressed in an analogy with the French Revolution: that the purpose of the October Revolution was not to supersede either the French Revolution or the February Revolution—both of which were bourgeois—but rather to complete them. This was apparently the conclusion Alexei Rykov wanted his fellow delegates to draw from remarks Lenin had made earlier about the French Revolution in which he seemed to deny the feudal roots of the French bourgeoisie; to Rykov this was a subtle way of suggesting that, in Russia, all Lenin wished to do was to 'alter the French Revolution', rather than go beyond it.[35] That Rykov's charge warranted a public response from Lenin attests to the importance and the centrality of the French Revolution in how the Bolsheviks conceptualized their own revolution. What Rykov actually meant by his accusation is unclear; the most plausible interpretation is that he objected on practical grounds as well as ideological ones to Lenin's implication that when the French Revolution began, the bourgeoisie was a *tabula rasa* and that that was the reason the policies pursued

---

[35] V. I. Lenin, 'Rech' o khoziaistvennom stroitel'stve', in Lenin, *PSS*, vol. XL, p. 269.

by some of its elements exceeded the boundaries otherwise imposed on it by its leaders having grown up under feudalism.

Whatever the reason for it, Rykov's charge, understandably, incensed Lenin, who replied that the French bourgeoisie acted differently after the French Revolution began from the way it did under feudalism because that was the way classes acted once the material circumstances that had previously circumscribed what they could do had finally changed—as they did in France in the late eighteenth century. Lenin then moved on to what was, as far as the French Revolution was concerned, his principal point. While originating under capitalism, the proletariat, he said, was now enjoying just as much freedom and autonomy after the October Revolution as the bourgeoisie in France possessed after the French Revolution. In other words, there was nothing now to prevent the proletariat from building socialism as quickly as possible—a point that Lenin may have considered essential to his efforts to sustain morale among the Bolsheviks in light of their inability, as of yet, to defeat the Whites and end the Civil War. But irrespective of what motivated it, Lenin's argument was significant both because it showed his sensitivity to the charge that the Bolsheviks were insufficiently radical—in contrast to the charge of the Mensheviks that they were excessively radical—and because it demonstrated how useful historical analogies could be to someone like Lenin with the tactical flexibility to alter the specific terms of an analogy, or even its foundational validity, in accordance with the political necessities and exigencies in any particular situation. For Lenin, analogies were a form of putty, to be moulded into whatever shape suited his purposes. In this particular instance, Lenin felt the need to show that the French Revolution and the October Revolution were practically identical.

One year later, not long after the Bolsheviks had suppressed the Kronstadt Revolt, Lenin felt compelled to emphasize, in a speech to a congress of transport workers then meeting in Petrograd, that the Bolsheviks' victory had been a 'close-run thing', and for precisely that reason they should never refrain from attacking their enemies with all the power they possessed; if they did anything less than that, the results could be catastrophic.[36] In expressing his fear that being driven from power was still a real possibility, he did what he had done on several earlier occasions when his customary self-confidence had yielded, if only temporarily, to fear and foreboding—namely to invoke the French Revolution for reassurance. But the Kronstadt Revolt, which transpired barely twenty miles from Petrograd, had frightened Lenin sufficiently so that not even the exploits of the Jacobins or the storming of the Bastille could lift his spirits. On the contrary, these iconic events of a distant revolution now suggested that all revolutions, including the Bolshevik, were susceptible to the same kind of threats, and that the dangers these

---

[36] V. I. Lenin, 'Rech' na vserossiiskom s"ezde transportnykh rabochikh', in Lenin, *PSS*, vol. XLIII, pp. 140–1.

posed could be fatal. Even though the French Revolution, until Thermidor, survived them, there was no guarantee that the Bolshevik Revolution would do the same. Revolutions, he said, were thwarted 'when the toilers, with temporary peasant support, establish short-lived dictatorships that have not consolidated power, so that after a brief period everything tends to slip back.... This was true of the Great French Revolution and, on a smaller scale is true of all revolutions.'[37] The same danger, Lenin continued, still faced the Bolsheviks: The 'petit-bourgeois-anarchist elements' that had revolted at Kronstadt still lurked in other parts of Russia, and unless the Soviet government hunted them down and destroyed them, the Bolsheviks 'would slide down as the French Revolution did'.[38] But if they mustered the strength and the force of will to defeat this element, 'the movement of the communist revolution that is growing in Europe will be further reinforced'.[39]

According to Lenin, revolutionaries could never be too vigilant. In April 1921, with the unpleasant memory of the Kronstadt Revolt still vivid, Lenin predicted that the Bolsheviks would either harness the petit-bourgeoisie for their own purposes or be destroyed by it, just the way the French Revolution had been betrayed by it when Napoleon came to power in 1799; in this instance he forgot that, in his version of the revolution, it had ended five years earlier, when Thermidor began.[40] Two months later, in an address to the Third Congress of the Communist International, Lenin singled out Miliukov, the SRs, and the Mensheviks for calling disingenuously for democracy and for 'Soviets without the Bolsheviks' during the Kronstadt Revolt; Miliukov, in particular, aroused Lenin's ire because, as the leader of the haute-bourgeoisie in Russia, he sought precisely what his counterparts in France had been able to achieve in 1794 and again in 1848–9, namely the destruction of a revolution that for all its limitations was progressive and beneficial.[41] In December, Lenin stated that 'the workers and peasants in France showed themselves capable of waging a legitimate, just, and revolutionary war against their feudal aristocracy when the latter wanted to strangle the Great French Revolution of the eighteenth century'.[42] But the same task was even easier now because not only France but almost all of Europe was still exhausted by the First World War and thoroughly balkanized by the Treaty of Versailles.[43]

It is quite appropriate that in this, the last statement Lenin made that concerned the French Revolution, he should have returned to the theme that runs like a

---

[37] Ibid., pp. 140–1.   [38] Ibid., p. 141.   [39] Ibid., p. 141.

[40] V. I. Lenin, 'O prodovol'stvennom naloge (znachenie novoi politiki i ee usloviia)', ibid., pp. 207–9.

[41] V. I. Lenin, 'Rol' 'chistoi demokratii' II i III/2 Internatsionalov, eserov i men'shevikov kak soiuznikov kapitala', in Lenin, *PSS*, vol. XLIV, p. 11.

[42] V. I. Lenin, 'O tezisakh po agrarnomu voprosu frantsuzskoi kommunisticheskoi partii', ibid., p. 277.

[43] Ibid., p. 277.

thread through his ruminations on the revolution, and indeed his entire career as a Marxist revolutionary, namely that individuals who engage in revolution as a profession need not be imprisoned by the limits ideology imposes. Revolutionaries sufficiently willing to take risks that could easily lead to their own defeat and annihilation should not shrink from exceeding these limits if there is a reasonable chance of success. And if exceeding these limits requires coercion and violence and bloodshed, so much the better: objectives are achieved and opponents of these objectives are eliminated simultaneously. What seems implicit in the totality of Lenin's career, not just it his various judgements of the French Revolution, is that the only law of revolutions that matters is a willingness to adopt whatever methods are necessary to achieve one's objectives. Finally, the French Revolution reinforced Lenin's inclination to trust his political instincts; the more audacious they were, the less prepared his enemies would be to oppose him. Danton might have been one of the losers in the French Revolution, but the audacity he recommended Lenin would adopt for his own purposes and thereby confer on Robespierre's ill-fated rival a form of posthumous vindication.

* * *

Unlike Lenin, who after the October Revolution seemed of two minds on the issue of terror, at times doubting its necessity but never its morality, Trotsky always pushed for the Bolsheviks to practise it. Any hesitation he said he felt was for rhetorical effect, a way of disguising as ambivalence an enthusiasm, exceeded by few other Bolsheviks, for mass terror on a scale surpassing that of the Jacobins'.[44] Its only defect when the Jacobins practised it, as far as Trotsky was concerned, was that technology in the eighteenth century had not advanced sufficiently to make possible the mass, institutionalized killing of the twentieth century.

On 1 December 1917, when Lenin was still temporizing on the issue of terror, Trotsky, after noting that some in Russia 'wax indignant' at its use, said that if the Bolsheviks could not succeed in defeating their class enemies by conventional means, terror would be the only alternative.[45] Any terror the Bolsheviks practised, he continued, should be 'modelled on the terror of the Great French Revolution. Not the fortress but the guillotine will await our enemies'.[46] On 2 December, after justifying the recent decree outlawing the Kadets, as a result of which many of their leaders were taken into custody, Trotsky offered a ritual *obeisance* to

[44] Pëtr Kropotkin may have had the Trotsky's willingness to practise terror in mind when asked, in December 1917, if the Paris Commune would be Lenin's model for the new Soviet state. After responding that the French Revolution provided a more likely antecedent, Kropotkin added (erroneously) that Lenin lacked 'revolutionary ideals', thereby suggesting that his commitment to the revolution could easily change. But Kropotkin said nothing comparable about Trotsky, commenting only that the French Revolution followed 'a pattern' congenial to him. Edgar Sisson, *One Hundred Red Days: A Personal Chronicle of the Bolshevik Revolution* (New Haven CT, 1931), p. 121.
[45] Quoted in Keep, *Debate on Soviet Power*, p. 177.
[46] Quoted in ibid., p. 178.

moderation by stating that 'we have not executed anybody and have no intention of doing so'.[47] But he went on to say, menacingly, that 'there are moments of popular anger and the Kadets themselves have been looking for trouble'.[48] To make certain that his threat was understood, Trotsky noted that 'during the French Revolution the Jacobins sent to the guillotine people more honest [than the Kadets] who obstructed the people's will'.[49] To reinforce the impression that the Bolsheviks would deal with their enemies without the slightest sentimentality, Trotsky called the guillotine 'a remarkable invention' that had the singular benefit of making men 'shorter by one foot'.[50]

Not only in 1917 but for several years afterward, Trotsky proudly compared himself to Robespierre and Saint-Just; partly to substantiate the comparisons, and the larger one between the French and the Russian Revolutions, he wanted the Bolsheviks to issue their own Declaration of the Rights of Man.[51] But Danton was the revolutionary Trotsky admired most (after Lenin), in part because he considered Danton's oratorical abilities equal to his own; in one account it was said that he imagined being Danton's reincarnation.[52] After a statue of the French orator and revolutionary was erected in Petrograd in 1919, Trotsky was photographed standing proudly alongside it. Of course Trotsky's pressing the comparison was not without its drawbacks; he had no wish to replicate Danton's fate, on the Place de la Concorde, where the guillotine worked its will at the hands of Robespierre.[53] However, the most appropriate comparison, after Trotsky's exploits in creating a Bolshevik army and commanding it effectively enough to defeat the Whites, was not to Danton, nor to Robespierre or Saint-Just, but to Lazare Carnot, who oversaw the organization and mobilization of the revolutionary armies that defended France and the French Revolution against external enemies in the mid-1790s.[54]

Not long after the October Revolution, Trotsky tried to persuade Lenin and the other leaders of the new regime to try Nicholas II publicly, and then, after his conviction, sentence him to death; a guillotine would already have been erected in Palace Square in Petrograd to achieve the prescribed result.[55] In arguing for this to

---

[47] L. Trotsky, 'Rech' na zasedanii petrogradskogo soveta ob otnoshenii k uchreditel'nomu sobraniiu i partii', *Delo naroda* (2 December 1917), in Trotsky, *Sochineniia*, vol. III: Part 2, p. 138.

[48] Ibid.   [49] Ibid.   [50] Quoted in Getzler, *Martov*, p. 176.

[51] Shlapentokh, *French Revolution and the Russian Anti-Intellectual Tradition*, p. 254.

[52] Pierre Fervacque, *La Vie Orgueilleuse de Trotski* (Paris, 1929), p. 125. In his PhD dissertation, 'Uses of the Past: Bolshevism and the French Revolutionary Tradition' (Harvard University, 1989), p. 189, Gabriel Schoenfeld speculates plausibly that Stalin's dictatorship, for all the bitter criticisms Trotsky levelled against it, served a positive role for Trotsky, enabling him, vis-à-vis Stalin, to be the Russian Danton.

[53] Eastman, 'Jacobinism and Bolshevism', p. 73.

[54] Nicolas Krasso, 'Trotsky's Marxism', in *Trotsky: The Great Debate Renewed*, edited by Nicolas Krasso (St Louis MO, 1972), p. 22.

[55] Shlapentokh, 'Images of the French Revolution in the February and Bolshevik Revolutions', p. 46; Lev Trotsky, *Dnevnik i pis'ma*, edited by Iu. G. Fel'shtinskii (Moscow, 1986), p. 100. In 1917 a rumour circulated in Petrograd that the guillotine could now be electrified, and thus would be capable of

happen, Trotsky, who imagined himself as the chief prosecutor in the trial, did not have to make explicit the parallel between what he hoped would be the fate of Nicholas II and what was actually the fate of Louis XVI. Trotsky's proposal, however, was not accepted, but that did not diminish his enthusiasm for the application of terror. In June 1918 he warned the Whites and all the other enemies of the Bolsheviks that 'Soviet power has still not employed the terror of the French Revolution . . . and that the patience of the Soviet government could run out'.[56] To underscore that he meant his threat seriously, he repeated his earlier observation about the guillotine reducing people's height by the length of their head.[57]

Even before the Civil War ended, Trotsky ascribed victory he expected to the terror he had recommended on the basis of the Jacobin Terror in the French Revolution.[58] In his essay, *Between Red and White*, written in 1922, Trotsky evoked the French Revolution yet again, this time, in a chapter entitled 'The Georgian Gironde', for the purpose of denigrating the Mensheviks in Georgia. The republic they had established there in 1917 was not a socialist one; its leaders were Wilsonian liberals masquerading as socialists.[59] Never one to acknowledge error, Trotsky expressed no qualms about annihilating class enemies regardless of their specific identity—the Whites, the kulaks (i.e. the most affluent peasants), and 'the bourgeoisie' were all the same to him—and he later condemned Stalin's Terror in the mid-1930s only because its victims included his supporters and one of his sons.

Trotsky and Lenin were not the only Bolsheviks to justify harsh measures against their enemies, and to do so by citing the Jacobins; their argument in reality boiled down to the notion that because the Jacobins practised terror in the French Revolution, and since the French Revolution, like the October Revolution, was progressive in furthering the course of history, for them to employ the same tactic for the same purpose was not only justified but politically prudent. This, no doubt, was what prompted other Bolsheviks, such as V. V. Osinskii, to argue in *Pravda* in September 1918 that the punishments the bourgeoisie deserved—in his mind these varied, depending on the degree to which its members posed a political threat to the new regime, from execution to forced labour to mere confinement in concentration camps—were justified because the Jacobins had likewise killed large numbers of evil people for equally virtuous reasons.[60] Other Bolsheviks were no

---

decapitating 500 people with only one movement of the blade. Julia Cantcuzene, *Revolutionary Days* (New York, 1970), p. 342.

---

[56] Quoted in Shlapentokh, *Counter-Revolution in Revolution*, p. 123.

[57] Ibid.

[58] L. Trotsky, 'Doklad na ob"edinennom zasedanii III s"ezda Sovnarkhozov i Moskovskogo Soveta Rab. i kr, Deputatov', *Ekonomikicheskaia zhizn'*, no. 18 (28 January 1920), in Trotsky, *Sochineniia*, vol. XV, p. 56.

[59] Leon Trotsky, *Between Red and White: A Study of Some Fundamental Questions of Revolution* (New York, 1975), pp. 68–72.

[60] V. V. Osinskii, 'Belyi i krasnyi terror,' *Pravda*, no. 192 (8 September 1918): p. 3.

less cold-blooded in how they believed enemies of the October Revolution should be neutralized, and similarly cited its French predecessor for moral corroboration and legitimacy.

But the French Revolution served other purposes in the years that followed the October Revolution. For Stalin, it was actually something to minimize. As a Georgian, Stalin saw the October Revolution more as the first step in the emancipation of the oppressed peoples of the East than as the culmination of the various revolutions, most of them in France, that had occurred in the West. This meant that the French Revolution was of only limited utility. As a bourgeois revolution, it did not speak to the interests of the proletariat. Nor, as a Western revolution, was it relevant to the peoples of the East. Stalin articulated the first of these axioms in a speech in January 1918 to the Third Congress of Soviets, in which he claimed that the French Revolution essentially defined what it meant to be French. France, he said, was 'that land of bourgeois democracy'.[61] In April 1920 Stalin again minimized the applicability of the revolution, this time to Russia itself. Both in time and space, it was fundamentally different from the Revolution of 1905 and the October Revolution: the French Revolution occurred when the proletariat was weak, while the two later revolutions occurred when the proletariat was stronger (in 1905) and stronger still (in 1917).[62] Stated simply, which is how Stalin usually expressed himself on issues involving Marxist ideology—not because he was unintelligent or ignorant of its intricacies, but because he wanted his readers to understand him—Stalin's position differed significantly from what by 1920 had become the Party Line: that the October Revolution was the inevitable successor to the French Revolution, and for that reason the two revolutions should be considered part of a larger unfolding of history, of which the Bolsheviks served as its current instrument and beneficiary.

Stalin, by contrast, was intent on establishing the self-sufficiency of the October Revolution, which in his mind lent to what the Bolsheviks were doing a different kind of virtue. To Stalin what legitimized the October Revolution, and lent to it its nobility of purpose, apart from the myth that it was carried out spontaneously by the proletariat, was that it succeeded without the assistance of other countries. In 1917 the Bolsheviks had acted alone, and the utility of their doing so was that it served to clarify Russia's relationship to the West—that it was the antithesis of the West, and largely *sui generis* in its history and culture. Indeed, if there was any part of the world to which the Bolsheviks should now be devoting special attention, it was the lands to their east. Indeed, in his 'theses' on 'the national question' presented to the Tenth Party Congress when it convened in March, Stalin took pains to clarify the reasons why countries in Western Europe were

---

[61] J. V. Stalin, 'Zakliuchitel'noe slovo po dokladu o natsional'nom voprose', in Stalin, *Sochineniia*, vol. IV, p. 36.
[62] J. V. Stalin, 'Lenin, kak organizator i vozhd' RKP', ibid., p. 311.

different—politically, economically, and ideologically—from those in Eastern Europe. In his mind, these boiled down to a single historical peculiarity: the states that emerged in Eastern Europe were uniquely affected by non-European peoples, among them the Turks and the Mongols, whose depredations ensured that the states that succeeded them, notably Austria, Hungary, and Russia, were multi-national.[63] Left unsaid, but clearly implicit in Stalin's analysis, was that the other parts of the world the Turks and the Mongols had once imperialized were also multinational—and thus equally unaffected by Western history and culture.

Like Stalin, Bukharin often viewed events in Russia from a global perspective. But whereas Stalin often excluded Western Europe from the parts of the world he considered susceptible to the Bolsheviks' message, Bukharin did the opposite. In his view the Bolsheviks could learn much from Europe—and from the French Revolution in particular. But unlike Trotsky, Bukharin did not consider the latter just a European phenomenon. In the model it presented to posterity, and in the ideas and moral values it introduced, the French Revolution had relevance well beyond both Europe and Russia. At its core, it was a supra-European revolution, indeed a prototype for revolution everywhere. In fact, the only thing that distinguished one country and one period of history from another was the time it took in each of them for socialism and communism to be achieved.

In much of what he wrote from 1917 to the mid-1920s Bukharin repeated what by then had become Leninist orthodoxy on the French Revolution. Like other Bolsheviks he practically deified the Jacobins as models of revolutionary valor; eulogizing Dzerzhinskii in 1926, he paid him the ultimate compliment by repeating Lenin's earlier description of the ruthless and morally uncompromising police chief as 'a proletarian Jacobin'.[64] In *The ABC of Communism*, co-authored with Evgenii Preobrazhenskii, he made clear his belief that the phraseology Lenin used to characterize the Jacobins also characterized the Bolsheviks—and that the reverse was also true. Of course, in Bukharin's Manichean view of the world, the Bolsheviks' enemies had to be demonized in the most damning rhetoric imaginable. For having supported Russia's involvement in the First World War, and for counselling leniency for the SR defendants in the first show-trial in Russia in 1922, Plekhanov, according to Bukharin, was just a latter-day Girondin, whose perfidy and hypocrisy in claiming falsely to be a genuine Marxist and socialist contrasted

---

[63] J. V. Stalin, 'Ob ocherednykh zadachakh partii v natsional'nom voprose. Tezisy k s"ezdu RKP(b), utverzhdennye TsK partii', ibid., pp. 15–16. Stalin's view of the French Revolution was also idiosyncratic, at least among the Bolsheviks, in that in contrast to Lenin and Marx, he praised their respective bêtes noirs, Blanqui and Ferdinand Lassalle, who he said were weak on theoretical and ideological matters, but strong on practical ones—in contrast to Plekhanov and Kautsky, for whom the reverse was true. Given Stalin's own penchant for the practical, one suspects that if forced to choose between the two sets of revolutionaries, he would have opted for the former, despite their denigration by Lenin and Marx, the only two persons in the Bolshevik and Marxist universe Stalin inhabited whom he considered his superiors. Stalin, 'Lenin, kak organizator i vozhd' RKP', ibid., p. 314.

[64] '"Rech" tov. N. I. Bukharina', *Pravda*, no. 168(3397) (24 July 1926): p. 3.

sharply with the honesty and valour of the Jacobins.[65] The French Revolution, in other words, could be seen as a struggle within a struggle, as the Jacobins fought the Girondins while the revolution they both claimed to personify was fighting desperately to beat back its foreign enemies.

But the French Revolution, in Bukharin's estimation, was more than a morality play in which the roles of the virtuous and the iniquitous were obvious to everyone. He cited it in *The ABC of Communism* not just to demonstrate that, as the archetypical bourgeois revolution, it could not possibly prefigure the October Revolution in any of the ways in which the latter, as a socialist revolution, was unique; in 1919, when the book was written, no revolutions similar to the Bolshevik had succeeded, and those that had occurred had failed. Rather, the French Revolution was invoked to demonstrate certain general laws of revolution; one of these was that the resistance they generate is bound in almost every instance to result in civil war. In addition, the revolution in France preached a message of opposition to political authority attractive to everyone suffering from oppression irrespective of their class or station in life:

> The revolutionary French bourgeoisie, as represented by Danton, Robespierre, and the other noted figures of the first epoch of the revolution, appealed to all the people of the world on behalf of deliverance from every form of tyranny; the *Marseillaise*, written by Rouget de l'Isle, and sung by the armies of the revolution, is dear to the hearts of all oppressed peoples.[66]

For Bukharin the French Revolution's influence on the course of history was potentially limitless. In an essay on historical materialism in 1921, he made clear that its principal achievement was not in bringing capitalism to France, but rather enabling it to develop everywhere. In that way, the French Revolution transcended the particular material circumstances that caused it. Indeed, its consequences were not confined to politics or the economy: '[The French Revolution] created a rich national literature; it produced numerous men of genius [who were] painters, prose writers, poets, and philosophers'.[67] More than other Bolsheviks, Bukharin embraced the notion that revolutions transformed the arts and aesthetic principles as well as politics, and that by substituting new genres and modes of expression for old ones, revolutions enrich the lives of everyone. Moreover, the very fact that Bukharin wrote knowledgeably about the arts shows that to him they had an intrinsic worth that transcended time and space. This, too, he seemed to suggest, was a universal law of revolution. Art had a way of projecting itself beyond what was possible in politics and in economic relationships, and for that reason Bukharin sincerely approved of the vocational freedom artists enjoyed under Lenin without repudiating his opinion that the only two-party system he would

---

[65] N. Bukharin and E. Preobrazhensky, *The ABC of Communism* (Monmouth, Wales, 2006), p. 154.
[66] Ibid., p. 198.   [67] Ibid., p. 197.

countenance in the Soviet Union was one in which one party ruled and the other was in prison.[68] This, in fact, was a fairly accurate description of the Soviet Union when its leaders were sponsoring extravagant pageants and celebrations designed to mimic the *fêtes* the Jacobins had produced to symbolize their transformational objectives.

In sharp contrast to Bukharin's vision of the French Revolution was the way two other Bolsheviks viewed it. For David Riazanov, whose principal contribution to Bolshevism was publishing a comprehensive collection of the works of Marx and Engels, the French Revolution might well have been two revolutions, the first a bourgeois revolution led by the bourgeoisie, the second one a bourgeois revolution led by classes and categories of the population less prosperous and powerful than the bourgeoisie; these included the workers of Paris, such as they were in 1792, when the Jacobins, 'as representatives of the petty bourgeoisie, came to power and pressed the demands of their class to their logical conclusions'.[69] While Riazanov did not draw any analogy between the French and the Russian Revolutions in his joint biography of Marx and Engels, where his analysis of the Jacobins appeared, one can easily imagine how he would have conceptualized it: the Provisional Government's equivalent in France would be the National and Legislative Assemblies that governed the country from 1789 to 1792, while the new Soviet government would be reminiscent of the Jacobins, though not its replica because the classes the Bolsheviks represented were even more radical than those the Jacobins had claimed to represent in France. The genuine ambivalence with which Riazanov viewed the Jacobins—more progressive than the feudal nobility, but not nearly enough to rival the proletariat—is readily apparent in the joint biography.[70]

Karl Radek hardly differed from Riazanov in how he viewed the French Revolution. However, he chose to emphasize its unfulfilled aspirations rather than its actual accomplishments. Radek was suspicious of arguments that the Jacobins themselves—in contrast to the classes they represented—were proletarian. In fact, as he explained in 1920 in a book entitled *Proletarian Dictatorship and Terrorism*, there were always revolutionaries to the left of the Jacobins, such as Jean-François Varlet and Jacques Roux, who, like the Jacobins, differed in their class origin from their particular political constituency. But because they and their supporters were more radical than the Jacobins, Varlet and Roux soon became political liabilities, and the Jacobins had no choice but to send them, in the spring of 1794, to the guillotine. This seemed, at first, to ensure the Jacobins' survival politically. Having completed the destruction of feudalism in France, there was nothing left for them

---

[68] Cohen, *Bukharin and the Bolshevik Revolution*, p. 201.

[69] David Riazanov, *Karl Marx and Frederick Engels: An Introduction to their Lives and Work* (New York and London, 1973), p. 19.

[70] Ibid., pp. 18–19.

to do given their origins in the petit-bourgeoisie. In fact, by eliminating the *sans-culottes* and the others to the left of them ideologically, they reduced their political base to such an extent that the success of the *coup d'état* on 9 Thermidor was a foregone conclusion.[71] But even if the Jacobins had not done things that were so manifestly self-defeating, because they had outlived their historical usefulness, they would have lost power no matter what they did; the only variable in their downfall was its timing.

None of what Radek wrote about the French Revolution differed significantly with what Lenin had already argued. Both men maintained that the Jacobins, for all their achievements, were in the end imprisoned by the times in which they lived, and when they tried to escape from their confinement, history and the Marxist dialectic brought them down. Moreover, Radek resembled Lenin in one other way, namely in his ability to assassinate the character of anyone who disagreed with him; the only difference was that the latter preferred the rhetorical equivalent of a sledgehammer to express his arguments *ad hominem*, while the former used cutting sarcasm.[72] Radek's book was intended as a response to the criticisms Karl Kautsky had recently levelled at the Bolsheviks, and it was entirely in keeping with Radek's contempt for the German socialist that he dismissed his criticisms, which included references to the French Revolution and to the Jacobins, as expressions of his 'castrated Marxism'.[73]

Intentionally or not, Kautsky's critique of the October Revolution was guaranteed, in the case of the Bolsheviks, to be met with a torrent of invective intended to destroy the author's credentials as a socialist. Although they had already done much to discredit them, one suspects that Radek, and also Lenin and Trotsky, believed still more had to be done to finish the job. Had Kautsky lost all credibility among European socialists, they probably would not have attacked him so relentlessly. But that is what they did. What triggered the assault was Kautsky's first extended denunciation of Bolshevism, *The Dictatorship of the Proletariat*, published in 1918. It was followed two years later by an even more thoroughgoing repudiation of Bolshevism in a book entitled *Terrorism and Communism*. In both works Kautsky invoked the French Revolution to clarify and strengthen his objections.

---

[71] Karl Radek, *Proletarian Dictatorship and Terrorism* (Detroit MI, n.d.), pp. 16–21.

[72] A typical example of Radek's modus operandi in that respect was his response, at the Twelfth Party Congress in 1923, to Voroshilov's comment, as Radek followed Trotsky towards the podium, that 'the lion (because Trotsky's first name in Russian was also the word for the animal) is followed by his tail'. Radek replied that it was 'better to be Trotsky's tail than Stalin's ass'. When the latter inevitably got wind of this, he asked Radek if his rejoinder was one of his jokes, to which Radek replied: 'Yes, but I did not invent the one about you being the leader of the international proletariat.' Ben Lewis, *Hammer & Tickle: A Cultural History of Communism* (New York, 2009), p. 60. One may safely infer that from that moment on, Radek, to Stalin, was a dead man walking.

[73] Radek, *Proletarian Dictatorship*, p. 19.

In the first of these works Kautsky reversed his view, first expressed after the 1905 Revolution, that the second, and presumably more successful bourgeois revolution in Russia that would follow it need not be carried to completion by the bourgeoisie; a coalition of the peasantry and the proletariat, which was what Lenin recommended, could act on its behalf. According to Kautsky, something similar had happened in the French Revolution, when the Jacobins, representing a coalition of elements of the urban and rural lower classes, took power from the bourgeoisie. But the Jacobins lost power before their more radical supporters could carry out a socialist revolution. This, however, need not be the fate of the Bolsheviks, who might take power and then proceed seamlessly to the construction of socialism.[74] Of course when Kautsky was contemplating these hypotheticals, no one in Russia or anywhere else in Europe had exercised his imagination to the same extent. Kautsky, in other words, was proceeding, if only in his own mind, where no other European Marxist, not even Lenin or Trotsky, had gone before.

By the time Kautsky was writing *The Dictatorship of the Proletariat*, however, reality, rather than mere possibilities, was what concerned him. The Bolsheviks had taken power in what they claimed to be a proletarian revolution. From his observations of the new Bolshevik regime, Kautsky felt compelled to acknowledge that the possibility of a proletarian revolution in Russia in 1917—and thus the possibility of a proletarian regime in Russia in 1918—was actually a fantasy. In reality, Russia in 1917 was ready only for a bourgeoisie revolution, and the only way the government it established could be proletarian was if this government was a dictatorship. The October Revolution, in other words, had been a hoax. Its perpetrators had taken power under false pretenses. The Bolsheviks had far exceeded the Marxist parameters of what was politically possible; given that capitalism in Russia had emerged only a quarter-century earlier, the only revolution in 1917 that could have produced a stable regime was a bourgeois revolution. In fact, the very prematurity of the October Revolution had made the application of terror a virtual necessity; without it the Bolsheviks would surely lose power—as the Jacobins did.[75]

By 1920 what the Bolsheviks had done since his writing *The Dictatorship of the Proletariat* only confirmed Kautsky's earlier objections to both the October Revolution and the terror he thought the Bolsheviks had no choice but to inflict because of it. But the very fact that the Bolsheviks had adopted that particular tactic—as Kautsky carefully explained in *Terrorism and Communism*—was proof they would soon lose power, and all one had to do to convince anyone who

[74] Karl Kautsky, *The Dictatorship of the Proletariat* (Ann Arbor MI, 1964), pp. 55, 101–2, 116, 148–9, and *passim*.

[75] Ibid., p. 57. In his analysis of Kautsky's condemnation of Bolshevism, Leszek Kolakowski recognized the role the Jacobins played in it, and made clear his agreement with the German socialist's analysis. Leszek Kolakowski, *Main Currents of Marxism: Its Rise, Growth, and Dissolution* (Oxford, 1978), vol. II, p. 45.

doubted it was to note that the Jacobins, who like the Bolsheviks were weak and felt the need to appear strong, had done the same thing and lost power anyway. Terror, in short, was morally wrong because there were no circumstances in which it could succeed in protecting governments like the Jacobins' whose objectives, considered on their merits, were progressive and therefore morally justified. Terror was detrimental to all that was best in the French Revolution because it could not prevent its betrayal by the Jacobins' successors.[76] And to underscore the point that mass killings of any kind, not just those involving premeditation, as was true for the Jacobins', were both counterproductive and morally wrong, Kautsky included in *Terrorism and Communism* his opprobrium of the massacres predating the Jacobins' in the French Revolution, in particular those that accompanied the storming of the Bastille. For revolutions to succeed, they must be consensual, or at least command sufficient popular support so that terror will not be required to perpetuate the new regimes that follow them.[77] In Kautsky's ethical calculus of the tactics revolutionaries could choose to achieve their objectives, terror was so morally corrupting and repugnant that it was alien even to animals, who killed only for survival.[78]

Kautsky failed to indicate if there were other circumstances in which terror, as a matter of policy, was morally justified, as, for example, in its application by a government that had come to power consensually but now was threatened by a minority that refused to acknowledge its legitimacy. But for the Bolsheviks, the meaning of Kautsky's exegesis on the morality of terror was undeniable. Its purpose was nothing less than to deny the moral legitimacy of the October Revolution, which for the Bolsheviks was tantamount to proclaiming that the nascent Soviet state did not deserve to survive. Kautsky's argument could be boiled down to a logical syllogism: like the Jacobins, the Bolsheviks took power prematurely; as happened to the Jacobins, this caused the Bolsheviks to practise terror, which was costing them what little popular support they had; thus they would be toppled by a contemporary equivalent of the Directory or Napoleon. In the book, which was written while the Civil War in Russia was still in doubt, Kautsky did not indicate if he thought the Whites were capable of defeating the Bolsheviks, but he clearly believed that if the Whites did not topple them, some other coalition of reactionary elements would do so—and for Kautsky that was an outcome even (or especially) socialists should wish for.

---

[76] Karl Kautsky, *Terrorism and Communism: A Contribution to the Natural History of Revolution* (London, 1920), pp. 38–43 and *passim*.

[77] Ibid., pp. 134, 137–8.

[78] Ibid., pp. 121–7. In explaining why the Jacobins practised terror, Stanley Hoffmann adopted a similarly 'functionalist' interpretation, arguing that while Robespierre and the others on the Committee of Public Safety thought their own moral virtue entitled them to kill people, they had no intention of practising mass terror before 'the hectic and heated circumstances in which France almost died in 1793' forced them to do so. Hoffmann, 'The French Revolution and the Language of Violence', p. 155.

Lenin and Trotsky of course were outraged by Kautsky's entire critique, which seemed to situate what they had done in 1917 and thereafter well beyond the bounds of what Marxism permitted. Trotsky, in particular, took umbrage at anyone who questioned his perspicacity in recommending a revolution that not even Marx—if one excluded his late flirtation with the notion of conflating the bourgeois and proletarian revolutions in Russia into one—believed could endure. And it was Trotsky, not Lenin, who in his rebuttal invoked the French Revolution, quite possibly in the belief that by refuting Kautsky's views on the French Revolution, he was casting doubt on the German socialist's credentials as an analyst of the Bolshevik Revolution.[79]

Early in his critique, which was published in 1920, Trotsky made clear that the two revolutions were really signposts on the road directing humanity to its own emancipation. Neither revolution could be understood without consideration of the other. The French Revolution was 'the greatest event in modern history', not to be surpassed, or even equalled until the Bolshevik Revolution.[80] The French Revolution, in other words, was not just an earlier analogue of the Bolshevik Revolution, but part of a larger unfolding of history in which the second revolution was an indication of how far humanity had progressed since the first one; for that reason the French Revolution had a special relevance to the Bolsheviks that nothing else in history, not even the 1905 Revolution, provided. The Red Army was a latter-day reincarnation of the French revolutionary armies, and the terror that was applied by the Jacobins was directed against enemies who had the same objective of obstructing the course of history as those the Bolsheviks currently faced in the Civil War. The fact that the Jacobins' enemies were both internal and foreign only heightened the danger they posed, and justified the means the Jacobins adopted to defeat them. Trotsky summarized the relationship between the two revolutions as follows:

> [T]he Russian Revolution, which culminated in the dictatorship of the proletariat, began with just that work which was done in France at the end of the eighteenth century. Our forefathers, in centuries gone by, did not take the trouble to prepare the democratic way—by means of revolutionary terrorism—for milder manners in our revolution.[81]

For Trotsky, terror was not some extraneous appendage to the two revolutions, in the moral evaluation of which it could be cavalierly ignored. Rather, it comprised their very essence. The audacity of what revolutions try to do makes resistance inevitable, and the fact that in the French Revolution things worsened for the

---

[79] Lenin's response was published as a pamphlet entitled *Proletarskaia revoliutsiia i renegat Kautskii* in Petrograd in 1918. It also appeared, greatly condensed but with the identical title, in *Pravda*, no. 219 (11 October 1918): p. 3.

[80] Leon Trotsky, *Terrorism and Communism: A Reply to Karl Kautsky* (Ann Arbor MI, 1969), p. 49.

[81] Ibid., p. 24.

Jacobins before they improved only underscored the wisdom of their not allowing any 'bourgeois' moral scruples to hold them back. Like Kautsky, Trotsky chose to rationalize the terror the Bolsheviks were then inflicting on their own enemies in the form of a syllogism. The French Revolution was a good thing for France and for humanity; the October Revolution was similarly beneficial; thus the tactics that were adopted in the French Revolution that enabled it to achieve its objectives were ones the Bolsheviks, no less legitimately, could employ.[82] In Trotsky's formulation of the relationship between means and ends in revolutions he considered morally virtuous, the moral value of the former was identical to that of the latter. This of course was contrary to the usual supposition that 'the ends do not justify the means'. Trotsky was not claiming that the moral virtue of communism justified tactics intended to achieve it, such as the mass extermination of real or potential enemies that were evil. Rather, he was arguing that terror was justified when it was adopted to achieve a virtuous objective, but morally abhorrent when used to achieve an objective that was immoral. Implicit in Trotsky's formulation was that there were no limits to the terror governments might justifiably inflict as long as their objectives remained virtuous.

Of course to Kautsky, Trotsky's logic was incomprehensible, which only further confirmed Trotsky's opinion that by criticizing the Bolsheviks, Kautsky was betraying socialism just as much as he did by supporting Germany's declaration of war in 1914. That Kautsky was still considered a socialist by many self-described socialists in Europe infuriated Trotsky because it implied support for Kautsky's charge that the tactics the Bolsheviks were employing to ensure the Soviet state's survival were unethical not just in the 'bourgeois' sense of the word, but also in the way socialists defined it.[83]

Another prominent socialist who cited the French Revolution in strengthening her critique of the October Revolution was Rosa Luxemburg. In an essay written shortly before her assassination in 1919, she began her critique in an unexpected way. Instead of stressing the dissimilarities between the two revolutions, so that the iniquity of the Bolshevik was accentuated by the virtue of the French, she stressed what she considered their similarity; the Bolsheviks, she said, were 'the historic heirs' of the Jacobins.[84] Moreover, the French Revolution did wonderful

[82] Ibid., pp. 23–5, 49–50, 55–9.
[83] Years later, the Soviet historian V. G. Revunenkov was more charitable than Trotsky, and far less given to rhetorical hyperbole, in cataloguing Kautsky's errors in his analysis of the French Revolution. While in Revunenkov's estimation Kautsky was correct in stressing its 'populist' aspects, personified most obviously in the *sans-culottes*, he was also, unfortunately, given to an overly 'schematised' view of the revolution that exaggerated the influence of the *sans-culottes* to such an extent that he ignored the degree to which the Jacobins, by the time their dictatorship ended, represented little more than a segment of the petit-bourgeoisie. Although he did not say so explicitly, it seems logical to conclude that to Revunenkov this was the reason—notwithstanding Kautsky's unfair condemnation of it—that the Jacobins were compelled to practise mass terror. Revunenkov, *Ocherki po istorii Velikoi frantsuzskoi revoliutsii*, p. 105.
[84] Luxemburg, *Russian Revolution*, p. 41.

things, and for that reason the Jacobins, who best embodied what it stood for, deserved enormous credit. Their seizure of power (and also the means they employed to remain in power, although Luxemburg did not make this point explicitly) was:

> the only means of saving the conquests of the revolution, of achieving a republic, of smashing feudalism, of organising a revolutionary defence against inner as well as outer foes, of suppressing the conspiracies of counter-revolution, and [of] spreading the revolutionary wave from France to all of Europe.[85]

In contrast to Kautsky, who considered the Girondins genuine revolutionaries and an acceptable alternative to the Jacobins, Luxemburg argued that whatever virtues the Girondins possessed, their moderation made chimerical any scenario in which they could have come to power and then avoid the ostensible excesses of which the Jacobins were culpable. In any revolution, she wrote, 'the golden mean' cannot be maintained.[86]

For Luxemburg a moderate revolution was an oxymoron, as impossible in France as in Russia. The French and Russian Revolutions, in fact, followed a remarkably similar trajectory even though France and Russia, in their histories and culture, were not at all alike. Russian peasants were far more distrustful of the Bolsheviks than French peasants were of the Jacobins. But none of that had any bearing on whether the Bolsheviks would remain in power and whether the policies they followed would facilitate rather than hinder the achievement of socialism. Where the Bolsheviks had gone wrong, in her opinion, was in not trusting the Russian people to see the wisdom in what the Bolsheviks intended. Disbanding the Constituent Assembly in January 1918 was foolish not because democracy was always and everywhere preferable. Exercised to benefit capitalists or reactionaries, it was harmful. But for a regime like the Bolshevik that had taken power without popular support, it was essential. For that reason the Bolsheviks should have allowed the assembly to function for its heuristic potential, because it was a forum in which the Bolsheviks could demonstrate their support for the peasantry while simultaneously persuading them that only by accepting socialism could their poverty and oppression disappear. In the process, the Bolsheviks would acquire badly needed credibility.[87] For Luxemburg this sequence of events had occurred once before, namely in France during the bourgeois monarchy of Louis Philippe, which was when the elements in the French population that still resisted the French Revolution finally accepted it.[88]

The message Luxemburg intended for the Bolsheviks was that unless they allowed the people the opportunity to express their opinions, the popular support they still enjoyed would be reduced to the point where they could only rule through the application of force. Lost would be governance by popular consensus,

---

[85] Ibid., p. 37.   [86] Ibid., p. 38.   [87] Ibid., pp. 60–2.   [88] Ibid., p. 62.

based not so much on agreement concerning the policies pursued in the present as on acceptance of the promise socialism held out of a society in which the material needs of the people were met and the spiritual contentment every human being was entitled to was enjoyed. In 1918, when Luxemburg was writing, the whole future of the Great Bolshevik Experiment—to which Luxemburg, for all her fears of Lenin's authoritarianism, was fundamentally sympathetic—still hung in the balance, its outcome a function of whether the Bolsheviks could impress upon the peasants how better off they were with the Bolsheviks in power to protect them and to instruct them in the virtues of socialism. Luxemburg issued her critique of the Bolsheviks cognizant that the ideological legitimacy of the October Revolution was based on the socialist credentials of the Bolsheviks, about which she was never in doubt. But she also recognized that the political legitimacy of the October Revolution—whether the Russian people would support it voluntarily— was very much in doubt because it had actually been an armed insurrection lacking the support a genuine revolution commanded. The regime that resulted was therefore a dictatorship—a proletarian dictatorship, to be sure, but a dictatorship nevertheless—and for that reason the Bolsheviks still had a great deal of work to do—not as oppressors but as propagandists for an ideology the benevolence of which she always assumed. Luxemburg did not object to proletarian dictatorships per se, but rather to those that were established without majoritarian support. For that reason, her acknowledgement that the regime headed by Lenin and Trotsky was in fact such a dictatorship might have generated a response from either or both of them as vitriolic and *ad hominem* as that which they directed at Kautsky. But Luxemburg's essay was not published until 1922, and her apotheosis as a martyr to the cause of communism following her murder in 1919—to which both Lenin and Trotsky added their condolences—made even a reasoned rebuttal impolitic.[89]

Other critics of the Bolsheviks were spared their rhetorical wrath. Among the fortunate few were Russian liberals. By 1920 they had long ceased influencing events in Russia, the vast majority of them either having left the country voluntarily after the October Revolution or forced to do so by the government. This was true of Pëtr Struve, who by 1917 had long abandoned Marxism and adopted a liberalism unusually attentive to peasants' needs and aspirations. In condemning actions of the Bolsheviks he considered politically unwise and morally objectionable, Struve on one occasion cited the French Revolution, which in one respect he considered analogous to the October Revolution. Both revolutions, he wrote, were

[89] V. I. Lenin, 'Rech' na mitinge protesta protiv ubiistva Karla Libknekhta i Rozy Liuksemburg 10 ianvaria 1919 g.', in Lenin, PSS, vol. XXXVII, p. 434. In 1932 Trotsky would minimize Luxemburg's criticism of the new Bolshevik regime while also exonerating her of Stalin's charge that she was a 'centrist' rather than a genuine communist. He also strongly suggested that the aspects of the Bolshevik regime she found objectionable were characteristic of Stalin's rule, rather than Lenin's. Leon Trotsky, 'Hands Off Rosa Luxemburg!' The Militant (6 and 13 August 1932), p. 4.

principally challenged not by forces external to them, but by their own internal dynamics. In the October Revolution these included a hypertrophied military and the authoritarianism in Bolshevism itself, with which Struve, who as a former Marxist knew Lenin well, was quite familiar. In the French Revolution the forces that challenged it—Struve did not name them but it is clear he meant the Directory, and possibly also Napoleon—halted the revolution but did not betray it by reversing the transformative changes it made. In that respect the October Revolution was radically different. According to Struve, the October Revolution contained within itself the seeds of its betrayal.[90]

Among the SRs, a comparable consensus emerged after the Treaty of Brest-Litovsk, which, by formalizing Russia's withdrawal from the First World War, caused the Left SRs, who had previously supported the Bolshevik regime, to join with the SR party in opposing it. Isaak Steinberg, a Left SR who had served as Minister of Justice in the new government before it ordered his arrest and penal incarceration, condemned the regime for its betrayal of socialism. In expressing his disgust, he singled out the Bolsheviks' infatuation with violence, which had given rise in Russia to what he called ironically 'the sacred guillotine'.[91] The mass arrests of Kadets, moreover, seemed to him a repetition of the mistakes of the French Revolution, which before his apostasy he wrongly thought the Bolsheviks had outgrown.[92] Following his arrest, Steinberg rued how easily and quickly in both the French and the Bolshevik Revolutions people could descend 'from the height of power to the gates of prison'.[93] Opinions critical of the Bolsheviks, such as Steinberg's, were of course nothing new to SRs like Viktor Chernov who had never supported the October Revolution, and several of them contributed articles to *Delo* and *Delo Naroda* condemning the Bolshevik terror and apotheosizing victims of the French equivalent, most notably Danton.[94] Pitirim Sorokin recalled later that when the Bolsheviks were harassing the SRs prior to their final prohibition and banishment, he felt especially empathetic to the Girondins.[95]

Not surprisingly, several French historians who had judged the February Revolution a worthy successor of the French viewed the October Revolution as a betrayal of both revolutions, and tangible evidence of history, as it were, going backwards. It took time for them to reach this conclusion. Alphonse Aulard gradually soured on the Bolsheviks after 1917, though not sufficiently, while the Civil War still raged, to prefer a White victory. He signed a petition, published in *L'Humanité* in 1919, opposing foreign intervention; in the same year, while standing for election to the French National Assembly, he summarized his

---

[90] P. Struve, 'Razmyshleniia o russkoi revoliutsii', *Russkaia mysl'* (January–February, 1921): pp. 35–6.

[91] I. N. Steinberg, *In the Workshop of the Revolution* (London, 1955), p. 137.

[92] Ibid., p. 59.   [93] Ibid., p. 158.

[94] Shlapentokh, *French Revolution and the Russian Anti-Democratic Tradition*, p. 274.

[95] Sorokin, *Leaves from a Russian Diary*, p. 93.

position on Russia in the form of a slogan, 'Neither Bolshevism nor Reaction'.[96] But by 1923 he was sufficiently disgusted with all things Russian that he disparaged Russian peasants, who he knew comprised a majority of the population, as contemplative, apathetic, and inclined to mysticism. Their insatiable hunger for land, moreover, had made them 'petit-bourgeois' in their politics, to the extent that they had any—a charge the editor of *Volia Rossii*, which published the article that contained Aulard's accusation, angrily denied.[97] By the time of his death in 1928 Aulard's objections to Bolshevism had hardened to the point where he deemed fascist Italy its illegitimate offspring.[98]

Despite the pungency of their criticism, because the threat they posed to the Bolsheviks politically was minimal or nonexistent, Struve, Aulard, and even the SRs, whose presence in Russia might have given their criticisms an immediacy and credibility foreigners and *émigrés* lacked, could all be safely ignored. If critics such as these required rebuttal, the task could be left to Soviet historians.[99] When the Mensheviks criticized the new Soviet state, however, the Bolsheviks realized that answering their charges was a priority. However weak politically, the Mensheviks' ideological proximity to the Bolsheviks, along with the fact that both Martov and Axelrod had a personal history with Lenin of roughly a quarter-century, meant that if Lenin and Trotsky were preoccupied with even more pressing obligations to respond themselves, others would have to do so in their place.

To the Bolsheviks, denying the ideological legitimacy of the October Revolution was perhaps the greatest sin Marxist socialists could commit. To do so was tantamount to rejecting the Soviet state the revolution produced. The Mensheviks of course were well aware of this, as they were of the similarities between the Bolsheviks and the Jacobins, which ensured that criticizing the latter could be a subtle way of criticizing the former. This was precisely the strategy lesser-known Mensheviks adopted. Familiar with the intelligentsia's stratagem while the monarchy existed of using 'Aesopian language' to express their opposition to it—that is to say, of disguising the true object of their opprobrium by criticizing something the censorship would not realize was comparable to it—they came to the tactic naturally. But the leaders of the Mensheviks drew the analogy directly. In December 1917 Fëdor Dan took to the pages of *Iskra* to attack Trotsky explicitly as 'a home-bred

[96] Ian H. Birchall, *The Spectre of Babeuf* (London, 1997), p. 110. Kondratieva claims that by 1919 Aulard had already become 'an enemy' of the Bolshevik regime and was collaborating with Russian *émigrés* for the purpose of eventually overthrowing it. Kondratieva, *Bol'sheviki-iakobintsy*, p. 174.

[97] A. A. Aulard, 'Dve revoliutsii', pp. 17, 20.

[98] Michel Vovelle, '1789–1917: The Game of Analogies', in *The French Revolution and the Creation of Modern Political Culture*, edited by Keith Michael Baker (New York, 1994), pp. 353–4.

[99] See, for example, A. Maletskii, 'Nasilovanie teorii ili teoriia nasiliia gospodina Olarda', *Kommunisticheskii internatsional*, no. 7 (1925): pp. 82–3, where the author berated Aulard for recently justifying the terror of the French Revolution as a 'functional' response to the requirements imposed by war. Because Maletskii considered the Jacobin terror analogous to the Bolsheviks', Aulard's justification, in his opinion, was not strong enough.

Robespierre'.[100] Iulii Martov, after writing privately to Axelrod on 1 December that 'only now has the "Jacobin" character in Leninism . . . been exposed in full measure', singled out Trotsky publicly three days later for his praising the guillotine's prowess as a means of execution.[101] To Martov, this particular instrument of revolutionary justice not only destroyed the innocent; it also coarsened and emboldened everyone who used it. He concluded his indictment with a plea to his readers to 'beware of the guillotine!'[102] Finally, when Iurii Larin, a professional historian also serving as a Bolshevik commissar, cited the French Revolution in *Pravda* justifying the exclusion of the Kadets from the Constituent Assembly, Martov, in *Vpered*, took Larin to task for applying the methods of the seventeenth and eighteenth centuries, which included terror, to the twentieth. Such methods, he wrote, were the result of political weakness and led directly to the betrayal of the revolution the Jacobins desired first by the Directory and then by Napoleon.[103]

Notwithstanding Martov's criticisms of the Jacobins, there were many aspects of the French Revolution he considered laudable. In its totality, its record was mixed. That caused him, in distinguishing the good from the bad, to contradict himself. In his letter of 1 December to Axelrod, he noted that before 1917 only a bourgeois revolution was possible in Russia and that it would resemble the French Revolution in its benevolence. But now that the October Revolution had occurred, he had to acknowledge his error: because he had never expected a second revolution to follow the first one so quickly, he could not possibly have predicted that the arrangements that resulted from the second resolution were neither bourgeois nor proletarian but rather something different, namely a pseudo-proletarian dictatorship—Martov could not come up with a less turgid designation—that was in fact emblematic of the less savoury aspects of the French Revolution, in particular its tendency to embolden, rather than to diminish, the forces it unleashed that were intent on ruling dictatorially.[104] But barely two weeks later, in *Novyi luch*, he condemned the Bolsheviks' attacks on the upcoming Constituent Assembly by citing how in 1792 the 'revolutionary vanguard'—by which Martov meant the Jacobins—did not force the Convention to adopt the Jacobins' radical policies, but instead achieved the same result by peaceful suasion.[105] In making sense of the clear contradiction between Martov's two assertions—the second one, on 15 December, essentially exonerated the

[100] Quoted in Shlapentokh, *Counter-Revolution in Revolution*, p. 121.
[101] Quoted in Ascher, *Pavel Axelrod*, p. 338.
[102] Quoted in Getzler, *Martov*, p. 176.
[103] Iu. Larin, 'Eshche o Kadetakh', *Pravda*, no. 200(131) (9 December 1917): p. 1; Martov quoted in Getzler, *Martov*, p. 173.
[104] Martov even described Lenin's followers as *sans-culottes*. Jane Burbank, *Intelligentsia and Revolution: Russian Views of Bolshevism, 1917–1922* (New York, 1986), p. 20.
[105] Iu. O. Martov, 'Revoliutsiia i uchreditel'noe sobranie', *Novyi luch*, no. 12 (15 December 1917), in Iu. O Martov, *1917–1922. Pis'ma i dokumenty* (Moscow, 2014), pp. 367–8. According to Martov the Girondins in the Convention were as amenable to this as the Jacobins were. This was because, in Martov's view, the Girondins and the Jacobins belonged to the same social class. Ibid.

Jacobins of the charge for which he had condemned them on 1 December—one might suggest that, to Martov, and to several other Mensheviks as well, the French Revolution was like Janus, the Roman god with two face: one virtuous, the other iniquitous. For that reason, in evaluating contemporary events, the temptation to invoke 'the face' of the French Revolution that supported one's particular interpretation or explanation was virtually irresistible.

Martov's ambivalence remained unresolved in 1918. In March, two months after the Bolsheviks had confirmed Martov's worst fears and disbanded the Constituent Assembly, he wrote in *Vpered* that the event reminded him of 9 Thermidor—quite possibly the first public reference in Russia after the October Revolution to this seminal event in the French Revolution that was generally agreed to have inaugurated a period of reaction and retrenchment.[106] But while reversing the policies of the Jacobins, Thermidor, according to Martov, did not lead directly and immediately to an actual counter-revolution. In fact, in Martov's description of the phenomenon, the Thermidorians who initially wielded power after the coup that toppled the Jacobins were genuine revolutionaries who simply believed Robespierre and Saint-Just had gone too far. To the extent that they dismantled much of the paraphernalia of the Jacobin Terror and reversed other extreme policies the Jacobins pursued, Thermidor was a good thing for France. But what made Thermidor, on balance, a tragedy was that, midway through it, moderates were succeeded by reactionaries, who proceeded to repress revolutionaries like Babeuf who threatened them; Martov did not say exactly when this happened but one suspects he had in mind the coup of 18 Fructidor (4 September 1797).[107] These Thermidorians, in contrast to the virtuous ones who preceded them in power, were 'duplicitous adventurists' who intended for France a dictatorship bent on reversing the advances that had been made since the revolution began nearly a decade earlier.[108] What made all of this relevant to Russia, Martov contended, was that the Bolsheviks, by imitating the Jacobins, were creating the conditions for a Russian Thermidor, in which 'gluttonous locusts' would take power in much the way the aforementioned adventurists had done in France.[109]

Martov's article, while clear in the analogy it posited between the Bolsheviks and the Jacobins, confused more than it clarified when it seemed to suggest a comparable analogy between the Mensheviks and Thermidor. If the former analogy was valid, one would think that for Martov the second analogy had to be valid as well. And if that were the case, it would suggest that the Mensheviks were destined to take power, just as the Thermidorians did. But the distinction Martov drew between good Thermidorians (1794–7) and bad ones (1797–9) called all of this in question, and one has to wonder whether an analogy between

---

[106] Martov, 'Nakanune russkogo termidora', *Vpered*, no. 22(9) (March 1918), cited in Kondratieva, *Bol'sheviki-iakobintsy*, p. 216, n. 40.

[107] Ibid., pp. 63–5.   [108] Ibid., p. 64.   [109] Ibid., p. 64.

the Mensheviks and the Thermidorians was one any Menshevik who accepted Martov's analysis of the French Revolution would want to pursue. The reason they would not is obvious: if, in the French Revolution, virtuous Thermidorians lost power to evil ones, and if the Mensheviks were analogous to the former, then it would follow, according to the terms of the analogy, that the Mensheviks were destined to take power but then sometime later to relinquish it—and to persons less virtuous than they. With such an outcome an integral part of the analogy, no Menshevik would want to accept it. Complicating matters further was Martov's failure to explain who precisely in 1918 was the Russian equivalent of the evil Thermidorians. One possibility was the military. Another was a socialist party gone astray (which could conceivably have been the Bolsheviks were it not for the fact that, in Martov's scheme of things, they were already Russian Jacobins). Yet another was Russian liberals, who, while not counter-revolutionary, nonetheless thought Russian socialists were too extreme and had taken the Russian Revolution too far. But Martov offered no guidance in this respect.

Martov's intellectual acrobatics were a product of his belief, shared universally by Marxist socialists, that history mattered—that, however obliquely and imperfectly, the present was prefigured in the past, and that invoking it to explain the present brought clarity and resolve rather than obfuscation and paralysis. Even in the last years of his life, he could not extricate himself from the abstract world of historical analogies that was more real to him than the history they purportedly explained. Specifically, he determined that the Bolsheviks could be admired for their resemblance to the Jacobins without admiring, or even considering inevitable, what followed the Jacobins in the French Revolution. In 1923 he wrote that the Jacobins ruled France as a dictatorship, and that the 'revolutionary committees' they established in 1794 to perpetuate themselves in power were 'absolutely identical' to those the Bolsheviks had been obliged to create in 1919.[110] Not surprisingly, other leading Mensheviks drew the same comparison. In articles written in 1918, Feodor Dan analogized the ongoing Bolshevik terror to that which the Jacobins had unleashed in France—but without invoking Thermidor, much less analysing it, as Martov did.[111] From Dan's analysis, one could easily draw the intended conclusion that the hypertrophied state Lenin was creating was oblivious to the needs and wishes of the people. Mixing his historical references freely, Dan also condemned the Bolsheviks for creating 'a Caesarist dictatorship' that might culminate in a reaction leading inexorably to a reversion to capitalism.[112]

In 1920 Pavel Axelrod, after Plekhanov's death the grey eminence of Menshevism, analogized the Bolsheviks to the Jacobins to demonstrate that Martov's analogy was incorrect. According to Axelrod, Martov had actually

---

[110] Martov, *Mirovoi bol'shevizm*, p. 40.
[111] Shlapentokh, *Counter-Revolution in Revolution*, p. 121.
[112] F. Dan, 'Bol'shevistskii bonapartizm', *Novaia zaria*, no. 3–4 (20 May 1918): p. 16.

202 THE FRENCH REVOLUTIONARY TRADITION

been too lenient in his condemnation of Bolshevism. However similarly the Jacobins and the Bolsheviks betrayed a revolution that until they each took power had been a virtuous one, in the attributes that really mattered they were dissimilar, and certainly not identical. Ethically, the Bolsheviks were far worse than the Jacobins. There was nothing even remotely progressive about the state they created, and Axelrod underscored how strongly he believed this by expressing his regret that he had ever claimed any analogy to the Jacobins.[113] Whatever resemblance there was was merely that which exists 'between an original and a clever parody, or between a grandiose, elemental event and a skillful imitation of it'.[114] Reiterating his belief that the Bolsheviks' commitment to Marxism was bogus, Axelrod included in his essay the comment that the Mensheviks, not the Bolsheviks, were the rightful custodians of the interests of the proletariat, and for that reason could never be analogized to the Girondins, who were capitalist.[115]

Axelrod's remonstrations, like Martov's lodged in books and articles published abroad, evoked nothing like the vituperation that followed Kautsky's. By then, Axelrod was elderly, and with Martov suffering symptoms of the cancer that would take his life a few years later, Lenin and Trotsky could reasonably expect their animadversions to stop soon. For that reason, and because Lenin and Trotsky were too preoccupied with other matters to take the time to refute the two Mensheviks themselves, the historian N. M. Lukin was selected to serve as their surrogate. Lukin was an appropriate choice. Having worked before the October Revolution on the Bolshevik newspaper *Nash put'*, he could be expected not to deviate from the party orthodoxy that the October Revolution was a proletarian revolution. And as a professor of history at Moscow University he could also be relied upon to substantiate his conclusions empirically.[116]

In his response, Lukin mostly agreed with Axelrod that the French and Russian Revolutions were different in fundamental ways. But he drew from this the very different conclusion that the October Revolution was ideologically legitimate. The difference between the two revolutions was ultimately a matter of timing. According to Lukin, the French Revolution occurred not only earlier than the October Revolution, but during an earlier stage of history. In France in the late eighteenth century, a proletariat did not exist. The Jacobin dictatorship was itself petit-bourgeois because that was the class to which the Jacobins belonged at birth, and as a result they were constitutionally incapable of carrying out policies beneficial to the lower classes even though they knew they would lose power

---

[113] 'Tov. P. B. Aksel'rod o bol'shevizme i bor'be s nim', *Sotsialisticheskii vestnik*, no. 6 (20 April 1921): pp. 3–7 & no. 7 (4 May 1921): pp. 3–5. The article includes excerpts from a letter Axelrod had written to Martov in 1920.

[114] Ibid., no. 6 (20 April 1921), p. 4.   [115] Ibid., no. 6 (20 April 1921), p. 5.

[116] In 1936 he was named director of the Institute of History of the Academy of Sciences. But instead of the position providing immunity from Stalin's Terror, it made him a logical target of it. In 1938 he was arrested and died in prison in 1940. Kondratieva, *Bol'sheviki-iakobintsy*, p. 217, n. 52.

without their support. This, in fact, was what happened in the spring and early summer of 1794, with the result that on 9 Thermidor the haute-bourgeoisie deposed the Jacobins and thereafter treated the lower classes with a malevolence consistent with what one would expect of the bourgeoisie whenever it held power. The Bolsheviks, however, were different. They were proletarian. While Lukin understandably did not explain how this could be the case given that the vast majority of the Bolsheviks were not themselves from the proletariat or even, with rare exceptions like Stalin, from the lower classes generally, the reader was expected to draw this conclusion, presumably because of everything the Bolsheviks had done, and were still doing, to benefit the proletariat since taking power just a few months before. The proletariat, for its part, was much larger than the lower classes that supported the Jacobins in the French Revolution, and Lukin was certain its support for the Bolsheviks would prevent anything even remotely resembling a Thermidorian reaction or counter-revolution. Support from the proletariat abroad made such a lamentable outcome even less likely. For that reason, Lukin concluded, enemies of the Bolsheviks at home, principally the SRs and the Mensheviks, should not expect support from any countries where the proletariat was powerful—by which he meant of course Western and Central Europe. There the capitalists had all they could handle from their indigenous working classes without involving themselves in a pointless effort to overturn the verdict of the October Revolution in Russia.[117]

Like virtually all Soviet historians prior to the Gorbachev era, Lukin believed that to classify historical events was tantamount to explaining them. This was evident in the biography of Robespierre he was writing when he was called upon to reply to Martov.[118] Many years later, A. Z. Manfred called the biography 'the first Marxist monograph in Russia on the great French bourgeois revolutionary'.[119] Given Manfred's ideological predilections, this was high praise, and Lukin's biography was followed by a similar one, in 1925 by Ia. M. Zakher, that also was well-received.[120] Among the arguments Lukin advanced was that the reason the Jacobins fell was because the coalition they represented was, at bottom, an artificial one. The Jacobins were not monolithic. They were divided into a right wing, personified by Danton, and a left wing, represented by supporters of Hébert and the *sans-culottes*, with Robespierre and his followers occupying the amorphous and often shifting middle ground between them. The rhetorical cross-fire Robespierre had to endure not only caused some confusion as to what he stood for and what he intended for France. It also, more significantly,

[117] N. Antonov [N. M. Lukin], 'Istoricheskaia ekskursiia Martova', summarized and analysed, but without attribution, in Kondratieva, *Bolsheviki-iakobintsy*, pp. 68–9.

[118] N. M. Lukin, *Robesp'er* (Petrograd, 1919); N. M. Lukin, *Izbrannye Trudy v trekh tomakh* (Moscow, 1960), vol. I, pp. 17–156.

[119] Manfred, *Velikaia frantsuzskaia revoliutsiia*, pp. 383–4.

[120] Ia. M. Zakher, *M. Robesp'er* (Moscow-Leningrad, 1925).

caused him to eliminate both of these deviations from the centrist orthodoxy he believed in and was attempting to impose. But since the Jacobins were also threatened by counter-revolutionary forces, in the form of actual armies intent on destroying them, after eliminating Danton and his followers Robespierre felt compelled to adopt many of their policy prescriptions. In addition, Lukin made the point that, deep in their hearts, Robespierre and the Jacobins preferred policies based on economic principles, such as free trade, that were advantageous to the bourgeoisie, but for purely political reasons enacted policies, such as the Maximum, that harmed it.[121] Were they to have remained in power beyond the summer of 1794, Robespierre and whoever still supported him would almost surely have eliminated the Maximum and restored at least a modicum of free trade domestically. In short, the Jacobins were petit-bourgeoisie forced by classes they did not belong to to pursue policies that were harmful to the class to which they did.[122] In the analysis Lukin provided in his Robespierre biography, he unintentionally illustrated a problem that all Marxist and Marxist–Leninist historians of the French Revolution had to resolve, namely whether the terminology they applied to the people they studied referred to the class into which they were born or to the class or classes that benefitted from the actions they took.

Because in much of what they wrote about the Jacobins these historians did not maintain this critical distinction between actions and social origins, the reader has no way of categorizing the Jacobins by class: were they petit-bourgeois because of their lineage, or plebeian or proto-proletarian by virtue of their policies? Lukin, in his writings, opted for the former: Robespierre was amoral and hypocritical, but as 'an ideologue of the petit-bourgeoisie', he sensed acutely the inevitability and historical necessity of capitalism; moreover he was also fearful of the proletariat it would inevitably create.[123] Cynically using emerging elements of the lower

---

[121] The Maximum was the short-form for the price controls the Jacobins imposed to keep unscrupulous profiteers from hoarding goods and then selling them at grossly inflated prices. They were abolished in December 1794, five months after the Jacobins lost power.

[122] Lukin, *Robesp'er*, especially pp. 118–42. Like Lukin, Zakher and Ts. Fridliand attributed the Jacobins' conservatism, relative to those to their left politically, to their origins in the petit-bourgeoisie. Ia. M. Zakher, *Parizhskie sektsii 1790–1795 godov* (Petrograd, 1921); Ts. Fridliand, 'Klassovaia bor'ba v iiune–iiule 1793 goda', *Istorik marksist* 2 (1926): pp. 159–209.

[123] What this characterization seemed to imply was that neither the Left Jacobins nor those on the Right whom Robespierre destroyed—for political reasons sequentially rather than simultaneously—were themselves petit-bourgeois: the former were plebeian or proto-proletarian, while the latter were of the haute-bourgeoisie. But Lukin did not state this explicitly, and a number of Soviet historians, including Manfred, who, despite his high opinion of Lukin's work, argued that the Jacobins, in reality, were part of a larger bloc that included the middle and petit-bourgeoisie, peasants, and urban plebeians (whom they sometimes called proletarians or proto-proletarians). Not until the Gorbachev era did Soviet historians try to emancipate themselves from the constraints of class analysis, and point out its inadequacies. See, for example, the proceedings of a conference of historians in Moscow in September 1988; the portions on the Jacobins are summarized in A. V. Chudinov, 'Nazrevshie problemy izucheniia istorii velikoi frantsuzskoi revoliutsii (po materialam obsuzhdeniia v Institute vseobshchei istorii AN SSSR)', *Novaia i noveishaia istoriia*, no. 2 (March–April 1989): pp. 65–74.

classes to take power, Robespierre had no choice but to dispense with them when they wanted to extend the French Revolution beyond the bourgeois, or petit-bourgeois limits history had imposed on it. Given also the omnipresent threat of counter-revolution aided by hostile forces abroad, Robespierre had no choice but to turn on these elements of the lower classes that supported him, and send their leaders to the guillotine. But this only weakened Robespierre further, and not long afterwards he lost power and was himself guillotined, in large part the victim of forces beyond his control. Implicit in all of this—and what made Lukin's biography so popular among the cognoscenti in the Communist Party—was its implication that the fate Robespierre and the Jacobins suffered could never befall the Bolsheviks. For that reason several Soviet historians of the revolution who followed Lukin were pleased to reiterate his argument that the Jacobins were petit-bourgeois and that that was what caused the coalition of lower classes they had created to disintegrate.[124]

* * *

The role the Jacobins played in the French Revolution was not the only issue Soviet historians addressed in the first years of Soviet rule. Another was 'Blanquism', the meaning and relevance of which one might think had been litigated among the Bolsheviks prior to the October Revolution, with the verdict Lenin affirmed—that Blanquism encouraged *coups d'état* lacking mass support and was thus a perversion of what the Jacobins had done—now etched firmly in Bolshevik stone. But this was not the case. In 1921, B. I. Gorev, in his biography of Blanqui, claimed that in his early years Marx had been a Blanquist, by which he meant that at that time in his life Marx shared Blanqui's conviction that revolution was both an art and a tactic requiring the same temperament as required in warfare. In addition, both Marx and Blanqui stressed the necessity for revolutionaries not to ignore opportunities in which the likelihood of gaining power was considerable even when popular support from the classes they claimed to represent and whose interests they wished to advance was insufficient. The last similarity Gorev noted was that both Marxists and Blanquists opposed the gradualism that, after both Marx and Blanqui were dead, re-emerged in Eduard Bernstein's evolutionary socialism.[125]

---

[124] Ts. Fridliand, *Zhan-Pol' Marat i grazhdanskaia voina XVIII v.* (Moscow, 1959), p. 86.

[125] B. I. Gorev, *Ogust Blanki* (Moscow, 1921), especially pp. 108–15. In the book Gorev argued that Plekhanov, despite his opposition to the terrorism of *Narodnaia Volia*—which he condemned precisely because those practising it lacked popular support—was no less a Blanquist than Marx. A Menshevik before becoming a Bolshevik, Gorev may have retained an admiration for Plekhanov inconsistent with the prevailing Leninist orthodoxy that the Father of Russian Marxism had been both a bad Marxist and an ineffectual revolutionary; lumping Plekhanov and Marx together might also have been a way of minimizing the differences between Menshevism and Bolshevisim on the issue of terror, which in turn would strengthen Gorev's shaky credentials as a loyal and legitimate Bolshevik and supporter of the Soviet state. But at least in this last respect Gorev had nothing to worry about. By 1921 Plekhanov was dead, and his opinions no longer consequential politically. For that reason Gorev's critics ignored what

Not surprisingly, Gorev's ideologically aberrant assertions produced an angry response. In an article in 1923, a Bolshevik writing pseudonymously as 'Sineira' took Gorev to task for his apparent deviations from the Leninist axiom that Blanquism was not only a perversion of Jacobinism but also, more significantly, a perversion of Marxism. Sineira stated flatly that Gorev was wrong—that Marx and Lenin always stressed that revolutions led by an elite required mass support, and that if they lacked it they were destined to fail. By denying this fundamental tenet of Marxism-Leninism, Gorev, in Sineira's estimation, showed the same lack of understanding of class struggle and its centrality in human endeavour of which Blanqui himself was plainly culpable. The fact that the October Revolution actually resembled what Blanqui preferred—rather than the mass upheaval the Bolsheviks claimed it was—made the need to dismiss his credentials as an estimable advocate and practitioner of revolution especially urgent.[126]

In another broadside, also in 1923, Sineira claimed, once again, that Gorev, erroneously, had turned Blanquism into a generic category encompassing all the ways class struggle manifested itself in political revolutions. After rejecting the criticism from Gorev's supporters that he had denied Blanqui's credentials as a revolutionary, Sineira argued that all he was suggesting was that Blanqui was not a Marxist revolutionary. In fact, the only attribute Blanqui shared with Marx was that they were revolutionaries and were both courageous. Moreover, the only arguable causal relationship between them was that Marx had influenced Blanqui, rather than the other way around, as Gorev had suggested. And once that was established, Sineira rejected Gorev's claim that Marx's support in the last years of his life of the terrorism of *Narodnaia Volia* revealed a fundamental affinity between the two men. According to Sineira, Marx never—not even when he wrote nice things about *Narodnaia Volia*—shared Blanqui's belief that the political transformation revolutions entailed need not be preceded by an economic transformation.[127]

After Gorev responded, fairly weakly, that Sineira, in maximizing differences between Blanqui and Marx that were actually inconsequential, was engaging in a form of 'scholasticism', the debate came to an end, with the orthodoxy Sineira had expressed reaffirmed.[128] But one aspect of it—that which concerned *Narodnaia*

he had written about Plekhanov, and focused their rhetorical fire on what he had written about Marx instead.

---

[126] 'Sineira', 'Est li v marksizme elementy blankizm?' *Pechat' i revoliutsii*, no. 5 (1923): pp. 112–115.

[127] 'Sineira', 'Zakliuchitel'noe slovo k diskussii ob elementakh blankizma v marksizme', *Pechat' i revoliutsiia*, no. 7 (1923), pp. 119–23.

[128] In 1928, however, those adhering to this view were the object of a mild rebuke. David Riazanov, who in 1921 had founded the Marx–Engels Institute and was generally considered the principal authority among the Bolsheviks on matters concerning Marx and Engels, noted (wrongly) in an article on relations between Marx and Blanqui that Lenin always held Blanqui in high regard. D. Riazanov, 'The Relations of Marx with Blanqui', *Labour Monthly: A Magazine of International Labour* 10, no. 8 (August 1928), p. 492.

Volia—re-emerged in the context of a somewhat different issue, which also involved the French Revolution—only this time what was at stake was whether the revolution had influenced the Bolsheviks directly, or whether its influence was transmitted by the so-called Russian Jacobins of the late nineteenth century, who unwittingly modified it to reflect Russian national history and culture. The question of the historical provenance of Bolshevism—whether it was Russian or French or, more broadly, Russian or non-Russian—had hovered over the Bolsheviks practically since their emergence in 1903 as a distinct and identifiable faction within the RSDLP. But it was not until the early 1920s, when the Bolsheviks' supremacy in Russia could no longer be doubted, and they finally had the security to ruminate about their ideological origins, that the debate was actually joined.

S. I. Mitskevich fired the first rhetorical shot. In 1923, in an article in *Proletarskaia revoliutstiia*, he argued that in their tactics and organizational principles, the Russian Jacobins of the late nineteenth century, most notably Zheliabov and Tkachev, strongly resembled Lenin and the Bolsheviks. However unrealistic, even utopian, their objectives given Russia's unreadiness for a workers' revolution, the Russian Jacobins shared Lenin's conviction that power in a revolutionary party had to be centralized if it was to survive in a repressive autocracy, much less destroy it once conditions had become more favourable. Moreover, the resemblance, according to Mitskevich, was not coincidental. Lenin inherited his desiderata on such matters from the Russian Jacobins, and the causal relationship that existed in that regard extended to programmatic issues as well, such as the confiscation of Church property and the immediate and rapid nationalization of land.[129] In his article Mitskevich failed to answer the question his argument suggested, namely why it was that a term borrowed from the French Revolution should be applied to prominent actors in the Russian revolutionary movement who did what they did because of observations and experiences having little or nothing to do with the French Revolution. The views shared by *Narodnaia Volia* and the Bolsheviks were the result of Russian realities, not French or European ones. Moreover, in light of this one might question whether the term 'Russian Jacobin' had any utility or relevance at all. It is true that the *narodovol'tsy* were cognizant of the original Jacobins in France, and greatly admired them; in certain ways they even tried to imitate them. But could one really believe that if the French Revolution had not occurred, the *narodovol'tsy*, whose memory Mitskevich honoured (incongruously) by calling them Jacobins, would have acted differently in any significant and meaningful ways? Mitskevich could conceivably have replied that using the term 'Jacobin' for the *narodovol'tsy* was warranted because the similarities between them and the Jacobins in France were real. But that

---

[129] S. I. Mitskevich, 'Russkie iakobintsy', *Proletarskaia revoliutsiia*, no. 6–7 (18–19) (1923): pp. 3–26.

response would still have not explained why the *narodovol'tsy* became revolutionaries in the first place. One cannot emphasize enough, in this particular context, that congruence and causality are different.

Not surprisingly in light of its failings, Mitskevich's article was not followed by others expressing agreement. But M. N. Pokrovskii, who after the October Revolution had served under Lunacharskii in the Commissariat of Education, and in 1921 had helped to establish the Institute of Red Professors, a post-graduate school for persons seeking additional training in the humanities, used the occasion of Lenin's death to express views remarkably similar to Mitskevich's. In a speech memorializing the founder of the Soviet state, Pokrovskii reiterated Mitskevich's argument that in matters concerning tactics and the distribution of political power within a revolutionary party, the Bolsheviks owed a great deal to the Russian Jacobins, who preceded them in the revolutionary movement.[130] Best exemplified by Zaichnevskii and Tkachev, the Russian Jacobins recognized the need for conspiracy just the way the Bolsheviks did several decades later; for that reason Pokrovskii lauded as 'the first document of Bolshevism' the proclamation Zaichnevskii had written in 1862 setting out the objectives of *Molodaia Rossiia*, which he founded.[131] In his confusion of means and ends, in believing that the tactics Russian Jacobins like Tkachev adopted justified calling them proto-Marxists irrespective of the fact that their objectives were not Marxist at all, Pokrovskii betrayed an inability to keep his categories straight. For that reason, it was easy, in the Stalin era, to attack him as ideologically deviant. But in 1924 this was still far in the future. The more relevant point, in terms of tracking the degree to which Pokrovskii's argument went beyond Mitskevich's, was that Pokrovskii seemed to extend the temporal limits of Russian Jacobinism backwards from the *narodovol'tsy* of the 1870s and 1880s to Zaichnevskii and *Molodaia Rossiia* in the 1860s. Intentionally or not, his doing so strengthened Mitskevich's central point that the roots of Russian Marxism were Russian.

Given its contents, Mitskevich's article was guaranteed to raise the hackles of many Bolsheviks. Lenin, just like Plekhanov and the other Russian Marxists who preceded him in the Russian revolutionary movement, had taken pains to distinguish the Bolsheviks from the *narodovol'tsy*, whose courage, while laudable, they all believed was wasted on attempts to perpetuate a peasant revolution that, according to orthodox Marxist theory, could never eliminate the poverty peasants experienced; this could only come about as a result of a proletarian revolution. What is more, Mitskevich's clear implication that the origins of Bolshevism could be found at least partly in Russia, specifically in Russian history and culture, contradicted the notion all Russian Marxists were obliged to accept and to affirm publicly that the origins of Bolshevism lay exclusively in

---

[130] M. N. Pokrovskii, 'Lenin v russkoi revoliutsii', *Vestnik kommunisticheskoi akedemii*, no. 7 (1924): pp. 8–21.

[131] Ibid., p. 13.

Marxism. In that spirit, N. N. Baturin, in 1924, also in *Proletarskaia revoliutsiia*, responded heatedly to what Mitskevich and Pokrovskii had alleged.[132] He began by stating why the term 'Jacobin'—the provenance of which he acknowledged was French rather than Russian—was nonetheless applicable to the Bolsheviks. In contrast to the Mensheviks, who preferred a form of 'organizational individualism and anarchism', the Bolsheviks shared the Jacobins' 'organizational centralism'. Temperamentally they were virtually the same.[133] Of course there were significant differences between the two sets of revolutionaries. The Bolsheviks, according to Baturin, were living at a time when, for reasons both political and technological, they had means of achieving their objectives far more powerful than any the Jacobins possessed. But as real as these differences were, they paled in comparison to those that distinguished the Bolsheviks from the Russian Jacobins, who resembled neither the Bolsheviks nor the French Jacobins, whose appellation was wrongly applied to them. The seizure of power the Russian Jacobins advocated was a palace coup; by contrast the October Revolution was a mass revolution. Moreover, the Bolsheviks and *Narodnaia Volia* were proceeding historically in opposite directions, the former towards socialism and communism, the latter from anarchism to liberalism. Finally, by calling Tkachev a proto-Bolshevik, Mitskevich proved that politically he was identical to the Russian Jacobins he described—neither socialist nor communist but rather petit-bourgeois, an accusation no Bolshevik who remained faithful to the tenets of Marxism-Leninism and the objectives of the October Revolution could possibly find congenial.[134] Although the debate over Russian Jacobinism showed that a genuine intellectual pluralism existed in the Soviet Union prior to the Stalin era, one can fairly consider Baturin's article, for the *ad hominem* manner in which it responded to arguments deemed incompatible with Marxism-Leninism, an argument for censorship.[135]

The back-and-forth between the two antagonists continued. In an article in *Katorga i Ssylka* (*Prison and Exile*), Mitskevich responded forcefully to Baturin's assault. In particular he tried to demonstrate that his earlier comments on Russian Jacobins had not exceeded what was ideologically acceptable. Russian Jacobins such as Pëtr Tkachev, while surely precursors of the Bolsheviks, were not committed to the Marxism the Bolsheviks professed. The socialist utopia Tkachev envisioned, which by its agrarian orientation would be less attentive than Lenin's to the proletariat, was a prime example of this. At the same time, Mitskevich

---

[132] N. N. Baturin, 'O nasledstve russkikh iakobintsev', *Proletarskaia revoliutsiia*, no. 7 (July 1924): pp. 82–9.

[133] Ibid., p. 87.   [134] Ibid., pp. 84–9.

[135] It should be noted that prior to 1927 even so-called bourgeois historians were allowed to write and to have their works published. George M. Enteen, 'Marxist Historians during the Cultural Revolution: A Case Study of Professional In-Fighting', in *Cultural Revolution in Russia, 1928–1931*, edited by Sheila Fitzpatrick (Bloomington IN, 1984), pp. 155–6.

endeavoured to distinguish Russian Jacobins from French ones. In his estimation the former suffered far more than the latter because in Russia capitalism was more rapacious than the forms it took in Western Europe. For that reason the objectives of the Russian Jacobins, while not identical to the Bolsheviks', were more radical than those of the French Jacobins—a conclusion consistent with Mitskevich's original point that the Russian Jacobins, irrespective of where the term that described them originated, were truly Russian, or at the very least more Russian than French.[136]

Baturin responded in kind.[137] After reiterating his earlier argument that Lenin and the Bolsheviks owed nothing to the Russian Jacobins, who in fact were mostly petit-bourgeois anarchists wishing they were liberals, Baturin made explicit what had been merely implicit in his earlier article, namely that while there were similarities between the Bolsheviks and the French Jacobins, those between the Russian Jacobins and the French Jacobins were just as real, perhaps even greater. To be sure, the Russian Jacobins were influenced by socialism, which emerged in France as a movement long after the French Jacobins had disappeared. But they were influenced by it only by their need to pretend they espoused it. Their origins in the petit-bourgeoisie were inescapable, and therefore only someone like Mitskevich, with his inadequate knowledge and understanding of Marxism, could consider the Russian Jacobins precursors of the Bolsheviks. He, Baturin, had examined the programmes of Zaichnevskii and Tkachev, and could report that

> in none of them could be found any of the elements of proletarian socialism. . . . Instead, they contained all the marks of petit-bourgeois socialist utopias. Between these reactionary utopias and Bolshevism it is impossible not only to place 'an equal sign', but also to deduce any analogy at all.[138]

Despite their genuine disagreements, Mitskevich and Baturin shared the same objective of clarifying the circumstances under which Marxism had emerged in Russia. For Mitskevich, this meant denying, or at least minimizing, the debt the Bolsheviks owed to *Chernyi Peredel.* Because the *chernoperedel'tsy* rejected terrorism in favour of mass agitation and propaganda, arguing against a causal relationship between the *chernoperedel'tsy* and Bolshevism was a convenient way of affirming one between the *narodovol'tsy* and Bolshevism.[139] As for Baturin, the

---

[136] S. I. Mitskevich, 'K voprosu o korniakh bol'shevizma', *Katorga i ssylka*, no. 3 (1925): pp. 92–101.

[137] N. N. Baturin, 'Eshche o tsvetakh russkogo iakobinstva', *Proletarskaia revoliutsiia*, no. 8 (1925): pp. 97–109.

[138] Ibid., pp. 395–6. In 1927, Baturin's conjunction of *Narodnaia Volia* and the French Jacobins would be repeated by Ia. Starosel'skii, who insisted that the true analogue to the Jacobins in Russia was not the Bolsheviks but the *narodovol'tsy*, the terrorism of which he considered subversive of the emerging proletariat. Ia. Starosel'skii, 'Burzhuaznaia revoliutsiia i iuridicheskii kretinizm. O rechi Olara, 'Teoriia nasiliia i Frantsuzskaia revoliutsiia', *Revoliutsiia pravda*, no. 2–3 (1927): p. 95. Starosel'skii, too, would perish in the Terror.

[139] Mitskevich, 'K voprosu', pp. 92–101.

vehemence with which he tried to discredit Mitskevich could not disguise completely his chagrin, which was shared silently by many Bolsheviks, that Marx had praised *Narodnaia Volia* so fulsomely, indeed that Marx had praised it at all, and in so doing suggested that Russia might avoid the capitalist stage of history entirely. This, of course, was contrary to the very essence of Marxism. But criticising Marx directly was *verboten* in the Soviet Union, and carried with it the risk of public chastisement, the loss of one's job, or worse. Baturin was shrewd enough not to do so. Instead, he made his point indirectly. By calling *Narodnaia Volia* 'Jacobin', and then by appending the prefix 'Russian' to the appellation, he could render nugatory any supposed link between Bolshevism and the non-Marxist revolutionaries that Marx, in defiance of his own ideology, had praised. In its place Baturin substituted the ideologically valid link he saw between the Soviet Union and the French Revolution, which he considered the first manifestation of a noble tradition of revolution beginning in France and concluding in Russia.

Not surprisingly, Soviet historians overwhelmingly supported Baturin and denounced Mitskevich.[140] But the *coup de grâce* was administered by Stalin himself, in a letter in 1931 to the editors of *Proletarskaia revoliutsiia*.[141] Devoted mostly to condemning heresies he had discovered in investigating the whole issue of a Soviet Thermidor, Stalin's letter included searing criticism not only of Mitskevich, but of the editors of *Katorga i Sylka* for having published the second of his two articles. In their grovelling response, which under the circumstances might fairly be excused on the grounds that their vocational survival, and possibly even their physical survival, was at stake, the editors wrote in a subsequent issue that 'we, like other historical journals, occasionally granted a rostrum to those who had no right to it, who used it to serve their own interests, which they concealed, and to engage in direct struggle against the proletarian revolution'.[142] Whether their apologia exempted the editors from imprisonment, execution, or consignment to a labour camp in Stalin's Terror is unknown.

* * *

The French Revolution figured prominently in the mythology the Bolsheviks constructed to invest the October Revolution with the legitimacy it needed. This was the result of a deliberate decision. Long before the October Revolution the Bolsheviks believed that revolutions like the French were integral to a temporal trajectory the Bolsheviks were privy to by virtue of their Marxist ideology. The

---

[140] See, for example, I. A. Teodorovich, 'Iz epokhi "Narodnoi Voli"', *Katorga i ssylka*, no. 57–8 (1929): pp. 7–44.

[141] J. V. Stalin, 'O nekotorykh voprosakh istorii bol'shevizma', *Proletarskaia revoliutsiia*, no. 6 (113) (October 1931): pp. 3–12. The letter also appeared, under the same title, in *Bol'shevik*, no. 19–20 (October 1931), pp. 10–18.

[142] Quoted in Cyril Black, ed., *Rewriting Soviet History* (New York, 1962), p. 313.

French Revolution in particular was significant because in France it ended feudalism while simultaneously inaugurating in Europe an age of industrial capitalism that would eventually yield socialism and communism; paradoxically, its significance for the Bolsheviks was heightened rather than diminished by its geographical and temporal distance from Russia in 1917. For that reason it would have been unthinkable for the Bolsheviks not to have analogized their revolution to the French, and on the basis of the analogies they drew to incorporate its mythology into their own. That the October Revolution resembled a *coup d'état* more than a mass revolution was yet another factor forcing the Bolsheviks to look elsewhere for much of the raw material for their foundational myth. More than any other event or series of events in history, the French Revolution provided what they needed.

One must bear in mind that the French Revolution, in 1917, was no longer a *tabula rasa* in Russian culture and politics. The 1905 Revolution had done much to imprint its multifarious meanings into public consciousness, and by 1917 educated and even semi-educated Russians were even more familiar with it. For that reason, invoking the French Revolution, and effectively fusing the mythologies of the two revolutions, the French and the Russian, into one was easy. A knowledgeable and attentive audience already existed, even if the hostility to the first revolution in some quarters ensured that the second one never gained universal support. Nevertheless, turning lukewarm supporters into enthusiastic ones was something for which the French Revolution was uniquely well-equipped, and making this process even easier was the fact that what most Russians knew of the French Revolution—in particular its most iconic events, such as the storming of the Bastille—had already been mythologized in France.[143] It was this mythologized iteration of the revolution, rather than a narrative adhering closely to historical reality, that Russians had absorbed and many now considered gospel truth.[144] Over the course of more than a century, the

---

[143] There existed a good deal of misinformation and incomplete information about this particular event; mythologies often bear only a loose relationship to the truth. Parisian *sans-culottes* stormed the Bastille not just because it symbolized monarchical oppression and tyranny. More prosaic considerations also applied. The prison was rumoured to contain stores of cartridges and bullets, which had not been included with the muskets demonstrators had earlier received. And it contained only seven prisoners, four of them forgers, one accused of incest, another, who was deranged, was thought an accomplice in a conspiracy to murder the king; yet another, also deranged, believed himself, depending on the day, to be either Julius Caesar or God. Finally, there had been a serious proposal in the spring of 1789 to close the prison and demolish it. Christopher Hibbert, *The Days Of The French Revolution* (New York, 1981), pp. 70–2. It seems safe to say that very few ordinary Russians knew much of this, or any of it, and that the Bolsheviks of course were not about to enlighten them. The storming of the Bastille was a useful myth irrespective of the facts. For a description of the mythology of the French Revolution as a whole, showing how long it took to develop fully, and the elaborations and emendations it underwent, see Elton, *The Revolutionary Idea in France, passim*; Maurice Agulhon, *Marianne into Battle: Republican Imagery and Symbolism in France, 1789–1881* (London and New York, 1981); and Robert Gildea, *Children of the Revolution: The French, 1799–1914* (Cambridge MA, 2008).

[144] The same was true for Europeans generally, for whom, by the twentieth century, the French Revolution had become 'a constituent part of [their] collective memory'. Peter Fritzsche, 'How

history of the French Revolution had been transformed into hagiography. But as far as the Bolsheviks were concerned, this only heightened its utility in fostering their own revolutionary mythology.

But the mythology of the French Revolution was like the proverbial double-edged sword. That the educated public was familiar with it meant it could be useful also to their enemies. Aspects of the revolution easily recognizable as analogous to policies the Bolsheviks followed provided instant fodder for those opposing these policies. The Jacobin Terror was a prime example. Of course it had its supporters and apologists, and not all of them were Bolsheviks or Soviet functionaries. But it was also cited to demonstrate that terror, no matter how virtuous its objectives, invariably degenerates into mindless and indiscriminate killings that call into question, and ultimately discredit, the motives of those who ordered it. To Sergei Kobiakov, who served as defence counsel for several defendants wrongly convicted in the revolutionary tribunals the Bolsheviks established immediately after the October Revolution, the public executions that followed reminded him of the September Days in 1792, and the corruption of the prosecutors he encountered in the courtroom he ascribed to their being infected by the scourge of 'Maratism'.[145] Among the most notorious of these was N. V. Krylenko, the chief prosecutor of the Soviet Union in the early 1920s who, as the first Minister of Justice, prescribed the death penalty for several of the persons Kobiakov defended. In Kobiakov's recollection, the ferocity with which Krylenko sent innocents to their deaths reminded him of Fouquier-Tinville's during the Jacobin Terror in the French Revolution.[146] In the opinion of Andrew Kalpashnikov, who had returned to Russia from the United States in May 1917 on the same boat carrying Trotsky, only to be incarcerated in the Peter-Paul Fortress two months after the October Revolution, Felix Dzerzhinskii, the exceptionally ruthless head of the Cheka, whom Kalpashnikov had met in April 1918, fully deserved the sobriquet, usually applied pejoratively, of 'the Robespierre of the Russian Revolution'.[147] The same hostility animated residents of Rostov, who, during the Civil War, sang 'a Russian Song of Liberty' that was set to the music of the *Marseillaise*.[148]

Nostalgia Narrates Modernity', in *The Work of Memory: New Directions in the Study of German Society and Culture*, edited by Alon Confino and Peter Fritzsche (Urbana IL and Chicago IL, 2002), p. 72.

---

[145] Sergei Kobiakov, 'Krasnyi sud: Vpechatel'niia zashchitnika revoliutsionnykh tribunalakh', in *Arkhiv Russkoi revoliutsii* (Moscow, 1922), vol. VII, p. 268.

[146] Ibid., p. 255.

[147] Kalpashnikov served as Trotsky's translator while both men, along with the other Russian *émigrés* and exiles on board, were detained in Halifax, Canada, for nearly one month before being allowed to continue their journey. Andrew Kalpashnikoff, *A Prisoner of Trotsky* (Garden City NY, 1920), pp. vii, xi, 224.

[148] Rhoda D. Power, *Under the Bolshevik Reign of Terror* (New York, 1919), p. 23.

The Bolsheviks, of course, were not about to allow their enemies to monopolize this mythology for what to them were nefarious purposes. Revolutionary mythologies resemble ordinary propaganda in that they are invoked to clarify, explain, and defend particular governments and the policies they pursue. But they also are intended to do much more than that. For revolutionaries like the French and the Bolshevik, the mythologies they created were meant to provide moral and ideological legitimacy not only for what they did, as a matter of policy, but also, and more importantly, for their reason for doing so, specifically to transform their own society, and eventually all societies, into something so superior to those that currently exist that it was beyond the ability of ordinary people even to imagine it. If one accepts Maxim Gorky's definition of a myth as 'a process of imagining', his assertion should perhaps be emended to take into account the myths revolutionaries foster for the purpose of realizing a vision that, to all those who do not share it initially, is quite literally inconceivable.[149]

For that reason the artistic instruments revolutionaries use in disseminating the mythology they create are many and varied. These include music, theatre, painting, sculpture, architecture, literature, poetry, the celebration of holidays, the anniversaries of significant events, public rituals, celebrations, commemorations, and even the language of public discourse itself. Their coordinated and deliberate mobilization for political objectives helps to create a shared folklore of revolution that presumably will survive the passage of time and the political vicissitudes every new political regime must endure. The Bolsheviks were aware of the power and political security this folklore, or common culture, provided, and they deliberately placed at its centre their foundational myth: that the October Revolution, which, by building on what the French Revolution began, made possible the construction of a communist society characterized by social justice and individual liberation on a scale heretofore nonexistent in history. Even before their revolution, the Bolsheviks—not just the more self-enamoured of them, such as Trotsky—had created for themselves a very theatrical self-image, in which they were actors on the largest stage imaginable, that of history itself. As a result, they turned to the task of infusing into the common culture in Russia the values and personal character traits they believed consistent with the task they expected the Soviet people to assume of creating New Soviet Men and Women, who, in the case of the former, have achieved the full development of their individual personalities. Among their most prominent personal qualities would be courage, self-confidence, and a willingness to take risks and to exceed what were thought to be the outer limits of human ability— but also a child-like obedience and deference to political authority.[150]

---

[149] Maxim Gorky, *On Literature* (Seattle WA, 1973), p. 244.
[150] Jay Bergman, 'The Idea of Individual Liberation in Bolshevik Visions of the New Soviet Man', *European History Quarterly* 27, no. 1 (1997): pp. 57–92; Jay Bergman, 'Valerii Chkalov: Soviet Pilot as New Soviet Man', *Journal of Contemporary History* 33, no. 1 (1998): pp. 135–52.

Most of all the Bolsheviks brought to this endeavour the belief, traceable to Marx and Engels, that progress is rarely easy, that it requires struggle, and that this struggle, while not ennobling in the way it was for Social Darwinists, nonetheless served the purpose of separating those who welcomed the opportunity to overcome adversity from those who shrank from it. In the latter category, according to the Bolsheviks, one found the Mensheviks, the SRs, the liberals, and every other rival of theirs that was left-of-centre on the political spectrum. For that reason revolutions were tailor-made for the mythology the Bolsheviks tried to create after the October Revolution, because it showed the Bolsheviks overcoming seemingly insurmountable obstacles in their struggle for social justice. In the October Revolution, in sum, practicality and pragmatism were harnessed in the service of a transformational ideology.

This Bolshevik mythology was, at bottom, didactic. It was intended to instruct and to inform, and to inculcate in people the values the Bolsheviks cultivated that had enabled them to take over a country and rule it effectively. To this heuristic endeavour, the French Revolution, along with the Revolution of 1905, provided much that was useful.[151] A prime example, replicated artistically countless times after 1917, was the storming of the Tuilleries, the Paris residence of the Bourbons, on 10 August 1792, which was memorialized by artists in Russia soon after the October Revolution; among the other critical turning points of the French Revolution Russian artists, writers, and poets chose to render was the insurrection in the spring of 1793 that eliminated the Girondins as a political force, thereby creating a vacuum filled by the Jacobins, and the murder of Marat by Charlotte Corday.[152] Other representations based on the French Revolution included a bas-relief of soldiers carrying a flag with the revolutionary triad—*liberté*, *égalité*, *fraternité*—emblazoned on it; one of these was a replication of a painting by Jacques-Louis David, 'The Oath of the Montagnards', under which was written the well-known aphorism of the artist: 'Once the enemies of the revolution are gone, they are no longer waiting for you'.[153] Surviving one's enemies, and then destroying them because they stood in the way of the revolution achieving its objectives, was a common theme in Bolshevik propaganda.

The most useful event in that regard, not surprisingly, was the storming of the Bastille, which perfectly encapsulated the Bolsheviks' image of themselves as the *avant-garde* of the proletariat storming the seemingly impregnable parapets of the bourgeoisie. Stalin neatly captured the Promethean essence of the tasks the

---

[151] The best known myth to which the Revolution of 1905 gave rise concerned the uprising on the battleship *Potemkin*, with the facts of which Sergei Eisenstein took considerable liberties in the film he produced and directed in 1925. Nicholas Reeves, *The Power of Film Propaganda: Myth or Reality* (London, 1999), pp. 70–3; Richard Taylor, *The Battleship Potemkin: The Film Companion* (New York, 2000), p. 54 and *passim*.

[152] N. T. Unaniants, 'Velikaia frantsuzskaia revoliutsiia v zhurnal'noi i prikladnoi grafike. 1917–1940 gg.', *Frantsuzskii ezhegodnik* (1989), p. 219.

[153] Ibid., pp. 211, 212.

Bolsheviks had set for themselves in his stated belief that 'there are no fortresses the Bolsheviks cannot storm'.[154] The Bolsheviks, in other words, would do symbolically what the Parisian *sans-culottes*, on 14 July 1789, had done literally. To be sure, building socialism and communism—which is what Stalin had in mind—was different from defeating the reactionary enemies of the Bolsheviks. But the Bastille, once its storming was mythologized, could symbolize any obstacle or impediment, and for that reason its replication in Russia after the October Revolution—in theatrical productions, placards and posters, and all kinds of literature, both highbrow and popular—was a common occurrence. The film directors Sergei Eisenstein and Vsevolod Meyerhold both directed productions replicating the event, the former in 1920, the latter in 1921.[155] Boris Pasternak, while never writing the novel on the French Revolution he long envisioned, nevertheless produced in the summer of 1917 two 'dialogues', the first between Saint-Just and Henrietta Leba, which was never published, the second between Saint-Just and Robespierre, which appeared in *Znamia Truda* (*The Banner of Labour*) in 1918.[156] Among the placards and posters with which the Bolsheviks adorned public spaces was one in 1920 depicting the storming of the Winter Palace in 1917. The artist's name was not provided, but the unattributed poem at the bottom described the official residence of the tsars as 'capitalism's Bastille'.[157]

Approximately two hundred theatres produced plays in the decade following the October Revolution that in one way or another were concerned the French Revolution.[158] Of these, by far the most influential was Romaine Rolland's, written in 1902, which in Russia was titled *Vziatie Bastilii* (*The Storming of the Bastille*) rather than by its original one, *Le 14 juillet*, almost certainly because it was more dramatic and captured the element of struggle the Bolsheviks found especially appealing and relevant to their ideological objectives.[159] The play was first performed in the summer of 1918 at a theatre in Petrograd run by the well-known director and actor, A. A. Mgebrov, who before the extended run the play enjoyed had supposedly submitted it to Lunacharskii, who approved it. Mgebrov emphasized the courage and *élan* of those storming the Parisian prison, which was clearly meant to symbolize all that was the reactionary and retrograde in pre-revolutionary France.

---

[154] J. V. Stalin, 'O rabotakh aprel'skogo ob"edinennogo plenuma TsK i TsKK (13 April 1928)', in Stalin, *Sochineniia*, vol. XI, p. 58.

[155] N. T. Unaniants, 'Velikaia frantsuzskaia revoliutsiia v spektaklaiakh sovetskogo teatra. 1917–1940 gg.', *Frantsuzskii ezhegodnik* (1989), p. 468.

[156] Ilina, 'Obraz evropeiskikh revoliutsii i russkaia kul'tura', p. 386.

[157] *Sovet politicheskii plakat: iz kollektsii gosudarstvennoi biblioteki SSSR imeni V. I. Lenina* (Moscow, 1984), p. 15. The title at the top of the poster reads, in translation: '1917 – October – 1920. Three Years Ago, Comrade – Do You Remember?'

[158] Unaniants, 'Velikaia frantsuzskaia revoliutsiia v spektaklaiakh sovetskogo teatra', p. 473.

[159] A concise explication and analysis of the French original is in David James Fisher's, *Romain Rolland and the Politics of Intellectual Engagement* (New Brunswick NJ, 2004), pp. 22–4. Rolland's play *Danton* was also performed in Russia, but to less effect. Huntley Carter, *The New Theatre and Cinema of Soviet Russia* (London, 1924), p. 15.

To heighten the collective nature of the heroism the play depicted, the cast, including extras, numbered one hundred and fifty.[160] In that way the play was a mass celebration, similar to, albeit on a smaller scale, the re-enactment, along the banks of the Neva River in Petrograd, of the same event, on 7 November 1918, to celebrate the first anniversary of the storming of the Winter Palace; in the festivities a replica of the Bastille was ignited just when ships of the Baltic Fleet, by pre-arrangement, were passing by. Not surprisingly, fireworks and searchlights were employed to heighten the drama.[161]

By 1927, however, Rolland's play had lost its allure. A production in that year was criticized publicly as an oversized caricature of reality that no longer spoke to the aspirations of the theatre-going public.[162] Left unsaid was that the play was unsuitable in the era of the NEP, which, in its implementation, entailed a cautious pragmatism inconsistent with the heroism central to the play; according to the official announcement, the play would not be included among those performed to commemorate the tenth anniversary of the October Revolution because it was frivolous and irrelevant to the occasion.[163] But barely two years later the Soviet Union was engaged in rapid industrialization, as called for in the first Five Year Plan, which resembled the storming of the Bastille in the heroism and persever-ance that were required to fulfil its prescribed quotas. Plays like Rolland's were therefore' relevant again, and were followed in 1939 by the publication of his laudatory biography of Robespierre.[164] By 1935 Rolland had become the Soviet Union's best known Western apologist, and for his slavish devotion was granted an audience with Stalin.[165]

The motif of storming enemy fortresses was common in Soviet culture even before Stalin used it as a metaphor for establishing socialism and communism. But the Bolsheviks at times reversed the normative values implicit in the metaphor, so that, in a mirror-image of the storming of the Bastille, the Soviet Union was itself a fortress protecting the Soviet people from voracious and duplicitous enemies attempting to storm it. Posters replicating this new dichotomy were common in Soviet cities and factories.[166] The Bolsheviks' fear of counter-revolution resulting from the enmity of the capitalist powers outside Russia was real, and before the Great Depression rendered nugatory any actual action to achieve this result, was to some degree justified. These circumstances suggested a state of siege similar to that which the French Revolution passed through in the 1790s, and the Bolsheviks found

---

[160] Unaniants, 'Velikaia frantsuzskaia revoliutsiia v spektaklaiakh sovetskogo teatra', pp. 467–8.
[161] Limonov. 'Prazdnestva Velikoi frantsuzskoi revoliutsii v 1789–93 gg.', pp. 403, 405, 407.
[162] Unaniants, 'Velikaia frantsuzskaia revoliutsiia v spektaklaiakh sovetskogo teatra', p. 473.
[163] Susan M. Corbesero, 'The Anniversaries of the October Revolution, 1918–1927: Politics and Imagery' (PhD dissertation, University of Pittsburgh, 2005), p. 189.
[164] Unaniants, 'Velikaia frantsuzskoi revoliutsii v knizhnoi grafike. 1917–1940 gg.', p. 414.
[165] Michael David-Fox, *Showcasing the Soviet Experiment: Cultural Diplomacy and Western Visitors to the Soviet Union, 1921–1941* (New York, 2012), p. 237.
[166] Stephen White, *The Bolshevik Poster* (New Haven CT, 1988) pp. 44, 45.

this, too, rich in symbolism they could utilize in impressing upon the Soviet people the dangers they faced from abroad even after internal enemies like the SRs, the Kadets, and the Mensheviks had all been routed. In 1921 the Soviet battleship that was called *Petropavlovsk* when it was launched in 1911 was renamed *Marat* after it was recovered from Kronstadt sailors holding its officers captive for the duration of the revolt. That these sailors formalized their demands on board the vessel probably figured in the government's decision to rename it quickly.[167] *Marat* remained on active duty for the next thirty-one years; in 1937 its presence in London at the coronation of King George VI was considered evidence of the Soviets' recognition of the solemnity and importance of the occasion—notwithstanding the sentiments of the monarchy-hating revolutionary for whom the ship was named—and in 1941 it was sunk by the Luftwaffe but soon raised, repaired, and recommissioned, this time as *Volkov* (obviously a Russian word and a common last name), because Stalin had decided the Soviet Union should fight the Nazis as a war of national liberation; ships once named for foreigners, even ones as illustrious in the ranks of revolutionary martyrs as Marat, now required monikers that were unmistakably Russian.[168] Another battleship, renamed *Mirabeau* in 1917, patrolled the Black Sea during the Civil War, in which capacity it may have engaged a French ship— because France was supporting the Whites—of the very same name.[169] It is not known if the Soviet *Mirabeau* participated in its subsequent sinking.[170]

Battleships were not the only things renamed with the French Revolution in mind. In its imitation, many of the trees planted in Russia in the 1920s and thereafter were called 'freedom trees'.[171] For the same reason, courts were renamed 'tribunals'.[172] Nikolaevskii Street in Moscow became Marat Street.[173] Moreover, borrowings such as these were not limited to inanimate objects. Babies were named for Marat, Robespierre, and Danton; some even received the monikers 'Giotin' and 'Bastil'.[174] Amazingly, this practice even extended into the animal kingdom. Either by felicitous coincidence or conscious decision, the horse pulling Stalin's sled on a portion of his trip to Siberia in January 1928 was named 'Marat'.[175]

Much of this appropriation of the French Revolution was spontaneous, even among the Bolsheviks, who needed no prompting from party officials to call

---

[167] Paul Avrich, *Kronstadt 1921* (New York, 1974), pp. 72–4, 213.

[168] M. J. Whitley, *Battleships of World War Two: An International Encyclopedia* (Annapolis MD, 1998), p. 217; Siegfried Breyer, *Soviet Warship Development 1917–1937* (London, 1992), vol. I, pp. 35, 228.

[169] A. V. Ado, 'Zhivoe nasledie velikoi revoliutsii: Predislovie k serii knig "Velikaia frantsuzskaia revoliutsiia. Dokumenty i issledovaniia"', in *Frantsuzskie rabochie: ot velikoi burzhuaznoi revoliutsii do revoliutsii 1848 goda*, edited by E. M. Kozhokin (Moscow, 1985), p. 9.

[170] General Loukomsky, *Memoirs of the Russian Revolution* (London, 1922), p. 224; Lobanov-Rostovsky, *Grinding Mill*, p. 320.

[171] Von Geldern, *Bolshevik Festivals*, p. 159.   [172] Kobiakov, 'Krasnyi sud', p. 246.

[173] Dalin, 'K istorii izucheniia Velikoi frantsuzskoi revoliutsii v SSSR', p. 107.

[174] Stites, *Revolutionary Dreams*, p. 111.   [175] Kotkin, *Stalin*, p. 679.

Dzerzhinskii 'the Saint-Just of the Russian Revolution', or Mikhail Larin, a member of the committee charged with nationalizing private property, 'the Saint-Just of Russian Economics'.[176] Nevertheless, in keeping with their Promethean ethos, which required them to change even the most mundane aspects of daily life, the Bolsheviks were not about to trust the Soviet people to remould themselves on their own. This task, so integral to the Bolsheviks' commitment to creating a new species of human being, necessitated their intervention. They ordered publishing houses to produce short, clearly written biographies suitable for a mass audience—Danton, Robespierre, and Marat were among the subjects— as part of a series called 'How the Proletariat Perpetuates Remembrance'.[177] N. M. Lukin, under the pen name N. Antonov, wrote a long essay of Charles I, Louis XVI, and Nicholas II.[178] Even more to the point, the Bolsheviks, in keeping with the Marxist assumption they shared that to name something was to define it, and that to rename something was to change it, called the old tsarist ministries 'commissariats', in obvious imitation of the *commissaires*, who played a critical role provisioning the armies of the French Revolution.[179] And because the customary term of address while the monarchy existed seemed to them too formal and evocative of still-existing class divisions, the Bolsheviks encouraged the continuation of the practice, common during the French Revolution and resumed in Russia after the collapse of the monarchy, of calling men *grazhdanin* and women *grazhdanka*; the difference was that these appellations were now infused with emancipatory and transformational implications.[180]

The ultimate objective of all of this was to create a new, distinctively 'proletarian' consciousness. This, in turn, would eventually inform the actions and behaviour of the New Soviet Man, the creation of whom was the ultimate objective of Bolshevism. All of the arts would be mobilized in this endeavour—especially the visual arts, which both in Russia and in Western Europe had by this time been reinvigorated and enriched by new modes of expression, such as Cubism and the many varieties of Futurism that, at least initially, were understandably incomprehensible to most Russians. Nevertheless, works of sculpture, even more than paintings, were thought to be especially effective in reaching the enormously large numbers of people whose consciousness the Bolsheviks sought to remould. If produced with weather-resistant materials, sculpture, unlike most paintings, could be displayed outdoors, where it could be seen, without the effort required to visit a museum, by literally millions of Soviet citizens. Placement outdoors also

---

[176] Liberman, *Building Lenin's Russia*, p. 22.

[177] N. T. Unaniants, 'Velikaia frantsuzskaia revoliutsiia v programme monumental'noi propagandy', in *Frantsuzskii ezhegodnik* (1989), pp. 148, 151.

[178] N. Antonov, [N. M. Lukin], *Karl I—Liudovik XVI—Nikolai II* (Moscow, 1918).

[179] Alan I. Forrest, *The Soldiers of the French Revolution* (Durham NC, 1990), pp. 131–7. The Bolsheviks were not the first to use the term. Kerensky had established 'people's commissariats' in the army, but did not apply the term to civilian institutions. Lobanov-Rostovsky, *Grinding Mill*, p. 211.

[180] Figes and Kolonitskii, *Interpreting the Russian Revolution*, p. 31.

meant that there was no limit on size. In keeping with their Promethean aspirations, sculpture produced under the Bolsheviks could be *bolshoi* ('big').[181]

To that effect, a formal decree of the Council of People's Commissars, dated 17 July 1918, and signed by Lenin, appeared in *Izvestiia* on the same day. It was also published a month later in *Iskusstvo* (*The Arts*). It called for the replacement of tsarist monuments by exactly sixty-six new ones, each honouring 'an outstanding person in the fields of revolutionary and social activity, philosophy, literature, science, and art'.[182] Although Lunacharskii was tasked with the implementation of the resolution, the press of his multifarious responsibilities required Lenin's intervention when he believed Lunacharskii derelict in fulfilling his obligation.[183] It should be borne in mind that the Soviet leader attached considerable importance to the creation and appropriate placement of this new 'monumental' art. Even though the Bolsheviks were themselves well-versed in European culture, and mostly appreciative of its artistic achievements, they also believed that the revolution in politics they had brought about in October 1917, and the transformation of the economy and society that would soon follow it, should be accompanied by a comparable revolution in the arts. Several organizations of writers and artists, such as *Prolekult*, tried quite deliberately to create works that were distinctively 'proletarian' in both style and subject matter. But no consensus existed on what exactly constituted proletarian art, and until the Stalin era the Soviet government did not consider its obligations to include the formulation of any binding requirements on writers and artists. In fact, the Sculptors' Union sponsored competitions, loosely overseen by Lunacharskii, to determine who would sculpt a particular personage: the participants submitted a bust or a bas relief; those deemed outstanding the sculptor would redo using stronger materials if that was necessary; apparently every sculptor, not just the winners, was paid 7,000 rubles for their efforts, half of which was provided in advance. Because the belief was common that Russian artists were incapable of producing 'monumental art' comparable to that of Delacroix and Daumier, there was no expectation that the works that were submitted would resemble

---

[181] There were of course painters who celebrated the October Revolution by infusing what they understood to be its emancipatory message into their depictions of figures in the French Revolution considered comparable to the Bolsheviks. M. K. Sokolov, for example, produced an entire cycle of works, mostly biographical, emphasizing the heroism of Mirabeau, Sieyès, Lafayette, Danton, Babeuf, Marat, and Saint-Just, among others. N. T. Unaniants, 'M. K. Sokolov. Tskil "Velikaia frantsuzskaia revoliutsiia"', *Frantsuzskii ezhegodnik* (1989), pp. 330–41.

[182] Christina Lodder, 'Lenin's Plan of Monumental Propaganda', *Sbornik: Papers of the Sixth and Seventh International Conferences of the Study Group of the Russian Revolution* (Leeds, 1981), p. 70; John E. Bowlt, 'Russian Sculpture and Lenin's Plan of Monumental Propaganda', in *Art and Architecture in the Service of Politics*, edited by Henry Armond Millon and Linda Nochlin (Cambridge MA, 1978), pp. 185–6; Lenin, in May 1918, had called for practically the same thing. V. V. Shleev, *Revoliutsiia i izobrazitel'noe iskusstvo* (Moscow, 1987), p. 270.

[183] Lodder, 'Lenin's Plan of Monumental Propaganda', pp. 69–70.

those of any particular sculptor. As a result, the viewing public, who adjudicated these competitions, enjoyed considerable latitude in their decisions.[184]

The results were quite eclectic; even monuments that were Cubist and Futurist stylistically were among those considered worthy of display.[185] The same was true of the sixty-six cultural luminaries whose achievements the monuments were intended to commemorate. These included the writers Voltaire, Gogol, and Lermontov; the painters Rublev and Cézanne; the composers Chopin, Scriabin, and Rimskii-Korsakov; rebels and revolutionaries thought to be precursors of the Bolsheviks, such as Spartacus; revolutionary *intelligenty* including Radishchev, Pestel', Herzen, and Chernyshevskii; and Stepan Khalturin and Sofiia Perovskaia of *Narodnaia Volia*. European revolutionaries whose busts would adorn Russia's cities and countryside included Lassalle, Garibaldi, and of course Marx and Engels. French revolutionaries were well-represented; among those singled out for commemoration were Robespierre, Danton, Marat, and even some criticized by Lenin and other Bolsheviks for not being Marxist, or not Marxist enough, such as Fourier, Saint-Simon, Blanqui, and Jaurès; whatever misgivings they had about their choices ideologically, the Bolsheviks nonetheless thought it prudent to include these 'renegades', at least visually, in the apostolic succession of revolutions and revolutionaries they believed had achieved its highest expression in 1917.[186] In that way, all memory of what had happened prior to the October Revolution would not be effaced, and history—as personified in these sixty-six extraordinary human beings—would become one long prologue to what the Bolsheviks had accomplished in 1917 and would soon accomplish in the future.

For some of the historical figures, their representation artistically was not easy. This was especially true for Robespierre. Commissioned by Lenin himself, his bust, which was sculpted by Beatrise Sandomirskaia, was placed in the Alexandrovskii Garden, not far from the Kremlin and on the route Lenin followed on foot to his office there. The formal unveiling was set deliberately for 7 November 1918.[187] Another bust, sculpted by N. A. Andreev, would by

---

[184] Ibid., p. 72; Nilsson, 'Spring 1918. The Arts and the Commissar', p. 46.

[185] Unfortunately, a number of these monuments collapsed, some only a short time after their completion. Among these was a statue of Danton, which stood in a public square in Moscow close to the Kremlin. Others, including several of Marat and Babeuf, were started but never completed. This should not be construed as evidence that the Bolsheviks did not care about them, or that their belief that the French Revolution played a central role in creating a mythology about their own revolution was flagging. The simplest explanation was the most likely: because some of the materials sculptors hoped to use, such as concrete, were needed for more important purposes, such as housing and the production of weapons, the less weather-resistant materials that were used instead caused the sculpture to fall apart, sometimes even before it was completed. Unaniants, 'Velikaia frantsuzskaia revoliutsiia v programme monumental'noi propagandy', pp. 150, 152.

[186] Bowlt, 'Russian Sculpture and Lenin's Plan', 186; Unaniants, 'Velikaia frantsuzskaia revoliutsiia v programme monumental'noi propagandy', p. 152; Mikhail Guerman, *Art of the October Revolution* (New York, 1979), pp. 10–12.

[187] Unaniants, 'Velikaia frantsuzskaia revoliutsiia v programme monumental'noi propagandy', p. 152.

prearrangement be unveiled simultaneously in Petrograd.[188] Because prior to 1917 not even the French had memorialized Robespierre in a work of sculpture, Sandomirskaia's and Andreev's were likely the first anywhere in the world to honour him in that particular fashion.[189] At the ceremonies in Moscow marking the occasion, at which, along with a large crowd of onlookers, a delegation of French socialists was present, Kamenev, among others, provided panegyrics appropriate for the occasion, lauding *l'Incorruptible* for 'crushing the counter-revolution in France with an iron hand'.[190] Lenin pronounced himself pleased with the results—he commented that the statue in Moscow deftly captured Robespierre's 'decisiveness'—and commissioned Lukin to write a tribute in the form of a pamphlet that would be widely distributed.[191]

But the statue was vandalized that very evening, and four days later, following driving rain, it broke into pieces, and was never repaired or replaced. The same fate befell the statue in Petrograd.[192] Surely one reason for this apparent indifference, which is especially incongruous given the tributes that were delivered when the two statutes had been unveiled, was the aforementioned shortage of materials, such as granite and bronze, sturdy enough to endure bad weather. Sculptors had to make do with gypsum, cement, and concrete—the last of these was what the statute in Moscow was made of—which caused many of the other monuments that were constructed with these materials to collapse.[193] Another possible reason was that there was a shortage of competent sculptors in Russia because the better ones had emigrated after the October Revolution.[194] If that was indeed the case, Lenin and Lunacharskii would almost certainly have been aware of it. But one suspects there was more to the failure to repair the shattered monuments, or to replace them with new ones, than just pragmatic considerations. Lenin evidently changed his mind on the efficacy of monumental art, at least insofar as prior revolutions like the French were concerned, and rebuffed later suggestions that another statue of Robespierre be built. According to Lunacharskii, writing many years later, Lenin concluded that the monuments still standing had not had their intended effect on the population, largely because the sculptors who created them

---

[188]   Ilina, 'Obraz evropeiskikh revoliutsii i russkaia kul'tura', 392.

[189]   John Hardman, *Robespierre* (London and New York, 1999), p. 214.

[190]   Quoted in Von Geldern, *Bolshevik Festivals*, p. 236; Bonch-Bruevich, *Izbrannye sochineniia*, vol. III, pp. 365–6.

[191]   Bonch-Bruevich, *Izbrannye sochineniia*, vol. III, p. 365; Unaniants, 'Velikaia frantsuzskaia revoliutsiia v programme monumnetal'noi propagandy', p. 152. I. Stepanov authored a comparable tribute, also in the form of a pamphlet, following the unveiling of a statue of Marat. Ilina, 'Obraz evropeiskikh revoliutsii i russkaia kul'tura', p. 392.

[192]   Von Geldern, *Bolshevik Festivals*, p. 236; Unaniants, 'Velikaia frantsuzskaia revoliutsiia v programme monumental'noi propagandy', p. 152.

[193]   Vsevolod Voinov, 'Zhivopos', in *Oktiabr' v iskusstve i literature 1917–1927* (Leningrad, 1928), p. 64. For the same reason a bust of Marat in Moscow met the same fate. Dalin, 'K istorii izucheniia Velikoi frantsuzskoi revoliutsii v SSSR', p. 152; Bonch-Bruevich, *Izbrannye sochineniia*, vol. III, p. 366.

[194]   Bonch-Bruevich, *Izbrannye sochineniia*, vol. III, pp. 365–6; Ia. Tugendkhol'd in *Nasha Rodina* (1918), cited in Nilsson, 'Spring 1918. The Arts and the Commissar', p. 46.

were ignorant of their propagandistic potential.[195] Finally, one suspects that politics played a role. Robespierre, while genuinely admired by the Bolsheviks for his personal qualities and for the prowess he showed politically in organizing the Jacobins before and after they took power, in the final analysis had led what amounted to a bourgeois revolution, not a proletarian one. For that reason, when his statue was unveiled Lenin still had qualms, or at least serious reservations, about the application of the kind of mass terror for which Robespierre, more than any other Jacobin with the possible exception of Saint-Just, had been responsible. Even if the institutionalized killing mass terror required could be morally justified in light of its purportedly noble objectives, there was no guarantee, at least not when Lenin first considered its application, that it would succeed. And if it failed, those responsible were likely to be among its victims. Robespierre's demise was an obvious example of that.

If one bears this in mind, then the similar fate of the monuments to his memory, and to those of other Jacobins such as Marat, can be understood as the result of a compromise: the Jacobin leaders deserved the Bolsheviks' respect and admiration, which should be given expression in the form of sculpted memorials, but should something happen to them, no measures to repair or replace them would be taken.[196] In fact, there is reason to believe that at least several of the Bolsheviks were initially reluctant, in the euphoria following their successful seizure of power, to emulate the imagery of the French Revolution. Before the October Revolution, Lunacharskii had indicated his awareness of the potential mass theatre possessed for spreading propaganda, but failed to mention in this context the *fêtes* of the French Revolution.[197] He may even have thought invoking the French Revolution to legitimize the October Revolution unnecessary.[198] In 1918 he suggested that the existing calendar be abolished and replaced by a new one, its first day being 25 October 1917, when the Congress of Soviets had formally legitimized the Bolsheviks' seizure of power.[199] While the same thing of course had occurred during the French Revolution, the Bolsheviks doing so would mean, in effect, that the French Revolution had never happened.

---

[195] Nilsson, 'Spring 1918: The Arts and the Commissar', p. 44; A. V. Lunacharskii, 'Lenin i isskustvo (1933)', in *Lenin o kul'ture i iskusstve* (Moscow, 1956), p. 526.

[196] As of 1999, there was still no monument to Robespierre anywhere in France that had been commissioned by the national government. Hardman, *Robespierre*, 214. The reason may be the lack of a national consensus on the morality and utility of the terror that remains inextricably a part of his legacy. On historical figures formally honoured by the creation of a monument to their memory there is almost always a national consensus that they did good things, or that the good things they did exceeded those that were bad. This evidently has not been the case in France concerning the Jacobins, although there is a station on the Paris *Métro* named for Robespierre and located, appropriately, under the street that bears his name (*Rue Robespierre*). Marisa Linton, 'Robespierre and the Terror', *History Today* 56, no. 8 (August 2006): p. 23.

[197] Von Geldern, *Bolshevik Festivals*, p. 23.

[198] Nilsson, 'Spring 1918, 'The Arts and the Commissars', p. 25.

[199] Von Geldern, *Bolshevik Festivals*, p. 236.

In the end, nothing came of Lunacharskii's suggestion—partly because he soon retracted it. The Bolsheviks never changed their calendar, and the French Revolution continued to inform the mythology the Bolsheviks' were creating about their own revolution. One must bear in mind that because the Provisional Government had offered virtually no resistance, the October Revolution, at least in Petrograd, was a largely bloodless affair in which the Bolsheviks, in Adam Ulam's apt phrase, did not seize power but rather 'picked it up'.[200] Even the so-called 'Storming of the Winter Palace' by cadres of Red Guards in reality had little about it that warranted its grandiloquent designation, with its intimations of heroic struggle. The palace was essentially undefended, and the ministers of the Provisional Government whose arrest was the reason for the operation offered no resistance.[201] In other words, the October Revolution was actually a rather pedestrian affair, quickly and easily consummated, without the drama inherent in a protracted Manichean conflict of good and evil, in which the Bolsheviks' enemies resisted them with a fortitude and perseverance overcome only by the comparable heroism and courage of the Bolsheviks and their proletarian supporters—thereby making the invocation of another, earlier revolution like the French superfluous.

In its mythological possibilities, the October Revolution was not sufficient. Time did not begin when it succeeded. The mythology of another revolution was required. In fact, the Bolsheviks occasionally admitted as much. In the decree of September 1920 establishing *Istpart*, a fully functional institution within the new Soviet government whose jurisdiction was 'the history of the October Revolution and the Russian Communist Party', one finds the rather remarkable statement that 'our revolution will be a beacon for communists of future generations just as the French Revolution was at the end of the eighteenth century for the bourgeoisie.... [In that way] the past would serve the present'.[202] In the words of a Russian who witnessed the emergence of this mythology and approved of it, 'our great emancipatory struggle was enhanced by the influence on it of the arts and literature of the French Revolution'.[203]

Many of the most illustrious novelists and poets lent their talents to this endeavour, and a goodly number of them employed motifs and images drawn directly from the French Revolution. N. I. Kareev hoped the works he produced that included references to the most iconic expressions of the French Revolution—the storming of the Bastille, the Declaration of the Rights of Man and Citizen, the

---

[200] Ulam, *The Bolsheviks*, p. 314.

[201] The 'bombardment' of the palace by guns on the battleship *Aurora* that preceded the assault damaged the building less than that which occurred during the filming of *Oktiabr'*, Sergei Eisenstein's classic film commissioned in 1927 to commemorate the revolution's tenth anniversary. Olga Romanova, 'Eisenstein's "October": Between Artistic Invention and the Myth of the Revolution, 2012', http://urokiistorii.ru/en/taxonomy/term/200/2822.

[202] Corney, *Telling October*, p. 100; *Ko vsem chlenam partii* (Moscow, 1920), p. 1.

[203] P. A. Pelshe, *Nravy i iskusstvo frantsuzskoi revoliutsii* (Petrograd, 1919), 5.

Marseillaise—would show the two revolutions, the French and the Russian, causally related; the mythology of the former not only prefigured the second but informed its meaning and larger significance.[204] In 1918 Demian Bednyi composed a poem, 'Kommunisticheskaia Marsel'eza', the very title of which suggested the same relationship between the two revolutions; in Bednyi's words, the French in 1789 and the Russians in 1917 were 'the fire of a universal blaze'.[205] For works such as these, 'the Court Poet of the Kremlin', as Bednyi was commonly referred to, was awarded the Order of the Red Flag in 1923.[206] Another sycophant who needed no prompting to produce works of which the Soviet leadership approved was Alexei Tolstoy. In 1919 he wrote a play, 'The Death of Danton', that in appealing to the less rational sensibilities of its audience, treated the facts of the revolutionary's life and death cavalierly. It showed him conspiring to kill Robespierre to stop the bloodshed for which the latter was responsible. But Danton did not succeed in this endeavour—of which Tolstoy makes clear he strongly approved—and shortly afterwards goes to his death. The entire play is pervaded by fatalism and a profound sense of helplessness. Because this was the opposite message to that which the Soviet government expected the play to convey, four years later Tolstoy solidified his reputation for artistic and ideological malleability by revising the play to the point where the original version was unrecognizable. No longer emphasizing Robespierre and Danton as prime movers of the revolution, it now depicted it as a conflict of social classes and categories in which the *sans-culottes*, in terms of their influence, were *primus inter pares*. Danton has been reduced very nearly to a nonentity. At best he was a genuine revolutionary paralysed by his timidity and indecision, at worst not a revolutionary at all. The tragic figure in the play was now Robespierre, who did not live to see the revolution's ultimate victory—which the play implied occurred in Russia, not France.[207]

Among the other writers and poets who did what the Soviet leadership expected of them were A. I. Bezymenskii, who penned a poem, entitled 'The Sans-Culottes', celebrating their heroism;[208] Andrei Globa, who wrote on the murder of Marat;[209] Vladimir Harbut, whose poem on the storming of the Bastille tried to make plain the connection between the events of 14 July and those of the Bolsheviks in October 1917;[210] and the always enigmatic Ilia Erenburg, whose novel, *Zagovor Ravnykh* (*The Conspiracy of Equals*), was appropriately ambiguous in its

---

[204] Kareev, *Prozhitoe i perezhitoe*, pp. 290–2.
[205] Quoted in N. T. Unaniants, 'Velikaia frantsuzskaia revoliutsiia v sovetskoi literature. 1917–1940 gg.', *Frantsuzskii ezhegodnik* (1989), p. 364.
[206] René Fueloep-Miller, *The Mind and Face of Bolshevism: An Examination of Cultural Life in the Soviet Union* (New York, 1965), p. 157.
[207] Unaniants, 'Velikaia frantsuzskaia revoliutsiia v sovetskoi literature', p. 364.
[208] Ilina, 'Obraz evropeiskikh revoliutsii i russkaia kul'tura', p. 387.
[209] Unaniants, 'Velikaia frantsuzskaia revoliutsiia v sovetskoi literature', p. 358.
[210] Ibid., p. 364.

message, initially describing the principal figures of the French Revolution dispassionately—which is to say in a fashion unbefitting a Soviet propagandist. By the end, however, any pretence to impartiality has long disappeared. The reader is expected to conclude that Babeuf was the archetypical revolutionary-martyr, who devoted his life to the betterment of the French people and paid for his efforts with his life.[211]

All of these works were intended for a mass audience, and written accordingly. But because the authors retained a measure of autonomy, the government thought it necessary to supplement them with others it issued itself, sometimes with expressive and even lurid covers and frontispieces; practically all of them were short and simple in the message they conveyed. Works written in foreign languages, such as *A Tale of Two Cities* and Victor Hugo's *1793*, were translated with the same considerations in mind.[212] Moreover, the Bolsheviks were aware that what remained of the old nobility—historically the most literate class in Russia— had already emigrated, and they accordingly stressed the art forms for which literacy was not required. Lenin considered film especially useful in infusing in the large percentage of the public that was still in varying degrees illiterate a proper appreciation of the Soviet regime and the goals to which it was committed.[213] In keeping with this requirement, Soviet filmmakers developed a new genre, called *agitki*, of films longer than newsreels but shorter than regular features, ranging from fifteen to thirty minutes long, which was considered enough time to focus on a particular theme and illuminate its contemporary relevance without unduly taxing the viewer's patience. Some of these films, such as 'Proletarians of the World Unite', released in 1919, included references to the French Revolution.[214] Other art forms accessible to the illiterate performed the same function film did, though on a much smaller scale. Several ballets about the French Revolution were produced; the most prominent were Vladimir Femelid's *Karman'ola* and Boris Asafiev's *Plamia Parizha* (*The Flame of Paris*).[215] Two orchestral overtures about the French Revolution by the French composer Henri Litolff—one about the Girondins, the other concerning Robespierre—were performed in Petrograd, Moscow, and other cities.[216] The Russian composer S. I. Pototskii never finished the opera he began that was based on Rolland's *Vziatie Bastilii*; nevertheless two scenes he had written were performed in September 1919 to an audience of Red Army soldiers.[217]

[211] Ibid., p. 365.
[212] Unaniants, 'Velikaia frantsuzskoi revoliutsii v knizhnoi grafike', pp. 413–14.
[213] Stites, *Revolutionary Dreams*, p. 98.
[214] Peter Kenez, *Cinema and Soviet Society, 1917–1953* (Cambridge, 1992), p. 32.
[215] Unaniants, 'Velikaia frantsuzskaia revoliutsiia v sovetskoi muzykal'noi zhizni. 1917–1940 gg.', *Frantsuzskii ezhegodnik* (1989), p. 445.
[216] Ibid., p. 443.   [217] Ibid., p. 443.

Theatrical productions for the purpose of inculcating the proper revolutionary consciousness were of course strongly supported by the Soviet government. One play intended to serve this purpose was Anton Amnuel's *Marat*. In the play Marat's oratory and his clashes with Lafayette were among the many aspects of his life that were depicted; especially significant was the stress on Marat's reluctance to employ indiscriminate terror. First performed in May 1919 in Petrograd, subsequent productions brought its message to Gomel and Archangel, and to other locations far from the then Russian capital.[218] Another play widely performed and highly esteemed by the educated elite in Petrograd and Moscow was M. E. Levberg's *Danton*. At its first performance in June 1919, such literary luminaries as Maxim Gorky and Alexander Blok were in the audience. Because the play stressed Danton's role in organizing resistance in 1792 against the external enemies intent on invading France and putting an end to the French Revolution, it was only natural for the audience to conjure in their minds the civil war in Russia that when the play was first performed, one could easily believe the Bolsheviks could lose.[219] Gorky so liked the play that he recommended it to others, and in comments on the play that would be published in 1921, Blok said that by seeing the play one 'realises what is near to us'.[220]

Yet another play intended to generate political consciousness was *Robespierre*. Written and directed by F. F. Raskolnikov, it depicted the period in 1794 between the celebration of the Cult of the Supreme Being and Robespierre's arrest and execution. A fatalism and a sense of the inevitability of things permeate the unfolding of events. Robespierre's views are those of a typical *bourgeois*, and thus incompatible with the requirements of the Hébertists and *les enragés*. As he becomes increasingly isolated politically, the audience comes to understand that this is why his support for the Maximum has diminished.[221] But the last words of the play, spoken by an ordinary artisan, underscored Raskolnikov's conviction that something superior to the system the Jacobins created has already emerged in Russia: 'This was not our regime. Ours will come. We will be victorious.'[222]

As effective as theatrical productions were in conferring on audiences the mentality the Bolsheviks considered essential in defeating foreign enemies and undertaking vast projects of social and economic engineering, such as industrialization and the elimination of private property, they also recognized that ordinary theatre, because it observed certain conventions, such as that the audience would be a passive recipient of what transpired on the stage, suffered from serious limitations. Accordingly, the Bolsheviks pioneered a different kind of theatre, which they preferred to classical productions partly because the latter were

---

[218] Unaniants, 'Velikaia frantsuzskaia revoliutsiia v spektaklaiakh sovetskogo teatra', p. 472. A production of the same play in 1920 directed by Sergei Eisenstein may have been his first experience in the role for which he would later become famous; not until 1923 would he direct a film. Ibid., p. 472.
[219] Ibid., p. 468.   [220] Ibid., pp. 468, 472.   [221] Ibid., p. 480.
[222] Ibid., p. 480.

performed indoors to a very small audience; even plays performed multiple times reached an infinitesimal percentage of the population. Performed outdoors, sometimes before several thousands of people, most of whom could not afford the cost of a ticket to an indoor production, the plays the Bolsheviks preferred quickly acquired their own taxonomical category, called *prazdnichestvo*, by which was meant the phenomenon of staging elaborate celebrations resembling those of holidays, but with political and ideological themes. In the Bolsheviks' mind, their purpose, in addition to helping create a legitimizing mythology of revolutionary heroism in the face of implacable opposition, was to reduce the distance between the party and the people, and between the powerful and the powerless; that the traditional distinction between participant and audience was blurred by the inclusion in the casts of literally thousands of ordinary citizens serving as extras gave credence to the notion that just by living in the Soviet Union, ordinary people were celebrating it.[223] Indeed, by celebrating historical events, past and present could be synthesized into a narrative suggesting nothing less than that living in the Soviet state was in some sense the culmination of history itself. But the roots of *prazdnichestvo* were actually traceable to the French Revolution, specifically to the gargantuan celebratory *fêtes* the Jacobins staged for the purpose of indoctrinating the French people in the virtues of their transformational ideology. The Bolsheviks were not the first to stage such celebrations in Russia. The Provisional Government preceded them, but because it lasted for only eight months, the most it could do, as mentioned earlier, was sponsor commemorations on the Champs de Mars in Petrograd.[224] The Bolsheviks, by contrast, had more time to experiment, to figure out which kinds of spectacles would have the greatest effect politically and ideologically.[225] But about the advisability of staging these spectacles in the first place, the Bolsheviks had no doubts. The very magnitude of the celebrations—in the number of participants, the size of the sets, and the universality and timelessness of the themes that were explored—would impress their audience with an intensity that traditional theatre, indeed no other art form, not even cinema, could match. The walls encasing the buildings where plays were traditionally performed would only trivialize the larger cosmic purpose for which these celebrations were intended, and by being performed outdoors could attract an audience that, at least in theory, was infinitely large. In that way, large numbers of people could draw the analogy the Bolsheviks intended between exceeding the conventional boundaries of the arts on the one hand, and achieving the transformational objectives they

---

[223] Malte Rolf, *Soviet Mass Festivals, 1917–1991* (Pittsburgh PA, 2013), pp. 1–5; Zh. Tierso, *Pesni i prazdnestva frantsuzskoi revoliutsii* (Petrograd, 1919), pp. 139–40.

[224] Corbesero, 'The Anniversaries of the October Revolution', p. 14.

[225] Christopher A. P. Binns, in 'The Changing Face of Power: Revolution and Accommodation in the Development of the Soviet Ceremonial System: Part I', *Man.*, vol. 14, no. 4 (1979), p. 587, notes that these Bolshevik spectaculars were the first in Europe since the French Revolution without any religious connotation. That he fails to mention those the Provisional Government produced does not vitiate the general accuracy of his observation.

considered prerequisites for the achievement of communism on the other. On occasion Lunacharskii quoted Robespierre on the ability of festivals like the Jacobins' to engender the moral and political improvement of participants and spectators alike:

> Gather people together and you will improve them because when grouped together, people will aspire to like one another, but can only like what they respect. Give this gathering a great moral and political theme—and love for all things worthy will grow together with pleasure in every heart because people will meet each other with pleasure.[226]

To reinforce this message, Lunacharskii and Kalinin sometimes delivered speeches before the action commenced, and even the orations of Desmoulins were repeated with great fanfare and sometimes followed by the singing of the *Marseillaise*, obviously to underscore the solemnity and universality of the occasion.[227]

In these mass celebrations, the traditional distinction between the actors and the audience, reflecting that between fantasy and reality, broke down. Spectators were sometimes seated onstage, thereby resembling, if only by their location, the classical Greek chorus.[228] Occasionally they were even enlisted as extras in productions requiring a large cast, such as those that re-enacted the storming of the Winter Palace.[229] It was important to Lunacharskii in particular that theatre be 'democratic', in the sense of involving the masses, and the many productions in which there were more extras than cast members might happily have served to impress upon the audience the conceit that the *coup d'état* that brought the Bolsheviks to power had actually been a mass revolution.[230] Because the Bolsheviks understood that they were neophytes in producing these spectacles, they found very helpful the instructions Jacques-Louis David provided the Jacobins for the *fêtes* they put on in Paris and elsewhere to gin up political support. The celebrations on May Day, 1918, for example, used music the way the French painter recommended, and those that included marching followed routes consistent with what he had prescribed in the 1790s.[231] Two years later, in front of the old stock exchange in Petrograd, some 4,000 actors, before an audience of 35,000, performed 'The Mystery of Liberated Labour', an extravaganza in which heroes the Bolsheviks considered their precursors, such as Stenka Razin, the *sans-culottes*, and Spartacus, were singled out for adulation.

---

[226] Quoted in Stites, *Revolutionary Dreams*, p. 98.
[227] Ilina, 'Obraz evropeiskikh revoliutsii i russkaia kul'tura', p. 401.
[228] Unaniants, Velikaia frantsuzskaia revoliutsiia v spektaklaiakh sovetskogo teatra, p. 468.
[229] Limonov, 'Prazdnestva Velikoi frantsuzskoi revoliutsii v 1789–93 gg.', p. 399.
[230] Corbesero, 'The Anniversaries of the October Revolution', p. 4.
[231] Limonov, 'Prazdnestva Velikoi frantsuzskoi revoliutsii v 1789–93 gg.', p. 398. In November 1918, on the first anniversary of the October Revolution, marchers carried banners of bare-breasted women, in the form of angels, with sheathed swords attached at their waists, in an obvious obeisance to Delacroix's iconic 'Liberty on the Barricades'. Corbesero, 'The Anniversaries of the October Revolution', p. 57.

In the opening scenes of the production, with Chopin's 'Funeral March' as musical accompaniment, these embodiments of revolutionary virtue try with no success to smash the obstacles preventing them from reaching territory where they will be free. The conclusion the audience is meant to draw from this is that further attempts will be no less futile. But just when it seems that progress is not possible, a red star appears in the east, which, as an obvious symbol of Bolshevism and socialism, heralds the liberation of humanity. Red banners and liberty trees like those in the French Revolution then emerge on the stage, as does an actor obviously meant to personify the liberation of labour. Upon his appearance, the soldiers directly in front of him demonstrably relinquish their weapons in belated, but nonetheless genuine recognition that the peace that now reigns will be permanent. In the last scenes of the play, spotlights on ships anchored in the Neva are directed towards the stage, sirens blow, and bands assembled alongside the audience play the *Internationale*, with both actors and the audience joining in.[232]

Two months later, another extravaganza was staged, also in front of the stock exchange in Petrograd, this one celebrating the convocation of the Second Congress of the Third International. Once again searchlights—this time positioned atop the Peter-Paul Fortress—highlight the action. Several thousand amateur actors, many of them workers, soldiers, and sailors, recapitulate the history of humanity as refracted through the revolutions that demonstrate the stages through which it passes on the way to communism. Over the course of the performance, first slaves and then Parisian *sans-culottes* try unsuccessfully to ascend a stairway at the top of which are evil rulers, their identity unspecified, defended by soldiers. But soon these rulers are forced to flee amidst great billows of smoke that enable them to escape with their lives. But new rulers appear, their identities no less difficult to divine; like their predecessors, they are intended to personify oppression generically. Their adversaries, however, are different. These are bald old men carrying impossibly large books, which are meant to show them utterly detached from reality. From both their appearance and what they say the audience recognizes them as the leaders of the long-ago discredited Second International. As expected, they, too, are driven from the stage, and a scene meant to suggest the First World War is followed quickly by a re-enactment of the October Revolution, in which the actors are intermingled among the spectators. Finally, soldiers appear, and ships approach on the Neva; both are meant to symbolize victory in the ongoing civil war.[233]

The spectacle that most thoroughly combined the elements that distinguished all of them from ordinary theatre was performed in 1920 on the third anniversary

---

[232] Additional details can be found in Stites, *Revolutionary Dreams*, pp. 94–5, from which much of the description has been taken.
[233] Fueloep-Miller, *Mind and Face of Bolshevism*, pp. 145–6.

of the October Revolution.[234] The largest of all, it called for 8,000 actors and 500 musicians. Remarkably, there were nine directors, each with a different degree of authority. Before an audience of 100,000, it had multiple stages both inside and outside the Winter Palace. Preceded by a musical overture named for Robespierre, the play took between four and five hours to perform. Although it was later made into a film, as a play it was performed only once. Thematically it reduced the events of 1917 to a linear progression of episodes that one of the directors considered analogous to the storming of the Bastille.

In ways both monumental and bombastic given the size of the audience, the number of actors, the grandeur of the setting, and the significance of the occasion, the production began with a cannon firing a blank. After trumpeters provide the equivalent of a call to arms, the action starts. On one platform, a figure easily recognizable as Kerensky is surrounded by generals, capitalists, and assorted courtiers, and goes about his business to the accompaniment of the *Marseillaise*. On another platform are ordinary people. Although their movements are at first haphazard and uncoordinated, gradually they come to act in unison, thereby suggesting how powerful they could be as a fighting force. Very soon they form one. To the strains of the *Internationale*, and amidst plaintive calls for Lenin, they are transformed miraculously into Red Guards, and while Kerensky and his entourage temporize, some of the soldiers defending him defect. On the opposite platform, as songs are sung, and speakers declaim the virtues of proletarian revolution, emotions reach a climax. Extras who heretofore have been standing motionless begin to move, and as they are joined by others driven by the same objective, they approach Kerensky. But he manages to elude them, and his supporters—though not Kerensky himself—take refuge inside the Winter Palace, where the remainder of the saga takes place. The Bolsheviks and their supporters pursue the now-powerless prime minister, and finally, after forcing their way into the palace, they take the ministers of the Provisional Government into custody. With the shooting of rockets and to songs sung by thousands, the Bolshevik spectacular finally comes to an end, its message clear: in just the way that, in the middle of the performance, the *Internationale* supersedes the *Marseillaise*, so, too, by the end of it the October Revolution has triumphed over the Provisional Government, and is poised to achieve for the Soviet people the liberty, justice, and happiness that not even the French Revolution obtained for the French. The audience presumably returns to their homes convinced that all of humanity will eventually partake of the blessings of the October Revolution, which they know has brought to power a totally new government that has accomplished in barely two years the equivalent of what it took the French Revolution a decade to achieve. With this in mind, the Soviet people can now turn away from the past and look to

---

[234] The description that follows draws heavily on that found in ibid., pp. 147–8.

the future, when everything they deserve but has been denied them for centuries will finally be theirs.

* * *

By the mid-1920s, the Bolsheviks had largely abandoned their belief that revolutionary consciousness could be instilled through the expedient of mass spectacles resembling those of the French Revolution.[235] But the revolution would remain relevant nevertheless—and in ways it had never been before. The whole issue of a Soviet Thermidor, which had hardly concerned the Bolsheviks either before the October Revolution or immediately after it, suddenly became a matter of utmost importance in the wake of the New Economic Policy Lenin imposed, for pragmatic reasons, on a reluctant Communist Party; the economic relaxation the NEP entailed suggested a retreat from the activism implicit in the October Revolution, and the spectre it evoked of ideological betrayal made analogies with the original Thermidor inevitable. Unlike the issue of Jacobinism, which, in the context of Russian Social Democracy, concerned the instrumentalities of revolution—tactics and organization more than objectives and intended results—invocations of Thermidor struck at the very heart of the whole Soviet Experiment. For that reason its mere mention was sufficient was raise the Bolsheviks' collective blood pressure. What could be more disturbing, more conducive to self-doubt and the anger it often gives rise to, than the possibility—even if raised only by analogy with a phase of another revolution, distant in both time and space—that the Bolsheviks were now betraying their own objectives? At the very least, the analogy with Thermidor raised fundamental questions about the nature of the economy and the political system the Bolsheviks had established, and about the way it was now developing. Was the Soviet Union evolving into something approaching socialism? Was it, in other words, advancing the course of history, as Marx and Engels had explained it in the mid-nineteenth century? Or was it regressing, the way the French Revolution did after the Jacobins' demise, to the arrangements that had existed in Russia prior to the monarchy's collapse? Moreover, the possibilities in what the future portended for the Soviet Union included outcomes neither Marx nor Lenin had seriously considered. Could the Soviet Union be changing, for example, into something resembling the Bonapartism that followed the French Revolution? Even worse, could it somehow be degenerating into something entirely new, for which there was no analogue in the French Revolution, or in any prior revolution in history?

---

[235] The meetings of workers that the Bolsheviks sponsored on a large scale beginning in the 1920s, at which the workers were encouraged to participate on an equal footing with the party functionaries running them, have been described as the intended successor to the theatrical spectaculars. Binns, 'The Changing Face of Power', p. 593.

These were questions of immediate ideological import when ideological enemies of the Soviet Union first raised them in the early 1920s to explain the nature of the Soviet system and why it seemed now to be jettisoning policies conducive to socialism in favour of others, most obviously the NEP, that seemed to put the country on a road that would lead it backwards to capitalism. As was the case when Lenin, in the early 1900s, took up the whole issue of Jacobinism, 'Thermidor' was first an epithet the Bolsheviks' enemies found useful in attacking them, and only later, in responding to the accusation, did the Bolsheviks confront the dilemma the term implied about the future of the state they had only recently established. Of course Thermidor was too enticing in its polemical potential for Lenin's putative successors in the mid-1920s not to employ it in bludgeoning one another rhetorically until one of them emerged triumphant. But irrespective of how Thermidor was used within the highest echelons of the Soviet Communist Party, the reason for the mortal threat its mere invocation posed to the Soviet system was the ideologically aberrant way this system began in 1917, when the Bolsheviks carried out what they claimed to be a proletarian revolution before its preconditions and prerequisites existed.

Thus the debate over the nature and the relevance of Thermidor in the late 1920s spoke to the very legitimacy of the October Revolution and to the enterprise of creating socialism in the Soviet Union. If the Soviets were to conclude, or somehow be forced to acknowledge, that the political and economic system they put in place in 1917 was now experiencing a regression even only a fraction as profound as that which had occurred in France from 1794 to 1799, then there would be good reason to believe that the Soviet Union, having betrayed its own objectives, was no longer the Soviet Union, but rather something else entirely. In short, the economic regression symbolized by Thermidor would likely lead to the political and ideological cul-de-sac personified by Napoleon, and if that happened, then the whole Bolshevik experiment in building socialism and communism would be at an end.

A great deal was at stake in the debate over Thermidor, and it is this new phase in how the French Revolution was received in Russia that now requires our attention.

8

The Phantom of the Soviet Thermidor

The possibility of the Soviet Union succumbing to a Soviet Thermidor was first raised by anti-Soviet Russian *émigrés*. In the 1920s, inside the self-contained world these *émigrés* inhabited, the word itself 'was on everyone's lips'.[1] In March 1921, shortly after the Kronstadt Revolt had been suppressed, the liberal and former Kadet, M. V. Mirkin-Getsevich, wrote pseudonymously that the revolt was one more piece of evidence that the Soviet Union was approaching its Thermidor, and would collapse soon after its arrival.[2] With the suppression of the revolt still vivid in his mind, Pavel Miliukov declared flatly that the Soviet Union was already experiencing a form of 'reaction' similar to that which had occurred in France in the late 1790s.[3] The Bolsheviks, of course, could not be pleased by such criticism, which suggested that the state they ruled might never achieve socialism. Moreover, by this time the Bolsheviks believed that, by continuing the emancipation of humanity the French Revolution had begun, they had acquired proprietary rights to its mythology. The French Revolution was theirs, and no one else's, to mine for raw material they could utilize in fashioning a mythology that would win for their regime the legitimacy they believed it needed. For that reason, the Bolsheviks were sensitive to attacks from enemies that used the revolution to defame them, and kept a watchful eye on the *émigré* press. But the liberal whose invocation of Thermidor most antagonised them was Nikolai Ustrialov. A former Kadet who during the Civil War edited the newspaper Admiral Kolchak's army published, he took refuge after the war ended in the Chinese city of Harbin, where he found other Russians in its large *émigré* community who shared his hostility to the new Soviet regime.[4] Even before the Kronstadt Revolt, Ustrialov believed that any 'economic Brest-Litovsk'—by which he meant a return to capitalism in Russia— would mean the end of the Soviet Union.[5] In 1921 he fleshed out this idea in his

---

[1] Quoted in Kondratieva, *Bol'sheviki-iakobintsy*, p. 70.

[2] B. Mirskii [M. V. Mirkin-Getsevich], 'Put' termidora'. *Poslednie novosti*, no. 266 (3 March 1921): p. 2. He expressed the same conclusion in '14 iiulia', *Poslednie novosti*, no. 330 (14 July 1921): p. 2.

[3] Cited in N. Ustrialov, 'Put' termidora', in N. Ustrialov, *Pod znakom revoliutsii* (Harbin, 1927), p. 41. Ustrialov used the same title Mirkin-Getsevich did to underscore his disagreement with the latter's notion of Thermidor as a specific event, rather than as a process.

[4] Kondratieva, *Bol'sheviki-iakobintsy*, p. 71. Ustrialov later made his peace with the Soviet regime, which he had come to believe was a hybrid of Bolshevism and nationalism. After working faithfully for the Soviet government in the agency that oversaw the Chinese Eastern Railway, he returned to the Soviet Union in 1935. In 1937 he was arrested and shot.

[5] Ibid., p. 219.

contribution to the collection of essays he edited, *Smena Vekh* (*Change of Signposts*), which was published in Prague in the same year, and in Smolensk one year later.[6]

Despite rejecting socialism and communism, the essays in the collection did not advocate resistance or opposition to the Soviet state. Rather, they counselled acceptance of it. Resistance was not necessary. The Soviet Union was destined to end up a state like those that preceded it in Russian history, which to the *smenovekhovtsy* was a good thing because the history of Russia was essentially the history of Russian nationalism. The Bolsheviks' reaction to this was not uniformly hostile. Although the Bolsheviks' claim to universality required them to reject the nationalism the *smenovekhovtsy* recommended, at the Eleventh Party Congress in 1922 Lenin nonetheless commended them for pointing out the growing danger petty corruption and a widespread commitment to personal enrichment posed to the regime as a whole.[7] One can be reasonably certain that that was the reason Lenin, who had read the collection carefully, approved its publication along with two volumes of essayscritically evaluating it.[8]

Ustrialov's contribution was consistent with the general argument of *Smena Vekh*. He agreed that the Soviet Union was destined to become a polity strongly resembling the bourgeois nation states of Western Europe. Where he differed was in invoking Thermidor to illustrate and to clarify his prediction. Because Thermidor, for the Bolsheviks, was the successor regime to the French Revolution, which ended when the Jacobin Terror did, the arrival in the Soviet Union of something resembling it would seem to suggest that the October Revolution had been for nothing, that it would never be the catalyst sparking socialist revolutions elsewhere in Europe or anywhere else. But Ustrialov did not consider the collapse of Bolshevism and the Soviet Union inevitable. The original Thermidor, he knew, did not entail the 'liquidation' of the French Revolution. Rather, it was only a later phase of it. For this reason there remained the possibility, should a Soviet Thermidor emerge, of the Soviet Union returning to its socialist roots. Regressing further into a Bonapartist dictatorship, as happened in the French Revolution, was by no means guaranteed. In fact, Thermidor might even be something the Soviet leadership would welcome, for it would make their ideological message more palatable to the Soviet people, who presumably desired 'normalcy' like that which the Thermidor in the French Revolution both engendered and reflected. Under

---

[6] The title of the collection was taken from the 1909 collection of essays, entitled *Vekhi* (*Signposts*) of which *Smena vekh* was intended as a corrective. Ustrialov's essay also appeared in *Novosti zhizni*, the newspaper he edited in Harbin. Ibid., p. 72.

[7] V. I. Lenin, 'Politicheskii otchet tsentral'nogo komiteta RKP(b)', in Lenin, *PSS*, vol. XLV, pp. 93–5. Of course Lenin feared the erosion of communism implicit in this corruption and greed while the *smenovekhovtsy* welcomed it as a harbinger of Russia's post-communist future.

[8] Edward Hallett Carr, *Socialism in One Country, 1924–1926* (New York, 1958), vol. I, p. 58.

such circumstances, they might even come to feel genuine enthusiasm for the Soviet regime.[9]

In assessing Ustrialov's critique of Bolshevism and the Soviet Union, it is important to remember that the 'National Bolshevism' he favoured did not mean he thought this new hybrid would be more Bolshevik (or socialist) than nationalist—or, for that matter, more nationalist than Bolshevik. Rather, he seemed convinced that its dichotomous elements would remain in an uneasy, but self-perpetuating equilibrium. But to the Bolsheviks themselves, such an amalgam was unacceptable. And far from mitigating their conviction that his motives were suspect and his intentions malevolent, Ustrialov's whole argument, corroborated as it was by the appropriation of terminology from the French Revolution, soon produced a reaction among the Bolsheviks much like a bull's after a red flag has been placed within his field of vision. Although Ustrialov never claimed that the Soviet Union had already reached the stage in its historical development that strongly resembled the French Thermidor, his prediction that it might soon do so was enough to make his argument—again from the perspective of the Bolsheviks—a threat. One must bear in mind that, to Ustrialov, the two Thermidors, the French and the Soviet, were a process, not a single event; the term signified degeneration towards a particular end point, rather than the end point itself, which, in the French case, was either Napoleon's dictatorship, which completed and stabilized the French Revolution before betraying it, or the explicit counter-revolution that began in 1815 with the return of the Bourbons. In other words, it did not mean an event or series of events that in the French Revolution inevitably resulted in a repudiation of some, but by no means all, of its original ideology. For Ustrialov Thermidor was a trend, and as such it might be managed successfully by the Soviet regime. In fact, it might even disappear on its own, thereby making unnecessary a revolution removing the Bolsheviks from power. If the Bolsheviks for some reason could not eliminate the Soviet Thermidor, they could grudgingly accommodate themselves to it in the hope that it would soon eliminate itself.

But Ustrialov also claimed that any Soviet Thermidor would be more subtle, and insidious, and thus more difficult to prevent, and later on more difficult to eliminate, than the Thermidor in France actually was. All that was needed for it to occur was 'an insignificant palace coup eliminating the most odious figures [of the regime] by the hands of their own associates, and in the name of their very own principles'.[10] The Soviet Thermidor, in other words, would destroy the Soviet system from within—which would seem to suggest that the supporters of a Soviet Thermidor could pose plausibly as supporters of the Soviet Union. Internal

[9] N. V. Ustrialov, 'Patriotika', *Smena vekh: sbornik statei* (Smolensk, 1922), pp. 52–65.
[10] Ibid., p. 70.

vigilance was therefore necessary if the Soviet leaders were to save the Soviet system, and perhaps also their own necks, from this particular threat.

The Mensheviks viewed the Soviet Thermidor differently. If, for Ustrialov and his acolytes, it was a reliable indication that the Soviet Union would end up a state little different from those that already existed in Western Europe, for the Mensheviks its presence, or even the mere possibility of its emergence, would prove their contention that the October Revolution had been premature. A Soviet Thermidor, in other words, would demonstrate not that socialism in Russia was impossible because the Russian people, as Ustrialov believed, were more nation-alist than socialist. Rather, a Soviet Thermidor would lead to the achievement of socialism, albeit in the distant future after the country had experienced the requisite oppression that always occurs under capitalism. Even before the NEP's emergence served as proof that Thermidor was already a reality, Iulii Martov, for example, was quick to argue, barely weeks after the October Revolution, that any attempt to achieve socialism in its immediate aftermath was hopelessly utopian and bound to fail. The prematurity of the revolution would make a dictatorship like the Jacobin necessary, but rather than ensuring the Bolsheviks' survival, it would accelerate 'petit-bourgeois tendencies' many Mensheviks, including Martov, considered Thermidorian.[11]

After the NEP was announced and began to be implemented, Martov, in November 1921, took up the issue again, this time claiming that the new policy permitting capitalism and market relations on a limited scale was in fact the proof he had been waiting for that Thermidor, in the Soviet Union, had already emerged.[12] Remarkably, the Bolsheviks themselves, by issuing the NEP, had 'thermidorianized' a not inconsiderable segment of the Soviet economy. But unlike Ustrialov, Martov saw Thermidor as exclusively an economic phenom-enon, albeit one that was likely to have significant political repercussions. In the French Revolution it had led to Napoleon's dictatorship, but in the Soviet Union it would lead to a genuinely proletarian regime, which the Kronstadt Revolt, despite its failure, had given Martov reason to believe might emerge sooner than he had originally anticipated. And once the proletariat took power, it would complete the bourgeois revolution the Bolsheviks had interrupted, and sometime later com-mence the construction of socialism.

According to Martov, now that Thermidor was a reality in the Soviet Union, its rulers, quite conveniently, would lose power no matter what they did. Should they abrogate the NEP and begin the massive projects of social and economic engin-eering considered essential to the establishment of socialism, insurrections like the Kronstadt Revolt would be commonplace, and the Bolsheviks would be compelled

---

[11] R. Abramovich, 'Martov i problemy russkogo bol'shevizma', *Sotsialisticheski vestnik*, no. 8–9 (24 April 1923): pp. 10–11.

[12] Iu. O. Martov, 'Na puti k likvidatsii', *Sotsialisticheskii vestnik*, no. 18 (15 October 1921): pp. 2–4.

to inflict terror the way the Jacobins did. But terror would not save the Bolsheviks any more than it did the Jacobins. The Bolsheviks would still be vulnerable to Thermidor, just as the Jacobins were; if it came about in the Soviet Union, it would lead to a military dictatorship, just like it did in France in 1799. But instead of this dictatorship being followed by the restoration of a retrograde class, as happened in France in 1815, the proletariat would eventually overthrow it, and in the end, all would be well.

In short, Martov was convinced that by eliminating the NEP, the Bolsheviks would lose power. But should the Bolsheviks do the opposite and continue the NEP, the result would be no different. An economy partly capitalist and partly socialist was inherently unstable, and whoever oversaw it would eventually have to choose one sector over the other. But before this happened, the prematurity of the October Revolution would weaken the Bolsheviks sufficiently for the proletariat to take power. Of course Martov in 1921 had no way of knowing that the Bolsheviks would do away with the NEP some years later, after Martov's death. But their doing so would not have altered the conclusion he had reached in 1921 that Bolshevism was doomed; like the Jacobins, they had taken power too early. In the French Revolution, the bourgeoisie, with the advent of Thermidor, regained in 1794 the power it lost in 1792, while in the still ongoing Russian Revolution, according to Martov, the bourgeoisie would at some point in the future regain the power it lost in October 1917, barely seven months after wresting it from the monarchy, which, for over a century, had been the political instrument of the landed nobility. But its prospective victory in Russia would be a pyrrhic one because the proletariat would soon take power itself.[13]

Another Menshevik, David Dallin, described Thermidor more as a political and psychological phenomenon than as a reflection of class relations. To him it entailed an absence of any interest in politics. To Dallin this resulted from a growing disenchantment with the Promethean imperative of achieving utopia

---

[13] Ibid., pp. 3–4. Of course Martov's overly schematic comparison ignored all sorts of complicating factors. The Jacobins were no more monolithic, tactically and ideologically, than the Bolsheviks. There were Left Jacobins and Right Jacobins in France, just the way there emerged a Left Opposition and a Right Opposition in the Soviet Union in the 1920s; within both dictatorships there were significant differences and serious debates over the direction the respective revolutions should take. Also, Martov failed to take into account the possibility that Thermidor in France, instead of following the Jacobin dictatorship, was prefigured in the economic policies the Jacobins followed after eliminating their own version of the Left Opposition in the spring of 1794, namely the Hébertists and the more radically inclined of the sans-culottes. In fact Soviet historians would argue strenuously in the 1920s, when debates and disagreement with the party's preferred opinions were still allowed, over whether it was actually the Jacobins, instead of the Directory and the political forces that established it, who introduced the policies generally subsumed under the rubric of Thermidor. Finally, Martov never indicated in any of his writings if he considered Thermidor, in purely economic terms, an actual counter-revolution or a form of 'backsliding' that left the basic accomplishments of the French Revolution intact. That he wrote of 'thermidorianization' suggests that he thought the whole issue meaningless, inasmuch as Thermidor could stand for a whole spectrum of policies from 'reactionary' to 'counter-revolutionary'.

either within a regime that valued property rights, as was the case in the French Revolution, or on behalf of a political system bent on eliminating private property entirely, as the Soviets, notwithstanding the NEP, intended. That in France Thermidor was carried out by erstwhile supporters of the Jacobin dictatorship it replaced—an assertion with which historians of the French Revolution might disagree—was particularly significant inasmuch as the Soviet Thermidor might emerge in a similar fashion, namely from within the Soviet leadership rather than in the aftermath of a revolution in which the Soviet Union itself was overthrown.[14] On this last point, other Mensheviks, including Fëdor Dan, agreed with Dallin. Significantly, they identified the so-called Right Opposition, headed by Bukharin and Rykov, that deemed it prudent economically to continue the NEP, as the unwitting instruments of the Soviet Thermidor, which these Mensheviks believed would entail the 'economic NEP' that already existed causing a 'political NEP' to emerge, in which the Right Opposition would rule the Soviet Union—but not for the purpose of achieving communism. Bukharin and Rykov and whoever else joined them in this new ruling elite would install in the Soviet Union something like the original Thermidor in France, and in that way vindicate the Mensheviks' decision not to support the October Revolution on the grounds of its prematurity. Moreover, agitating for a counter-revolution in this particular scenario would be unnecessary. All the Mensehviks had to do to ensure that the Soviet system collapsed was to wait.[15] Of course the Mensheviks' support was the last thing Bukharin and the Right Opposition wanted or needed, and indeed unscrupulous supporters-turned-enemies such as Stalin were fully capable of using it to defame them.

The Mensheviks always had trouble understanding Stalin. Prior to his embark-ing in 1928 on policies that, in purely economic terms, rendered any notion of a Soviet Thermidor ridiculous, several had concluded that the ongoing terror for which Stalin was partly responsible was not actually a means for achieving a counterrevolution.[16] Pëtr Garvi argued in 1927 that the NEP had already caused

[14] D. Dallin, 'O termidore', *Sotsialisticheskii vestnik*, no. 165 (1 December 1927): pp. 3–10; and D. Dallin, 'NEP i anti-NEP', *Sotsialisticheskii vestnik*, no. 5(195) (8 March 1929): pp. 2–3. Dallin planned to write more on the themes of these articles in a book he started that was tentatively titled *The Russian Thermidor and the Degeneration of Communism*, but he never finished it. André Lieblich, *From the Other Shore: Russian Social Democracy after 1921* (Cambridge MA, 1999), p. 377. Ironically, the scenario Dallin sketched out in these articles of how a facsimile of the original Thermidor would emerge in the Soviet Union was strikingly similar to the argument a number of Soviet historians were making simultaneously that by imposing Thermidorian policies before Thermidor actually began, the Jacobins were blurring the distinction between their own rule and that which followed it. In this view, the events of 9 Thermidor served merely to accelerate the course of events in the revolution, rather than reversing them.

[15] Lieblich, *From the Other Shore*, pp. 147–8.

[16] See, for example, the editorial in *Sotsialisticheskii vestnik*, no. 154 (20 June 1927): pp. 1–2, entitled 'Ko vsem sotsial-demokraticheskim rabochim Sovetskogo soiuza'. Dallin was particularly averse to the notion that Stalin was not the Thermidorian he seemed to be, but rather the very opposite, and the transformational policies Stalin announced in the winter of 1928–9 must have come as a considerable shock. Dallin, 'NEP i anti-NEP', *passim*.

an 'economic Thermidor' in the Soviet Union, and that if it continued, it could easily generate a 'political Thermidor' leading inexorably not to socialism but to capitalism.[17] In fact, the recent defeat of the Left Opposition, which to Garvi was the only counterweight within the Soviet Communist Party to the forces that were driving it rightward to Thermidor, suggested that the process might already be underway, impelled as it was by the Right Opposition—which then included Stalin. But Garvi implied that should the Right Opposition be defeated, Stalin would likely emerge as its undisputed successor.[18] Garvi, like most Mensheviks, misunderstood Stalin; in that respect he was like Trotsky. But unlike Trotsky, he did not underestimate him.

Because the Mensheviks never quite acknowledged Stalin's credentials as a genuine revolutionary committed to communism, they persisted in believing throughout his rule that the Soviet Union was on the verge of Thermidor or had already succumbed to it. In 1945, Boris Nikolaevskii, undoubtedly impressed by Stalin's adoption during the Second World War of more moderate policies designed to convince the Soviet people that Soviet rule was preferable to rule by the Nazis, argued that Thermidor was an inevitable and universal result of revolutions that occurs when the generation that made the revolution is succeeded by one that is sceptical of many aspects of it, and therefore seeks to freeze existing class relationships on the basis of the new, but now familiar and accepted economic system. As a result, the fulfillment of any earlier, still unkept promises is no longer possible, as is any chance of the revolution regaining its original energy and radicalizing its programmatic objectives beyond what those who made the revolution intended.[19] In March 1956, undoubtedly influenced by Khrushchev's heartfelt but incomplete denunciation of Stalin at the Twentieth Party Congress one month earlier, Oreste Rosenfeld wrote that, in the Soviet Union 'Thermidor is in full swing'.[20] Not long afterwards, Lydia Dan, whose Menshevism, like that of her husband, had been watered down to the point where it was practically indistinguishable from a kind of Leninism, decried the de-Stalinization that Rosenfeld celebrated, and expressed her fear that Khrushchev's descent into Thermidorian reaction might lead to the dissolution of the collective farms, along with the other defining institutions of the Soviet system.[21]

---

[17] P. Garvi, 'Pod znakom termidora', *Sotsialisticheskii vestnik*, no 159–60 (22 September 1927): p. 6.

[18] Ibid., p. 5. The so-called Left Opposition, when it emerged in 1923, consisted mostly of supporters of Trotsky, who was the object of attacks from Zinoviev and Kamenev, his one-time allies against Stalin. In the spring of 1926, however, the latter joined forces with Trotsky's to form what is sometimes called the Joint Opposition or the United Opposition.

[19] B. Nikolaevskii, 'Termidor' russkoi revoliutsii', *Sotsialisticheskii vestnik*, no 15–16 (573–4) (6 September 1945): pp. 171–5.

[20] Quoted in Liebich, *From the Other Shore*, p. 286.

[21] Ibid., p. 285. Though not himself a Menshevik, nor even Russian, Milovan Djilas, in his influential analysis of Soviet Communism, *The New Class*, claimed that the bureaucrats and party functionaries still ruling the Soviet Union had been installed during what he called 'the Soviet Thermidor', the

Although Dan did not say so explicitly, the ultimate outcome of her scenario of the Soviet Union's ideological degeneration was the Soviet Union's collapse, followed by a Russian equivalent of the Bourbon Restoration in France. Unlike the French originals, however, these Russian Bourbons would hold onto power, rather than lose it in a Russian version of the 1830 Revolution in France.

* * *

Predictions of a Soviet Thermidor were just about the last thing the Bolsheviks wanted to hear once the NEP, which seemed uncannily to resemble it, was implemented.[22] In 1927 Garvi wrote correctly that the Bolsheviks were as much annoyed by his ability, in emigration, to write openly about Thermidor as they were by his application of the term to the Soviet Union.[23] For this reason the term was never mentioned publicly or in the Soviet press until 1925. But the Bolsheviks, as mentioned, had access to *émigré* publications, and their familiarity with the French Revolution made comparisons, mostly sotto voce, inevitable. Trotsky even admitted that, during the Kronstadt Revolt and the first years of the NEP, he had had 'more than a few' conversations with Lenin about Thermidor and its possible relevance.[24] He also acknowledged in his autobiography, written many years after the fact, that the analogies liberals and Mensheviks drew in emigration, which at the time he had derided as 'superficial' and 'unsubstantiated', were not so ridiculous that he and other Bolsheviks did not draw similar analogies themselves, albeit privately.[25] Lenin, of course, was well-versed in the history of the French Revolution, and the resemblance between its Thermidorian phase and the NEP was not lost on him. Nor, for that matter, was he oblivious to the possibility of the Soviet Union experiencing something analogous to Thermidor without its leadership being overthrown; in the spring of 1921 he spoke almost flippantly about it while preparing a report to the Tenth Party Conference on the tax in kind he intended to propose.[26] Along with noting the difficulties of governing peasants reluctant to part with their produce, Lenin made a point in the report itself that even though

responsibility for which he assigned primarily to Stalin. Milovan Djilas, *The New Class* (San Diego CA, 1983), p. 51.

[22] According to Michel Vovelle, in '1789–1917: The Game of Analogies', p. 369, Lenin coined the term 'autothermidorization' in 1921 to signify the process whereby revolutionary regimes reverted to conventional ones. I have been unable to find any instance of Lenin using the term in his *Polnoe sobranie sochinenii*—though he could have done so in ordinary conversation. In any event, no other leading Bolshevik, to the best of my knowledge, used the term or attempted to define it.
[23] P. Garvi, 'Ot sud'by ne uidesh', *Sotsialisticheskie vestnik*,no. 161 (7 October 1927): p. 5.
[24] *Arkhiv Trotskogo. Kommunisticheskaia oppozitsiia v SSSR, 1923–1927* (Moscow, 1990), vol. IV, p. 14.
[25] In 1927, in the course of vouching, disingenuously, for Trotsky's loyalty to the Soviet Union and his commitment to communism, Bukharin referred specifically to Trotsky's statement denigrating these analogies. N. I. Bukharin, 'Doklad na sobranii aktiva Leningradskoi organizatsii VKP(b) (26 October 1927)', in N. I. Bukharin, *V zashchitiu proletarskoi diktatury: sbornik* (Moscow, 1928), p. 234.
[26] V. I. Lenin, 'Materialy k X vserossiiskoi konferentsii: plany doklada o prodovol'stvennom naloge', in Lenin, *PSS*, vol. XLIII, p. 403.

the Civil War was over, the Soviet state still had to do something about the 'bureaucratic distortions' from which many of its leading institutions suffered.[27] In other words, the Soviet leader was all too cognizant that the symptoms of a Soviet Thermidor—corruption, careerism, and what would soon be referred to as 'bureaucratism'—already existed. By the early 1920s 'careerists' with no particular commitment to Marxist ideology had joined the party in such numbers that the Old Bolsheviks, who remembered the October Revolution fondly while ignoring the failures and fratricidal conflict that preceded it, were suddenly a small minority; Stalin's ability to articulate the resentment of this new generation of communists for the Old Bolsheviks—the intellectual snobbery and the condescension many of them showed Stalin himself caused him to feel the same resentment acutely—was a significant factor in his rise to power. But when the party referred formally, in a resolution at the Eleventh Party Congress in 1922, to the specific failings they believed conducive to a Soviet Thermidor, the term itself was conspicuous in its absence. The most Lenin was willing to acknowledge was that the red tape and corruption he knew was rampant were indicative of bourgeois decadence and degeneration. The Soviet leader also shelved plans he had for responding publicly to Ustrialov, probably because doing so would have required him to explain at length why the latter's application of the term to the Soviet Union was unwarranted.[28] In that event, refuting the charge of Thermidor would likely have had the paradoxical effect of giving it greater credibility.

The course of action Lenin wanted the Bolsheviks to follow was to eliminate the attributes of Soviet politics and society that might cause Thermidor to occur—or might be plausible evidence that Thermidor was occurring already—without ever using the term publicly. But by the mid-1920s, after Lenin's death, the symptoms of Thermidor were so obvious, and the temptation to use the term as a political expletive so enticing, that this strategy proved untenable. The whole issue of a Soviet Thermidor soon became a defining one: from what a Soviet leader thought about it could be inferred his opinions on a variety of other issues. The first Bolshevik of any prominence to raise the issue publicly was Pëtr Zalutskii, a supporter of Zinoviev, at the Fourteenth Party Congress in 1925.[29] Significantly, he used the term to signify a species of counter-revolution, in which a onetime revolutionary government established an economic system much like the one it had previously abolished. The effect of this was to make the charge that the

---

[27] V. I. Lenin, 'Zakliuchitel'noe slovo po dokladu o prodovol'stvennom naloge (27 May 1921)', ibid., p. 327.

[28] Kondratieva, Bol'sheviki-iakobintsy, pp. 89–91.

[29] Zalutskii was a worker but also an autodidact, which may explain his knowledge of French history. Deutscher, Prophet Unarmed, p. 244. His having once been an SR, and then a supporter of Zinoviev, was sufficient reason for him to perish in the Terror. But raising the spectre of Thermidor, possibly at the instigation of Zinoviev, as Tomskii claimed shortly afterwards, certainly did not improve his chances of survival. Kondratieva, Bol'sheviki-iakobintsy, p. 223, n. 72; XIV s"ezd vsesoiuznoi kommunisticheskoi partii (b). 18–31 dekabria 1925 g.: stenograficheskii otchet (Moscow, 1926), p. 281.

Soviet Thermidor existed, or might soon exist, even more explosive than if he had used the term instead as a synonym for a mere 'reaction'.[30] Reversing a counter-revolution was of course more difficult than reversing a mere reaction to a revolution. For that reason, accusing someone of advocating the former was a more serious charge than accusing someone of the latter, but either could be deemed grounds for public condemnation, expulsion from the party, imprisonment, or even worse. The wisest thing a Bolshevik concerned for his career could do, under the circumstances, was to make certain the word 'Thermidor' never passed his lips.

But the Bolsheviks, if nothing else, were loquacious, and very often excessively so; that Stalin could hold his tongue better than his rivals played a role in his eventual success. Moreover, once the struggle to succeed Lenin began after the Soviet leader had suffered the first of what would be a series of strokes in May 1922, the temptation to stigmatize one's rivals as advocates of a Soviet Thermidor was irresistible, and now that Zalutskii had lanced the proverbial boil, the debate about its existence in the Soviet Union would rage virtually until the struggle for power itself ended in 1929 with Stalin triumphant.

* * *

There was one Soviet leader in whom the term generated intrinsic interest, and in whose opinion historical analogies generally, and those involving the French Revolution specifically, deserved dispassionate analysis. This was Leon Trotsky, who analysed the analogy with Thermidor at considerable length beginning in the mid-1920s. Of course Trotsky always claimed his analysis was based entirely on empirical evidence and was impervious to political considerations. But as his political fortunes declined, politics increasingly influenced his conclusions. It was politics, rather than any self-contained reconsideration of the French Revolution, that eventually caused him, in 1935, to redefine the term itself to enhance its utility in diatribes against his political enemies. Despite the polemical sleights-of-hand this required, the evolution of Trotsky's view of Thermidor deserves attention.

Notwithstanding a single mention of the term in 1903, in which Thermidor was cited in explaining the gap in the French Revolution between the Jacobins and Napoleon, Trotsky wrote almost nothing about its possible applicability to the Soviet Union before Zalutskii raised the issue in 1925.[31] Over the next two years, as Zalutskii's original speculation was the pretext for attacks aimed at Zinoviev and others, such as Kamenev, who were aligned with him, Trotsky was not among those who responded critically. The reason for this was that Trotsky's concept of Thermidor was similar to Zalutskii's. But any sympathy he may have felt for Zalutskii was not sufficient to cause him to come to Zalutskii's defence. Instead, he remained silent. Perhaps Trotsky thought responding to these attacks was

---

[30] *XIV s"ezd*, p. 358.   [31] Trotsky, *Vtoroi s"ezd RSDRP*, p. 30.

beneath his dignity. Perhaps he also still took seriously his earlier admonition that historical analogies were no substitute for historical analysis. He might even have refrained, albeit temporarily, from raising the analogy because he thought his doing so would dishearten the international proletariat even more than he believed it already was because of capitalism's survival in Western and Central Europe even after a socialist revolution in Russia. However one defined the original Thermidor, whether as a form of counter-revolution or merely as a reactionary phase within a revolution that would resume its course once the phase ended, the fact remained that applying the term to the Soviet Union implied that something had gone very wrong, that the October Revolution had stalled, or perhaps even reversed itself, and that the proletariat's hold over the political institutions of the state was, at the very least, precarious.[32] Whatever the reason or reasons for Trotsky's silence, by 1927 they no longer mattered. Trotsky lustily joined the debate. The reason he gave for his reversal was his recent discovery that one can and should seek analogies with and learn from the past—a lesson he repeated two years later, when he wrote grandiloquently that 'not [resorting] to analogies with the revolutions of past epochs [is] simply to reject the historical experience of mankind'.[33]

Having sanctioned in principle the investigation of historical analogies, Trotsky now examined the specific validity of the Thermidorian one. His verdict was that the analogy was inappropriate because the original Thermidor was a genuine counter-revolution, changing not only class relations, but the political arrangements that arose from them. Even under the NEP, by contrast, the Soviet Union remained a proletarian state both politically and, for the most part, economically. Thermidor was certainly a danger, and the fact that the Soviet Union had developed a large and increasingly autonomous bureaucracy unaccountable to anyone made possible—if not yet likely—a system comparable to that which existed in France from 1794 to 1799.

What Trotsky did, in effect, was to accept the definition of Thermidor Ustrialov and the Mensheviks had offered while rejecting their conclusion, shared by the German Communists, Ruth Fischer and Arkadi Maslow, that the Soviet Thermidor, as a species of counter-revolution, already existed.[34] Yes, Trotsky admitted, economic deprivation, cultural backwardness, and the failure of proletarian revolutions in Western Europe had made the Soviet Union susceptible to what he and others concerned about a Soviet Thermidor often called 'bureaucratism'.

[32] Tamara Kondratieva implies that this last consideration was what caused Trotsky to speak of 'Thermidorian tendencies' in the Soviet Union rather than of Thermidor actually existing in the country. *Bol'sheviki-iakobintsy*, p. 187. While this was surely one reason for Trotsky's choice of words, there were other, even more pressing ones.

[33] Leon Trotsky, 'Thermidor (Summer 1927)', in Trotsky, *CLO* (1926–7), p. 263; Leon Trotsky, 'A Letter to the Italian Left Communists (25 September 1929)', in *WLT* (1929), p. 322.

[34] Isaac Deutscher, *The Prophet Outcast: Trotsky 1929–1940* (London, 1963), pp. 53–4.

This particular phenomenon directly threatened the Soviet Union's legitimacy as a socialist and proletarian entity. Unchecked, it would result in the bureaucracy controlling the means of the production, making decisions on its own instead of implementing those of the party. But Trotsky and his supporters did not draw from this unpleasant prospect the pessimistic conclusion it suggested. Instead they offered a convenient extenuation: because a bureaucracy could not own property, much less pass it on generationally, it was not a class, and so even if it did somehow take power, the means of production would remain in the hands of the proletariat.[35]

But the proletariat in the Soviet Union could no longer count on all the factions within the Communist Party to represent it. The forces for Thermidor that Trotsky thought emanated from the kulaks and institutions such as the army and the diplomatic corps were assisted by elements within the party that, whatever their 'subjective' intentions, were by their actions making a Soviet Thermidor 'objectively' more likely.[36] Trotsky's vivid metaphor for this was of a Thermidorian dragon whose tail (by which he meant the openly counter-revolutionary forces outside the party) was wagging a head (i.e. the Communist Party) that had lost control over its body.[37] On some occasions in the mid-1920s when Trotsky addressed the issue of Thermidor, he included Stalin and his supporters among the forces within the party unconsciously promoting counter-revolution.[38] On other occasions, however, he described the Stalinist faction as 'a centrist' body, positioned precariously between the Bukharinists on the right and his own supporters (or what remained of them) on the left, while occasionally oscillating between them on the various questions that arose to bedevil the party as it grappled with problems it never anticipated.[39] Whatever the configuration of forces in the Soviet Union that were either oblivious to, or actually abetting the emergence of a Soviet Thermidor, for Trotsky the threat it posed to everything he had worked to achieve in the Soviet Union was real:

> To deny the danger of bourgeois restoration for the dictatorship of the proletariat in a backward society under capitalist encirclement is inconceivable. Only a

[35] Trotsky, 'Theses on Revolution and Counter-Revolution (26 November 1926)', in *CLO* (1980), pp. 169–72; Trotsky, 'Thermidor', in *CLO* (1926–7), pp. 258–63.

[36] Leon Trotsky, 'The Fear of Our Platform (23 October 1927)', in *CLO* (1926–7), pp. 446–7; Leon Trotsky, 'The Danger of Bonapartism and the Opposition's Rule (21 October 1928)', in *CLO* (1928–9) (New York, 1981), p. 275; Leon Trotsky, 'Where is the Soviet Republic Going? (25 February 1929)', in *WLT* (1929), p. 46; Leon Trotsky, 'To the Bulgarian Comrades (4 October 1930)', in *WLT* (1930–1) (New York, 1973), p. 45.

[37] Leon Trotsky, 'Declaration to the Sixth Comintern Congress (12 July 1928)', in *CLO* (1928–9), pp. 139–42; Leon Trotsky, 'Defence of the Soviet Republic and the Opposition (7 September 1929)', in *WLT* (1929), p. 280.

[38] Leon Trotsky, 'Reply to an Ultimatum (16 December 1928)', in *CLO* (1928–9), p. 362; Leon Trotsky, 'The Bolshevik Opportunists Need Help (1 June1929)', in *WLT* (1929), p. 150.

[39] Leon Trotsky, 'At a New Stage (December 1927)', in *CLO* (1926–7), pp. 489–90; Leon Trotsky, 'The Sino-Soviet Conflict and the Opposition (4 August 1929)', in *WLT* (1929), p. 216.

Menshevik or a genuine capitulator who understands neither the international nor the internal resources of our revolution could speak of the *inevitability* of a Thermidor. But only a bureaucrat, a windbag, or a braggart could deny the *possibility* of Thermidor.[40]

Moreover, the consequences of a Soviet Thermidor would be extremely serious:

Thermidor . . . does not signify a period of reaction in general, i.e. a period of ebb, of downsliding, or a weakening of revolutionary positions. Thermidor has a much more precise meaning. It indicates the direct transfer of power into the hands of a different class, after which the revolutionary class cannot regain power except through an armed uprising. The latter requires, in turn, a new revolutionary situation, the inception of which depends upon a whole complex of domestic and international causes.[41]

How, then, could a Soviet Thermidor become a reality? Here, too, Trotsky seemed unable to make up his mind. Sometimes he speculated that Thermidor could occur incrementally, in stages, or, in Trotsky's words, 'on the instalment plan', with the *kulaks*, the bourgeoisie, and their objective allies within the party and the bureaucracy gradually reducing the protectors of the proletariat, Trotsky and his allies, to political impotence'.[42] At that point, the Soviet Union would cease to be a workers' state, and the Thermidorian counter-revolution would be complete. But on other occasions Trotsky insisted that Thermidor could emerge only as the result of civil war, which meant that as long as a civil war did not occur in Russia, Trotsky could continue to argue that Thermidor had not yet occurred.[43] Finally, Trotsky argued at times that Thermidor could be ushered in by a coup of the army, with Voroshilov or Budenny as the eventual Bonapartist dictator.[44] Only at the very end of the 1920s, when Stalin's power, which Trotsky had consistently underestimated, could no longer be minimized, did Trotsky come to see his Georgian rival as the most likely candidate for the Soviet Bonaparte.[45] Indeed, as Stalin's power continued to grow in the early 1930s, despite the turmoil caused by industrialization and collectivization, Trotsky speculated that the Thermidorian and Bonapartist stages of counter-revolution might be merged, or, the

---

[40] Trotsky, 'Thermidor', in *CLO* (1926–7), p. 260.

[41] Trotsky, 'Defence of the Soviet Republic and the Opposition', in *WLT* (1929), p. 279.

[42] Trotsky, 'Thermidor', 263; Leon Trotsky, 'The July Plenum and the Right Danger (22 July 1928)', in *CLO* (1928–9), p. 175; Leon Trotsky, 'Speech at the Joint Plenary Session of the CC and the Central Control Commission (1 August 1927)', *Stalin School of Falsification*, p. 172.

[43] Trotsky, 'At a New Stage', in *CLO* (1926–7), p. 489.

[44] Trotsky, 'The Danger of Bonapartism and the Opposition's Rule', in *CLO* (1928–9), p. 275.

[45] Leon Trotsky, 'What is the Immediate Aim of Exiling Trotsky (4 March 1929)?' in *WLT* (1929), p. 61; Leon Trotsky, 'Communists and the Bourgeois Press (March 1929)', in *WLT* (1929), p. 96; Leon Trotsky, 'Jacob Blumkin Shot by the Stalinists (4 January 1930)', in *WLT* (1930) (New York, 1975), p. 25.

alternative, that the Thermidorian stage might be skipped entirely, largely because the forces Trotsky thought were supporting Stalin in Russia were considerably more powerful than those that had supported Napoleon in France.[46]

About all of this several observations are appropriate. First, Trotsky's concern, which at times came close to being an obsession, that the Soviet Union might experience its own Thermidor, changed the way he viewed the Jacobins. Before Thermidor became an issue, Trotsky had not only lauded the Jacobins for their willingness to overcome any moral scruples about killing people, which were now just outdated remnants of an earlier age, and to apply as much force and coercion as they deemed necessary to achieve their objectives. He also identified with the Jacobins, considering himself a 'neo-Jacobin' whose efforts to assist the proletariat were comparable to those of the original Jacobins to assist the *sans-culottes* and the other lower-class elements in France who took control of the French Revolution after the bourgeoisie, out of cowardice and an absence of will, had relinquished it. By the late 1920s, however, Trotsky was no longer the valorous conquistador who had subdued the Provisional Government, the Whites, the SRs, the Kronstadt Rebels, the Mensheviks, and all the other duplicitous and malevolent enemies of progress, social justice, and individual emancipation. Instead, he was a defeated, or nearly defeated oppositionist, who after 1927 was no longer in European Russia, where all the important political and economic decisions were made, and after 1928 no longer in Russia at all, but rather a stateless exile without the wherewithal to avenge the enemies in the Kremlin who had emasculated him politically. As a result, the Jacobins, in his own mind, changed from winners to losers, from victors to victims. And their defeat was as much a personal insult to Trotsky, because it so closely resembled his own defeat, as it was a setback for all that was progressive and hopeful in France after feudalism and the *ancien régime* had been destroyed. By sending Robespierre and his confederates to the guillotine, the Thermidorians eliminated from the earth 'the most revolutionary force of their time'.[47] And because Trotsky himself had been brought down by forces within the Communist Party who only pretended to be genuine communists, he could not help but depict the Thermidorians in France as Jacobins who, prior to 9 Thermidor, had pretended to share their noble vision. The result was what he called a second chapter in the history of the Jacobins, one that emitted an odour so foul that it 'assail[ed] one's nostrils'.[48] In the testimony he gave in a quasi-trial the party prescribed in 1927 to provide a legal basis for his expulsion from the party and for the additional

---

[46] Leon Trotsky, 'On the Question of Thermidor and Bonapartism (November 1930)', in *WLT* (1930–1), p. 71; Leon Trotsky, 'Thermidor and Bonapartism (26 November 1930)', in *WLT* (1930–1), p. 76.

[47] Trotsky, 'Speech at the Joint Plenary Session of the CC and the Central Control Commission (1 August 1927)', *Stalin School of Falsification*, p. 145.

[48] Ibid., p. 146.

punishments it inflicted in 1928 and 1929, Trotsky described the depredations the ersatz Jacobins had inflicted on the genuine Jacobins as follows:

> The party regime stifles everyone who struggles against Thermidor. In the party the mass worker, the man of the mass, has been stifled. The rank and file is silent. Recall the history of the Jacobin Clubs.... A regime of terror was instituted; for silence was made compulsory; 100% votes and abstention from all criticism were made compulsory; thinking in accordance with orders from above were made obligatory; men were compelled to stop thinking that the party is a living, independent organism, and not a self-sufficient machine of power.... The Jacobin Clubs, the crucibles of revolution, became the nurseries of future functionaries of Napoleon. We should learn from the French Revolution. But is it really necessary to repeat it?[49]

Second, it must be said that if Trotsky's views on the French Revolution clouded his political judgement, the requirement that he absolve himself (and, by implication, Lenin and the October Revolution) of any responsibility for the current predicament of the Soviet Union surely hampered his understanding of the French Revolution. For one thing, one might question his holding the Jacobins, or a goodly number of them, responsible for Thermidor. For another, he romanticized the Jacobins who resisted Thermidor as martyrs despite their having sent literally hundreds of innocent Frenchmen to their deaths. But the most convincing evidence that his understanding of the French Revolution left something to be desired was his notion that the original Thermidor constituted a genuine counter-revolution. The evidence that it was not is considerable. Thermidor did little to disturb the agrarian property settlement of the revolution, and it left intact enough of what the National Assembly, the Legislative Assembly, the Convention, and the Committee of Public Safety had accomplished, such as the substitution of departments for provinces, the adoption of the decimal system, and the creation of France as a republic, so that Napoleon could essentially complete the revolution by his codification of French civil law and other reforms.[50] In sum, Trotsky was wrong. The counter-revolution he believed France to have experienced in the late 1790s did not begin until the last years of Napoleon's rule and the return of the Bourbon monarchy in 1815. Permitting history to limit one's political choices while allowing the requirements of politics to distort one's reading of history was probably not what Trotsky had in mind when he said that one should analyse historical events and learn from them.

---

[49] Ibid., p. 146.

[50] Denis Woronoff, *The Thermidorean Regime and the Directory 1794–1799* (New York, 1984), pp. 192–5. To some historians of the French Revolution, the Directory, when considered as the political expression of the phase of the revolution commonly considered Thermidorian, was characterized by a non-ideological moderation—neither royalist nor revolutionary—that was the ultimate cause of its downfall. See, for example, Palmer, *Age of Democratic Revolution*, vol. II, 212–19.

Third, and last, Trotsky's acknowledging the threat of a Soviet Thermidor while rejecting the reality of it seems another instance of his optimism tempering his powers of analysis. The Soviet Union, he never tired of insisting even after his own political demise in the mid-1920s, remained a workers' state, and even as Trotsky became alarmed by Stalin's accumulation of power in the early 1930s, he was not entirely displeased by the way Stalin used his power to transform Soviet industry and agriculture.[51] Of course it is difficult to understand, as Robert McNeal has pointed out, how a regime as ossified by bureaucracy as Trotsky said the Soviet Union was in the mid-1920s could have embarked on policies as politically risky, indeed as Promethean, as those that Stalin chose to pursue a few years later.[52] Equally preposterous, given Trotsky's powerlessness in exile, is Isaac Deutscher's explanation that Stalin collectivized Soviet agriculture because of pressure from Trotsky.[53] But the most relevant point in this respect is that Trotsky's analysis of Thermidor reinforced his belief that, in the end, all would be well, the proletarian revolution and Trotsky's reputation intact. However real was the danger that the Soviet bureaucracy might come to own the means of production as well as controlling it, and thereby nullifying the October Revolution, Trotsky could still look to the French Thermidor and proclaim—as he had in the case of the Jacobins—that for all the similarities he discerned between the two revolutions, Russia's would never be analogous to France's. The bourgeois revolution in France was stopped on 9 Thermidor and did not resume (in Trotsky's Marxist scheme of things) until well into the next century. But the proletarian revolution in Russia, while threatened by Thermidorian counter-revolution, would survive it, and continue constructing socialism. Trotsky's analysis of Thermidor was an example of bad history producing shortsighted policies, but at least it proved psychologically comforting.

In contrast to Trotsky, Stalin did not look to the French Revolution for psychological solace. In evaluating his comments on the Soviet Thermidor, one must bear in mind that by the late 1920s he had the wherewithal, as the nearly undisputed leader of the Soviet Union and the successor to Lenin, to prevent it, and given his ideological objectives, good reason for doing so. The reversion to an economic system that previously existed—which was precisely what Thermidor entailed wherever and whenever it came about—was the antithesis of the radical transformation of the Soviet economy and society he believed his extraordinarily ambitious policies would bring about. Of course there were some in the party who wanted the NEP, at least for the foreseeable future, to continue. Bukharin, with his

[51] Trotsky, 'Thermidor and Bonapartism', in *WLT* (1930–1), p. 73.

[52] Robert McNeal, 'Trotsky's Interpretation of Stalin', *Canadian Slavonic Papers*, no. 5 (1961): p. 95. See also his 'Trotskyist Interpretations of Stalinism', in *Stalinism: Essays in Historical Interpretation*, edited by Robert C. Tucker (New York, 1977), pp. 30–52. I draw on McNeal's shrewd analysis in my own explication of Trotsky's views on Thermidor and on the French Revolution itself.

[53] Deutscher, *Prophet Unarmed*, p. 466.

call for peasants to 'enrich themselves', was the most ardent and eloquent proponent of this opinion. To Trotsky and other in the Left Opposition, however, continuing the NEP, irrespective of its benefits economically, was dangerous politically. However limited it was, the economic freedom the NEP permitted might engender demands for political freedom, which to a regime like the Soviet, which came to power in what was essentially an urban insurrection lacking majoritarian political support, could easily lead to a counter-revolution reversing everything the Bolsheviks had accomplished.

Stalin, however, had no such concerns. His intention to collectivize Soviet agriculture and to resume the rapid industrialization the First World War and the October Revolution had interrupted precluded any possibility of a Soviet Thermidor. Of course there were political advantages to pretending that the threat it posed was real. Anyone who raised the issue could be attacked because its implications were so injurious of the Bolsheviks' pride and sense of accomplishment— not to mention how completely the economic retrenchment and regression a Soviet Thermidor implied contradicted the transformational imperatives inherent in Bolshevism and Soviet communism. But about its becoming a reality in the Soviet Union, Stalin believed there was no reason to be concerned.

The tactic he adopted rhetorically and for exclusively political purposes was to claim that merely raising the possibility of Thermidor increased the likelihood of its occurrence, and that anyone who did so was an enemy of the Soviet Union who should be dealt with severely. In December 1925, after Zalutskii stated the concerns shared by many others within the party that the danger of a Soviet Thermidor was real, Stalin responded that the whole notion was preposterous— and then made clear that the real threat to the party and the country was from Trotsky and the Left Opposition.[54] In December 1926, an editorial in *Pravda*—for the publication of which Stalin's approval was now required—excoriated Trotsky and the Opposition for their 'fetid and insipid lies about Thermidor', which blinded many in the party, even committed Bolsheviks and communists, to the very real threat posed by genuine counter-revolutionaries, the most dangerous of whom, in the considered opinion of the editors, were Trotsky and his closest confederates.[55]

In other words, it was not Thermidor, but those who deliberately conjured it for the purpose of destroying the Soviet Union, with whom honest communists, according to Stalin, should be concerned. In September 1927, after dismissing 'the foolish and ignorant charges about degeneration and *termidoriastvo* which the oppositionists sometimes level against the party', he declared that he would not deal with them 'because they are not worth analysing'—and then ended his polemic by replicating his earlier syllogism that to warn against a Soviet

---

[54] J. V. Stalin, 'K istorii raznoglasii', in Stalin, *Sochineniia*, vol. VII, p. 385.
[55] 'Za T. Zinov'evym—T. Trotskii', *Pravda*, no. 286(3515) (10 December 1926): p. 2.

Thermidor was reveal oneself as a supporter of it, and that to support a Soviet Thermidor was to reveal oneself as an enemy of the Soviet Union.[56] The Trotskyist opposition, he said, '[was] a hotbed and nursery of degeneration and Thermidorian tendencies'.[57] In October 1927 he declared all talk of Thermidor 'twaddle', and two months later, at the Fifteenth Party Congress, in the course of responding to his own, obviously rhetorical question of whether the Soviet Union was currently a proletariat dictatorship—which according to the stenographic account of the congress produced laughter among the assembled delegates—he repeated his earlier charge that raising the danger of Thermidor was tantamount to advocating its arrival. He formulated his argument as follows:

> The opposition says that we are in a state of Thermidorian degeneration. What does this mean? It means that we do not have a dictatorship of the proletariat, that both the economy and our politics have collapsed and are going backwards, that we are advancing not towards socialism, but towards capitalism. This, of course, is strange and foolish. But the opposition insists on it..... Clearly there is nothing Leninist in this 'line'....It is Menshevism of the purest sort. The opposition is slipping into Menshevism.[58]

In June 1930, in a report to the Central Committee at the Sixteenth Party Congress, Stalin finally acknowledged the depth of the danger a Soviet Thermidor would pose to both the party and the state. But he now defined Thermidor differently. No longer just a reactionary phase in a revolution that the revolution would probably survive, it was now a species of counter-revolution that would be difficult, or perhaps even impossible, to reverse. But he quickly reassured his audience that presently there was no cause for alarm. Thanks to his own vigilance and that of the police—or so Stalin implied—the danger was now safely in the past. 'Trotskyism', he reported, has collapsed. And the Soviet Union, far from having degenerated into Thermidor, was continuing its long march to socialism.[59]

Stalin's objections to the very possibility of a Soviet Thermidor were obviously self-serving and politically motivated. But there seems to have been an additional consideration. To establish his credentials to lead a country that was still demographically Russian, albeit with large numbers of non-Russians of whom Stalin, being Georgian, was obviously one, he had to proclaim publicly that Russia was *sui generis*—that its history, culture, political institutions, and everything else that constituted its collective identity owed nothing to the rest of the world. This meant

---

[56] J. V. Stalin, 'Politicheskaia fizionomiia russkoi oppositsii', in Stalin, *Sochineniia*, vol. X, pp. 165–6.
[57] Ibid., p. 166.
[58] J. V. Stalin, 'Trotskistskaia oppozitsiia prezhde i teper', ibid., p. 202; J. V. Stalin, 'Partiia i oppozitsiia', ibid., p. 342.
[59] J. V. Stalin, 'Voprosy rukovodstva sotsialisticheskim stroitel'stvom', in Stalin, *Sochineniia*, vol. XII, pp. 343–4.

that drawing analogies between anything Russian and anything non-Russian was improper; in the 1930s Soviet historians would be shot for doing so. Accordingly, in *The Foundations of Leninism*, the first work of his that was written and published after Lenin's death, Stalin proclaimed the self-sufficiency of the October Revolution.[60] It owed nothing to the bourgeois revolutions in Western Europe that preceded it—the English, the French, the German, and the Austrian. Stalin was quick to explain how Russia's revolution was unique—because 'the bourgeois revolution [had] unfolded in Russia under more advanced conditions of class struggle than in the West'—but he said nothing about why it was unique.[61] This did not mean he had no opinion. He did. It was that the Russian proletariat—and thus also the Russian peasants from the ranks of whom the proletariat emerged— was instinctively more class-conscious and radical politically than its counterparts in supposedly more advanced countries in Western Europe.[62] While Stalin's opinion was driven by the conviction that expressing it would redound to his political advantage, it also seems the genuine sentiment of a Georgian seeking satisfaction in a country, that, for all its current government's claims to respect the autonomy of its ethnic minorities, in essence remained Russian, and would continue to be Russian even after socialism and communism had been achieved. According to Stalin, analogies with the French Revolution, indeed analogies with anything neither Soviet nor Russian—no matter how illuminating or politically useful in providing moral and ideological legitimacy—could not be tolerated, much less incorporated into party orthodoxy, for to do so was to undermine the centrality of the Soviet Union in history's inexorable advance to socialism and communism. In October 1927, in the same speech in which he dismissed all talk of Thermidor as 'twaddle', he enlarged his critique to include the French Revolution as a whole. No matter what aspect of it one might analogize to the October Revolution, the very act of doing so was evidence of disloyalty, even treason, and for that reason—and also because any such analogies were factually inaccurate— should be avoided entirely.[63] 'Historical analogies with the French Revolution', Stalin warned, 'have been and continue to be the main argument of all the various Mensheviks and *smenovekhovtsy* against the preservation of the proletarian dictatorship and the possibility of building socialism in our country'.[64]

As it happened, Stalin's dictum on the inadmissibility of historical analogies allowed for exceptions. In November 1927, in an article in *Pravda* marking the tenth anniversary of the October Revolution, he began by stating that the revolution differed 'in principle' from earlier revolutions in England, France, and Germany; the progressive nature of their objectives, and the heroism they

---

[60] J. V. Stalin, *The Foundations of Leninism* (New York, 1932), *passim*.   [61] Ibid., p. 62.
[62] Ibid., especially pp. 58–72.   [63] Stalin, 'Trotskistskaia oppozitsiia prezhde i teper', pp. 201–2.
[64] Ibid., p. 201.

demanded of their protagonists, Stalin readily acknowledged.[65] But the long-term effects of these non-Russian revolutions were limited. All they did was substitute one class of exploiters for another. The October Revolution was different. The Bolsheviks who carried it out successfully promised that that would never happen again, at least not in Russia, and the record of the Soviet Union in the decade that followed showed that their promise had been kept. Nevertheless, there was one respect in which the French Revolution and the October Revolution were analogous: they each produced cadres of committed revolutionaries, the Jacobins and the Bolsheviks respectively, capable of generating legitimate fear among their enemies.[66] As a result, neither faced the degree of resistance from abroad that might have led to military defeat, and as a result they both had the opportunity—which in the Soviet Union has continued to the present day—to perform inestimable services for their respective revolutions. Stalin expressed this idea in the following way:

> History is repeating itself, though on a new basis. Just as before, during the period of the downfall of feudalism, the word 'Jacobin' evoked terror and loathing among the aristocrats of all countries, so, too, now, in the period of the downfall of capitalism, the word 'Bolshevik' evokes terror and loathing among the bourgeoisie in all countries. And just as Paris, earlier, was the refuge and the school for the revolutionary representatives of the rising bourgeoisie, so, too, is Moscow now the refuge and the school for the revolutionary representatives of the rising proletariat.[67]

The other exception Stalin allowed to the general principle of eschewing analogies concerned the respective agencies of repression in revolutionary France and Soviet Russia:

> The GPU, or Cheka, is the punitive organ of the Soviet state. It is an organ more or less analogous to the Committee of Public Safety, which was created during the Great French Revolution. It punishes primarily spies, conspirators, terrorists, bandits, profiteers, and counterfeiters. It is something in the nature of a military-political tribunal established for the purpose of protecting the interests of the revolution from the counterrevolutionary bourgeoisie and their agents.[68]

What these particular exceptions suggested was that when it came to political power—acquiring it, holding onto it, and applying it on behalf of ideological objectives that were transformational—Stalin would not be bound by any of the

---

[65] J. V. Stalin, 'Mezhdunarodnyi kharakter Oktiabr'skoi revoliutsii', ibid., pp. 239–40.

[66] Ibid., pp. 240, 247.

[67] Ibid., p. 247. Also in 1927, Stalin reproached the Kuomintang in China, warning them that if they did not learn to act like Jacobins, and demonstrate a willingness to use violence and coercion, they would never take power. K. McDermott and J. Agnew, *The Comintern: A History of International Communism from Lenin to Stalin* (New York, 1999), p. 177.

[68] Stalin, 'Beseda s pervoi amerikanskoi rabochei delegatsiei', in Stalin, *Sochineniia*, vol. X, p. 234.

strictures or limitations he had previous expostulated. And just as he justified policies that sacrificed the interests of international communism to those of the Soviet Union on the grounds that these two sets of interests were actually identical, so, too, did he eliminate in his own mind the apparent contradiction between a maxim on the inadmissibility of historical analogies and the exceptions to it he not only acknowledged but proudly affirmed.

* * *

As Trotsky and Stalin were propounding their very different views on using analogies to clarify the Soviet Union's development, the debate within the party over the specific issue of the Soviet Thermidor quickly became primarily a political one. Under the circumstances, it is hard to see how this could have been otherwise. The French Revolution and the analogies to its Thermidorian phase were an integral aspect both of the struggle to succeed Lenin in the mid-1920s and of the simultaneous debate on the NEP, which irrespective of its positive effect on the Soviet economy was never meant to be anything more than a temporary expedient. Politically, ideologically, and even (or perhaps especially) psychologically, it was, in the final analysis, incompatible with Bolshevism. The policies that virtually all of the Bolsheviks believed would follow it, namely rapid industrialization and the collectivization of agriculture, were intended to eliminate any remnants of the capitalism the NEP allowed, and would satisfy the Promethean imperative in Bolshevism, of which the NEP, with its moderation and economic backsliding, was the antithesis. What is often forgotten in accounts of this so-called Second Revolution is that it was intended to preclude a Soviet Thermidor. But until these transformational policies could be initiated, a Thermidorian reaction in the Soviet Union was a real possibility, and for that reason the political benefits of raising the issue remained. Smearing those within the party who warned of a Soviet Thermidor as its advocates was too tempting for many Bolsheviks not to do so. And so, in the late 1920s, the debate within the party continued.

Further emboldening Bolsheviks to use the issue for political purposes was the publication, in 1925, of a new collection of Ustrialov's essays, to which the Bolsheviks had access and with which many of them were soon familiar. In these essays Ustrialov reiterated his earlier arguments that the Soviet Union was approaching the equivalent of Thermidor and that it was a very good thing that it was.[69] The reaction of the Bolsheviks to this was predictable. Zinoviev was the first to respond. Writing in *Pravda* in September 1925, he freely acknowledged Ustrialov's claims that the Soviet Union was experiencing 'degeneration'.[70] But he also rejected the conclusion Ustrialov drew that the Soviet system was suffering

---

[69] Ustrialov, 'Put' termidora,' pp. 41–7.
[70] G. Zinoviev, 'Filosofiia epokhi. K s"ezdu partii', *Pravda*, no. 214(3145) (19 September 1925): pp. 2–3, and *Pravda*, no. 215(3146) (20 September 1925): pp. 2–3.

from problems so severe and intractable that it would likely disintegrate at some point in the foreseeable future. With his customary bravado, Zinoviev reassured his readers, seemingly ad nauseum for Bolsheviks who had heard such reassurances many times before, that, notwithstanding Ustrialov's prediction, everything would be fine in the end. The NEP, which Zinoviev acknowledged might have eventuated in a genuine counter-revolution, in which the Bolsheviks would either lose power or preside over a complete regression to capitalism, would soon be abolished, its positive effect on the Soviet economy exhausted, and replaced by policies conducive to socialism. Thus anyone who argued, or even merely suggested, that the NEP should be permanent—here Zinoviev clearly had Bukharin and the Right Opposition in mind—was guilty not only of opposing Lenin, whom Zinoviev reminded his readers had originated the NEP, but of supporting Ustrialov, an émigré and an implacable enemy of Bolshevism.[71] Two months later, Bukharin replied to Zinoviev. In *Pravda* he quite deliberately confused Zinoviev's description of the Soviet Union for his prescription for the Soviet Union; by acknowledging the reality of the NEP, Zinoviev was actually indicating his preference for it. Bukharin then went on to argue, disingenuously, that the bureaucratism Zinoviev had decried as a form of degeneration that, if not attended to, could lead to Thermidor was proof that he now believed the Soviet Thermidor already existed.[72]

The public exchange between the two men, each claiming to be Lenin's rightful successor, was just one of many in the weeks preceding the Fourteenth Party Congress. So often was it alleged that the Soviet Union was approaching its Thermidor, and that those who spoke of it actually welcomed it, that by the time the Party Congress convened in December, *termidor* and *termindoriantsy* had entered the Russian language; in fact *termidorianstvo* had practically become a formal deviation from ideological orthodoxy.[73] Further raising the rhetorical heat in debates about these terms was the fact that their provenance was traceable to enemies of the Soviet Union like Ustrialov and the Mensheviks. To claim that Thermidor was approaching was therefore to call, in effect, for the destruction of the Soviet Union. But it was Zalutskii's invocation of a Soviet Thermidor that was ultimately responsible for the issue assuming an importance sufficient to warrant the party as a whole rendering a formal judgement of it. That he chose the Fourteenth Party Congress as his venue—rather than an article in *Pravda* that many Bolsheviks might not read, and to which they could only respond directly in letters to the editors, or days later in an article of their own—suggests that that was precisely his objective, and possibly also that of Zinoviev, his political sponsor and

[71] Ibid.

[72] N. I. Bukharin, 'Tsezarizm pod maskoi revoliutsii', *Pravda*, no. 259(3190) (13 November 1925): pp. 2–4, and *Pravda*, no. 261(3192) 15 (November 1925): pp. 2–3.

[73] A. M. Selishchev, *Iazyk revoliutsionnoi epokhy: iz nabliudenii nad russkim iazykom (1917–1926)* (Moscow, 2003), p. 17.

protector. If that was in fact the case, Zalutskii miscalculated badly. Raising the issue publicly served only to underscore its gravity. The attacks that followed his remarks were strident, impassioned, and *ad hominem*. In purely political terms, it made no sense even to raise the possibility of a Soviet Thermidor. It was too easy for political enemies to confuse analysis for advocacy, and in that way malign honest communists as traitors. Bukharin, whose artistic and literary sensibilities have been lauded as evidence of his humanism, and considered evidence that, had he taken power instead of Stalin, he would have avoided the worst excrescences of Stalinism, in 1926 spoke bluntly of 'the bottomless stupidity of the analogy [with Thermidor]'.[74]

Zalutskii's comments on the Soviet Thermidor were not the result of any epiphany at the party congress itself. Nor were his comments hastily conceived. Prior to the party congress he had written a pamphlet in which he laid out his arguments carefully. His thesis was that given certain realities in the Soviet Union, it could conceivably end up a new species of 'state capitalism', which he said was indistinguishable from 'Thermidorian degeneration'.[75] While not yet a reality either in the Soviet Union or in the Communist Party, a Soviet Thermidor might emerge in the future because some in the party, perhaps unintentionally and with the best of intentions, were advocating policies conducive to it. But in the event this occurred, an expanding stratum of state bureaucrats, rather than the Communist Party itself, would be responsible for it. At the party congress, Zalutskii under-scored the urgency of the problem about which he had written earlier, and with considerable passion implored the delegates to address it. 'The Thermidorian route of the development of the Great French Revolution', he said, 'must be for us the object of our attention', and steps should be taken immediately to prevent it.[76] One of these, in his opinion, was avoiding calls like Bukharin's for the peasantry to enrich itself. Zalutskii did not cite Bukharin by name, but anyone conversant in Soviet politics could easily have figured out whom he was referring to. Like Zinoviev, Zalutskii believed the principal threat to Leninism was Bukharin, whose political skills he then considered superior to those of the plainspoken and seemingly ideologically illiterate Georgian who in the end would triumph over, and subsequently liquidate, all of his rivals. But Zalutskii added that objective factors, too, such as the continued growth of the *kulaks*, made the emergence of a Soviet Thermidor more likely, and perhaps also imminent.[77]

To Zalutskii, the threat of a Soviet Thermidor was real, and its chances of actually occurring were increased by unnamed party leaders who 'glossed

---

[74] N. I. Bukharin, 'Na poroge desiatogo goda', *Pravda.*, no. 258 (7 November 1926): p. 2.

[75] Robert Vincent Daniels, *The Conscience of the Revolution: Communist Opposition in Soviet Russia* (New York, 1960), p. 255. In fact, Zalutskii's analogy could not be valid because Thermidor in France occurred when capitalism was just beginning—in contrast to full-blown capitalism, of which 'state capitalism' is a derivative or a descendant.

[76] *XIV s"ezd vsesoiuznoi kommunisticheskoi partii (b)*, p. 358.   [77] Ibid.

over' issues instead of dealing with them substantively; the result could be 'a petit-bourgeois state'.[78] Even with the qualifications Zalutskii included in his presentiments of the future, which he clearly intended as a warning rather than a simple prediction, much less a prediction he would be pleased to see realized, his comments touched a nerve among the assembled delegates. Just to speculate that the Soviet Union might become the kind of regime Trotsky in 1917 had consigned to 'the dust-bin of history' was to call into question everything the delegates had fought for throughout their political lives. To conjoin the term 'petit-bourgeois' with predictions of the Soviet Union's future was to play with political and ideological dynamite, and the fact that Zalutskii had used the term as a synonym for Thermidor—which the Bolsheviks believed was what ended the French Revolution prematurely and led inexorably to a restoration of the *ancien régime* in 1815—made it even more of a pejorative and political expletive than it would otherwise have been. It now hardly seemed to matter that the French Thermidor and any Soviet one would have to be different: while Thermidor in France returned the haute-bourgeoisie to power, its Soviet incarnation would bring the petit-bourgeoisie to power; presumably qa less affluent strata of the bourgeoisie could be more easily neutralized by a post-Thermidorian Soviet regime than an affluent one. But in moments of high drama—of which Zalutskii's speech certainly qualified as an example—fine ideological and semantic distinctions lose their salience. Intentionally or not, Zal;utskii was questioning the very legitimacy of the October Revolution and the Soviet state, and persons in the party whose loyalty one might think were irreproachable found themselves accused either of considering a Soviet Thermidor possible, or of actually advocating it, or even of having taken concrete steps to ensure its arrival. Before the Fourteenth Party Congress convened, even Felix Dzerzhinskii, who had ordered the execution of thousands and fully deserved the sobriquet 'Iron Felix', had been forced to admit, in a letter to Stalin, to joining a conspiracy with Zinoviev and Kamenev that, by splitting the party, might lead to Thermidor.[79]

The result, for Zalutskii and Zinoviev, was just what one would have expected. They were subjected to rhetorical fusillades the ferocity of which revealed simultaneously how threatened the Bolsheviks were by any mention of Thermidor, but also the political opportunities that merely mentioning it provided. As far as the other leading Bolsheviks were concerned, Zalutskii and Zinoviev might just as well have had targets on their foreheads. Mikhail Tomskii, who at the time controlled Soviet trade unions and was also a supporter of Bukharin, praised Zalutskii for saying publicly what others were whispering privately.[80] But the speakers who

[78] Ibid.
[79] 'Pis'mo F. E. Dzerzhinskogo Stalinu i Orzhonikidze (5-6 October 1925)', in *Politicheskii dnevnik* (Amsterdam, 1970), pp. 238–41. Under pressure, the Soviet police chief disavowed any further involvement just prior to the Fourteenth Congress in December.
[80] *XIV s"ezd vsesoiuznoi kommunisticheskoi partii (b)*, p. 281.

followed him made clear that their intentions were not so benign. P. G. Petrovskii, the president of the Ukrainian Central Committee, stated flatly that by raising the issue of a Soviet Thermidor publicly, Zalutskii had betrayed the October Revolution.[81] Alexei Rykov, who had succeeded Lenin in 1924 as the formal head of the Soviet government, accused Zalutskii of creating 'an atmosphere of panic' at the party congress and in the Communist Party, and called for his expulsion from the Central Committee; because Rykov held Zinoviev ultimately responsible for Zalutskii's apostasy, he prescribed for Zalutskii's mentor and superior within the party the identical punishment—as did Lazar Kaganovich, who cited Zinoviev's article in *Pravda* as the source of the disputation currently roiling the party congress and the Communist Party.[82] Kliment Voroshilov limited his denunciation to calling Zalutskii's views 'criminal from the perspective of Communist unity'.[83] But a delegate from Tula, cited in the stenographic record of the congress simply as 'Kabakov', called the threat posed by Thermidor greater than earlier ones such as 'defeatism, liquidationism and *Aksel'rodshchina*'.[84] One of the reasons that was the case, according to Kabakov, was that the *smenovekhovtsy* and the followers of Miliukov were the first to raise the issue. Although the delegate from Tula did not indicate why the current danger exceeded the earlier ones he mentioned, his claim that the Thermidorian threat was now both domestic and foreign, personified by Zalutskii and others inside the Soviet Union as well as by persons and organizations outside of it, could be considered the reason for it.[85] That people opposed to the Soviet Union were accusing it of succumbing to Thermidor was proof that Thermidor in the Soviet Union existed.

This was also the gist of a letter composed by the party leadership in Moscow. It alleged that any analogy with the original Thermidor was suspect because the Mensheviks and Ustrialov had earlier raised it. Moreover, because Thermidor meant nothing less than a bourgeois restoration and the end of the whole Soviet experiment, punitive action of some sort was required against any and all party members who favoured it, predicted it, or simply warned against it. But these three deviations from party orthodoxy, in the considered opinion of the authors of the letter, were not equally dispositive of treason. Zalutskii's apostasy far exceeded that of the Trotskyites, who merely raised the possibility of a 'growing over' into Thermidor. Zalutskii, to his eternal shame, had gone further. By claiming a Soviet Thermidor likely, he had embraced a view so at odds with communist ideology that his capitulation rendered him one of a number of 'bourgeois ideologues' who were bent on the Soviet Union's demise.[86]

---

[81] Ibid., p. 169.   [82] Ibid., pp. 238, 414–15.   [83] Ibid., p. 393.
[84] Ibid., p. 358.   [85] Ibid., p. 358.
[86] 'Otvet MK-RKP (b)—na pis'mo leningradskoi partkonferentsii', in *Partiia i novaia oppozitsiia. Materialy k prorabotke resheniia i XIV s"ezda VKP (b)* (Leningrad, 1926), p. 201.

Chastened by the torrential invective he had to endure, Zalutskii recanted his views, and begged his colleagues' forgiveness in an article in *Leningradskaia Pravda* written even before the congress ended.[87] One could not be certain, from the article alone, what exactly Zalutskii now regretted having said, and in any event it did not prevent his expulsion from the Central Committee, nor Zinoviev's removal as chairman of the Leningrad Soviet.[88] But it was sufficient, at least for the immediate future, to preclude his expulsion, and Zinoviev's as well, from the Communist Party. In fact, the general consensus in the party, in the aftermath of the party congress, was that public discussion of Thermidor did more harm than good, and the only other formal action it took in connection with the entire matter was to establish a special commission, headed by Kuibyshev, to investigate it—which of course turned up no new information that would warrant additional action.[89] In the spring of 1926, after Zinoviev and Kamenev joined with Trotsky to form what would be called, pejoratively by their rivals, the Left Opposition, all three and their supporters refrained from invoking any analogy with the Thermidor in France, or any predictions or warnings about a Thermidor in the Soviet Union.

But debate continued sotto voce within the party, and in the fall of 1926, at the Fifteenth Party Conference, it became public once again, this time at the instigation of Bukharin. In the aforementioned article in *Pravda* that appeared shortly after the conference had convened, he pointedly quoted Goethe's maxim that only those who live through history were competent to discuss it.[90] At the conference itself, Bukharin condemned as 'unsubstantiated slander' the mere mention of a Soviet Thermidor; those raising the issue were violating 'the spirit and the letter and the very essence of Leninism'—a verbal assault for which Stalin praised Bukharin in terms from which the assembled delegates, had they possessed prophetic powers, would have immediately recoiled.[91] Bukharin, Stalin announced with genuine pleasure and admiration, 'does not argue with [his enemies]. He slaughters them.'[92] The conference marked the first time the party acknowledged formally that in its ranks were members claiming that the Soviet Union was already experiencing Thermidor, which in practical terms meant that making the claim was just as contrary to Leninism and Bolshevism as was Thermidor itself.[93] According to Bukharin, those using the term were up to no good. Their intention was to shock rather than to inform, and by doing so demonstrated not only a lack of loyalty to the party and to communism but a lack

---

[87] *XIV s"ezd vsesoiuznoi kommunisticheskoi partii (b)*, p. 230; *Novaia oppozitsiia: sbornik materialov o diskussii 1925 goda* (Leningrad, 1926), p. 45.

[88] Leonard Schapiro, *The Communist Party of the Soviet Union* (New York, 1971), p. 300; Daniels, *Conscience of the Revolution*, p. 271.

[89] Kondratieva, *Bol'sheviki-iakobintsy*, p. 111.

[90] Bukharin, 'Na poroge desiatogo goda', p. 2.   [91] Ibid.

[92] *XV konferentsiia vsesoiuznoi kommunisticheskoi partii (b). 26 oktiabria–3 noiabria 1926 g.: stenograficheskii otchet* (Moscow, 1927), pp. 600–1.

[93] Kondratieva, *Bol'sheviki-iakobintsy*, p. 128.

of intelligence itself. But for all of this, Bukharin, speaking not only for himself but also for the party as a whole, professed himself not terribly concerned for the future. 'We will go forward and achieve victory irrespective of the prediction of Thermidor, in spite of it and against it!'[94] According to the stenographic account of the conference, his comments were followed by the highest compliment the party censors, in describing the reaction of the audience, could pay a speaker, namely that his comments was followed by 'fervent, prolonged applause culminating in an ovation'.[95]

At the Seventh Plenum of the Communist International, meeting in Moscow in late November and early December, 1926, Bukharin resumed his assault. 'Historical analogies', he cautioned once again, 'must be used extremely carefully', and for that reason, he said, he could not imagine anything more ignorant and contrary to Marxism than applying the notion of 'Thermidorian degeneration' to the Soviet Union.[96] He reminded his audience that Thermidor in the French Revolution was far from peaceful; in fact it was 'an open act of counterrevolution' carried out by the Girondin bourgeoisie and supported by errant Jacobins against the Robespierre's dictatorship, which, as a dictatorship of the petit-bourgeoisie, was destined, in any event, to collapse.[97] Only an embryonic proletariat existed in France in the late eighteenth century, and understandably had no sense of itself as an independent and self-willed entity capable of acting in its own interests, which Bukharin said consisted of protecting the petit-bourgeoisie (i.e. the Jacobins even after they had rid themselves of the Hébertists and *les enragés*) from the haute-bourgeoisie (i.e. the Thermidorians).[98] At another session of the plenum, Bukharin elaborated on his earlier analysis as follows:

> Thermidor was victorious [in the French Revolution] because it had to be victorious, because in the era of the Great French Revolution the haute-capitalist bourgeoisie was stronger than the petit-bourgeoisie, which was represented politically by the Jacobin dictatorship. And the Jacobin dictatorship fell because the proletariat was not strong enough to sustain it, much less to act on its own behalf, and to thus play an independent role in the revolution.... It is absolutely absurd to say that the economically illiterate [within the party] should raise the whole issue of Thermidor. Even an elementary familiarity with the French Revolution and our own history is sufficient to see that raising this issue is ridiculous and that doing so is to engage in simplification and smacks of vulgarity and absurdity.[99]

---

[94] *XV konferentsiia vsesoiuznoi kommunisticheskoi partii (b)*, p. 604.   [95] Ibid.

[96] 'Doklad tov. Bukharina', *Puti mirovoi revoliutsii. Sed'moi rasshirennyi plenum ispolnitel'nogo Komiteta Kommunisticheskogo internationala, 22 noiabria–16 dekabria 1926: stenograficheskii otchet* (Moscow, 1927), vol. I, p. 80.

[97] Ibid., p. 81.   [98] Ibid., p. 81.

[99] 'Preniia po dokladu t. Stalina', *Puti mirovoi revoliutsii*, vol. II, pp. 118–19. Bukharin repeated his argument in print, adding only that by raising the analogy the Oppositionists had 'broken ranks' with

At the same plenum, Stalin, even more than Bukharin, eschewed arguments based on history in favour of *ad hominem* invective. The rhetorical device he used was a familiar one: Oppositionists who invoked the analogy were assisting enemies of the Soviet Union, while Oppositionists who considered it valid but refrained from invoking it were cowards and hypocrites.[100] Foreign communists at the plenum argued much the way Stalin did. The French Communist Jacques Doriot accused the Opposition of avoiding the whole issue of Thermidor—but then proclaimed himself prepared to flagellate the Opposition should it raise the same issue in the future.[101] Palmiro Togliatti, who would soon become the leader of the Italian Communist Party, chided the Oppositionists for losing their 'revolutionary faith', the most obvious proof of which was their 'confusion' in their consideration of the analogy.[102] Ernst Thälmann, the leader of the German Communist Party, called Thermidorianism a form of defeatism and capitalism, and at the end of the plenum supported a resolution that was passed overwhelmingly stating that raising the analogy with Thermidor advanced the interests of 'the enemies of the proletariat and renegades from communism'.[103]

Clearly the Soviet leadership and the Opposition reached diametrically opposite conclusions on the political utility of raising the possibility of a Soviet Thermidor. Stalin and Bukharin saw how easily the term could be used to stigmatize their opponents, while the latter, finally realizing how easily using the term analytically could be misconstrued as evidence of supporting it, decided to use the term as little as possible. The fury with which they were attacked convinced Zinoviev and some of Trotsky's supporters—though not Trotsky himself, who remained fascinated by historical analogies and used them to impress other Bolsheviks with his erudition—to use euphemisms for Thermidor, such as 'bureaucratism'; others claimed that their whole notion of Thermidor had been misconstrued as identical to that of Ustrialov and his supporters, the danger from which they termed, pejoratively, *ustrialovshchina* ('the work of the Ustrialovites'); still others downplayed the danger posed by any analogy to the original Thermidor or stopped mentioning it altogether. A variation on the strategy of distinguishing an acceptable examination of the Soviet Thermidor (e.g. Trotsky's) from an unacceptable one (e.g. Ustrialov's) was the statement of one of Trotsky's supporters, I. N. Stukov, who, when asked at the Fifteenth Party Congress in November 1927 if he was accusing the Central Committee of *termidorianstvo*, replied that

Marxist-Leninist orthodoxy. N. Bukharin, 'Vystuplenie na VII rasshirennom plenume IKKI', *Pravda*, no. 289 (14 December 1926): pp. 3–4.

---

[100] J. V. Stalin, 'Eshche raz o sotsial-demokraticheskom uklone v nashei partii', in Stalin, *Sochineniia*, vol. IX, pp. 48–51, 58.

[101] Quoted in Kondratieva, *Bol'sheviki-iakobintsy*, p. 134.

[102] Ibid., p. 134.   [103] Ibid., pp. 134–5.

the danger it posed was minimal because only persons outside the party, in the country at large or abroad, were discussing it.[104]

But such contrivances fooled no one, and they certainly did not deter Stalin and Bukharin and their supporters from assailing the Opposition with the same gusto and *joie de vivre* they had shown earlier. By 1927 the attacks had escalated to the point where calm and rational reconsideration of the issue, and of the loyalty (or lack of it) of those still raising it, was impossible. In two speeches in the beginning of August, Stalin again angrily denounced all talk of Thermidor. To speak of tendencies towards its realization in the party was 'foolish' and 'unserious'.[105] Presumably, with Trotsky, Zinoviev, and Kamenev now removed from their positions of leadership in the party and in the Soviet government, the danger to the Soviet Union the term implied had largely passed. But supporters of the three men were still causing the leadership trouble. In the same speech, Stalin even averred that the only way the Soviet Union could experience its own Thermidor was by renegade party members constantly talking about it. But even if they did so, they did not really believe a Soviet Thermidor had already come about or even that such a thing was likely; these ersatz communists therefore raised the issue only to strengthen the war they were still waging to destroy the Soviet state, though with less and less chance of success.[106] Confessing in the first of these speeches his inability to comprehend 'how there remains in our party people who say it has become Thermidorian', by the time he delivered the second one four days later his bewilderment had turned to contempt: the arguments supporting the charge were simply 'stupid'.[107] In fact, if those now levelling it would simply desist, the chance of Thermidor ever existing in the Soviet Union would be zero.

As for Bukharin, he preferred the public role of Thermidor's analyst, defining it as basically a synonym for a particular kind of 'bourgeois counterrevolution' that occurred in France and for which there was some support in the Soviet Union, though not, he reassured his readers, within the Communist Party, much less in the Central Committee'.[108] The historian Alexander Slepkov eschewed the scholarly analysis one might have expected of a member of his profession, and simply attacked the Opposition for their 'Menshevik theories about Thermidor', while Dmitrii Maretskii, another historian and supporter of Bukharin, made clear in *Pravda* that while the differences between the French and Russian Revolutions were too great for any analogy with the original Thermidor to withstand scrutiny, the accusation, by itself, was dangerous and required refutation, which Maretskii,

[104] *XV s"ezd. Vsesoiuznoi kommunisticheskoi partii (b). Stenograficheskii otchet* (Moscow, 1935), vol. I, p. 277.

[105] J. V. Stalin, 'Rech' 5 avgusta', in Stalin, *Sochineniia*, vol. X, p. 80.

[106] Ibid., p. 81; J. V. Stalin, 'Rech' 9 avgusta', ibid., pp. 85–91.

[107] Stalin, 'Rech' 5 avgusta', ibid., pp. 80–1; Stalin, 'Rech' 9 avgusta', ibid., p. 88.

[108] 'Doklad tv. Bukharina na sobranii partaktiva Leningradskoi organizatsii VKP (b) 9 avgusta 1927 goda', *Pravda*, no. 186 (18 August 1927): p. 3.

having already written on the subject, obligingly provided.[109] 'The historical Thermidor', he intoned in a pamphlet published in 1927, in no way resembled 'the sugary-vegetarian Ustrialovite-Oppositionist description'.[110] In fact, 'all analogies, from a Marxist point of view, [were] nonsensical, absurd, and illiterate'.[111]

By the time the Fifteenth Party Congress convened, the Trotskyites, with nothing more to lose, had gone back to talking openly of 'the Thermidorian danger' and of the need to eliminate it.[112] The 'Proposed Platform' the Opposition had made public prior to the congress spoke explicitly of *termidorianstvo* outside the party and condemned all those within the party, concentrated in its right wing, who, by mindlessly repeating Stalin's rhetoric, were unwittingly assisting in its realization. The platform also claimed that Lenin's clairvoyance on the issue somehow proved the validity of its arguments. Lenin, it claimed, had recognized the danger a Soviet Thermidor posed to the party long before anyone else did, and in the early 1920s had even identified the constituencies in the Soviet population most likely to support it—the *kulaks*, the NEP men, and 'careerists' within the party guilty of bureaucratism.[113] Karl Radek, ostensibly an Oppositionist and supporter of Trotsky, nonetheless equivocated when he had to choose between the platform's view of Thermidor, which was basically that it was now everywhere, and that of Stalin and Bukharin, which was that it existed only in the minds of party renegades and traitors. Thermidor existed, Radek acknowledged, but the Communist Party, while not uninfected by it, nonetheless included elements capable of fighting it.[114]

After the Congress convened, some Oppositionists tried to make amends. The Soviet Union, they admitted, remained a workers' state, and the threat of a Soviet Thermidor was negligible; in fact the term itself was a meaningless verbal construction, a conjunction of historical phenomena, namely Bolshevism and its reactionary or counterrevolutionary negation, that were incompatible. Thermidor had not arrived in the Soviet Union, and likely never would. But that was not enough to stop Stalin and Bukharin and their allies from hurling anathemas at anyone who opposed them on the issue. Stalin's response was to claim that even the Oppositionists who in 1917 had carried signs in Moscow and Leningrad and in

---

[109] A. Slepkov, *Oppozitsionnyi neomen'shevizm. O 'novoi platforme'*, (Moscow, 1927), pp. 29–30, quoted in Kondratieva, *Bol'sheviki-iakobintsy*, p. 137; D. Maretskii, 'Tak nazyvaemyi 'termidor' i opasnosti pererozhdeniia', *Pravda*, no. 166(3698) (24 July 1927): p. 3 and no. 170(3702) (29 July 1927), pp. 2–4.

[110] D. Maretskii, *Tak nazyvaemyi 'termidor'* (Moscow/Leningrad), 1927, p. 33.

[111] Ibid., p. 39.

[112] *Proekt platforma Bol'shevikov-Lenintsev k XV s"ezdu VKP (b), krizis partii i puti ego preodoleniia*, quoted in Kondratieva, *Bol'sheviki-iakobintsy*, pp. 120–1.

[113] Ibid., pp. 120–2.

[114] K. Radek, *Termidorianskaia opasnost' i oppozitsiia* (Moscow, 1927), cited in Kondratieva, *Bol'sheviki-iakobintsy*, p. 122. By 1929 Radek had changed his mind and now believed the Soviet Union was on the verge of Thermidor. The Central Committee, he said, resembled the Convention on the eve of 9 Thermidor. Deutscher, *Prophet Outcast*, p. 67.

other cities supporting socialism and the Bolsheviks could not be trusted; to any sentient person their defects of character were obvious. Even worse was that they still favoured what they were now denouncing; their current affirmations of political loyalty and ideological orthodoxy should, for that reason, be ignored. To this kind of character assassination the Oppositionists could only deny that they had any intention of harming the Soviet Union or of obstructing the construction of socialism, and that they yielded to no one in their hatred of the *ustrialovtsy*. But by this time Trotsky had been expelled from the Communist Party, and the only relevant measure of any argument about Thermidor, or about any other issue of concern, was whether those making the argument were either powerful or powerless. In reality, the Opposition had no means of escaping their earlier embrace of the analogy. Recantations like Zalutskii's had already been shown to be useless and, because they smacked so obviously of political calculation, were counterproductive.[115] But to accept the reality of the analogy, to acknowledge honestly that 'Thermidor has begun', was no less destructive of the Opposition, because the admission was tantamount to acknowledging that the Soviet Union no longer was a workers' state, and that their life's work might actually have been for nothing.

The Opposition, in short, had boxed itself in—although one is hard pressed to conjure a strategy that would have avoided the political cul-de-sac in which it now found itself. For Adolf Ioffe, a longtime supporter of Trotsky and the only oppositionist to state publicly that Thermidor had begun, the gravity of the predicament and that of the Soviet Union was reason to take his own life, which he did in November 1927.[116] By that time Stalin and Bukharin were determining party orthodoxy in all matters of history, not just those concerning the French Revolution, and Bukharin's subsequent demise made Stalin the only 'historian' in the Soviet Union whose opinions mattered. All that was left for the latter to do was to make certain that professional historians in the country understood this and altered their views accordingly.

* * *

The first indication that something was wrong, that the autonomy Soviet historians enjoyed was in jeopardy, came at the first Pan-Russian Conference of Marxist Historians, which met in Moscow from 28 December 1928 to 4 January 1929. Albert Mathiez was condemned for predating the original Thermidor from 9 Thermidor to the destruction of the Hébertists and *les enragés* in the last months of the Jacobin dictatorship, and for attacking the NEP as a contemporary equivalent; his prominence as a historian of the French Revolution, combined with his ideological and political apostasy, made necessary a concerted campaign

---

[115] *XIV s"ezd vsesoiuznoi kommunisticheskoi partii (b)*, p. 230.
[116] Mariia Ioffe, 'Nachalo', *Vremia i my*, no. 20 (1977): p. 178.

against him that even acquired its own name: *matezovshchina*.[117] This ended a longstanding debate among Russian historians about the nature, timing, evolution, and consequences of the original Thermidor in the French Revolution, and whether or not something similar to it was already emerging, or would soon do so, in the Soviet Union. This debate was just as vigorous as that within the party, but the degree to which opposing views were dealt with without the ad *hominem* vituperation manifested by the likes of Stalin and Bukharin is striking, and stands in stark contrast to the intellectual sterility that followed in the Stalin era itself.

Before 1929, as long as they did not attack Lenin or deny the legitimacy of the October Revolution, the freedom Soviet historians were granted was real. M. N. Pokrovskii, who had joined the party only after the October Revolution, and in the 1920s professed a position on Russian Jacobinism that the party found unacceptable, nonetheless remained Rector of the Institute of Red Professors, and retained a measure of intellectual independence.[118] Similarly, while French historians, in addition to Mathiez, such as Aulard and Jaurès, were criticized for emphasizing insufficiently the role of class and material interests in history, their writings were not forbidden, and the same was true for historians in the Soviet Union whose views deviated even more significantly from the tenets of Marxism-Leninism. The ambivalence with which the party viewed these French historians is epitomized in allowing new translations of their works—but only with introductions by Soviet historians criticizing them, sometimes severely.[119]

Nevertheless, in the 1920s a Party Line on the French Revolution existed, even when, for much of the decade, it was not enforced. The revolution as a whole was unmistakably bourgeois both in its original intentions and in its eventual effects. But it was carried out by the bourgeoisie, as a class, only until 1793, when the Girondins and other members of the haute-bourgeoisie concluded that their objectives of eliminating feudalism and abolishing the monarchy had been accomplished. At this point, elements of the petit-bourgeoisie, principally the Jacobins, emboldened by classes below them who found the status quo insufficiently protective of their interests, tried to radicalize the revolution beyond the limits France's historical development in the late eighteenth century would permit. The terror the Jacobins inflicted domestically and the defeats French armies inflicted on foreign armies intent on restoring the *ancien régime* in France enabled the revolution to continue. But the reprieve it enjoyed was short-lived, and the French Revolution ended on 9 Thermidor. This was essentially Lenin's view of

---

[117] Vovelle, '1789–1917: The Game of Analogies', pp. 363, 371–2, 377. The anathema pronounced on Mathiez did not last long. In 1930 he was made a foreign associate member of the Soviet Academy of Sciences.

[118] Enteen, 'Marxist Historians during the Cultural Revolution', pp. 155–6.

[119] N. I. Kareev, '"Frantsuzskaia revoliutsiia v marksistskoi istoriografii v Rossii". *Vstuplenie i publikatsiia D. A. Rostislavleva*', in *Frantsuzskii ezhegodnik: stat'i i materialy po istorii Frantsii 1989* (Moscow, 1989), pp. 203–4, 209.

the French Revolution, which had the inestimable political advantage of analo-gizing the French Revolution (in which the Jacobins and their allies did what the bourgeoisie as a whole refused to do) to the Russian Revolution (in which the Bolsheviks carried out the proletarian revolution that the Provisional Govern-ment, representing the bourgeoisie, was unable to do).

It was in differentiating subdivisions within the coalitions that formed in the course of the French Revolution that disagreements arose. The most divisive of these concerned the Jacobins. Soviet historians proposed two very different interpretations of who the Jacobins were and what they did. While some sharply distinguished their dictatorship from the Thermidorian reaction that followed it, others maintained that the Jacobins put in place or continued policies similar to those pursued under Thermidor; in some instances, according to proponents of the latter view, the Thermidorians simply continued what the Jacobins began. Often cited as proof of this was the Jacobins' refusal to abrogate the *Loi Le Chapelier*, promulgated in 1791, that forbade workers from forming guilds for the protection of their collective interests. The reason for this, in this interpret-ation, was that the Jacobins sought programmatically to benefit neither the petit-bourgeoisie, which was the class to which the Jacobins belonged, nor the urban and rural lower classes, whose leaders the Jacobins eventually sent to the guillo-tine. Rather, they advanced the interests of the haute-bourgeoisie, which led the revolution from 1789 to 1793, and would lead the reaction to it that would begin, seemingly very abruptly, on 9 Thermidor. But appearances were deceptive. On that day, only the political leadership changed. The more consequential changes were in the economy, and these, in fact, were quite gradual, beginning before 9 Thermidor and continuing long after it. This evolution was what prompted Soviet historians to speak of a 'growing over' from the Jacobins to Thermidor. Taken literally, this notion meant that the French Revolution ended twice: polit-ically (and abruptly) on 9 Thermidor, but economically (and gradually) over several months.

The most determined and consistent proponent of the orthodox position—that the French Revolution ended in every way, not just politically, on 9 Thermidor—was N. M. Lukin. Throughout the 1920s and for some years thereafter his opinion of the Jacobins remained what it had been in 1918, when he served as a surrogate for Lenin and Trotsky in condemning Martov's animadversions on the October Revolution. The Jacobins, he always argued, were petit-bourgeois, and once in power the majority of them served the economic interests of their class.[120] Lukin was not oblivious to the so-called Left Jacobins, who were sympathetic to the Hébertists and others claiming to represent the urban and rural lower classes;

---

[120] N. Lukin, 'Lenin i problema iakobinskoi diktatury', *Istorik marksist* 1 (1934): pp. 99–146, constitutes the most complete explication of Lukin's views on the Jacobins and on the French Revolution as a whole.

these Jacobins were actually hostile to capitalism, and profoundly sympathetic to the interests of the classes and categories of the population below them. In fact the latter were remarkably similar to those the Bolsheviks represented in 1917.[121] But the contradiction between the Jacobins' class and the opinions they espoused ensured their political defeat; those who survived the purge of the so-called Left Jacobins in the spring of 1794 lost the political leverage they had over 'centrist' Jacobins like Robespierre and Saint-Just. But in their class origin, which to Lukin was the ultimate determinant of the distribution of political power in the French Revolution, the Jacobins, despite their disagreements over policy, were all, and always, petit-bourgeois.[122]

Lukin was not the only Soviet historian to take this position. V. Kolokolin and S. Monosov, who had studied under Lukin, did so as well.[123] In their view, the difference between the Jacobins, who were petit-bourgeois, and the Bolsheviks, whom they insisted were the political instrument and vanguard of the proletariat, was so enormous that analogies between them, and between the French Revolution and the October Revolution, would necessarily be 'superficial', 'trite', and worst of all, 'unscientific'.[124] As for Thermidor, to Kolokolin and Monosov it was an integral part of the historical process in which capitalism replaced feudalism, but it was also a cul-de-sac, a temporary regression or reaction that only slightly delayed capitalism's inexorable development. The Jacobins were brought down, in the end, by divisions within their own ranks, which made them easy prey for the haute-bourgeoisie after both the Left and the Right within their party had been purged in the spring of 1794. The reaction that followed it was inescapable, and the distinctive term that was applied to it, and to it alone, captured its distinctiveness in the French Revolution. Indeed, Thermidor or something resembling it was possible only in a bourgeois revolution. And since the revolution in 1917 that established the Soviet Union was a proletarian revolution, a Soviet Thermidor was impossible.[125]

---

[121] Ibid., pp. 100–2. Lukin even went so far as to argue that it was peasant support for the plebeians in Paris and other cities that enabled the coalition they formed with elements of the petit-bourgeoisie to advance the revolution before the Jacobins took power as well as afterwards. But once the peasants acquired land, the wealthiest among them sided with counter-revolutionaries—a betrayal Lukin underscored by terming them *kulaks*. Ibid., pp. 109–12.

[122] Ibid., especially pp. 117–18, 125–7, 132–6. It may not have been a coincidence that the triangular internal division of the Jacobins into Left, Centre, and Right was seen to prefigure the tripartite division within the Soviet Communist Party during Stalin's rise to power into a distinguishable Left (which included Trotsky, Zinoviev, and Kamenev after the latter two had reconciled with the former in 1926), Centre (Stalin, for a time) and Right (Bukharin, Tomskii, and Rykov). Perhaps because the struggle for power in the Soviet Union lasted longer than the Jacobins remained in power in France, contenders like Stalin, as circumstances changed, altered their views for political advantage and moved from one of the three subdivisions to another.

[123] Kòndratieva, *Bol'sheviki-iakobintsy*, pp. 144–5.

[124] V. Kolokolkin and S. Monosov, *Chto takoe termidor?* (Moscow, 1928), quoted in ibid.

[125] Kondratieva, *Bol'sheviki-iakobintsy*, pp. 145–6. The same argument, of course, was useful politically to discredit everyone in the Soviet Union who warned of a Soviet Thermidor or claimed it already existed. The historian A. Zaitsev argued that Thermidor, which he defined as a restoration of

Other Soviet historians disagreed. While not contesting the axiom Lukin and others had affirmed (that the Jacobins were petit-bourgeois and thus different from the *sans-culottes* and the other 'proto-proletarians' who for a time supported them), they maintained that the Jacobins, once in power, adopted economic policies so similar to those adopted later during Thermidor that their subsequent downfall had little or no effect on France economically.

The most articulate proponent of this viewpoint was Ts. Fridliand. In 1926, he wrote, for example, that 'on all the basic questions of social and economic policy the Jacobins offered a distinct programme that was in the interests of the bour-geoisie'.[126] In 1927 he was more specific, writing that the Jacobins were pursuing policies supported by, and beneficial to the industrial and commercial bourgeoisie—from which he drew the conclusion that Thermidor was more a continuation than a reversal of what preceded it.[127] Although he used the term sparingly, Fridliand had no doubt there had been a 'growing over' both in the economic policies the Jacobins pursued and in the particular stratum of the bourgeoisie that benefitted from them. But there was a corollary to his argument, of which he seemed unaware, that robbed the Jacobins of the moral superiority nearly all Soviet historians, including Fridliand, customarily ascribed to them in relation to their adversaries. Since very little distinguished the Jacobins program-matically from the elements of the haute-bourgeoisie that later introduced Thermidor, and since the Girondins, before losing power to the Jacobins, had acted objectively in the interests of this same stratum of the bourgeoisie, there was really very little difference politically between the Jacobins and the Girondins (and between both of them and the Thermidorians), and certainly no reason, apart from personal ambition, for their struggle for power in May–June 1793 to have been so tumultuous. According to Marx—to whose theories of history Fridliand claimed to be totally faithful—class struggles were always more bitter, more protracted, and more energetically pursued than those motivated by personal pique or, in this particular instance, by ambition and a simple lust for power.[128]

the bourgeoisie to political power and economic dominance, could only be conceived of by persons who themselves were bourgeois. For that reason Trotsky, Zinoviev, and everyone else in the Soviet Union who were speaking about a Soviet Thermidor were members of the bourgeoisie. His argument was a variation on the fallacy of *cui bono*: since a Soviet Thermidor will benefit the bourgeoisie, those predicting it must be bourgeois themselves. A. Zaitsev, *Ob ustrialove, 'neonepe' i zhertvakh ustrialovsh-chiny* (Moscow/Leningrad, 1928), pp. 14–15, 37.

---

[126] Ts. Fridliand, 'Klassovaia bor'ba', p. 167.

[127] Ts. Fridliand, 'Perepiska Robesp'era', *Istorik marksist* 3 (1927): p. 89.

[128] In the article Fridliand also noted that 'nothing in the ideas of Jacques Roux [a leader of the *sans-culottes* and *les enragés*] was foreign to Jacobin ideology', and that, Kropotkin notwithstanding, neither Roux nor those he led were communists. Rather, they were Left Jacobins. Ibid., p. 195. This of course muddies Fridliand's argument considerably, to the point where the Jacobins, the Girondins, and the urban poor of Paris were ideologically indistinguishable.

Nevertheless, several prominent Soviet historians agreed with Fridliand's original argument. In 1927, N. P. Freiberg argued that *les enragés*, who desired a revolution more democratic in its objectives than that which the Jacobins had actually created, successfully forced the Jacobins, if not to transform their dictatorship into a democracy, at least to support policies they originally opposed. The most obvious example of this was the Maximum, which was antithetical to the laissez-faire economics Robespierre and most of the other Jacobins favoured.[129] What the Jacobins preferred—but which for a time they could not implement because of political pressure from the left—were policies that benefitted the bourgeoisie. In that sense, the Jacobins were proto-Thermidorians.[130] This view was shared by K. P. Dobroliubskii, who argued that Thermidor continued what the Jacobins began. Like Fridliand, Dobroliubskii claimed that the latter, once in power, advanced the interests of the haute-bourgeoisie.[131] For that reason 9 Thermidor merely 'realigned' the political arrangements in France so that they coincided once again with preexisting economic realities.[132] Ia. M. Zakher agreed with Dobroliubskii in that respect, but was even more precise in determining when the Jacobins abandoned the interests of their own class, the petit-bourgeoisie, and began to serve the interests of the haute-bourgeoisie. According to Zakher, this occurred after the elimination of both the Dantonists, who were to Robespierre's right politically, and the Hébertists, who were to his left. This gave *l'Incorruptible* the political freedom and security to lead what was now unabashedly and undeniably a petit-bourgeois government that served the interests of the haute-bourgeoisie. To the extent that that was the case, Thermidor was a continuation of what preceded it.[133] In agreement with Zakher, Dobroliubskii, and Freiberg was P. P. Shchegolev, who in 1927 noted simply that, by the summer of 1794, the Jacobins had moved decisively to the right, thereby betraying their lower-class supporters.[134]

This practice of predating Thermidor was first attacked, with the full imprimatur of the Communist Party, in the winter of 1928, at a meeting of the Society of

---

[129] Doyle, *History of the French Revolution*, p. 229; Stone, *Anatomy of Revolution Revisited*, p. 359; Palmer, *Twelve Who Ruled*, pp. 70, 311.

[130] N. P. Freiberg, 'Dekret 19 vandem'era i bor'ba beshenykh za konstitutsiiu 1793 goda', *Istorik marksist* 6 (1927): p. 144. At the same time, Freiberg cautioned that *les enragés*, while considerably to the left of the majority of the Jacobins (i.e. those to the right of the Hébertists), were not themselves proletarians or socialists, let alone communists. Rather, they were urban, petit-bourgeois artisans, like Babeuf and the Babouvists. Ibid., pp. 172–3.

[131] Kondratieva, *Bol'sheviki-iakobintsy*, p. 151.

[132] K. P. Dobroliubskii, 'Novaia ekonomicheskaia politika termidorianskogo reaktsii', in *Zapisky Odesskogo Institutu Narodnoi Osviti* (Odessa, 1927), vol. I, *passim*.

[133] Ia M. Zakher, *Deviatoe termidora* (Leningrad, 1926), p. 17.

[134] P. P. Shchegolev, 'K kharakteristike ekonomicheskoi politiki termidorianskoi reaktsii', *Istorik marksist* 4 (1927): pp. 75–6.

Marxist Historians in Moscow.[135] But afterwards, there were still dissenters, notably Shchegolev, who persisted in his apostasy, and it was not until the aforementioned First Pan-Russian Conference one year later that the party, now entirely Stalin's political instrument, made clear that no dissent on the whole matter of Thermidor would be tolerated. One wonders why it took so long for the party to act. One possible reason is that Lenin had embedded in party orthodoxy the judgement he first expressed in 1905 that Russian Social Democrats—by whom of course he meant the Bolsheviks—were 'the Jacobins of today'. Since then, the Bolsheviks had come to impute, almost reflexively, a purity of motive and a hardness of will to the Jacobins that, notwithstanding their ideological limitations as members of a retrograde class in comparison to the proletariat, immunized them against charges from within the ideological universe the Bolsheviks inhabited that otherwise would have brought down on them the full weight of the Bolsheviks' disapproval and contempt.[136] One such charge was the betrayal of allies, especially those to one's left. This, of course, was precisely what the Jacobins were accused of, however indirectly and implicitly, by Fridliand and the other Soviet historians who agreed with him.

For that reason, excuses had to be made. Zakher, who saw the proverbial handwriting on the wall before most others did, reversed himself in 1927, arguing now that, in light of evidence of which he had previously been unaware,

> the historical Thermidor was not part of an evolutionary—or more precisely, a counterrevolutionary—unfolding of history prepared by [most immediate] the events of the Great French Revolution that preceded it. The 'growing over' into Thermidor did not precede 9 Thermidor. Instead it followed it. It was not the cause of 9 Thermidor, but rather the result of it.[137]

To demonstrate his bona fides as a loyal Bolshevik and communist, Zakher cited Bukharin's opinion on Thermidor, which was that the Jacobins and the Thermidorians had nothing in common economically, and that that was why they were so easily distinguishable morally, politically, and ideologically. But he also claimed that the congruence between his views and Bukharin's was entirely coincidental, because he based his (new) conclusion solely on the historical record.[138]

In the very same way, and almost certainly out of an instinct for professional self-preservation, Fridliand, at the same meeting of the Society of Marxist Historians, followed suit. There, before a packed auditorium, he termed Thermidor 'a

---

[135] Kondratieva, *Bol'sheviki-iakobintsy*, p. 153.

[136] Lenin, *Shag vpered, dva shaga nazad*, p. 370.

[137] Ia. M. Zakher, 'Problema 'termidora' v svete noveishikh istoricheskikh rabot', *Istorik marksist* 6 (1927): p. 242.

[138] Ibid., p. 239. To solidify his credentials Zakher also excoriated Mathiez for still subscribing to the thesis of 'growing over' despite its having been thoroughly discredited. Ibid., pp. 237–41.

transformational event' in the French Revolution, when one class deposed another and then pursued policies that were qualitatively different.[139] From this particular aspect of the revolution he went on to reject the drawing of more general analogies between the French and the Bolshevik Revolutions on the grounds that they were fundamentally dissimilar. The French Revolution, being bourgeois-democratic, could not possibly be similar in any significant way to the October Revolution, which of course was proletarian and socialist. The differences between them were so obvious and fundamental that comparing them was 'vulgar analogising' and generally a waste of historians' valuable time.[140] Among the very few who still predated the original Thermidor before 9 Thermidor was Shchegolev, who wrote as late as 1930 that the continuities between the Jacobins and the Directory, which served the economic interests of the haute-bourgeoisie, were more numerous and more consequential than what distinguished them politically.[141] On this he was challenged by both Lukin and S. A. Lotte, neither of whom was about to let themselves be stigmatized by anything the party had condemned.[142]

In light of the party's belated, but nonetheless forceful denunciation of the thesis that the transition from the Jacobins to Thermidor was economically evolutionary, rather than something that occurred suddenly and comprehensively, one is left wondering not only why it took so long for the party to denounce it, but also why so many Soviet historians persisted in expressing it. Presumably those who did were aware of Lenin's personal identification with the Jacobins; no doubt they also realized that describing them as proto-Thermidorians significantly diminished the Jacobins, perhaps to the point where their own credentials as revolutionaries could be legitimately questioned, or even denied. The best explanation one can come up with is that describing the Jacobins in this fashion was to suggest that, at least in France, Thermidorian policies came about by stealth—that they were put in place by revolutionaries who either did not realize that by doing so they were betraying the revolution to which they still believed themselves to be committed, or knew exactly the implications of their actions; if the latter was the case, then the Jacobins were not revolutionaries at all, but rather reactionaries intent on returning power to the haute-bourgeoisie, a class less

[139] Kondratieva, Bol'sheviki-iakobintsy, pp. 153–4; Ts. Fridliand, '9-e termidora', Istorik marksist 7 (1928): pp. 158–9.

[140] Fridliand, '9-e termidora', p. 158.

[141] Kondratieva, Bol'sheviki-iakobintsy, pp. 164–6. Shchegolev adhered to the newly established orthodoxy to the extent to which he disparaged Mathiez, whose views on the Jacobins he now claimed 'could not withstand criticism'. P. P. Shchegolev, Posle termidora. Ocherki po istorii termidorianskoi reaktsii (Leningrad, 1930), p. 4. But he did not disavow his original thesis that, in their economic policies, the Jacobins prefigured the Thermidorians and, as corroboration, cited the Maximum, claiming that the changes it underwent after 9 Thermidor were 'superficial'. Posle termidora, p. 74.

[142] Dalin, 'K istorii izucheniia Velikoi frantsuzskoi revoliutsii v SSSR', pp. 112–13; S. A. Lotte, 'Protiv "matezovshchiny" i "ustrialovshchiny" v istoricheskoi literature', Problemy marksizma, 2 (1931): p. 210.

progressive than the petit-bourgeoisie, the class they belonged to by birth. More-over, by concealing both their motive and their intentions, the Jacobins were guilty of unconscionable mendacity.

* * *

Superimposed on the political realities in the Soviet Union in the mid-1920s, this seemingly arcane debate over the meaning of the original Thermidor in the French Revolution had serious political and ideological implications. What the notion of a 'growing over' seemed to suggest, if one applied it in the Soviet context, was that Thermidor could come about in the Soviet Union furtively and incre-mentally, as it had in the French Revolution, and in the absence, until it had already sunk deep roots in the Soviet economy, of any signal event like Robe-spierre's arrest and execution. As the prospect of a Soviet version of the phenom-enon became plausible after the institution of the NEP, many Bolsheviks believed it could come about through actions by persons within the Communist Party itself, who, while pretending to have the interests of the party at heart, in actuality were intent on harming it, perhaps even on bringing down the entire Soviet system. The Soviet Thermidor, in short, might resemble a malignancy, metaphor-ically eating away at the Soviet Union from within, its existence, much less its deleterious and even catastrophic effects, recognized too late for any surgical intervention to succeed. This view of how a Soviet Thermidor could arise would serve the interests of those who would welcome it as well as those who feared it. For the former it would be a prediction of what hopefully would come true; for the latter it would be a stark and undeniable warning.

In the end, the Soviet leadership, which by the end of 1928 consisted of Stalin and his now thoroughly Stalinist entourage, concluded that this particular explanation of how a Soviet Thermidor might arise was not wrong so much as irrelevant. What made it so was the Second Revolution Stalin initiated involving industrialization on a scale and with a rapidity none of the other Bolsheviks could have anticipated, along with the collectivization of agriculture, which required brutality and coercion of such magnitude that not even Lenin, at his most vindictive and ruthless, or Trotsky, who favoured rapid industrializa-tion before Stalin did, could ever have imagined. Both of these policies, in their objectives, motivation, and implementation, made impossible any kind of Thermidorian retrenchment, reaction, or counter-revolution. What had been a real danger in the 1920s, when NEP existed, simply vanished once Stalin had determined he would transform the Soviet economy so that it would finally, after a hiatus of just over a decade, be consonant ideologically with the trans-formation of politics the October Revolution had brought about in 1917. For that reason any and all analogies with the French Revolution emphasizing the commonality of a regression or even of merely a breathing spell would be at best irrelevant, and at worst harmful. The virtues Stalin wanted the Soviet people to emulate were those of a conqueror and a warrior. 'There are no fortresses', he said, 'that Bolsheviks cannot storm.'[143] One is hard pressed to conjure an ethos more different from this Promethean one and more injurious of it, than the psychology of self-enrichment and the eschewal of political activism implicit in the original Thermidor in France, at least as the Bolsheviks conceived of it.

---

[143] Quoted in Sheila Fitzpatrick, *Education and Social Mobility in the Soviet Union 1921–1934* (Cambridge, 1979), p. 181.

9

Stalin

The Jacobins as Proto-Stalinists

Stalin never personally attacked Soviet historians for claiming that in the French Revolution there was a growing over from the Jacobins to Thermidor. But it was hardly a coincidence that in 1930, this notion, which just a few years earlier was propounded by several of the finest historians in the country, was not only declared incorrect; just expressing it was considered evidence of criminality.[1] Stalin's notorious attack in 1931 on Soviet historians generally for their all-too-frequent expressions of 'rotten liberalism' made no mention of the issue, and included nothing about the French Revolution.[2] But statements he made in the early 1930s had the effect of restoring the Jacobins to the pantheon of revolutionaries Lenin said should be admired, if not always emulated. Stalin also added new reasons for the Jacobins to occupy their pride of place.

Stalin's natural inclination was to denigrate the French Revolution to the point where no Soviet citizen would consider drawing analogies to it. In 1930, Soviet historians prudently followed suit. In addition to calling mere discussion of a Soviet Thermidor a criminal act, V. Ia. Kirpotin parroted the new party line: analogies to the French Revolution 'obscured the differences between a bourgeois transformation and a socialist one'.[3] In the interview Stalin gave to Emil Ludwig in December 1931, he responded to a question about the role 'wage equalization' would play under socialism by attacking 'the primitive communists' in both the English and French Revolutions who favoured it, and cited Marx and Engels to

---

[1] Kondratieva, *Bol'sheviki-iakobintsy*, p. 172.

[2] J. V. Stalin, 'O nekotorykh voprosakh istorii bol'shevizma', *Proletarskaia revoliutsiia*, no. 6 (113) (October 1931): pp. 3–12. Stalin's attack, which, to give it greater visibility, was published also in the journal *Bol'shevik* , was triggered by an article by an obscure historian who had argued, incorrectly in Stalin's opinion, that Lenin underestimated the 'opportunism' of the leaders of the Second International prior to the outbreak of the First World War. But its underlying purpose was to force historians—the most odious of whom Stalin disparaged in the letter as 'archive rats'—to follow whatever 'line' the political leadership considered expedient. As a result, historians were purged, albeit peacefully, and among those who suffered this fate, which included expulsion from the party, was Fridliand, who upon his subsequent arrest was denounced as a 'Trotskyite'. Also among those purged—perhaps surprisingly given his unwavering opposition to the proponents of 'growing over'—was Lukin, who suffered the indignities of being condemned as a Zinovievite and of his ostensible errors exposed publicly. John Barber, 'Stalin's Letter to the Editors of *Proletarskaya Revolyutsiya*', *Soviet Studies*, no. 1 (January 1976): pp. 21–2, 39, 40–1; Anatole Mazour, *Modern Russian Historiography* (Princeton NJ, 1958), p. 201. Like Lukin, Fridliand perished in the Terror.

[3] V. Ia. Kirpotin, *Ideinye predshestvenniki marksizma-leninizma v Rossii* (Moscow, 1950), p. 101.

corroborate his opinion that strict equality of wages—as opposed to their being determined equitably and fairly—had no place in a socialist state; in fact, it had 'nothing in common with Marxism'.[4] While citing Cromwell in the English Revolution as the prime exemplar of this opinion, Stalin did not specify who in the French Revolution made the same mistake. However, it is likely that he was thinking of Babeuf and the Babouvists, of whom he had never been especially fond, and perhaps also of Hébert and the Hébertists. In November 1927, almost certainly on Stalin's orders, a play entitled 'The Conspiracy of Equals' that depicted its participants favourably was banned after only one performance.[5] Quite apart from his opposition to the extreme egalitarianism the Babouvists favoured, Stalin, who then still lacked sufficient power to ensure his political security, would not want any *coup d'état*, even one that failed, depicted on stage in a favourable light.

But Stalin did not merely denigrate several of the leading figures in the French Revolution, or reject as contrary to Marxism the ideas they espoused. In response to Ludwig's next question about whether the October Revolution was 'in any sense the continuation and culmination of the Great French Revolution', Stalin responded that it was not; in fact his response was so emphatic and categorical that one is inclined to consider what he said his genuine belief, rather than a reflection of any political considerations:

> The October Revolution is neither the continuation nor the culmination of the Great French Revolution. The goal of the French Revolution was to liquidate feudalism in order to establish capitalism. The goal of the October Revolution, however, is to liquidate capitalism in order to establish socialism.[6]

The significance of what Stalin said to Ludwig should not be underestimated. By his words, Stalin did nothing less than repudiate, even if only inferentially, the mythology about the French Revolution Lenin and the Bolsheviks had constructed since 1905. Where Lenin saw the differences between the French and the October Revolution as an indication of historical continuity, in which the later revolution superseded the earlier one without denying its historical necessity, Stalin considered these differences evidence of discontinuity; because the two revolutions, in their essence, had little in common, any similarities between them were superficial. For Stalin, history was purposeful and providential, in the sense of its having a final resting place, but its phases were distinct, and certainly not transcended by any 'growing over' from one to another. Aristocracies did not relinquish economic and political supremacy to capitalists voluntarily, any more than capitalists did the

---

[4] J. V. Stalin, 'Beseda s nemetskim pisatelem Emilem Liudvigom', in Stalin, *Sochineniia*, vol. XIII, pp. 118–19.

[5] Unaniants, 'Velikaia frantsuzskaia revoliutsiia v spektaklaiakh sovetskogo teatra', p. 473.

[6] Stalin, 'Beseda s nemetskim pisatelem Emilem Liudvigom', p. 123.

same for the proletariat, which in the Soviet Union was now beginning the stupendously difficult task of constructing socialism in the face of continued resistance from capitalists both at home and abroad. But the second of these transitions owed little to the first one. While sharing an instinct for self-preservation, aristocracies and capitalists were fundamentally different—and henceforth this assertion was not debatable in the Soviet Union. In short, Stalin's contribution to the conversation about the relationship between Jacobinism in France and Bolshevism in Russia was to end it. In Stalin's opinion, which by 1930 was the only one in the Soviet Union that mattered, history was the exact antithesis of the seamless web it was to many liberals and Social Democrats in the West, in which its discernible phases offered remarkably little resistance to those that followed them. At the same time, by stressing the discontinuities in history to the extent that he did, Stalin was coming dangerously closely to rejecting the Marxist view of history in its totality.

Stalin's subsequent pronouncements on the French Revolution either denigrated its importance or proclaimed its irrelevance. That its objectives were bourgeois instead of socialist and its actors foreigners instead of Russians were unpleasant facts for Stalin, and he usually mentioned them when it suited his purposes politically to mention the revolution or even, albeit rarely, to praise it. In Stalin's first public statement after the Nazi invasion—in which, to rally public resistance, he referred to the Soviet people as 'brothers and sisters'—he cited Napoleon's intervention in Russia and ensuing defeat as proof that Hitler's would meet the same fate.[7] To be sure, the French Revolution itself had been a progressive phenomenon, advancing industrial capitalism—which was one reason Stalin was favourably inclined to Napoleon; his undeniable gifts as a military strategist and tactician were another. But during the Second World War Stalin felt compelled to make clear that these were utilized on behalf of a country that—notwithstanding Napoleon's month-long occupation of Moscow—never really threatened Russia's survival. By contrast, the threat the Nazis posed was a mortal one; any comparison of Napoleon's campaign with the Nazis', he commented publicly in 1942, on the eve of the anniversary of the October Revolution, 'will not bear criticism'.[8] In the same speech, he noted the numerical disparity between the three million Soviet soldiers fighting the Nazis and the pitifully small number, at least by comparison, who fought for Napoleon and France at the battle of Borodino in the fall of 1812.[9] Stalin, in other words, felt confident enough by 1942 to acknowledge the Nazis' military strength—to which he contrasted Napoleon's

---

[7] J. V. Stalin, 'Vstuplenie po radio 3 iiulia 1941 goda', in Stalin, *Sochineniia* (Moscow, 1997), vol. XV, p. 56. Subsequent references to this later edition of Stalin's works will be rendered as *Sochineniia* (1997), followed by the volume and page number.

[8] J. V. Stalin, 'Doklad na torzhestvennom zasedanii Moskovskogo Soveta deputatov trudiashchikh-sia s partinymi i obshchestvennymi organizatsiiami goroda Moskvy (6 November 1942)', ibid., p. 122.

[9] Ibid., p. 123.

military weakness—in a speech intended to convince his listeners that the Nazis were doomed to defeat. Irrespective of whether the German forces were strong or weak, in the history lessons his speeches during the Second World War were intended to impart, one thing never changed—Napoleon's weakness and, by implication, that of France as well. Stalin fashioned Soviet resistance of the Nazis as a patriotic crusade to which all Russians who venerated their country's heroics against earlier invaders should pledge their allegiance, and for this reason alone analogies with foreign countries and their revolutions would not be helpful.

In Stalin's last years, he had little to say publicly about the French Revolution. In 1950, in his articles in *Pravda* on linguistics, he included the comment that there were limits to what the French Revolution had accomplished: even as it was transforming politics and the economy, it was powerless to achieve a revolution in linguistics, which, as an aspect of the ideational 'superstructure' that Marx believed had no existence independent of material reality, Stalin now considered a tool in moulding the New Soviet Man. By this time, Stalin had convinced himself that the human personality was infinitely malleable, and could therefore be altered independently of changes in the material bases of society.[10] For that reason the Soviets need not wait for the full effects of industrialization and the collectivization of agriculture to take effect. A new species of human being could be created without them.[11] But two years later, in *Economic Problems of Socialism*, his last work before his death in 1953, the Prometheanism that was so seamlessly integrated into the Marxist ideology he had believed in for the entirety of his public life prompted him to re-evaluate his previous position that the October Revolution, in relation to the French Revolution and all other revolutions that preceded it, was *sui generis*, and that the only revolutions that might resemble it were future socialist revolutions elsewhere in the world.[12] 'Society is not powerless against the laws of science' was perhaps the most revelatory statement of the essay, and to underscore its centrality, Stalin cited the bourgeoisie of the French Revolution to make clear his belief that the Soviet people were perfectly capable of changing anything that to others seemed immutable.[13]

---

[10] Rolf, *Soviet Mass Festivals*, p. 143. The *prazdniki* the Bolsheviks staged was one way of instilling the personal attributes people would manifest under communism before communism existed; Malte Rolf has aptly called the process of instilling these attributes a form of 'inner sovietisation', while also noting that it yielded mixed results, largely because pre-soviet attitudes, especially where these concerned Christianity, could not be extirpated entirely. Ibid., pp. 146–50.

[11] Using Pavlovian conditioning to change human behaviour radically was another 'short-cut' Stalin hoped would yield the loyal Soviet citizens he wanted before the material preconditions for their emergence existed. Robert Tucker's article, 'Stalin and the Uses of Psychology', in *The Soviet Political Mind*, edited by Robert C. Tucker (New York, 1972), pp. 143–72, is illuminating in this regard. Stalin's intense desire to accelerate the course of history suggests that Piatakov's statement about Lenin making a proletarian revolution before the preconditions for it existed applies equally to Stalin if one substitutes 'building socialism' for 'making a proletarian revolution' as that which occurred prematurely in Russia.

[12] J. V. Stalin, *Ekonomicheskie problemy sotsializma v SSSR. Otvet tovarishchu Notkinu, Aleksandru Il'ichu*, in Stalin, *Sochineniia* (1997), vol. XVI, p. 188.

[13] Ibid.

However laconic his comments on the French Revolution, and notwithstanding the infrequency with which he uttered them, in the last years of his life Stalin was simply too impressed by the Jacobins not to consider their example relevant to his own political requirements as the leader of a country still surrounded, at least in his own mind, by enemies intent on destroying it. That he himself was losing some of the mental acuity he had enjoyed as a younger man made the vigilance he had manifested earlier in his career even more necessary now. Stalin, in a sense, had become his own enemy. But because the frailties of old age had been precluded by the guillotine in 1794, the Jacobins were forever youthful, and worthy of emulation in perpetuity. According to Dmitrii Volkogonov, Stalin esteemed Robespierre in particular for originating the whole notion of ideological crime, of which entire categories of the population could be guilty simply by virtue of their existence.[14] Sheila Fitzpatrick notes his admiration of the Law of Suspects the Jacobins decreed in September 1793; its proviso permitting apprehension for mere suspicion of criminality was of course consistent with what the Soviet police were allowed to do for virtually the entirety of Stalin's rule.[15] Eric Van Ree even claims that Stalin's notions of 'revolutionary dictatorship' and 'revolutionary patriotism' originated in his understanding of how the Jacobins exercised power once they had acquired it, and in his study of Stalin's political thought defines it explicitly as a form of 'Marxist Jacobinism'.[16]

One need not go as far as Van Ree to acknowledge that the Jacobins personified a regime Stalin looked to for guidance now that what was originally a revolutionary party in Russia had become, under Lenin and Stalin, a ruling elite. Of course neither the Jacobins nor the French Revolution as a whole provided a template for ruling the Soviet Union in a manner consistent with Stalin's needs and objectives. Nevertheless, there were two aspects of the Jacobin dictatorship he found especially useful, even though the Jacobins had at their disposal nothing like the modern machinery of coercion and propaganda that was available to Stalin, which he continued to refine in the last years of his life.

The first of these concerned the application of terror. Emboldened by what he knew about how the Jacobins had applied it in the 1790s, Stalin increasingly ordered the elimination of people not just for any ideological recalcitrance they had supposedly manifested towards the construction of socialism and communism, but simply because he deemed them personal enemies, and by virtue of that fact alone, enemies of the Soviet state and the Soviet people.[17] One could even say that whatever Stalin may have believed about the irrelevance of the French

[14] Volkogonov, *Stalin*, p. 279.
[15] Sheila Fitzpatrick, *The Russian Revolution* (New York, 1994), p. 179.
[16] Van Ree, *Political Thought of Joseph Stalin*, pp. 230–54, 283.
[17] Matthew Lenoe draws this distinction in his article, 'Fear, Loathing, Conspiracy: The Kirov Murder', in *The Anatomy of Terror: Political Violence under Stalin*, edited by James Harris (Oxford, 2013), p. 201.

Revolution, he nonetheless admired the Jacobins for the alacrity with which they killed people. If, in the end, they killed ineffectively and insufficiently, which caused them to lose power less than two years after acquiring it, he would simply take care to avoid their mistakes. But to Stalin the similarities with the Jacobins were just as obvious as the differences. While they might only have had at their disposal primitive means of execution like the guillotine and slow-firing rifles, the enemies these weapons eliminated were actually much like those Stalin had to eliminate in the 1930s in their cunning, their malevolence, and their unsurpassable duplicity. Robespierre and Saint-Just would have found nothing untoward and unrecognizable in the charges in the Show Trials that perfidious communists inside the Soviet Union were conspiring to destroy the Soviet state at the behest of foreign intelligence agencies and Trotsky, who, after his exile from the Soviet Union in 1929, might have reminded the two Jacobins of the *Comte de Provence*, the Bourbon Pretender and future Louis XVIII.

The second reason the Jacobins appealed to Stalin was that he could easily construe them as the personification of French nationalism and patriotism. Notably absent in Stalinist pronouncements on the French Revolution is any acknowledgement of its international and universalist pretensions. Far from its being the first step in the emancipation of humanity, as Marx, Engels, and Lenin perceived it, the French Revolution in Stalin's estimation acted to protect the interests of a nation state and the economic interests of several of the classes that comprised it. Paradoxically, Stalin's espousal of Soviet patriotism, especially during 'the Great Patriotic War', instead of precluding admiration for the Jacobins, and by implication for the French Revolution as a whole, had the effect of increasing it.

Moreover, Stalin never fully jettisoned Marxist ideology in explaining the French Revolution. An unsigned tribute in 1939 in the issue of *Pravda* on the sesquicentennial of the storming of the Bastille dutifully reiterated the Leninist view that 'the French Revolution [was] the most significant event of the modern era prior to the October Revolution'.[18] Although the bourgeoisie was its principal beneficiary, the revolution was actually galvanized by the lower classes and thus truly a popular movement. 'With the iron fist of terror', the political instrument of these classes [i.e. the Jacobins] 'mercilessly smashed [the revolution's] antagonists—the counterrevolutionaries, the opportunists, and the traitors.'[19] In fact, the Jacobins were the best the French bourgeoisie could produce. But in the end, the revolution could not transcend its historical limits, and the working class was still too weak to do what the bourgeoisie was unwilling to do. The result, as inescapable as it was regrettable, was the Jacobins' and the revolution's defeat by the Thermidorians.

---

[18] '150-letie frantsuzskoi burzhuaznoi revoliutsii', *Pravda*, no. 193(7878) (14 July 1939): p. 1.
[19] Ibid.

After 1917 all of the Bolsheviks could have written this without contradicting anything else they had written on the Jacobins and the French Revolution. But there were aspects to this article that were distinctively Stalinist. The anonymous author or authors made much of the external threat to the revolution posed by counter-revolutionary monarchies actively seeking its destruction; that these instruments of feudalism in Europe were aided in their effort by traitors inside France only made the danger more insidious, and for that reason more difficult to detect. The Jacobins, while they soon fell victim to it, nonetheless set an enviable standard of defiance in the face of overwhelming resistance that posterity would look back to with admiration. Robespierre, Marat, and Saint-Just were just the most prominent of the actors in the French Revolution 'to inspire the revolution-aries of the working class with their massacres of obsolete forces of the old order', and in that way set an example the proletariat in Russia in 1917 would emulate because the Jacobins were not really responsible for their subsequent defeat.[20] History was the culprit, rather than any insufficiency of courage, will, and determination. For that reason the proletariat, who were the pupils of the Jaco-bins, were now—through the instrument of Stalin's terror—actually exceeding their teachers in destroying their enemies once and for all and on behalf of a regime, which they themselves had established in 1917 and had long since exceeded the lifespan of the Jacobin one.

Still, as the same article clearly implied, the proletariat in the Soviet Union had to remain vigilant even after defeating its enemies. Fascism—which was how Nazism was always referred to in the Soviet Union because 'National Socialism' suggested a similarity with socialism itself—always posed a genuine threat to the Soviet state. What made this warning remarkable was that Stalin, through his epigones in the press, linked it to the French Revolution, even though fascism, as 'the most frenzied and the most reactionary circles of finance capital', was the political expression of the last stage of industrial capitalism prior to a proletarian revolution.[21] The French Revolution, of course, had ushered in the earliest pre-cursor of this particular kind of capitalism. Nevertheless, the author or authors of the *Pravda* article in 1939 claimed that fascism threatened not just the Soviet Union but also 'the principles of 1789'.[22] This is a remarkable statement for any Marxist, Marxist-Leninist, or Stalinist to make. It shows loyal Stalinists—after Stalin had proclaimed as the irrefutable truth that any analogy between the French and the October Revolutions was not only false but ridiculous because the revolutions occurred under vastly different circumstances—nonetheless implying, in the newspaper of the Soviet Communist Party—that this was simply not the case, indeed that the opposite of what Stalin had said was true. The French and the October Revolutions were comparable, and any comparison will show them to be

[20] Ibid.   [21] Ibid.   [22] Ibid.

similar. Even more remarkable was the implication that not only the Soviet Union and socialism, but all existing bourgeois regimes—which by definition were based on 'the principles of 1789'—were threatened by fascism. Even though fascists belonged to the bourgeoisie, they were also, paradoxically, a mortal threat to it.[23] Threatening capitalists and socialists, the bourgeoisie and the proletariat, equally and with the same ferocity it had manifested in coming to power in the countries it ruled, fascism, in 1939, was far from the last expression politically of 'finance capital', despite the fact that Stalin a decade earlier believed it was destined soon to disappear, and said so publicly.

The author or authors of the article in *Pravda* seemed of two minds about the Jacobins and about the French Revolution generally. They apparently accepted that the revolution was essential to the development of industrial capitalism, and then, many years later, to its replacement in the Soviet Union by an economy that Stalin, in 1936, had publicly termed 'socialist'. But the article also argued that the Jacobins, who were indisputably the most consequential of all the parties that led the revolution during its multiple phases, were concerned most of all with their own country. In the litany of things the article claimed the Soviet people admired about the French Revolution, such as the hatred its leaders manifested for the Catholic Church, it was the Jacobins' struggle to destroy the foreign enemies of the revolution, to discover the traitors in their midst and to destroy the foreign governments that were directing them, that they admired most. When the author or authors asked what exactly it was that explained the courage and unstinting dedication the Jacobins mustered in fighting their multifarious and diabolical enemies, the answer they provided was simple: 'their love for their *rodina*'.[24] Though usually rendered in English as 'the motherland', the word has always had mystical connotations for Russians, who consider them specific to Russia. That in this instance the word was applied to a foreign country testifies to the role the French Revolution and France played in Stalinist politics and culture, despite Stalin's own efforts, at times, to minimize it.

Other articles in the same issue of *Pravda* contained similar arguments. F. Kheifets termed the Jacobins 'the most decisive representatives of the revolutionary bourgeoisie', which from 1789 to 1794, endeavoured to destroy 'all of the

---

[23] That fascism and the French Revolution are incompatible in the principles each espoused is an assertion with which most historians of modern European history would agree. To my knowledge, only one Western historian of any prominence has claimed the opposite—that fascism ideologically is a continuation of the French Revolution, namely George Mosse, in his article, 'Fascism and the French Revolution', in *The Fascist Revolution: Towards a General Theory of Fascism*, edited by George L. Mosse (New York, 1999), 69–93. In the article Mosse makes much of the Nazis' mobilizing the German people on behalf of an extreme nationalism that he identifies as a 'civic religion' traceable historically to the Jacobins. In the abstract, the similarity Mosse argues for may be plausible. But one suspects that there are more direct antecedents of this aspect of Nazi ideology and practice in German history that owed little or nothing to the French Revolution.

[24] '150-letie frantsuzskoi burzhuaznoi revoliutsii', p. 3.

remnants of feudalism [and] to establish in France a democratic republic'.[25] But the bourgeoisie in those years was hardly monolithic. In fact, it was riven by a split between the Jacobins and the Girondins that might have ended the French Revolution prematurely had the former not been able to neutralize the latter politically. There was nothing extraordinary about an article in a Soviet newspaper asserting this. Leninist orthodoxy since 1905 held that the Jacobins were them-selves from the petit-bourgeoisie and thus more progressive than the Girondins, who were from the haute-bourgeoisie. Like the other authors who were writing, in effect, as Stalin's surrogate, Kheifets contended that the Girondins were even worse than how Soviet historians and political leaders had described them prior to the commencement of Stalin's rule. Above and beyond their ideological crimes, the Girondins were traitors to the country of France—which meant that the Jacobins, among their other virtues, were patriots. Moreover, the reason for such a stark dichotomy was that the Girondins and the Jacobins came from the two principal factions of the bourgeoisie: the haute-bourgeoisie in the case of the Girondins, the petit-bourgeoisie in the case of the Jacobins. Politics, in other words, was a function of class. This, of course, is a fundamental axiom of Marxism and Marxism-Leninism. But the corollary, which Stalin seemed to use surrogates in the Soviet press to express, was that under capitalism, and even during the transition from feudalism to capitalism, the more advanced the class, or the subset of a class, the more patriotic it would be. Because of the subclass of the bourgeoisie they belonged to, the Girondins could not help but betray the revolution and render assistance to its foreign enemies, while the Jacobins—not only because of the different subclass they represented, but also because they were committed personally and politically to the survival and welfare of France—could not help but try to preserve the revolution by defeating these same foreign enemies. The French Revolution was the Great French Revolution not just because it was the first bourgeois revolution in history. According to Stalin, again through the medium of surrogates' articles in the Soviet press, it was a Great Revolution also because the Jacobins, like Stalin, recognized that, for a revolution to succeed, its leaders had to feel a special commitment to their own country, causing them to place its welfare over any other value or principle they might happen to profess, because without it, their enemies would destroy not only their own revolution, but also their own country.

But honouring and protecting and defending their country were not the only things the Jacobins had to do so that the revolution they supported survived. In Stalin's view of history and of human events generally, victors could never rest on their laurels. Defeated enemies, unless they were eliminated entirely, were always lurking, intent on avenging their own defeat and destroying all those responsible

---

[25] F. Kheifets, 'Iakobinskaia diktatura', *Pravda*, no. 193(7878) (14 July 1939): p. 3.

for it. Successful rulers had to be just as vigilant as their enemies were duplicitous. In Kheifets' words, they had 'to extend their hand against the counterrevolutionary imperialists'.[26] In the case of the Jacobins, this necessitated destroying not only foreigners who threatened them, but also the Girondins and former supporters of the Jacobins who had betrayed them; among the traitors the Jacobins eliminated— with an absence of mercy Kheifets clearly approved of—was Charles Dumouriez, the French general who in April 1793 had defected to the Austrians because he feared he would be punished for having lost a battle one month earlier, and also, though less obviously, for having opposed the execution of Louis XVI two months before that.[27] But the good sense that caused the Jacobins to recognize the links between their foreign enemies and those inside France was not enough, according to Kheifets, to save them. Paradoxically, the very steps the Jacobins took to assist the lower classes—such as allowing peasants to take back land they believed the aristocracy had wrongly seized years or even decades earlier—accelerated the transformation of the peasantry into a class of satiated small property owners who no longer wanted or needed the revolution to continue.

Another policy, according to Kheifets, that had the same effect was the Maximum, which the Jacobins put in place, despite their longstanding belief in laissez-faire economics, to win the support of classes and categories of the population that were beneath them, most notably the *sans-culottes*. But among the Jacobins' supporters were other elements of the population that wanted the Maximum to end. Forced to choose, the Jacobins, fatefully, chose the latter, and dropped their support of the Maximum. In the end, the Jacobins lost power anyway, and Kheifets leaves the reader with the clear impression that no matter what the Jacobins did, nothing they could have done would have ensured the long-term continuation of their regime. Having unified France in the face of external danger, the Jacobins, their historical mission completed, were helpless to prevent the unity they created dissolve once the danger had passed. But unlike the Jacobins, the leaders of the Soviet Union—as Kheifets implied strongly at the end—would triumph over any enemies, foreign or domestic, foolish enough to seek its destruction. If the Jacobins, in the final analysis, were defeated, more than anything else, by history itself, the Soviet Union under Stalin transcended history, which, along with Stalin's own incomparable abilities, effectively rendered the Soviet Union omnipotent.[28]

Other contributors to same issue of *Pravda* touched on many of the themes Kheifets stressed. A. Molok described the French Revolution as a patriotic revolution, the enormity of which facilitated the creation of revolutionary armies that

---

[26] Ibid.

[27] Valerie Mainz, *Days of Glory? Imaging Military Recruitment and the French Revolution (War, Culture, and Society, 1750–1850)* (London, 2016), p. 238; Ian Davidson, *The French Revolution: From Enlightenment to Tyranny* (New York, 2016), pp. 149–53.

[28] Kheifets, *Iakobinskaia diktatura'*, p. 3.

defeated the external forces intent on destroying it.[29] In Molok's description, there was nothing international or supranational about the revolution. The Jacobins were its best exemplars, and among the Jacobins, Marat exemplified what made them, to all intents and purposes, proto-Stalinists—even though Molok himself did not apply that particular appellation. But he extolled Marat for attacking 'the new bourgeois aristocracy', which, 'by ripping off the mask of the idols of the liberal bourgeoisie, the most egregious of whom were Necker and Lafayette, he exposed the treason of the royal court'.[30] Then, fully cognizant of the fact that the enemies of the revolution were like a hydra, reappearing no matter how many times they seemed to have been defeated, Marat fought the Girondins—'the new masters of the bourgeois republic'—and after them 'the counterrevolutionaries', against whom he directed 'merciless rhetorical attacks'.[31] Adopting the phraseology of Stalinism, Molok concluded his paean by crediting Marat, and by implication the other Jacobins who continued what he had been doing after his untimely death at the hands of Charlotte Corday, for unmasking 'enemies of the people'—the same term that was applied in the Soviet press and in official pronouncements to the millions of victims of Stalin's Terror.[32]

Molok praised Robespierre even more effusively than he did Marat: 'Only with love do patriots and democrats say his name [because] they know that no other interests existed for him except serving his country.'[33] His greatness and that of the Jacobins consisted primarily in what they did on behalf of the Committee of Public Safety in 1793–4, when they led 'the progressive classes of the time' and fought their enemies both internally and abroad. In that respect, and also in carrying out needed but difficult reforms that benefitted the classes in France that most needed them, the Jacobins did the dirty work of the revolution, from which the haute-bourgeoisie had recoiled. But once the Jacobins enacted the agenda of what was, and had to remain, a bourgeois revolution, they became expendable, their historical mission accomplished. 9 Thermidor was of course regrettable, but it could not be averted.[34]

Also joining in the celebration in *Pravda* was the eminent Soviet historian Evgenii Tarlé. That someone of his notoriety was called upon to lend his talents to honouring the French Revolution in the most prestigious and powerful newspaper in the Soviet Union attested to the significance of the occasion. Tarlé did not disappoint.[35] He paid the requisite attention to the enemies of the revolution, particularly the *émigrés*, whose resemblance to Trotsky and his followers, in Tarlé's estimation, was unmistakable. But what made these enemies of the revolution especially diabolical was their enlistment of foreign governments in their nefarious schemes, which showed these *émigrés*' contempt not just for the French

[29] A. Molok, 'Tribuny Konventa', *Pravda*, no. 193(7878) (14 July 1939): p. 3.
[30] Ibid.   [31] Ibid.   [32] Ibid.   [33] Ibid.   [34] Ibid.
[35] E. Tarlé, 'Bor'ba s interventsiei', *Pravda*, no. 193(7878) (14 July 1939); p. 3.

Revolution but for France itself. Absent the Jacobins' vigilance and single-minded determination to stop them, Prussian officers, in Tarlé's description, would not only have torched Paris after conquering it; they would also have massacred its children, because if they had failed to do so, '[these children] would all grow up to be Jacobins'.[36] Tarlé singled out Robespierre for special commendation: in the essential enterprise of 'killing enemies and traitors', he was nothing short of 'indomitable'.[37] In that respect, as well as in many others that Tarlé evidently did not think it necessary to enumerate, the French bourgeoisie in 1939 was hardly worthy of its illustrious predecessor in the French Revolution. But the Soviet Union, which had recently unmasked and destroyed its own traitors even more ruthlessly and effectively than the Jacobins did, was nonetheless pleased to honour a revolution that inaugurated a new chapter in the history of humanity, the beneficent repercussions of which, after unfolding first in Western Europe and then a century or so later in Russia, would soon be felt even further eastward, in Asia.[38]

During the Stalin era, the French Revolution was not only on Stalin's mind. It also figured prominently in the sensibilities of the Stalinists who shared the milieu the dictator inhabited that became even more insular after the suicide of Stalin's second wife in November 1932, which left the Soviet dictator virtually bereft of family life.[39] As Simon Montefiore has amply demonstrated, a genuine subculture emerged at that time around Stalin to which his subordinates could not remain oblivious on pain of exclusion from the dictator's good graces, or worse.[40] Lazar Kaganovich, whose limited education and provincial outlook presumably had rendered him largely ignorant of history other than that of the Bolsheviks, nevertheless knew enough about the French Revolution to speak coherently, if superficially and in the self-identifying phraseology of Stalinism, about how the Jacobins dealt with their enemies. His verdict was that they did so effectively but lacked the ruthlessness needed to kill all of them, the morality and the practical necessity of which Kaganovich never questioned. In May 1991, less than three months before his death, he stated in an interview that while the Jacobins were justified morally and as a matter of expediency in physically eliminating the Girondins, they failed to do the same to 'the swamp', by which Kaganovich meant the delegates to the Convention who refused to align themselves with either the Jacobins or the Girondins. While at times they supported what the Jacobins did, they never forgot their original enmity, and soon betrayed them.[41] According to Kaganovich, the reason the Jacobins did not defend themselves was

---

[36] Ibid.   [37] Ibid.   [38] Ibid.

[39] The first volume of Svetlana Alliluyeva's memoirs, *Twenty Letters to a Friend* (New York, 1967), are illuminating in this regard, even though her ascription of responsibility of the Terror mostly to Beria should cause the reader to treat them very carefully.

[40] Simon Sebag Montefiore, *Stalin: The Court of the Red Tsar* (New York, 2003).

[41] G. A. Kumanev, *Riadom so Stalinym* (Moscow, 1991), p. 78.

because 'the swamp was linked to them by many threads'—in other words because its members had insinuated themselves into the ranks of the Jacobins, thereby rendering them defenceless.[42] One can easily imagine Kaganovich at this point in the interview silently congratulating himself and Stalin for not making the same mistake.[43]

* * *

By the mid-1930s, it was clear that the controversy over the 'growing over' thesis had ended with the victory of those who rejected it, and the harsh derogation of those who had once espoused it was consistent with the larger hardening of an ideological orthodoxy not only in history but in most matters cultural and intellectual. Another indication of this was the posthumous denunciation of Mathiez. Triggered by his intervention on Tarlé's behalf when the latter's credentials as a loyal supporter of the Soviet Union were under attack, the campaign against the much-admired French historian captured perfectly the intermingling of the personal, the political, and the historical in the litany of errors of which he was presumably guilty. Among the most-often cited were his signing a petition protesting the death penalty for forty-eight intellectuals recently convicted of various crimes, and continuing to maintain that the Jacobins adopted Thermidorian policies while still in power. The attacks these transgressions generated were followed by pronouncements, with the party's approval either explicit or strongly implied, that Mathiez was once again espousing the views of the imperialist bourgeoisie.[44]

To be sure, the debate about the Soviet Thermidor continued among the Mensheviks. In 1929 Rafael Abramovich had argued, counterintuitively, that industrialization, because of its rapidity and attendant social and economic dislocation, actually made *termidoriastvo* more likely.[45] By 1935 Fëdor Dan had gone further. The Soviet Union, he said, had already entered the stage of Thermidor.[46] Its industrialization was the most obvious proof of this. In fact, the very existence of Thermidor in the Soviet Union, he wrote in 1936, meant that its transformation into a genuine social democracy was possible, perhaps even likely.[47] In fact, several other Mensheviks considered the Soviet Union's joining the League of Nations in 1933, and its promulgation in 1936 of a constitution with explicit (but entirely fraudulent) guarantees of civil liberties and free elections,

---

[42]   Ibid., p. 79.
[43]   French communists and other apologists in France during the Stalin era not surprisingly viewed the Jacobin terror in much the way Kaganovich did. Jean Brubat, *Le châtiment des espions et des traîtres sous la Révolution française* (Paris, 1937), is a prime example.
[44]   Vovell, '1789–1917: The Game of Analogies', p. 364 and *passim*.
[45]   R. Abramovich, 'Termidor i krest'ianstvo', *Sotsialisticheskii vestnik*, no. 7–8 (12 April 1929): p. 5.
[46]   F. Dan, 'Protiv terrora – za revoliutsiiu', *Sotsialisticheskii vestnik*, no. 1 (10 January 1935): p. 3.
[47]   F. Dan, 'Puti vozrozhdeniia', *Sotsialisticheskii vestnik*, no. 14–15 (14 August 1936): pp. 9–10.

visible proof that this transformation had already begun.[48] But for some, the Nazi–Soviet Pact in 1939 and the Winter War against Finland three months later dashed these hopes for good—or, as happened in Trotsky's case in 1935, prompted a re-evaluation of the term itself.[49] In 1940 Dan acknowledged that Thermidor in the Soviet Union was irreversible, but now he thought it precluded, rather than facilitated, the Soviet Union's becoming a social democracy; indeed it confirmed that the Soviet Union, in its politics, was Bonapartist, or perhaps even fascist.[50]

But by the mid-1930s Stalin no longer cared what the Mensheviks wrote, and in the criminality the defendants in the show trials were accused of, they figured hardly at all; Trotsky and foreign intelligence agencies, not the Mensheviks in emigration, were deemed the masters of the dastardly plots in which the defendants had allegedly participated.[51] Moreover, neither the French Revolution nor the Jacobins in particular played a role in the trials, and Stalin himself barely mentioned them as the Terror that ensued reached its apogee in 1937–8. This did not mean, of course, that he was prepared, in the case of the French Revolution—or of other matter on which he had expressed himself publicly—to allow any challenge or disagreement. While the trials and the Terror continued, Stalin's claims to a monopoly of wisdom not just in politics but in virtually all areas of Soviet life was more emphatic and absolute than it was previously.

But this did not mean that Soviet historians were either totally silent on the revolution or were in agreement on every aspect of it. Rather, they trod carefully, 'pulling their punches' when it seemed the politic thing to do, and generally focusing their attention on aspects of the revolution on which the Party Line was unambiguous and unmistakable, thus making deviations from it easy to avoid. Accordingly, most no longer concerned themselves with the relationship between the Jacobins and Thermidor, focusing instead on the role the Jacobins played in the French Revolution as a whole—a role that they, like Stalin, considered a mostly positive one. The first indication of this shift in emphasis was N. M. Lukin's article, 'Lenin and the Problem of the Jacobin Dictatorship', which appeared in *Istorik marksist* in 1934.[52] Of all the Soviet historians who wrote about the French Revolution during the Stalin era, Lukin may have most faithfully replicated Stalin's own views. However much Stalin may have claimed—as he did in his interview with Emil Ludwig in 1931—that the October Revolution was not only not analogous with the French Revolution but owed precious little to it, his views on the earlier revolution still mattered, and Lukin may have deliberately altered

---

[48] B. Dvinov, 'Na pochve deistvitel'nosti', *Sotsialisticheskii vestnik*, no. 3 (15 February 1940): pp. 32–3.
[49] B. Dvinov, 'K partiinoi platforme', *Sotsialisticheskii vestnik*, no. 6 (24 March 1940): pp. 71–5. On the change in Trotsky's view, see pp. 428–9.
[50] F. Dan, 'Dva puti', *Novyi mir*, nos. 1 & 2 (1940), cited in Kondratieva, *Bol'sheviki-iakobintsy*, p. 186.
[51] Fourteen Mensheviks still living in the Soviet Union had been tried in 1931; all were found guilty, but none were executed.
[52] Lukin edited *Istorik marksist* from 1933 to 1938, when he was arrested.

his own opinions to coincide with them. Of course neither his article nor his prior services to the Bolsheviks prevented his subsequent arrest and elimination in the Terror. But this was not for any lack of effort on his part.

Of course there was much in Lukin's article that could have been written before Stalin came to power. In many ways it adhered to the strictures Lenin had placed on how the French Revolution should be interpreted, particularly as these pertained to the Jacobins. The Jacobins, as Lukin described them, were themselves petit-bourgeois revolutionaries attempting to make real in France the desiderata of a bourgeois revolution after the haute-bourgeoisie made clear it was unwilling to do so. With the support of persons who could only aspire to be bourgeois, such as the Parisian *sans-culottes*, the Jacobins were nonetheless able to fashion a coalition, not unlike that which Lenin advocated in 1905 and actually assembled in 1917, that brought them to power. For that reason the dictatorship the Jacobins established could properly be considered 'bourgeois-democratic'.[53] But by 1794 they had gone as far as they could. The bourgeois revolution to which they were committed had reached its limits.

Where Lukin's views were different from those he had expressed in the 1920s was in the emphasis he now placed on class distinctions within the French peasantry in explaining the Jacobins' demise, and the end of the French Revolution itself, on 9 Thermidor.[54] Specifically—so went his argument—affluent peasants in France, who earlier in the revolution had received the land they demanded, were simply too strong and too numerous for the 'rural proletariat'—sometimes Lukin called them 'rural *sans-culottes*'—to overcome, and as a result, the French Revolution ended when Thermidor began. But nothing comparable to this had happened, or would ever happen, in the Soviet Union. While in the French Revolution poor peasants were largely bypassed or used to advance the interests of other classes, in the Soviet Union their interests were duly considered, their needs met, and their principal enemies, the *kulaks*, destroyed. Indeed, in an article in 1930 Lukin had seemed to suggest, through an analogy with the Jacobins, that by destroying the *kulaks*, the Soviet government was doing precisely what the Jacobins should have done to ensure their survival. For that reason, the Soviets

---

[53] Kondratieva, *Bol'sheviki-iakobintsy*, pp. 166–7. This particular argument, which Lukin had made in works written prior to 1934, was criticized in 1933 by S. A. Lotte, who stressed that the Jacobins made certain that the coalitions they dominated advanced their own interests, rather than those of the plebeians and others who supported them. This was why they did not grant the lower classes any rights or allow their representatives to help the Jacobins make policy. S. A. Lotte, *Velikaia frantsuzskaia revoliutsiia* (Moscow/Leningrad 1933), p. 217. But Lukin never suggested that they did. For this reason Lotte's criticism was disingenuous. In the end, none of this mattered. Both historians, not just Lukin, perished in the Terror.

[54] Lukin, 'Lenin i problema iakobinskoi diktatury', pp. 135–6. To be sure, in his 1934 article Lukin in no way rejected or even qualified his earlier contention that the weakness of the urban lower classes in France, which he said included a primitive industrial working class, played a major role in the genesis of the Jacobins' demise.

would avoid their own Thermidor.[55] For the lower classes, the Jacobins were only lukewarm and inconsistent advocates: they stopped enforcing the *Ventôse* decrees confiscating and redistributing *émigrés'* estates, and retained the *Loi Le Chapelier* banning guilds and the equivalent of unions.[56] Even when the 'plebeian' elements that supported the Jacobins were most influential, namely from September 1793 to March 1794, the Jacobins did not exceed the limits their class identity prescribed.

In another departure from earlier writings, Lukin, in 1934, claimed that had the Hébertists somehow been able to take power from Robespierre and the other 'centrist Jacobins', they would have done to their lower-class supporters what the centrist Jacobins actually did to them, namely destroy them politically and physically, and in that way ensure their own survival. But constraints imposed by class, rather than pragmatism, would explain the Hébertists (hypothetical) behaviour. The Hébertists, no less than the Jacobins, were from the petit-bourgeoisie. Hébert himself was by profession a journalist. In short, no revolution in France in the late eighteenth century could have satisfied the needs of any class other than the bourgeoisie.[57] In fact, of all the revolutionaries in the French Revolution, Babeuf and the Babouvists—or so Lukin's analysis implied—had the *least* chance of improving the lives of the lower classes. Although, in contrast to the Jacobins and the Hébertists, the Babouvists understood that private property was the ultimate cause of the lower classes' impoverishment, publicising their conviction would have cost them support instead of increasing it. That was why, as if in recognition of this unpleasant reality, they remained an underground conspiracy, and made no discernible effort to gain popular support. While the Babouvists' condemnation of private property during the French Revolution was certainly morally valid and empirically descriptive, because of the historical circumstances in which the revolution occurred, they could never have gained the power necessary to abolish it.

There were other ways in which Lukin's article was distinctively Stalinist. Prior to the Stalin era, Soviet historians had not singled out one foreign enemy among the many that sought the Jacobins' destruction. But Lukin, while dutifully citing Lenin in justifying the Jacobin's terror and identifying the Girondins as its principal object, stressed that the treason that prompted it consisted primarily of the Girondins' support for France's arch enemy, Great Britain.[58] In addition, Lukin emphasized the role military force played in preventing foreign governments from defeating France, ending the revolution, and ensuring the return of

[55] Ibid., p. 136; Alexander Tchoudinov, 'The Evolution of Russian Discourse on the French Revolution', in *The Routledge Companion to the French Revolution in World History*, edited by Alan Forrest and Matthias Middell (New York, 2016), p. 289. According to Lukin one of the principal flaws in Mathiez's interpretation of the French Revolution was his minimizing the disparity between rich peasants and poor ones. Lukin, 'Lenin i problema iakobinskoi diktatury', pp. 135–6.
[56] Lukin, 'Lenin i problema iakobinskoi diktatury', p. 137.
[57] Ibid., pp. 135–6.   [58] Ibid., pp. 107, 130.

the Bourbons. Stalin would make Soviet historians stress both of these themes later in the same decade, when he deemed Nazi Germany the Soviet Union's principal enemy, and prescribed the application of military power in stopping its expansionism.[59]

One can understand why in the Stalin era Soviet historians would have to cultivate the ability to alter their views as circumstances warranted. One senses that for historians like Lukin, whose Marxism-Leninism was a matter of conviction, rather than the result of abject servility, it was difficult, perhaps even heart-rending, to make the requisite adjustments. In the end, none of this mattered. Stalin did not need a reason to have historians—or persons in any other profession or sphere of Soviet intellectual life—shot or sent to a labour camp. For those whose intellectual roots were in an ideology other than Bolshevism, their actuarial prospects were especially precarious. That said, expressing an opinion inconsistent with, or even contrary to the Party Line was not in every instance conducive to imprisonment, exile to a labour camp, or execution. Some were better than others in anticipating objections or changes in the party line, and modulating their opinions accordingly. One of the most adept in navigating the ideological land mines to which so many other historians fell victim in the Terror was Evgenii Tarlé, who not only survived the Terror but was still active professionally at the end of it.

Tarlé's career was a series of peregrinations between respectability and virtual oblivion.[60] His earliest political views were nebulous, and his interest in French history predated service to with the Soviet regime.[61] But the views he expressed in the 1920s did not deviate in any significant way from Marxist ideology, and he did not suffer professionally or personally for espousing them. Although not a member of the Communist Party, he became a 'corresponding member' of the Academy of Sciences in 1921, and joined the Society of Marxist Historians soon after it was established in 1925. However, Pokrovskii, who was the founding president of the society and the editor of its journal, *Istorik marksist*, attacked Tarlé in 1929, accusing him specifically of ignoring the role of the individual in history; Pokrovskii even impugned him as a traitor who harboured the desire to become the foreign minister in any capitalist government that might replace the Soviet one. Of course Tarlé's 'unsavory' past ideologically helped to make such an unfounded and absurd accusation plausible.[62]

---

[59] Of course this prescription ended in August 1939 with the signing of the Non-Aggression Pact—only to be revived after Nazi Germany attacked the Soviet Union in June 1941.

[60] Ann. K. Erickson, 'E. V. Tarlé: The Career of a Historian under the Soviet Regime', *American Slavic and East European Review* 19, no. 2 (April 1960): pp. 202–16. I have drawn on this article for biographical information and also for insights into Tarlé's historical works.

[61] A. E. Manfred claimed that, at the time of the Bolshevik Revolution, Tarlé was not yet a Marxist. Erickson, 'Tarlé', p. 203.

[62] Erickson, 'Tarlé', pp. 203–4; Enteen, 'Marxist Historians during the Cultural Revolution', pp. 156–7.

As expected, Tarlé was arrested in 1930 and a year later sent into internal exile in Kazakhstan. But Stalin considered his talents as a historian useful in disseminating Soviet propaganda—in much the way he valued Maxim Gorky's abilities as a writer—and Tarlé returned from exile in 1934. Chastened by the experience, he published works fulsomely praising Mikhail Kutuzov and Pëtr Bagration, the Russian commanders principally responsible for driving Napoleon out of Russia in 1812. In 1936 he published a full-scale biography of the French emperor (which appeared in English translation in 1937).[63] Cognizant that the biography would be published only if it conformed to the strictures of Marxism-Leninism while also substantiating Stalin's belief in the singular role individuals (like himself) played in history, Tarlé knew he had to tread carefully. Should he stress human agency at the expense of economic determinism, he would be denounced no less severely than if he had viewed the French emperor as a mere captive of impersonal forces beyond his control. But Tarlé threaded this ideological needle successfully. In the biography he readily acknowledged Napoleon's singular prowess as a military tactician and strategist. But he also described the French emperor as the unwitting instrument of the capitalist bourgeoisie that had come to power in the French Revolution. Napoleon's attempts to subordinate the rest of Europe to his will and dominion marked 'the birth of the stubborn conflict of new social and economic forces, a conflict which did not begin with Napoleon or end with him, and whose basic significance consisted in the victorious assault of the middle class against the feudal and semi-feudal order in France and Europe'.[64] The wars he fought with England were at bottom a struggle between 'commercial and industrial groups' in both countries, each of which was seeking control over more backward ones: hence Napoleon's incursion into Russia in 1812.[65]

As for Napoleon's relationship to the French Revolution, Tarlé rejected the claim that by completing the revolution, he confirmed its victory *ex post facto*. Instead, Tarlé described the French Emperor as a transitional figure who, after extinguishing in France the revolutionary flame that had burned so fiercely, nonetheless carried the message of the French Revolution to the rest of Europe.[66] But in both of these endeavours Napoleon never represented the interests of any segment of the bourgeoisie other than its uppermost echelons, which, in Tarlé's schematization of the revolution, took power not in 1789, as most Bolsheviks and virtually all Soviet historians insisted, but in 1794, when Thermidor began.[67] Napoleon's *coup d'état* on 18 Brumaire confirmed its supremacy, which the

---

[63] Eugene Tarlé, *Bonaparte* (London, 1937). Because Tarlé and the Soviet historians who criticized him all evaluated Napoleon at least partly on the basis of his relationship to the French Revolution, and because none considered his rule emblematic of a uniquely Bonapartist regime, I am analysing their views here, in the section of the book concerned with the French Revolution, rather than in that which is concerned with Bonapartism, a concept that emerged later in the nineteenth century in the context of Louis Napoleon's dictatorship.

[64] Ibid., p. 10.   [65] Ibid., pp. 10–11.   [66] Ibid., p. 407.

[67] Ibid., p. 406.

prospective French emperor did nothing to diminish despite the fact that for political reasons he claimed to champion the peasantry, who provided the majority of the recruits for his army.

But Tarlé's biography suffered from a serious defect that caused its author, for good reason, to fear for his life. By 1936 Stalin had already conceptualized in his own mind the hybrid of Marxism-Leninism and Russian nationalism first expressed in 1924 in his theory of 'Socialism in One Country', which held that the Bolsheviks could by themselves construct a socialist society even if its completion and subsequent evolution into communism still required proletarian revolutions elsewhere in Europe.[68] Although it is not known if Stalin actually read Tarlé's biography, there is no doubt that he knew of it, and approved the attacks to which its author was subjected by Soviet historians, the principal claim of whom was that it downplayed the role peasant resistance had played in Napoleon's defeat.

Rather than contest these attacks or simply ignore them—to do either would have been suicidal professionally and possibly even physically—Tarlé, prudently, took them seriously, and produced another, very different biography. Published in 1938, it reserved for the Russian people a good deal of the credit for the victory the Russian army achieved; in the author's estimation, they fought with 'heroic fortitude'.[69] In this new iteration of Napoleon's life and career, Tarlé singled out the peasantry for commendation. The assistance it rendered the partisans fighting the *Grand Armée* from the rear was crucial in weakening it, so that after withdrawing from Moscow, it could not contest Kutuzov's forces pushing it westward towards the border with Prussia. Not even serfdom, in Tarlé's estimation of the peasantry's resistance, diminished its sense of national identity.[70] As for Napoleon himself, he was no longer the progressive figure he was in the original biography. Instead, Tarlé now depicted him as an insatiable imperialist for whom the Russian campaign was the most 'predatory' of all those he embarked on in a long career as a conqueror.[71] To underscore the obvious similarities between Napoleon and Hitler, and to reassure his readers that Russia would defeat the latter with the same determination that had enabled it to repulse the former, Tarlé stressed that the lessons Soviet generals could draw from Napoleon's defeat would ensure the Soviet Union's victory in the event that Hitler would be foolish enough to attack it. Conversely, German generals could not find in 'the Hitlerite textbooks' they studied any comparable insights concerning Russia's military strategy in 1812 that might still be relevant to any forthcoming Nazi invasion.[72]

For all of this, there were passages in the book in which Tarlé ascribed Napoleon's defeat to factors other than the personal qualities of Kutuzov on the

---

[68] Kotkin, *Stalin*, p. 555.
[69] Eugene Tarlé, *Napoleon's Invasion of Russia* (New York, 1942), p. 4.
[70] Ibid., p. 352.   [71] Ibid., p. 405.   [72] Ibid., p. 407.

one hand, and the collective virtue of the Russian peasantry on the other. Rather, what ensured Napoleon's defeat was simply the fact that his forces were overextended militarily, and were fighting in a climate that was literally unendurable and in political terms extraordinarily unfavourable. But the book was sufficiently stocked with the triumphalist clichés redolent of the Russian nationalism Stalin had found lacking in the original version for its author to be awarded the Stalin Prize in 1942 for his contribution, which concerned Kutuzov and the objectives Alexander I hoped to achieve by defeating Napoleon, to an official history of diplomacy.[73] Moreover, Stalin refraining until 1947, in an article in *Bol'shevik*, from publicly praising Kutuzov for employing the same tactics against Napoleon that Stalin himself had ordered his generals to pursue against the Nazis, and which the Soviet dictator said were responsible for both victories, the first in 1812 over the French, and the second in 1945 over the Germans.[74] By 1947 Tarlé was working on a very different project, a biography of the French diplomat Talleyrand, which, after it appeared in 1948, was praised in *Voprosy istorii* for refuting unnamed 'bourgeois historians' who ascribed the wily Frenchman's success to his personal qualities, rather than to objective conditions.[75] It was also lauded for making Talleyrand's 'bourgeois' diplomacy accessible not just to historians of France but to ordinary people, who might otherwise be ignorant of the degree to which his diplomacy informed the policies of the bourgeoisie in the twentieth century, including and especially the 'fascist German barbarians' who in 1941 had attacked the Soviet Union.[76]

But none of the praise Tarlé received immunized him against future attacks on his second, and presumably more ideologically acceptable account of Napoleon's Russian campaign. In 1951 it was attacked—thirteen years after its publication—in the journal *Bol'shevik* for using 'bourgeois' and non-Russian source materials instead of ideologically reliable Russian ones, and for exaggerating the role of weather and the geographical spaciousness of Russia to the detriment of Kutuzov ('the outstanding military leader of his era'), and of the Russian army as a whole.[77] Tarlé responded in a letter to the editors of the journal that in the book he was currently writing on the Napoleonic era he would rectify his earlier errors and incorporate the insights he gained from his corrections, along with those Stalin had shared with the Soviet people in his 1947 article, into his analysis of Kutuzov's abilities as a military strategist.[78] But because Tarlé still rejected several of the

[73] Erickson, 'Tarlé', p. 215.

[74] 'Otvet tov. Stalina na pis'mo tov. Razina', *Bol'shevik*, no. 3 (February, 1947): pp. 7–8.

[75] A. Molok, 'Obzor, E. V. Tarlé, *Taleiran* (Moscow/Leningrad, 1948)', *Voprosy istorii*, no. 10 (1948): p. 158.

[76] Ibid.

[77] S. Kozhukhov, 'K voprosu osenke roli M. I. Kutuzova v obshestvennoi voine 1812 goda', *Bol'shevik*, no. 15 (August 1951); p. 23.

[78] E. V. Tarlé, 'Pis'mo v redaktsiiu zhurnala "Bol'shevik"', *Bol'shevik*, no. 19 (October 1951): pp. 72, 76–7. Tarlé never finished the book.

criticisms reviewers had levelled against his second biography, the editors judged his recantation insufficient.[79] The result of all of this was that in an article in 1952, Tarlé tried again to make amends. He compared Napoleon's generalship unfavourably with Kutuzov, who he now insisted was also the superior diplomat; most important of all, the Russian commander was a Russian patriot and properly suspicious of foreigners. His only failing was his personal modesty. Because of it, even many who knew him were insufficiently appreciative of his talents.[80] In the article Tarlé—who could play the fulsome sycophant whenever it was warranted— even blamed Napoleon (falsely) for the fires just prior to his arrival in Moscow in 1812 that had burned much of the city to the ground.[81]

After the Second World War, both Napoleon and the French Revolution itself were reinterpreted, but well within ideological limits that had previously been prescribed. In 1946 A. L. Narochnitskii challenged the prevailing view, articulated originally by Lukin, that the Jacobins, notwithstanding their lower-class supporters, were exclusively bourgeois.[82] Narochnitskii did not disagree, but argued that the Jacobins, politically and programmatically, were not monolithic. Nor were they indistinguishable in terms of their class origin. There was a discrete and distinguishable right wing in the Jacobin dictatorship, which Narochnitskii said was drawn not from the lower ranks of the bourgeoisie, but rather from higher strata within this class, which were bent on self-enrichment; the most prominent Jacobins so inclined included Danton, Carnot, and Bertrand Barère. In fact Robespierre and Saint-Just were more apt to satisfy their demands and to protect their interests than Lukin and most other Soviet historians had been willing to admit. But in the end the political threat the Right Jacobins posed had to be neutralized, and their leaders guillotined. Nevertheless, the most dangerous enemies of Robespierre and Saint-Just were beyond the ranks of the Jacobins, among the plebeians who sought a property settlement which, while not entailing the abolition of private ownership, would nonetheless threaten the bourgeois interests of Robespierre and his allies. However, the Babouvists, in Narochnitskii's jaundiced opinion, were so far to the left of these centrist Jacobins that not even he, who believed that the homogeneity of the Jacobins had long been exaggerated, thought to include them within the Jacobins' ideological orbit.

In articles written in 1949 and 1964, Narochnitskii more or less repeated himself, although in the second of these, he took pains to distinguish the Jacobins, whom he still described as bourgeois, from *les enragés*, the *sans-culottes*, and the

[79] 'Ot redaktsii zhurnala "Bol'shevik"', ibid., pp. 78–80.
[80] E. V. Tarlé, 'Mikhail Illarionovich Kutuzov—polkovodets i diplomat', *Voprosy istorii*, no. 3 (March 1952): pp. 81–2.
[81] Ibid., p. 55.
[82] A. L. Narochnitskii, 'Raskol sredi iakobintsev i vneshniaia politika iakobinskoi respubliki s ianvaria do aprelia 1794', in *Uchenie zapiski Moskovskogo pedagogicheskogo instituta im. V. I. Lenina* (Moscow, 1946), vol. XXXVII, p. 120, cited in Revunenkov, *Ocherki po istorii Velikoi frantsuzskoi revoliutsii*, p. 110.

other plebeian elements who temporarily supported the Jacobins when they wrongly believed their own interests and those of the Jacobins coincided. But once this particular fiction could no longer be sustained, the two erstwhile allies in the struggle to eliminate feudalism and the monarchy became deadly enemies. Although the Jacobins managed to eliminate the threat from these lower-class elements, their victory was a pyrrhic one. Without their support, Robespierre was powerless to resist the charge that he was conspiring with Great Britain, and his downfall, which followed quickly, was preordained.[83]

In everything he wrote about the Jacobins, Narochnitskii—in contradistinction to most Soviet historians—seemed to recognize that how one characterized and classified them was a matter of perspective. Viewing the Jacobins from within their own ranks, they appeared, not altogether implausibly, as heterogeneous; indeed throughout much—but by no means all—of his analysis Narochnitskii situated himself so that that was how he viewed the Jacobins. But he also recognized that when he viewed them from a vantage point beyond their own ideological, geographical, and temporal limits, and specifically from that of a Soviet historian in the twentieth century, the Jacobins were indubitably bourgeois. For Narochnitskii this was hardly a pejorative. Once they had shed the 'deviationists' both to their right and to their left, the remaining Jacobins were 'the most courageous and decisive representatives of the revolutionary class of their time—the bourgeoisie'.[84]

What so bedeviled Soviet historians when they wrote about the Jacobins was that they could fairly be described as monolithic and heterogeneous simultaneously. When Narochnitskii, for example, considered the Jacobins in isolation from the world beyond them, he ascribed the policy differences he perceived to subdivisions with the bourgeoisie. There were Right, Centre, and Left Jacobins, whose political preferences reflected their origins in the haute-, middle, and petit-bourgeoisie respectively. These differences were real, and because the terminology used to describe them in no way contradicted Marxist ideology, Narochnitskii had no reason to question them. But when he considered the Jacobins in relation to the rest of France, which in the 1790s was teeming with extremists like the Babouvists on the left and royalists and *faux* revolutionaries like the Girondins on the right, the Jacobins were transformed, in his analysis, into a discrete and ideologically self-contained entity. He did this, one suspects, partly in the interest of clarity, partly out of a visceral commitment to the concepts and categories of Marxist

[83] A. L. Narochnitskii, 'Voprosy voiny i mira vo vneshnei politike iakobinskoi respubliki letom 1793 r.', *Uchenie zapiski Moskovskogo pedagogicheskogo instituta im. V. I. Lenin* (Moscow, 1949), vol. LVIII, p. 87, cited in Revunenkov, *Ocherki po istorii Velikoi frantsuzskoi revoliutsii*, p. 111; A. L. Narochnitskii, 'Voprosy voiny i mira v politike iakobintsev nakanune 9 termidora', in *Mezhdunarodnye otnosheniia politika, diplomatiia XVI–XX veka* (Moscow, 1964), especially pp. 469–70, 475, 511.

[84] Narochnitskii, 'Raskol sredi iakobinstev', cited in Revunenkov, *Ocherki po istorii Velikoi frantsuzskoi revoliutsii*, pp. 110–11.

analysis, and partly because, in comparison to everyone who was not a Jacobin, the Jacobins were monolithic. Thus the contradiction in his descriptions of the Jacobins was more apparent than real, a matter of perspective rather than of any failing or mistake in what he wrote. When everything external to them was excluded, the Jacobins were heterogeneous; when it was included, they were monolithic.

As long as this fundamental distinction is borne in mind, the debates among Soviet historians on the Jacobins are more easily understood. One can also comprehend why these debates occurred in the first place. Soviet historians writing on the French Revolution assumed from the Marxist-Leninist ideology they accepted that the Jacobins had to belong to a particular class, and that what the Jacobins believed, said, and did had to reflect that inescapable fact. But as historians they also could not help but notice differences in belief, oratory, and action, and felt compelled to incorporate these differences into their analysis by introducing tripartite distinctions based on class (haute, middle, and petit-bourgeoisie) and ideology and politics (Right, Centre, Left). Whom they included in these categories was at times problematic—should the Hébertists, for example, be considered Left Jacobins, or were they beyond the outer limits of Jacobinism entirely? Soviet historians, understandably, differed in how they answered such questions.

As long as Stalin was alive, this kind of ideological hair-splitting did not really matter. Stalin himself seemed unconcerned by it, and at any rate wrote nothing about it. For him it was sufficient that Soviet historians consider the Jacobins French patriots as well as 'progressive' in the policies they pursued. Most important of all, the Jacobins should be praised for their valour in unmasking and destroying domestic traitors intent on facilitating the efforts of foreign enemies to end the revolution and bring back the *ancien régime*. Once the vast projects of social transformation that had been launched in the late 1920s had been accomplished—albeit at an appalling cost in human lives—any sympathy Stalin may have harboured for the left-wing elements in the French Revolution that wished to go beyond what the Jacobins desired, and in Leninist fashion transform a bourgeois revolution into a socialist one, disappeared for good. The Soviet Union, he declared in 1936, was now socialist, and there was no longer any need for Soviet Babouvists to cajole Soviet Jacobins to go further. The Soviet Jacobins—of whom Stalin was the paradigmatic example—were fully capable of proceeding to communism on their own.

*   *   *

Throughout the Stalin era, the themes Soviet historians stressed in their analysis of the French Revolution were reflected in the arts and in the popular culture. E. O. Burgunker's frontispiece to a collection of poems published shortly before the first show trial in Moscow in August 1936 depicted Robespierre's downfall vividly, and with the clear message that it was the work of malevolent and duplicitous conspirators.[85] Significantly, it showed Robespierre at a lectern, presumably on the floor of the Convention. Two of the conspirators are trying to pull Robespierre to the floor, but without success. The third conspirator, who can see his colleagues' predicament, is about to stab Robespierre with a knife. That the latter cannot see the man who will shortly murder him underscores the conspirators' cowardice and duplicity. Of course Burgunker has deliberately compressed Robespierre's arrest and execution—which in fact occurred over an entire day—to a matter of seconds.[86] In fact, there is nothing in what is depicted to indicate that Robespierre's enemies are acting in the name of any law. Instead of arresting the Jacobin leader and adjudicating his criminal culpability, they are simply killing him—with the result that he does not have the opportunity to die publicly with a look of defiance that might shame his executioners and memorialize his courage in the minds of any spectators. In this respect it is noteworthy that, in Burgunker's creation, the audience to which Robespierre had been orating is omitted. This has the effect of underscoring the Jacobin's vulnerability; three men are engaged in killing just one man, which of course only heightens his martyrdom, even if, unfortunately, there is no one watching to confirm it. Burgunker's frontispiece, in fact, was intended as a morality play in miniature, in which the moral polarity between the Jacobin leader and his murderers is stark and unmistakable. Anyone viewing it in the Soviet Union in the mid-1930s with even just a rudimentary knowledge of the French Revolution would understand that what was depicted was harmful to the revolution, and that what happened to Robespierre should never happen to Stalin.

Another aspect of the frontispiece worth mentioning, in light of the absence of any spectators or of anyone other than the murderers and their victim, is the degree to which the French Revolution was personalized in the figure of Robespierre. This, one suspects, was not accidental. A good deal of the visual art that appeared during the Stalin era that pertained to the revolution was 'biographical'. In much the way the Stalin cult ascribed virtually everything that was virtuous and praiseworthy in the Soviet Union to Stalin himself, events, especially historical events, were personalized, and not just to make them more easily understood. In Stalinist culture and social mores, the complexities of modern life were simplified into the terms of the longstanding paternalism in Russian history and culture that presumably would increase the respect, admiration, and obedience Stalin expected from the Soviet people.[87] In the Stalin era, the traditional dichotomy in Russian

---

[85] Unaniants, 'Velikaia frantsuzskaia revoliutsiia v knizhnoi grafike. 1917–1940 gg.', p. 420.

[86] Palmer, *Twelve Who Ruled*, pp. 375–81.

[87] Pipes, *Russia under the Old Regime*, especially pp. 281–318. Sheila Fitzpatrick, in *Everyday Stalinism: Ordinary Life in Extraordinary Times: Soviet Russia in the 1930s* (New York, 1999), p. 15, notes that low-level officials deliberately fostered this paternalism. But she also argues that after the famine in the early 1930s, many peasants rejected the illusion the government fostered of Stalin as 'a good tsar', ibid., p. 28.

culture between father and son was deliberately replicated in analogous relationships between teacher and student, mentor and neophyte, and most critical of all,
between ruler and subject.[88]

In much of what artists and writers produced during the Stalin era that touched
on the French Revolution, one can see this same distinction refracted through the
image of the eloquent, courageous, resourceful, and heroic revolutionary acting in
the interests of ordinary people who have the good sense to defer to their betters
and follow their orders unquestioningly; in this respect, they might as well be
children properly obeying their parents. One finds this motif, for example, in
E. I. Kogan's frontispiece, entitled 'Robespierre on the Rostrum', that preceded the
text in a 1939 republication of Rolland's play.[89] Quite deliberately Kogan positioned the rostrum so that Robespierre is elevated in relation to his listeners, who
are obvious enthralled by what he is saying. Even when rendered in strict
portraiture, without onlookers or supporters demonstrating their admiration—
as was the case in the series of drawings M. K. Sokolov produced of Mirabeau,
Sieyès, Lafayette, and Danton—the avuncular, almost Stalin-like wisdom the
leaders of the French Revolution seemed to personify is obvious despite their
relative youthfulness.[90]

Among the other qualities artists stressed when depicting the French Revolution were heroism and struggle. For that reason, the individuals they selected to
personify the revolution were depicted as larger than life—idealized, romanticized,
and poeticized in varying degrees depending upon the artist's estimation of them.
A 1940 lithograph of Marat orating before an attentive crowd skillfully imparted
the message that the French Revolution was accomplished by outstanding individuals far more than by ordinary people, who, when they act, are motivated more
by rhetorical exhortation than by grievances grounded in material exploitation.[91]
Even Babeuf, whose communism Stalin considered premature, was accorded the
honour of his bust standing prominently in Minsk in the headquarters of the
Belorussian Communist Party.[92]

Yet another theme Stalinist artists developed in explicating the deeper meaning
of the French Revolution was its militarization. Above and beyond the application
of force and coercion by civilian leaders intent on extirpating their enemies, the
revolution was notable for the degree to which its iconic moments were military or
quasi-military affairs. This, at any rate, was how artists in the Stalin era depicted
them. Among the lithographs Iu. P. Velikanov produced in the 1930s was one

[88]   Bergman, 'Valerii Chkalov', pp. 147–52.
[89]   Unaniants, 'Velikaia frantsuzskaia revoliutsiia v knizhnoi grafike. 1917–1940 gg.', p. 421.
[90]   N. T. Unaniants, 'M. K. Sokolov. Tsikl "Velikaia frantsuzskaia revoliutsiia"', pp. 330–47.
[91]   Unaniants, 'Velikaia frantsuzskoi revoliutsii v knizhnoi grafike. 1917–1940 gg.', p. 425.
[92]   N. T. Unaniants, 'Velikaia frantsuzskaia revoliutsiia v sovetskom izobrazitel'nom iskusstve', in
Frantsuzskii ezhegodnik (1989), p. 262.

showing *sans-culottes* bombarding the Bastille with cannons.[93] In the actual event, the defenders of the fortress, now serving as a prison, were the ones with cannons; the *sans-culottes* were armed only with muskets and swords.[94] In a similar vein, a frontispiece A. D. Goncharov drew in 1933 for a score François-Joseph Gossek had composed attempting to replicate the revolution musically, depicted civilians marching in neat rows behind musicians as if they were soldiers, and the revolution itself a military campaign.[95] Finally, in the frontispiece K. I. Rudakov drew for a new edition of Rolland's plays entitled *Théâtre de La Révolution*, one sees the Bastille assaulted by what appear to be troops carrying flags and armed with cannons, and led by their commander, who is on horseback and brandishing a sword.[96] In Rudakov's rendition, this event—which encapsulates for Frenchmen the spirit, message, and larger meaning of the revolution—is nothing less than a full-scale military operation. To those viewing it the way Rudakov described it, the storming of the Bastille was not at all spontaneous—a quality Stalin, no less than Lenin, generally abhorred in politics and in most other aspects of life.

*   *   *

In the way it was depicted during the Stalin era—not only by Stalin himself, but also by historians, writers, and artists—the French Revolution differed significantly from how the Bolsheviks had viewed it immediately after the October Revolution. With Stalin's rise to power, its universalist aspirations—its claim to speak on behalf of all people irrespective of their time and place—receded into the background. What replaced it was a morality play on the virtues of patriotism and strict obedience to one's superiors, and on the absolute necessity of ferreting out, unmasking, and physically destroying one's country's enemies. In short, the utility of the French Revolution did not diminish. But its meaning and its practical relevance changed considerably. It is certainly true, notwithstanding Stalin's protestations to the contrary, that he continued to consider the revolution relevant to his political needs, and for that reason it remained an integral aspect of the mythology the original Bolsheviks had begun constructing about their own revolution even before it actually occurred. And after their revolution brought the Bolsheviks to power, the earlier revolution in France they considered a precursor and a precedent retained an immediacy and a relevance that make the history of the Soviet Union from 1917 to 1953 inexplicable absent any consideration of its influence.

---

[93] N. T. Unaniants, 'Iu. P. Velikanov. Seriia "velikaia frantsuzskaia revoliutsiia"', in *Frantsuzskii ezhegodnik* (1989), p. 271.

[94] To be sure, the cannons were fired only on ceremonial occasions, and evidently were directed so that their cannon balls would land precisely where there was little that could be damaged. Frantz Funck-Brentano, *Legends of the Bastille* (London, 1899), p. 256.

[95] Unaniants, 'Velikaia frantsuzskaia revoliutsiia v knizhnoi grafike. 1917–1940 gg.', p. 418.

[96] Ibid., p. 424.

This was not the case, however, for most of the remaining years of the Soviet Union's existence. From Stalin's death in 1953 to the advent of *perestroika* ('reconstruction') and *glasnost'* ('openness') in the late 1980s, the French Revolution, while remaining a subject of interest and considerable controversy for historians, receded in Soviet politics and culture into the background. Indeed, one could plausibly argue that when Khrushchev and Brezhnev ruled the Soviet Union from 1953 to 1982, and Iurii Andropov and Viktor Chernenko presided over it from 1982 to 1985, the French Revolution hardly mattered at all.

But such an argument would not be correct. After 1953 the example of the French Revolution was still invoked, albeit not nearly as often, and certainly not with the same intensity, as it was when the Soviet Union was in its ascendancy. Neither its survival nor its status as a socialist regime was any longer in doubt, at least as far as its leaders were concerned. Moreover, the distinction the Soviet Union could justifiably claim for itself as the victor over the Nazis who raised the Red Flag over the Reichstag in Berlin in 1945, did much to confirm the conviction of the Soviet leadership that the Soviet system to which the October Revolution had given birth would endure, and that no other revolutions were needed to confirm its legitimacy. At last, the October Revolution could be decoupled from the French Revolution and be considered, to all intents and purposes, *sui generis*. But that did not occur, and when the Soviet Union, in the late 1960s, first showed outward signs of decline, and in the late 1970s of actual decay, the relevance and the utility of the French Revolution increased. Precisely how it did so must now be determined.

10

Returning to the Leninist Line under Khrushchev and Brezhnev

Soviet leaders invoked the French Revolution infrequently between Stalin's death and the Gorbachev era. Neither Khrushchev nor Brezhnev nor the hapless Konstantin Chernenko was intellectually curious, much less an intellectual. The French Revolution spoke to nothing in their personal or political lives. Only Iurii Andropov, probably because his portfolio before becoming general secretary included the surveillance of political dissidents, knew enough about the revolution to have an opinion of it. While in charge of the KGB, he publicly lauded Felix Dzerzhinskii—one of his predecessors in the position he held—as a 'proletarian Jacobin' on the centenary of his birth in 1979.[1] But Andropov said nothing about the revolution, at least not publicly, after becoming general secretary three years later. In the Soviet press, the revolution did not go unnoticed in these years, but references were limited mostly to anniversaries of the storming of the Bastille. Entries in authoritative reference works, most notably the *Bol'shaia Sovetskaia Entsiklopediia*, still called the revolution, in imitation of Marx and Lenin, 'the Great French Revolution', and implicitly justified its adjectival honourific on the grounds that it inaugurated the age of industrial capitalism in France and in the other parts of Europe that were exposed to its progressive agenda.[2] The entries also repeated the relevant tenets of what long ago had become Leninist orthodoxy. In 1978, for example, the encyclopaedia reiterated Lenin's sharp distinction between the original Jacobins and the so-called Russian Jacobins of the late nineteenth century, denigrating the latter as hopelessly 'utopian' and as ideologically anomalous as the Blanquists in France.[3] In the visual arts, the same inattention prevailed. Painters and sculptors reproduced many of the principal figures of the revolution, and after Stalin's death the censorship was relaxed sufficiently so that personages previously denigrated as tools of the haute bourgeoisie, such as Mirabeau, could be given the same recognition accorded longstanding heroes

---

[1] Iu. O. Andropov, *Kommunisticheskaia uvezhdennost'—Velikaia sila stroitelei novogo mira: Doklad na torzhestvennom sobranii v Moskve, posviashchennom 100 letiiu so dnia rozhdeniia F. E. Dzerzhinskogo* (Moscow, 1977), p. 4.

[2] For example, *Bol'shaia sovetskaia entsiklopediia*, 3rd edn (Moscow, 1971), vol. IV, p. 405.

[3] *Bol'shaia sovetskaia entsiklopediia* (Moscow, 1978), vol. XXX, p. 483.

such as Robespierre, Saint-Just, and Marat.[4] Although there were still no public monuments to any of the above-mentioned revolutionaries, Marat enjoyed the distinction of both a chocolate factory and a street in Leningrad bearing his name, although a play about his life that was written in 1954 was never performed.[5]

In short, despite the fact that in the three decades between Stalin and Gorbachev, editions of Victor Hugo's *1793* still sold well, interest in the French Revolution waned.[6] Khrushchev, Brezhnev, Andropov, and Chernenko all prized the privileges from which they and the rest of the so-called *nomenklatura* benefitted, even though these privileges were not heritable. In that sense, there remained in the Soviet Union a self-contained and easily identifiable ruling elite, even though its composition changed generationally and was not distinguishable from ordinary Soviet citizens by the possession of wealth. Like the Thermidorians of the late 1790s—of the existence of whom one suspects only Andropov, of all the Soviet leaders cited above, was aware—these leaders had no interest in vast projects of social and economic engineering on the scale to which Stalin was accustomed.

As a result, the French Revolution, in the post-Stalin Soviet Union, became something of an anachronism, its exhortatory message relevant more to earlier, more 'transformational' periods of Soviet rule, and its role in the mythology the regime still needed to justify itself considerably diminished.[7] But it did not disappear entirely. Rather, the particular message the Soviet leadership wanted to impart about the revolution required that its leaders be depicted differently. This was most apparent in the visual arts. The painter X. A. Avrutis, for example,

[4] N. T. Unaniants, 'Velikaia frantsuzskaia revoliutsiia v sovetskom iskusstve i literature', in *Frantsuzskii ezhegodnik* (1989), p. 509.
[5] Schoenfeld, 'Uses of the Past' (PhD dissertation), p. 221; Unaniants, 'Velikaia frantsuzskaia revoliutsiia v sovetskogo iskusstve i literature', p. 511.
[6] Unaniants, 'Velikaia frantsuzskaia revoliutsiia v sovetskom iskusstve i literature', p. 504.
[7] In other, less ossified communist regimes, the influence of the French Revolution remained strong—as it did among their increasingly emboldened opponents. In most of the regimes, the lesson their leaders gleaned from the revolution was that the Jacobins possessed the toughness necessary to kill their opponents, and that their virtuous objectives were justification enough. Suong Sikoeun, a leading figure in the Khmer Rouge, wrote that 'Robespierre is my hero. Robespierre and Pol Pot: both of them share the qualities of determination and integrity'. Fidel Castro, according to some who knew him well, 'loved comparisons to the French Revolution'. Ho Chi Minh, who had attended the founding congress of the French Communist Party in 1920, wrote in 1945 that 'French imperialists were abusing the standard of Liberty, Equality, and Fraternity', and by doing so were 'acting contrary to the ideals of humanity and justice'. Sikoeun quoted in Jean-Louis Margolin, 'Cambodia: The Country of Disconcerting Crimes', Stéphane Courtois et al., *The Black Book of Communism* (Cambridge MA, 1999), p. 624; Pascal Fontaine, 'Communism in Latin America', ibid., p. 651; Jean Lacouture, *Ho Chi Minh: A Political Biography* (New York, 1968), pp. 26, 111. The French Revolution also inspired anticommunists. Students in Tiananmen Square in Beijing in May 1989 sang the *Marseillaise* to underscore their opposition to communism and their demand for democratic government. Doyle, *History of the French Revolution*, p. 422. On 4 November 1989 some of the 500,000 marchers in East Berlin calling for an end to the communist regime in East Germany carried signs with the inscription '1789–1989'. Gale Stokes, *The Walls Came Tumbling Down* (New York, 1993), p. 140. Contrary to a popular misconception, Zhou Enlai was not referring to the French Revolution when, in 1972, he said it was too early to assess it definitely. What he was referring to was the turmoil in France in the spring of 1968. Richard McGregor, 'Zhou's Cryptic Caution Lost in Translation', *The Financial Times* (10 June 2011): p. 8.

produced portraits of most of the major figures of the revolution, including Danton, Saint-Just, Desmoulins, and Robespierre, in his 'Cycle of the Great French Revolution'.[8] But none was depicted as a resolute and strong-willed advocate of transformational change whose passionate commitment to progress was leavened by rational calculation of what was, and what was not, politically possible. In one rendition, painted in 1975, Desmoulins appears frivolous and even effeminate, which were hardly qualities Brezhnev, who was in power when the portrait was produced, or any of his predecessors prized or considered appropriate in a political leader. Another portrait Avrutis produced of Desmoulins, and the one he did of Danton, seem more like caricatures than depictions consistent with contemporary descriptions. While the explicit brush strokes Avrutis used might suggest emotional identification, neither of these legendary avatars of modern revolutionary oratory comes across as especially attractive or impressive. Danton, in fact, appears to be practically screaming, his teeth bared and his eyes aflame. But it was Avrutis's depictions of Robespierre that best captured the post-transformational exhaustion pervasive in the post-Stalin era. In one of his paintings, Robespierre's severity, arrogance, and coldness—all traits contemporaries ascribed to him—are unmistakable.[9] In another portrait of Robespierre, the French Jacobin comes off even worse.[10] Avrutis portrays him immediately after his decapitation. Nothing about the now-deceased leader suggests heroism or courage in the face of adversity. The onlookers—only their feet are depicted—appear eager to trample the remains. Robespierre is not a martyr, only a loser, and anyone observing the painting without foreknowledge of the event it depicted could reasonably infer that the French Revolution was a dismal failure as well.

Another painter drawn to the revolution, B. A. Tolbert, denigrated Robespierre differently. One of his paintings of the Jacobin leader is part of a triptych, with portraits of Thomas More and Tomas Campanella on either side of him; the impression this leaves is that Robespierre, who lived after both of these men, was nonetheless part of the period of history to which they belonged.[11] This central figure in the French Revolution—and by implication the French Revolution itself—are thus not forerunners of future revolutions such as the October Revolution, but rather the last personification of a pre-modern fervour bearing little, if any, resemblance to the contemporary Soviet Union, or even to the younger, more aspirational regime that took power in 1917. Moreover, Robespierre is shown on the scaffold, minutes, or perhaps mere moments, from his execution. Motionless and staring straight ahead, with his lips compressed, *l'Incorruptible* is stoical in the face of death; there is no intimation of defiance befitting a committed revolutionary. What appear to be French soldiers are standing behind him, which suggests that Tolbert saw Robespierre as the defeated combatant he was for Avrutis.

---

[8] Unaniants, 'Velikaia frantsuzskaia revoliutsiia v sovetskom iskusstve i literature', pp. 508–9.
[9] Ibid., p. 508.   [10] Ibid., p. 508.   [11] Ibid., p. 507.

Robespierre, in this rendition, has no supporters; he is, in essence, a solitary and monumental figure rather than one whose death will chagrin the masses he previously led. In fact it is difficult to imagine—if this painting is the only piece of evidence about the Jacobins to which a viewer has access—the French people caring, one way or the other, about Robespierre's fate.

One might think that the Soviet dissidents, because their condemnation of the Soviet system was based on moral principles mostly traceable to the Enlightenment, would write a great deal about the French Revolution, the intellectual origins of which were identical to their own. But only a few actually did. A possible reason for this was that since the Soviet Union based its own legitimacy on the French Revolution, the dissidents could hardly do the same. In addition, dissidents like Alexander Solzhenitsyn who rejected Soviet Communism because they believed its rationalism and secularism originated in the Enlightenment, considered the French Revolution—the vehicle that carried its message to the rest of Europe—counterproductive of the principles found exclusively in Russian Orthodoxy that they preferred.[12] Finally, many of the dissidents may simply have considered the specific origins of their opinions unimportant. That their opinions, in their own minds, were expressive of natural law, and therefore timeless as well as universally valid, may have made unnecessary, and potentially misleading, the task of tracing them historically to the French Revolution, or to any other event specific to any particular time and place.

Among the few who cited aspects of the revolution, if only fleetingly, was Roy Medvedev. In his critique of Stalinism, *Let History Judge*, he compared Stalin to Napoleon, and Stalin's psyche to that of Napoleon's police chief, Joseph Fouché.[13] Another was Dmitrii Volkogonov, who, depending on definitions, may not even have been a dissident at all; prior to the Gorbachev era, Volkogonov, in contrast to the dissidents, did not condemn the Soviet system publicly. Nevertheless, his views on Stalinism, which were as harshly critical as Medvedev's, were germinating when the dissident movement existed, and may have been influenced by it. But however one defines him, Volkogonov's belief in the French Revolution's salience in evaluating the Soviet Union is clear. In an interview during the Gorbachev era, he noted that every revolution contains within itself 'the seeds of Thermidor', and then, referring to the Stalin era, said that the October Revolution was no exception.[14] But not every revolution, he continued, need experience a Thermidor like the original

---

[12] Perhaps the definitive statement and exposition of these principles are the collection of essays, *From under the Rubble*, edited by Alexander Solzhenitsyn et al. (New York, 1976). Solzhenitsyn's hostility to all things Western, not just its philosophical rationalism and liberalism, is most apparent in the commencement address he delivered at Harvard University in 1978, reprinted as *A World Split Apart* (New York, 1988).

[13] Roy Medvedev, *Let History Judge: The Origins and Consequences of Stalinism* (New York, 1989), pp. 571–2, 596–7.

[14] 'O Staline i Stalinizme: beseda D. A. Volkogonym i R. A. Medvedevym', *Istoriia SSSR*, no 4 (1989), p. 102.

one, and revolutions can mitigate or otherwise modify its effects so as to avoid the harm it caused France.[15] But every Thermidor, he said, involved some version of bureaucratism, and Stalin's regime in that regard was no exception. But according to Volkogonov, this did not mean—as Trotsky famously insisted—that the Georgian dictator was a mediocrity and a tool of the bureaucracy, whose growth he fostered. Rather than look to the French Revolution for explanations of Stalinism, Volkogonov believed that the Roman Empire offered a far better basis for comparison. Stalin, he said, was like Caesar, and the system Stalin created a form of Caesarism. But without the opportunity, during the interview, to explain precisely how the two means of rule were analogous, Volkogonov further muddied the conceptual waters by claiming in the interview that Stalinism was also an expression of totalitarianism—which to exist requires the modern technology Caesar and the Romans obviously lacked.[16]

Andrei Sakharov, the dissident most indebted intellectually to the Enlighten-ment, was among the few who affirmed the causal relationship between the Enlightenment and the French Revolution, and understood that the moral abso-lutism that helped to define the dissident movement reached Russia first by means of the French Revolution and then through the refractory lens of the pre-revolutionary intelligentsia. That his dissidence was grounded in the Enlightenment truly warrants his description as a Russian *philosophe*.[17] For Sakharov the French Revolution was a milestone in the history of humanity, which he truly believed was the history of progress. In contrast to Solzhenitsyn, Sakharov considered reason not the cause of the evils both men decried, but rather the best corrective of them. Far from corrupting the moral virtue of the Russian people, reason was for Sakharov the essential prerequisite to the rule of law, without which a truly just and humane society that sanctified the individual personality cannot exist. But perhaps because the dissidents were understandably preoccupied with explaining those aspects of the Soviet Union they found morally repugnant, they lacked the time or the inclination to answer the questions Sakharov and Solzhenitsyn addressed, namely whether the Enlightenment and the French Revolution contributed to the moral improvement of humanity, and whether these two signal events in Western Civil-ization were the repository of the moral virtue that suffused the dissidents (as Sakharov believed), or the ultimate source of the crimes against humanity of which the Soviet Union was undeniably guilty (as Solzhenitsyn believed).

*   *   *

---

[15] Ibid., pp. 102–3.   [16] Ibid., pp. 102–3, 105.
[17] A biography of Sakharov that ascribes his dissidence to the intelligentsia (as well as to the requirements of science) is Jay Bergman, *Meeting the Demands of Reason: The Life and Thought of Andrei Sakharov* (Ithaca NY, 2009). On the dissidents' indebtedness to the intelligentsia, and their awareness of it, see Jay Bergman, 'Soviet Dissidents on the Russian Intelligentsia, 1956–1985: The Search for a Usable Past', *Russian Review* 51, no. 1. (January 1992): pp. 16–35. Also tracing the origins of the intelligentsia to the Enlightenment is Shatz, *Soviet Dissent*, especially pp. 12–63. The work of Sakharov that mostly clearly reveals the Western origins of his dissidence is his most famous one, *Progress, Coexistence, and Intellectual Freedom*, edited by Harrison E. Salisbury (New York, 1968).

Soviet historians, of course, lived in a very different world, philosophically and morally, from that which the Soviet dissidents inhabited, a world still shaped by Marxist beliefs about the primacy of class struggle and its role in causing history to unfold as a series of increasingly progressive stages leading ultimately to eternal happiness and the satisfaction of all material and spiritual needs.[18] In brief, everything in history was preparation for what followed it, and for that reason Soviet historians, unlike the dissidents, had no choice but to believe the French Revolution worthy of their continued consideration. Of course there were limits to how far they could deviate from Leninist orthodoxy before transgressing it. But in the post-Stalin era, these did not preclude debate and disagreement.

Although the official ideology of the Soviet Union was an amalgam of Marx's thought and Lenin's, the two men differed significantly on the French Revolution. While they both called it a Great Revolution, and agreed that its greatness inhered in its role as the first bourgeois revolution, they disagreed on the role the bourgeoisie played in it. For Marx the French Revolution was a bourgeois revolution because the bourgeoisie was both its instrument and principal beneficiary. For Lenin, the bourgeoisie was more the latter than the former; by 1793 the bourgeoisie had taken the revolution as far as it could, and a surrogate was needed to continue it. This turned out to be a hybrid strikingly similar to 'the democratic-dictatorship of the proletariat and the peasantry' that, in Lenin's ideologically self-serving scheme of things, succeeded the Provisional Government in Russia in October 1917. But while the first of these hybrids could not survive once it completed the French Revolution, there were no limits on how far the second one could go because by 1917 history had reached the point at which the proletariat was ready to assume the role history assigned it of replacing capitalism with socialism, and then socialism with communism.

As for the Jacobins in the French Revolution, Marx and Lenin agreed that they had emerged from the bourgeoisie, only to replace it in power and then drive the revolution to completion. But Lenin went well beyond anything Marx had written about the lower classes the Jacobins represented politically. Lenin stressed that the dictatorship the Jacobins established included elements of the population that were not bourgeois, and that for a few months in the winter and spring of 1794 the Jacobins' objectives far exceeded what was historically possible. According to Lenin, that was the reason the Jacobins lost power in the summer of 1794; whether those responsible for imposing these more radical objectives on the Jacobins were other Jacobins or persons from other classes entirely, Lenin never made clear. But about one aspect of the Jacobin dictatorship, and about the French Revolution

---

[18] Roi and Zhores Medvedev were the most prominent of the dissidents who considered Marxist-Leninism indispensable both in explaining the Soviet Union and in prescribing the principles they thought would best reform it. But most dissidents were not Marxists or Marxist-Leninists, and a clear majority of them were hostile to both.

generally, he was certain—that their principal beneficiary was the bourgeoisie, and for that reason the French Revolution remained a bourgeois revolution. The principal losers in the revolution, apart from the aristocracy and the monarchy that had served as the political instrument of the aristocracy, were the plebeians and the peasants—and also the more radical Jacobins who supported them—who sought objectives that were unachievable. This in turn emboldened reactionary and counter-revolutionary enemies of the revolution both at home and abroad, and the French Revolution stopped with the advent of Thermidor. To be sure, the radical objectives of the plebeians and the peasants, and of the elements within the petit-bourgeoise that shared them, were not socialist or communist. To be so was impossible. The plebeians were not a proletariat. But their ideological successors would be, and those in Russia have been engaged since 1917 in the task of creating a society more radical—and therefore more just and more conducive to the total liberation of the individual—than anything the Babouvists, the plebeians, and the Jacobins—in descending order in terms of their radicalism—could have hoped to establish.

This, at any rate, was what passed for the party line in the post-Stalin Soviet Union. Nearly all Soviet historians accepted it. But how they expressed it varied greatly. In 1972 B. G. Veber, after faithfully reiterating it, noted the 'fierce hatred' the Great French Revolution still inspired among reactionaries, which, to Lenin years earlier, proved 'the vitality and the force of its influence on humanity' in the nineteenth and early twentieth centuries.[19] V. S. Alexeev-Popov, also in 1972, after quoting Lenin on the obligation Marxism imposed to respect the French Revolution 'most profoundly', singled out the Jacobins for supporting what Lenin had once described most as 'the revolutionary people among the revolutionary progressive classes of their time'.[20] The Jacobins were the embodiment of revolutionary virtue— and thus the Girondins, their implacable opponents, could not be anything other than the opposite.[21] Ten years earlier, he and Iu. Ia. Baskin had written that while the dictatorship the Jacobins had established was, for a short time, a makeshift coalition of all the lower classes in France, the Jacobins were always in charge of it; indeed the Jacobins themselves, in contrast to their supporters, were either bourgeois or, more specifically, petit-bourgeois, depending upon which part of the article one was reading. But no matter where one located the Jacobins on any spectrum within the bourgeoisie, there should be no doubt that the French Revolution was a bourgeois revolution because it ushered in the supremacy of the bourgeoisie.[22]

[19] Veber, 'V. I. Lenin i istoricheskoe nasledie iakobintsev', p. 6.

[20] V. S. Alexeev-Popov, 'Znachenie opyta velikoi frantsuzskoi revoliutsii dlia russkogo rabochego dvizheniia nakanune i v period revoliutsii 1905–1907 gg.', in *Frantsuzskii ezhegodnik* (1970), p. 35.

[21] Ibid., pp. 36–7.

[22] V. S. Alexeev-Popov and Iu. Ia. Baskin, 'Problemy istorii iakobinskoi literatury v svete trudov V. I. Lenina', in *Iz istorii iakobinskoi diktatury 1793–1794*, edited by V. S. Alexeev-Popov, A. Ia. Gansov, and K. D. Petriaev (Odessa, 1962), pp. 25–9.

In this bedrock assumption one detects the logical fallacy of *cui bono*—of confusing the beneficiaries of something, in this case the French Revolution, for those responsible for it. But irrespective of whether the bourgeoisie carried out the revolution or merely benefitted from it, Soviet historians were in agreement that its ultimate beneficiary would be the proletariat. While ratifying politically the new economic dominion of the bourgeoisie, the French Revolution was also responsible, in the words of K. E. Dzhedzhula, for 'preparing objectively the conditions for the rapid development of the proletariat . . . and for the formation and development of socialist ideas' not only in France and in Europe, but also elsewhere in the world.[23] For A. V. Ado, who produced detailed studies of the peasantry in France, Lenin deserved the prestige he enjoyed among historians because he pointed out the contributions the peasantry and the plebeians made to the revitalization of the French Revolution after the haute-bourgeoisie had tired of it.[24] Lenin's recognition of this, and of the Jacobins' ability, as 'the most consequential bourgeois democrats', to help the lower classes achieve their objectives, was why the Soviet leader's explanation of the French Revolution was superior even to that of Marx and Engels.[25]

Several Soviet historians applied the paradigm Lenin had derived from the French Revolution to other European revolutions. In 1960 B. F. Porshnev, after reiterating that the French Revolution benefitted the bourgeoisie even though large elements of it rejected it or simply remained inert, claimed that the same thing was true for revolutions in Germany in the sixteenth century, England in the seventeenth century, and of course Russia in the twentieth century.[26] These revolutions demonstrated what Porshnev, following in Lenin's footsteps, considered an iron law of revolutions, namely that when a class does not want to make the revolution to which it is assigned by history to make, classes whose own revolution has not yet happened can serve as its surrogate. Partly because Plekhanov, Kautsky, and Jaurès were all, in Porshnev's estimation, incapable of recognizing this, they were inferior to Lenin not only as theorists and students of history, but also, more importantly, as political leaders.[27]

Most Soviet historians, however, eschewed *la longue dureé*, avoiding broad pronouncements on revolutions generically. Instead they focused on the French Revolution itself, devoting a good deal of their time to clarifying the Jacobins' relationship to the classes and social categories of the population that were below

---

[23] Dzhedzhula, *Rossiia i velikaia frantsuzskaia burzhuaznaia revoliutsiia*, p. 3.

[24] A. V. Ado, 'Zhivoe nasledie velikoi revoliutsii', p. 12.

[25] Ado's opinion was that Lenin 'developed profoundly the basic views of Marxism [on the French Revolution]', ibid.

[26] B. F. Porshnev, 'V. I. Lenin o rannikh burzhuaznykh revoliutsiiakh', *Novaia i noveishaia istoriia*, no. 2 (1960): pp. 55–6. Porshnev's proof that the class that benefitted from the French Revolution had hardly participated in it was simply to quote Lenin's statement that that was the case.

[27] Ibid., p. 52. In this litany of blinkered theorists, Porshnev could have included Marx, but of course did not. He did, however, fault Engels, albeit only tacitly, for not recognizing, as Lenin did, that the scenario common to revolutions in Germany, England, and France was applicable to all revolutions. Ibid., p. 55.

them both politically and economically, and thus unable to radicalize further a revolution that the Jacobins, with their support, had already radicalized to the fullest extent the Marxist dialectic would permit given the conditions that prevailed in France in the late eighteenth century. Alexeev-Popov and Baskin, for example, focused on the bloc the Jacobins led after taking power in the spring of 1793. For them, the relationship between the parties that comprised it was a microcosm of the revolution as a whole, explaining why, for a time, it succeeded, only to fail not long afterwards, as its leaders were supplanted by elements in France intent on either stopping it or reversing it. The authors began by stressing their rejection of even the slightest intimation that the *sans-culottes* supporting the Jacobins were themselves petit-bourgeois. What they were—both for better and for worse—were plebeians. As such, they lacked the political acumen to run a government. But they also more than made up for this deficiency in their enthusiasm, courage, and fortitude. As a result, they served admirably as the instrument of the Jacobins in the events that brought the Jacobins to power.[28]

In their analysis, the two authors stressed that there were actually two instances in the French Revolution in which one class or stratum of the population acted on behalf of another: the first in August 1792, when the bourgeoisie as a whole could not continue the revolution and the Jacobins, who were from the petit-bourgeoisie, had to do so in their place; and then in 1793, when the Jacobins needed the plebeians to defeat the anti-Jacobin elements in the Convention; had the plebeians not been able to do this, the Jacobins could not have taken power, and the French Revolution would have ended not in 1794 (on 9 Thermidor) but in 1793.[29] In fact, it was pressure from the plebeians that forced the Jacobins to direct the terror they initiated not only against royalists, who had always loathed the revolution and sought the restoration of the *ancien régime*, but also against the Girondins and other former supporters of the revolution who turned against it as it became more radical after the Convention's establishment in 1792.[30]

To the extent to which Soviet historians came to a consensus on the Jacobins, it consisted, more or less, of what Alexeev-Popov and Baskin had written in 1962: while the assistance of the plebeians was critical to the Jacobins taking power, their influence after they did was limited. The Jacobins were always in charge of the bloc that was the social basis for their political supremacy.[31] For better or for worse, that reality was unchangeable. Because conditions in France in the late eighteenth century could never generate a revolution sufficiently radical to satisfy the needs and serve the interests of the plebeians, they could never find satisfaction in any coalition or bloc the Jacobins led. The French Revolution could be radicalized to the extent to which its objectives were those of the Jacobins. But it could never be

---

[28] Alexeev-Popov and Baskin, 'Problemy istorii iakobinskoi literatury', p. 87.
[29] Ibid., pp. 116, 130.   [30] Ibid., p. 137.
[31] The two authors traced of provenance of this view through earlier Soviet historians to Lenin. Ibid., pp. 21–3 and *passim*.

radicalized to the extent to which its objectives were those of the plebeians. For that reason the plebeians were destined to suffer disappointment, disenchantment with the revolution, and ultimately a loss of what little political influence they possessed. But the fate of the Jacobins would not be, and could not be, much better. Their victory over the plebeians turned out to be a pyrrhic one, because without the plebeians' support, the Jacobins could not by themselves hold off the forces of counter-revolution that had rejected the revolution practically from the moment it began, and gathered strength as the radicalization of the revolution turned erstwhile supporters into enemies. To be sure, the Jacobins, in the spring of 1794, rejected the plebeians (by sending their leaders to the guillotine) before the plebeians could reject the Jacobins. But the result would be the same irrespective of the sequence of events. Without the allies the Jacobins needed to take power and to hold onto it, it was only a matter of time before the Jacobins lost power—which they did on 9 Thermidor. Under the circumstances, the French Revolution could not have ended in any other way, or at any other time, give or take a few weeks or months, than it did.

The larger conclusion post-Stalinist Soviet historians drew from all of this was that while the October Revolution resembled the French Revolution, and the Soviet Union the Jacobin dictatorship, the two revolutions and the two regimes were not identical. In fact, the respective differences between the governments each revolution brought to power determined why one of them, the Jacobin, collapsed and the other, the Bolshevik, endured. In the end, Lenin's 'democratic-dictatorship' reflected a genuine confluence of interests among its tripartite elements—the Bolsheviks, the proletariat, and the peasantry—that was not the case for the bloc the Jacobins created. Lenin, looking back at the Jacobins, knew exactly which parts of their legacy he should adopt, and which he should ignore. This, in fact, was one of the reasons he succeeded. Writing during the lengthy *interregnum* between Stalin and Gorbachev, when the Soviet Union achieved an uneasy equilibrium between Stalinism on the one hand, and radical reform on the other, Soviet historians had no way of knowing that not terribly far in the future their confidence in Lenin's judgement, which caused them to believe the Soviet Union would last forever, would be shown to have been unwarranted.

But while it lasted, this consensus was very broad, and the part of it that stressed the inherent instability of the Jacobin dictatorship achieved nearly unanimous support. Among those who shared in it was V. P. Vol'gin, who in remarks delivered at a conference celebrating the fortieth anniversary of the October Revolution, stressed that the Jacobins represented politically the most revolutionary classes of the eighteenth century, namely the urban and rural poor.[32] But because of their unshakeable commitment to the preservation of private property,

---

[32] V. P. Volgin, 'Lenin i revoliutsionnye traditsii frantsuzskogo naroda', in *Frantsuzskii ezhegodnik: stat'i i materialy po istorii Frantsii 1958* (Moscow, 1959), p. 10.

the Jacobins could not imagine, much less advocate, the socialism that offered the only real solution to the poverty and oppression that afflicted these classes. As a result, the Jacobins lost power.[33]

In the same camp as Vol'gin was A. E. Manfred, who wrote more about the French Revolution than any other Soviet historian in the post-Stalin era.[34] On the Jacobins, Manfred was concise: though petit-bourgeois themselves, they had to rely on classes below them, which made the bloc they led unstable. But while the bloc existed, it was truly 'the party of the French people', and more than anything else in the revolution was what made the Jacobins precursors of the Bolsheviks, and the French Revolution a harbinger of the October Revolution.[35] The class divisions the bloc transcended were real, but the Jacobins proved sufficiently adroit in fashioning economic policies, such as the Maximum, that addressed the most vital economic interests of the plebeians, so that the revolution could continue beyond the limits it had reached in 1792. But the Jacobins could not alter the fact that these policies were, at bottom, anti-capitalist, and thus incompatible with the 'pro-capitalist' role history had chosen the French Revolution to play. That the Jacobins would eventually lose power was therefore inevitable. But Manfred stressed that the principal reason for their fall was not any conflict of interests between the Jacobins and the plebeians, but rather the congruence of their interests. Whatever the Jacobins might believe about the Maximum in the privacy of their own deliberations, their continued public support for the measure linked them even more closely to the plebeians, and according to Manfred it was this perceived identity of interests that drove the middle and haute-bourgeoisie to overthrow the Jacobins on 9 Thermidor.[36] Whether, in the Jacobins' demise, this identity of interests was the result of conviction or political calculation was irrelevant. The objective conditions that pertained in France in 1794 permitted no other outcome.[37]

Manfred's analysis thus corroborated the orthodox view in these years that the French Revolution was analogous to the October Revolution, and that the principal reason for this was that the coalition the Jacobins created was comparable to

[33] Ibid., p. 11.

[34] His views on the Jacobins are most easily accessed in his article, 'O prirode iakobinskoi vlasti', pp. 92–103.

[35] Ibid., p. 100. To describe the coalition the Jacobins led, Manfred used the same words Lenin did after the 1905 Revolution—'a revolutionary democratic-dictatorship'—for the regime he intended establish in 1917. Ibid., p. 102.

[36] Bailey Stone describes as 'irrefutable' the evidence indicating that the Jacobins always favoured laissez-faire economics in principle, and supported measures like the Maximum only as an expedient they would be removed once its political necessity no longer existed. Stone, *Anatomy of Revolution Revisited*, p. 359.

[37] Manfred, *Velikaia frantsuzskaia revoliutsiia*, *passim*. This is also one of the points V. M. Dalin stressed, on pp. 10–12, in his introduction to Manfred's history of the revolution, and it was also supported by E. V. Kiselev in 'Parizhskaia Kommuna i sektsii 9 Termidora', in *Frantsuzskii ezhegodnik: Stat'i i materialy po istorii Frantsii 1981* (Moscow, 1983), pp. 106–26.

the 'democratic-dictatorship of the proletariat and the peasantry' that was Lenin's lodestar prior to 1917. Manfred, of all the Soviet historians who wrote about the French Revolution, was perhaps the most sensitive to Lenin's need for inclusivity. It was for that reason, one suspects, that Manfred took Babeuf and the Babouvists seriously, rather than simply disparaging them, as most Soviet historians did, for their naiveté. While conceding that the Babouvists were wrong to believe that communism could be established in what was still a pre-industrial country, in which a genuine proletariat did not yet exist in numbers sufficient to make them a political force, Manfred linked them, nevertheless, to the Jacobins. In his view, Babeuf was just a more extreme version of Robespierre.[38]

While Manfred's deviation from the party line on Babeuf hardly vitiated the orthodoxy of everything else he wrote about the French Revolution, it did constitute an instance of genuine originality—of which, in the post-Stalin era, there were several others. Based on extensive research on the *Vendée* and other instances in the revolution in which the peasants played the principal role, A. V. Ado argued that what occurred in the countryside beginning in 1789 was a genuine *jacquerie*—by which he meant a spontaneous, 'pre-modern' uprising of peasants directed against the aristocracy, which was the principal oppressor class under feudalism.[39] In fact, this uprising was the last of its genre in European history. In Ado's estimation peasants' grievances and aspirations were qualitatively different from those of the plebeians in French towns and cities, and while it would be wrong to deduce from this that the French Revolution was actually two separate revolutions occurring simultaneously, one would not be incorrect in viewing this particular *jacquerie* as a revolution occurring within a larger revolution. The bourgeoisie was the beneficiary of both of these revolutions, in many cases using the profits it acquired in commercial capitalist activities in towns and cities to purchase land previously owned by the aristocracy and the Church.[40] What made Ado's idiosyncratic interpretation politically suspect was that it called into question, if only by implication, and only for those cognizant of the analogy Lenin had drawn between the Jacobins and the Bolsheviks, the identity of interests Lenin claimed to exist between the Russian proletariat and the Russian peasantry. But Ado was not punished or even reprimanded for his ideological deviation.

Soviet historians had always been critical of other historians, French or otherwise, who rejected Marxism and were hostile to the Soviet Union. Magnifying small differences into large ones, they were especially critical of French historians, such as Mathiez, who were sympathetic to the Soviet Union but whose methods of analysis they deemed insufficiently Marxist. Under Stalin this tendency intensified, and

---

[38] A. Z. Manfred, *Ocherki istorii Frantsii XVIII–XX vv.* (Moscow, 1961), p. 75.
[39] A. Ado, *Krestianskoe dvizhenie vo Frantsii vo vremia velikoi burzhuaznoi revoliutsii kontsa XVIII veka* (Moscow, 1971), *passim.*
[40] Ibid., pp. 5–6.

after his death it did not disappear entirely. In 1966 V. G. Revunenkov reproved Jaurès for idealizing the Jacobins while simultaneously denying the bourgeois character of the Convention, claiming wrongly that it represented the nation, rather than discrete classes.[41] But while criticism continued under both the Khrushchev and Brezhnev regimes, Soviet historians were also free to acknowledge any debt they owed to French historians who earlier had been attacked, such as Mathiez and Jaurès, and even to Alexis de Tocqueville, who, unlike the historians who could now be lauded for their perspicacity, had never pretended to be a Marxist or a socialist.[42] Credit was accorded also to contemporary French historians of the revolution whose views could be considered quasi-Marxist, or at least consistent with Marxist tenets, such as the ubiquity of class struggle. Those receiving such recognition included Albert Soboul, George Rudé, and Richard Cobb; in 1981 Moscow State University awarded Soboul an honorary doctorate, and two years later the Soviet government approved the publication of Jaurès's multi-volume history of the French Revolution.[43] Only François Furet, whose disapproval of the Soviet Union and disparagement of Marxist interpretations of the French Revolution seemed mutually reinforcing, remained the object of relentless and bitter criticism.[44]

Of the Soviet historians who in the post-Stalin era deviated from the orthodox Leninist interpretation, V. G. Revunenkov most actively explored what they could write without transgressing the limits of what the government permitted. He rejected the prevailing notion that the dictatorship the Jacobins established resembled Lenin's democratic-dictatorship of workers and peasants.[45] In his opinion, it was nothing of the sort, and the reason Lenin made such an egregious error was that he wrote about the Jacobins before previously unknown writings of Marx and Engels, showing he was wrong, had been discovered.[46] Had Lenin known of these materials, Revunenkov reassured his readers, he would have considered them seriously, and altered his opinion accordingly.

According to Revunenkov, the Jacobins did not lead a bloc that included Hébertists and lower-class elements variously described as plebeians, *sans-culottes*,

[41] Revunenkov, *Marksizm i problema iakobinskoi diktatury*, pp. 58–62. Revunenkov was no less candid in registering his objections to Kautsky's, Plekhanov's, and Kropotkin's views on the revolution. Ibid., pp. 51–7, 68–72.

[42] See, for example, Ado, 'Zhivoe nasledie velikoi revoliutsii', pp. 10–13. There is no way of knowing if 1985 volume containing Ado's article was published before Gorbachev's ascension to the position of general secretary in March of that year. But one can be sure that Ado wrote his contribution sometime before then.

[43] Ibid., p. 13; P. A. Pimenova, 'O sovetskoi istoriografii Velikoi frantsuzskoi revoliutsii (1979–1986 gg.)', in *Frantsuzskii ezhegodnik: stat'i i materialy po istorii Frantsii 1989* (Moscow, 1989), p. 125.

[44] Ado, 'Zhivoe nasledie velikoi revoliutsii', p. 14. One suspects that Furet's criticisms of Marx, most prominently in his *Marx and the French Revolution*, written in the late 1980s, infuriated Soviet historians even more than his criticisms of the historians themselves.

[45] Revunenkov presented his argument most comprehensively in 'Problema iakobinskoi diktatury v noveishikh rabotakh sovetskikh istorikov', in V. G. Revunenkov, *Problemy vseobshchei istorii* (Leningrad, 1967), pp. 83–92, and in his *Marksizm i problema iakobinskoi diktatury*.

[46] Revunenkov, 'Problema iakobinskoi diktatury', p. 91.

and *les enragés*. In fact such a bloc never existed. Lenin and the Soviet historians who believed it did were wrong. Rather, the Jacobin dictatorship was like an umbrella, under which the multifarious elements of the lower classes found shelter, which in the context of the 1790s in France meant that their lives were protected, their needs addressed, and their interests advanced, albeit to a far lesser degree than Soviet historians maintained. The Jacobins were not the equals of those among the lower classes who supported them. In Revunenkov's opinion they were not even *primus inter pares*. Rather, they were the leaders. For that reason it was essential that the Jacobins be restored to their rightful place at the very centre of the events in France once the monarchy was abolished, the Girondins routed, and the Convention reduced virtually to very nearly a rubber stamp for what the Jacobins did, which was determined on the basis of the Jacobins' interests, rather than on those of the categories of the population they protected. To be sure, the Jacobins should not be idealized, as Manfred and post-Stalin era historians were doing, any more than they should be 'canonized', of which Lukin and the Stalinist historians who followed him in the 1930s had been guilty when they erroneously located what made the Jacobins virtuous in their centralizing political power in France.[47] Revunenkov believed there was nothing especially praiseworthy about the Jacobins in that respect, and while he was careful not to compare the Jacobin Terror to Stalin's, his readers could easily infer that he considered these two episodes of enormous and excessive bloodletting not just historically analogous but also morally comparable, even though Stalin's, by mobilizing more technologically advanced means of repression, took more lives. But the point Revunenkov stressed most strongly about the Jacobins was that their interests were their own, and that the alliance they formed with other classes and strata of French society was, and could only be, a matter of convenience. In fact, the Jacobins were right to dissolve the alliance, as they did in the spring of 1794, when their interests and those of their allies diverged. In the end, the mental universe the Jacobins inhabited was not accessible to the *sans-culottes* and the others who looked to the Jacobins for protection because the Jacobins and their followers belonged to different classes. The Jacobins, in contrast to their supporters, came from the bourgeoisie, and no amount of rhetoric about commonalities of interest could alter that essential fact.[48]

Revunenkov could not have been oblivious to the challenge his opinions posed not just to Soviet historians specializing in the French Revolution, but to the historical profession as a whole. Like others in the Soviet elite, historians were entrusted with the task of perpetuating Leninist orthodoxy within their area of

---

[47] Revunenkov, 'Problema iakobinskoi diktatury', p. 83.

[48] Although Revunenkov criticized Albert Soboul for minimizing the role played by the *sans-culottes* in the elimination of feudalism in France, he praised him for distinguishing their interests from those of the Jacobins. Revunenkov, 'Novoe v izuchenii velikoi frantsuzskoi revoliutsii', p. 125; Revunenkov, *Marksizm i problema iakobinskoi diktatury*, pp. 137–47. See also Tchoudinov, 'The Evolution of Russian Discourse on the French Revolution', pp. 290–1.

professional expertise. For that reason the response to his work was overwhelmingly critical, and remained so into the 1980s.[49] Alexeev-Popov attacked Revunenkov for his emphasis on the Jacobins' 'egoism' and their 'anti-democratic' tendencies, and for claiming wrongly that was what had caused the Jacobins to stand 'against the people' instead of 'with the people'.[50] V. M. Dalin attacked him for rejecting Lenin's view of the 'class basis of the Convention' and for condemning the regime the Jacobins established as a 'terrorist bourgeois dictatorship'.[51] Additionally, Revunenkov was wrong in asserting that, by ignoring the interests of the lower classes Robespierre and the other Jacobins disallowed 'democracy for the people'—which in the orthodox Soviet lexicon had nothing to do with elections or any of the other paraphernalia of popular rule; rather it implied a strictly hierarchical party or society in which decisions by the leaders might or might not reflect the wishes of those below them but, once made, were accepted unquestioningly. According to Dalin, democracy was precisely what the Jacobins practised, and for doing so they should be praised instead of condemned.[52]

Revunenkov's view of the Jacobins was even condemned formally in 1970 at a symposium sponsored by the Academy of Sciences that one suspects was convened to do precisely that.[53] What the symposium revealed was that while historians expressing ideologically unorthodox opinions were no longer shot or sent to labour camps, as was the case under Stalin, they were still subjected to the formal obloquy of the state, which could ruin reputations as successfully as Stalin's terror destroyed lives. Revunenkov's apostasy was dealt with in a matter that reflected the larger compromise Khrushchev adopted and the Brezhnev regime continued between a continuation of the harsh repression of the Stalin era on the one hand, and the allowance of genuine freedom of expression on the other.

On the issues on which historians could write freely, there remained limits, even as the punishment for exceeding them was considerably milder. Historians could not malign Lenin or deny the legitimacy of the October Revolution. Nor could they write about Menshevik critics of Leninism such as Plekhanov and Martov unless they included the requisite quotations of Lenin that refuted them. In the end, Soviet historians still had to accept the philosophical principles of Marxism-Leninism, even if, in rare cases, they disagreed, as Revunenkov did, on the specific conclusions they drew from the application of these principles to a

---

[49] Iu. F. Kariakin and E. G. Plimak, in *Zapretnaia mysl' obretaet svobodu. 175 let bor'by vokrug ideinogo naslediia Radishcheva* (Moscow, 1966), pp. 286–95, were among the very few whose opinion of the Jacobins resembled Revunenkov's.

[50] Alexeev-Popov, 'Znachenie opyta velikoi frantsuzskoi revoliutsii', p. 46.

[51] Dalin, *Istoriki Frantsii XIX–XX vekov* (Moscow, 1981), p. 81.

[52] Ibid.

[53] Ibid.; Gabriel Schoenfeld, 'Uses of the Past: Bolshevism and the French Revolutionary Tradition', in *The French Revolution of 1789 and its Impact*, edited by G. W. Schwab and John R. Jeanneney (Westport CT, 1995), p. 302. Schoenfeld's article and his 1989 PhD dissertation, on which his article was based, provide a cogent analysis of Revunenkov's views and those of his critics.

particular historical issue. What is striking about the dispute Revunenkov's work triggered was the degree to which he and his critics were in agreement, most significantly on the primacy of class and economic interests, not just in the French Revolution, but in history generally. The question at the core of the dispute—were the Jacobins' actions a reflection of their class origins in the bourgeoisie (or in a particular segment of it), or were they a consequence of leading a coalition with other classes with whose economic interests those of the Jacobins were temporarily congruent—was such a difficult one that answering it had the effect of obscuring the larger assumption Revunenkov shared with his critics that economic interests and class relations were the prime movers of history. In this respect, there were limits beyond which no Soviet historian who wished to keep his job would go as long as the philosophical constraints of Marxism and Marxist-Leninism remained in place. Indeed, one suspects that Soviet historians literally could not imagine writing history, or at least history they thought worthy of serious consideration, that did not accept the philosophical assumptions of Marxism-Leninism that were an integral aspect of every intellectual discipline, not just history, in the Soviet Union from 1953 (or really 1917) to the Gorbachev era.

*   *   *

Reading what Soviet historians wrote about the French Revolution during these years does not leave one with the impression that they were straining to escape the ideological and philosophical straitjacket constricting them. One senses instead that, with few exceptions, they were unaware of it. To return to Marxism-Leninism after many years in the intellectually airless atmosphere that was Stalinism—with its virtual replacement of economic class by Soviet patriotism, which changed the Jacobins from pre-socialist radicals too enthusiastic for their own good into proto-NKVD agents rooting out subversives—was to liberate oneself intellectually. To go beyond Marxism-Leninism, however, was to confine oneself to an intellectual ghetto, with no chance of escaping it short of renouncing one's convictions on the one hand, or taking the almost unimaginable and exceedingly dangerous step of becoming a dissident on the other. For that reason even French historians like Mathiez, Soboul, and Lefebvre, who were sympathetic to socialism and the October Revolution, could not be considered entirely reliable guides in ascertaining historical truth.[54] To be sure, there were some historians during the Khrushchev and Brezhnev eras, such as Iurii Afanasiev, who silently wished to write history in

---

[54] Soviet historians' criticisms under Lenin and Stalin have already been cited. It should also be noted that Alexeev-Popov and Baskin, in 'Problemy istorii iakobinskoi literatury', pp. 46–8, criticized Soboul and Lefebvre for considering the *sans-culottes* 'petit-bourgeois'. A. V. Ado, in *Krestianskoe dvizhenie vo Frantsii*, p. 12, upbraided Lefebvre for considering the French Revolution actually two revolutions, one urban, the other rural.

defiance of Marxist-Leninist ideology.[55] But for their numbers to increase significantly, a different kind of Soviet leader, who either rejected Marxism-Leninism or
was willing to tolerate other types of history that contradicted it, would have to
emerge. Change, in short, would have to be imposed, or at least strongly encouraged, from above.

The question that remained for Soviet historians of the French Revolution after
Mikhail Gorbachev became general secretary of the Communist Party in 1985,
and two years later told them 'to fill in the blank pages of the Soviet Union's
history', was whether they would use their new freedom to write a different kind of
history.[56] This question was important for a reason that transcended the French
Revolution and how historians in the Soviet Union considered it. Since 1917 the
revolution had been an integral aspect of the mythology of the October Revolution, legitimizing it by having prefigured it, while also leaving behind a legacy of
heroism, perseverance, and determination that the revolutionaries who took
power in Russia over a century later pledged themselves not just to match, but
to exceed; in doing so these French revolutionaries would be demonstrating not
just their own virtues, but, in embryonic form, the virtues of communism. But the
Soviet Union, during the slightly more than three decades since Stalin died, had
begun to show signs of stagnation, for which the institutions and practices of the
Soviet system itself could plausibly be held responsible.

Thus the larger question that remained unanswered when Gorbachev came to
power was whether the mythology the Soviets had so laboriously constructed to
sanction the Soviet system would continue to do so, or be used by critics of the
Soviet system to show how far it had betrayed the promises and expectations
implicit in its foundational mythology. The role the French Revolution played in
this mythology was therefore something that not just Soviet historians, but all
those with a stake in the future of the Soviet Union itself, including and especially
the new general secretary and his advisors, would have to consider.

---

[55] This is easily gleaned from an interview Afansiev gave in the late 1980s, reprinted as 'The Agony
of the Stalinist System', in *Voices of Glasnost: Interviews with Gorbachev's Reformers*, edited by Stephen
F. Cohen and Katrina vanden Heuvel (New York, 1989), especially pp. 97–100.

[56] M. S. Gorbachev, 'Ubezhdennost'—opora perestroika', *Izbrannye rechi i stat'i* (Moscow, 1987),
vol. IV, p. 373. Gorbachev's exhortation, translated literally, would be: 'We must value our Soviet
history of seventy years.' But it is usually rendered in English as it is here.

11

Transgressing the Leninist Line
in the Gorbachev Era

During his first two years as the leader of the Soviet Union, Mikhail Gorbachev said nothing about the French Revolution. But in 1987 he began to make clear his agreement with the long-standing dictum in Soviet mythology that the October Revolution was the rightful successor of the French Revolution: that the second revolution resumed what the first revolution began but left unfinished, namely the installation of a new and radically different means of organizing society that provided not only social justice through the transformation of property relations, but also the possibility of the individual's achieving his full potential in whatever way he defined it. But Gorbachev also believed—although for political reasons he could not state it publicly—that the Soviet system suffered from serious deficiencies that were ethical as well as economic and political. If the October Revolution brought to power a government that was superior to the governments the French Revolution had produced, that did not mean, in his opinion, that it could rest on its laurels. For the Soviet Union to achieve the humane and efficient socialism that was the ultimate justification for the October Revolution, another revolution would be needed—only this one would be peaceful, non-confrontational, and leave untouched the basic institutions and economic arrangements of the Soviet system. The Communist Party would retain its monopoly of power, and like a father who knows what is best for his children, guide the Soviet people in their efforts to create a better life for themselves.

The constellation of policies Gorbachev believed would repair the mistakes and redress the inadequacies previous Soviet leaders had been unwilling or unable to prevent was quickly dubbed *perestroika*—which, in English translation, is usually rendered as 'reconstruction'—to indicate that the Soviet Union would be reconstructed rather than transformed entirely. Not long afterwards, when it appeared that these policies were not achieving the intended results, the general secretary inaugurated another policy, called *glasnost'*, that entailed telling the truth about the Soviet Union no matter how unpalatable or unflattering it might be. Ideally, glasnost' would facilitate *perestroika*, and *perestroika* would constitute the third revolution—after the French and the Bolshevik Revolutions—that would finally realize the noble objectives each of its predecessors had aspired to, but in the end could not make real. Just as the October Revolution marked the beginning of a stage in the moral improvement of humanity higher than that which the French Revolution had achieved over a century earlier, so, too, would the achievement of *perestroika* signify the attainment of an even more advanced state of human existence than that which the Soviet Union had reached—but from which it recently seemed to be retreating when *perestroika* began.

Instead of dissolving the links Soviet mythology claimed to exist between the French and the October Revolutions, Gorbachev, in sum, sought to reinforce them, while at the same time extending the teleology between the two revolutions to include the third one, which in the Soviet Union was about to commence. That *perestroika* was hardly revolutionary in either its means, which would remain peaceful, or its objectives, which instead of transforming the Soviet system would improve those aspects of it that were worth salvaging, did not deter him from claiming that the policies he was implementing would change the Soviet Union just as radically as the October Revolution had changed Russia and the French Revolution had changed France.

*　*　*

Gorbachev expressed this amended teleology on several occasions in the late 1980s. In 1987, in his first extended exegesis on how exactly he thought *perestroika* would improve the Soviet Union, he noted that revolutions in France in 1830, 1848, and 1871 had been required to complete the revolution that began in 1789. The obvious inference he wanted his readers to draw was that the October Revolution was no different from the French Revolution in requiring additional revolutions—or policies like those Gorbachev was implementing peacefully and incrementally— to make everything it promised real. In 1988, in a speech to the General Assembly of the United Nations, he stated flatly that the French Revolution was one of the two historical events that had most shaped the modern world; to this he hardly needed to add—though he did so anyway—that the October Revolution was the other one.[1] 'Each in its own way', he argued, had 'contributed to the progress of humanity'.[2] But the world, he concluded, was different today, and for that reason *perestroika* should supersede the October Revolution the way the October Revolution had superseded the French Revolution.[3] In 1989, in remarks to members of a visiting delegation from France, the general secretary stated that he and the Soviet people 'take pride in the French Revolution' because they can trace to it 'the roots of *perestroika*'.[4] That his praise was precisely what one would expect from a politician seeking to ingratiate himself with his audience should not obscure the fact that, in this particular instance, he was expressing what he actually believed.

---

[1] 'Vystuplenie M. S. Gorbacheva v organizatsii Ob"ediennykh Natsii', *Pravda*, no. 344 (9 December 1988): pp. 1–3.
[2] Ibid., p. 1.　　[3] Ibid., p. 1.
[4] 'Vstrecha M. S. Gorbacheva s predstaviteliami frantsuzskoi obshchestvennosti', *Pravda*, no. 273 (30 September 1989), p. 1.

Because Gorbachev's comments on the French Revolution were few and mostly fragmentary, one must look to Alexander Yakovlev, the Central Committee Secretary in charge of ideology and the intellectual architect of *perestroika*, for a lengthier and more carefully considered exposition of the view the two men shared that the revolution was a precursor of *perestroika*, its influence mediated by the October Revolution, which chronologically was roughly equidistant between them. In July 1989, at a conference in Moscow commemorating the bicentennial of the French Revolution, and with the reform-minded foreign minister, Eduard Shevardnadze, in the audience, Yakovlev delivered the keynote address.[5] Mixing Marxist-Leninist phraseology with language more typical of a Western intellectual than a Soviet politician, Yakovlev spoke like a *philosophe* seeking to escape the ideological constraints imposed by living one's entire life in the Soviet Union and absorbing its Marxist-Leninist ideology, which since childhood one was told was impervious to refutation.

He began by claiming that Voltaire, Rousseau, Montesquieu, and Helvétius, whatever their differences, 'intellectually "ploughed the soil" that produced the [French] Revolution by destroying faith in traditional authority and morality'.[6] *Perestroika*, he said, would do the same. So clearly that even the most inattentive listener would be aware of it, Yakovlev stated his agreement with Gorbachev that, by reforming the Soviet Union, *perestroika* would render the Soviet economy more efficient than the capitalist economies in the West. Once Western elites were convinced of this, the ideological competition of the Cold War would lose its purpose, and Western governments would join with their Soviet counterpart in ending it. In fact, these governments would be so impressed by the humane socialism Gorbachev was introducing (or more precisely, reproducing) in the Soviet Union that they would adopt it themselves. By demonstrating the moral and practical superiority of socialism to capitalism, *perestroika*, in other words, would by example cause the enemies of the Soviet Union not just to stop hating it, but also to emulate it.

But as his speech makes amply clear, Yakovlev's break with ideological orthodoxy remained tantalizingly incomplete. He described the French Revolution as fundamentally a bourgeois revolution, and reiterated the Soviet shibboleth that the October Revolution was a proletarian revolution. Like Gorbachev, he still revered Lenin as the prototypical Social Democrat and Marxist humanist. And like Soviet historians from Lenin to Brezhnev, he saw the two revolutions as sequentially related: 'The impulse of the [French] Revolution, its influence on the historical process, to no small degree predetermined the form and content of the [October] Revolution.'[7]

[5] Schoenfeld, 'Uses of the Past' (PhD dissertation), p. 4. Yakovlev's remarks were published four days later, as an article entitled 'Velikaia frantsuzskaia revoliutsiia i sovremennost', in *Sovetskaia kultura* (15 July 1989): pp. 3–4.
[6] Yakovlev, 'Velikaia frantsuzskaia revoliutsiia i sovremennost', p. 3.
[7] Ibid., p. 4.

Like a magnetic field preventing iron filings from escaping it, Marxist orthodoxy still limited how far Yakovlev was willing to go in violation of it. Nevertheless, what he said about the French Revolution and about its relationship to
perestroika demonstrated that since 1985, when Gorbachev became general secretary, his principal advisor's opinions on matters of ideology had changed
significantly and in a way that Gorbachev himself might well have considered
close to heretical. The very fact that Yakovlev ascribed to the *philosophes* a share of
the responsibility for the French Revolution showed how tenuous now was the
hold Marxist orthodoxy exerted on him. According to Marx, events like the
French Revolution that were political were part of an ideational 'superstructure'
reducible to an interplay of classes reflecting primarily the material conditions in
which people lived. Ideas were a reflection of these material conditions rather than
what determined them. In the case of the Enlightenment, the ideas of Voltaire,
Montesquieu, Helvétius, and the other *philosophes* were themselves a manifestation of the class relations in France in the eighteenth century—the same relations
that at the end of the same century caused the French Revolution to commence.
But to Yakovlev this revolution, while certainly the result of conflicts among
classes, was also driven by ideas and moral principles, the most influential of
which was 'the striving for a harmonious society freed of the inequality between
estates and of monarchical tyranny, in which private interests would be compatible with society's interests'.[8] Indeed, what made the October Revolution worthy
of emulation everywhere was not just its commitment to the political supremacy
of the proletariat, to the abolition of private property, and to the creation of a
classless society, but also its application in Russia in the twentieth century of the
ethical principles of the French Revolution of the late eighteenth century,
the intellectual impetus to which was the Enlightenment, with its belief in the
liberating properties of reason.

To Yakovlev, the French Revolution, grounded as it was in the Enlightenment,
was the original inspiration both for the October Revolution and for the reforms
Gorbachev was currently implementing under the aegis of *perestroika*. But it was
also much more than that. Of all the revolution's benefits, the most enduring was
its vision of human existence based on the liberation of the individual personality,
with reason as the principal tool for determining the institutional arrangements
that would codify this vision and thereby ensure its survival. The values the French
Revolution embodied were eternal. They transcended class, national boundaries,
and time itself. While Yakovlev did not use the term 'natural law' in describing the
moral principles he believed were discoverable through the application of reason,
natural law, in fact, was what he was referring to.

[8] Ibid., p. 3.

But the speech Yakovlev delivered showed that while he resembled a *philosophe* espousing moral principles he considered timeless, absolute, and universal, there coexisted in his intellectual armoury a Burkean reverence for what he called in his speech 'the accumulated wealth of civilization'.[9] For Yakovlev, this inheritance was not something any rational human being would dispose of the way one would a piece of used clothing. For that reason he looked askance at the tendency among the Jacobins, which they shared with Burke's intellectual nemesis, Thomas Paine, to think that they could 'begin the world over again', and symbolize their absolute rejection of the past by substituting a new calendar for the old one.[10] In his speech Yakovlev made clear that *perestroika* did not entail a wholesale repudiation of the past. For him, Gorbachev's reforms afforded the Soviet people the chance to resurrect the legacy of the French and the Bolshevik Revolutions, which Yakovlev truly considered among the most enduring and impressive achievements of humanity, enriching the Soviet people with a moral capital they should now invest in improving their own lives, which required not just the rejuvenation of already existing institutions, but also a process of moral self-improvement. As far as Yakovlev was concerned, in these two revolutions alone there was enough of this moral capital so that the Soviet people did not have to look anywhere else to find it. The only historical events that really mattered were 1789 and 1917.

To be sure, these two revolutions were not identical; the October Revolution was even, in certain respects, a negation of the French Revolution. It intended the abolition of an inherently oppressive system of class relations that the earlier revolution had ushered in. But it was also an enrichment of it. Thus from both revolutions, not just the Bolshevik, there emerged what Yakovlev considered a commitment to 'the democratisation of social life'; with that as its guiding principle, there began in the Soviet Union 'the construction of a society of justice and equality' that would finally be completed through the application of *perestroika* and *glasnost'*.[11] For Yakovlev, these two lodestars in the eventual emancipation of all of humanity entailed in the Soviet Union both the government and the people 'mobilising the spiritual possibilities inherent in a socialist society', and in that way fulfilling the original agenda of what Yakovlev, in orthodox Marxist-Leninist fashion, still referred to as 'the Great French Revolution'. But its legacy was not primarily new and different class relations.[12] Yakovlev acknowledged, but downplayed considerably, the Marxist-Leninist notion of the French Revolution as a bourgeois revolution. Rather, its legacy was ideational, spiritual, and ethical. It marked the first time in human history when 'anarchy and force yielded to reason, conscious will, and a high morality based on humanism and social responsibility'.[13]

---

[9] Ibid., p. 4.
[10] Thomas Paine, *Common Sense*, edited by Isaac Kramnick (New York 1976), p. 120.
[11] Yakovlev, 'Velikaia frantsuzskaia revoliutsiia i sovremennost'', p. 4.
[12] Ibid.   [13] Ibid.

At the end of his oration, Yakovlev left his audience with the clear impression that there was hardly any aspect of Soviet politics and culture deserving of respect and admiration that was not influenced by, or did not benefit from, the French Revolution.

Of course there were aspects of the revolution that he counselled all right-minded citizens of the Soviet Union to reject. Yakovlev came down very hard on the Jacobins, in whom 'impatience was replaced by intolerance', thereby causing 'class struggle to degenerate into hatred'.[14] Ethical objectives, he cautioned, could not be achieved by unjust methods, which, as the Jacobins applied them, were counterproductive of the goals they were intended to advance. The French Revolution would have been better without the Jacobin Terror, just as the October Revolution would have been better without the terror Lenin inflicted in its immediate aftermath, and that which Stalin inflicted after Lenin's. In this respect Yakovlev parted company with Gorbachev. In his opinion Lenin was hardly the socialist humanist that Gorbachev clearly (and incorrectly) considered him. In Yakovlev's words, the Bolsheviks—who took their cue from their leader, who of course was Lenin until his death in 1924—were guilty of 'idealising terror and of repeating 1793'.[15] But the political freedom and civil equality the French Revolution guaranteed survived the Jacobins, and in the late twentieth century it remained a precious inheritance no less relevant than it was at its inception in 1789. In fact, Yakovlev even traced to the French Revolution the notion central to *perestroika* that governments have an obligation to provide not just abstract rights, but also a measure of material security and comfort, without which these rights would be meaningless. Should the Gorbachev regime succeed in achieving these objectives, it will have fulfilled the highest aspirations not only of the October Revolution but of the French Revolution, which for Yakovlev was the original repository of all that was best in socialism, Soviet communism, and *perestroika*. With Gorbachev guiding the Soviet people the way a father does his children, they could find in the past a virtual template for the future it was Gorbachev's and Yakovlev's obligation, but also their crowning glory, to create.

The bicentennial of the French Revolution prompted others in the Soviet leadership and in the educated elite to evaluate it. Many of the conclusions they drew mirrored Yakovlev's. And because much of what they wrote appeared in the Soviet press, the revolution's relationship to the Soviet Union became a matter of public concern. In a collection of articles in the journal *Novoe vremia* (*New Times*) written for the same occasion, the editors, in their unsigned introduction, reaffirmed that the French Revolution was rightly called 'The Great French Revolution' because it was 'the watershed [in history] between the past and the present'.[16] Quoting Lenin, they stressed its civilizing properties. But they made no mention

---

[14] Ibid.   [15] Ibid.
[16] '1789 + 200 = 1989', *Novoe vremia*, no. 28 (1989): p. 38.

of the bourgeoisie or the proletariat, and after acknowledging that the revolution ended privileges based on caste and feudal obligations, while also abrogating the legal division of France into three estates, they went on to credit it with establishing 'a democratic tradition' and introducing to the world the concept of 'the self-determination of nations'. Of the canonical authorities usually invoked on such occasions, Marx and Engels (though not Lenin) were conspicuous in their absence, as was, remarkably, the October Revolution itself.[17] The legacy of the French Revolution transcended it, according to the editors, because its message was universal: 'the whole of mankind', rather than any single country or class benefitted from it, and its legacy, which changed the history of countries as far removed from France as those in Latin America, was in fact mostly cultural and political.[18] The only reference to the Soviet Union was in the context of noting the coincidence of the bicentennial with 'the social awakening' precipitated by *perestroika* and *glasnost*.[19]

The contributors themselves focused on various aspects of the French Revolution. Because of the freedom they enjoyed, their conclusions varied. None reflected any preexisting orthodoxy or party line. Alexander Sogomonov, for example, cited the results from a recent poll in France on the French Revolution; he also noted that, under Stalin, and even during the regimes of Khrushchev and Brezhnev, these would never have seen the light of day.[20] But now anyone in the Soviet Union who read the journal knew what they were. Lafayette, whom Soviet historians prior to the Gorbachev era had generally condemned as a traitor to the revolution, was the most admired, far more than Marat, while Robespierre was the most hated. Sogomonov made a special point of noting that only committed communists admired and respected *l'Incorruptible*—a finding consistent with a large majority of respondents condemning the execution of Louis XVI.[21] Another contributor, Evgenii Kozhokin, focused instead on why the Jacobins fell, arguing that they were brought down by subordinating social interests to the imperatives of philosophical absolutes.[22] In the French Revolution, ideas mattered more than class, and Kozhokin made clear that he considered this anomaly—which is what a Marxist or Marxist-Leninist would have to consider it—applicable not just to the Jacobins, but to the entire revolution. The inference Kozhokin wanted his readers to draw was that the revolution reflected the changing relationship in France in the late eighteenth century between the individual and the state, and that what caused this relationship to change—far more than class struggle—was ideology.

---

[17] Ibid.   [18] Ibid.   [19] Ibid.
[20] Alexander Sogomonov, 'Lafaiet ili Marat', *Novoe vremia*, no. 28 (1989): pp. 39–40.
[21] Ibid.
[22] Evgenii Kozhokin, 'Diktatura i demokrtiia', *Novoe vremia*, no. 28 (1989): pp. 38–9.

Another contributor, Alexei Salmin, went even further than Kozhokin in eschewing Marxist concepts and categories.[23] For him the French Revolution was a struggle of ideas—a contest between 'state-organised Christianity' and what he termed 'the Republican principle'.[24] Instead of stressing Leninist shibboleths about a feudal aristocracy initially superseded by a bourgeoisie that soon found itself a spectator as lower classes led by the Jacobins did the necessary dirty-work of the revolution, Salmin saw the revolution as a multi-faceted phenomenon, its animating principles being theological, ideological, social, and political all at once. The revolution was the result of French society, in all its splendid diversity, rising up spontaneously against the state and its allied institutions, most notably the Catholic Church. At the same time, Salmin singled out individuals and particular periods of the revolution for commendation, while conversely singling out for condemnation both Napoleon and the Jacobin Terror for the horrific and mostly unnecessary loss of life of which they were both guilty. Employing understatement effectively, Salmin fastened on Marat as the worst of the Jacobins, whose behaviour in certain situations he described dryly as 'not particularly meritorious'.[25] By way of comparison, Salmin situated the Marquis de Lafayette, both for his admirable personal qualities and for the inestimable support he gave the Americans in their war of independence, at the opposite end of the ethical spectrum from Marat and the Jacobins. Salmin's high praise for the French aristocrat, whose social class had caused Soviet historians either to denigrate him or to acknowledge his services to the French and American Revolutions only with the utmost reluctance, was certainly notable. Even more surprising, however, was Salmin's designation of the Americans' struggle against the British as a war for democracy.[26] While to a Western reader Salmin's contention would not seem outlandish or even unusual, to his Soviet counterparts his ascription of America's founding to an idea, rather than to the interplay of material circumstances and economic forces, was nothing short of astonishing.

In the Soviet press, a number of articles on the bicentennial were almost as unorthodox politically and ideologically. In *Pravda* B. Bolshakov was moved by the occasion to describe the French Revolution as 'the Great French Revolution'.[27] But that was his only serious concession to ideology. Unlike those in *Novoe vremia*, his article included no exhortations to emulate Marxism-Leninism. Nor did he couple plaudits for the October Revolution with similar ones for the French. Instead he referred to recent comments of Margaret Thatcher that the latter brought with it terror and eventually Napoleon, but also the Declaration of the Rights of Man, which she traced not to anything French, but rather—perhaps not surprisingly in light of her nationality—to the Magna Carta. One must bear in

[23] Alexei Salmin, 'Zhazhda samoochishcheniia i terror', *Novoe vremia*, no. 28 (1989): pp. 40–1.
[24] Ibid., p. 40.   [25] Ibid., p. 41.   [26] Ibid., p. 41.
[27] B. Bolshakov, 'Nakanune Iubeleia', *Pravda*, no. 195 (14 July 1989): p. 7.

mind how remarkable it was that, in the pages of the newspaper of the Communist Party of the Soviet Union, the then prime minister of Great Britain—and a staunch conservative, no less—was cited approvingly in an article that, by its silence on the virtues of Soviet ideology, might cause its readers to question the legitimacy, or at least the continued beneficence, of the Soviet Union.

In *Izvestiia*, the official newspaper of the Soviet government (and therefore second in authority and prestige only to *Pravda*), one could read much the same thing. Iurii Kovalenko, writing in Paris, described the actual preparations for the bicentennial celebration.[28] But the author also included his own opinions. He berated the French people, albeit mildly, for their nationalism—for not situating their most illustrious and consequential revolution within the context of the larger, supranational history of progress that included in England both the Magna Carta and the Glorious Revolution. Even more significantly, Kovalenko failed to mention, much less to describe in orthodox Marxist fashion, the class structure of France prior to the French Revolution or as a result of it. Instead he pronounced the revolution a signal event in the ongoing quest for 'social justice', which he said included the current quest in the Soviet Union for human rights.[29] But for all of these encomiums, there were also subtle indications—such as the burial, on an inside page in the next day's edition of *Izvestiia*, of a small photograph of a celebratory gathering on the Place de la Bastille in Paris—that not everyone in the Soviet leadership agreed with Kovalenko's positive, albeit ideologically unorthodox commendation of the French Revolution, and might even have opposed his article's publication.[30]

The willingness to examine the French Revolution anew, and to do so, thanks to Gorbachev, without fear of anything worse than verbal admonishment, extended to academia. The Soviet economist Nikolai Shmelov stated in 1989, during the first session of the Congress of People's Deputies, that history in certain instances was repetitive, and that in the case of the French Revolution the economic problems faced by the governments it produced prefigured the budget deficits and hyperinflation characteristic of the Soviet economy.[31] Just a few years earlier, comments like Shmelov's could not have been uttered publicly. That they contained an accusation reprinted in the most influential newspaper in the Soviet Union was even more remarkable: the specific problems Shmelov pointed to in Soviet society were caused, in his opinion, by 'the administrative-command system', which was Gorbachev's customary appellation for the Soviet system established by Stalin in the early 1930s.[32]

---

[28] Iu. Kovalenko 'Parizh, 14 iulia...: Frantsiia otmechaet 200-letie revoliutsii', *Izvestiia*, no. 196 (14 July 1989): p. 4.
[29] Ibid.   [30] *Izvestiia*, no. 197 (15 July 1989): p. 4.
[31] His comments were reprinted in *Pravda*, no. 160(25878) (9 June 1989), p. 2.
[32] Ibid.

It took time for Soviet historians to utilize fully the freedom they enjoyed in the Gorbachev era to re-examine issues about which they and their predecessors had drawn conclusions strictly within the limits imposed by Marxism-Leninism. This was certainly true of what was written about the French Revolution. In 1986, after Gorbachev had come to power but before his policies had advanced from the purely improvisational to those that would soon be codified under the rubric of *perestroika*, N. Molchanov publicly admonished the French people for not commemorating the French Revolution favourably enough.[33] Citing Benjamin Franklin's observation that everyone of sound mind and benevolent intentions had two fatherlands—his own and France—he bemoaned the absence in the latter of any monument or street named for Robespierre. Up to the spring of 1794, he argued, the Jacobins reflected in their policies the 'democratic tendencies' of the people they represented.[34] The Terror they practised was by no means a precursor of recent instances of genocide. Rather, the most apt analogy was to the Saint Bartholomew's Massacre in France in August 1572—a derogation which for Molchanov was a subtle way of reassuring his readers that nothing like what the Jacobins wrongly did was even remotely possible in the Soviet Union. Molchanov was particularly critical of François Furet for having trivialized the French Revolution, thereby transforming it into something that bore no resemblance to the actual event. 'The French Revolution', he wrote, 'lives on, but many want to prevent it from living.'[35] Their principal sin, of which Molchanov made clear he believed other Western historians to be culpable, was to consider the revolution a forerunner of totalitarianism, which, for Molchanov, was an especially defamatory characterization not only of France, but also of the Soviet Union.

Not all historians used the freedom the government now allowed to denounce it. Nor was the orthodoxy on the French Revolution that had prevailed since 1917 always challenged. Some historians simply repeated the by-now hackneyed clichés. In B. S. Itenberg's 1988 analysis, the French Revolution remained 'The Great French Revolution'.[36] In his opinion it marked in political terms the victory of the bourgeoisie over feudal absolutism, and thus had a profoundly progressive influence on countries on both sides of the Atlantic. The Jacobins were the most revolutionary-minded members of the bourgeoisie, so much so that they advanced the interests of a different social stratum, the plebeians, whose support protected them against the retrograde and pernicious forces of absolutism and counter-revolution.[37] As for the meaning the French Revolution left for posterity, Itenberg

---

[33] N. Molchanov, 'Revoliutsiia na gil'otine: takov smysl diskussii v sviazi s priblizheniem 200-letiia vziatiia Bastilii', *Literaturnaia gazeta*, no 28(5094) (9 July 1986): p. 14.

[34] Ibid.   [35] Ibid.

[36] Itenberg, *Rossiia i velikaia frantsuzskaia revoliutsiia*, *passim*.

[37] The lingering popularity of opinions such as this may help to explain why the chocolate factory that prior to *perestroika* had been named for Marat still bore his name as late as 1989. Schoenfeld, 'Uses of the Past' (PhD dissertation), p. 221.

expressed the hope that the bicentennial would be a global event marked by the solidarity of all progressive people, and a way of reminding those insufficiently enamoured of the French Revolution that, despite its temporal distance from the present, it nonetheless made possible everything in their lives that was worth-while.[38] In the case of the Soviet Union, a good deal of what happened in the revolution that was good 'has often been repeated in the events of Russian life'.[39]

But for all the ways in which Itenberg remained faithful to the old, and by now increasingly antiquated Leninist orthodoxy, he expressed his views without the *ad hominem* denigration of other historians who disagreed with him that was required in the Stalin era, and standard practice when Khrushchev and Brezhnev led the Soviet Union.[40] One reason for this was that Gorbachev's invitation to Soviet historians to investigate Soviet history honestly and openly had the effect of lowering the rhetorical temperature of the inevitable disagreements that ensued. It also provided legitimacy to the efforts of historians to write a new kind of history while still drawing on the old. More than a few tried to reconcile the orthodoxies they had once accepted with contrary arguments that were now defensible in light of new evidence. Some went even further, jettisoning Marxism-Leninism entirely. The result was that, for the first time since the mid-1920s there existed in the Soviet Union genuine diversity of opinion not only on the French Revolution and its relationship to the October Revolution, but also on the relevance of the two revolutions to the various challenges the Soviet Union was facing in the late twentieth century. Unless they condemned the October Revolution as morally illegitimate, Soviet historians could argue—and some did argue—that either or both of the two revolutions were *sui generis*, and that the teleology socialists and communists since Marx, Engels, and Lenin believed existed, in which the later revolution continued what the earlier one began, was in fact chimerical. It was now politically acceptable to argue, in other words, that the French Revolution and the Russian Revolution were discrete events and should be evaluated accordingly.

Mikhail Gefter, in an interview in 1988, seemed intent on synthesizing the longstanding Leninist orthodoxy on the French Revolution with his own idiosyn-cratic interpretation of it.[41] Thermidor, he said, was something all revolutions experienced. With this no Leninist could disagree. Lenin had said the same thing himself. But Gefter went on to argue that the course the Soviet Union had followed in reaching Thermidor was particular to it, and that the Stalinism it entailed still powerfully afflicted the Soviet people.[42] In an article in 1989, S. F. Blumenau and Iurii Afanasiev, who was by training a historian of France, repeated Lenin's

---

[38] Itenberg, *Rossiia i velikaia frantsuzsaia revoliutsiia*, p. 231.   [39] Ibid., p. 63.

[40] Jaurès, Aulard, and Mathiez—all of them convenient targets of rhetorical fusillades in the past— go unmentioned in Itenberg's book, which exceeds two hundred pages.

[41] Mikhail Gefter, 'Stalin umer vchera', in *Inogo ne dano* edited by Iu. N. Afanasiev (Moscow, 1988), pp. 297–322.

[42] Ibid.; Giuseppe Boffa, *The Stalin Phenomenon* (Ithaca NY, 1992), pp. 184, 187.

assertion, without including any rejoinder of his own, that the French Revolution was 'a bourgeois democratic revolution'.[43] But they also cited dissenting opinions, even François Furet's, fairly and non-polemically, and showed considerable familiarity not only with what historians in France had written about the French Revolution but also with the contributions some of them, such as Fernand Braudel, had made to the study of European history generally.[44] Yet another Soviet historian, V. P. Smirnov, while lauding the French Revolution the way earlier historians had done for its progressive effects on the subsequent course of European and Russian history, also called on his colleagues to apply to it the 'new thinking' Gorbachev wanted the Soviet people to apply to all aspects of life.[45] This meant that the elevated ethical pronouncements of the revolution, such as the Declaration of the Rights of Man, were more than empty rhetoric to disguise simple greed. The rights the declaration proclaimed existed independently of the material circumstances that Smirnov still believed gave rise to them. In fact, they were the ultimate progenitor of the United Nations Charter, the Universal Declaration of Human Rights, and the Final Act of the 1975 Helsinki Accords, which, in the case of the Helsinki Accords, imposed unambiguous moral obligations on Soviet Union for having signed it.[46] The French Revolution was therefore not just the paradigmatic bourgeois revolution; it was also, in its ethical aspirations, a universal revolution, its uplifting message applicable everywhere. In sum, it was 'one of the greatest achievements of civilization'.[47]

Of course not everyone who played a significant role in the revolution was of high moral character. Babeuf, according to Smirnov, was actually a forerunner of the 'barracks communism' that often deformed the Soviet Union by prescribing a form of 'artificial egalitarianism' that required the regulation of the minutest details of everyday life.[48] This in turn necessitated unrelenting surveillance and an extreme centralization of political power not dissimilar to that which Jacobins preferred. Smirnov did not refrain from citing the relevant statistics on the Jacobin Terror, including not only the number of lives it extinguished, which he estimated at 17,000, but also the number of arrests, which he surmised to have been roughly a half-million. Quoting Saint-Just's demand that the government prosecute not only traitors but the much larger number of Frenchmen who were merely indifferent to the revolution, Smirnov ascribed the slaughter Saint-Just and his

---

[43] Iu. N. Afanasiev and S. F. Blumenau, 'Diskussii vokrug Velikoi frantsuzskoi revoliutsii', in *Frantsuzskii ezhegodnik*, p. 33.

[44] Ibid., p. 11.

[45] Smirnov, 'Velikaia frantsuzskaia revoliutsiia i sovremennost', pp. 55–65.

[46] Ibid., p. 58. The accords were the first document on human rights the Soviet Union signed. By doing so it also tacitly acknowledged the legitimacy of the Universal Declaration, in the original vote on the adoption of which in the United Nations in 1948 the Soviet Union had abstained. Mary Ann Glendon, *A World Made New: Eleanor Roosevelt and the Universal Declaration of Human Rights* (New York, 2001), p. 228.

[47] Ibid., pp. 55, 59.   [48] Ibid., p. 60.

compatriots on the Committee of Public Safety carried out to their belief that they were acting virtuously, that they intended a more just and equitable society, and thus believed that any method they employed to achieve it was justified.[49]

When Smirnov turned to the Soviet Union, however, his allegiance to Lenin and Leninism returned with a vengeance. He allowed that, for a long time, human rights had not been observed in the Soviet Union. But Stalin, not Lenin, was responsible for that lamentable fact.[50] In that respect, as well as in others, Stalinism was a betrayal of Leninism, and for that reason there was nothing wrong in Stalinism that the resurrection of the original ideals of the October Revolution could not eliminate. That the Soviet Union, under Stalin, had taken a wrong turn did not mean Soviet historians today could not assist the Gorbachev regime in its efforts to resume the heroic endeavour the French Revolution had begun and the October Revolution continued of creating a humane and just society—by which Smirnov meant one that was socialist—wherever it was possible to do so. In his conclusion, he even predicted that since proceeding from capitalism to socialism could be peaceful, the violence both of these revolutions required to succeed could be avoided.[51]

V. G. Revunenkov also changed his views on the French Revolution in the Gorbachev era, embracing in 1989 a position he had previously rejected.[52] Revunenkov's earlier view was that the bloc the Jacobins led in the mid-1790s provided protection for classes and categories of the population that were not bourgeois, as the Jacobins were. Despite the confluence of interests that caused the two principal entities in the bloc to agree to it, the relationship was not based on any kind of equality. The Jacobins were clearly dominant. In 1989, however, Revunenkov wrote that 'the bloc of popular plebeians, workers, and peasants' who joined forces with the Jacobins were not their junior partners but rather 'the driving force of the revolution itself'.[53] In fact, in Revunenkov's revised rendition of the French Revolution, the plebeians rather than the Jacobins were its galvanizing force, even while the latter were in power. He even quoted from an article Marx had written in 1848 to make the point that the Jacobins were not the only ones in France effectuating a bourgeois revolution after the bourgeoisie, consumed by its own cowardice, refused to continue it. The lower classes played a role in this endeavour no less essential, or perhaps even more essential, than that of the Jacobins. Confronted by enemies all around them, these revolutionary elements of the lower classes

> fought only for the realization of the interests of the bourgeoisie, albeit by non-bourgeois means. The French terror in its entirety was nothing more than the

---

[49] Ibid., pp. 61–3.   [50] Ibid., p. 59.   [51] Ibid., p. 65.

[52] V. G. Revunenkov, 'Velikaia frantsuzskaia revoliutsiia i traditsii izucheniia i novye podkhody', *Voprosy istorii*, no. 5 (May 1989): pp. 98–116.

[53] Ibid., p. 99.

application of plebeian means of dealing with the enemies of the bourgeoisie, with absolutism, feudalism, and *meshchantsvo* [the narrow-minded elements of the petit bourgeoisie].[54]

In the same article, Revunenkov made clear his (partial) rejection of the conventional wisdom that had prevailed before the Gorbachev era by including Mirabeau and Lafayette with Robespierre and Marat in the pantheon of heroes the Bolsheviks had established even before the Soviet Union existed.[55] Even more heretical was his acknowledgement that Stalinist historians 'canonised the Jacobin dictatorship, glossed over its internal contradictions, and idealised the Jacobin terror'.[56] But one can also find judgements in the article with which Lenin could have agreed. One example was the author's acknowledging Napoleon's destruction of the French republic but nonetheless pronouncing the emperor's influence on history progressive because he helped to transmit the ideals of the French Revolution to the rest of Europe.[57] There are several others as well. But these did little to enhance Revunenkov's reputation among Soviet historians. The problem was not inaccuracies or omissions. Rather, it was one of timing. Revunenkov rejected the Leninist orthodoxy when it prevailed among Soviet historians prior to the Gorbachev era, but then accepted large aspects of it just when Soviet historians, in the Gorbachev era, were questioning it and even, by 1988 and 1989, openly rejecting it.

In the case of the French Revolution, there were many examples of this. In 1988, V. Sergeev wrote openly that Robespierre was a hypocrite and an opportunist, compared to whom even the Girondins—the bête noir of Soviet historians for decades—were morally preferable.[58] At the same time, Sergeev argued that the Jacobin terror was best understood not as a political manifestation of class struggle, but as an effort to curb simultaneously the waning domination of the aristocracy and the growing domination of the bourgeoisie. But if the principal consequences of the terror were economic, its origins, because they were traceable to Rousseau, were political and ideological. In other words, Sergeev was openly reversing the causality central to Marxist and Marxist-Leninist ideology between ideas and the material conditions in which people live.

It was one thing for Soviet historians, as individuals, to write articles implying that they harboured reservations about the way history had been written earlier in the Soviet Union. It was another thing for them to repudiate Marxism entirely. But perhaps the most extreme manifestation of their intellectual independence

---

[54] Ibid., p. 103. The article Revunenkov quoted from is K. Marx, 'Burzhuaziia i kontrrevoliutsiia (1848)', in K. Marx and F. Engels, *Sochineniia*, 2nd edn (Moscow, 1955), vol. VI, p. 114.

[55] Revunenkov, 'Velikaia frantsuzskaia revoliutsiia i traditsii isucheniia i novye podkhody', p. 116.

[56] Ibid., p. 109.   [57] Ibid., p. 116.

[58] V. Sergeev, 'Tigr v bolote', *Znanie-sila* no. 7 (1988), pp. 65–74. The tiger in the title comes from Pushkin, who once called Robespierre 'a sentimental tiger'. Manfred, *Velikaia frantsuzskaia revoliutsiia*, p. 392.

and professional autonomy was organizing conferences and symposia in which judgements were rendered on subjects of their own choosing, rather than the government's.

One such conference, in Moscow in September 1988, was sponsored by the history section of the Academy of Sciences. Just a few years earlier sponsorship by the academy would have imposed an ideological straitjacket on the participants. But now things were different. Thirty historians of the French Revolution gathered for the explicit purpose, in the words of its official announcement, of freeing the history that will henceforth be written on the revolution from 'dogmatic schematizations and stereotypes'.[59] Given the mindset that years of political indoctrination had created among historians, one might think that the historians at the conference, after rejecting the prevailing dogma on the revolution, simply substituted another one. But this was not the case. While most participants rejected both what Lenin and the Bolsheviks had believed about the French Revolution and the Marxist conceptual framework that was used to explain it, the variety and multiplicity of the presentations at the conference belied the conclusion that, in this particular instance, the cure was just as bad as the disease it was intended to ameliorate.

H. H. Bolkhovitinov, for example, rejected the Bolsheviks' ritualized idealization of the Jacobins, especially of Robespierre, Marat, and Saint-Just, as 'knights without fear or any reason for reproach'.[60] The Jacobins, he reminded his colleagues, practised terror not only against reactionaries and counter-revolutionaries, but against the plebeians and the *sans-culottes*, whom he described as 'the true avant-garde of the revolution'.[61] In Bolkhovitinov's description, the Jacobins were revolutionaries and counter-revolutionaries simultaneously. To consider them with anything other than ambivalence was to reduce the practical complexities of history to an unrealistic simplicity. In fact, the ascription of historical events to economic factors alone was profoundly misleading. What drove the Jacobins to do what they did was their ideology, which Bolkhovitinov traced intellectually to the Enlightenment.[62] Another participant, D. A. Rostislavlev, stated that the differences separating the Parisian plebeians from the most radical Jacobins were intellectual, political, and programmatic, and had little to do with class and class interests.[63] This, in fact, was why the overthrow of the Jacobins on 9 Thermidor was so easy and bloodless. Echoing Rostislavlev, but adducing different evidence for the primacy he placed on ideas at the expense of economic considerations, both Ye. E. Guseinov and S. Ia. Karp, in separate presentations, argued against any neat schematization of the traditional Jacobin–Girondin dichotomy: in Guseinov's opinion, the Girondins

---

[59] Chudinov, 'Nazrevshie problemy izucheniia istorii velikoi frantsuzskoi revoliutsii', p. 65.

[60] Quoted in ibid., p. 66. The reader will recall that the Bolsheviks applied the same encomium, after his death, to Felix Dzerzhinskii, the first head of the Soviet political police.

[61] Quoted in ibid., p. 66.   [62] Ibid., p. 66.   [63] Ibid., p. 68.

welcomed support anywhere on the spectrum of economic classes they could find it, while in Karp's neither the Jacobins nor the Girondins were politically or ideologically monolithic.[64] Yet another participant, E. V. Kiselev, enlarged Karp's conclusion to describe the bourgeoisie as a whole.[65]

Other participants were even more direct in rejecting the fundamental tenets and vocabulary of Marxist-Leninist history as it pertained to the French Revolution. L. A. Pimenova said she much preferred calling the *ancien régime* an 'old order' rather than a 'feudal order' because the latter descriptive implied an overly schematized view of French history.[66] N. Iu. Plavinskii went even further, arguing that calling the Enlightenment a reflection of bourgeois class relations was simplistic.[67] Rather, he said, it was a self-contained intellectual movement from which counter-revolutionaries could extract as much that was congenial to their conservatism as revolutionaries could find that was supportive of their radicalism. Both sides in the French Revolution, in other words, had a valid claim to be the true heirs and executors of the Enlightenment. Moreover, they both changed the ideas they received from the Enlightenment to conform to their dichotomously opposite needs and aspirations. But perhaps the most emphatic and direct repudiation, in the context of the French Revolution, of the entire schemata of Marxist-Leninist history was A. V. Gordon's.[68] In the course of criticizing the orthodox view, as articulated by E. B. Cherniak, that the Jacobins' 'utopianism' was what made their dictatorship vulnerable to a Thermidorian reaction, he rejected the whole notion of the French Revolution as a bourgeois revolution.[69] The reason for his rejection was that the revolution unleashed forces that, instead of reflecting class distinctions, transcended them. Sometimes these forces were favourable to the bourgeoisie; other times they were not. But whatever their provenance, their effects were not reducible to the overly abstract concept of class.

Because the Soviet leadership, prior to Gorbachev, had always considered history a form of politics, and in the last years of Stalin's life a means of transforming the very mental apparatus with which the Soviet people received and interpreted the world around them, what was at stake at the conference transcended history.[70] Even if only implicitly, the moral legitimacy of the Soviet Union, based as it was on a mythology in which the French Revolution played an essential and central role, was challenged, refuted, and even rejected. While accepting the Leninist truism that the two revolutions and the regimes they established were related teleologically, more than a few of the historians at the conference reversed the ethical gloss communists since Lenin had placed on it.

---

[64] Ibid., p. 72.   [65] Ibid., p. 72.   [66] Quoted in ibid., p. 71.

[67] Ibid., p. 71.   [68] Ibid., p. 69.

[69] E. B. Cherniak, '1794-I god. Nekotorye aktual'nye problemy issledovaniia velikoi frantsuzskoi revoliutsii', *Novaia i noveishaia istoriia*, no. 1 (1989): pp. 77–95; Gordon also disparaged Cherniak's view as 'overly schematic'. Ibid.

[70] Tucker, 'Stalin and the Uses of Psychology, especially pp. 151–66.

Instead of prefiguring, in its own moral virtue, that of the October Revolution, the French Revolution was a precursor of the horrors the October Revolution made possible by creating the Soviet system that was responsible for them. One such historian, V. P. Smirnov, stated openly that 'the Jacobins created, for the first time in history, a system of mass terror organised by the state'.[71] His implication that the terror Lenin and Stalin later unleashed was a more effective and comprehensive replication of what the Jacobins had done was unmistakable and, one suspects, deliberate. Explicit agreement with what Smirnov had merely implied, namely that the presence in France's economy before 1789 of distinctly capitalist elements showed that the revolution merely changed the political context in which these elements were evolving, came from A. V. Ado. History itself, he suggested, was evolutionary, rather than a series of stages punctuated by rapid and transformational upheavals—an opinion that, if applied to France in the eighteenth century, implied that the revolution that began in 1789 was unnecessary: the economic and social trends discernable in the late eighteenth century would have continued into the nineteenth even without it.[72]

In and of itself, Ado's implication was heretical enough. But in his remarks he went even further. The Terror of the Jacobins, he said, was nothing less than 'the older brother', of Stalin's.[73] Of course Soviet historians had said precisely that, albeit in different ways, practically for the duration of Stalin's rule. But their judgement of Stalin's Terror—that it was not only necessary but also the most obvious manifestation of the moral virtue both the Jacobins and Stalin embodied—Ado rejected completely. What Soviet historians and occasionally Stalin himself had praised, he now condemned. Indeed, one year later, V. Sergeev, in the aforementioned article in which he eviscerated Robespierre as a hypocrite and flayed the Jacobins for perverting Rousseau's ideas in how they applied them to governance, condemned the Jacobins not simply for establishing a model Stalin followed and then quickly surpassed. In addition, he held Robespierre and the Jacobins responsible—along with Stalin, Lenin, and the October Revolution itself—for Stalinism. The Jacobins, in other words, had helped to cause Stalin's Terror even though it occurred over a century after the Jacobins had lived and died. It was in this context that Sergeev coupled his condemnation of Stalinism with an expression of hope that, by learning about the French Revolution, the Soviet people would come to understand better the most morally egregious aspects of the October Revolution.[74]

* * *

One could easily write a history of modern France—or even a history of modern Europe—that considered much of what followed the French Revolution a

---

[71] Chudinov, 'Nazrevshie problemy izucheniia istorii velikoi frantsuzskoi revoliutsii', p. 66.
[72] Ibid., p. 70.   [73] Quoted in ibid., p. 66.
[74] Sergeev, 'Tigr v bolote', p. 74.

commentary on it, in which three broad opinions would be discernible: some judging the revolution excessive, others considering it sufficient, and still others viewing it as insufficient, and thus requiring additional revolutions either to complete its agenda or to improve on it. Those espousing in France the last of these three opinions got their wish. Revolutions erupted there in 1830, 1848, and 1871.[75] The revolutionaries responsible for these upheavals were well aware of their provenance in the original revolution, and the result was not farce—in keeping with how Marx famously encapsulated the historical relationship between the two Napoleons—but rather, paraphrasing Eugen Weber, the creation of a 'revolutionary tradition'.[76] The phrase itself might seem oxymoronic, but historically it was not. The revolutions in France in the nineteenth century were distinctively conservative, even though what was being preserved was the conviction that the country required radical change for social justice to be achieved, and that the first steps towards the realization of a government and a society that provided it had been taken in the late eighteenth century, beginning in 1789.

The question that now must be addressed is whether the Bolsheviks and their successors, the Soviets, saw these later revolutions as comprising, with the original one, a larger tradition of revolution, and if that was the case, whether these later revolutions were as useful as the first one in conceptualizing a mythology legitimizing the October Revolution and the Soviet system that emerged as a result of it. These later nineteenth-century revolutions will be treated separately and in chronological order, and hopefully without obscuring what made each of them unique. But they are included here primarily to demonstrate that together with the first one they left behind a tradition, established and confirmed in France but sufficiently applicable elsewhere in time and space to be adapted in the Soviet Union in order to confer additional legitimacy—above and beyond what Marxism-Leninism provided—on the intrinsically ennobling enterprise of building socialism and communism. Within this revolutionary tradition, in other words, could be found not only a veritable panoply of mistakes to be avoided, but also tactics and strategies to be adopted, policies on taking power to be pursued, and characterological traits, as these were manifested by particular French revolutionaries, to be emulated.

---

[75] One can fairly consider the establishment of the Paris Commune a French revolution even though it occurred only in one city—albeit the most populous and the most politically consequential in the entire country—because its repercussions extended well beyond Paris to the rest of France.

[76] Eugen Weber, 'The Nineteenth-Century Fallout', in *The Permanent Revolution: The French Revolution and its Legacy: 1789–1799*, edited by Geoffrey Best (London, 1988), p. 181. Marx's exact words, in *The Eighteenth Brumaire of Louis Bonaparte*, p. 15, were: 'all facts and personages of great importance in world history occur, as it were, twice...the first time as tragedy, the second as farce'. In the first part of the statement, Marx was paraphrasing Hegel.

PART II
1830

12

The Revolution That Stopped Too Soon

The French Revolution did not 'cause' the revolutions that followed it. But by providing them a mythology their leaders could draw on in expressing, defending, and justifying their own particular actions and objectives, the French Revolution helped to legitimize these revolutions for millions of Frenchmen. When Lafayette, to sanction the overthrow of the Bourbons and their replacement by the Duc d'Orléans in 1830, embraced the new king on the balcony of the Hôtel de Ville in Paris, someone in the approving crowd below the two men passed to them a large tricoleur.[1] In February 1848, the newly created Provisional Government formally established the Second Republic precisely where the Bastille had once stood; shortly afterwards the throne of the former king was transported to the same location and unceremoniously burned.[2] And in March 1871 Parisians called the new government they established a commune, in imitation of the institution of the same name in the French Revolution; two months later the Communards put in place a new institution of governance and called it a committee of public safety because they still thought that replicating the vocabulary of the French Revolution might inspire their defenders to protect them successfully.

But these *obeisances* were intended not just to safeguard the revolutions that followed the original one. They also were meant to demonstrate that programmatically and ideologically these revolutions were its successor—that having solved only some of the problems afflicting France, the original revolution of 1789 required additional revolutions to finish what it had begun; for some this required emending the original revolution's agenda, which, to a significant degree, was what the Revolutions of 1830, 1848, and 1871 intended. What these revolutions were not intended to create—but which they created anyway—was a coherent revolutionary tradition transferable to other countries, such as Russia, where it could be infused into 'native' mythologies legitimizing objectives no less grandiose, adventurous, and all-encompassing in their applicability than anything that had been envisioned in France. That in Russia the ideology determining these objectives came from Germans, not Frenchmen, and was mediated in its

---

[1] David H. Pinckney, *The French Revolution of 1830* (Princeton NJ, 1972), p. 162.
[2] Agulhon, *Marianne into Battle*, p. 67; Mike Rapport, *1848: Year of Revolution* (New York, 2008), p. 56.

application by Russian national history and culture, in no way diminishes what France's revolutions and revolutionaries contributed to it.

* * *

That the Revolution of 1830 failed to capture the Bolsheviks' imagination to the extent to which the other revolutions in this revolutionary tradition were able to do is undeniable. Neither they nor their predecessors in the Russian revolutionary movement wrote much about it, and what they wrote showed a singular lack of passion. This is understandable. Compared to 1789, 1848, and 1871, 1830 lacked high drama. There was nothing in the revolution comparable to the storming of the Bastille or to the June Days in 1848, when the lower classes battled French army soldiers valiantly but to no avail, or to the martyrdom the Paris Commune projected because so many Communards lost their lives defending it. The over-throw of Charles X and his replacement by Louis Philippe were too easy. Fighting was limited to three days, and only four days elapsed between its cessation and Charles' abdication; one week after that Louis Philippe was proclaimed the King of the French. Moreover, the latter enjoyed sufficient legitimacy, at least during the first years of his reign, so that no lavish coronation was considered necessary, and once the king took power, nothing like the Jacobin Terror was required to protect it.[3] Indeed, the king resisted calls to execute ministers who had served the Bourbons.[4] Finally, the Revolution of 1830 lacked the supranational and univer-salist aspirations of the French Revolution. European monarchs, most of them conservative, concluded correctly that it posed no threat serious enough to require the application of military force to defeat it. Instead, an uneasy equilibrium prevailed, as neither Louis Philippe nor Prince Metternich, perhaps the most visible symbol of political conservatism in Europe, saw fit to challenge the de facto political division of Europe between liberal regimes like France and conser-vative ones like Austria.[5]

It is not surprising that the only art and literature the revolution inspired that resonated with future generations, and became part of a seemingly timeless revolutionary mythology in France and elsewhere, were Delacroix's iconic 'Liberty on the Barricades' and Victor Hugo's *Les Misérables*.[6] But the events of the revolution itself—their alacrity, the relatively prosaic way in which they unfolded, and the fact that they occurred predominantly, if not entirely, in Paris, leaving other Frenchmen either ignorant of them or mere observers—were not the only

---

[3] Rapport, *1848*, 23. Later in the decade the situation changed, and there occurred the first of eight assassination attempts on the king's life, all unsuccessful, until his abdication in 1848. Tombs, *France 1814–1914*, pp. 21, 366.

[4] Tombs, *France 1814–1914*, p. 11.

[5] Jonathan Sperber, *Revolutionary Europe 1780–1850* (New York, 2013), p. 366.

[6] That Hugo's novel was published in 1862, thirty-two years after the revolution, and that much of it takes place well before it began, would seem to qualify severely any claim that the 1830 Revolution was the only reason for the novel's fame. Nor should there be any doubt that many who read the novel appreciated it more for its literary merit than for its political message.

reasons it failed to appeal to the non-rational aspects of the mind so conducive of the passions from which mythologies of any kind, not just revolutionary ones, are able to emerge. There was another reason the 1830 Revolution, at least in comparison to the other French revolutions, failed to stir emotions. The Revolution of 1830 was not much of a revolution at all. Despite the transformational implications of the word itself, this particular revolution did not change very much. Louis Philippe was aware of the symbolism implicit in his eschewing the royal robes and crowns of the Bourbons for an ordinary business suit. But his regime, as François Furet has pointed out, was more like the Bourbon Restoration that preceded it than supporters of either dynasty, the Bourbon or the Orléanist, were willing to acknowledge.[7] Other historians have noted that the revolution, other than substituting one royal family for another, did not precipitate dramatic changes in the kinds of people running the government.[8] Both before and after 1830 the institutions of governance were staffed predominantly with the so-called *notables*—the amorphous but nonetheless distinctive social stratum that had emerged in the French Revolution from the economic fusion of the landed upper classes and the urban bourgeoisie.[9] What changed in 1830 was that *notables* who rejected the French Revolution and accepted the restoration that followed it were replaced by *notables* for whom the opposite was the case.[10] Because by 1830 industrialization in France had barely begun, the crowds that participated in the July Days consisted of artisans and skilled workers rather than an actual proletariat.[11] For this reason the revolution that occurred in 1830 was not, in Marxist terminology, a proletarian revolution, nor even a true bourgeoisie revolution. The members of the Chamber of Deputies who were elected after the revolution were remarkably similar in their economic status to those who had served in its pre-revolutionary predecessor.[12] Fully 90 per cent were landowners, and as late as 1846, almost one-third were titled nobility.[13]

The Revolution of 1830, in sum, was a predominantly political affair, driven mainly by a widely shared desire to be rid of the Bourbons once and for all. Louis Philippe seemed cognizant of his lacking a mandate for transformational change, and as ruler seemed guided by his sense of a *juste milieu*.[14] Content to 'muddle through', in much the way the Directors had tried to do in the late 1790s, the new king's moderation alienated the political extremes in France no less than the Directors did, while the coterie of moderates that supported him shrank in

---

[7] François Furet, *Revolutionary France 1779–1880* (New York, 1988), p. 327.

[8] Christopher H. Johnson, 'The Revolution of 1830 in French Economic History', in *1830 in France*, edited by John M. Merriman (New York, 1975), p. 147.

[9] Pinckney, *French Revolution of 1830*, p. 277.   [10] Tombs, *France 1814–1914*, p. 358.

[11] David H. Pinckney, 'The Crowd in the French Revolution of 1830', *American Historical Review*, 70, no. 1 (October 1964), pp. 1–17.

[12] Pinckney, *French Revolution of 1830*, p. 280.   [13] Tombs, *France 1814–1914*, p. 123.

[14] Gordon Wright, *France in Modern Times: From the Enlightenment to the Present* (New York, 1981), p. 109.

numbers, so that another revolution seemed inevitable. But its occurrence in 1848 should not obscure the fact that the Orléanist regime he headed lasted eighteen years, which, compared to other French governments of the nineteenth-century prior to the Third Republic, was a long time.

For all of these reasons, the 1830 Revolution showed the Bolsheviks that not all revolutions were equal, and that some were more useful than others. The 1830 Revolution was certainly one of the latter. But the Bolsheviks did not ignore it entirely, and it influenced their thinking to the extent to which it strengthened conclusions drawn from other, more stirring French revolutions. Moreover, it helped them, in conjunction with what they knew about the Revolution of 1848 and the Paris Commune, to combine all three revolutions with the original one to create in their own minds a genuine tradition of revolutions, of which their own revolution would be the next one.

Having emerged out of the Russian intelligentsia of the nineteenth century, the Bolsheviks of course were influenced by what certain *intelligenty* had written about the Revolution of 1830. Bakunin, who, until his last years, remained an incorrigible optimist about all matters political, noted that the 1830 Revolution confirmed the supremacy of the bourgeoisie in France, thereby consigning to oblivion 'the vestiges of feudal and clerical domination' that still existed when the French Revolution ended.[15] As a result, the French nobility, after 1830, lost what little chance it still had of taking power and holding onto it. According to Bakunin, this was because the bourgeoisie, which by 1830 had become not just the dominant social class but also 'the defender and preserver of the state', simply would not allow this to happen.[16] In fact, by turning on the lower classes that had initially assisted it, the bourgeoisie seemed to ensure its political supremacy for the immediate future. But in reading Bakunin's comments on the revolution, one senses that notwithstanding the evidence he himself provided of the lower classes' political passivity and immaturity, he still harboured the secret desire for another revolution, in which these classes would consign the bourgeoisie to well-deserved oblivion. For Bakunin, a victorious revolution was always destined to follow whatever event or series of events that left him, momentarily, disappointed.

Other *intelligenty* were not so optimistic. The 1830 Revolution showed Chernyshevskii that not all revolutions benefitted the lower classes. The problem, as he later diagnosed it, was that in 1830 they engaged on the side of the middle classes, who cared nothing for their interests or their needs.[17] But to Chernyshevskii the problem was not just that the lower classes had made a bad decision. Rather, their decision reflected a broader aversion, a pervasive indifference to politics generally,

---

[15] Bakunin, *Statism and Anarchy*, p. 125.

[16] Bakunin, *God and the State* (New York, 1970), p. 83.

[17] N. G. Chernyshevskii, 'Iiul'skaia monarkhiia', in N. G. Chernyshevskii, *Izbrannye sochineniia* (Moscow/Leningrad, 1928), vol. I, pp. 316–453.

which explained why the lower classes had at one time supported the First French Republic, only to embrace 'Napoleon's absolute monarchy' a few years later.[18] Even the striking workers in Lyon in the early 1830s, he noted ruefully, lacked the requisite political sophistication to achieve their objectives, or at least to establish an equilibrium in which neither side enjoyed any significant advantage. Only when the lower classes embraced socialism would they have a real chance of eliminating the political institutions that, acting as the agents of the bourgeoisie, oppressed them. The only solace Chernyshevskii found in the entire debacle was that the cluelessness of the lower classes was not their fault. In 1830 socialism barely existed in France, but once it did, the liberals who had emerged victorious in that same year would soon find their political and economic supremacy challenged, and not long after that, finally ended.

For Alexander Herzen, 1830 was as much a disappointment as it was for Chernyshevskii, with whom he shared the conviction that socialism was the only remedy for the exploitation peasants and workers were destined to endure wherever an Industrial Revolution occurred. Where he differed was in not finding fault in the lower classes. Their passivity did not cause the Revolution of 1830 to fail. Rather, the reason was that it was a political revolution that merely substituted one ruling dynasty for another. Accordingly, it left the underlying economic realities in France unchanged. The poverty that existed in France before the revolution continued after it—which caused Herzen to profess his lack of surprise when workers in Lyon and Paris actively protested their plight shortly after the revolution ended.[19] And since Herzen read about the revolution long after its occurrence, its failure did not have the transformational effect on his ideology that the failure of the next revolution in France would have eighteen years later.

For revolutionary *intelligenty* of the generation after Herzen's, the 1830 Revolution was part of a larger epoch in the emergence and early development of socialism. Nothing about the revolution was *sui generis*, or even particularly distinctive. Rather, in the opinion of Tkachev, it was a political revolution that, by failing to remedy the economic hardships that caused it, made another revolution inevitable. The changes the 1830 Revolution produced were beneficial, but insufficient and, in the end, inconsequential.[20] In Tkachev's analysis there was little with which Kropotkin, who usually differed with Tkachev on tactical matters, disagreed. The most complimentary observation Kropotkin could make about the revolution was that it contributed to the Revolution of 1848. But that—no doubt to Kropotkin's regret—was the extent of its influence.[21]

For Marx and Engels, however, the Revolution of 1830 had special significance. Marx learned of it at a young age from his father Heinrich, who sang not just the *Marseillaise* but also *Parisienne*, the unofficial anthem of the revolution; once

[18] Ibid., p. 415.   [19] Malia, *Alexander Herzen*, pp. 101–2, 189.
[20] Tkachev, 'Retsenziia no knigu A. Rokhau', p. 193.   [21] Kropotkin, *Conquest of Bread*, p. 6.

when the former was sung, someone, possibly Heinrich, waved a handkerchief made to resemble the *tricoleur,* with scenes of Parisians fighting on the barricades in 1830 depicted as well.[22] Marx's first extended comment on the revolution was in *The Holy Family,* in which he wrote that, after 1830, the liberal bourgeoisie continued the progressive changes the French Revolution inaugurated but that the Restoration had rudely interrupted.[23] The result was that the bourgeoisie no longer saw the state as the instrument for achieving the liberation of everyone. Instead, it now 'acknowledged the state as the official expression of its own exclusive power and the political recognition of its own special interests'.[24] For that reason, and because the revolution did nothing to change the underlying economic conditions that had prevailed since the late eighteenth century, a subsequent revolution—a proletarian revolution—would still have to happen before the exploitation from which the proletariat suffered first diminished and then disappeared entirely.

One of Marx's earliest comments on the revolution was that it changed France from a system in which the king was the source of political authority to one in which the king's authority was henceforth given to him by the people.[25] While this might fairly be considered a progressive development, according to Marx it actually did nothing to lessen the proletariat's oppression. But once the proletariat realized this, its sense of betrayal would precipitate another revolution—and in 1848 it did. Marx fleshed out this idea in articles written two years after the revolution in that year had been crushed.[26] Looking back on its closest precursor chronologically, Marx stressed that the 1830 Revolution did more than substitute Orléanists for Bourbons. It also ratified politically a change in the respective influence and power of the various subclasses within the bourgeoisie: those engaged in commerce and industry—'railway kings', along with the owners of coal mines, iron works, and forests—joined with bankers and landed aristocrats— which he said comprised a 'finance aristocracy'—to form an haute-bourgeoisie more powerful politically than the mostly petit-bourgeois Jacobins in the French Revolution.[27] Strong enough to exercise power, if only fleetingly, in the last decade of the eighteenth century, this petit-bourgeoisie, while strengthened in the early nineteenth century by a large influx of urban professionals, was still too weak in 1830 to resist the growing dominance of the haute-bourgeoisie, which managed to turn the July Monarchy of Louis Philippe into 'a joint-stock company for the exploitation of (France's) national wealth'.[28]

---

[22] Sperber, *Karl Marx,* p. 28. It is not known if the handerkerchief was his possession.
[23] Marx and Engels, *The Holy Family,* p. 140.   [24] Ibid.
[25] Rubel, 'The French Revolution', p. 21.
[26] The articles were published in a journal, *Neue Rheinische Zeitung, Politisch-Oekonomische Revue,* that Marx produced and edited in London in 1849–50. In 1895 the articles were published as a discrete essay, with an introduction by Engels, under the title *The Class Struggles in France 1848 to 1850.* Personal communication with Jonathan Sperber (5 November 2018).
[27] Marx, *The Class Struggles in France,* pp. 33–5.   [28] Ibid., p. 36.

By the time the Paris Commune was destroyed in the spring of 1871, its bloodletting easily exceeding that which had occurred in 1830 and 1848, Marx could look back on these earlier revolutions not only with the benefit of extended hindsight, but with the memory of the Commune still vivid in his mind. In the second draft of *The Civil War in France*, his magnum opus on the Commune, Marx described what happened in France in 1830 not so much as a change in the balance of power within the bourgeoisie as a transfer of political power 'from the landowner to the capitalist, and thus from a distant to an immediate opponent of the workers'.[29] Moreover, the Orléanists the revolution brought to power were one of the many 'parties of order' in France in the nineteenth century that used the state as 'an undisguised instrument of civil war'; the others that did so were successively 'Legitimist, bourgeois republican, and Bonapartist'.[30] Writing in 1871, Marx was able view the 1830 Revolution over *la longue durée*: he could now situate it historically relative both to the revolution that preceded it and to the revolutions that followed it, and determine how precisely it differed by virtue of its occurrence at a different point in the larger history of industrial capitalism.

Central to everything Marx wrote about the 1830 Revolution was that by the time it occurred, the bourgeoisie had advanced sufficiently since the French Revolution so that, in any subsequent revolution, it would not, in the middle of it, transfer to another class the responsibility history conferred on it of safeguarding the emergence of industrial capitalism. This, of course, was what he thought had happened in the French Revolution. By 1830, however, the ongoing economic transformation of the French economy from one based on feudalism to a capitalist one rendered a similar substitution unnecessary. In that year, workers helped the bourgeoisie make a revolution of which the bourgeoisie was the principal beneficiary, just as they had done in the French Revolution beginning in 1792. But ending a dynasty in France was easier in 1830 than ending the monarchy itself had been in 1792 and the bourgeoisie could more easily ignore the wishes and interests of the lower classes—which by 1830 included an industrial working class growing in size and becoming increasingly radical politically—and still not lose power. Paradoxically, the bourgeoisie had an easier time of it in establishing (or re-establishing) its political supremacy in 1830 than it did in 1789.[31]

---

[29] Quoted in Furet, *Marx and the French Revolution*, p. 229.

[30] Ibid., p. 230. By 'Legitimist' Marx meant supporters of the now powerless Bourbons.

[31] In his 1895 introduction Engels described the 1830 Revolution in much the way Marx did—as a political revolution that did nothing to change the material conditions in which the proletariat lived. In that respect, according to Engels, it differed from the French Revolution, which, both in France and in many other parts of Europe, ended one epoch in history, namely feudalism, and replaced it with another, namely industrial capitalism. The 1830 Revolution, by contrast, substituted one subclass within the bourgeoisie for another. But both of these revolutions were bourgeois revolutions, and as such could not bring about the only thing that would eliminate the proletariat's exploitation, namely communism. F. Engels, Introduction to Marx, *Class Struggles in France*, p. 12.

What Marx and Engels learned from the 1830 Revolution and its aftermath was that revolutions do not end when the participants retreat or are driven from their proverbial battle stations, which in the nineteenth century consisted mostly of barricades. Setbacks occur, and that was what happened in France during the three revolutions that followed the first one. But later generations would eventually resume the struggle, which Marx and Engels were certain would continue until the oppression that caused revolutions to occur in the first place had been eliminated. Viewed retrospectively, they could consider these revolutions, along with their eighteenth-century progenitor and antecedent, organically related. This, in itself, was cause for optimism. In the progression 1789–1830–1848–1871 there was the comforting implication of inevitability. No revolution short of the proletarian one yielding socialism and communism was self-contained. Each one, for its own objectives to be achieved, required another one. And because Marx and Engels believed that the progressive changes the dialectic made inevitable were universal, there was no reason this teleology of revolutions could not cross the borders between countries or even the seas between continents. As a result, later revolutionaries in far-off Russia could easily convince themselves that to these four distinct paroxysms of popular anger and discontent in France they would add a fifth one of their own making. In sum, what the 1830 Revolution contributed to the creation of this revolutionary tradition was in providing Marx and Engels an early and very concrete manifestation of their view of history as the unfolding of one economic system after another, with successful revolutions sounding the death knell for one that was about to expire, and seemingly unsuccessful ones, like that in 1830, silently weakening those that survived, thereby delaying their destruction but not preventing it.

By both temperament and conviction the Mensheviks were inclined to follow Marx and Engels faithfully. This was especially the case in deciding when exactly revolutions should be attempted, and which classes should lead them. For Martov, about whom it could be said, paraphrasing Shakespeare, that he loved Marxism not wisely but too well, this meant that the 1830 Revolution demonstrated the limits beyond which the bourgeoisie, in the early nineteenth century, was unwilling to go in reforming France. Pseudonymously reviewing a book on Lafayette, Martov called him 'an ideologue of the bourgeoisie', and implied strongly that what was true of the Marquis was true of the class whose interests he had committed himself to protect.[32] For his part, Plekhanov thought more deeply about the revolution. In the article written in 1889 to mark the centenary of the French Revolution, he coupled 1830 with the unrest in Lyon in 1831, compared both to the English revolutions of the seventeenth century (1642–51 and 1688–9), and concluded that while in England the earlier revolution was the more influential of the two, in

---

[32] Iu. Kedrov [Iu. Martov], 'Obozrenie V. Ia. Bogucharskogo, *Markiz' Lafaiet: deiatel' trekh revoliutsii*', *Zhizn'* 9 (September 1900): p. 359.

France the reverse was true: 1830 did little more than ratify what began in 1789, but the events in Lyon were a harbinger of the proletarian revolution Plekhanov was convinced would eventually destroy bourgeois democracies wherever they existed and make possible the construction of socialism and communism.[33] That his prediction had not yet come true a full century after the French Revolution did nothing to temper Plekhanov's confidence in his own powers of prognostication and, even more importantly as far as he was concerned, in those of Marx and Engels. In 1889 Plekhanov was politically powerless, and thus could do little but issue intellectual dicta that were empirically untestable. For this reason the elaborate structure and vocabulary Marxism provided for interpreting historical events acquired, in his own mind, a reality that diminished his ability to comprehend the realities that existed outside his own mind, in the world around him. This of course was case for practically all Russian Marxists, with the partial exception of Lenin and Trotsky, for whom political considerations sometimes overrode ideological constraints. Until Russia experienced its bourgeois revolution, and thereby reached the stage of history France had achieved over a century earlier, Mensheviks like Plekhanov let their minds run free, the conceptual webs they weaved limited only by the rigid concepts and categories of the Marxism they professed.

* * *

For many years Lenin wrote nothing about the 1830 Revolution. In the spring of 1905, he did not think to mention it when asking in an article if the ongoing revolution in Russia resembled 1789 or 1848.[34] In 1906, in a speech to the Unity Congress of the RSDLP, he finally referred to it, but only in explaining why the proletariat in France in the early and mid-1840s might conclude that any revolution the bourgeoisie led would work to its own disadvantage.[35] In 1830, according to Lenin, the bourgeoisie split economically between its more prosperous elements, which he described as 'Legitimist', and those that comprised the petit-bourgeoisie, which in its political affiliation was Orléanist.[36] Lenin saw no need to state that the republic that was established in 1848 failed. But he did promise his audience that should the Bolsheviks find themselves in a situation resembling France's in 1848, they would not allow the bourgeoisie to destroy the proletariat; instead they would seize power the way the Jacobins did in 1793 by taking over the Convention. In 1909 Lenin once again mentioned 1830; this time he wrote that in Russia another revolution was imminent, and for that reason Russian socialists should not 'liquidate' their underground apparatus; Stolypin's ongoing efforts to de-radicalise the Russian peasantry the way Bismarck had tried to do was bound

---

[33] Plekhanov, 'Stoletie velikoi revoliutsii', p. 56.
[34] V. I. Lenin, 'Revoliutsiia tipa 1789 ili tipa 1848', in Lenin, *PSS*, vol. IX, pp. 380–2.
[35] V. I. Lenin, 'Zakliuchitel'noe slovo po voprosu o sovremennom momente i klassovykh zadachakh proletariata', ibid., vol. XII, pp. 374–5.
[36] Ibid., vol. XII, p. 375.

to fail. In fact, the future revolution would likely be followed by later ones, thereby creating a teleology of revolution resembling the French, which included 1830 along with 1848 and 1871.[37] Lenin did not say what he would recommend once this sequence in Russia was complete, but it seemed to follow that preparations for a proletarian revolution should then commence.

Finally, in an article in 1911 Lenin explained what he considered the causes of the 1830 Revolution, and how its results increased the gap between France and the German states regarding the influence and power of their respective middle and upper classes.[38] The 1830 Revolution, he affirmed, made France a bourgeois monarchy, and to the extent to which it ensured that no other kind of monarchy could ever emerge in France, it eliminated any chance of a second Bourbon Restoration. (Here Lenin momentarily forgot about Louis Napoleon's empire—which in some ways resembled a monarchy—or did not think it prudent to mention it.) The reason the revolution succeeded was that the Bourbons, by 1830, could no longer conceal the fact that they were supported by the nobility, and that its support, rather than that of the 'liberal bourgeoisie'—by which Lenin meant the haute-bourgeoisie—was critical to the continuation of the dynasty. The Revolution of 1830, however, was the result of the nobility's increasing economic obsolescence, and the revolution's success in ending the Bourbon Restoration ensured that this liberal bourgeoisie thereafter did not have to share power with anyone. The implication in Lenin's argument was that Louis Philippe was essentially its puppet or, at the very least its political instrument. But this did not mean that between 1830 and 1848 the bourgeoisie in France did not evolve. Because it did, the result in 1848 was a government led by what Lenin called 'a republican bourgeoisie', which he described as 'a retrained, re-educated, and reborn' version of the original bourgeoisie that first gained power in the French Revolution.[39] Again Lenin compared France to the German states, where the aristocracy, prior to Bismarck, never relinquished its hegemony, and the elements of the bourgeoisie that were 'liberal' endeavoured to imitate it rather than to overthrow it, as happened in France in 1830.[40]

In all of these instances prior to 1917 in which Lenin directly or indirectly addressed the 1830 Revolution, he considered it on its own terms and within its own context. But in the celebratory speech he delivered to the Congress of Soviets on 27 October 1917, as the Bolsheviks were completing their remarkably efficient (and largely bloodless) insurrection in Petrograd, Lenin viewed it differently.[41] After asking the proletariat in Great Britain, Germany, and France for their support, to increase the likelihood of their doing so he mentioned the labour

---

[37] V. I. Lenin, 'I. I. Skvortsovu-Stepanovu', ibid., vol. XLVII, p. 224.
[38] V. I. Lenin, 'Printsipal'nye voprosy izbiratel'noi kompanii', ibid., vol. XXI, pp. 83–4.
[39] Ibid., vol. XXI, p. 84.   [40] Ibid., vol. XXI, p. 84.
[41] V. I. Lenin, 'Doklad o mire', ibid., vol. XXXV, pp. 16–17.

movements in each country, specifically the Chartists in England and the workers in Germany who had sought the revocation of Bismarck's anti-socialist laws. In the case of France, he mentioned its workers, who 'in uprisings repeatedly revealed the strength of their class-consciousness'.[42] Undoubtedly Lenin included the 1830 Revolution among these uprisings, and by the phraseology he used made clear that he was referring to the quartet of revolutions in France that by 1917 had become, in his considered opinion, a tradition with a collective meaning and mythology.

Although Lenin himself never again referred to the 1830 Revolution in his writings and public statements, his opinion of it influenced other Bolsheviks. That the Communist Party imposed no particular interpretation of it, nor thought to include it in the grandiose theatrical productions in which the French Revolution figured prominently, made the expression of one's sincerely held opinions easier. Nevertheless, Lenin's opinions on practically everything were too imposing and formidable for the Bolsheviks to ignore, and what was written about 1830 in the Soviet Union prior to the Gorbachev era was basically a facsimile of the Leninist original.

Among the first statements after Lenin's death were David Riazanov's. As director of the Marx–Engels Institute since its creation in 1919, Riazanov was uniquely qualified to opine on matters on which Marx and Engels had expressed opinions. In his joint biography of Marx and Engels that was published in 1927, he commented that the 1830 Revolution had occurred when both men were young, and thus well before their political views had coalesced. For that reason it exercised an outsized influence that earlier and later events lacked.[43] In fact, Riazanov seemed aware that revolutions, because of the emotions they stirred, were especially appealing to individuals with sensibilities like those of Marx and Engels, whom he lauded for their insatiable curiosity about history.

As for the revolution itself, Riazanov described it as an event that transcended its original time and place. Although it began in France, it 'swept all over Europe from West to East', even inspiring an insurrection in Russia.[44] In its economic effects, the Revolution of 1830 emancipated 'the industrial, commercial, and financial bourgeoisie' from the hegemony of the old nobility, which had enforced its waning, but nonetheless considerable economic supremacy throughout the Restoration.[45] But instead of establishing a republic in 1830, which Riazanov implied was the objective of the non-bourgeois elements of the population, without whose support and participation the revolution would undoubtedly have failed, the victorious bourgeoisie opted instead for a constitutional monarchy. The bourgeoisie, in other words, was the principal beneficiary of the revolution even though the proletariat and impoverished peasants were its principal instrument. The treachery and hypocrisy the bourgeoisie displayed that

[42] Ibid., vol. XXXV, p. 17.   [43] Riazanov, *Karl Marx and Frederick Engels*, p. 14.
[44] Ibid., p. 14.   [45] Ibid., p. 25.

made possible such an advantageous outcome were characteristic of the class not just in France but everywhere. But the advantage the bourgeoisie gained in France in 1830 would soon be challenged by lower classes embittered by the events of that year and increasingly aware that the bourgeoisie was the source of their own exploitation.

The first significant expression of the radicalism this new awareness engendered occurred in 1831, in Lyon, among workers in the silk industry. For a few days, workers controlled the city, and while their demands were entirely economic, their example prompted another revolt, also in Lyon, three years later. Unfortunately, the workers who seized control of the city showed a lamentable, but entirely understandable lack of ideological consciousness; their demands remained economic, thereby demonstrating their ignorance of the imperative essential to a successful proletarian revolution that the capitalist system as a whole had to be destroyed before any appreciable improvement in their living conditions could occur. But this in no way diminished the sense of betrayal the workers experienced when the insurrection failed, and for that reason it was only a matter of time before they would erupt in violence again.[46]

As for Trotsky, who always viewed revolutions as a form of theatre in which the participants played roles assigned to them by history itself, the Revolution of 1830 was the equivalent of a sideshow, its trajectory not long enough for its actors to reveal the full extent of their heroism and bravery, and its consequences not significant enough to warrant more than a few cursory references in his writings. Trotsky, of course, was an aficionado of revolutionary bravura, and for him there were other revolutions in Europe, most notably the Paris Commune, more closely approximating in their theatricality the pathos he believed made for effective propaganda, in which struggle led to victory, only to be followed by final defeat and tragic martyrdom. In his 1925 treatise on what he believed would be the future evolution of England, he commented that the 1830 Revolution was an impetus to the Reform Bill the Parliament approved shortly afterwards—which for Trotsky was hardly an encomium given his disdain for the political gradualism the reform bill embodied; it graphically violated not only Trotsky's ideological commitments, but also his aesthetic sensibilities about how people engaged in politics should act.[47] Twelve years later, in The Revolution Betrayed, written long after losing power himself, the most Trotsky could say about the 1830 Revolution was that, by substituting one 'ruling upper crust' for another, it transferred power not from one class to another but within the bourgeoisie, thereby precluding any serious challenge to the latter's economic supremacy until 1848.[48] In fact, the particular stratum within the bourgeoisie that benefitted from the 1830 Revolution would

---

[46] Ibid., pp. 25–6.   [47] Leon Trotsky, Where is Britain Going? (Ann Arbor MI, 1960), p. 22.
[48] Leon Trotsky, The Revolution Betrayed: What is the Soviet Union and Where is it Going? (New York, 1972), p. 288.

survive the revolution in 1848, and so dominate the country's economy in the second half of the nineteenth century that Trotsky, in 1917, considered it the paradigmatic example of how high finance under capitalism could determine a country's politics and economy: 'France is the classic land of finance-capital which leans for its support on the petty bourgeoisie, and for that reason it was 'the financial interests of the French Bourse' that prompted France to go to war in 1914.[49]

Unlike Lenin, who valued the 1830 Revolution as an integral component of the revolutionary tradition that began in France in 1789, Trotsky seemed to consider it, if not *sui generis*, then certainly an event explicable on its own terms, rather than as a transitional phase between the French Revolution that preceded it and the revolutions in 1848 and 1871 that followed it. In Trotsky's description, the only lesson the 1830 Revolution imparted was to underscore the need, after the French Revolution ended, for subsequent revolutions to consolidate the victory the bourgeoisie had secured in 1789. But for Trotsky, 1848 and 1871, far more than 1830, were linked organically to the original French revolution. While the elements within the bourgeoisie that emerged victorious in the late eighteenth century soon afterwards applied capitalist methods and principles in administering their newly acquired land, they remained a landed class. Not until 1830 would they yield primacy within the bourgeoisie to more urban and commercial elements—but even without the 1830 Revolution, this change in the relative power of subclasses within the bourgeoisie was, to all intents and purposes, inevitable. More broadly, one senses from Trotsky's analysis that nothing that happened in 1830 had to happen in order for another, more radical revolution to occur.

Soviet historians, with few exceptions, adhered to a Marxist, or at least a class-based, interpretation of the 1830 Revolution. N. I. Kareev, a Kadet who served in the Duma but like many Russian liberals was radicalized by reading Cherny-shevskii, Dobroliubov, and Lavrov, wrote a multi-volume history on how historians in France interpreted the French Revolution in the first half of the nineteenth century. Not surprisingly, he saw the 1830 Revolution as a turning point in the evolution of France from 1789 to 1848. He argued that 1830 marked 'a new France [that] was victorious over an old one'.[50] By this he meant the end of the conflict between the aristocracy and the bourgeoisie that began in 1789. In the compromise the 1830 Revolution brought about, the aristocracy retained its property but lost its political power, and for that reason all hope of ever reversing the French Revolution vanished. Like it or not, the supremacy it yielded to the bourgeoisie

---

[49] Leon Trotsky, 'Democracy, Pacifism, and Imperialism', *Vpered* (30 June 1917), in Vladimir Lenin and Leon Trotsky, *The Proletarian Revolution in Russia*, edited by Louis B. Fraina (New York, 1918), pp. 195, 196.

[50] N. I. Kareev, *Frantsuzskie istoriki pervoi poloviny XIX veka* (Leningrad, 1924), vol. I, pp. 13–14.

was permanent. At first, the bourgeoisie had reason to believe that its interests would be protected by the new Orléanist regime. But it soon recognized that what it really wanted politically was democracy like that which later informed the Second Republic until Louis Napoleon used it to create the Second Empire. In that respect, the bourgeoisie was greatly influenced by histories of the French Revolution such as Thiers', which suggested that history was only rarely repetitive, that the renunciation of power that cost the bourgeoisie so dearly in the French Revolution at the hands of the Jacobins need not happen again, and that after taking power in a future revolution, the bourgeoisie, instead of renouncing it as it did in 1792, would retain it, and thereby ensure its long-term supremacy.[51] In addition, France had changed sufficiently since 1789 to render obsolete the democracy the French Revolution practised after Louis XVI was guillotined and the monarchy abolished. By 1830 the most appropriate system of government for France, in the sense of meeting the needs of the dominant social classes, was the 'bourgeois monarchy' of Louis Philippe. In Kareev's analysis, the Orléanist king advanced the interests of the bourgeoisie because he shared its growing fear of the lower classes. This in turn solidified the king's credentials as a class monarch, which enabled him to rule until 1848, long after one might think that changes in French society had made his abdication and the end of the class monarchy he had established inevitable.[52]

In the Stalin era, history was made to serve the interests of the government to an extent greater than it was when Lenin was alive, and also during the struggle to succeed him after his death, when a party line did not exist or was difficult to discern in the rise and fall of competing blocs based more on political interests than ideology. This was certainly true for historians concerned with France. In their works, references to the Revolution of 1830 were few. For Stalinist historians as well as Leninist ones, the later revolution did not exude the universality that had characterized the French Revolution. But it contained lessons relevant to present-day politics that prompted Evgenii Tarlé, for one, to point them out. He included in his aforementioned article in *Pravda* on the sesquicentennial of the French Revolution a comparison between supporters of the 1830 Revolution in France, who sought foreign assistance, and elements in France in the late 1930s who betrayed their country by supporting Hitler and rejecting the Popular Front against 'German fascism', which, when Tarlé was writing, the Soviet Union still supported.[53]

In the post-Stalin era, historians fortunate enough to have survived Stalinist Terror resumed their endeavours unimpeded unless they violated specified canons

---

[51]   Ibid., p. 140.   [52]   Ibid., pp. 141–2.
[53]   Tarlé, 'Bor'ba s interventsiei', p. 4. Tarlé's article appeared on 4 July 1939; the Soviet Union and Nazi Germany did not sign the Non-Aggression Pact, with a secret protocol attached to it, until 23 August.

of Marxist-Leninist ideology as it applied to history. In reality, virtually everything not forbidden was allowed. Among historians of France, even V. M. Dalin, who had spent seventeen years in a labour camp, once again reiterated, seemingly voluntarily, the Leninist mantra on the 1830 Revolution, writing in 1981 that it marked a change in class relations above and beyond that for which the French Revolution, four decades earlier, had been responsible. More broadly, 1830 completed the transfer of political power from the aristocracy to the bourgeoisie that had begun in 1789. But the bourgeoisie in 1830 confronted the opposition of a class, the proletariat, which barely existed when the French Revolution began. Although the struggle between the two classes remained unresolved for the next decade and for most of the one after that, in 1848 the bourgeoisie crushed the proletariat's heroic attempt, with assistance from impoverished peasants, to take power itself. By destroying the Paris Commune, it did the same thing in 1871. But because the supremacy of a retrograde class over a progressive one was never permanent, the victories the bourgeoisie enjoyed in 1830, 1848, and 1871 were pyrrhic ones. The October Revolution, while not sparking a proletarian revolution in France, was nonetheless the first indication that a revolution there was inevitable; the only uncertainty concerned when exactly it would occur.[54] Similarly, A. Z. Manfred, in 1983, described the 1830 Revolution as a moment in French history, and in the history of the bourgeoisie in Europe, when a segment of the class took power and thereby made permanent the gains its antecedents had made in the French Revolution. After 1830 there would be no more restorations in French history, at least none that were committed to the interests of the aristocracy. While acknowledging that to achieve its objective in 1830 the bourgeoisie required the assistance of 'the monied aristocracy', Manfred made clear, if only by implication, that that requirement did not make the Revolution of 1830 a counter-revolution.[55]

* * *

To the Bolsheviks, the 1830 Revolution was a success. Replacing Bourbons with Orléanists, notwithstanding that they both were royal families, was not without significance in the inexorable ascendency of humanity from feudalism to capitalism. Nor, for that matter, was the change the revolution caused in the relationship between the elements of the bourgeoisie, which benefitted from the revolution more than it contributed to it, a trivial one. The revolution confirmed in France (though not in other parts of Europe, including and especially Russia) the legitimacy of the first French revolution—while also demonstrating that by 1830 the classes involved in that revolution had changed considerably. The bourgeoisie

---

[54] Tchoudinov, 'The Evolution of Russian Discourse on the French Revolution', p. 291. Dalin, *Istoriki Frantsii*, pp. 38–41 and *passim*. One can glean Dalin's views on the 1830 Revolution from his comments on the French historians who described and interpreted it.

[55] Manfred, *Velikaia frantsuzskaia revoliutsiia*, p. 368.

the lower classes confronted in that year and decades afterwards was not the professionally minded bourgeoisie that had started the French Revolution. Rather, it was now a commercial class engaged in finance, and increasingly, with the passage of time, an industrial class. As such, it was more protective of its own interests, and more willing to use military force—as it would in 1848—to ensure its continued economic supremacy. In fact, the reason the bourgeoisie called on the military to suppress the proletariat in 1848 was because the lower classes in France had also changed dramatically since the late eighteenth century: the artisans and craftsmen, whose support as *sans-culottes* was as critical to the Jacobins' victory in 1793 as the lack of it was to the Jacobins' defeat in 1794, had surrendered pride of place among the oppressed elements in France to a small but growing industrial working class, the exploitation of which made it potentially a stronger political force than that the *sans-culottes* had even showed themselves to be in the 1790s.

Viewed retrospectively through the prism of Marxism-Leninism, the 1830 Revolution, which confirmed existing economic realities without creating any new ones, was nonetheless an augury of better things to come—not only in France, but also in Europe. To be sure, that was not the case for the revolution eighteen years later. Viewed through the same lens, the Revolution of 1848 in France could not plausibly be considered anything other than a disaster. Precisely because expectations when it began of what it might accomplish were so high, its ignominious end in the semi-tragic, semi-farcical Second Empire of Louis Napoleon seemed a cruel trick history had played on its supporters. The only solace one could draw from the debacle was that the dialectic was not finished with France in 1848, that it would continue to cause economic conditions for the proletariat to worsen until a proletarian revolution occurred either there, or somewhere else in the world (as happened in Russia in 1917), and made things right. The defeat the forces of virtue suffered in France in 1848 was a genuine tragedy, its pathos underscored by the extravagant and utterly unrealistic hopes its outbreak had generated. In the minds of the Bolsheviks, the Revolution of 1848 easily overshadowed the Revolution of 1830, which by comparison remained a mere episode in the larger mythology French historians of the French Revolution, such as Guizot, were already constructing when the revolution occurred, and of which the Bolsheviks, years later, were well aware.

From the revolution that contributed the least to the French Revolutionary Tradition—of which it was, nevertheless, an integral part—we now advance in this teleology of revolutions to 1848, when there occurred a revolution of far greater significance in the mythology the Bolsheviks constructed about their own revolution and the regime it brought to power.

PART III
1848

13

The Revolution That Failed

The 1848 Revolution in France was a disappointment to those who had hoped it would yield a socialist government. Nevertheless, the revolution did not lack for a legacy radicals and revolutionaries of later generations found useful, even if it was mostly a negative one, illuminating mistakes to be avoided rather than successes to be emulated. But for Russian revolutionaries in particular there was another reason to consider the revolution carefully. James Billington has described the revolutions in Europe in 1848 as the last great upheaval on a continent that was still, socially and economically, pre-industrial.[1] In much of Europe an Industrial Revolution had not yet occurred, and in countries like France where it had already begun, the working class still consisted to a large extent of self-employed artisans and craftsmen, rather than a true proletariat labouring in outsized factories. In this respect France was not so different from Russia that its revolutions had nothing Russian revolutionaries might find useful in devising strategies for taking power in their own country. Moreover, conditions in the countryside in France bore some resemblance to those in Russia. Much of the peasantry in France, while assuaged considerably by the property settlement of the French Revolution, was by no means satisfied by the status quo as France approached mid-century; the 1848 Revolution was not limited to Paris. Nor was it limited to urban elements of the population. Peasants participated in such large numbers and over such a large expanse of the country that Peter Amann has described the revolution, in its rural incarnation, as a peasant *jacquerie*, the last one in France until the Fifth Republic.[2] From this, too, revolutionaries living in Russia, which was even more rural than France, found both solace and encouragement, for it gave them grounds for believing, optimistically, that Russian peasants, properly indoctrinated—or perhaps without indoctrination at all—might prove at least as active politically as their French counterparts in 1848.

Finally, as several French historians have pointed out, the revolution the French experienced in 1848 was the result of rising expectations, triggered by rapid industrial growth in the first half of the 1840s, followed by their rapid extinction as poor harvests coincided with a financial and industrial slump; these events all at

---

[1] Billington, *Fire in the Minds of Men*, p. 235.
[2] Peter Amann, 'The Changing Outlines of 1848', *American Historical Review* 68, no. 4 (July 1963): p. 947.

once caused agricultural prices to rise, consumer spending to drop, and unemployment in towns and cities to ensue.[3] The result was a 'crisis of modernization' culminating in 1848 in a revolution driven not by those who had benefitted from industrialization, but rather by those it harmed—urban artisans and craftsmen unable to compete with an industrial labour force, and peasants in the countryside, whose numbers were increasing faster than the number of jobs in factories for those who had abandoned agriculture in favour of something more reliable and remunerative.[4] For this reason, the 1848 Revolution had special meaning for Alexander Herzen and the Russian populists, who deemed industrial capitalism an avoidable evil and looked instead to the peasant commune, with its implications of socialism, as the instrument of Russia's moral and political rejuvenation. As for the Bolsheviks, who welcomed industrialization under the auspices of a capitalist economy as a necessary prerequisite of socialism, the fact that the 1848 Revolution was the first one in Europe to include elements intent on establishing socialism was enough to obscure, if not to block out completely, its origins in what was still a pre-industrial society.[5] Although the 1848 Revolution did not yield victories like those the French Revolution had achieved a half-century earlier, or fail as poignantly as the Paris Commune would a quarter-century later, it was not without its attractions for Russians intent on transforming their own country radically and, if necessary, through violence.[6]

Of all the Russian revolutionaries prior to the Bolsheviks who ascribed the failure of the 1848 Revolution in France to the treachery and hypocrisy of the bourgeoisie, Herzen was the most directly affected by this ostensible betrayal. Indeed, his furious denunciations both shortly after the revolution ended and in works written long afterwards would cause later revolutionaries in Russia to make his antipathy to the bourgeoisie their own. Herzen arrived in Paris in May 1848, in time to witness the June Days, the brutality of which seemed to him emblematic of the moral bankruptcy not just of France but of Western Europe as a whole. Far from an isolated incident unreflective of the unethical depths to which Western Civilization had descended, the June Days, for Herzen, were its microcosmic reflection. Thereafter he would dichotomize Europe ethically as well as geographically, condemning its Western core as irredeemable, while apotheosizing its Eastern periphery, specifically Russia, as the embodiment of all that was morally pure and socially just. The element of betrayal loomed large in Herzen's

---

[3] The harvest in 1846 was the worst in a quarter-century. Tombs, *France, 1814–1914*, pp. 367, 371.

[4] Rapport, *1848*, p. 32.

[5] Malia, *History's Locomotives*, p. 218. The Bolsheviks might also have found off-putting the refusal of the Second Republic—excepting only its efforts to foster Polish independence—to export its revolutionary principles to other parts of Europe by means of military force, considering its mere example sufficient to achieve the same objective.

[6] Robert Gildea, '1848 in European Collective Memory', in *The Revolutions in Europe 1848–1849: From Reform to Reaction*, edited by R. J. W. Evans and Hartmut Pogge von Strandmann (New York, 2002), pp. 234–5.

explanation of the killings he condemned, for which he held primarily responsible the liberals who had established the Second Republic and issued the orders to Cavaignac's troops to use all necessary force to disperse the Parisian lower classes defending themselves: 'The men who proclaimed the republic became the assassins of freedom.... The liberal names that had resounded in our ears for a score of years or so are today those of reactionary deputies, traitors [and] inquisitors.'[7] Although Herzen continued to believe in the original principles of the French Revolution, after 1848 he deemed them incompatible with the 'statism' he perceived in the Second Republic, and considered Europe, not just France, politically retrograde because of it.[8]

To be sure, Herzen had not liked everything he saw in Paris and in the rest of France before the revolution began; his observations of the French countryside while travelling to Italy in December 1847 convinced him that not everything in the West was morally uplifting, and his description of Paris in the fall of 1847 as 'unbearably oppressive' because of 'the unbelievable decadence' surrounding him makes clear that his seemingly sudden and unprecedented rejection of the West in the summer of 1848 did not emerge *ex nihilo*.[9] In addition, the failure of lower-class Parisians in May to overthrow the National Assembly, which had been established the month before, perturbed Herzen greatly; in his words, it 'tore the bandage from my eyes'.[10] That said, the June Days profoundly affected Herzen emotionally, unleashing paroxysms of anguish and despair that his earlier disappointment in France had not come close to approximating, and he reacted to the events in June with an anger suggestive of the moral and philosophical absolutism characteristic of the Russian intelligentsia as a whole. Herzen described these events in the ornate language to which he was often given when writing about matters that produced an emotional response:

> Paris! How long did that name burn as a lodestar for the nations; who did not love it, did not bow to it? But now its time is past; let it disappear from the stage.... Paris has grown old, and youthful dreams no longer become her.... [T]he June Days did not revive Paris; and so the decrepit vampire draws still more blood, the blood of the just, that same blood which on 27 June reflected the fire of the torches lit by the exultant hands of the bourgeoisie.... What will come of this blood? Who knows, but no matter what the issue, it is enough if in this paroxysm of madness, revenge, discord, and retribution, the world that oppresses the new man while keeping him from living, and thereby preventing the future from being born, simply disappears. This would be magnificent, and so I say: long live chaos and destruction.[11]

[7] Alexander Herzen, *From the Other Shore* (New York, 1956), p. 59.   [8] Ibid., p. 61.
[9] Malia, *Alexander Herzen*, pp. 365, 367.   [10] Ibid., p. 371.
[11] A. I. Herzen, 'Posle grozy', *S togo berega*, in Herzen, *Polnoe sobranie sochinenii*, vol. V, 417–18.

Herzen's emotions in 1848—from the exhilaration that followed the overthrow of the monarchy in February, through the disillusionment, and then the despair, that ensued when it dawned on him that the moral bankruptcy and decadence of the West could not be eliminated by political revolution alone—followed the same parabolic trajectory that would ensue a decade later, after Tsar Alexander II promised to abolish serfdom but then established in its place a system in which most former serfs were still tied to the land.[12]

In short, Herzen took the defeat of the 1848 Revolution as a personal affront, an insult to his moral and aesthetic sensibilities; as a result of it, France could never again be worthy of his affection and respect. 'Place any sort of military insignia on a Frenchman's cap', he wrote not long after the June Days, 'and he becomes an oppressor'.[13] Fortunately for Herzen, in the years that followed the revolution he discovered what he considered the moral and political antithesis of everything he found abhorrent in France, namely the *obshchina*, the uniquely Russian variant of the peasant commune that, by providing for regular redistribution of the lands peasants tilled, somehow imbued in them an egalitarianism Herzen considered evidence of an instinctive rejection of private property. To all intents and purposes, Russian peasants were, unwittingly, socialist, and Herzen's conviction that they practised social justice without consciously intending it only heightened their moral superiority over the urban middle classes he observed in France.

Of course Herzen was not the only *intelligent* in the aftermath of 1848 to draw the same comparison and to reach, more or less, the same conclusion. For Bakunin, the class conflict between the working class and the bourgeoisie that the June Days brought into unmistakable focus showed that compromise or reconciliation between them was impossible; for that reason the June Days served a useful purpose notwithstanding the many lives it extinguished.[14] In Bakunin's vivid prose, two forces confronted each other in France in 1848: 'the savage face of the people' and 'a savage military force' bent on the people's total annihilation.[15] The very brutality Cavaignac exhibited when he turned his killers loose was not the result of cynicism, but of conviction. He was, in Bakunin's estimation, 'a very sincere republican', and the fact that an ostensibly democratic government had resorted to extra-democratic means to survive was proof that such governments could not, under any circumstances, serve as effective and ethical instruments of revolutionary change.[16] Instead, they should seek the improvements they desired by activating the revolutionary potential of the peasantry, which in Russia possessed the additional virtue of being inherently anarchist, their commune tangible evidence of their instinctive distrust of political authority.

---

[12] Herzen was so infatuated with Alexander before the harsh reality of the emancipation set in that he called the tsar, with his customary hyperbole, the 'Galilean'. Quoted in Adam B. Ulam, *Prophets and Conspirators in Pre-Revolutionary Russia* (New Brunswick NJ, 1998), p. 44.

[13] Quoted in Malia, *Alexander Herzen*, p. 378.   [14] Bakunin, *Statism and Anarchy*, p. 148.

[15] Ibid., p. 157.   [16] Ibid., p. 159.

As for Chernyshevskii, who while the 1848 Revolution was still in progress recognized its necessity after reading Guizot's history of France, the joy he experienced after the overthrow of Louis Philippe and the Orléanists, which he believed would bring both power and material security to the lower classes, was quickly dashed by what he considered the bourgeoisie's unconscionable perfidy.[17] Culminating in the June Days, it convinced him that the lower classes had made a mistake not so much in allying with the bourgeoisie—in reality it could not eliminate the monarchy by itself, and the bourgeoisie was its only conceivable ally—but by maintaining the alliance long after it had lost its utility.[18] Once Cavaignac had killed so many of them, and in doing so had broken their backs politically, the lower classes, in Chernyshevskii's opinion, should have recognized the virtue and the necessity of socialism, which was precisely what he himself did one year later.[19] But Chernyshevskii differed from Herzen and Bakunin in his conviction that the Russian peasantry, while more amenable to socialism than any of its Western European equivalents, was not yet ready for a socialist revolution; when it would be, he gave no indication. Chernyshevskii's contemporary, Pëtr Zaichnevskii, who was also familiar with the events in France in 1848, was even more critical of the French lower classes, stating flatly in his 1862 pamphlet, *Molodaia Rossiia*, that only a dictatorship could have saved the revolutionaries of 1848, whom he denigrated as 'pitiful' for not having established one.[20]

Later Russian revolutionaries developed further the notion Herzen and Chernyshevskii propounded that the 1848 Revolution was intended only to change the political arrangements in France, and that by ignoring more fundamental economic ones—the lower classes in France were no better off after the revolution than before it—its failure was assured. This, at any rate, was the lesson the *chernoperedel'tsy* drew from their collective analysis of the revolution; Plekhanov and Axelrod, prior to their conversion to Marxism in the early 1880s, included it among the revolutions in Europe that they considered evidence of a sort that by seeking political change (through the assassination of government officials) instead of spreading propaganda among the masses (for the purpose of inciting a peasant revolution as soon as the objective preconditions for such a revolution existed), *Narodnaia Volia* was reversing the proper sequence of events. Economic change precedes and is a prerequisite of political change, not the reverse.[21] The revolutionaries in France in 1848, in other words, had made the same mistake the terrorists in Russia were committing, even though the former engaged in mass politics while the latter adopted a tactic that was essentially a substitute for it.

---

[17] Dalin, *Istoriki Frantsii*, p. 17.   [18] Venturi, *Roots of Revolution*, pp. 161–2.

[19] He also proclaimed himself an admirer of Pierre Leroux and a supporter of Louis Blanc. William F. Woehrlin, *Chernyshevskii: The Man and the Journalist* (Cambridge MA, 1971), pp. 55–6.

[20] P. Zaichnevskii, 'Molodaia Rossiia', in *Politicheskie protsessy v Rossii 1860-x gg (po arkhivnym dokumentam)*, edited by Mikhail Lemke (Moscow/Petrograd, 1923), vol. II, p. 513.

[21] Itenberg, *Rossiia i velikaia frantsuzskaia revoliutsiia*, pp. 109, 133.

Pëtr Kropotkin came to the same conclusion. The downfall of the monarchy in 1848 was of course a progressive development, but those responsible for it were derelict in eliminating the economic inequalities the Orléanists, no less than the Bourbons before them, had allowed to continue. The result was that for more than a decade after 1848 French socialists were either silent or so disillusioned by the failure in that year to address these issues that some of them rejected socialism and settled on something less radical. The problem was not that the revolutionaries of 1848 failed to recognize the primacy of economic interests. Rather, it was that they trivialized them, focusing on matters of tertiary importance, such as prison labour and military pensions, instead of providing the lower classes with food, which in Kropotkin's idiosyncratic lexicon was a short-form for economic interests generally. For all of this, however, Kropotkin continued to consider 1848 one of the three years in French history—1793 and 1871 were the others—when the ethical abyss between centralized government and the people it exploited was most apparent.[22] By expressing his conviction in this respect, he was implicitly affirming the existence of a French revolutionary tradition—a tradition he believed would continue until this exploitation finally ended with the establishment of socialism. Having risen up to smite their oppressors unsuccessfully no less than three times in the past—in 1793, 1848, and 1871—the people of France could be counted on to do the same thing in the future, and as many times as might be necessary to achieve, at last, their own emancipation.

Finally, Pëtr Tkachev, who believed that using terrorism to change the political arrangements in Russia would lead inexorably to a peasant revolution transforming the entire economy, acknowledged that in France in 1848 the same sequence of events did not occur. Politics changed, but the existing economic realities, which were inherently unfair and exploitative, continued. Not even 'the barbaric cruelty' the bourgeoisie revealed during the June Days could force the lower classes to radicalize what had been a political revolution by making it an economic one.[23] Even the plans Louis Blanc had developed for the social transformation of France were impractical.[24] Nevertheless, the history of France from Napoleon Bonaparte to Louis Napoleon contained lessons Tkachev believed Russian revolutionaries would do well to study carefully. Both in 1830 and 1848 the ruling monarchy seemed impregnable. But 'in one night, it lost all its power, and was left without a roof and shelter, supine near the feet of those whom only yesterday it could shoot or hang publicly'.[25] This particular phase of French history, in short, demonstrated the positive possibilities of conspiratorial politics.

*   *   *

---

[22] Kropotkin, *Conquest of Bread*, pp. 7–8, 28, 52.
[23] P. N. Tkachev, 'Retsenziia na knigu A. Rokhau', in Tkachev, *Izbrannye sochineniia*, vol. V, p. 191.
[24] Ibid., p. 192.   [25] Ibid., p. 193.

All these revolutionaries left behind ideas, perceptions, theories, and recommendations on which the Bolsheviks would draw, adopting and adapting some, but not
others, in accordance with their own requirements at any particular time. But the
influence of Marx and Engels was more profound; the Bolsheviks were Marxists,
and perforce had to take seriously what Marx, and to a lesser extent Engels, had to
say about the 1848 Revolution in France. It is true that Marx and Engels spent
little time in Paris in the spring of 1848. After arriving in the French capital in
March, after which they established a branch of the Communist League, the
manifesto of which they had written earlier in Brussels, they left for Cologne in
April. To Marx and Engels the uprising in the German city seemed to them a
bourgeois revolution, like that in France a half-century earlier.[26] Their decision is
understandable. They were of course both German, and what they thought they
would witness would surely abide by the strictures of their ideology, and in doing
so confirm its validity. Prior to 1848 they were exceedingly sceptical that that
would happen soon. The most laudatory comment Marx had mustered in that
regard was in 1843, when he allowed that Germany 'had barely reached [its]
1789'.[27] But once there, it took some time for Marx, at least, to realize that all the
German revolutions would likely fail. Not until July would he denigrate them, in
their totality, as a mere 'parody' of the original French Revolution.[28]

One might think that Marx's and Engels' absence from Paris during the months
following their arrival in Cologne robbed their impressions of the events that were
occurring simultaneously in the French capital of a certain immediacy and an
intensity of emotion; the most notable of these were the June Days, the suppression by the National Guard one month earlier of demonstrations intended to force
the replacement of the existing assembly by one more sympathetic to the lower
classes, and the events that followed in the late summer and autumn culminating
in Louis Napoleon's victory in the presidential election in December. But perhaps
surprisingly, that was not the case. In fact, the emotions stirred up by the events in
France in 1848 far exceeded in their intensity those engendered by the other three
French revolutions the two men either observed or analysed retrospectively. One
finds in Marx's writings on 1848 in particular a degree of personal identification
and involvement, albeit more vicarious than real, that only increased as the initial
jubilation occasioned by the fall of the monarchy in February yielded to anger
after the June Days.

[26] Sperber, *Karl Marx*, pp. 214–7. Neither the Communist League nor the manifesto Marx and
Engels wrote for it had any discernible influence on the course of events in France (or anywhere else in
Europe, for that matter) in 1848. Billington, *Fire in the Minds of Men*, p. 279; Rapport, *1848*, pp. 212–3.
[27] Karl Marx, *Critique of Hegel's Philosophy of Right* (New York, 1970), p. 128.
[28] Gerhard Kluchert, 'The Paradigm and the Parody: Karl Marx and the French Revolution in the
Class Struggles from 1848 to 1851', *History of European Ideas*, no. 14 (January 1992): pp. 85–99. In
1909 Lenin used the identical word in expressing his agreement with Marx's mordant dismissal of these
German revolutions. V. I. Lenin, 'Tsel' bor'by proletariata v nashei revoliutsii', in Lenin, *PSS*, vol. XVII,
p. 388.

But before Marx's somewhat belated recognition that a proletarian revolution in France was hopelessly premature could sink in and become the basis for more rational calculations in the future, he and Engels beseeched the proletariat to take advantage of what they both considered to be 'the death throes' of capitalism, and carry out the task that history and the dialectic had conferred on it. Even the June Days were not irreversible. In November 1848, in one of the many articles Marx wrote for the *Neue Rheinische Zeitung*, the newspaper he had established the previous spring and continued to edit until it was shut down on orders of the Cologne police in May 1849, he advocated the establishment in France of a revolutionary dictatorship based politically on the proletariat; should the proletariat take power, it would not shrink from employing terror as 'the only way in which the murderous death agonies of the old society and the bloody birth throes of the new society [could] be shortened, simplified, and concentrated'.[29]

By 1850, Marx had finally achieved the detachment necessary to explain why the revolution in France two years earlier had failed, and why any effort to repeat it would only yield the same desultory result.[30] In articles in the *Neue Rheinische Zeitung*, he ascribed the defeat the proletariat suffered in Paris to several factors, all of them, for different reasons, beyond the capability of the proletariat to have vitiated sufficiently for the outcome of the revolution to have been different.[31] For one thing, universal male suffrage in elections to the National Assembly in April worsened class antagonisms, making impossible the revival of any alliance between the bourgeoisie and the proletariat based on a perceived convergence of interests (which, in fact, did not exist); this was confirmed in June when the government closed the National Workshops, which had provided employment for many workers and others. For another, while the revolutions in 1789 and 1848 included the replacement of a monarchy by a republic, what followed it differed significantly in the two revolutions. In contrast to the French Revolution, where the *fraternité* engendered by foreign invasion transcended class distinctions, enabling the Jacobins to form a coalition attentive to the needs of the lower classes, in 1848 no such invasion occurred. In fact, the June Days essentially precluded France from assisting revolutionaries in other parts of Europe, as it did in the 1790s, which Marx now considered absolutely essential to the survival of any future revolution in France. From this he drew the larger conclusion that, for any subsequent revolution to succeed in France, it also had to succeed in other

---

[29] Quoted in Michael Evans, *Karl Marx* (London, 2004), p. 137.

[30] It took longer for Engels to do the same. In 1851 he was still calling Louis Blanc 'a pious little swindler', and in 1852 still writing that 'the defeats in Paris in June 1848, and of Vienna in October', certainly did far more to 'revolutionize the mind of the people of those two cities than the victories of February and March'. 'Letter, Engels to Ernst Dronke (9 July 1851)', in Marx and Engels: *Collected Works*, vol. XXXVIII, p. 381; Engels, *Revolution and Counter-Revolution in Germany in 1848*, p. 96.

[31] All of the citations in the analysis of these articles are to *Class Struggles in France*, a compendium of Marx's articles in the *Neue Rheinische Zeitung* on the 1848 Revolution that was published in 1895 with an introduction by Engels.

countries, especially those that bordered it. In 1848, by contrast, the proletariat and the bourgeoisie were on their own and thus the latter had no compunctions about turning on the former four months after the revolution began and effect-ively destroying it as a political force.[32] In Marx's own words, 'the Paris proletariat was forced into the June insurrection by the bourgeoisie. In this lay its doom.'[33]

But even absent the licence the bourgeoisie rightly concluded it possessed to destroy the proletariat as a political force in France, Marx believed it would have found the wherewithal to crush the proletariat anyway. This was because in June it could call upon 24,000 National Guardsmen—most of them criminals and others beneath the proletariat in the existing class structure of French society, often referred to as 'lumpenproletarians'—to do its dirty work.[34] The proletariat, in other words, faced two enemies, not one, in the summer of 1848. The only class with which the proletariat could have forged an alliance, and thereby avoided the predicament in which it found itself, was the peasantry. But Marx, after raising the possibility of such an alliance, quickly dismissed it, as his longstanding prejudice against the peasantry, whose way of life he famously termed a form of idiocy, undoubtedly re-emerged. The peasantry, he stated flatly, was 'the class that represents barbarism within civilization'.[35]

However grudgingly, Marx finally admitted in 1850 that he and Engels and scientific socialists everywhere should settle in 'for the long haul'. In his address to the Communist League in March of that year, he focused almost entirely on Germany, where the treachery with which the proletariat had been betrayed two years earlier he ascribed not to the bourgeoisie as a whole, as he had in his analysis in 1848, but to what he termed 'a democratic petit-bourgeoisie'.[36] In fact, in its perfidy this German petit-bourgeoisie far exceeded the French bourgeoisie.[37] But Marx's prescription remained the same: a proletarian revolution in the immediate future could not succeed, and therefore the best thing for the proletariat to do, indeed the only thing it could do, was to prepare quietly, beyond the auditory capabilities of its enemies and under the tutelage of mature professional revolu-tionaries like Marx himself, for the day in the distant future when circumstances would finally be more propitious. In sum, there were no shortcuts to socialism.

Engels, however, disagreed. In the last years of his life, Marx's longtime collaborator rejected his formulation of the problem. Although not so sanguine

[32] Marx, *Class Struggles in France*, pp. 44–6, 54.   [33] Ibid., pp. 57–8   [34] Ibid., p. 50.
[35] Ibid., p. 71.
[36] Marx, 'Address of the Central Authority to the League', in Marx and Engels, *Collected Works*, vol. X, p. 279.
[37] In the 1850s and through most of the 1860s, Marx, unlike Herzen, still considered Paris the most likely venue in Europe for a successful revolution. In addition he continued to believe that the precedent of the French Revolution still applied—that a revolution in France would trigger revolutions elsewhere in Europe. Only in the late 1860s did Marx come to consider Ireland and the German states, and in the late 1870s Russia, as likely sites for the first significant and serious revolutions in Europe since 1848. That it came about in Paris in 1871 was thus, for Marx, a pleasant surprise. Sperber, *Karl Marx*, pp. 369, 375.

or naïve to consider proletarian revolutions imminent, he nonetheless recalled the exploits of the Russian terrorists and reiterated what he had first articulated in the late 1870s, namely that the peasant commune in Russia could serve as the basis for socialism; whether it might do so elsewhere was not clear. However, in the introduction he wrote in 1895 to *The Class Struggles in France*, Engels allowed that there was also reason for cautious optimism concerning France and Germany. Of course there were countervailing tendencies in the two countries that he had to acknowledge could not be ignored. Louis Napoleon's Second Empire, for one, provided proof of 'the unripeness of the proletarian aspirations of that time'.[38] But Marx's longtime collaborator also suggested that the consequences of historical events had to be considered over *la longue durée*; in the case of France that meant its longstanding revolutionary tradition could not be ignored. He and Marx, he wrote, were always cognizant of the effect the mere existence of this revolutionary tradition in French history had already had on French politics, and for that reason 'our conceptions of the nature and the path of the "social" revolution proclaimed in Paris in February 1848, of the revolution of the proletariat, were strongly coloured by memories of the models of 1789 and 1830'.[39]

Implicit in Engels' introduction was that any pessimism one might rightly consider a normal reaction to the crushing of revolutions in Germany and in France in 1848 should now give way to optimism; several decades had passed, and since then conditions in the two countries had changed considerably. In keeping with his high opinion of the socialist and revolutionary credentials of the Russian peasantry, Engels took pains to include the absence of peasant support among the reasons for the proletariat's defeat, at least in France, in 1848. But unlike Marx, for whom the peasantry was mostly useless politically and largely extraneous to the scenario he conjured in which the proletariat would eventually take power, Engels, in 1895, made clear he believed peasants could play a role in these proletarian revolutions.

By writing the introduction Engels provided two ways of untying the Gordian knot in which Marxist orthodoxy had constricted Russian Marxists with its inescapable imperative (if one ignores Marx's private statement to Vera Zasulich in 1881 to the contrary) that proletarian revolutions can only be successful in countries where the proletariat is capable of taking power by itself. One of these options was to seek peasant support. The other was for the proletariat (led presumably by Russian Marxists) to make a bourgeois revolution, from which the bourgeoisie would be excluded so that a proletarian revolution would follow it; this would inspire the proletariat in more advanced countries in Europe, such as Germany, France, or Great Britain, to take power itself. Once its power was secure, it could then assist any regime the Russian proletariat had established until the

---

[38] Engels, 'Introduction' to Marx, *Class Struggles in France*, p. 17.   [39] Ibid., pp. 12–13.

THE REVOLUTION THAT FAILED   367

latter was strong enough to ensure its own regime's survival. As it happened, Lenin availed himself of both of these options, with the result that a regime claiming itself committed to socialism and communism emerged in Russia in 1917, and remained in power for nearly three-quarters of a century.

But the majority of Russian Marxists were not as daring or as flexible ideologically as Lenin proved to be. For Plekhanov and the Mensheviks, Marxism was sacred doctrine, to be followed faithfully, rather than a smorgasbord of principles, insights, and historical analysis from which one could pick and choose in deciding what to do when tactical imperatives conflicted with what the ideology seemed to suggest, or even clearly required. This was certainly the case for Plekhanov's pronouncements on the 1848 Revolution in France. In the article he wrote on the centenary of the French Revolution, he argued, with respect to 1848, that that was when France experienced for a second time the sequence of events that had first occurred in 1830 and 1831, when an inconsequential revolution in 1830 was followed a year later by a rebellion (in Lyon) that while a failure, was predictive of a future proletarian uprising in the entire country—an uprising Plekhanov believed would end the ersatz democracy through which the bourgeoisie had exploited the proletariat. When Plekhanov was writing, this uprising, of course, had not arrived, but he was certain it eventually would, because the ideology predicting it was irrefutable.[40]

As for the 1848 Revolution itself, Plekhanov argued that it had the same effect that the Revolution of 1830 had on the insurrection in Lyon in 1831. The only difference was that in 1848 the sequence of a consequential event (the June Days) following a relatively insignificant one (Louis Philippe's abdication in February that left class relations unchanged) occurred within the span of one year, rather than two. But in every other way, the pattern was the same. The overthrow of the Orléanists in February 1848 was no more consequential than their ascension to power in 1830. These were both political changes that did little or nothing to change the material circumstances in which the French people lived and worked. The June Days, however, were the equivalent of the Lyon rebellion seventeen years earlier. While they obviously failed to catapult the proletariat to power, they left behind a legacy of heroism and martyrdom from which future generations of workers would find the inspiration to redouble their efforts to establish socialism in the unlikely event their spirits sagged.[41]

What Plekhanov left unsaid in the article—probably because it contradicted what Marx had written in 1848, when the outcome of the revolution was still uncertain—was that the workers really had no business rising up in the June Days

---

[40] Plekhanov, *Stoletie velikoi revoliutsii*, pp. 56, 63–4.

[41] In the article, Plekhanov claimed that the same sequence applied in the French Revolution, in the course of which less consequential events in 1789 were followed by more consequential ones in 1793. Ibid., pp. 56–7.

against the bourgeoisie, the political dominance of which, backed up by the army and the National Guard, was so overwhelming that trying to end it was pointless. For Plekhanov, it was practically a generic rule of revolutions that whenever the proletariat was its principal instrument and intended beneficiary, a failed revolution was worse than no revolution at all. This maxim informed Plekhanov's analysis of the 1848 Revolution in an article in 1915, in which he cited approvingly the comparison Marx had drawn in *The Eighteenth Brumaire* between the French Revolution and the Revolution of 1848: whereas in 1789 and thereafter 'the rule of the Constitutionalists was followed by the rule of the Girondins, and the rule of the Girondins by the rule of the Jacobins', in 1848 the reverse was the case: 'the proletarian party appeared as an appendage of the petty-bourgeois democratic party. It was betrayed and dropped by the latter on April 16 [when large demonstrations of lower-class Parisians occurred], on 15 May [when an attempted insurrection failed in Paris], and in the June Days'.[42] In 1848, in other words, the revolution, when compared to that which began in 1789, ran backwards. The former, from February to June, regressed while the latter, from 1789 to 1793, progressed. This, of course, was consistent with the dictum Plekhanov drew from Marx concerning the temporal relationship between a bourgeois and a proletarian revolution: the former must always precede the latter, and a decent interval must pass—Plekhanov did not provide a rough estimate of its duration—for the second revolution to succeed. The failure of the proletariat in 1848 to take power was not the result of any moral, intellectual, or political failing or deficiency. Rather it was the inevitable consequence of its violating what to Plekhanov was an iron law of history, namely that its stages can never be compressed, much less skipped entirely. While sufficiently flexible to conjure a variant of Oriental Despotism to clarify aspects of Russia's historical evolution that were inexplicable within the context of Western feudalism, Plekhanov remained committed to Marxist ideology to the point of tactical rigidity, which was why he was a better theorist than a practical politician.[43] Lenin, by contrast, was able to harness his tactical flexibility in the pursuit of ideological objectives.[44] In short, Plekhanov thought the history of France was destined to repeat itself for quite some time. In 1848 the French proletariat tried to seize power, first in May and then in June, and in both instances the bourgeoisie defeated it. Should the Russian proletariat attempt the

[42]   Marx, *Eighteenth Brumaire*, p. 42. Lenin laid out Plekhanov's argument in detail before attacking it in V. I. Lenin, 'O dvukh liniakh revoliutsii', in Lenin, *PSS*, vol. XXVII, pp. 76–7.

[43]   Samuel H. Baron, *Plekhanov in Russian History and Soviet Historiography* (Pittsburgh PA, 1995), pp. 95–115. Marx and Engels had raised the possibility of a peculiarly Asian equivalent of feudalism in discussions they had about India in the 1850s. Sperber, *Karl Marx*, p. 401.

[44]   In 1906 Rosa Luxemburg, in her own analysis of 1848, combined Plekhanov's decidedly low opinion of the political consciousness and tactical acumen on the proletariat in France with her belief, which resembled Lenin's after 1905, that the proletariat in Russia was capable of mounting another revolution fairly soon, and that, despite its imminence, it would succeed. Luxemburg, 'Blankizm i Socjałdemokracia', *passim*.

same thing, the same result would ensue—and the reason it would was that history had not progressed sufficiently (at least not in Russia in the late nineteenth or early twentieth century, where an Industrial Revolution began far later than it did in Western Europe) for the result to be otherwise.

Other Mensheviks agreed with him. In June 1917 Martov professed his alarm that the Provisional Government might summon 'its praetorian guard from the front [and] play the role of a Cavaignac'.[45] This, he conceded, would have the beneficial practical effect of eliminating the Bolsheviks as a political force in Russia. But it would also destroy the Soviets, and in particular the Petrograd Soviet—to which Martov, not coincidentally, was addressing when he evoked the precedent of Cavaignac's betrayal, of which he knew everyone in his audience would be cognizant. After Martov finished, Irakli Tsereteli assured him that neither he nor the Mensheviks nor the Russian proletariat had anything to worry about. Martov's analogy, he explained, was mistaken:

> Comparing our revolutionary army with the soldiers of Cavaignac, you forget that the nineteenth-century revolutionary stereotype is quite inapplicable to our revolution. Then the bourgeoisie, relying on a conservative peasantry and an army composed of such peasants, disposed of the proletariat and paved the way for the victorious counter-revolution. But the army of revolutionary Russia is part of the revolutionary peasantry, and is at one with the working class in the soviet... in consolidating liberty.[46]

Tsereteli may well have been correct in dismissing the chance of a Russian Cavaignac marching on Petrograd, disbanding the Petrograd Soviet and the Provisional Government, and instituting a military dictatorship. That Kornilov, who was the closest (albeit still distant) equivalent of both Cavaignac and Napoleon Bonaparte in Russia in 1917, was unable to do this—if that in fact was his actual intention—suggests that he was. But the Georgian Menshevik, who had no illusions about Lenin's benevolence (or about Stalin's), fell prey to a different delusion when considering the Mensheviks' options should a genuine Russian Cavaignac appear. In that instance, he assured the Bolsheviks, 'we shall fight in the same ranks with you'.[47] Such a scenario, one can suggest with some confidence, would have been an excellent example of the cure being worse than

---

[45] Quoted in Victor Chernov, *The Great Russian Revolution* (New Haven, 1936), p. 29.

[46] Quoted in ibid., pp. 29–30. German socialists in the late nineteenth century, like their Russian counterparts, honoured the French who fell in 1848 in the June Days, and also the Communards who were massacred in Paris in 1871. Beatrix Bouvier, 'On the Tradition of 1848 in Socialism', in *Europe in 1848: Revolution and Reform*, edited by Dieter Dowe et al. (New York, 2001), pp. 891–915. One reason they did may have been that because the German 1848 had been such a disaster, they could find solace only in revolutions in other countries. And since their ostensible allegiance was to an international phenomenon instead of a strictly German one, their admiration of some things French did not carry with it any sense of betrayal of their own country and culture.

[47] Tsereteli quoted in V. I. Lenin, 'Iz kakogo klassovogo istochnika prikhodiat i "pridut" Kaven'iaki', in Lenin, *PSS*, vol. XXXII, p. 345.

the disease. The misperception of non-Bolshevik socialists in Russia, even one as level-headed as Tsereteli, of *ne pas l'ennemis de la gauche*, was a common one and, as it turned out, a dangerous one.

* * *

By its very failure, the 1848 Revolution in France showed Lenin why a proletarian revolution in Russia, under very different conditions, might succeed. This was particularly apparent in 1905, when the Russian masses finally eschewed their longstanding inertia and took action which, under more sagacious leadership, might have destroyed the monarchy once and for all, and then done the same to any bourgeois-democratic regime that followed it. This, at any rate, was what Lenin believed through the entirety of the revolution. Moreover, at no other time prior to 1917 did Lenin improvise ideologically to the extent that he did in 1905, in considering how a proletarian revolution in Russia might soon ensue. The adage that guided him in that year was truly Napoleon's: *On s'engage et puis on voit*. But the scenarios he entertained, and the tactical options he considered, were grounded in the lessons he drew from the grim realities of the 1848 Revolution in France.

In March and April 1905, as the revolution gained momentum, in large part the result of increasingly prevalent anarchy in the countryside, Lenin composed an article, 'A Revolution of the 1789 or the 1848 Type', that was in many ways a balance sheet comparing Russia in 1905 to France when each of its four modern revolutions was occurring.[48] The 1789 and 1848 examples were the most relevant, Lenin averred, because the differences between what their most radical elements intended determined their respective outcomes: 1789 was a moderate revolution that succeeded, while 1848 was a radical revolution that failed. It was obvious which one Lenin, for psychological reasons as much as for ideological ones, preferred. The heroism and martyrdom in 1848 appealed to him more than the half-hearted radicalism of the Jacobins, however admirable they were in charac-terological terms. He also included a rhetorical swipe at Martynov for preferring the opposite.[49] The question for Russia while its revolution was still raging was whether it should be limited to the curtailment of tsarist authority and the establishment of a constitution institutionalizing the monarchy's continuation (which would resemble 1789), or go beyond that and replace the monarchy with a republic (which would resemble 1848 prior to the June Days), which might be followed quickly by a proletarian revolution. Lenin's article argued for the latter. But he also took pains to stress that replicating 1848 with a happier ending would not be easy in Russia. Of course there were good reasons why any revolution in Russia in 1905 would fail—and why a failed revolution would be worse than no revolution. These included improved means of communication, compared to

[48] Lenin, 'Revoliutsiia tipa 1789 ili tipa 1848', ibid., vol. IX, pp. 380–2.   [49] Ibid., vol. IX, p. 382.

those existing earlier in France, which, during a revolution, according to Lenin, would benefit the government more than it would the revolutionaries. Also, there were no concurrent revolutions in Europe or anywhere else to inspire the revolutionaries in Russia. Finally, the antagonism between the bourgeoisie and the proletariat in Russia in 1905 was greater than it was in France in 1848; for that reason the bourgeoisie would support the proletariat in Russia, if it did so at all, for an even shorter time than it did in France in 1848.

But Lenin also specified the reasons why the 1905 Revolution might nonetheless succeed. The brevity of bourgeois support, or even its complete absence, could be advantageous in the event it eliminated quickly any illusions the Russian proletariat entertained about the bourgeoisie's benevolence. What is more, 'the revolutionary party' in Russia—by which Lenin meant either the Bolsheviks or Russian socialists generally—was more advanced ideologically than any of the revolutionaries in France in 1789, 1848, or 1871. Finally, the grievances of the lower classes were greater and more varied in Russia than in France; in the latter there was nothing analogous to the restive nationalities and ethnic minorities in the former; and the concurrent war with Japan was radicalizing the Russian people at least as much as the wars France fought in the 1790s radicalized its people, and made them more, not less, supportive of the French Revolution.[50] In 1848, by contrast, there were no foreign enemies that had to be repelled militarily, and therefore no *union sacrée* to unify the country and galvanize enthusiasm for the revolution.[51]

A few weeks later, in a report to the Third Congress of the RSDLP, Lenin returned to the 1848 Revolution, this time to emphasize the treachery not just of the bourgeoisie in France, but also, more bitingly and at much greater length, of the petit-bourgeoisie in Germany, about which Marx had written a great deal in the *Neue Rheinische Zeitung*.[52] Like Marx, Lenin was even more disappointed and chagrined by the failure of the German 1848 than by the failure of the French—though in Marx's case, the fact that he was German made it almost a personal affront. In an article in September1905, Lenin once again invoked both the German and the French 1848, this time juxtaposing their respective results with those of the French Revolution.[53] On a spectrum with complete success at one end and abject failure at the other, Lenin situated the French Revolution and the German 1848 as if they were polar opposites, with the French 1848 roughly equidistant between them, leaving his readers to infer that it might had achieved more than

[50] Ibid., vol. IX, pp. 380–2.
[51] This last point Lenin was content to make indirectly and obliquely, probably because his Marxist ideology looked askance at any juxtaposition of nationalism and socialism, or at least any that retarded the realization of the latter.
[52] Lenin, 'Doklad ob uchastii sotsial-demokratii vo vremennom revoliutsionnom pravitel'stve', ibid., vol. X, especially pp. 132–3.
[53] V. I. Lenin, 'Chego khotiat i chego boiatsia nashi liberal'nye burzhua?', ibid., vol. XI, pp. 225–7.

merely ending the Orléanist Monarchy had circumstances been different or the workers' leaders more resourceful, more imaginative, and more tactically shrewd.

The articles Lenin wrote in 1905 that addressed the 1848 Revolution in France bear a striking resemblance to what Marx had written a half-century earlier when the revolutions in France and Germany were still in progress and their outcomes uncertain. Both men succumbed to a euphoria that dulled their judgement— although Marx soon calmed down and came to his senses, recognizing that the German bourgeoisie for quite some time would be even less able to make a bourgeois revolution than the French proletariat would be to make a proletarian one. Lenin, however, was incorrigible, for several years after the 1905 Revolution anticipating its repetition and possibly even its radicalization. In fact, one senses that Lenin prized the Revolution of 1848 in France for its effect on Marx— primarily to radicalize him, to sharpen his political instincts, and to open his eyes to the need for a rapid seizure of power much like what Lenin would engineer in Russia in 1917. For that reason one might speculate that, on an emotional level, the Marx who soon concluded reluctantly that industrial capitalism in Europe was not in its death throes but rather surviving its birth pangs disappointed Lenin profoundly—and that Marx's later dalliance with Russian terrorism and *Narodnaia Volia* heartened Lenin and disappointed him simultaneously: Marx once again seemed open to the notion of an imminent revolution, albeit in Russia rather than in France, but wrongly placed his hopes on the Russian peasantry rather than on the Russian proletariat, perhaps because the latter was still too small for any alliance of the two classes to be effective.

One would think that the failure of the Moscow uprising in December 1905 would cause Lenin's optimism to dissipate. The uprising was not only the last significant event in the revolution, but it was also the only aspect of the revolution in which the Bolsheviks, in any numbers, participated. But that did not happen. If anything, the fact that socialists in other countries were just as confident that another bourgeois revolution in Russia was imminent, and that shortly after it began it would morph seamlessly into a proletarian one, was cause for genuine optimism; not even the issuance of the Fundamental Laws in Russia prescribing the procedures in accordance with which the new parliament (or Duma) would function, dampened Lenin's spirits—and the fact that Kautsky—whom the future Soviet leader would continue to revere until August 1914—shared his confidence was confirmation that Lenin's optimism was warranted. In fact, in March 1906, in an article on 'The Russian Revolution and the Tasks of the Proletariat', Lenin mostly let the German socialist speak on his behalf—which was something Lenin did only rarely in his speeches and writings—in explaining why the Moscow uprising, unlike the June Days in 1848, should not be considered an irreversible defeat.[54] Among the

---

[54] V. I. Lenin, 'Russkaia revoliutsiia i zadachii proletariata', ibid., vol. XII, pp. 213–16.

differences, as Kautsky explained them, were that the defeat in Moscow occurred nowhere else in Russia, while the June Days (in his opinion and Lenin's) was a nationwide disaster; that the peasants in Russia supported the 1905 Revolution as a whole, while the peasantry in France, much of which was more affluent than the peasantry in Russia, opposed the 1848 Revolution; that the 1905 Revolution was followed, at least initially, by famine and other problems that predated the revolution and indeed were what had originally ignited it, while the 1848 Revolution was followed by prosperity, which made its repetition impossible; and finally, that the barricades the Bolsheviks erected in Moscow, while obviously not effective enough to prevent tsarist troops from breaching them, were nonetheless superior to those the Parisian proletariat had constructed in 1848.

Also in March 1906, Lenin offered yet another argument—this time in his own voice—for why the Bolsheviks should actually be happy despite the recent defeat they had suffered in Moscow.[55] The mental gymnastics he had to perform to reach his conclusion were considerable. Lenin freely acknowledged that the calm Europe enjoyed after the suppression of its revolutions in 1848 was real. But that only proved that changes were occurring *sub rosa*—and because the same was true in Russia, a revolution there was actually imminent. The very strength the tsarist monarchy mustered that enabled it to survive a revolution that lasted for nearly an entire year was actually proof of its weakness—and to bolster the shaky empirical foundation on which his argument was based, Lenin noted that the Kadets, on whose political support the peaceful transformation of Russia into a constitutional monarchy depended, were destined to collapse as ignominiously as French socialists did, much to Lenin's retrospective consternation, in 1848 and 1849. Applied to Russia, Lenin's argument that sometimes the best things that happen happen silently seemed to guarantee the Bolsheviks' success. If the Kadets collapsed, the Bolsheviks would replace them, thereby making another bourgeois revolution more likely—only this time the revolution would not only succeed in deposing the monarchy; it would thereafter be quickly transmogrified into a proletarian revolution. But if, contrarily, the Kadets by some chance succeeded in taking power, they would soon lose it, thereby creating a political vacuum the proletariat and the peasantry would fill. In other words, no matter what the Kadets did, the Bolsheviks would benefit.[56]

This was not the only argument Lenin mustered in the aftermath of the 1905 Revolution that was based on his understanding of what had happened in France in 1848. In 1906, in a letter to St Petersburg workers, he lambasted Alexander Vinogradov, a Menshevik, who, in keeping with his relative moderation, had recently argued that any future revolution in Russia should 'follow the lines of 1848–49 and not 1789–93'. In other words, Vinogradov preferred that the future

[55] V. I. Lenin, 'Pobeda Kadetov i zadachy rabochei partii', ibid., vol. XII, pp. 329–32, 352.
[56] Ibid., vol. XII, *passim.*

revolution fail.[57] To Lenin, Vinogradov's notion was the most odious form of defeatism. Lenin wanted conditions to improve in Russia because he believed that that would make a bourgeois revolution, and therefore any proletarian revolution that might follow it, more likely rather than less so. But whatever the Kadets did or did not do, their 'treachery' was a permanent component of their politics and collective persona, and Lenin's conviction was strengthened by his believing their treachery having been prefigured in France in 1848, when the 'liberal bourgeoisie' did so much to ensure that the closest approximation to a proletarian revolution that was possible at that particular moment in history—namely the agitation resulting in the June Days—would fail.[58]

Lenin stressed this point even more emphatically in a report to the Fifth Congress of the RSDLP in 1907. In the context of attacking Tsereteli for what Lenin considered the Georgian Menshevik's 'political vacillation', which seemed to Lenin emblematic of the weakness and political cowardice of the Mensheviks generally, he rejected Tsereteli's invocation of the 1848 Revolution to support the view not only that 'the conditions for socialism were not yet ripe', but also that 'it is impossible to fight for freedom without some sort of alliance with bourgeois democracy'.[59] To Lenin this was idiocy of the highest order, and he invoked what he considered the real lesson of the 1848 Revolution to refute it:

> Both the revolution of 1848 and subsequent historical experience taught international Social Democracy the very opposite [of Tsereteli's contention] namely, that bourgeois democracy stands more and more against the proletariat, that the struggle for freedom is waged consistently only when the proletariat leads it. The year 1848 teaches us not to seek alliances with bourgeois democrats. Rather it teaches us that we need to free the least developed sections of the masses from the influence of bourgeois democracy, which is incapable of fighting for democracy.[60]

Lenin's head was often at war with his heart when evaluating the bourgeoisie in general, and the French bourgeoisie in 1848 in particular. He could accept rationally that its perfidy in the long run only worsened its chances for survival—and for that reason should be welcomed. But on an emotional level he could not help but deride the class both generically and whenever he viewed its actions in a particular time or place in the most derogatory and defamatory terms. Articles he wrote in December 1911, March 1913, and June 1914 revealed the same visceral hatred of the French bourgeoisie of the mid-nineteenth century

[57] Lenin, 'Doklad ob obedinitel'nom s"ezde RSDRP (Pis'mo k Peterburgskim rabochim)', *PSS*, vol. XIII, pp. 20–1.

[58] Ibid., p. 21.

[59] V. I. Lenin, 'Rech' o doklade o deiatel'nosti dumskoi frak`tsii', in Lenin, *PSS*, vol. XV, p. 322.

[60] Ibid., vol. XV, p. 322.

that he expressed throughout his political life for the French 'imperialists' and 'capitalists' of his own generation.[61]

Lenin and the other Bolsheviks called the revolution that began in 1789 the Great French Revolution because, irrespective of its provenance in the discontent of classes beneath the bourgeoisie such as the *sans-culottes* and impoverished peasants, it was, nevertheless, in its essentials, a bourgeois revolution, the first one in history in which the bourgeoisie was its principal beneficiary. No less critical to its outsized reputation—neither Marx nor the Bolsheviks applied to any other revolution (except of course, in Lenin's case, the October Revolution), the adjectival designation of greatness they applied to the French Revolution—was that it succeeded. As a result, Lenin expected more of the French bourgeoisie in the nineteenth century than he did, say, of the German bourgeoisie, which had shown itself in 1848 to be especially reprehensible in its abject refusal to fight feudal principalities effectively and energetically. But conditions in the German states were still fairly primitive compared to those in France in 1848, so the Germans, whatever their personal deficiencies, could cite these conditions to explain away their failure. The French bourgeoisie, however, could not do so. In fact, Lenin's outrage was partly a function of his belief that the French bourgeoisie in 1830, 1848, and 1871 was even more hostile to the lower classes than it had been in the French Revolution. By 1911 he cited this hostility in an article explicating the relationship in Russia that he said existed between genuine socialists like himself and other Bolsheviks on the one hand, and retrograde and perfidious socialists and liberals on the other.[62] What makes the article noteworthy is that, by referring in the article to 'the four revolutions in France between 1789 and 1871', and writing about them in a way that suggested they had a collective meaning above and beyond the legacy each one left behind, Lenin showed that, in his mind, these revolutions had come to comprise a genuine revolutionary tradition.[63] By 1911, in other words, Lenin was invoking a generic category of revolutions both to corroborate his diagnosis of the present-day political realities in his own country and to provide guidance on how best to use the insights it provided to the advantage of the Bolsheviks and of the Russian proletariat.

The outbreak of the First World War, among its other effects on Lenin, caused him to enlarge this revolutionary tradition to encompass European history as a whole. In the winter of 1915 he responded to the argument of Alexander Potresov, one of the first Russian Marxists in Russia but now a committed Menshevik and opponent of the Bolsheviks, that the war marked the point in Europe's evolution in which 'national isolation' was superseded by 'internationalism' in the relations

[61] V. I. Lenin, 'O lozungakh i o postanovke dumskoi i vnedumskoi s.-d. raboty', ibid., vol. XXI, p. 14; V. I. Lenin, 'Istoricheskie sud'by ucheniia Karla Marksa', ibid., vol. XXIII, p. 2; V. I. Lenin, 'Priemy bor'by burzhuaznoi intelligentsii protiv rabochikh', ibid., vol. XXV, p. 321.
[62] V. I. Lenin, 'Reformizm v russkoi sotsial-demokratii', ibid., vol. XX, p. 310.
[63] Ibid., vol. XX, p. 310.

between the countries within the two wartime alliances. This notion, Lenin insisted, was incorrect. True, the recent outbreak of war signified something larger than the commencement of hostilities. But what it ushered in was not a benign internationalism but rather an age of rapacious and exploitative imperialism, which Lenin would ascribe during the war to the need for the bourgeoisie to find markets in other parts of the world for the goods the proletariat in Europe had become too impoverished to purchase.[64]

In placing this new age of imperialism in historical context, it is not surprising that Lenin should have divided European history into discrete phases since the time when the bourgeoisie had emerged as a political force. That its power increased from phase to phase suggested it might also eventually diminish. What is noteworthy about Lenin's periodization is that the dates he provided corresponded directly to revolutions in France. The first of these phases, he wrote, was from the Great French Revolution to 1871, during which the bourgeoisie, after ending feudalism, was politically and economically ascendant. Lenin noted that his choice of 1871 to mark the end of this bourgeois ascendancy was dictated by the Franco-Prussian War, which catalysed German unification, without which the First World War would not have happened—although as a consequence of imperialism, something like it would have happened anyway.[65]

The second epoch in European history Lenin delineated was from 1871 to 1914, which he described in his polemic against Potresov as an age when the bourgeoisie declined. According to Lenin, this caused it to become more oppressive of the proletariat rather than less so. But by immiserating the proletariat to satisfy its insatiable thirst for profit, the bourgeoisie impoverished itself—or rather would have done so but for the opportunities that beckoned in lands outside Europe, where the existing polities could not resist European armies sent by governments beholden to the bourgeoisie to depose them or to make them dutiful puppets. In light of Lenin's description of this second epoch in Europe's modern history, the brutality with which the bourgeoisie suppressed the Paris Commune made it an apt symbol for this second epoch's commencement.[66]

The role the Revolution in 1848 played in this periodization Lenin explained in 1916 in an article on the self-determination of minorities such as the Poles. Instead of considering 1848 symbolic of a subdivision within the first phase of capitalism he claimed was dominant in Europe from 1789 to 1871, Lenin abruptly changed the years bracketing this phase in the history of capitalism, claiming now

---

[64] V. I. Lenin, 'Pod chuzhim flagom', ibid., vol. XVI, p. 143; V. I. Lenin, *Imperialism: The Highest Stage of Capitalism* (London, 2010).
[65] Lenin, 'Pod chuzhim flagom', in Lenin, *PSS*, vol. XVI, pp. 142–3. In a later article co-authored with Zinoviev, Lenin stated explicitly that it was the Paris Commune—not the Franco-Prussian War (which of course helped to trigger the establishment of the Commune)—that signified the end of this period, which, the article made clear, still began with the French Revolution in 1789. V. I. Lenin and G. Zinoviev, 'Sotsializm i voina', ibid., vol. XXVI, pp. 311–12.
[66] Lenin, 'Pod chuzhim flagom', ibid., vol. XVI, p. 143.

that it began in 1848. If Lenin had explained the substitution because he now realized that it was in 1848 when many of the stateless nationalities in Eastern Europe had first expressed their opposition to the Russian, Austro-Hungarian, and Ottoman Empires, one could understand the substitution. But Lenin did not do that. He simply changed dates without supplying a different term for the period from 1789 to 1848, or any iteration of his reason or reasons for doing so.[67] Perhaps he thought his readers would recognize that the change he made only applied to Eastern Europe because they knew that the French Revolution, notwithstanding its transformational effects on Western Europe, changed Eastern Europe only marginally, if at all. Whatever Lenin's reasoning, his invocation of 1848 showed that it now played a significant role in his thinking at a time when the outcome of the war Europe was fighting remained uncertain and, in 1915 and 1916, showed no signs of stopping anytime soon.

In the years immediately preceding 1917, Lenin had a good deal of time on his hands, and could indulge his penchant for disguising the degradation of political enemies as dispassionate historical analysis. In 1915, he took exception to Plekhanov's argument, which the latter had recently claimed was based on Marx's comparison of the revolutions of 1789 and 1848, that the proletariat and the Marxist revolutionaries who currently supported them had no choice but to desist from making an actual revolution until the bourgeoisie, which would resist it, could no longer do so successfully.[68] This particular argument, whenever the Mensheviks or any other opponent of the Bolsheviks articulated it, touched a raw nerve in Lenin, because the passivity it prescribed was so contrary to the 'voluntarist' component of his temperament. In 1915 his reaction was particularly harsh in light of the vehemence with which, just a few months earlier, he had attacked socialists he previously admired, such as Kautsky and Plekhanov, for supporting their own country's decision to go to war in 1914. In fact, in January 1917, Lenin was so embittered by the political paralysis he was experiencing that he lashed out at the bourgeoisie for the death and destruction its warring factions had caused since 1914. Minimizing as mere 'sops' recent concessions the combatants had made to improve material conditions for their own people, he analogized them to concessions 'the executioners of the 1848 and 1905 Revolutions' had agreed to vitiate the murderous effects of their own rapacity and bloodlust.[69] In short, the First World War did nothing to soften the hard edges of Lenin's combative rhetoric when ideological allies turned enemies made an argument with which he honestly and strongly disagreed.

In refuting Plekhanov's argument in 1915, Lenin accurately recapitulated Marx's argument, on which Plekhanov had relied in claiming that for the time

[67] V. I. Lenin, 'Itogi diskussii o samopredelenii', ibid., vol. XXX, p. 21.
[68] V. I. Lenin, 'O dvukh liniakh revoliutsii', ibid., vol. XXVII, pp. 76-7.
[69] V. I. Lenin, 'Povorot v mirovoi politike', ibid., vol. XXX, p. 345.

being proletarian revolutions anywhere in Europe would fail. He duly noted Marx's contention that in the French Revolution moderate governments were succeeded by more radical ones, but that in 1848 this sequence was reversed. Lenin did not contest Marx's assertions; instead he reaffirmed them. But he personalized his disagreement with the conclusion Plekhanov had drawn from them by disparaging it as evidence of the latter's 'vulgar idealism'.[70] That was why, according to Lenin, Plekhanov (and by implication the Mensheviks) could no more be trusted to protect the interests of the proletariat presently or in the future than the French petit-bourgeoisie could have been trusted to do so in 1848. In short, the 1848 Revolution had the effect on Lenin during the First World War not only of prescribing what he and the Bolsheviks should not do if they decided to make a revolution in Russia but it also provided fodder for Lenin's instinctual belligerence that, in the absence of outlets for his political aspirations, became an even more prominent part of his personality.

Once the collapse of the monarchy in Russia made practical politics possible for revolutionaries previously confined to Western Europe, Lenin, after his arrival in Petrograd at the Finland Station in April, referred to 1848 only infrequently during the rest of the year, and even less so afterwards. None of the *fêtes* and other celebrations the Bolsheviks sponsored to legitimize the October Revolution referred to it or re-enacted any aspect of it. But the revolution remained, as it were, just beneath the surface of his politics, to be elevated to consciousness as political and ideological requirements dictated. Disinclined to invoke a failed revolution while trying to convince his fellow Bolsheviks to carry out a successful one, Lenin nevertheless used 1848 as a kind of exclamation point in *ad hominem* attacks against his political enemies. To show that in a failed revolution one could find the inspiration necessary to make a successful one, Lenin invoked the Paris Commune, rather than the events of 1848, because its suppression, by all accounts, took more lives.[71] Instead, Lenin invoked the socialists who he claimed had betrayed the French proletariat in 1848 to underscore the iniquity of the socialists he thought were doing the same to the Russian proletariat in 1917. In March he attacked Alexander Kerensky as the Russian Louis Blanc, who for Lenin was the archetype of the moderate socialist whose incomprehension of the political realities at any particular time was exceeded only by an absence of will, discipline, decisiveness, integrity, and courage. Blanc's utter unfitness as a socialist and

---

[70] Lenin, 'O dvukh liniakh revoliutsii', ibid., vol. XXVII, p. 77.
[71] The number of insurgents killed in the June Days was 'at least 1,500'. Rapport, *1848*, p. 208. By comparison, estimates of the deaths caused by the suppression of the Commune range from 10,000 to 20,000. The smaller figure is cited in Arno Mayer, *The Furies: Violence and Terror in the French and Russian Revolutions* (Princeton NJ, 2002), p. 109, the larger in D. W. Brogan, *The Development of Modern France (1870–1939)* (New York, 1966), p. 73. In *Massacre: The Life and Death of the Paris Commune* (New York, 2014), p. 255, John Merriman argues for a death toll of 15,000; he also considers the killings a precursor of genocides in the twentieth century because of the degree to which they were organized and systemic.

revolutionary Lenin considered evidence that anyone who resembled him in the Russian revolutionary movement, such as Kerensky, should by rights be excluded from its ranks; neither man, he sniffed, even understood what socialism was.[72] In June Lenin cautioned the Russian proletariat not to listen to the Mensheviks or the SRs because, like Blanc, they were 'petit-bourgeois socialists'—which in Lenin's lexicon of insults meant they were *faux* socialists pretending to be real ones.[73] And in August he grouped Blanc ethically, politically, and ideologically with 'Chernov, Tsereteli, and the rest of that contemptible crew'.[74] When, in *State and Revolution*, written after the failure of the Bolshevik-led insurrection in July had forced Lenin to seek refuge in Finland (which retained the autonomy it had enjoyed under the monarchy), he attacked the 'sham socialists' he considered responsible for his predicament, and compared them to their counterparts in 1848 and 1871, who similarly betrayed the working class by claiming a bogus harmony of interests between the workers and their capitalist oppressors.[75]

That Lenin directed his wrath at Cavaignac, rather than at the civilian leadership whose orders he followed, in the only article he wrote in 1917 that was devoted to the 1848 Revolution, revealed his fear of the Russian army preventing a proletarian revolution or overthrowing any regime a proletarian revolution might ensconce in power. In an essay entitled 'The Class Origins of Present-Day and "Future" Cavaignacs', which appeared in *Pravda* on 16 June, he advised his readers at the outset to 'remember the class role played by Cavaignac'.[76] 'The bourgeois republicans' who came to power in February 1848 were like the Kadets in objectively pursuing 'the interests . . . of the ruling class' irrespective of any kind words they uttered about the lower classes.[77] But the proletariat in Paris in 1848 'aspired not to "reconcile itself" to the bourgeoisie, but to defeat it', which prompted the latter to order the army, under General Cavaignac, 'to disarm the Paris workers and to shoot them *en masse*'.[78] Such an atrocity would have constituted little more than a footnote in the history of socialism and communism were it not for the fact, according to Lenin, that the identical sequence of events was occurring in Russia. He quickly followed this assertion by professing his ignorance as to the identity of the Russian Cavaignac; neither Tsereteli nor Chernov nor even Kerensky was strong enough to play the role of the gravedigger of the Russian Revolution. But all three were currently 'pursuing petit-bourgeois policies that make possible and necessary the appearance of a Cavaignac'.[79] What Lenin did make clear in his article was that this Russian Cavaignac—whoever he

---

[72] V. I. Lenin, 'Pis'ma iz daleka (pis'mo 2)', in Lenin, *PSS*, vol. XXXI, pp. 30, 32.

[73] V. I. Lenin, 'Velikii otkhod', ibid., vol. XXXII, p. 311.

[74] V. I. Lenin, 'Za derev'iani ne vidiat lesa', ibid., vol. XXXIV, p. 82.

[75] Lenin, *State and Revolution*, pp. 22–3.

[76] V. I. Lenin, 'Iz kakogo klassovogo istochnika prikhodiat i 'pridut' Kaven'iaki?', in Lenin, *PSS*, vol. XXXII, p. 343.

[77] Ibid., pp. 343–4.   [78] Ibid., p. 344.   [79] Ibid., p. 345.

turned out to be—would not alter existing class relations. Having no political interests of his own, he would be merely a tool, albeit an effective one, of counter-revolution.

But fortunately for the proletariat's political prospects in 1917, the analogy Lenin took pains to elucidate was a limited one. France in 1848 and Russia in 1917 were different. The Russian proletariat—as he insisted in many other articles he wrote in 1917—was politically sophisticated, instinctively revolutionary, and inclined to follow leaders—such as Lenin—cognizant of their own best interests. Compared to the French proletariat, the Russian was immeasurably better equipped to make a proletarian revolution: it had more time to come to the proper conclusion about the causes of its own exploitation. Moreover the social-ists, or so-called socialists, contesting the Bolsheviks for their loyalty and allegiance—most egregiously the Mensheviks and SRs—were deficient personally, politically, and ideologically; among the shortcomings Lenin mentioned were weakness, unreliability, credulity, timidity, and an inability to make up their minds.[80] Although Lenin did not say so explicitly, the reader could readily infer from his article that the principal reason for the failure of the 1848 Revolution in France was that there was no French equivalent of either Lenin or the Bolsheviks.

After the October Revolution, Lenin yet again expressed his fear of a Russian Cavaignac. As in earlier writings, he noted that whoever would assume that persona would be acting as an instrument of the bourgeoisie, without interests or aspirations of his own. Nevertheless, the Bolsheviks' trepidation of this par-ticular contingency obstructing history's progress was well-founded. Lenin took up the matter in July 1918, as the Civil War still raged and the Bolsheviks' political and physical survival was far from assured. The best deterrent to the scenario he feared, in which the Bolsheviks were succeeded by a bourgeois dictatorship kept in power by military force, was the Bolsheviks' continuing their policy of 'bringing the small bourgeoisie under our control', because not doing so would encourage 'millions of small [peasant] proprietors' to take for themselves property previously nationalized by the state. Should they do so, 'Napoleons and Cavaignacs [were] bound to develop'.[81] Lenin was concerned, for good reason, that the external threat the White armies posed might cause a rebellion within the territory the Bolsheviks controlled, and that such a rebellion, should it occur, would embolden the Whites to redouble their efforts even if, in the end, the rebellion was destined to fail. But once the Bolsheviks won the Civil War, this scenario was no longer applicable, and references to Russian Cavaignacs in Lenin's writings disappeared, even though David Riazanov, the new director of the Marx–Engels Institute, included materials on the 1848 Revolution, many of them tracked down by

---

[80] Ibid., p. 346.
[81] Quoted in James Bunyan and Harold Henry Fisher, eds, *The Bolshevik Revolution, 1917–1918: Documents and Materials* (Stanford CA, 1961), p. 685.

Boris Nikolaevskii, in the voluminous archives of documents on European social-ism and Marxism he had assiduously assembled in the 1920s.[82]

*   *   *

Given his penchant for historical analogies, it is hardly surprising that, of all the Bolsheviks, Trotsky was the only one who thought it necessary to describe in detail the meaning and relevance of the 1848 Revolution in France. For Trotsky, just as for Lenin, the failure of the 1905 Revolution was what triggered his investigation. He laid out his initial explanation for the revolution's failure in 1906 in *Results and Prospects*. He began by asserting that economic backwardness was the reason why the proletariat had emerged in Russia to challenge the bourgeoisie politically even before a bourgeois revolution had succeeded. To Plekhanov and the Mensheviks, economic backwardness was the most powerful external impediment—an absence of political consciousness was its internal equivalent—to a proletarian revolution. Only the dialectic, by generating changes that were as time-consuming as they were effective, could overcome it. But to Trotsky economic backwardness was not an obstacle to revolution but an incentive to it. In his mind it held out all sorts of intriguing possibilities, the most enticing of which, from his perspective, was for a proletarian revolution either to evolve directly out of a bourgeois revolution—which in his mind almost happened in 1905—or to occur even before a bourgeois revolution had begun. That in both scenarios Trotsky violated Marx's strictures on when, at what rate, and in which order these revolutions would occur did not really bother him, because he believed nearly simultaneous revolutions in Western Europe, carried out by workers inspired by what their colleagues in Russia were doing, could render Russian workers assistance should they require it.[83]

This, in short, was what Trotsky meant by a 'permanent revolution'. It is commonly believed that he took the idea from the German Social Democrat Alexander Helphand (who adopted the revolutionary pseudonym of 'Parvus'), with whom Trotsky had lengthy conversations in Munich before they both found themselves in St Petersburg in 1905.[84] Strictly speaking, this was true. But it was

---

[82] Arup Banerji, *Writing History in the Soviet Union* (New Delhi, 2008), p. 30.

[83] On the first page of the essay, Trotsky pronounced Russia's historical development 'distinctive' and claimed optimistically that it 'opens up before us completely new historical prospects'. The only other country whose history he considered similar to Russia's—specifically in the political impotence of its bourgeoisie—was Germany. But because Russia's bourgeoisie and proletariat in 1905 were more advanced—though not advanced enough to take power—than Germany's in 1848, the duration of the revolutions the two countries experienced was different: Germany's revolution was suppressed more quickly and efficiently, and thus with fewer lives lost, than Russia's. Trotsky, *Itogi i perspektivy*, pp. 11, 28.

[84] Deutscher, *Prophet Armed*, p. 101; Z. A. B. Zeman and W. B. Scharlau, *The Merchant of Revolution: The Life of Alexander Israel Helphand (Parvus)* (London, 1965), pp. 65–6. In his autobiography, Trotsky himself credited Helphand with transforming proletarian revolution 'from an astronomic "final" goal to a practical task of our own day'. Leon Trotsky, *My Life* (New York, 1970), p. 167.

also the case that Trotsky found corroboration of Helphand's scenario in his own understanding of the Revolution of 1848 in France and in the German states, which together served as a template for everything that should not be done if any future revolution in Russia was to succeed. Trotsky did not think the differences between the two countries, and between the revolutions they each experienced in 1848, precluded their being analysed, and compared to the 1905 Revolution in Russia, as if they were one.

Trotsky believed the 1848 Revolutions failed in France and in the German states because the grievances the lower classes in these two countries had come to believe could be redressed in a political revolution were simply too disparate and even contradictory for these classes to join together and fight the princes and monarchs opposing them as a cohesive bloc. Fighting their opponents separately, instead of working together, the proletariat and the impoverished elements of the peasantry capable of overcoming their natural conservatism were destined to fail. In reality, the revolutions that began in France and Germany in 1848 failed not only also because such an alliance never lasted long enough for a permanent government reflecting the interests of its participants to be established. They also failed because liberals in both countries acted perfidiously, successfully disguising their unalterable commitment to the pursuance of their own material interests. For that reason it was a grievous mistake for the lower classes to have aligned with them initially—and by the time they realized it, the liberals had called on the army (in the case of France), or worked out political arrangements with feudal princes (in the German states), that made a repetition of the June Days in France, or some facsimile of them in Germany, suicidal. In both parts of Europe order and the status quo ante were quickly restored. In contrast to the French Revolution, which notwithstanding the disparate economic interests of its participants was a national revolution, the 1848 Revolutions were class wars, in which the classes that were oppressed were not sufficiently oppressed to recognize that the differences between them were less than those between all of them and the class above them.[85]

But all was not lost. The capitalists exploiting the proletariat would themselves soon diminish in number and eventually become so weak politically that the proletariat would destroy them and replace capitalism with a proletarian dictatorship that itself would melt away with the elimination of classes. Socialism and then communism would be the happy result. But the activist in Trotsky rebelled against the patience this scenario required. One senses, in reading everything Trotsky wrote about the 1848 Revolution in France, that, in contrast to Germany, where the proletariat was significantly weaker, and the bourgeoisie correspondingly more powerful, than they were in France, he considered the defeat of the revolution in France a close-run thing. If circumstances, or the actions of

---

[85] Trotsky, *Itogi i perspektivy*, pp. 25–9.

particular individuals had been just slightly different—if, for example, there had been someone like Trotsky himself who could have explained to peasants and workers why their disagreements were trivial in comparison to their grievances, and that the only way their grievances could be redressed was by overthrowing the newly established Second Republic or, better yet, by establishing their own republic before a liberal bourgeois republic hostile to their interests could be established—the Revolution of 1848 would have succeeded. Specifically, it would have set in motion, greatly accelerated, the chain of events leading ultimately to perpetual peace, prosperity, social justice, artistic creativity, and the emancipation of the individual Trotsky described so eloquently in 1924 in *Literature and Revolution*.[86] Russian revolutionaries could learn much from the Revolutions of 1848, especially the revolution in France. Should they do so, he concluded, 'the nineteenth century would not have passed in vain'.[87]

In *1905*, which was written between 1907 and 1909, when there were no events in Russia to distract Trotsky from calmly explicating the reasons the 1905 Revolution had failed, he began by recapitulating the analysis that informed *Results and Prospects*. What distinguished *1905* from the earlier work was Trotsky's explicit admission that the 1905 Revolution failed—and thus could not evolve seamlessly into a proletarian revolution—because the circumstances that prevented it were nearly identical to those that prevailed in 1848, when the bourgeoisie was not yet powerful enough in Germany to withstand the forces defending feudalism, or in France to preclude a dictatorship relying for its survival on the army and adopting, if only symbolically, many of the attributes of military rule; while not himself a soldier, Louis Napoleon dressed like a general and was the nephew of the most illustrious military figure in France's history. At the same time, however, the bourgeoisie was strong enough in both countries to subdue the proletariat and any other elements of the lower classes that challenged it. In Trotsky's formulation, the 'liberal bourgeoisie' triumphed over the proletariat and the peasantry because 'radical urban elements' in French and German cities and towns were still socially and politically amorphous, and thus incapable of convincing the peasantry to join them in a common effort to depose their respective oppressors.[88]

For this reason the revolutions of 1848 failed, and for the same reason the same fate befell the revolution in Russia in 1905. But far more than in the earlier work, Trotsky in *1905* made clear that the French 1848 and the German 1848, while similar in many ways, were different in the chances each had had of succeeding. Germany in 1848 had still not experienced its 1789, and accordingly its bourgeoisie in 1848 was far weaker than the French. For that reason the optimism about Russia's future Trotsky gained by believing that the proletariat in France had a decent chance of gaining power in 1848, and failed to do so only because of

---

[86] Leon Trotsky, *Literature and Revolution* (Ann Arbor MI, 1960), especially pp. 253–6.
[87] Trotsky, *Itogi i prospekty*, p. 25.   [88] Trotsky, *1905*, p. 49.

the actions (or the inaction) of specific individuals, was vitiated by the pessimism suggested by the impossibility of a bourgeois revolution—not to mention a proletarian one—succeeding in Germany in the very same year. Trotsky's rueful acknowledgement of this imparted to *1905* a measure of realism absent in *Results and Prospects*. For Trotsky in 1906, the German 1848 was only slightly less disheartening than the French. By the time he was writing *1905*, however, only a complete suspension of disbelief could have caused him to replicate his earlier analysis. Only the French revolution in 1848 had any real chance of success, and in that respect Trotsky was finally at one with Marx and Lenin, for whom the German Revolution in 1848, once it ended, offered revolutionaries of later generations absolutely nothing inspirational or even worthy of admiration. In fact, the subsequent unification of Germany under Bismarck, whose adroit manipulation of concessions and crackdowns enabled the Hohenzollern monarchy to remain in power, left France as the only major European country with a revolutionary tradition worth exploring.

By the time Trotsky became a Bolshevik in the summer of 1917—which was the next time he took up the 1848 Revolution—his optimism about the prospects for a proletarian revolution in Russia caused his opinion of the French proletariat in 1848 to improve. In his retelling of the revolution, he made clear his conviction that French workers had made 'heroic efforts for independent action'.[89] But he still had to qualify his praise by noting that they possessed neither 'a clear revolutionary theory nor an authoritative class organization', and for that reason '[their] importance in production [was] infinitely lower than the present economic function of the Russian proletariat'—which was Trotsky's way of saying that the latter was ready to transform the bourgeois revolution that in February had overturned the monarchy into a proletarian revolution overturning the Provisional Government.[90] He did permit himself a cautionary note: that the proletariat failed in France in 1848 because the property settlement the first French revolution applied successfully in the countryside had made the peasantry politically conservative, and thus oblivious through most of the nineteenth century to the continued suppression of the urban lower classes. In short, the alliance between the proletariat and the peasantry that according to Trotsky was the only means by which a bourgeois revolution and a proletarian one could be sequential, with only days or at most a few weeks between them, was impossible in France in 1848.[91] But in 1917 in Russia such an alliance was not only possible; the Bolsheviks, now acting with the benefit of Trotsky's counsel, were helping to create it. Indeed, their doing so was perhaps the most convincing evidence he could offer that the

---

[89]   Leon Trotsky, 'Character of the Russian Revolution', in Lenin and Trotsky, *Proletarian Revolution in Russia*, p. 272.
[90]   Ibid.
[91]   Trotsky reiterated this particular explanation for the proletariat's defeat in 1848 in *Between Red and White*, p. 79.

'productive power' of the Russian proletariat would soon exercise 'revolutionary power' greatly exceeding its numerical strength.[92]

Largely because of its treachery in 1848—and in 1871 in its suppression of the Paris Commune—the French bourgeoisie occupied a special place among the villains in history Trotsky never tired of excoriating. His belief that the French bourgeoisie practised an imperialism more rapacious than that of any other country is reflected in the sheer number of defamatory references in Trotsky's writings (exceeded only by similarly derogatory references in Lenin's) to French capitalism and French imperialism. During the Civil War both he and Lenin singled out France for its support of the Whites, and at times their animus seemed to exceed even that which they still harboured towards Kautsky and the other German socialists for repudiating their pledge to oppose German involvement in war in 1914, which to Lenin and Trotsky was prima facie evidence that they were no longer socialists.[93]

Once the Civil War ended, Trotsky was more inclined to consider the 1848 Revolutions in Europe successful—this was true even, to a limited extent, in Germany—if judged by their long-term results. These included 'sweeping away the remnants of the regime of guilds and serfdom, and thereby extending the framework of capitalist development'.[94] In fact, by 1925 Trotsky was including 1905 in the apostolic sequence of revolutions that began in France in the late eighteenth century, continued there through the nineteenth century, and culminated in Russia in 1917.[95] To justify Russia's inclusion in this now supranational revolutionary tradition, Trotsky cited the Decembrist Revolt in 1825, which he knew was shorter than the four revolutions in France, and because the Decembrists could not prevent the continuation of the monarchy in the person of the newly installed tsar Nicholas I, even less consequential than the Revolution of 1830, which at least ended one dynasty before installing another.[96] For all his faults, Trotsky knew too much history not to acknowledge that what the Decembrists had engaged in was more an urban insurrection than a mass revolution; the Russian people were merely its intended beneficiary.[97] But the distinction he

[92] Trotsky, 'Character of the Russian Revolution', p. 271.

[93] A typical example of his special animus were his comments in a speech delivered in Red Square in 1920 honouring the commanders of the Bolshevik forces fighting the Whites. L. Trotsky, 'Rech' na parade v chest' krasnykh komandirov na Krasnoi ploshchadi', in L. Trotsky, Kak vooruzhalas' revoliutsiia (na voennoi rabote) (Moscow, 1921), vol. II, pp. 285–7.

[94] Leon Trotsky, 'Report on the World Economic Crisis and the New Tasks of the Communist International (June 1921)', https://www.marxists.org/archive/trotsky/1924/ffyci-1/ch19b.htm.

[95] L. Trotsky, '1905. Cherez dvadtsat' let', Pravda, no. 6(3235) (8 January 1926): p. 5.

[96] Albeit with misgivings and without great enthusiasm, the Decembrists wanted Constantine, Nicholas' older brother, to rule after Alexander I, the oldest brother, had died in November, because they believed, wrongly, that Constantine shared their liberalism. Mazour, First Russian Revolution, pp. 158–9.

[97] The Decembrists did not think to appeal to the crowd observing their 'standing revolution' to join them. Ibid., pp. 175–6.

established was meant to underscore the centrality of the real revolutions he cited in the ongoing progression of history that had reached a new plateau, unattained in any of the French revolutions, with the Bolsheviks' gaining power in 1917 as the designated agent of the Russian proletariat; indeed he considered the Bolsheviks the proletariat's embodiment.

Trotsky extolled the revolutions he considered part of this larger tradition of revolution not just for assisting 'history' in its long march to the secular nirvana of communism. He esteemed them also for the transformation they produced in the revolutionaries who carried them out, sometimes successfully, sometimes not. To Trotsky there was something ennobling in each revolution—1793, 1848, 1871, and 1905—that future revolutionaries would look back to for examples of the personal qualities they would need if the new society they established would be a virtuous one. The personal virtues Trotsky believed revolutionaries needed to make a successful revolution were the same virtues enabling them, once in power, to achieve their revolutions' objectives. In the speech delivered on the twentieth anniversary of the Bolsheviks' insurrection in Moscow in December 1905, Trotsky summoned all of the eloquence of which he was capable in elucidating what he considered the essence of each of these revolutions and why together they formed a tradition that should inform the Bolsheviks' ongoing pursuit of social justice through the establishment of socialism:

> The history of human society included a series of convulsive upsurges of the oppressed masses against oppressors and oppression. Years and decades of apparently hopeless servitude have been, are, and will continue to be burst open by explosions and insurrection.... These are the years in human history which, not only in the memory of revolutionaries, but in that of each thinking individual in the camp of the oppressed, seem to be forever cast in bronze, sharply separated from the endless years devoid of personality and shape.
>
> 1793 has remained in the memory of humanity as one of those 'metallurgic' years, when under the leadership of the Jacobins, those Bolsheviks of the eighteenth century, plebeians, *sans-culottes*, artisans and semi-proletarians—the ragamuffins of the Paris suburbs—established an iron dictatorship and meted out unforgettable punishment to the crowned and privileged rulers of the old society.
>
> 1848 lives in the memory of humanity, not so much because the backward bourgeoisie attempted in that year to get power, but because from under the cowardly and thieving bourgeoisie the young head of the proletarian lion was already raising itself.
>
> 1871 has been engraved in the memory of workers as the year when the heroic proletariat of Paris made an attempt, unforgettable in its lessons, to take into its hands the reins of government of a new civilised society.
>
> 1905 is another of those years in human history, particularly ours, that is cast in bronze.... Only 1905 gives us a revolution with a familiar native element. New generations pass through it. They experience in their flesh and blood its

experience, its initial semi-victories, its blows, and its stern lessons. The inner fabric of the people is transformed. Only by experiencing the Revolution of 1905 could our country, twelve years later, write into history the greatest of all years— 1917![98]

*   *   *

Stalin's silence on the 1848 revolutions speaks volumes about his opinion of them. Martyrdom was not something he aspired to, nor did he consider it ennobling, much less confirmation of moral superiority. Achieving one's objectives was far more important; in most of the issues that concerned him, no other considerations mattered. The whole issue of 'Bonapartism' spoke to his legitimacy as the ruler of a state formally committed to achieving socialism and communism. For that reason, he addressed it. But the events of 1848 preceding Louis Napoleon's ascension to power and the establishment of the Second Empire had no utility for him. Nor, for much the same reason, did they attract the attention of Khrushchev or Brezhnev, or any of the Soviet rulers, excepting Gorbachev, who followed them. And for Gorbachev the 1848 Revolution mattered mainly as part of a tradition of revolutions in France in which the revolution that began it in 1789 and the revolution that ended it in 1871 had far more salience to the issues he dealt with than did the two intervening revolutions in 1830 and 1848.

Once the shackles of Stalinism were removed in the mid-1950s, Soviet historians, however, wrote a good deal about the 1848 Revolutions in France and Germany. None deviated from the Leninist orthodoxy that in France the proletariat failed to achieve its objectives because without the support of the peasantry it could not defeat the bourgeoisie, which stopped at nothing to prevent the proletariat from radicalizing the political revolution in February ending the Orléanist monarchy, and carrying out an economic revolution committed to the socialization of private property. But the way Soviet historians expressed this orthodoxy—the evidence they chose to corroborate it, the aspects of it they either emphasized or minimized, and the larger lessons they drew from it—varied considerably. In 1959 V. P. Volgin stressed the political and ideological immaturity of the proletariat, arguing that the absence of support it needed from the peasantry was the principal reason it failed to wrest power from the bourgeoisie.[99] To Volgin, 1848 in France encapsulated perfectly the hypocrisy, dishonesty, and duplicity of the bourgeoisie—the corrective of which in practical terms was an industrial working class possessing 'a scientific understanding of its class interests', by which, of course, Volgin meant Marxism-Leninism.[100] In 1960 B. F. Porshnev quoted Engels on the degree to which the bourgeoisie needed the

---

[98] Trotsky, '1905. Cherez dvadtsat' let', p. 5.
[99] V. P. Volgin, 'Lenin i revoliutsionnye traditsii frantsuzskogo naroda', pp. 13–14.
[100] Ibid., p. 14.

masses to defeat monarchies opposed to it; while in France it succeeded in this endeavour, in the German states it failed.[101] But Porshnev focused on the heroism of the German proletariat to the virtual exclusion of the French, and the reason for this was because the German proletariat spoke through the imposing figure of Marx himself. It was 'in the pages of the *Neue Rheinische Zeitung*', according to Porshnev, that '[the German proletariat] unmasked the readiness of the bourgeoisie...to make a deal with the monarchy and the landowners'.[102] In 1962, V. S. Alexeev-Popov and Iu. Ia. Baskin emphasized that through much of the year, the proletariat in France acted as part of a radical bloc that included elements of the petit-bourgeoisie; for that reason it resembled the blocs that had emerged in 1793 in the French Revolution, and would do so again in 1830 and 1871. However, in contrast to the French Revolution, in which the haute-bourgeoisie's betrayal in 1792 was what a caused a bloc of the lower classes that also included the petit-bourgeoisie to emerge in 1793, the bloc that coalesced in 1848 did so before the bourgeoisie betrayed it. But the objective conditions that existed in France in 1848 vitiated any chance of this bloc actually defeating the bourgeoisie and coming to power itself. For that reason the political unity it possessed was useless. France in 1848 was simply not ready for any class or bloc of classes that excluded the bourgeoisie and ruled itself.[103]

A. Z. Manfred was especially sensitive to the causal relationship between the revolutions comprising this tradition. He paid special attention to the way histor-ians of the French Revolution in nineteenth-century France, most notably Lamar-tine and Louis Blanc, misapplied in 1848 the revolution's tactical lessons, and in doing so made an already difficult task impossible. Louis Blanc, he sniffed, was as poor a historian of the French Revolution as he was a political leader of the 1848 Revolution. The reconciliation between the Girondins and the Jacobins Blanc believed would have strengthened the French Revolution would actually have weakened it, and one of the reasons the proletariat was crushed in 1848 was because it followed Blanc's advice in that year to do what he thought the Girondins and the Jacobins should have done a half-century earlier. But the alliance Blanc recommended in 1848 would have been no more advantageous to the proletariat than a similar arrangement would have been in 1789 for the Parisian *sans-culottes*.[104] Hardly more constructive in this respect was Lamartine, like Blanc an ersatz revolutionary, whose preference for the Girondins over the Jacobins disqualified him from speaking authoritatively on the French Revolution and acting efficiently and ethically in 1848: for all his animadversions of the bourgeoisie, Lamartine was never a reliable ally of the proletariat.[105] Betrayed by both liberals and pseudo-socialists, the proletariat, in 1848, lacked the means to

---

[101] Porshnev, 'V. I. Lenin o rannikh burzhuaznykh revoliutsiiakh', p. 51.   [102] Ibid.
[103] Alexeev-Popov and Baskin, 'Problemy istorii iakobinskoi literatury', p. 131. The authors' com-ments on 1848 are elliptical and much of their argument must be inferred.
[104] Manfred, *Velikaia frantsuzskaia revoliutsiia*, pp. 371–2, 381.   [105] Ibid., p. 368.

overcome the sundry forces intent on defeating it, and Manfred concluded from his analysis that, for the proletariat, the 1848 Revolution, like the revolutions in France in 1830 and 1871, was a premature revolution; for that simple reason only the French Revolution deserved its appellation as a Great Revolution.[106] Manfred's comments would be echoed in the Gorbachev era, when the implication in Manfred's attacks on Blanc and Lamartine that individuals affect the course of events as much as objective conditions do was stated explicitly. In 1989 V. A. Gavrilichev cited approvingly Herzen's derogation of the same two leaders of the 1848 Revolution in France as 'short-sighted, weak-willed dilettantes', fully deserving condemnation for 'ruining' it'.[107]

Of the Soviet historians who took up the 1848 Revolution in their scholarship, B. S. Itenberg's views most closely tracked Lenin's. What happened in France in 1848, in his opinion, was that a bourgeois revolution morphed temporarily into a proletariat one. The proletariat, like the bourgeoisie, was intent, in the spring of 1848, on transforming France into a democratic republic. But fear among other classes in France that sought an economic transformation to accompany a political one caused the class it most directly threatened economically, the bourgeoisie, to suppress it—first in the June Days, and then in December, when Louis Napoleon, supported by monarchists and a large percentage of the bourgeoisie, came to power; that he won the presidency of France in a genuinely free election did not diminish the illegitimacy of the political supremacy he thereafter enjoyed.[108]

More than most Soviet historians, Itenburg analysed the 1848 Revolution as a self-contained historical event, its larger significance limited to the role it played in linking earlier revolutions in France to the Paris Commune twenty-three years later. Other Soviet historians, however, were not so reticent. B. G. Veber seemed to study the revolution for the role he believed it played in the political education of the Bolsheviks, who were cognizant of the pitfalls it prefigured in the dicey enterprise of conducting a revolution and replacing an old regime with a new one. According to Veber, Marx and Engels enjoyed the inestimable advantage, in comparison to other political theorists and advocates of socialist and communism, of 'involving themselves in the mass revolutionary struggle of 1848–49'.[109] That gave them the perspective 'from which to ascertain the future pattern of the workers' movement and democracy in different countries'—which for Veber was a roundabout way of saying that their temporal proximity to the Revolution of 1848 enabled them, once the revolution ended, to produce a generic template of

---

[106] Ibid., pp. 368, 405–6.
[107] Gavrilichev, 'Velikaia frantsuzskaia revoliutsiia v publitsistike revoliutsionnykh demokratov', p. 376.
[108] Itenberg, *Rossiia i velikaia frantsuzskaia revoliutsiia*, pp. 47–8.
[109] Veber, 'V. I. Lenin i istoricheskoe nasledie iakobintsev', p. 25.

revolution that Lenin and the Bolsheviks would subsequently rely on in establishing the Soviet Union.[110] But Weber also credited the French revolutionary tradition as a whole for the role it played by itself—apart from its value after passing through the interpretive prism of Marxism—in clarifying Lenin's thinking at critical points in his own political and ideological maturation. In 1905, for example, Lenin, in Veber's estimation, knew enough French history to recognize that the choice Russia faced in that year was whether the bourgeois revolution that was underway would resemble 1789 or 1848, and when Lenin realized that the ongoing revolution in Russia would resemble the latter rather than the former and that the revolution in Russia would therefore fail, the lessons he drew from that regrettable, but perhaps inescapable outcome were the right ones. In short, the success of the October Revolution and the emergence of the Soviet Union depended considerably on how Lenin interpreted the 1905 Revolution, and how Lenin interpreted the 1905 Revolution depended considerably on how he interpreted the revolutions that preceded it in France.[111]

*   *   *

For all of this, the 1848 Revolution in France, considered as a discrete event, did not inflame and inspire to the degree to which other French revolutions were able to do. Its success was brief and ephemeral, its defeat seemingly permanent. For sheer drama, it offered nothing comparable to the storming of the Bastille. Nor, for that matter, did it harbour any universal aspirations or objectives revolutionaries elsewhere in Europe or in another part of the world might find congenial. The socialists and liberals who led the 1848 revolution considered it primarily a French affair, made by Frenchman in the pursuit of objectives from which the French people, more than any other, would benefit. Absent in 1848—not just in France but in Europe as a whole—was any overarching sense of common purpose, much less any grandiloquent conviction, as there was in the French Revolution, that what they were engaged in were just the initial steps in the emancipation of humanity. Moreover, while industrialization in France was certainly accelerating by the mid nineteenth-century, the working class remained mostly pre-industrial, consisting mainly of artisans and craftsmen, rather than a genuine proletariat employed in factories that by their size alone would have increased the magnitude of strikes and other expressions of discontent. The class consciousness Marxists were convinced would cause the working class to resist entreaties from the bourgeoisie to join it in an alliance that, as it happened in 1848, would bring the working class nothing but misfortune, remained primitive in France. Moreover, the 'proletarian internationalism' that would remain an article of faith

[110] Lenin quoted in ibid.   [111] Ibid., p. 8.

for a later generations of socialists until its claim to prevent wars was shown in 1914 to be chimerical was still, in 1848, a mere figment of the inflamed imaginations of Marx and Engels. Finally, the fact remained that, viewed retrospectively from the perspective of twentieth-century revolutionaries like the Bolsheviks, the Revolution of 1848 in France could not match, for sheer pathos, the Paris Commune of 1871, the destruction of which took longer and required a far larger number of troops, thereby increasing exponentially the potential martyrdom of the Commune's defenders.

For these reasons the Revolution of 1848, by itself, had precious little to recommend it when the Bolsheviks had to legitimize their own revolution to the majority of the Russian people who rejected it. But the Revolution of 1848 in France was far from irrelevant. Its consideration seemed to generate among the Bolsheviks the realization that there existed in the history of France a revolutionary tradition, that the Revolution of 1848 was a part of it, and that this tradition had a meaning different from—one might even say greater than—that of the particular revolutions comprising it.

Moreover, the Revolution of 1848 happened to have a *dénouement* in the rise to power of Louis Napoleon and his transmogrification of the Second Republic into the Second Empire. Among the Bolsheviks, this gave rise to what for them was a fearful spectre, no less threatening than Thermidor, in its demoralizing and delegitimizing imputation that any regime they created might degenerate into a hypertrophied state, ruling ostensibly on behalf of all classes and thus impervious to its own ideological bankruptcy. This hypertrophied state stood at the apex of a political system that came to be known among the Bolsheviks as 'Bonapartism'; that it emerged in France when the economy was still capitalist did not diminish the fear among the Bolsheviks of its emerging in Russia even after—or especially after—the economy there had become socialist. While there was much about Louis Napoleon's persona that could be easily satirized, and about his ultimate demise as a Prussian prisoner of war to make him an object of contempt, he possessed a *savoir faire* in matters political without which not even his venerable lineage as the nephew of the original Napoleon could have ensured his rise to power. But the Bolsheviks were actually afraid of *both* Napoleons, the first one just as much as, and, at times, even more than the second one. Louis Napoleon may have adopted some of the affectations of the military, such as wearing a uniform on ceremonial occasions, and also, it seems, whenever his portrait was painted, but the most likely gravedigger of any proletarian revolution, in the overheated imaginations of the Bolsheviks, would more likely be someone like Napoleon Bonaparte: an actual general, or at least an officer, more illustrious, more imposing, and more successful in running a military and winning wars than the nephew of his, whose success in destroying the Second Republic was what initially sparked the Bolsheviks' concern about the larger phenomenon that bore the family name the two French rulers shared.

However, regardless of which Napoleon the Bolsheviks considered the real precedent for the military dictatorship they feared might destroy them, it seems proper, in this study, to consider the whole phenomenon of Bonapartism an integral aspect of the French Revolutionary Tradition. After all, the original Napoleon consolidated and codified the French Revolution before betraying it, and by doing so made possible a synthesis of two traditions in French history, the Napoleonic and the Revolutionary, once there emerged in the 1870s a consensus in France on what Gordon Wright has called 'the republican ideal'.[112] However amorphous it might be conceptually, and however indeterminable its provenance in French history given its applicability to two rulers and two periods of history separated by more than a half-century, Bonapartism had nonetheless become an integral aspect of the French Revolutionary Tradition by the time the Bolsheviks discovered this tradition, explored it, and determined its temporal and ideological limits. An analysis of Bonapartism, as the Bolsheviks perceived it, is therefore essential in ascertaining the relationship between this tradition and the larger history of Bolshevism and the Soviet Union.

[112] Wright, *France in Modern Times*, p. 205.

14

The Phantom of the Russian Bonaparte

Marx and Engels introduced to the Bolsheviks the concept commonly called 'Bonapartism'.[1] Russian *intelligenty*, by and large, were aware of the term and occasionally used it to clarify—for themselves, one suspects, as much as for others—political systems and methods of rule not explainable in the terminology to which they were accustomed. But their influence on the Bolsheviks, in this respect, was minimal. Chernyshevskii confined his analysis of Bonapartism to reaffirming that it could issue from a successful revolution, as it did in the French Revolution as well as from a failed revolution, as it did in the case of the Revolution of 1848.[2] The phenomenon was never uppermost in his mind, and for that reason he never specified its attributes, much less the ways in which the regimes the two Napoleons established differed from other authoritarian regimes that resembled them. Mikhail Bakunin, with his consummate fear of political power concentrated in a central government, spoke of the French government under Gambetta as 'Bonapartist' by virtue of its 'administrative apparatus'.[3] But like Chernyshevskii he did not explain why this particular regime, but not others that exercised political power similarly, should be given this particular designation. Finally, Alexander Herzen used the term mostly as a pejorative; that he applied it to Heinrich Heine's views on the Revolution of 1830, but to no government or political leader of any significance, makes clear its irrelevance to his formulation and conceptualization of his own politics.[4] When discussing the

---

[1] That Marx and Engels usually applied the term to the regimes of the two Napoleons does not mean that they considered the term inapplicable to others. Over the course of their lifetimes, imitators appeared; in fact Louis Napoleon was an imitator himself, consciously adopting some of the persona of his uncle in the hope of achieving his own renown. Marx and Engels had no trouble labelling as 'Bonapartist' the policies Bismarck pursued in Germany in the 1870s to appease the lower classes with material benefits, such as old-age insurance, while perpetuating a political system designed to keep them powerless. Bismarck's policies, and the political calculations that produced them, were, in fact, remarkably similar to Louis Napoleon's. In 1866 Engels explicitly characterized the system Bismarck created as 'a Bonapartist semi-dictatorship'. 'Letter, Engels to Marx (13 April 1866)', Marx and Engels, *Selected Correspondence*, p. 206. While Marx never developed an actual theory of Bonapartism, after his surprise that someone so supposedly foolish and stupid as Louis Napoleon could come to power in France had subsided, he accepted the notion that regimes like his could emerge in other countries of Europe provided their economies were capitalist. Marx never denied explicitly that Bonapartism could exist under socialism because he did not think it was necessary to do so. To Marx 'Bonapartist socialism' (or 'socialist Bonapartism') was an oxymoron.

[2] Plimak and Khoros, 'Velikaia frantsuzskaia revoliutsiia i revoliutsionnaia traditsiia v Rossii', p. 243.

[3] Quoted in K. J. Kenafick, *Michael Bakunin and Karl Marx* (Melbourne, 1948), p. 168.

[4] Herzen, *Past and Thoughts*, p. 597.

two Bonapartes, he mostly disparaged them, and his only comment suggesting that dictatorships like those the two men established were prototypical of a generic category was that 'every revolution creates its own Napoleon'.[5]

It fell to Marx and Engels to explain what a Bonapartist regime consisted of, and why it should appear in a country such as France that had already experienced a capitalist revolution elevating the bourgeoisie to power. One must bear in mind that the two men explained the phenomenon, at least initially, while still disappointed by the failure of the 1848 Revolution. Like Herzen and Bakunin, they witnessed Louis Napoleon's ascension to the presidency of France in December 1848, its transformation in 1851 into the power base for a future dictatorship, and finally, in obvious imitation of his uncle, his proclaiming France an empire and himself its emperor in 1852.[6] Because their ideology could not explain, much less have predicted these events, Marx and Engels both reacted initially to Louis Napoleon's triumphs more emotionally than rationally. Beneath the genuine contempt they harboured for the man himself—'a serious buffoon' and 'a crafty *roué*' were among the less disparaging descriptions Marx proffered in *The Eighteenth Brumaire*—there was an undercurrent of anger and resentment, borne, one suspects, out of genuine bewilderment, in what they first wrote about the man.[7] Only after passions had cooled, and Louis' policies could be evaluated empirically, were Marx and Engels capable of evaluating his regime calmly and rationally, and determining whether it warranted the creation of a new generic category of political regimes to understand it.

Their first response to Louis' coup was sheer invective. In contrast to the original Bonaparte, who was a serious and historically consequential figure, his nephew, according to Engels, was 'stupid', the means by which he took power 'ludicrous', and the proclamation he issued explaining it 'fatuous'.[8] The likelihood of his government surviving more than a few months was minimal. For all of these reasons Engels wondered

> how much longer the World Spirit, clearly much incensed at mankind, is going to continue this farce, whether with the year we shall see Consulate, Empire, Restoration and all pass by before our eyes, whether, too, the Napoleonic dynasty must first be thrashed in the streets of Paris before it is deemed impossible in France, the devil only knows. But it strikes me things are taking a remarkably lunatic turn and that the *crapauds* [i.e. philistines] are heading for an astonishing humiliation.[9]

---

[5] Quoted in Mayer, 'Lenin and the Jacobin Identity', p. 130.

[6] The title of Marx's influential essay on Louis' seizure of power, *The Eighteenth Brumaire of Louis Bonaparte*, refers to the date according to the old Jacobin calendar still in effect when Napoleon Bonaparte seized power in France on 9 November 1799.

[7] Marx, *The Eighteenth Brumaire of Louis Bonaparte*, pp. 75–6.

[8] 'Letter, Engels to Marx (3 December 1851)', in Marx and Engels, *Collected Works*, vol. XXXVIII, p. 504.

[9] Ibid., vol. XXXVIII, pp. 505–6.

Two years later, in a letter to Joseph Wedemeyer, Engels was still emphasizing the personal element in history, denigrating Louis implicitly by praising the military campaigns of his uncle; the latter were the classic exemplar of how a revolutionary army, indeed any army, should fight.[10] Engels seemed to recognize that Louis' success could not be explained either by Marxist ideology or by any exceptional personal attributes other than reptilian cunning. But rather than soften his earlier disparagement, he continued his *ad hominem* invective towards Louis Napoleon, which he seemed to believe had greater resonance when coupled with *ad hominem* praise for Napoleon Bonaparte.

Unlike his longtime collaborator, however, Marx felt compelled to explain Louis' rise to power ideologically. The result was *The Eighteenth Brumaire of Louis Bonaparte*. Marx began writing it in December 1851, mere days after the coup that made Louis Napoleon a dictator; he finished it in April 1852. It was published first in New York, also in 1852, in the first issue of the German *émigré* newspaper *Die Revolution*. In the essay, Marx offered two explanations, one for Louis' gaining power, the other for his holding onto it. Both required Louis' success to be depersonalized. In explaining Louis' rise to power, Marx reduced him to the political instrument of two social strata within the French bourgeoisie; Louis' political intelligence, or lack of it, was irrelevant. In the first stratum were wealthy landowners—in the essay Marx called them Legitimists—who originally favoured the Bourbons, then resisted the Orléanists, and finally settled on Louis Napoleon because he was politically malleable. The second consisted of *nouveaux-riches* from the financial and industrial elite who had once favoured Louis Philippe and subsequent Orléanist pretenders, but after 1848 though it wiser, in light of the first Napoleon's universally accepted greatness, to support the second one; that he was a pale imitation of his much-beloved uncle, and thus unlikely to offer resistance once in power, seemed to confirm the sagacity of their decision.[11]

At this point in the essay, Marx included among the social classes and sub-classes of the population that brought Louis Napoleon to power the 'small-holding peasants', whose involvement he now made clear he considered crucial to Louis Napoleon's success.[12] Their attraction to him was, at bottom, irrational: despite tilling land their ancestors had received in the French Revolution, the poorest peasants, who comprised a majority of the class as a whole, were instinctively monarchist and therefore susceptible to seductive authoritarians like Louis Napoleon who promised them everything.[13] Later in the essay, however, Marx changed his mind, now claiming that the essential prerequisite for Louis Napoleon's continuation in power had nothing to do with the class identity of his supporters, and everything to do with his creation of a state so much more powerful than the

---

[10] 'Letter, Engels to Joseph Wedemeyer (12 April 1853)', ibid., vol. XXXIX, p. 305.
[11] Marx, *The Eighteenth Brumaire of Louis Bonaparte*, pp. 46–9.   [12] Ibid., p. 123.
[13] Ibid., pp. 46–9, 123–4.

bourgeoisie and the landed proprietors whose support, along with that of the peasants, had made its establishment possible. Marx describes this hypertrophied state the second Napoleon established as follows:

> Only under the second Bonaparte does the state seem to have made itself completely independent. As against civil society, the state machine has consolidated its position so thoroughly that the chief of the Society of 10 December [i.e. Louis Napoleon], suffices for its head, an adventurer blown in from abroad, raised on the shield by a drunken soldiery, which he has bought with liquor and sausages, and to which he must continually ply with sausages anew. Hence the downcast despair, the feeling of most dreadful humiliation and degradation that oppresses the breast of France and makes her catch her breath. She feels dishonoured.[14]

One suspects that the contumely Marx harboured for peasants made it easier for him to believe that, irrespective of his characterological deficiencies, once Louis Napoleon was secure as Emperor of the French, he could do pretty much as he wished. The state machine of which he was its most public and tangible expression would remain hypertrophied, and neither peasants nor any other class or stratum of the population could destroy it absent some internal or external catastrophe befalling France—as it finally did in 1870.[15]

One should not underestimate Marx's contempt for 'this princely *lumpenproletarian*'.[16] One suspects that at some level he thought Louis would remain in power because peasants were even bigger idiots than their leader. But one should also not ignore the inescapable contradiction between Louis Napoleon's ostensible lack of political intelligence and his political success. Becoming president, dictator, and emperor of France in quick succession was no mean feat. That he did so hardly more than a decade after two failed attempts to seize power (in 1836 and 1840) had resulted, respectively, in his living in exile in several countries, including the United States, and being convicted in court of sedition and sentenced to life imprisonment in a castle (from which he later escaped) only increased the enormity of his achievement. Louis Napoleon was not at all the 'manageable cretin' not only Marx, but many others, such as Adolph Thiers, imagined him to be, and the ignominy he endured as a prisoner of the Prussians in 1870 should not obscure his very real political intelligence.[17] In explaining Marx's personal derogations of Louis Napoleon, which were even more intemperate than those of

---

[14] Ibid., pp. 122–3.
[15] Of course many of those who voted for Louis in December 1848 had no idea about his beliefs and what he stood for—which was partly the result of Louis' own indecision. But peasants entertained actual delusions. Some thought he was his uncle, Napoleon Bonaparte—who by then had been dead for three decades and whose body had long ago been placed in a marble sarcophagus in Les Invalides in Paris in conspicuously public ceremonies. Others who voted for Louis thought that, once he was president, he would pay their taxes. Sperber, *The European Revolutions*, p. 152.
[16] Marx, *The Eighteenth Brumaire of Louis Bonaparte*, p. 85.
[17] Quoted in Gildea, *Children of the Revolution*, p. 58.

other persons he personally disliked, it must be borne in mind that Louis Napoleon's success—which was what had forced him and Engels to conceptualize a new generic category of political systems—was not supposed to happen. Dictators in an age of industrial capitalism could not come to power largely because peasants supported them. Nor could they remain in power by transcending classes entirely—as Louis Napoleon was able to do quite successfully until the last years of his rule.[18]

There was another factor causing Marx to underestimate Louis Napoleon when he was writing *The Eighteenth Brumaire* and still believed a revival of the 1848 Revolution was possible. Louis Napoleon, notwithstanding Marx's animadversions on his character, effectively dashed his hopes—as it happened, for the rest of his and Engels' lives. But unlike other 'gravediggers' of revolutions that might otherwise have succeeded, Louis adopted the persona of a politician genuinely committed to assuaging the concerns and ameliorating the grievances of the lower classes. To Marx this was mere political posturing, and for that reason he concluded that Louis had not rejected the Revolution of 1848 so much as betrayed it, which made his success in taking power especially infuriating. The 1848 Revolution was for Marx and Engels an opportunity that was lost, rather than an opportunity that never was. Notwithstanding the determinism implicit in their dialectical materialism, Louis Napoleon's victories were by no means preordained. One can easily imagine a scenario in which, at least until he assumed the title and the role of emperor, he could have been stopped had either his supporters or his enemies acted differently.

After the emotional revulsion Marx and Engels felt towards Louis Napoleon diminished, their new-found moderation caused them to disagree about what Bonapartism actually was. In a letter in 1868 to François Lafargue (not to be confused with Marx's son in-law Paul Lafargue), Marx claimed that 'Napoleonic regimes' were founded on the weariness and [political] impotence of 'the two antagonistic classes of society'—by which he meant, of course, the bourgeoisie and the proletariat.[19] This was consistent with what Marx had written six years earlier in a letter to Engels, in which he denigrated his fellow German socialist Ferdinand Lassalle, whom he considered a rival for the affection and support of German workers, as 'an enlightened Bonapartist' for the 'fantasies' he ostensibly harboured about the state encouraging and even sponsoring the establishment of 'producer

[18] For a mostly positive evaluation of the emperor, see Jasper Ridley, *Napoleon III and Eugénie* (New York, 1979), p. 573; Albert Guérard, *Napoleon III* (Cambridge MA, 1943), pp. 281–93; and Theodore Zeldin, 'The Myth of Napoleon III', *History Today* 8, no. 2 (February, 1958): pp. 103–9. A very critical one even locates in the Second Empire the theoretical basis for the totalitarian police states of the twentieth century. Howard C. Payne, 'Theory and Practice of Political Police during the Second Empire in France', *Journal of Modern History* 30, no. 1 (March 1958): p. 23. A more recent and balanced appraisal is Alain Plessis, *The Rise and Fall of the Second Empire 1852–1871* (Cambridge, 1985).

[19] 'Letter, Marx to Lafargue (12 November 1868)', in Marx and Engels, *Collected Works*, vol. XLII, p. 334.

cooperatives' beneficial to the working class.[20] Obscured by Marx's customary sarcasm was the conviction that Bonapartism was a transitory form of statism that could exist only after the entire edifice of industrial capitalism had collapsed in a proletarian revolution, but before a proletarian dictatorship could be established. The hypertrophication of the state Bonapartism entailed was itself morally and politically neutral, and if that was all the phenomenon implied, it would be little different from a proletarian dictatorship. But what distinguished the former from the latter was the particular class or classes it existed to protect. A proletarian dictatorship would benefit the proletariat by nationalizing private property, and in doing so reduce the number of classes to one. This would mean, in effect, that no classes existed, and once a classless society existed, there would no longer be any need for government, which would wither away. Communism would replace socialism, and its arrival would mark the end of history itself.

A Bonapartist dictatorship was different. It was not a virtual facsimile of a proletarian dictatorship. It existed to benefit classes that were not on the 'right side' of history and would do everything in its power to protect their interests and thereby ensure its own survival. In fact, in 'The Civil War in France', Marx's essay on the Paris Commune that appeared less than a month after its suppression, he described a Bonapartist regime as one that treated the people it ruled with a severity that far exceeded that which the bourgeoisie, by means of a bogus democracy that promised the lower classes political power but never provided it, normally needed to maintain its supremacy. In Marx's own phraseology, state power in Bonapartist empires like Louis Napoleon's 'soared high above society'—a formulation suggesting that whoever ruled Bonapartist regimes might have originated in the bourgeoisie but had managed, but in the political power he accumulated had managed to transcend it.[21]

In Engels' later references to Bonapartism one finds a different vision of the relationship between the ruler and the people. While Marx believed this relationship consigned the bourgeoisie to a status only marginally superior to that of all the other classes of society, Engels saw the relationship approximating that between equals. In Engels' conception, the Bonapartist dictator not only remembered the class from which he emerged, but he also perpetuated its privileges. By a process of elimination, the only class capable of producing such rulers was the bourgeoisie. In fact, in a letter to Marx in 1866, Engels described a Bonapartist regime as simply a partial dictatorship in which the dictator remained the political instrument of the bourgeoisie.[22] The dictator clearly had more power than that which a democratically elected leader exercised under capitalism. But the purpose

[20] 'Letter, Marx to Engels (30 July 1862)', ibid., vol. XLI, p. 390; George Lichtheim, *Marxism* (New York, 1969), p. 95.
[21] Karl Marx, 'The Civil War in France', in K. Marx and V. I. Lenin, *Civil War in France: The Paris Commune* (New York, 1968), p. 56.
[22] 'Letter, Engels to Marx (13 April 1866)', in Marx and Engels, *Selected Correspondence*, p. 205.

THE PHANTOM OF THE RUSSIAN BONAPARTE 399

for which this power was employed was effectively the same in both forms of government—not to transcend classes but to benefit one class, the bourgeoisie. In that respect the difference between a bourgeois democracy and a Bonapartist dictatorship was, for Engels, one of degree rather than of kind. The former had less power than the latter, and that, rather than the goal it was employed to achieve, was why the two governments required different names. In the letter, Engels went so far as the characterize Bonapartism as 'a religion of the modern bourgeoisie'—by which he meant an arrangement whereby the bourgeoisie happily acquiesced in the transfer of power from a (bogus) legislature or president to an avowed dictator because he was no less committed than bourgeois democrats to maintaining the bourgeoisie's economic supremacy.[23] Another reason for the bourgeoisie's insouciance was because the Bonapartist dictator, once his political security and prerogatives were assured, would be uniquely able to neutralize the proletariat's hostility by redirecting it onto some other entity, which need not be an economic class; another country would be preferable. As he wrote in 1865, these arrangements were feasible only in certain conditions, which were precisely those that pertained in France after the failure of the 1848 Revolution, namely when the bourgeoisie was too weak and insecure to rule directly, but the proletariat was not yet powerful enough to supersede it by means of a socialist revolution.[24]

In short, there was a quid pro quo in Engels' notion of Bonapartism that was absent in Marx's: in the former, the bourgeoisie relinquished political power to the Bonapartist dictator because it recognized that the dictatorship he personified would refrain from destroying or in any way tampering with the economic advantages capitalism had conferred on it. In Marx's scenario, in other words, the Bonapartist dictator transcended the bourgeoisie, and presumably was more powerful and autonomous as a result, while in Engels' the Bonapartist dictator, for reasons of his own, allowed himself to be the political instrument of the bourgeoisie. Of course the difference in the two men's notions of Bonapartism over the long run was irrelevant to the ultimate result, which remained a proletarian revolution that would destroy both the bourgeoisie and the political arrangements, ranging from bourgeois democracy to a Bonapartist system like Bismarck's or Louis Napoleon's, it contrived to protect its economic dominance. But the inexorable contradictions the dialectic was constantly introducing into history ensured that this dominance could never be permanent. Not even the application of overwhelming military force—which neither Marx nor Engels considered necessary for a Bonapartist regime to exist, though they both thought it might be

[23] Ibid.
[24] Friedrich Engels, *The Prussian Military Question and the German Workers' Party*, cited in Jost Dülffer, 'Bonapartism, Fascism and National Socialism', *Journal of Contemporary History*, no. 11 (1976): p. 111.

necessary in suppressing the proletariat, could achieve this objective. Bonapartism was for Marx and Engels what imperialism was for Lenin, namely a means by which the continuation of capitalism beyond earlier predictions of when it would collapse could be explained.[25] Each was an ad hoc addendum to a theory purporting to explain the future of capitalism. Instead of jettisoning the theory when its predictive powers seemed to have diminished, first Marx and Engels and then, a half-century or so later, Lenin, looked for easy answers that would repair the damage empirical reality had inflicted on the theory they all subscribed to, and reconfirm the inevitability of the glorious end of history in socialism and communism. In sum, Bonapartism domestically and imperialism abroad were expedients enabling industrial capitalism to continue long after its anticipated expiration date.

*   *   *

Of the Mensheviks, Plekhanov was the only one daring enough, prior to the October Revolution, to speculate on the ramifications of Bonapartism somehow manifesting itself either within a socialist party or in a socialist state. Both scenarios, if they came to pass, would cast doubt on Marxism itself. Marx and Engels, it is true, were willing to tamper with their life's work when the terrorists in Russia in the late nineteenth century seemed to offer a means of accelerating the life-cycle of industrial capitalism. But for Marx and Engels the terrorism the Russians practised, by inspiring the peasants to revolt, was a means of achieving socialism and communism more quickly. Bonapartism, by contrast, would delay this or even preclude it. For this reason the two men approached the whole matter of Bonapartism reluctantly; it is also why prior to 1917 the Mensheviks, excepting Plekhanov, avoided it entirely.

In 1904, in the aftermath of Lenin's actions at the Second Congress, in which he called for the creation of a workers' party, in which political authority was centralized and its rank and file expected to follow its dictates unthinkingly, Plekhanov thought it necessary to address the issue. He did so in an essay in *Iskra* published also as a pamphlet entitled *Centralism or Bonapartism*.[26] Its purpose was to distinguish the forms of government each concept implied, and explain why he preferred the former to the latter; in fact, he proudly proclaimed himself its advocate. Plekhanov wrote the essay just when he had begun to harbour doubts about Lenin's commitment to a socialist party based on the eventual dominance of the workers over professional revolutionaries like himself and Lenin once the latter had instilled in the former the revolutionary consciousness necessary for a proletarian revolution to succeed. Prior to that time, these

---

[25] Lenin, *Imperialism.*
[26] G. V. Plekhanov, 'Tsentralizm ili Bonapartizm', *Iskra*, no. 65 (1 May 1904), in Plekhanov, *Sochineniia*, vol. XIII, pp. 81–93.

professional revolutionaries, despite their constituting only a small fraction of the party's membership, would run the party until they had taught the workers everything they needed to know. When that happened, the workers would take over the party. In fact, Lenin—and every Soviet leader that followed him with the partial exception of Gorbachev—never allowed this transfer of power to occur while ruling the Soviet Union, and in the article Plekhanov posited a dichotomy between centralism, which he favoured, and Bonapartism, which he said was what Lenin preferred, as a way of expressing his growing concern that Lenin would rule dictatorially should he ever have the opportunity to do so.

The Bonapartism Plekhanov said Lenin favoured was essentially a means of establishing political dominance by perpetual 'plebiscites' of party members.[27] Paradoxically, this entailed, in Plekhanov's opinion, not so much a rejection of democratic norms as an overuse of them. What Lenin defended as the mere 'canvassing' of members for the purpose of ascertaining their opinions on particular issues Plekhanov considered a de facto form of dictatorship that would inevitably tempt the person leading it to falsify the results of these plebiscites. The result would be a party—and by implication a government should the party come to power in a revolution—that far exceeded the degree to which its power, to be employed successfully, had to be centralized. In 1903 Plekhanov had agreed with Lenin that because a workers' party had no choice but to operate in Russia clandestinely, its leaders in exile in Western Europe had to enjoy a monopoly of political power enabling them to establish policy and to ensure that party cells back in Russia, which were able to communicate with one another only with difficulty or not at all, received word of it. In fact, a party that was functionally Bonapartist stood a far better chance of overcoming this particular obstacle, and generally speaking would function effectively even if it had to do so clandestinely. But the downside of a Bonapartist party was the chance, perhaps even the likelihood, that the dominance of the professional revolutionaries over the workers within the party would be even greater than it would be in a party the structure of which had been 'merely' centralized. Moreover, by 1904 Plekhanov had known Lenin long enough to know that he preferred a Bonapartist party to a centralized one, and for that reason alone any manifestation of an incipient Bonapartism within the recently established RSDLP should be squelched immediately. In Plekhanov's pithy summation of the distinction between the two kinds of parties Russian socialists were considering, a Bonapartist party, in which there was too much centralization, would likely establish 'a dictatorship *over* the proletariat', while a party in which there was just the right degree of centralization would establish 'a dictatorship *of* the proletariat'.[28] For that reason, Plekhanov proudly proclaimed himself 'a centralist, but not a Bonapartist'.[29]

---

[27] Ibid., p. 93.   [28] Ibid., p. 91.   [29] Ibid., p. 92.

For Lenin, Bonapartism and its adjectival derivative were mostly epithets useful in demeaning and defaming political opponents. But this does not mean these words had no substantive meaning for him or that the enemies of his against whom they were directed did not share certain political attributes and aspirations that could plausibly be considered Bonapartist. Lenin's first mention of the term was in a letter in February 1905 to S. I. Gusev and Alexander Bogdanov, the former a strong supporter of Lenin, the latter an eccentric and not entirely reliable one whose belief in the rejuvenation of the deceased tested the limits of Lenin's patience as much as it exceeded the outer limits of Marxist orthodoxy.[30] In the letter, Lenin attacked unnamed enemies as 'Bonapartists' for their recycling calls for a unity congress at which supporters of *Vpered*, the newspaper the Bolsheviks produced, would resolve their differences with supporters of *Iskra*, the official newspaper of the RSDLP, once controlled by Lenin but now run by Mensheviks; the result of all of this would be the restoration of party unity. To Lenin these differences, while more tactical than ideological, were irreconcilable. But that, in his opinion, was actually a virtue as far as the proper functioning of a socialist party was concerned. In addition, the existence within the RSDLP of two separate newspapers, with the Bolsheviks using one of them to express their own opinions, enabled them to remain a discrete and distinguishable faction within the party. By 1905 Lenin's penchant for 'splitting' errant Bolsheviks for their ostensible deviations from Marxist orthodoxy had become a major factor, perhaps the decisive one, in preventing the unity that many within the party desired. Lenin, however, damned them collectively as Bonapartist, presumably because they claimed to transcend the differences within the party the way both Bonapartes had done in France.[31] Their supposedly noble intentions Lenin dismissed as a form of moral preening inconsistent with the hard-nosed realism he preferred; whether this was a quality the two French emperors shared was not something Lenin considered appropriate for discussion.

One month later, in an article in *Vpered* entitled 'The Tricks of the Bonapartists', Lenin went further, claiming now that the elements within the party that wanted a party congress were intent on holding one even without the Party Council's approval—which under the rules of the party would be illegal. But the Party Council, for its part, was hardly blameless. According to Lenin, it sought to rig the process by which delegates to any forthcoming party congress would be accredited. Indeed, both of these party organs—and by implication the party as a whole—were acting in violation of their own procedures, and for that reason, presumably, warranted the appellation Lenin used in the title—but nowhere in the text—to condemn them.[32] As a result, the reader, while finding abundant evidence for the presumption that all Bonapartists, for one reason or another, were bad,

[30] V. I. Lenin, 'Pis'mo A. A. Bogdanovu i S. I. Gusevu', in Lenin, *PSS*, vol. IX, pp. 244–8.
[31] Ibid., vol. IX, p. 245.   [32] V. I. Lenin, 'Prodelki Bonapartistov', ibid., vol. IX, pp. 362–6.

could not glean from the article any understanding of what Bonapartism actually was. Finally, in an article three years later on why the agrarian reforms proposed by Pëtr Stolypin would make the radicalization of the Russian peasantry more likely rather than less so, as the tsarist minister intended, Lenin supplied a definition. That it now had a specific meaning, however, did not mean that Lenin no longer considered it useful as an all-purpose political epithet:

> Bonapartism [Lenin wrote] is the manoeuvring on the part of a monarchy which has lost its old patriarchal or feudal, simple and solid foundation—a monarchy which is obliged to walk a tightrope in order not to fall, to make advances in order to govern, to bribe in order to please, and to fraternise with the dregs of society, with outright thieves and swindlers, in order not to rely only on bayonets. Bonapartism is the objectively necessary evolution of the monarchy in any bourgeois country, traced by Marx and Engels through an entire series of events in the modern history of Europe.[33]

Bonapartism, in other words, was for Lenin a generic phenomenon, not limited to France or Russia, even though these were the two countries where it manifested itself most clearly. Nor was it particular to revolutionary politics. Governments, even reactionary ones like Stolypin's, could manifest it. But for Lenin its application always reflected the primacy he ascribed in politics to treachery and betrayal, which for him were as much a reflection of an intensely personal duplicity and mendacity as it was generic behaviour informed by the requirements of class. In this instance, however, it was meant to suggest the practice—which Lenin obviously believed Louis Napoleon had originated in France—of tricking people impoverished by their own reactionary government into believing any reforms it proposed were designed to help them, rather than to ensure their obedience when these reforms, inevitably, made their lives worse rather than better. But with more than a hint of bravado, Lenin then reassured his readers that this kind of massive deception could not be effective indefinitely, and that in Russia it would not save the monarchy—which was Stolypin's underlying objective—no matter how attractively his reforms were packaged and presented to the Russian people. In fact, Stolypin, quite unintentionally, was bent on carrying out the equivalent of a bourgeois revolution in the Russian countryside, and while like bourgeois revolutions in Western Europe his reforms might improve conditions temporarily, over the long run they would worsen them to the point where the peasants would willingly support urban workers in a proletarian revolution. According to Lenin, after promising a legislature in 1905 to defuse the passions the revolution in that year had unleashed, the monarchy was now using the actual legislature it had created in 1906 to legitimize agrarian reforms designed to trick the peasants into supporting a government that actually loathed them. This kind of mendacity,

---

[33] V. I. Lenin, 'Ob otsenke tekushchego momenta', ibid., vol. XVII, pp. 273–4.

Lenin concluded, was the essence of Bonapartism, even though oppressive governments that were configured differently might act just as perfidiously. In his words, 'the Russian autocracy wanted to be covered up, dressed up, and decked out with the help of the Duma'.[34] But the repression the Duma was intended to conceal could not mask the autocracy's real objectives indefinitely. In fact, 'each day of [the Duma's] existence revealed, exposed, and uncovered the true character of our state power, its actual class foundations, and its Bonapartism'.[35] What made this particular reference to Bonapartism distinctive was that Lenin mentioned it separately from the whole issue of class, implying that Bonapartism had more to do with how a government functioned—in this instance in a fashion that was especially, even uniquely, deceitful and prevaricating—than with its social composition.

But describing the class or classes of which Bonapartism was a political manifestation was not the reason Lenin wrote the article. His objective was more political than analytical. In 1908 the fortunes of the Bolsheviks were perhaps at their lowest point during the twelve years between the two revolutions Russia experienced in the beginning of the twentieth century, and the future Soviet leader felt a special obligation to conjure a scenario promising imminent rather than long-term success. Accordingly, Lenin sketched out in the article the sequence of events that had already begun in Russia that he believed would occur in any country—excluding of course those that were already socialist—where the government, like Louis Napoleon's in France in the mid-nineteenth century, was making a concerted effort to save itself. But the feudalism the Russian monarchy existed to preserve was destined soon to collapse, and there was nothing Stolypin could do to prevent it. The most Bonapartist policies like Stolypin's could achieve was delay. Of course whether Lenin actually believed this is a matter of pure conjecture. Nevertheless, one can plausibly speculate that he excoriated Stolypin's reforms—which were Bonapartist both because they were imposed on Russian peasants unilaterally and because they were intended to perpetuate a reactionary regime in power—because he feared they might actually work. Had Stolypin lived to a ripe old age instead of falling victim to an assassin's bullet three years after Lenin's article appeared, he might well have been the first Bonapartist in power to have avoided the total defeat his prototypical predecessors had suffered at Waterloo and Sedan respectively. It was not for nothing that Lenin, who habitually disparaged Nicholas II as 'the idiot Romanov', genuinely, if grudgingly, respected Stolypin and at some level feared him for recognizing that a peasantry that was 'sobre and strong' might allow the Russian monarchy to endure.[36]

---

[34] Ibid., vol. XVII, p. 276.   [35] Ibid., vol. XVII, p. 276.
[36] V. I. Lenin, 'Rech' v Moskovskom sovete rabochikh, krest'ianskikh i krasnoarmeiskikh deputatov 12 marta g.', ibid., vol. XXXVI, p. 85; Wolfe, *Three Who Made a Revolution*, p. 359. The latter phrase was Stolypin's.

Several months after Lenin had identified Stolypin's reforms as a species of Bonapartism, he commented on a draft resolution on 'the tasks of the party' at a party conference—not to be confused with the party congresses, which were better attended and dealt with more consequential matters—and once again used the same sobriquet to render them, in his mind at least, ineffectual and ephemeral. This time, however, he called them 'bourgeois Bonapartist' rather than simply 'Bonapartist'.[37] By doing so Lenin seemed to be suggesting—regardless of whether the adjective was applicable in the case of Stolypin—that Bonapartism was descriptive not only of a feudal government like Russia's attempting to carry out a bourgeois revolution without its attendant violence, but other kinds of governments ruling countries at different stages of historical development. But like his earlier articles on the same subject, this one stressed that Stolypin's reforms could never work, and instead would actually accelerate the political radicalization of the poorest peasants, mostly by increasing the distance economically between affluent peasants and impoverished ones. In the end, the monarchy, ironically, would be Stolypin's reforms' most obvious casualty—or so Lenin believed despite his isolation as a powerless exile in Western Europe.

In the years prior to 1917, Lenin provided a fairly detailed and easily understandable description and analysis of Bonapartism. But there was one aspect of his definition of the term that was conspicuous in its absence. Nowhere in his writings of those years did Lenin ever suggest that Bonapartism had a military component: that Bonapartist regimes, to warrant their adjectival descriptive, had to be headed either by a member of the military—in all likelihood a general or, at the very least, an officer—or by a civilian who needed the military's support to come to power and remain in power. However, in the very different political environment that pertained in 1917, the military would occupy a prominent place in both Lenin's conception of the term and his use of it for political purposes.

*   *   *

Lenin did not arrive at his newfound conclusion that Bonapartism, to be taxonomically distinct, required the involvement of the military—and that Napoleon Bonaparte rather than Louis Napoleon was therefore the more appropriate precedent of a Bonapartist dictator—in a vacuum. In Russia in 1917, after the monarchy fell, there was talk, much of it grounded in fear, of a Russian Bonaparte, and when Russians spoke about the imminence of Bonapartism, the precedent they had in mind was not the second Napoleon—the Napoleon of Marx and Engels, and until recently of Lenin himself—but rather the first one.[38]

---

[37] V. I. Lenin, 'Proekt rezoliutsii o sovremennom momente i zadachakh partii 21–7 dekabria 1908 g.', in Lenin, *PSS*, vol. XVII, p. 325.

[38] Beatty, *Red Heart of Russia*, p. 155; Pauline Crosley, *Intimate Letters from Petrograd* (New York, 1920), p. 58. Not surprisingly, some in the army hoped a Russian Napoleon would emerge from their ranks even before the monarchy collapsed. Shlapentokh, *Counter-Revolution in Revolution*, pp. 31–3.

Alexander Kerensky, after becoming prime minister of the Provisional Government in the summer, was the political figure most commonly thought to aspire to that particular role. That he had adopted some of the accoutrements of military service, such as suspending one of his arms in a sling, which wrongly suggested that he had been wounded in combat, was certainly a factor in sustaining this perception.[39] But concern that the February Revolution would be betrayed in much the way the two Napoleons turned against the revolutions that had made their rise to power possible long preceded Kerensky's elevation from the Ministry of Justice. In fact, the infamous Order Number 1—issued by the Petrograd Soviet almost immediately after its creation calling on soldiers and sailors to contravene duly-issued orders of their officers—was intended to preclude a military dictatorship many thought would resemble Napoleon's.[40] In reality, there was good reason for concern. The anarchy that engulfed Russia in the spring and summer of 1917 created a political vacuum that the Russian military, either on the orders of one of its own leaders or at the behest of a civilian using the army to advance his own interests, could easily have filled—if it did not itself disintegrate as peasants in uniform seeking land simply left their units and journeyed home in the expectation of a monumental 'black repartition'. To be sure, the substitution of the first Napoleon for the second as the original inspiration for the dictatorship many in Russia considered the only alternative to anarchy, made it possible for much of the left in Russia to view a Bonapartist dictatorship favourably, seeing it as a continuation and a deepening of the February Revolution, rather than a betrayal of it. Bonaparte, in the minds of most Russian liberals and socialists, had done much that was progressive and beneficial before becoming an incorrigible imperialist brought down, in the end (after his generalship had deteriorated just as his belief in his own infallibility was reaching megalomaniacal dimensions) more by his successes than by his failures.[41]

Viktor Chernov, the leader of the SR Party, was the most prominent of those on the left who, in the summer of 1917, stated his preference for a 'Russian Bonaparte' replacing the Provisional Government and taking steps to eliminate, or at least to reduce significantly, the anarchy engulfing Russia; that the Russian army was suffering defeats that threatened to cause its complete disintegration

---

But trepidation at the same prospect was more prevalent. In the summer of 1917—to cite just one example—Bolsheviks in Saratov saw 'Napoleonic tendencies' in the Mensheviks there. Donald J. Raleigh, *Revolution on the Volga: 1917 in Saratov* (Ithaca NY, 1986), p. 147.

---

[39] Sukhanov, *Russian Revolution*, p. 362. In fact Kerensky suffered from bursitis in his shoulder, which does not exclude his using his condition for political purposes.

[40] Allan K. Wildman, *The End of the Russian Army: The Old Army and the Soldiers' Revolt (March–April 1917)* (Princeton NJ, 1980), vol. I, p. 3. Wildman does not mention Napoleon as the model of a presumptive military dictator, but many in Petrograd considered him as such irrespective of whether they favoured a military dictatorship or opposed it.

[41] Andrew Roberts, *Napoleon: A Life* (New York, 2014), especially pp. 555–802.

failed to lessen his enthusiasm for such an outcome.[42] In Chernov's preferred scenario, a Russian replica of the original Napoleon would come to power in a 'a dry putsch', by which he meant a *coup d'état* blessed, incongruously, by the government it deposed; that Napoleon's coup in 1799 came close to approximating such an unusual transfer of political authority may have inured Chernov to the oxymoronic implications of a legal *coup d'état*, and more importantly the unlikelihood of an army beset by mass desertions and discredited by battlefield defeats having the wherewithal to come to power legally or in any other way.[43] But this was what Chernov believed. Once in power, whoever was playing the role of the Russian Bonaparte would proceed to take steps Chernov believed would eventuate in socialism. Bonapartism, in sum, was a good thing and Russian socialists would be wise to do what they could to assist in its realization.

But for most Russian socialists the prospect of a Napoleonic *dénouement* to the February Revolution, whether in the form of a military dictatorship like Napoleon Bonaparte's or a civilian-led regime resembling Louis Napoleon's, was perhaps the worst possible outcome. Like their French precursors, such a ruler in Russia would mouth progressive rhetoric to mask policies that were mostly or uniformly reactionary. The element of trickery that for Lenin was an essential element of Bonapartism was present in how many others on the left conceived it. V. I. Talin, writing in June in *Rabochaia gazeta*, warned his readers that aspiring dictators in Russia might claim to represent ordinary people, but should they do so, they would be no more truthful and honest than Louis Napoleon had been before becoming the emperor of France.[44] Other than Kerensky and General Alexei Brusilov, who briefly was feared to be the Russian Bonaparte in the weeks preceding the October Revolution, only General Lavr Kornilov, who lacked the political intelligence necessary to play the role successfully, came to mind after his army's marching northward from Ukraine to Petrograd in August seemed the first step towards supplanting the Provisional Government; as it happened, his army was quickly disarmed by forces loyal to the government in the beginning of September.[45] It remains unclear what his intentions were: he might have ordered his army to Petrograd not to overthrow the civilian government, but to assist it in defending the capital against an anticipated German offensive, the fear of which caused Kerensky to request assistance from Kornilov (and to permit the Bolsheviks to form the semi-military detachments that would eventually overthrow him) in the first place.

What this not-so-humorous comedy of errors revealed, as far as Russian Bonapartism was concerned, was how minimal a threat it actually posed to the

---

[42] Chernov, *The Great Russian Revolution*, p. 336.   [43] Ibid.
[44] V. I. Talin, 'Ulitsy', *Rabochaia gazeta*, no. 80 (14 June 1917): p. 2.
[45] Shlapentokh, *Counter-Revolution in Revolution*, p. 77; Beatty, *Red Heart of Russia*, p. 148. Whether Lenin, who at times showed discernment in his evaluation of people, considered Kornilov a potential Napoleon, is not known. Stefan T. Possony, *Lenin: The Compulsive Revolutionary* (Chicago IL, 1964), p. 237.

Provisional Government and to the February Revolution. One is struck by Kerensky's political ineptitude in 1917, exaggerating the threat the army posed to his government, while minimizing the threat posed by the Bolsheviks, and through all of this acting and speaking in ways that caused himself to be considered, in the guise of the Russian Bonaparte, the most likely gravedigger of the revolution. That the prime minister never actually harboured any desire or intention to carry out a Russian equivalent of 18 Brumaire was beside the point in light of the political situation that existed in Russia in 1917. Kerensky was perceived as willing and able to do precisely that, and when Lenin, despite his repeated denigrations of the prime minister as 'a tiny Bonaparte', vowed publicly in late September 'to drive out the Bonapartist gang' of Kerensky with its fake 'pre-parliament', the threat Lenin was referring to seemed to many Russians, especially those on the political left, a credible one.[46] That Tsereteli, in September, felt compelled to defend Kerensky in the pages of *Izvestiia* against Trotsky's charge that the prime minister was 'the mathematical centre of Russian Bonapartism' attests to the fear of a coup engineered with the support of the military that, despite the absence of empirical evidence to sustain it, was pervasive in the Russian capital.[47] The result was that an exaggerated threat, namely that of a Russian 18 Brumaire, to the February Revolution and the Provisional Government caused many to minimize or ignore a very real threat, namely that from the Bolsheviks. Among those who did so was Kerensky himself. Cognizant of his own intentions, which precluded any illusions that he was somehow a Bonaparte in waiting, he nonetheless considered very seriously the likelihood of someone else in Russia emerging to play that particular role. By doing so, he rendered himself virtually oblivious to Lenin's public threats to overthrow him.

The role the fear of Bonapartism played in the Russian Revolutions of 1917 was not inconsiderable. For some, such as Kerensky, it affected their political judgement, specifically their calculations about which of the real dangers to the February Revolution and the Provisional Government threatened them the most. That the fear afflicting Kerensky and those who shared his trepidation might prove debilitating, and work to the advantage of their political enemies, only increased its potential in causing the Provisional Government itself to unravel. Lenin, for one, was well aware of how much the spectre of Russian Bonapartism haunted the non-Bolshevik left—mainly liberals, Socialist Revolutionaries, and the Mensheviks—in 1917. Always the political opportunist, he knew exactly how to take advantage of it. The result was that a year that began with a liberal revolution ended with a

[46] Quoted in Chernov, *The Great Russian Revolution*, p. 305; quoted in Leon Trotsky, *History of the Russian Revolution*, unabridged edition (Chicago IL, 1932), p. 607.
[47] 'Rech' Tsereteli', *Izvestiia*, no. 176 (20 September 1917): p. 3. In May 1917 Trotsky had implied that this description of Kerensky, while 'superficial', was nonetheless accurate; there is no reason to believe he changed his mind in the months that followed. Leon Trotsky, 'The Revolution in Crisis', in Lenin and Trotsky, *Proletarian Revolution in Russia*, p. 249.

regime in power in Russia led by illiberal Marxist ideologues committed to the establishment of communism not only in Russia but everywhere, and irrespective of the cost in human life.

*   *   *

One should not assume that Lenin's understanding of Bonapartism, as a means of seizing power, emerged *ex nihilo* in 1917. Nor should one infer that the events of that year had no effect on it. Lenin's notion of what Bonapartism was—and what it was not—was dynamic. It evolved in response to the ever-changing political realities in Russia in that year, with the result that by autumn he could propose an insurrection reasonably confident there was no one in Russia capable of acting as a Russian Bonaparte and suppressing it. Lenin's first attempt, albeit brief, to explain what the term suggested and whether it was applicable to Russia in 1917 was in May, when, in an article in *Pravda* entitled 'In Search of Napoleon', he pointed to Kerensky's recent call for 'iron discipline' in the army as evidence that either he or an unnamed general might 'take upon himself the role of a Napoleon, the role of a strangler of freedom, the role of an executioner of the workers'.[48] On whether that was likely or not, Lenin was silent. But it is notable that his conception of a Russian Bonaparte was capacious enough to include both a civilian (like Louis Napoleon) and a general or military officer (like Napoleon Bonaparte) taking power against little or no opposition and then betraying the lower classes who supported them.

In considering Lenin's evolving views on Bonapartism, one must bear in mind that many articles of his predicting the course of events in Russia did not include the word itself, which might plausibly be considered evidence that he did not consider a Bonapartist regime a possibility in Russia before the Bolsheviks seized power themselves. Another explanation, less plausible than the first, is that he thought an attempt to establish such a regime so obviously inevitable that he felt no need to use the term to inform his readers of this. Yet another explanation is that he refrained from using the term because he was not entirely sure in his own mind what was meant by it.

But when Lenin did use the term, it was always in derision, not just of the individual playing the role of the Russian Napoleon, who was almost always Kerensky, but of those who foolishly supported him. That was certainly the case in an article Lenin wrote at the end of July, in which he denigrated Kerensky as a Bonapartist but directed most of his rhetorical fusillades at the liberals, the SRs, and the Mensheviks supporting him.[49] The only politically sophisticated and perspicacious individuals or group of individuals in Russia who were doing so, according to Lenin, were the capitalists, who recognized that while Kerensky's

---

[48] V. I. Lenin, 'Ishchut Napoleona', in Lenin, *PSS*, vol. XXXII, p. 61.
[49] V. I. Lenin, 'Uroki revoliutsii', ibid., vol. XXXIV, pp. 55–69.

Bonapartism required him to proclaim mendaciously his intention to benefit all classes in Russia, it also ensured that only the capitalists would benefit from his actual policies. Accordingly, Kerensky's recent establishment of a coalition government, which presumably precluded its advancing the interests of a particular class, was actually a subterfuge concealing his commitment to the interests and welfare of the bourgeoisie. Since 1848 the capitalists had shown themselves adept at 'fooling, dividing, and weakening the workers' in this particular way whenever they realized that ruling the workers directly would be counterproductive and even conducive of a proletarian revolution that would destroy them.[50] In that respect, Bonapartism, was effective in delaying—but not preventing indefinitely—its own demise.

The title of another article written at the end of July—'The Beginning of Bonapartism'—was all one needed to know that Lenin believed an effort to establish Bonapartism in Russia was already underway.[51] Kerensky, of course, was leading it, and Lenin specified the actions the prime minister was taking with the approval of his cabinet that warranted the application of the term: 'the manoeuvring of state power, relying on a military clique (that is, on the worst elements of the army) for support, between two hostile classes and forces [here one presumes Lenin means the bourgeoisie and the proletariat] which more or less balance each other out'.[52] The recent July Days, during which Lenin, on the spur of the moment, tried unsuccessfully to transform street demonstrations in Petrograd into a coordinated seizure of power were surely what prompted his disquisition. In Lenin's scenario, the leader of a Russian 18 Brumaire need not have been an army officer; a civilian supported by the army was sufficient to warrant the application of Bonapartist terminology.

What distinguished the article from earlier ones was Lenin's statement that 'Bonapartism in Russia is no accident but a natural product of the development of class struggle in a petit-bourgeois country with capitalism considerably developed and also a revolutionary proletariat'.[53] This, it would seem, was Lenin's way of expressing his pessimism about the Bolsheviks' prospects after the fiasco earlier in the month, which required him to seek refuge in Finland, the semi-independence of which within the Russian empire afforded him a measure of protection after the extent of his collaboration with Germany, which had enabled his return to Russia several months earlier, became known. But once having acknowledged that Bonapartism was a natural concomitant of capitalism, rather than the aberration Marx and Engels had considered it, Lenin felt compelled—perhaps to restore his own peace of mind even more than that of his readers'—to predict that any incipient Bonapartism in Russia was likely to disappear; all that was needed for that to happen was for 'the working class and the people as a whole ... to wage a

[50]   Ibid., vol. XXXIV, p. 63.   [51]   V. I. Lenin, 'Nachalo Bonapartizma', ibid., vol. XXXIV, pp. 48–52.
[52]   Ibid., vol. XXXIV, p. 49.   [53]   Ibid., vol. XXXIV, p. 50.

struggle on a large political scale and based on far-reaching class interests'.[54] The very fact that 'the Russian Bonapartism of 1917 differed in several respects from the beginnings of French Bonapartism in 1799 and 1849' was for Lenin reason enough to conclude that the former would last not nearly as long as the latter.[55] Because Bonapartism in France had emerged, in Lenin's conception of the French Revolution, five years after the revolution ended (on 9 Thermidor), it was strengthened by the reforms the revolution had put in place. Bonapartism in Russia, by contrast, emerged barely months after Russia's revolution had begun, and thus had no real achievements it could point to or promise to continue in gaining the political support it needed to succeed.

In the articles mentioning Bonapartism written closer to the October Revolution, Lenin made clear his growing confidence in the Bolsheviks taking power—thereby ending quickly and decisively the incipient or proto-Bonapartism that, in the person of Kerensky, was the political instrument of the Russian bourgeoisie, and supported 'objectively' by ersatz socialists like the SRs and the Mensheviks. In an article written for *Rabochii put'* near the end of September, Lenin noted that Kerensky was 'revealing himself more and more as a Bonapartist'.[56] But his policies by now were indistinguishable from those of the Kadets. Even worse—but advantageous to the Bolsheviks because their essence as *faux* revolutionaries was now apparent—was that 'the Plekhanovs, the Breshkovskaias, and the Potresovs' had finally revealed, by the identity of their views with Kerensky's and those of the Kadets, the full extent of their own ideological degeneration.[57] The ultimate result of this kind of Bonapartism in Russia, Lenin seemed to be saying, was an ideological cesspool containing the refuse of an illiberal liberalism and the putrid remains of socialists who, by not supporting the Bolsheviks, had shown themselves not to be socialists at all.

After the October Revolution, the question Lenin had to address was not whether the Bolsheviks' opponents manifested evidence of Bonapartism, but whether the government he was establishing did so. This elevated the stakes in the debate. Marx and Engels had made clear they considered Bonapartism a phenomenon existing only under capitalism; acknowledging that it could appear under socialism, or even during the proletarian dictatorship that preceded it, was to provide the proletariat's enemies an easy way of questioning the legitimacy of its revolution and the interim arrangements immediately following it. Moreover, the appearance of Bonapartism after the demise of capitalism would be proof that Marx and Engels had been wrong—that their description of history as linear and progressive was deficient. It was one thing for the Bolsheviks to call Kerensky the

[54] Ibid., vol. XXXIV, p. 51.   [55] Ibid., vol. XXXIV, p. 51.
[56] V. I. Lenin, 'O geroiakh podloga i ob oshibkakh Bol'shevikov', ibid., vol. XXXIV, p. 250.
[57] Ibid., vol. XXXIV, p. 250.

Russian Bonaparte. For non-Bolshevik socialists to call Lenin the Russian Bonaparte and his regime a form of Bonapartism was something else entirely.

Lenin was well aware of this, and his naturally combative nature did not fail him in rejecting the charge whenever it was levelled in the aftermath of the October Revolution. In fact, he had sufficient confidence that the new regime he was stablishing bore no resemblance to a Bonapartist one that he freely indulged in comparisons with the original Bonaparte when he considered them conducive to optimism about the new Soviet state. In his report to the Seventh Congress, barely days after the Bolsheviks had signed the treaty at Brest-Litovsk ending hostilities with Germany, in which they lost large amounts of territory rich in natural resources, Lenin analogized the treaty to that which Napoleon and Alexander I had agreed to at Tilsit in 1809.[58] The Bolsheviks, he freely admitted, would violate the treaty with the Germans just as Alexander did the agreement he signed with Napoleon. The difference was that while Napoleon became aware very quickly of the tsar's mendacity, Lenin would make sure that, in the case of Brest-Litovsk, the Germans would be unaware, at least for a while, of the Bolsheviks' violations of it. Lenin's confidence in his ability to outwit his enemies was not, however, unlimited. In the same report, Lenin acknowledged that the survival of the new Soviet regime was by no means certain, and that the Germans, if sufficiently provoked, could 'reduce the Soviet people to slavery'.[59]

By April 1918, Lenin's confidence that the Bolsheviks would not be overthrown militarily, in a *coup d'état* or in any other fashion, had returned. At a session of the Executive Committee of the Communist Party, he angrily rejected as 'verbal trickery' the charge levelled against him by Martov from outside the party, and by Bukharin and the Left Communists inside it, that a dictatorship like Louis Napoleon's or Julius Caesar's was possible.[60] In a subtle portent of the prosecutor demonizing defendants in the Show Trials of the 1930s, Lenin insinuated that Martov and the Bolsheviks supporting Bukharin might be coordinating their actions for maximum effect, namely by 'providing materials for a hundred historical issues that no one will read'.[61] Nevertheless, the Bolsheviks loyal to Lenin had to be especially vigilant. In '"Left-Wing" Childishness', published in *Pravda* and as a pamphlet in May 1918, the Soviet leader cautioned readers— without using the term itself—that the threat of Bonapartism, in the form of either a military dictatorship or a civilian dictatorship supported primarily by the military, should not be taken lightly. Potential Napoleons, he wrote, might find support from 'petty-proprietors' like those in France that supported Louis Napoleon and General Cavaignac, the latter of whom by that time having replaced

[58]   V. I. Lenin, 'Politicheskii otchet tsentral'nogo komiteta 7 marta', ibid., vol. XXXVI, pp. 22–3.
[59]   Ibid., vol. XXXVI, p. 23.
[60]   V. I. Lenin, 'Zakliuchitel'noe slovo po dokadu ob ocherednykh zadachakh sovetskoi vlasti', ibid., vol. XXXVI, p. 270.
[61]   Ibid., vol. XXXVI, p. 271.

Julius Caesar in Lenin's mind as an antecedent whose successful ascent to power might inspire the nefarious forces currently threatening the Bolsheviks.[62] In 1918 Lenin's animus towards French imperialism and capitalism descended to even lower depths of rhetorical vituperation. In an article in July Lenin included twenty-two calumnious references in what was nineteen pages of text when the article was republished in the fifth edition of his *Complete Collected Works*.[63] In the article, Lenin identified France, after the treaty the Bolsheviks had signed at Brest-Litovsk, as their most dangerous external enemy, and after the civil war began a few months later, as the Whites' most reliable and helpful supporter. The iniquity implicit in this was, to Lenin, especially reprehensible because the country responsible for it had previously generated an entire tradition of revolution, the mere existence of which presaged the day when the capitalism and imperialism causing wars like the First World War and the Russian Civil War were a thing of the past.

During the civil war, Lenin's fears of a Bonapartist coup or insurrection were to some extent a function of the Bolsheviks' fortunes. By March 1919, when the Eighth Party Congress convened in Petrograd, these had deteriorated considerably. In the theses the congress adopted, which could not have been approved had they not replicated Lenin's opinions, what henceforth will be referred to as Soviet Bonapartism was the object of some attention and cause for considerable concern:

> The agitation carried on from the camp of the bourgeois democrats (the SRs and Mensheviks) against the Red Army, as a manifestation of 'militarism' and the basis for creeping Bonapartism, is only an expression of political ignorance or charlatanism, or a mixture of both. Bonapartism is not a product of military organization as such, but a product of particular social relations. The political rule of the petit-bourgeoisie, standing between the reactionary big-bourgeois elements and the revolutionary proletarian lower orders, are not yet capable of playing an independent political role or of exercising political rule, provided the necessary prerequisite for the rise of Bonapartism, which found its bulwark in the prosperous peasantry and rose about the class contradictions which had not been solved by the revolutionary programme of petit-bourgeois democracy.[64]

But while the threat Bonapartism posed to the Soviet regime was real, there was reason to believe it could be neutralized and then eliminated entirely:

> In so far as the foundation of Bonapartism is the *kulaks* [the stratum of slightly more affluent peasants adept at capitalist practices], to that extent the very social

[62] V. I. Lenin, 'O "levom" rebiachestve i o melkoburzhuaznosti', ibid., vol. XXXVI, p. 298.

[63] V. I. Lenin, 'Rech' na ob"edinennom zasedanii VTsIK, Moskovskogo Soveta, fabrichno-zavodskikh komitetov i professional'nykh soiuzov Moskvy 29 Iulia 1918 g.', ibid., vol. XXXVII, pp. 1–19.

[64] L. Trotsky, 'Our Policy in Creating the Army', in *The Military Writings and Speeches of Leon Trotsky* (Moscow, 1979), vol. I, pp. 252–3.

composition of our army, from which the kulaks are excluded and have been driven out, furnishes a very effective guarantee against Bonapartist tendencies. The Russian parodies of Bonapartism, in the form of the Krasnov movement, the Kolchak movement, and so on, emerged not from within the Red Army but in direct and open struggle against it.[65]

In light of how both the Bolsheviks and their ideological and political enemies on the left, most notably the Mensheviks, would define and describe Soviet Bonapartism in the 1920s and thereafter, it is worth noting that Lenin clearly considered Bonapartism not just a reactionary phase within the life-cycle of a socialist country, from which it could easily recover, but in certain circumstances a form of counter-revolution requiring for its elimination a revolution like that in Russia in 1917. While for Lenin Bonapartism could be avoided if the Bolsheviks listened to him and followed his counsel, the consequences of their not doing so would be severe, and remediable only with great difficulty and at considerable cost.

*   *   *

Any analysis of Lenin's views on Bonapartism after the October Revolution must take into account the fact that non-Bolshevik socialists in both Russia and Western Europe were already attacking the regime he was establishing on precisely the grounds that it was, in one way or another, Bonapartist. Of course these socialists did not agree on what Bonapartism was any more than they did on the institutional arrangements a Bonapartist state would adopt. But for all of them the term was a pejorative, usually invoked to explain or corroborate their assertion that the Bolsheviks had betrayed the goal that as socialists they presumably aspired to, namely the creation of a society in which authoritarianism of any kind, not just that resembling the dictatorships the two Napoleons had established, was absent. Where they differed was in ascertaining the causes and consequences of this particular form of authoritarianism. More specifically, these non-Bolshevik socialists considered it especially necessary to ascertain if Bonapartism, as they defined it, advanced the interests of one class, several classes, or no classes. And when it came to determining what should be done to halt or reverse the Bonapartism that might exist or be imminent in the Soviet Union, there was no more agreement than there was on why it would appear in the Soviet Union in the first place. Nevertheless, in what these critics wrote about Bonapartism one could find insights into what they thought of the Soviet Union itself— which, in turn, often prompted angry rebuttals and denunciations from the Bolsheviks themselves.

In January 1918 the Bolsheviks, after only one day's deliberations, disbanded the Constituent Assembly—in the elections for which the year before, they finished second, behind the SRs, who won a plurality. Several SRs thought that that would cause the new Bolshevik government to fall—thereby precluding any need to overthrow it—and that they would form the government that followed it. But others in the SR party were not so optimistic. Some thought a form of Bonapartism, with its leadership drawn from the military, would emerge instead. Others feared that the hypertrophied state the Bolsheviks were constructing would enable it to survive the dissolution of the assembly and might even cause the Bolsheviks to become, to all intents and purposes, Bonapartists themselves. In assessing which of these two forms of Bonapartism was the lesser evil, some SRs preferred non-Bolshevik Bonapartism because they believed it would be less effective than Bolshevik Bonapartism in suppressing what the SRs considered the peasants' innate predisposition to socialism. But others disagreed. In fact, some of the SRs in Samara stopped opposing the Bolsheviks because they believed that 'a right-wing dictatorship' would be worse.[66]

Other critics of the Bolsheviks, who offered different alternatives to the nascent Soviet state, had no difficulty concluding it was Bonapartist or would likely become so in the future. Nikolai Ustrialov predicted flatly that once the Soviet Union had degenerated into a form of Jacobinism, it would degenerate further into 'Napoleonism', which he said would carry out what in *Smena vekh* he called 'an economic Brest-Litovsk' to underscore the degree to which Bonapartism entailed a betrayal of Bolshevism.[67] Karl Kautsky, in 1918, thought that what Ustrialov predicted was already happening: because the Bolsheviks represented only a portion of the proletariat—the Mensheviks and the SRs enjoyed the allegiance of the remainder of it—they had no choice but to rule through a one-party dictatorship that might eventuate in a Bonapartist form of government because, like the Jacobins in 1793, it was centralizing political power in Russia to the requisite degree.[68] In his words, 'the dictatorship of the lower classes gives way to the dictatorship of the sword'.[69] Three years later he stated flatly that this process was complete, and that the Soviet Union was de facto a Bonapartist regime. The coercive institutions of the Soviet state, most obviously the Cheka, were now even more powerful than they were at the height of the Civil War, and had so insinuated themselves into every aspect of personal life in the Soviet Union that they were deciding the kinds of food and how much of it people ate. But they still bore a striking resemblance to the police Napoleon had used to root out

---

[66] Leonard Schapiro, *The Origin of the Communist Autocracy: Political Opposition in the Soviet State—First Phase 1917–1922* (Cambridge MA, 1977), p. 355. Shlapentokh, *Counter-Revolution in Revolution*, p. 110.

[67] Quoted in Peter J. S. Duncan, 'Changing Landmarks? Anti-Westernism in National Bolshevik and Russian Revolutionary Thought', in *Russian Nationalism Past and Present*, edited by Geoffrey Hosking and Robert Service (London, 1998), p. 57; Ustrialov, 'Patriotika', p. 63.

[68] The other outcome Kautsky considered possible was a government like Cromwell's in England. Kautsky, *Dictatorship of the Proletariat*, p. 58.

[69] Ibid.

traitors and crush political dissent.[70] In 1930, Kautsky reaffirmed his earlier analogy between Bolshevism and Bonapartism, claiming now that 'if one wants to establish parallels between the last Russian Revolution and the first French one, then the Bolsheviks should be compared not to the Jacobins, but to the Bonapartists.'[71] In 1931, Kautsky went further, proclaiming that Bolshevism and Bonapartism were not morally comparable. Bolshevism was worse. Whereas Bonapartism in France had defended and maintained the economic status quo it inherited from the Directory, in the Soviet Union the Bolsheviks not only have destroyed 'the political conquests of the revolution', but by subjugating the trade unions and factory councils, they have 'enveloped the entire apparatus of production within the straitjacket of a bureaucracy as incompetent as it was corrupt and arbitrary. As a result the economy is condemned to complete ruin.'[72]

But the critics to whom the Bolsheviks responded most vehemently whenever the issue of their ostensible Bonapartism was raised were the Mensheviks, many of whom had known Lenin for many years, even decades in the case of Martov and Pavel Axelrod. For that reason their criticisms, however ineffectual in turning public opinion in the Soviet Union against the Bolsheviks, stung them sufficiently to warrant rhetorical reprisals, and after the suppression of the Kronstadt Revolt in 1921, the formal suppression of their political party. The Mensheviks were also among the first to attack the Bolsheviks for their ostensible Bonapartism. In a letter to Axelrod in June 1918, V. O. Levitskii proclaimed the new Bolshevik state 'a genuinely Bonapartist regime'.[73] In the same month B. Gorev asked in an article in *Novaia zaria* if the Bolsheviks intended 'socialism or Bonapartism?'[74] His answer was that Lenin resembled Napoleon in caricature because the Bonapartism he intended was a parody of socialism, and the separate peace he signed with the Germans a parody of Bonapartism.[75] Also in 1918 Fëdor Dan attacked Lenin for a very different reason, but his conclusion was essentially the same. Lenin, Dan wrote, was establishing a hypertrophied state, oblivious to the material interests of the Russian people, that ruled through a 'bureaucratised police apparatus' intent on preserving its own working class, which required for their satisfaction the continuation of the Bolsheviks in power.[76] The result was a form of 'Bolshevik Bonapartism [of which] the proletariat was its principal enemy'.[77]

---

[70] Karl Kautsky, *Georgien, eine sozialdemokratische Bauernrepublik* (Vienna, 1921), p. 68; Karl Kautsky, *Von der Demokratie zur Staats-Sklaverei. Eine Auseinandersetzung mit Trotzki* (Berlin, 1921), pp. 42–3.
[71] Quoted in Salvadori Massino, *Karl Kautsky and the Socialist Revolution, 1880–1938* (London, 1979), p. 287.
[72] Quoted in ibid., p. 288.
[73] 'Pis'mo Akselrodu (16 June 1918)', in *Martov i ego blizkie: sbornik* (New York, 1959), p. 64.
[74] B. Gorev, 'Sotsializm ili Bonapartizm?' *Novaia zaria*, no. 5–6 (10 June 1918): pp. 14–19.
[75] Ibid., p. 15.
[76] Fëdor Dan, 'Bol'shevistskii Bonapartizm', *Novaia zaria*, no. 3–4 (20 May 1918): p. 16.
[77] Ibid., p. 17.

Finally, in 1922, in one of the most incisive critiques any Menshevik directed at the nascent Soviet state, Martov accused its Bolshevik rulers of establishing a government antithetical to the interests and the welfare of the proletariat. Whatever commitment to socialism the Bolsheviks might have retained after the NEP was established had now dissipated because the NEP had shown itself to be, in fact, a latter-day Thermidor, which necessitated a political dictatorship increasingly resembling Napoleon Bonaparte's—but sustained by a police more powerful than anyone could have imagined, much less created, in France in the beginning of the nineteenth century. From a regime that, in its ideological aspirations, was 'utopian and communist', Lenin had caused it to degenerate into one that Martov termed 'Thermidorian-Bonapartist' because he believed the principal attributes of both of these phases in the history of France informed the present-day anomaly that was the Soviet Union. Where the latter differed from these two stages in the history of France was in its compressing them to the point of simultaneity.[78]

To reproach the Bolsheviks for their Bonapartism, incipient or otherwise, was to call into question the moral, political, and ideological legitimacy of the Soviet state. This of course was the reason the Mensheviks did so—and also the reason the Bolsheviks took such pains to refute them. Where the Mensheviks disagreed among themselves was on what exactly had triggered the degeneration of the Soviet state so soon after its creation. In 1922 Martov made the perfectly plausible argument that the civil war in Russia after the October Revolution—even more than the NEP—was what started the Soviet Union on its path to Bonapartism; its leader, should Bonapartism be its final destination, would be either Trotsky, the Red Army's founder and still the Commissar of War, or someone else, probably in the Communist Party, succeeding Lenin and acting in a fashion reminiscent of Napoleon.[79] Pëtr Garvi, by contrast, located the roots of Soviet Bonapartism not just in the Civil War, which had thoroughly militarized the Communist Party, but also in the NEP, which, by permitting the limited application of capitalism and free market principles in the economy, made necessary the suppression not only of opposition parties like the Mensheviks but also, by the prohibition on factions in 1921, on dissenting opinions within the party itself. What made the Soviet Union resemble a Bonapartist regime, rather than just a generically authoritarian one, according to Garvi, was that it concealed its baseness beneath a veneer of humanitarian rhetoric about its concern for the welfare of its people.[80]

---

[78] Iu. O. Martov, 'Problema "edinogo fronta" v Rossii', *Sotsialisticheskii vestnik*, no. 13/14 (20 July 1922): p. 4.

[79] Ibid., pp. 4–6. The principal *émigré* Menshevik newspaper, *Sotsialisticheskii vestnik*, was published in Berlin until the Nazis came to power in 1933 and forced its relocation to Paris, from which it moved to New York in 1940 shortly before France surrendered to Nazi Germany.

[80] P. Garvi, 'Bonapartizm ili demokratiia', *Sotsialisticheskii vestnik*, no. 23–4 (17 December 1923): pp. 2–7. In the article Garvi used the term as a verb ('to Bonapartise') and as a participle ('to be Bonapartised'). He was the only Russian socialist I am aware of having done that. In 1927 Garvi made clear that the transformation of the Soviet regime into a Bonapartist one was 'irrepressible', even as the

For all of that, however, Lenin was probably angered most of all by Pavel Axelrod's fulminations. After Plekhanov's death in 1918 Axelrod became the senior and most respected non-Bolshevik Marxist in Russia. His first condemnation of Lenin as a Russian Napoleon appeared in *Iskra* in 1904, just months after the schism at the Second Party Congress had revealed the tactical and temperamental differences separating the Bolsheviks and Mensheviks.[81] In 1919, cognizant that recapitulating his earlier disputes with Lenin would strengthen his current argument that by taking power in 1917 the Bolsheviks had perverted both the spirit and the letter of Marxism, Axelrod did so with considerable *élan*, which may have been what prompted Pëtr Garvi in 1925 to credit him with identifying Lenin's 'Bonapartist habits' earlier, and denouncing them more emphatically, than any other non-Bolshevik socialist.[82] According to Axelrod, Lenin's political personality informed the government he headed and for that reason the latter was just as much a manifestation of Bonapartism as the former; for the same reason, the Soviet Union was not merely a perversion of socialism but its antithesis.

For the Mensheviks, Stalin's rise to power and the policies he pursued once it was complete made the question of whether the Soviet Union was a Bonapartist state or in the process of becoming one more pressing. While the NEP existed, Rafael Abramovich thought the Soviet Union was Bonapartist because it had restored a measure of capitalism while perpetuating itself politically. But by 1929, after the NEP ended, he had changed his mind: the Soviet Union was not, as yet, a Bonapartist state—although its having become Thermidorian as a result of the NEP made its evolving eventually into Bonapartism very likely.[83] In 1930, however, Abramovich altered his definition of the phenomenon so he could argue that Stalin's economic policies were actually making Bonapartism in the Soviet Union less likely rather than more so. Bonapartism, in the context of the Soviet Union, he now defined as the replacement of a workers' state by classes that had recovered not only any property their members had lost in the preceding revolution, but the political power they had once exercised by virtue of their economic supremacy. But collectivization and industrialization in the Soviet Union, far from strengthening these classes, were currently destroying them,

base of the Soviet economy remained 'genuinely socialist'. He did not make clear if the latter would later degenerate into something else and, more broadly, if Bonapartism included a particular set of economic policies to accompany its fairly clear desiderata on how the state itself should be organized. Garvi, 'Pod znakom termidora', p. 5.

[81] P. B. Axelrod, 'K voprosu ob istochnike i znachenii nashikh organizatsionnykh raznoglasii. Iz perepiska s Kautskim', *Iskra*, no. 68 (15 June 1904): p. 3.
[82] P. B. Axelrod, *Kto izmenil sotsializmu? (Bol'shevizm i sotsial'naia demokratiia v Rossii)* (New York, 1919), especially pp. 21–2; Garvi, 'P. B. Aksel'rod i Men'shevizm', pp. 11–12.
[83] Sergei Melgunov, *Kak Bol'sheviki zakhvatili vlast'; oktiabr'skii perevorot 1917 goda* (Paris, 1953), p. 185; Abramovich, 'Termidor i krestianstvo', p. 5.

with the result that the Soviet Union under Stalin was actually more socialist—and therefore less Bonapartist—than it had been under Lenin.[84] Also in 1930, Abramovich seemed to abandon entirely the task of determining whether the Soviet Union was already Bonapartist, tending towards Bonapartism, or tending away from it. Having now determined that because analogies with earlier manifestations of the phenomenon were necessarily superficial, the term itself, if not the larger questions about the Soviet Union it raised, should be avoided in explaining the Soviet Union's evolution.[85] For Abramovich, and for the Bolsheviks and Mensheviks generally, Bonapartism—like much of the other terminology they all adopted from France's tradition of revolutions—was like the element mercury, capable of expanding or contracting its outer limits to conform to the requirements of whoever happened to be observing it, and in the process eluding all efforts to ascribe to it a fixed meaning.

To be sure, some Mensheviks could keep their categories straight and stick to one definition of the phenomenon. In contrast to Abramovich, Fëdor Dan maintained for most of his life a consistent view of Bonapartism—of what it was and whether the Soviet Union embodied it. In 1918, he argued that the 'petit-bourgeois property relations [leading to] beastly interpersonal conflicts in the [Russian] countryside' worked decisively to the disadvantage of the proletariat, not least because they made the restoration of capitalism in the country as a whole more likely.[86] Those policies, moreover, emanated from a political dictatorship that, by denying not just the proletariat but everyone in Russia political rights and civil liberties, transcended class. For that reason, and because Dan believed a regime attentive to the needs of the proletariat and intent on establishing socialism could never be Bonapartist, he concluded that the Soviet regime, which did not really care about the working class, was in fact a Bonapartist one. But Bonapartist regimes were not stable, and those that like the Soviet one thought themselves impervious to internal opposition were especially vulnerable.[87]

Despite the dramatic changes Stalin mandated in the Soviet Union in the early 1930s—principally the collectivization of agriculture and crash industrialization under the auspices of a planned economy—Dan did not alter his views on Soviet Bonapartism. Nor did he do so during the Terror later in the same decade. But in 1940 he did. He now believed Bonapartism could emerge in the Soviet Union even

---

[84] Lieblich, *From the Other Shore*, pp. 192–3.

[85] R. Abramovich, 'Bol'shevizm v tupike. O knige Kautskogo togo zhe naznaniia', *Sotsialisticheskii vestnik*, no. 20 (25 October 1930): pp. 4–5. His counsel in 1930 notwithstanding, Abramovich returned to the analogy in 1943, this time delineating three types of Bonapartism—the first being that of Napoleon himself, the second like that which existed when the Soviet Union had become Thermidorian in the 1920s, and the third a military dictatorship or an ostensibly civilian dictatorship that was actually controlled by the military. Ultra-nationalism, he wrote, was also a component of Bonapartism. Although the Soviet Union was Bonapartist without its being ultra-nationalist, he predicted that its anticipated victory over Nazi Germany would make it so. R. Abramovich, 'Bonapartizm i russkaia revoliutsiia', *Sotsialisticheskii vestnik*, no. 523–4 (8 July 1943): pp. 145–7.

[86] Dan, 'Bol'shevistskii bonapartizm', p. 15.   [87] Ibid., pp. 15–17.

after the bourgeoisie (and the intelligentsia along with it) had been destroyed. In fact, he now called the Soviet Union fascist as well as Bonapartist, though without distinguishing these two types of political leadership and organization.[88] Perhaps Dan refrained from doing so because he considered it more important to stress that the Soviet Union was not socialist, and that one of the reasons it was not socialist was because it was not democratic. Although capitalism no longer existed—on this Dan agreed with Stalin—the Soviet Union, because it was ruled by a ruthless dictatorship, had not yet advanced into socialism. This would seem to preclude Dan, or any other democratic socialist, from supporting it. But in 1940 he came very close to doing precisely that, and the reason was not that he considered the Soviet Union, compared to Nazi Germany, the lesser of two evils. Because the two countries, at that time, were not at war, comparing them for the purpose of distinguishing Bonapartism from fascism, or for any other reason, might not even have occurred to him. His argument—which was only implied rather than stated explicitly—was different. From his assumption that any democratic regime that succeeded Stalin's would probably be capitalist (because Stalin had discredited socialism in the minds of most Russians), he concluded that democratic socialists should support Stalin's regime because capitalism was worse. In other words, the Soviet Union was the lesser of two evils not because the only alternative to it was Nazism but because the only alternative to it was capitalism.[89] It was left to Boris Nikolaevskii and the little-known Iu. Denike to argue that the Soviet Union in the 1940s was actually a totalitarian dictatorship (and thus demonstrably more powerful than the regimes of the Bonapartes in the nineteenth century), and thus unlikely to be replaced anytime soon, or possibly forever. For that reason, arguments about whether its successor would be capitalist or socialist or base its politics and economy on some other ideology were just an intellectual exercise and a waste of valuable time.[90]

However opaque the reasoning that buttressed them, the Mensheviks' attacks hit the Bolsheviks where they were vulnerable. As ideologues themselves, the Bolsheviks were susceptible to ideological challenge, especially when it came from persons claiming to be socialist. Even more dangerous were criticisms inside the Soviet Union and from within the Communist Party that concerned issues of Marxist–Leninist ideology. For this reason, invoking the spectre of Bonapartism, even when the reason was purely political, was a double-edged sword. This of course was also true for Thermidor. Both terms, while effective when used purely

---

[88] In the mid-1930s Dan had begun calling the Soviet Union 'totalitarian' even though the term, taken literally, implies that regimes to which the term applies will never retreat to the democratic socialism Dan favoured, or to any other system in which the government does not enjoy total power. Dan, 'Puti vozrozhdeniia', p. 7. Absent defeat in war, totalitarian regimes, by definition, last forever.

[89] Dan, 'Dva puti', cited in Kondratieva, Bol'sheviki-iakobintsy, p. 186.

[90] Nikolaevskii, '"Termidor" russkoi revoliutsii', pp. 171–5; Iu Denike, 'Revoliutsiia bez termidora', Novyi zhurnal, vol. 7 (1943): pp. 202–19.

to defame other Bolsheviks politically, inevitably raised the larger issue of the Soviet Union's ideological legitimacy—or the lack of it. But since many Bolsheviks considered Thermidorianism reversible, condemning another Bolshevik for predicting it was not nearly as destructive of his ideological bona fides as it was to accuse him of Bonapartism, which, because it was stronger and had more 'staying-power' than any Thermidorian reaction or counter-revolution, conjured a scenario in which the Soviet Union itself was destroyed totally and permanently.

The Soviet leader against whom the charge of Bonapartism was most effective was Trotsky. His role in creating the Red Army and then leading it to victory in the Civil War, along with an ego and sense of self-importance he hardly bothered to conceal, made Trotsky virtually the personification of Russian Bonapartism: his military exploits were reminiscent of the first Napoleon, his personal vanity of the second. Nevertheless, when Lenin, in December 1922, suffered the first of several strokes that would end his life thirteen months later, Trotsky's enemies, who considered him Lenin's most likely successor, began a whispering campaign that reached a fever-pitch at the Twelfth Party Congress in December 1923.[91] Alfred Rosmer reports in his memoirs that the typical complaint was that Trotsky 'thinks he is Bonaparte [and] wants to play at being Bonaparte'.[92] Because the charge of Bonapartism implied that Trotsky had forsaken socialism or had never truly believed in it, it resonated among Bolsheviks who recalled his not joining the party until the summer of 1917; coupled with other defects Trotsky suffered from in the context of Soviet politics, such as his Jewish heritage, it had the potential to end his political career entirely. To render the accusation nugatory, Trotsky resigned as Commissar of War in 1925, but by that time the damage it had already inflicted on his credentials as a loyal Bolshevik and Communist was irreversible.[93]

After assisting in Trotsky's political destruction, Bonapartism played only a minor role in the struggle to succeed Lenin that ended with Stalin's ascendancy. Moreover, if one looked to French revolutions for analogies that might be useful in explaining the NEP and alerting the party to the dangers of continuing it, it made more sense—both politically and as a matter of simple logic—to raise an analogy with Thermidor than to conjure the whole conundrum of Bonapartism. Neither the Bolsheviks nor the Mensheviks really knew what Bonapartism might consist of in the context of a presumptively socialist society, or even how it would come about in the first place; Marx and Engels offered no guidance because to them, such an outcome was impossible. For that reason, from 1924 to 1929 the Bolsheviks spoke of Bonapartism infrequently, and when they did, it was in the context of explaining what might follow a Soviet Thermidor rather than what might appear instead of it.

---

[91] Kotkin, *Stalin*, p. 825, n. 182.
[92] Alfred Rosmer, *Lenin's Moscow* (New York and London, 1971), p. 207.
[93] Deutscher, *Stalin*, p. 297; Trotsky, *My Life*, p. 518.

One of the few Bolsheviks who during these years endeavoured to describe how Bonapartism might come about in the Soviet Union, and how precisely it would transform it, was Alexander Slepkov, a supporter of Bukharin and a member of the so-called Right Opposition. In 1927, Slepkov attacked the Left Opposition not for claiming that Bonapartism was a threat to the Soviet Union (which in fact was what certain members of the Left Opposition had alleged), but for claiming that it was close to becoming a reality in the Soviet Union (a claim that no one in the Left Opposition had made). In his indictment, Slepkov stressed that, according to the Left Opposition, the Red Army was the instrument by which Soviet Bonapartism would be established.[94] In reality, the Left Opposition, and Trotsky in particular, described the current threat to the Soviet Union as Thermidorian rather than Bonapartist, and that the two stages in the French Revolution, were they both to be replicated in the Soviet Union, would be sequential rather than simultaneous—as they were in France. Bonapartism could not exist in the Soviet Union, or anywhere else for that matter, until Thermidor existed. Moreover, Trotsky's notion of the Soviet Thermidor in the 1920s was that it was a species of counter-revolution that, regardless of its origins—either in elements within the party that had betrayed it, or in bourgeois states external to the Soviet Union itself—would mean the end of the union and the entire enterprise of creating socialism and communism. Thus there was no reason, according to Trotsky, to worry much about Soviet Bona-partism, even when acknowledging the danger of a Soviet Thermidor.

But such distinctions meant nothing to Slepkov, who was engaged in political defamation, not historical analysis. What made his accusation significant in the evolution of the Bolsheviks' conception of Bonapartism was that it considered it an exclusively military phenomenon, in which the military determined which civilians would rule, or ruled itself. It is true that the Bolsheviks earlier had been among those attacking Kerensky and Kornilov as potential Russian Bonapartes. But it was also the case that the Bolsheviks—along with the Mensheviks and the various other elements comprising the anti-Bolshevik left in Russia both before and after the October Revolution—considered Bonapartism through the mid-1920s a particular type of authoritarianism, rather than as a form of governance absolutely requiring the military's involvement. Indeed, nearly all of the Bolsheviks who addressed the issue knew that the French precursor both Marx and Engels and they themselves usually had in mind was Louis Napoleon rather than Napoleon Bonaparte.[95]

In the late 1920s this changed. Thereafter, the consensus in the Soviet Communist Party was that Bonapartism, if it emerged, would be the result of the

[94] Slepkov, A. *Oppozitsionnyi neomen'shevizm. O novoi platforme* (Moscow, 1927), p. 33.
[95] It bears repeating that Louis Napoleon, who, while donning military garb for political purposes as Emperor of the French, never served at any rank in the French army (although he did attain the rank of captain in the Swiss army). F. A. Simpson, *The Rise of Louis Napoleon* (London, 1968), p. 90.

intervention of the Red Army in civilian politics, either by providing critical support for a civilian aspirant to power or by taking power directly. The only aspect of this consensus that changed in the 1930s was that it narrowed considerably. Since all putative Bonapartists had been ousted from the entirely civilian Soviet leadership, Bonapartism could only mean the Red Army ruling Russia. The threat it posed to the Communist Party, in other words, was external to it. And while it is true that, in the Gorbachev era, Bonapartism regained a good deal of its original meaning as a generic category of dictatorships that betrayed the noble intentions of the political system it replaced, this cannot change the fact that for most of the time the Soviet Union existed—specifically from the Stalin era to the advent of Gorbachev's policy of *perestroika*—the term signified nothing more nor less than a military dictatorship.[96]

Explaining why the Soviets were so fearful of a military coup requires consideration of the circumstances in which Bolshevism emerged. For the original Bolsheviks, and for those who preceded them in the revolutionary movement, the Russian military was an abstraction. Most engaged in radical politics from an early age, so few actually served in the military, and even fewer were acquainted with its upper echelons, from which any Russian or Soviet Bonaparte would presumably emerge. For this reason the Bolsheviks were prone to exaggerating the cohesiveness and political acumen of the Russian officer corps, and understandably developed an exaggerated fear of it. This would explain the need after the October Revolution to keep a close eye on the army, and on its officers and generals in particular—which the Bolsheviks believed could best be done through the institution of the political commissars; these were essentially loyal party *apparatchiki* sent to spy on the leaders of the Red Army. Another factor generating this fear was the NEP, which by providing a measure of economic freedom in the Soviet Union, made demands for political freedom more likely. Not surprisingly, the Bolsheviks, having come to power without the support of a majority, or even a plurality, of the Russian people, could never permit such freedom unless they somehow lost entirely their well-honed instinct for political survival. Revolutionaries who take power in a *coup d'état* do not relinquish it voluntarily. Moreover, because the conscripts in the Red Army were largely peasants, the depredations they and their families endured in the collectivization

---

[96] The term was also useful in the Soviet system in advancing one's own career—and in destroying others. On one occasion it was even reduced to an ineffectual style of administration inconsistent with Bolshevik governance. Marshal Tukhachevskii, whom some thought harboured Bonapartist aspirations himself, once derided the chief of staff of the Soviet armed forces, Boris Shaposhnikov, as 'an office Napoleon'. Stephen Kotkin, *Stalin: Waiting for Hitler, 1929–1941* (New York, 2017), p. 995, n. 206. To be sure, the two men disagreed on how the Red Army should fight future wars—Tukhachevskii's emphasis on tanks and armoured warfare required a much larger force than Shaposhnikov thought economically feasible. Sally W. Stoecker, *Forging Stalin's Army: Marshal Tukhachevsky and the Politics of Military Innovation* (New York, 2018), p. 44.

of agriculture—in which, according to some estimates, more than fourteen million Soviet citizens, most of them peasants, were killed or died of starvation—made the Red Army, as an institution, especially dangerous.[97] Hence the fear, after the 1920s, of a military dictatorship, rather than of dictatorship generically.

The centrality the original Napoleon henceforth enjoyed in the Soviet leadership's discussions of Bonapartism caused Soviet historians to explore his rule more intensively, usually for the purpose of determining whether Napoleon's rule was progressive or not, and in the Stalin era whether over the long run it helped Russia or harmed it. In the 1920s, the prevailing opinion was M. N. Pokrovskii's, namely that Napoleon's regime was the political expression in France of incipient industrial capitalism. As such, his regime advanced the course of history in both France and Russia. Because the latter had not yet experienced a bourgeois revolution when Napoleon attacked it in 1812, his campaign, despite the death and devastation it caused, would have been a good thing for the country had it succeeded and caused the replacement of the Russian monarchy by a bourgeois regime.[98] As additional justification, Pokrovskii cited Russia's serial violations of Napoleon's Continental System.[99]

Pokrovskii's dominance of the historical profession in the Soviet Union ended with the government denouncing him three years after his death in 1932, for a variety of ideological deviations, among them an excessively schematized (i.e. class-based) view of history. Nevertheless, at least one Soviet historian persisted in writing about Napoleon. S. A. Piontkovskii, in 1935, even went so far as to justify Napoleon's Russian campaign as morally justified in a war for which the Russian nobility, who were increasingly intent on producing for profit, were responsible. As landed capitalists, they needed to sell their grain and any timber they could salvage to England, but Napoleon's Continental System precluded it. Moreover, Russian peasants in territory occupied by Napoleon in 1812 were as hostile to the Russian nobility—to which, as serfs, they had performed labour or had made payments in kind or in money—as they were to the French.[100]

But Piontkovskii was put on notice in 1936 that history like his, where it concerned Napoleon, was no longer acceptable. That he was liquidated in 1937 underscored the seriousness of his deviation. Perhaps appropriately, the new line was announced by the publication of a biography of Napoleon felicitously edited by Karl Radek, whose ability to conform to whatever the prevailing orthodoxy happened to be at any particular time was considerable. Radek's principal target, as it happened, was not Piontkovskii but rather Tarlé, virtually all of

---

[97] Robert Conquest, *The Harvest of Sorrow: Soviet Collectivization and the Terror-Famine* (New York, 1986), p. 306.

[98] Leo Yaresh, 'The Campaign of 1812', in Black, *Rewriting Russian History*, pp. 264–5.

[99] M. N. Pokrovskii, *Diplomatiia i voiny tsarskoi Rossii v xix stoletiia* (Moscow, 1923), p. 33.

[100] S. A. Piontkovskii, *Ocherki istorii SSSR xix i xx vv.* (Moscow, 1935), pp. 13–15.

whose opinions on Napoleon's Russian campaign Radek not only rejected, but condemned.[101] With the publication of books like Radek's, discussion of Napoleon's rule, and of Bonapartism in general, was limited, with one very significant exception, to the Mensheviks in exile. The exception was Trotsky himself, who was able to continue his ruminations about the French Revolution, Thermidor, and Bonapartism, and to publish them without being arrested or losing his life, because after his expulsion from the Soviet Union in February 1929, he was, and would remain until his assassination in 1940, a political exile, forced to flee from one country to another whenever political pressure on the host country caused it to expel him. But throughout his peregrinations, Trotsky was free to continue his intensive study of the French Revolution and its nineteenth-century successors not only to help him understand why Stalin had defeated him, but also for any optimism these revolutions might provide about the chances of Stalin's regime collapsing, and one headed by Trotsky replacing it.

*   *   *

Trotsky, more than any other Russian Marxist, Bolshevik or Menshevik, enlarged the notion of Bonapartism from a particular kind of bourgeois or petit-bourgeois dictatorship, with its political base predominantly in the peasantry, into one that transcended parties, classes, and even the state itself. But he did not define the phenomenon this way until the events of 1917 prompted him to do so. Immediately following his emergence as a Marxist revolutionary in the early 1900s, Trotsky's interest in French revolutions was mostly limited to the Jacobins and ascertaining whether Lenin resembled them. On the rare occasions when he mentioned Bonapartism, it was in polemics to score debating points, rather than to explain what he meant by the term in a calm and reasonable fashion. For example, in the fall of 1905 he attacked the Russian bourgeoisie, personified by the onetime Marxist-turned-liberal Pëtr Struve, for espousing a 'gold-plated liberalism' that made it an implacable enemy of the peasantry and the proletariat.[102] Even worse was its susceptibility to 'the lure of Bonapartism', which he described simply as 'a bloody and iron order' no less hostile to the masses than the monarchy; what made Russian liberals like Struve so contemptible was true also of Sergei Witte, the minister of finance under Alexander III and Nicholas II.[103] Not until 1914 did he even use the term as an adjective descriptive of Louis Napoleon's regime.[104] For Trotsky, Bonapartism was more a figure of speech than

---

[101] K. Radek, ed., *Napoleon* (Moscow 1936), pp. 378, 419, 420. Radek would be arrested in the same year the book was published, and killed three years later either in prison or in a labour camp, possibly by ordinary criminals. Warren Lerner, *Karl Radek: The Last Internationalist* (Stanford CA, 1970), pp. 170–1.

[102] L. Trotskii, 'Toskuiut po Bonapartu', in Trotsky, *Sochineniia*, vol. II, part 1, p. 322.

[103] Ibid., p. 323.

[104] Trotsky first used the term in *The War and the International 1915* (n.p. 1971), pp. iii, 34, 37, which he wrote in 1914 after the outbreak of the First World War.

a generic term for a particular kind of authoritarianism possessing any explanatory or predictive value.

In 1917, however, allegations that Kerensky and Kornilov were putative Bonapartists were too widespread for Trotsky to ignore the term or to use it merely as an epithet. He now sought to ascertain its deeper meaning. But the task was harder than he anticipated. In an essay, entitled, 'Elements of Bonapartism', he could not decide if Bonapartism was the political instrument of the petit-bourgeoisie or a term descriptive of a government that, by representing all classes, transcended it.[105] After denigrating Kerensky as bearing only a superficial resemblance to the original Napoleon, and his government as the embodiment of 'sophomoric Bonapartism'—presumably to distinguish it from a genuinely Bonapartist regime—Trotsky went on to describe Kerensky's government as if there was really no difference between the two.[106] Kerensky's government, in other words, was not a parody of a Bonapartist regime—in the way Marx and Engels considered Louis Napoleon's government a parody of Napoleon Bonaparte's—but the genuine article. This was how Trotsky, at the critical point in his essay, described it:

> The Kerensky government, exercising no control, is in its very nature a government without a social foundation. It was consciously constructed between two possible foundations: the working masses and the imperialist classes. In that lies its Bonapartism.[107]

But having achieved, finally, a measure of clarity, Trotsky followed this succinct description with speculation about the degree to which 'the new czarism'— Trotsky's new epithet for the Provisional Government now that it was headed by Kerensky—would have to rely on 'the passive inertia' of a single class, the peasantry, for its survival.[108] Confusing his readers further, Trotsky went on to state that the principal instrument of Bonapartism was a trained and disciplined army.[109] But since, in Trotsky's opinion, the Russian army currently failed to fit this description, and also because class antagonisms in Russia were too intense for any ruler to transcend them in the guise of a personal dictatorship, the reader could only conclude that Russia was not currently Bonapartist under any reasonable definition of the term.

Looking back on Kerensky's government in his history of the Russian Revolution, written fifteen years after the events it described, Trotsky seemed at last to have contrived a definition he could live with. Bonapartism, he wrote, was

---

[105] Leon Trotsky, 'Elements of Bonapartism', in Lenin and Trotsky, *Proletarian Revolution in Russia*, pp. 247–54.

[106] Ibid., p. 252.   [107] Ibid., p. 253.   [108] Ibid., p. 254.

[109] Ibid., p. 254. In a separate article, written at the same time as 'Elements of Bonapartism', Trotsky characterized the Provisional Government as 'socialist Bonapartist' without explaining what kind of hybrid he meant by this apparent confluence of socialism and Bonapartism. Leon Trotsky, 'What Next?', in Lenin and Trotsky, *Proletarian Revolution in Russia*, p. 263.

'the idea of a master of destiny rising above all classes'.[110] Kerensky, he now maintained, aspired to the role of the Russian Bonaparte, but could not rise above the possessing classes on whose support the Provisional Government depended to survive, and in transcending these classes become as much of a Bonaparte as the two Bonapartes in France. The reason he could not do this was because his support was too dependent on the petit-bourgeoisie—just the way Kornilov could not be a genuine Bonaparte because his support was too dependent on the haute-bourgeoisie.[111] In Trotsky's analysis, this 'structural' impediment to Kerensky's becoming a Bonaparte, and thereby surviving the Bolsheviks' attempts to overthrow him, was the first of three reasons Trotsky offered for his failure in 1917. The other two were Kerensky's deficiencies as a political leader, and the equilibrium that existed in the fall of 1917, after both he and Kornilov had discredited themselves personally and politically—the latter by his futile attempt to seize power in a military *coup d'état*, the former by his pathetic response to it. The result was a political vacuum that the Bolsheviks, led by Trotsky, found easy to fill.[112]

Trotsky's open contempt for Kerensky, fully shared by Lenin, was especially pronounced because of Trotsky's equally obvious admiration, despite the ideological abyss between them, of Napoleon Bonaparte. Trotsky may have modelled the Red Army on the democratic armies Napoleon inherited from the French Revolution when he came to power in 1799, and Napoleon's modest origins in Corsica precluded Trotsky's condemning him as a typical representative of an increasingly affluent bourgeoisie. In a speech in 1918, Trotsky quoted the well-known dictum, often ascribed to Napoleon, that in the knapsack of every recruit there is a marshal's baton.[113] That he did so approvingly was consistent with his subsequent statement that effectively justified coups like Napoleon's in 1799: 'In a revolutionary country, every energetic and steadfast soldier may and must, in a moment of danger, take over the post of command, however high'.[114] What is more, Napoleon was right to draw from all classes, not just the upper ones, for his officers and generals. Several of his greatest commanders—Trotsky felt no need to name them—were so low-born that they could not even write their own names. In an exegesis on military doctrine published as a pamphlet in 1921, Trotsky judged 'the Bonapartist military tradition of the bold offensive' precisely that which revolutionary armies should adopt, and in the same year he rejected Kautsky's charge that the Bolsheviks' recent conquest of Georgia and its reabsorption into Russia were somehow evidence of Bonapartism.[115]

[110] Trotsky, *History of the Russian Revolution*, unabridged edition, p. 469.   [111] Ibid., p. 472.
[112] Ibid., pp. 456–73.
[113] Leon Trotsky, 'The Non-Commissioned Officers', in Trotsky, *Military Writings*, vol. I, p. 233.
[114] Ibid., vol. I, p. 233.
[115] Leon Trotsky, 'Military Doctrine or Pseudo-Military Doctrinairism', ibid., vol. V, p. 321; Trotsky, *Between Red and White*, pp. 19–30.

Prior to the mid-1930s, Trotsky's view replicated Marx's. Bonapartism was something to which only capitalist countries, like France in the nineteenth century, were vulnerable. But by having nationalized the means of production, the Soviet Union could never degenerate into Bonapartism, and anyone who claimed the opposite—that the Soviet Union was becoming Bonapartist, was already Bonapartist, or might become Bonapartist in the future—was wrong. In 1933, when the German Communist Hugo Urbahns called the Soviet Union Bonapartist, Trotsky strongly objected, reminding his readers that Bonapartism existed only when private property remained in the hands of the bourgeoisie, and since in the Soviet Union private property was already nationalized and the means of production in the hands of the proletariat, Bonapartism was not a viable option. The Soviet Union was not Bonapartist because it could not be Bonapartist.[116]

With this conviction firmly in mind, Trotsky could press for the adoption of specific policies Napoleon followed without worrying that this increased the chances of the Soviet system succumbing to Bonapartism. In fact, having excluded the Soviet Union from the regimes in his Marxist-based taxonomy that might degenerate into Bonapartism, Trotsky could use the term and its variants as epithets in condemning anyone or anything he found objectionable. In 1920 he disparaged the Pilsudskii regime in Poland for its 'third-rate Bonapartism', and in 1923 he dismissed Pilsudskii himself as 'a Polish Kerensky, only made up to look like Napoleon'.[117]

In 1935, however, Trotsky changed his mind on the whole question of Thermidor. This caused him to refine what he believed Bonapartism to be, and to reconsider the chances of it emerging organically in the Soviet Union from within the Communist Party itself. In the 1920s Trotsky had defined Thermidor as a form of counter-revolution and acknowledged that its appearance in the Soviet Union would mean the end of the entire enterprise of establishing communism and creating the New Soviet Man. But when Trotsky and his supporters regained power—about the inevitability of which Trotsky almost never doubted—a Soviet Thermidor would be precluded; should it exist, it would be extinguished quickly. But the persistence of Stalin's rule in the Soviet Union, coupled with his own powerlessness and inability to alleviate its most pernicious effects, caused Trotsky to reverse each of his conclusions concerning a Soviet Thermidor: what it was and what its presence in the Soviet Union would signify, and whether it existed already in the Soviet Union or might emerge there in the future.[118]

---

[116] Leon Trotsky, 'The Class Nature of the Soviet State (1 October 1933)', in *WLT* (1933–4) (New York, 1975), pp. 107–8.

[117] Leon Trotsky, 'The Polish Front', in Trotsky, *Military Writings*, vol. III, p. 141; Leon Trotsky, 'From a Report', ibid., vol. V. p. 145.

[118] Leon Trotsky, 'The Workers' State, Thermidor, and Bonapartism (April 1935)', in *WLT* (1934–5) (New York, 1971), pp. 166–84.

In short, Trotsky now admitted that Thermidor was a reality in the Soviet Union, but, in mitigation of the dire conclusions that seemed to follow his admission, redefined the term to signify merely a reactionary phase in an ongoing revolution, as it was in the French Revolution, rather than a counter-revolution, which of course would be more difficult to reverse. In France, he wrote, the years from 1794 to 1799 had been a time in which political power changed hands from the radical Jacobins to 'the more moderate and conservative [ones], the better-to-do elements of bourgeois society'.[119] The coup that deposed Robespierre and his followers in the summer of 1794 was only a political revolution, and thus left intact the social and economic reforms of the French Revolution. But Trotsky's new definition of Thermidor allowed for the possibility of an even more salubrious outcome, namely that a reactionary phase within a progressive revolution, unlike a counter-revolution, might disappear on its own, without any internal revolution or foreign intervention. The reason for Trotsky's optimism was obvious. If Thermidor, as a generic phenomenon, was deleterious but nevertheless impermanent, then its presence in the Soviet Union made it possible for Trotsky to continue to call the Soviet Union a workers' state—or to argue that if it was no longer a workers' state it might easily become a workers' state again—and to believe that the possibility, even the likelihood, of creating socialism and communism there remained real.

Trotsky, however, was not willing to predict that this Soviet Thermidor would soon disappear and that it would do so on its own—despite the fact that his new definition permitted it. In fact, he wrote in this same article that the Soviet Union was not only Thermidorian in some of its economic and social arrangements, but simultaneously Bonapartist in its political ones.[120] Notwithstanding his earlier statements reassuring his followers that Bonapartism was a concomitant of capitalism and that socialist states were immune to it, in 1935 he affirmed that, as an essential attribute of Stalinism, it existed in Russia. In fact, after condemning as 'banal pedantry' the attempt to analogize the different stages of the Russian Revolution to those in the French Revolution, Trotsky characterized Stalin's regime in the Soviet Union as analogous to Bonaparte's at the end of the Consulate; so obvious was this analogy he was 'hit between the eyes by it'.[121] While in the five years that remained before his assassination in Mexico in 1940 Trotsky would claim that the Soviet Union resembled other phases of the original Bonapartist regime in France, he never retracted his initial claim that in the way political power was exercised and in the relationship between the political leadership and Soviet society, the Soviet Union, in its totality, was Bonapartist.[122]

[119] Ibid., p. 174.   [120] Ibid., p. 178.   [121] Ibid., p. 175.
[122] Trotsky even contradicted himself in the 1935 article, claiming at the end of it that the current Soviet regime, in the terminology used to distinguish the various phases of Napoleon's dictatorship, was 'closer in type to the Empire than the Consulate'. Ibid., p. 182.

What, then, according to Trotsky, did Bonapartism in the Soviet Union consist of? As he explained it, Bonapartism was an expedient the Soviet bureaucracy employed to perpetuate itself and to perpetuate the political power it exercised through the person of Stalin, whose political supremacy was buttressed by the police and the military. Stalin's rule, moreover, transcended the class structure of the Soviet Union, and for that reason the bureaucracy of which Stalin was its political instrument could more easily dominate the country and thwart any attempt by the proletariat to regain control of the party and the government. By essentially 'separating' politics from society, Bonapartism was able to pulverize Soviet society to such an extent that the Soviet bureaucracy could continue to embezzle from the proletariat the rewards of what remained a proletarian economy. This separation, in other words, worked both ways: while it ensured the continued supremacy of the bureaucracy, of whom Stalin was its principal political instrument, it also afforded a measure of protection to the Soviet economy, which, thanks to Lenin and Trotsky, remained proletarian in the absence of a capitalist bourgeoisie owning the means of production. In Trotsky's words:

> Stalin guards the conquests of the October Revolution not only against the feudal-bourgeois counterrevolution but also against the claims of the toilers, their impatience and their dissatisfaction; he crushes the left wing that expresses the ordered historical and progressive tendencies of the unprivileged working masses; he creates a new aristocracy by means of an extreme differentiation in wages, privileges, ranks etc. Leaning for support on the topmost layer of the new social hierarchy against the lowest—sometimes vice versa—Stalin has attained the complete concentration of power in his own hands. What else should this regime be called if not Soviet Bonapartism?[123]

The conclusion Trotsky drew from the separation of politics and economics he believed existed in the Soviet Union, and constituted irrefutable proof of its Bonapartism, was, again, a cautiously optimistic one. Bonapartism, as he defined it, was powerful but unstable. Soviet Bonapartism, in fact, was like a sphere balanced on the point of a pyramid, ready to fall—at this point Trotsky's metaphor loses its value—either in the direction of a regime whose polity was genuinely and unalterably proletarian, or in the direction of a regime, probably a fascist one, that openly restored bourgeois property.[124] Indeed, Trotsky acknowledged that

---

[123] Ibid., p. 181. This passage also reveals that Trotsky on occasion described Stalin not as a mere tool of the bureaucracy but as a more or less independent and self-contained political actor wielding power that derived from no one else and from no particular class or stratum in Soviet society, not even a hypertrophied bureaucracy that, in its size, bore no relation to the one the Bolsheviks inherited in 1917.

[124] Ibid., pp. 181–2. Complicating matters was Trotsky's multiple descriptions of the Soviet Union under Stalin as 'totalitarian', which would seem to preclude the possibility of its reversion, presumably after Stalin's overthrow, to a genuinely proletarian state. See, for example, Trotsky, *Revolution Betrayed*, pp. 100, 108, 183, 276, 279. Trotsky, who was familiar with what the Mensheviks wrote in emigration after their expulsion from the Soviet Union (which Trotsky supported), probably knew that his views

fascism and Soviet Bonapartism were similar in that both were 'crisis regimes', with fascism protecting the conquests of 'finance capital', and Bonapartism those of a 'permanent bureaucracy'.[125] But both regimes were condemned by the perseverations of the Marxist dialectic to collapse, and the result would be an incipient workers' state in the case of fascism, and a revived and resurgent workers' state in the case of Soviet Bonapartism.[126]

Over the next several years Trotsky tinkered with his views on Soviet Bonapartism without significantly revising them, though in 1939 he speculated briefly that the Soviet Union could degenerate further into a 'bureaucratic collectivism' unlike any previous despotism in history, a possibility he rejected almost immediately after raising it.[127] When, in 1936, Stalin allowed (rigged) elections and promulgated a new Soviet constitution, Trotsky took these developments to mean that Soviet Bonapartism was now 'plebiscitary', and thus dependent for its legitimacy (though not its power) on the results of balloting and on the clauses of a document that were both meaningless.[128] As for the show trials and the terror that began in the same year, Trotsky saw them as further proof of the instability of Soviet Bonapartism: threatened by the proletariat, the ruling bureaucracy was responding with terror. This view of the Terror, however, grossly minimized Stalin's role in it, and Trotsky never explained why the Soviet government should have cannibalized itself instead of limiting the terror it inflicted to the classes that ostensibly threatened it. Trotsky failed to explain, in other words, why the victims of Stalin's Terror included loyal Stalinists, who were presumably just as much a product of Soviet bureaucracy as Stalin himself, as well as enemies of Stalin and the Soviet bureaucracy who were genuine advocates of the proletariat and socialism, among whom Trotsky's supporters (and until his assassination, Trotsky himself) were the most ardent and articulate. The only conceivable and logically consistent explanation for such obvious irrationality is that Stalin, or more meaningfully those who constituted the ruling bureaucracy and presumably made clear to Stalin what exactly he should do, were clinically insane. But Trotsky

---

on totalitarianism in the Soviet Union closely resembled Fëdor Dan's, as expressed in 'Puti vozrozhdeniia'. Of course Trotsky would never acknowledge the similarity publicly.

---

[125] Ibid., pp. 169, 180–3; Leon Trotsky, 'Bonapartism and Fascism (15 July 1934)', ibid., pp. 53–4. Ironically, Trotsky's notion of fascism was also Stalin's. Indeed, the prevailing orthodoxy in the Soviet Union in the Stalin era and afterwards—excluding only the twenty-two months between the Non-Aggression Pact in 1939 and the Nazi invasion of the Soviet Union in 1941—was that fascism was 'the open, terroristic dictatorship of the most reactionary, most chauvinist and most imperialist elements of finance capital'. Georgii Dimitrov at the Seventh Comintern Congress in 1935, quoted in Robert O. Paxton, *The Anatomy of Fascism* (New York, 2005), p. 8.

[126] Trotsky, 'The Workers' State, Thermidor, and Bonapartism', pp. 170–1; Trotsky, 'Bonapartism and Fascism', p. 57.

[127] Leon Trotsky, 'The USSR in War (25 September 1939)', in Leon Trotsky, *In Defense of Marxism* (New York, 1973), pp. 13–15.

[128] Leon Trotsky, 'The New Constitution of the USSR (16 April 1936)', in *WLT* (1935–6) (New York, 1977), p. 311.

could not even entertain this possibility. For one thing, it contradicted Marxism's dogma on the material origins of everything ideational. For another, it might be considered obviation of Stalin's responsibility for the Terror.

As the Terror intensified and it became increasingly clear that Trotsky's death would be its logical culmination and climax, Trotsky, quite understandably, used the word Bonapartism and its adjectival derivative as a convenient pejorative for everything from Stalin's egomania to his personal sadism and abuse of power. His last writings are filled with references, none of them particularly illuminating, to 'Bonapartist gangsterism' and 'Bonapartist riff-raff'.[129] But in more reflective moments he regained the serenity that enabled him to predict the eventual demise of Soviet Bonapartism. In March 1939 he speculated that civil war in Russia might follow the conclusion of the Eighteenth Party Congress, and that war with Japan would result in the collapse of the entire regime.[130]

All of this, however, was far in the future when Trotsky first proclaimed his views on Soviet Bonapartism in 1935. Far more important than speculating on when and how it might be destroyed was clarifying the circumstances that had allowed it to emerge. This required his clarifying the relationship between Soviet Bonapartism and the Soviet Thermidor, which he had conveniently redefined to preclude the conclusion that the October Revolution had been betrayed and that socialism in the Soviet Union was no longer possible, at least not in the foreseeable future. If, as Trotsky now argued, the development of the Russian Revolution was roughly analogous to that of the French, and if, as Trotsky also argued, the Soviet Union was currently at a stage in its development corresponding to that of the first Napoleonic dictatorship in France, claiming now that the Soviet Thermidor was real but that it only signified a phase in a revolutionary process suggested that the same was true for the Soviet Bonapartism that had succeeded it, namely that it, too, only signified a phase in a revolutionary process. But while the successor to Soviet Thermidor was something worse, namely Soviet Bonapartism, the succes- sor to Soviet Bonapartism might be something better, namely the Soviet Union's reversion to the path to socialism it had been following before Trotsky's political demise, which he believed was triggered by Lenin's final illness and death. What was new in Trotsky's analysis of his own demise was that he now made it coterminous with both Lenin's death and the beginning of the Soviet Thermidor. In the same article in which he proclaimed the existence of Soviet Bonpartism, he also stated that the Soviet Thermidor that preceded it had begun in 1924.[131] By doing that, Trotsky shielded Lenin's actions, most notably the suppression of the

[129] Leon Trotsky, 'The Bonapartist Philosophy of the State (1 May 1939)', in WLT (1938–9) (New York, 1974), p. 325; Leon Trotsky, 'Again and Once More Again on the Nature of the USSR (18 October 1939)', in In Defence of Marxism, p. 24.
[130] Leon Trotsky, 'Stalin's Capitulation (11 March 1939)', in WLT (1938–9), p. 218; Leon Trotsky, 'Only Revolution Can End War (18 March 1939)', ibid., p. 235.
[131] Trotsky, 'The Workers' State, Thermidor, and Bonapartism', p. 174.

Kronstadt Revolt, the inauguration of the NEP, and the elimination of political parties like the Mensheviks that had criticized and condemned the Bolsheviks, from the stigma attached to the Thermidorian analogy. And by proclaiming the Soviet Union Bonapartist, he could explain—at least to his own satisfaction—why Stalin had defeated him (because he had the full weight of the Soviet bureaucracy behind him), but still hold out hope for Stalin's eventual defeat and his own victory and vindication. However powerful Soviet Bonapartism, in the person of Stalin, might be at the present time, it had yet to wrest from the Soviet proletariat control over the means of production. In fact, it might never do so, and for that reason remained vulnerable to a proletarian revolution against it.

This, at any rate, was what Trotsky understood by Soviet Bonapartism. His analysis helps to explain why he considered it a cause for great concern, but it also enabled him to remain at least cautiously optimistic about the future. Nevertheless, there were serious problems in Trotsky's entire post-1934 analysis of the Soviet Union. By characterizing it specifically as Bonapartist, he was effectively elevating Stalin—whom he always considered a mediocrity—to the level of a historical actor as significant as Napoleon. Trotsky seemed aware that his readers might draw such a conclusion, which was almost certainly why he explicitly rejected any personal comparison between Napoleon and Stalin, blithely remarking in one of his writings on the subject that 'whenever the social conditions demand it, Bonapartism can consolidate itself around axes of the most diverse calibre'.[132] But even without explicitly analogizing Stalin to Napoleon, applying to the Soviet Union under Stalin a term that inevitably evoked the image of the French revolutionary emperor would always work to Stalin's advantage. Trotsky, however, was so eager to categorize the events that had been unfolding in the Soviet Union since 1917—partly because for Marxists categorizing something was tantamount to explaining it—that he could not refrain from doing so in the case of Stalin. And because of his near-obsession that the Bolsheviks might recapitulate in their own history the history of the French Revolution, the analogue he chose for Stalin's regime was, understandably, Napoleon's.

Another problem with his calling the Soviet Union Bonapartist was that he followed it by proclaiming little more than a year later, in a chapter in *The Revolution Betrayed*, that the Soviet Union was still in its Thermidorian phase, leaving any reader cognizant of Trotsky's earlier designation to wonder if it was still applicable.[133] In that regard one should note Trotsky's speculation in the early 1930s that somehow Thermidor and Bonapartism might merge in the Soviet Union, and more broadly that there need not be in the Soviet Union a literal repetition of the phases of the French Revolution. Thermidor and Bonapartism, after all, were both expressions, the former economic and the latter political, of the

---

[132] Ibid., p. 181.   [133] Trotsky, *Revolution Betrayed*, pp. 86–114.

same reactionary impulses. But there were other flaws and failings in Trotsky's analysis that could not be explained away so easily. Trotsky seems to have assumed that a state whose means of production were nationalized was *ipso facto* a workers' state. This, however, was theoretically dubious and historically false. Max Shachtman, a supporter of Trotsky who later rejected him, noted in the early 1940s that after nationalizing private property and the means of production, the proletariat, unlike the bourgeoisie under capitalism, could not exercise economic ownership without having political power, and since, according to Trotsky, the Soviet proletariat after 1934 had no political power (because it was wielded exclusively by the Soviet bureaucracy through Stalin himself), it could not own the means of production.[134] The Soviet Union, in other words, could not be a workers' state, and the long list of governments that since the 1930s have nationalized (or 'socialized') their economies without transferring power to their working class, or to any other class, provides corroboration of a sort for Shachtman's argument.

In assessing Trotsky's argument that after 1935 the Soviet Union manifested the essential attributes of Bonapartism, one must bear in mind that the Soviet Union was not the only regime, or even the first regime, that Trotsky identified as Bonapartist. In the early 1930s he had viewed with alarm the growing menace of fascism in Europe, and endeavoured to explain the transition to it with terminology borrowed from the history of France. In articles written at the time, Trotsky proclaimed that the Papen and Schleicher governments in Germany, the Doumergue government in France, and the Dolfuss regime in Austria were all Bonapartist to one degree or another. All were extraordinary governments brought into existence by the forces of finance capital for the purpose of protecting the bourgeoisie from the proletariat. Ruling through the police and the military, these regimes created and perpetuated a stalemate, if only a temporary one, between the two classes.[135] The following description of the Dolfuss government in 1933 can be taken as applicable to the other Bonapartist governments he identified:

> [The Dolfuss government] veers between two irreconcilable camps; [it is] forced to an ever-increasing degree to substitute the military-police apparatus for the social support that is ebbing away from under its feet. Expressed in the tendency towards Bonapartism are the urge of the possessing classes, by means of

---

[134] McNeal, 'Trotskyist Interpretations of Stalinism', p. 45.

[135] For example, Leon Trotsky, 'The German Puzzle (November 1932)', in Leon Trotsky, *The Struggle against Fascism in Germany* (New York, 1971), pp. 268–9; Leon Trotsky, *The Only Road* (New York, 1933); Trotsky, 'Bonapartism and Fascism', pp. 51–7. Until 1935 Trotsky did not imagine that a similar stalemate could exist after a proletarian revolution as well as before it, and that that would be reason enough to consider the result a form of Bonapartism. The stalemate in this case would not be between the bourgeoisie and the proletariat, but between a ruling bureaucracy and the proletariat. In *The Revolution Betrayed* and in other writings of his describing this bureaucracy, Trotsky always called it a 'stratum' or a 'caste' rather than a class to preserve the notion—to many it was actually a fiction— that the Soviet Union, in its economic arrangements, remained a workers' state.

military-police measures that are kept under cover, in the reserve paragraphs of democratic institutions, to avoid an open break with legality; a long period of civil war; and a bloody fascist dictatorship.[136]

But such regimes, because their social base was so precarious, could not prevent the inevitable: either they would succumb to proletarian revolution (the outcome Trotsky obviously preferred) or they could seek the support of the petit-bourgeoisie and become fascist. In the latter instance the Bonapartist regime would acquire a social base, and in its fascist incarnation would be blessed with 'a degree of social and political stability'.[137] But Bonapartism and fascism were both the result of the failures and the decline of capitalism, and to distinguish this kind of Bonapartism from its French original, Trotsky coupled his explanation with periodic reminders that the Bonapartism of Napoleon was an expression of capitalism in Europe when it was just emerging.[138]

But Trotsky, having discerned what he was now calling 'a Bonapartism of capitalist decay', seemed not to be satisfied with it.[139] In 1933 he muddied the taxonomical waters considerably by allowing that the governments of Poland, Yugoslavia, and Austria were actually 'quasi-Bonapartist,' without indicating what distinguished this ersatz Bonapartism from the genuine Bonapartism of Napoleon and Stalin.[140] On other occasions Trotsky complicated his taxonomy even more by predicting that fascist regimes, while more stable than their Bonapartist precursors, would likely revert to a form of Bonapartism before the proletariat had the opportunity to destroy them once and for all. As Trotsky explained in 1934:

Just as Bonapartism begins by combining the parliamentary regime with fascism, so triumphant fascism finds itself forced not only to enter into a bloc with the Bonapartists but, what is more, to draw closer internally to the Bonapartist system. The prolonged domination of finance capital by means of reactionary social demagoguery and petit-bourgeois terror is impossible. Having arrived in power, the fascist chiefs are forced to muzzle the masses who follow them by means of the state apparatus. By the same token, they lose the support of broad masses of the petit-bourgeoisie. A small part of it is assimilated by the bureaucratic apparatus. Another sinks into indifference. A third, under various banners, passes into opposition. But while losing its social mass base, by resting

---

[136] Leon Trotsky, 'Austria's Turn Next (23 March 1933)', in *WLT* (1932–3), (New York, 1972), p. 148.
[137] Trotsky, 'Bonapartism and Fascism', pp. 54–5.
[138] Leon Trotsky, 'German Bonapartism (30 October 1932)', in *Struggle Against Fascism*, pp. 330, 333; Leon Trotsky, 'Class Nature of the Soviet State', p. 107.
[139] Trotsky, 'Class Nature of the Soviet State', p. 107.
[140] Leon Trotsky, 'An Interview by Georges Simenon (6 June 1933)', in *WLT* (1932–3), p. 263. As already noted, Trotsky in 1920 had called Poland, then ruled by Pilsudski, an example of 'third-rate Bonapartism'. But that did not prompt any effort to define Bonapartism or to explain its emergence in Poland.

upon the bureaucratic apparatus and oscillating between the classes, fascism is regenerated into Bonapartism.[141]

Trotsky used the same argument to explain the 'Night of the Long Knives' in Nazi Germany in 1934, as a result of which, according to Trotsky, the Nazi regime could be considered Bonapartist.[142] But this 'Bonapartism of fascist origin', he added, was distinguished from the pre-fascist variety by its much 'greater stability'.[143]

Trotsky's typology thus came to consist of six, and possibly seven, kinds of Bonapartism: the Napoleonic original, pre-fascist Bonapartism, fascist Bonapartism, post-fascist Bonapartism, the Bonapartism of the Soviet Union under Stalin, and the quasi-Bonapartism of Yugoslavia and Poland. (The seventh variety, if one chose to include it, was the 'senile Bonapartism', that in 1940, shortly before his death, Trotsky believed to be the essence of Vichy France, its 'senility' reflecting what Trotsky considered the greater ease with which it could be overthrown.)[144] Faced with so many varieties of the same phenomenon, each of them different from one another and from the prototype that gave them all their name, one could reasonably question whether a single term could properly be used to define them. By invoking the spectre of Bonapartism so promiscuously and carelessly, Trotsky robbed it of its analytical value. Moreover, the Bonapartist regime of Napoleon lasted for nearly sixteen years, much longer than the brief duration Trotsky predicted for most of its modern analogues. More broadly, there was something seriously amiss in an analogy that depended for its validity on similarities between an essentially pre-industrial society and industrial ones. Napoleon's Russia may have been analogous in certain ways to Papen's Germany, Stalin's Russia, and Dolfuss' Austria, but the similarities implicit in these analogies were minimal in comparison to what distinguished the three regimes from Napoleon's, and one from the others.

Similar objections could be raised about Trotsky's claim for an analogy with Thermidor. Even a cursory comparison of the French and Soviet Thermidors (accepting that the latter existed as a form of reaction rather than of counter-revolution) suggests that while there were aspects of both that could be considered 'reactionary', the forms this reaction assumed in the two situations were radically different. In the case of France, the decentralization of power, the petty corruption, and the looser morality that prevailed in the late 1790s might be fairly

---

[141] Trotsky, 'Bonapartism and Fascism', p. 55.
[142] Ibid. Although, as Timothy Mason pointed out, there was some truth to the argument, which was Trotsky's, that the Nazis to some degree separated politics from the German economy, it hardly followed logically—nor is there empirical evidence to support the contention—that Hitler and the Nazis, as both Trotsky and Stalin believed, were the unwitting instruments of German big business. T. W. Mason, 'The Primacy of Politics—Politics and Economics in National Socialist Germany', in *The Nature of Fascism*, edited by S. J. Woolf (New York, 1965), pp. 165–95; Henry A. Turner, Jr, *German Big Business and the Rise of Hitler* (New York, 1985).
[143] Trotsky, 'Bonapartism and Fascism', pp. 55–6.
[144] Leon Trotsky, 'Bonapartism, Fascism, and War (August 1940)', in *WLT* (1939–40), p. 417.

considered a reaction to the austerity and the centralization of political authority under the Jacobins.[145] So, too, could the social and cultural conservatism in the Soviet Union in the Stalin era be considered a reaction to the experimentation in the 1920s in the arts and in a wide variety of sexual and social mores.[146] But surely a society characterized by opulence, corruption, and the gratification of private impulses is significantly different from one that officially sanctifies the family, productivity, and the subordination of the individual to collective entities like a political party and the state. Perhaps a more appropriate counterpart to Thermidor in Soviet history was the NEP, but even here the analogy is inexact, inasmuch as the NEP led to economic growth in a nation at peace, while the original Thermidor depressed the economy of a country at war.[147]

There were other differences, several of them critically important, between the two societies. One was that Stalin altered the tone and substance of Soviet foreign policy far more than the Directory altered the foreign policy of the Jacobins.[148] Another was that the Directory faced genuine challenges from both royalists and counter-revolutionaries, some domestic but others foreign, that assumed the form of actual conspiracies and rebellions, while the threats to Stalin were either trivial (Trotsky's Fourth International) or more potential than real (perhaps from Sergei Kirov) or entirely imagined.[149] Yet another was that the Soviets, because of their more advanced technology, could impose a degree of cultural and political homogeneity that the Thermidorians, with more primitive means of control at their disposal, could not.[150]

Finally, one is struck by how much of the history of the Soviet Union had no real analogue or equivalent in the French Revolution—or, for that matter, in 1830, 1848, and 1871. One looks in vain for any French Comintern, or for anything comparable to Lenin's Twenty-One Conditions binding foreign communist

---

[145] See, for example, Woronoff, *Thermidorean Regime*, pp. xx, 1–10, 38–9, 64–7.

[146] Stites, *Revolutionary Dreams*, especially pp. 225–41; Nicholas Timasheff, *The Great Retreat: The Growth and Decline of Communism in Russia* (New York, 1946); Fitzpatrick, *Russian Revolution*, pp. 158–63. Of course this cultural conservatism in no way vitiated the radicalism that was evident simultaneously in the economy.

[147] Woronoff, *Thermidorean Regime*, pp. 113–16.

[148] Adam Ulam, *Expansion and Coexistence: The History of Soviet Foreign Policy, 1917–1967* (New York, 1968), pp. 183–208; J. Godechot, *La Grande Nation: expansion révolutionnaire de la France dans le monde de 1789 à 1799* (Paris, 1956). That the Directory enlarged the objectives of Jacobin foreign policy, instead of reversing them, is the conclusion Martyn Lyons draws in *France under the Directory* (Cambridge, 1975), pp. 204–14.

[149] That there was a conspiracy in 1934 to replace Stalin with Kirov was Robert Conquest's conclusion in *Stalin and the Kirov Murder* (New York, 1989). More recently, in *The Kirov Murder and Soviet History* (New Haven CT, 2010), Matthew Lenoe has argued that no such conspiracy existed and that Kirov was killed by a lone, mentally unbalanced assassin. That Stalin used Kirov's murder for his own purposes, irrespective of his possible complicity in the matter, has never been seriously disputed.

[150] Woronoff, *Thermidorean Regime*, pp. 118–42; Gail Warshovsky Lapidus, 'Educational Strategies and Cultural Revolution: The Politics of Soviet Development', in Fitzpatrick, *Cultural Revolution*, pp. 78–104.

parties to the Soviet. Indeed, there was nothing in how the Soviet Union dominated Eastern Europe during the Cold War comparable to the Sister Republics in Europe in the 1790s, which retained a degree of autonomy that enabled French generals like Napoleon to develop the political skills needed to take power in France.[151] Also, there was missing in the French Revolution a Promethean vision of the state transforming nature through violence and coercion that found its fullest expression in the Soviet Union in industrialization and the collectivization of agriculture. The closest the French came in that regard was in the Jacobins' short-lived attempt to create a Republic of Virtue by changing external aspects of daily life such as the calendar, and holding the much-noted *fêtes* for the purpose of generating political consciousness.[152]

For purely political reasons, Trotsky would have been better off writing nothing about the French Revolution or Bonapartism. His treatment of these phenomena was marred by factual inaccuracies and a tendency to misread historical evidence, such as his erroneous assertions, all in his *History of the Russian Revolution*, that Danton was the leader of the insurrection of 10 August 1792—when in fact his role was no greater than that of others—and that the diary of Louis XVI could be considered evidence of 'spiritual emptiness'—when in fact Louis considered his diary a record of his prowess as a hunter, rather than a vehicle for stating privately his version of political events.[153] But even if one accepts the validity of everything Trotsky wrote about the French Revolution and Bonapartism, and acknowledges that the analogies he drew between the French and the Russian Revolutions were completely accurate, the fact remains that all of this was extraneous to his defence of the Soviet Union under Stalin as 'a degenerated workers' state'.[154] In other words, Trotsky could have characterised the Soviet Union as reactionary or counter-revolutionary, or in the throes of a 'plebiscitary dictatorship' without employing the vocabulary and the categories of another revolution and another revolutionary tradition. Instead, by explaining one revolution in the terms of others, Trotsky seriously underestimated the factors peculiar to each revolution—and to the history and national culture of the countries where they occurred—that help to explain the different path each of them followed. As a result, Trotsky's career-long meditation on the relationship of the Russian Revolution to the French Revolution and to the revolutionary tradition it inaugurated,

---

[151] R. R. Palmer, *The World of the French Revolution* (New York, 1971), pp. 149–62; Lyons, *France under the Directory*, pp. 146–58, 189–203; Roberts, *Napoleon*, pp. 74–104.

[152] In the case of the latter, one could say that the Bolsheviks got the idea of using them as political propaganda from the French Revolution, but infused those they sponsored with content that was *sui generis*.

[153] Trotsky, *History of the Russian Revolution*, unabridged edition, pp. 69, 881. These and other instances where Trotsky got his facts wrong are enumerated and discussed in Louis Gottschalk, 'Leon Trotsky and the Natural History of Revolution', *American Journal of Sociology* 44 (1938): pp. 339–54.

[154] Trotsky, 'The Workers' State, Thermidor, and Bonapartism', pp. 172–3.

marred as it was by factual errors, abrupt reversals, and imprecision of language, sheds more darkness than light.

Trotsky, who did not lack intelligence (though he seemed constitutionally incapable of introspection), was oblivious to all of this. In fact, he seemed so impressed by the intellectual gymnastics required to articulate the analogies he proffered that they eventually lost their original purpose. If, in the beginning, Trotsky intended the analogies he drew to illustrate, clarify, or corroborate a conclusion he had already arrived at, very soon they became more real in his mind than the phenomena they were intended to explain. From a tool of political analysis, Trotsky's analogies became a substitute for it. In fact, by the mid-1930s Trotsky had transformed Thermidor and Bonapartism into universal historical categories, descriptive not just of the French Revolution and the Russian Revolution, but of a pattern of degeneration, albeit a reversible one, to which no revolution in the future could be considered immune, not even (or perhaps especially not) socialist and proletarian ones.

Why Trotsky did this remains a matter of speculation. Apart from infatuation with his own intellectual and rhetorical pyrotechnics, there was also, perhaps, the unstated, but nonetheless undeniable fact that Marxist ideology could not explain the October Revolution, which by its lights was an aberration, and thus of no help when the Soviet Union after Lenin developed in ways that Trotsky could not have predicted and of which he wholeheartedly disapproved. In Trotsky's expectations of what the October Revolution would generate in Russia, Stalin and Stalinism were not among them. Finally, one might suggest that the misuse of historical analogies (and of history generally) is certainly not limited to revolutionaries, though the tendency of revolutionaries like Trotsky to justify their actions by appealing to history in the form of analogies with earlier revolutions may make them more prone than others to underestimate the singularity and the uniqueness of historical events. It may even be the case that the misuse of historical analogies is a consequence, unfortunate but unavoidable, of the tendency in Western civilization, traceable to its origins in Judaism and Christianity, to view history as linear and progressive, and thus an ongoing process in which the past was always a prelude to the future.

Whatever the reasons causing Trotsky to make such a mess of things when he looked to history for guidance, the fact remains that he continued to do so long after someone in his position less enamoured of his own powers of cerebration might have stopped and considered other ways of achieving the clarity about the Soviet Union's evolution he clearly needed and desired. Trotsky certainly knew the pitfalls of drawing analogies. In 1919, in a new introduction he wrote for *Results and Prospects*, he argued that most analogies, especially those by his political opponents, were the result of 'thoroughgoing [intellectual] superficiality'; the obvious inference he wanted his readers to draw from his comment was that they themselves should eschew historical analogies entirely, because the insights they provided were in almost every instance illusory.[155] But Trotsky seemed constitutionally incapable of taking his own advice in this regard, and as a result made the same mistakes he criticized his personal and political enemies for committing.

*   *   *

When Stalin drew historical analogies, in contrast to Trotsky he always seemed cognizant of the limits of their explanatory and predictive capability. When he used them, his motives were always political—usually to defame an enemy or some impersonal entity he considered hostile and dangerous either presently or in the future. Moreover, he could evaluate historical issues and the individuals involved in them without referencing the Marxist ideology that purported to explain them. This was true of what he wrote about Thermidor in the 1920s, and it was true of what he wrote about Bonapartism in the late 1920s and 1930s.

Stalin first invoked the spectre of Soviet Bonapartism in September 1927 in a speech to the Executive Committee of the Comintern. He began by stating that it was the opposition led by Trotsky that raised the whole issue. As Stalin continued, it became clear that what he objected to was not Bonapartism itself, but rather the opposition's ascription of it to the Soviet Union, a charge the general secretary indignantly rejected. In so doing, he provided a definition of the term, and thereafter never rejected his definition or altered it in any discernible way. For Stalin, Bonapartism was 'the forcible seizure of power in a party, or in a country, by a minority in opposition to the majority'.[156] But since 'an overwhelming majority in both the Communist Party and the Soviets' did not harbour Bonapartist tendencies, much less any inclination to transform them into deliberate and immediate action, the danger Bonapartism posed was practically nil.[157] In fact, the idea that it could do so was absurd: 'Has there ever been a case in history when the majority has imposed its own will upon itself by the use of force? Who but lunatics could believe that something so inconceivable [was] possible'.[158] The only circumstance, according to Stalin, in which the Soviet system would succumb to a Bonapartist dictatorship was if the opposition somehow imposed it over the objections of the Communist Party and the Soviet proletariat. It is true that Stalin did not address the possibility of Bonapartism, or something closely approximating it, succeeding a Soviet Thermidor should it ever exist. But by minimizing the danger of a Soviet Thermidor, which he said was advocated by 'degenerate opportunist elements' comprising only a small minority within the party, he effectively reduced to a nullity the chance of the Soviet Union becoming Bonapartist. In Stalin's mind, historical stages repeated themselves only in the

---

[155] Trotsky, *Itogi i perspektivy*, p. 3.
[156] J. V. Stalin, 'Politicheskaia fizionomiia russkoi oppozitsii', in Stalin, *Sochineniia*, vol. X, p. 164.
[157] Ibid., vol. X, p. 164.   [158] Ibid., vol. X, pp. 164–5.

order in which they originally occurred: because Bonapartism had followed Thermidor in France, it would do the same—were it to appear at all—in the Soviet Union. But in reality the issue was moot. Since Stalin and his supporters would prevent a Soviet Thermidor, Soviet Bonapartism would never exist.

In the same speech, which marked the only time Stalin ever explained what Bonapartism was (in contrast to minimizing its prospects in the Soviet Union), he did not ascribe to it any military dimension; nowhere did he indicate or imply that the dictatorship it entailed would either be supported by the military or led by it. Nor did he mention Napoleon himself, who, for anyone whose definition of Bonapartism included a military component, would be the quintessential Bona-partist ruler. Stalin's refusal to do so, one might suggest, was because he had a high opinion of Napoleon both as a ruler and military strategist, and would have no need to alter it as long as his notion of Bonapartism did not require its political manifestation to be a military dictatorship like Napoleon's.

In Marxist terms, Napoleon, as the political instrument of an incipient indus-trial bourgeoisie, was progressive and reactionary simultaneously, to be praised for advancing capitalism at the expense of feudalism, but also condemned as an enemy of the proletariat and socialism. Stalin had no reason to reject this particular aspect of Marxist orthodoxy, and nothing in his writings and speeches suggests that he did. But for all his military prowess and political acumen, Napoleon, in Stalin's estimation, would always bear the onus of attacking Russia in 1812 and nearly defeating it. In some sense, Stalin's ambivalence about the French emperor reflected the admixture, in his own mind, of Marxist ideology and the Russian nationalism he espoused, possibly in compensation for his non-Russian origins in Georgia. If, at certain times, Stalin could think well of Napoleon for his indubitably impressive political skills and military achievements, which were put to good use eliminating the last remnants of feudalism in France, at other times Stalin seemed to shrink from his conviction, as if remembering that the emperor also put his formidable abilities at the disposal, so to speak, of a bourgeoisie that intended for both the proletariat and the country of Russia nothing but harm.

In 1934, in an article on Engels written originally as a letter to the Politburo of the Communist Party, Stalin seemed intent on resolving his ambivalence and making sure his readers knew his real opinion of Napoleon. While certainly 'loathsome and filthy', his conquests, Stalin noted, were nonetheless no worse ethically than those of other rulers, including the tsars.[159] Moreover, 'the intrigue, deceit, treachery, flattery, brutality, bribery, murder, and incendiary politics' Napoleon brought to the political and military struggles he engaged in were absolutely essential to his success.[160] In the article, Stalin chastised Engels for criticizing the tsars excessively: by doing so, Marx's collaborator, according to

[159] J. V. Stalin, 'O stat'e Engel'sa "Vneshniaia politika russkogo tsarizma"', ibid., vol. XIV, p. 20.
[160] Ibid., vol. XIV, p. 20.

Stalin, ignored the role imperialism played in causing Napoleon to wage war on Russia in 1812. For that reason, Napoleon's campaign was a forerunner of the wars of the twentieth century, which, according to Stalin, were the result of imperialism. But a reader might be forgiven for concluding that, for all of Stalin's criticisms, Napoleon was really not so bad, and in light of his heroics on the battlefield, was actually, at least by Stalinist standards, quite impressive.

Even when nefarious comparisons to Napoleon were appropriate, Stalin stopped short of condemning him for everything he did. In a speech in 1941, on the eve of the anniversary of the October Revolution, when the danger to Moscow was so palpable that soldiers marching in Red Square the next day would continue directly to the frontlines mere miles beyond the city limits, Stalin managed to analogize Napoleon to Hitler so that the former seemed the antithesis of the latter, even though both were guilty of attacking Russia. In Stalin's comparison, 'Hitler resembled Napoleon no more than a kitten resembled a lion'.[161] And if Stalin's choice of animals worked to Napoleon's advantage in the personal qualities it suggested each man possessed, Stalin enlarged the comparison to include the respective historical forces the two rulers personified. Here, too, Stalin made his preferences clear: 'Napoleon fought against the forces of reaction while relying on progressive ones, whereas Hitler, by contrast, relied on the forces of reaction while fighting against progressive ones.'[162] For that reason, Hitler's defeat was inevitable.

Stalin referenced Napoleon next in a speech in 1942, when he simply noted the disparity in the number of troops Napoleon and Hitler ordered into Russia, which for Stalin was a way of demonstrating the enormity of the task the Red Army still faced even after inflicting on the *Wehrmacht* its first defeat in the battle for Moscow in December 1941. But Stalin said nothing more about Napoleon until 1947, when he intervened in the aforementioned dispute involving Tarlé. By praising the tactics Kutuzov employed against Napoleon, Stalin, for the first time, seemed intent on diminishing the latter's ability as a military strategist.[163] As a result, Bonapartism, in its Stalinist incarnation, acquired an explicitly military connotation. No longer a mere expedient concocted by the bourgeoisie to ensure its continued economic supremacy, it had become, by the late 1940s, a real danger to the future health, and possibly even the survival, of the Soviet Union, which, according to Stalin, had become completely socialist in 1936. In 1950 Bonapartism was defined formally in *The Large Soviet Encyclopedia* as:

> one of the forms of the counterrevolutionary dictatorship of the big bourgeoisie, relying on the militarists, and manoeuvring in the conditions of an unstable

---

[161] Stalin, 'Doklad na torzhestvennom zasedanii Moskovskogo Sovet', ibid., vol. XV, p. 80. In a printed edition of Stalin's speech, one reads that this particular comment evoked 'laughter and loud applause'. While these reactions were often entirely fabricated for political purposes, in this instance one can easily imagine Stalin's audience reacting in exactly that way.

[162] Ibid., vol. XV, p. 80.   [163] 'Otvet tov. Stalina na pis'mo tov. Razina', pp. 7–8.

equilibrium of class forces. [Bonapartism] appears when the class struggle is reaching its limits... when the bourgeoisie is unable to cope with the revolutionary movement, while the proletariat is still weak and cannot win the struggle [with the bourgeoisie].[164]

Bonapartism, in other words, could only emerge under capitalism, and while this revised definition explicitly cited 'militarists' as its principal bulwark, left unsaid was the identity of whoever exercised political power once Bonapartism existed. About this, one can only speculate that Stalin thought silence was best: saying nothing about Bonapartism in a purportedly socialist society might reduce, perhaps to a nullity, the chances of it actually emerging. Stalin's fear of Bonpart-ism was real, as his demotion of Marshal Zhukov and reassignment to a provincial command after the conclusion of the Second World War amply demonstrated.[165] That his fear was unwarranted, or at least greatly exaggerated, was evidenced by the fact that, over the twenty-four years of Stalin's rule, no one in the upper echelons of the Soviet armed forces, as far as one can tell, ever questioned its legitimacy, much less tried to remove Stalin from power, even though the Soviet generals and marshals who dealt personally with him had good reason to murder him, especially after Stalin decimated the Red Army's High Command in 1937. They also had the means and the opportunity to do so. But there were sound reasons for doing nothing. An unsuccessful attempt on Stalin's life would of course have guaranteed immediate execution, while a successful attempt, if it ushered in a regime hostile to the conspirators, might have produced the same lethal result. The irony in all of this is that, whatever the outcome of any hypothetical Soviet 18 Brumaire, Stalin, by purging the upper echelons of the Soviet armed forces, effectively precluded its actual occurrence.

But the fear of a Bonapartist *coup d'état* engineered by the military did not disappear after Stalin's death, and in 1957 it re-emerged in public discourse.[166] In October of that year Bonapartism was among the reasons stated publicly for Nikita Khrushchev's removal of Marshal Georgii Zhukov as Minister of Defence. Despite his having approved Zhukov's appointment two years earlier, Khrushchev

---

[164] *Bol'shaia sovetskaia entstiklopediia* (Moscow, 1950), vol. V, p. 556.

[165] On 10 March 1952, *Pravda* printed a photograph, taken in February 1950, of Stalin, Mao, and Georgii Malenkov, a Politburo member and thought by many to be Stalin's chosen successor. Because Malenkov, in the photograph, had affected the iconic Napoleonic pose—one of his hands was behind the opposite side of the suit he was wearing—he was strongly criticized by various members of the Central Committee, who would not have done so without Stalin's approval. There is also good reason to believe that Malenkov's unfortunate pose served as a convenient excuse for his rivals to attack him in the struggle for power that followed Stalin's death in 1953. Jan Plamper, *The Stalin Cult: A Study in the Alchemy of Power* (New Haven CT, 2012), p. 84.

[166] The term itself remained a useful political epithet. At a Central Committee Plenum in July 1953, V. M. Andrianov joined with others in justifying Beria's prior arrest and prospective trial and execution, describing the former police chief as 'a Bonaparte, ready to climb to power over mountains of bodies and rivers of blood'. 'The Beria Affair: Plenum of the Central Committee CPSU: The Fourth Session—July 4, 1953', in *Political Archives of Russia* 3, no. 2/3 (1992), p. 145.

had come to consider the Soviet general a potential threat, and acted decisively to neutralize it. After the Second World War Zhukov was the closest equivalent in the Soviet Union to a war hero; like his American counterpart, Dwight Eisenhower, he received much of the credit for the operational decisions enabling the Red Army to drive the *Wehrmacht* out of Russia and, in May 1945, to force Germany to surrender. Like Stalin, Khrushchev was jealous of Zhukov, but unlike Stalin he had reason to fear him. Zhukov's willingness during the war to speak to Stalin with none of the deference to which the Soviet dictator was accustomed seemed to Khrushchev sufficient proof of Zhukov's political ambitions, which might include, by 1957, his gaining power at Khrushchev's expense, and then possibly overturning the entire Soviet system.[167] In 1955, however, Khrushchev's fear was not yet sufficient to deter him from approving Zhukov's appointment. In fact, his doing so made political sense: with Zhukov in Moscow, the new Soviet leader could keep an eye on him. Moreover, Zhukov might prove to be politically useful. This was certainly the case in June 1957, when he provided the military transport planes needed to fly Khrushchev's supporters in the Central Committee to Moscow to meet in an emergency session after Presidium members hostile to Khrushchev and his policy of partial de-Stalinization had secured a majority favouring his dismissal.[168]

The Central Committee, as Khrushchev expected, overruled the Politburo, thereby ensuring his continuation in power—and also vindicating his original decision to appoint Zhukov defence minister. But once that happened, Zhukov became expendable, and in the context of Soviet politics, a potential enemy. That Khrushchev could not have overcome his rivals (condemned publicly as 'the Anti-Party Group') without Zhukov's support and assistance revealed a degree of dependence that the first party secretary, lacking Stalin's enormous power, could not endure—hence Zhukov's dismissal. But unlike Stalin's victims in the 1930s who were liquidated immediately or consigned to labour camps, where most of them died, Zhukov, in the more relaxed atmosphere of the Khrushchev era, was allowed to live, his lenient punishment of forced retirement eerily similar to Khrushchev's after the coup deposing him in 1964.

What made Zhukov's dismissal noteworthy was the accusation of Bonapartism that served to justify it. The charge did not emerge *ex nihilo*. Even when Zhukov was appointed defence minister, figures in the uppermost echelons of Soviet politics and the military warned of his ostensibly Bonapartist aspirations. In 1955, at a dinner in Khabarovsk, in the Soviet Far East, with Khrushchev present,

---

[167] Montefiore, *Stalin*, pp. 373, 394. One of Zhukov's biographers, however, claims that Zhukov was always 'in awe' of Stalin. Geoffrey Roberts, *Stalin's General: The Life of Georgy Zhukov* (New York, 2012), p. 86.

[168] In 1952 the Politburo was renamed the Presidium and would be called that until 1966. From 1953 to 1966 the position of General Secretary of the Communist Party, previously held by Stalin, was officially renamed First Party Secretary, and would also be called that until 1966.

Marshal Rodion Malinovskii, who would be Zhukov's successor at the Ministry of Defence, described the one-time war hero as 'an incipient Bonaparte' and 'a dangerous man who must be stopped'.[169] At the same dinner, Malinovskii warned Khrushchev and everyone else in attendance to 'watch out for Zhukov', and gave as his reason the marshal's Bonapartist ambitions.[170]

It was only natural, then, that the same charge be levelled afterwards. Publicly Zhukov was condemned after his dismissal for 'adventurism' and for violating the Leninist principle requiring the party's control of the military. Both were formal deviations—there were twenty-nine in all—from party orthodoxy. In ordinary language, this meant that Zhukov was guilty of conspiring to establish a military dictatorship in the Soviet Union, with himself as the dictator. This of course was the essence of Bonapartism, as the Soviets since the Lenin era had defined it, and one can be certain that Khrushchev and the other Presidium members who wanted Zhukov gone were aware of this. In his memoirs, written many years later, Khrushchev claimed that Zhukov had articulated his 'Bonapartist ambitions' in conversations with Soviet army officers, presumably in the course of enlisting them in a plot to overthrow the civilian leadership; whether Khrushchev believed this was the case remains problematic and, in terms of the politics of the matter, irrelevant.[171] The public campaign to defame Zhukov immediately following his dismissal was approved at the highest levels of the Soviet leadership, and reaffirmed at subsequent party congresses. While largely confined to Moscow, it also required party leaders and government officials elsewhere in the country to denounce him—which they did. For example, on 31 October 1957, N. G. Ignatova, the party secretary of the Gorkii *obkom* (region), claimed in a speech delivered to party activists that Zhukov had sought to establish 'a personal dictatorship' and for the Bonapartism that that entailed was justly condemned. In fact, in his enormously inflated self-regard, Zhukov, according to Ignatov, was even worse than Napoleon.[172]

By the end of the decade, Bonapartism had become a formal deviation from party doctrine in everything but name. Zhukov, of course, was its personification.

---

[169] V. Naumov, ed., *Georgii Zhukov: Stenogramma oktiabr'skogo (1957g.) plenuma Tsk KPSS i drugie dokumenty* (Moscow, 2001), p. 637.

[170] Ibid., p. 539. Because no date for the dinner is provided in the stenographic account of it that was published two years later, it is possible that Malinovskii's comments were delivered at two separate dinners. But it is unlikely that Presidium members—according to one account Nikolai Bulganin was present along with Khrushchev and Georgii Malenkov—would gather at a location so far from Moscow twice in the same year absent a crisis or a sudden emergency. Ibid., p. 637.

[171] Nikita S. Khrushchev, *Khrushchev Remembers: The Last Testament* (New York, 1976), p. 14. Several generals and at least one marshal in the army opposed Zhukov's dismissal. Timothy J. Colton, *Commissars, Commanders, and Civilian Authority: The Structure of Soviet Military Politics* (Cambridge MA, 1979), p. 181. But that, by itself, was hardly evidence of Bonapartism, which in the Soviet sense of the phenomenon implied that those guilty of it form an actual conspiracy to seize the government in a *coup d'état*, which none of these military officials intended.

[172] Naumov, *Stenogramma obkiabr'skogo (1957g.) plenuma*, p. 455.

In 1959, at the Twenty-First Party Congress, Malinovskii called Zhukov 'a latter-day Bonaparte' whose intention to 'separate the army from the Communist Party' was sharply rebuffed, and at the Twenty-Second Party Congress two years later, Khrushchev himself cited as evidence of the Soviet general's Bonapartism his ostensible 'aspirations to seize power personally'.[173] Also at the congress, Marshal F. I. Golikov cited Zhukov's 'Bonapartist course' among the reasons for his dismissal.[174] Understandably, none of this sat well with Zhukov himself. In a letter he sent in February 1964 to Khrushchev and Anastas Mikoyan, he angrily denied any intention of becoming 'a new Napoleon', among the other 'fables' that had been repeated about him in memoirs, journals, and other published material.[175] Eight months later Khrushchev himself lost power in a coup not dissimilar to that which he claimed Zhukov had earlier plotted against him; the result, as far as Zhukov was concerned, was that his public rehabilitation was now a real possibility. In March 1965, he formally applied for it, and two months later, on the eve of the twentieth anniversary of the end of the Second World War in Europe, received a standing ovation after entering the hall where Leonid Brezhnev would shortly deliver a speech praising him explicitly.[176] The following day he joined Brezhnev and the other Soviet leaders reviewing the Victory Parade on top of the Lenin Mausoleum.[177]

Zhukov's ostensible Bonapartism was the public face of the concept when both Khrushchev and Brezhnev ruled the Soviet Union. Limiting the term to an exclusively military affair confirmed the Stalinist view of the phenomenon; for that reason Louis Napoleon, in the way he came to power and how he ruled the Second Empire, still did not figure in it at all. Moreover, there was nothing in the public condemnations of Zhukov to suggest any desire to transcend classes once he had overthrown the Soviet system and installed a military dictatorship; after 1936 it was official dogma that the country was socialist and that only one class, the working class, existed. Nor was anything said or written about Zhukov's ostensible intention to deceive the Soviet people by claiming disingenuously—as Louis Napoleon had in France a century earlier—that the material benefits he would dispense reflected a desire to improve their material welfare. Under Stalin, Khrushchev, and Brezhnev, Bonapartism was something to which only errant generals and marshals were susceptible, and power for its own sake was its only reward. As a result, Zhukov was not stigmatized as a budding capitalist, much less

---

[173] Quoted in *Vneocherednoi XXI s"ezd Kommunisticheskoi Partii Sovetskogo Soiuza: Stenografi-cheskii otchet* (Moscow 1959), vol. II, p. 127; quoted in *Vneocherednoi XXII s"ezd Kommunisticheskoi Partii Sovetskogo Soiuza: Stengraficheskii otchet* (Moscow, 1961), vol. II, p. 120.

[174] 'Rech' tovarishcha F. I. Golikova', *Pravda*, no. 304(15794) (31 October 1961): p. 3.

[175] 'Pis'mo G. K. Zhukov N. S. Khrushchevu i A. I. Mikoianu (27 February 1964)', in Naumov, *Stenogramma obkiabr'skogo (1957 g.) plenuma*, p. 496.

[176] Roberts, *Stalin's General*, p. 294. At the first mention of Zhukov's name, the audience applauded.

[177] Ibid.

or a proto-fascist. Nor was he condemned—as one might malign Napoleon Bonaparte—for seeking continental domination.

To be sure, Soviet historians in both the Khrushchev and Brezhnev eras continued their serious study of the phenomenon, secure in the knowledge that they would not be shot or sent to a labour camp for drawing conclusions unpalatable to either Soviet leader, neither of whom likely cared much about whether the policies of the two Napoleons were expressive of an entire category of deviant regimes. In the matter of Bonapartism, Soviet historians could say what they wished. As a result, much was said about it between the Stalin era and Gorbachev's rise to power in the mid-1980s. In 1959 V. P. Volgin came close to blaming Louis Blanc for Louis Napoleon, arguing that the duplicity of the former accustomed the proletariat in 1848 to demagogues from the petit-bourgeoisie like the latter.[178] In 1975 Iu. A. Krasin went so far as to claim that there were aspects of Stalinism that could plausibly be considered evidence of Bonapartism: a single ruler and his public exaltation, the supremacy of the state over society, and a rough equality in the strength of the two largest and most antagonistic classes. But Krasin followed his assertion with the disclaimer that Stalinism and Bonapartism were not the same thing, and that any resemblance was largely obviated by the fact of Stalin's taking power after the bourgeoisie in Russia had been destroyed, rather than before it. But this did not mean that Stalin's power was absolute. Not only could he not destroy everything in the Soviet Union Lenin had established, but he also could not physically eliminate everyone who sought to continue 'the Leninist tradition'.[179]

For his part, V. G. Revunenkov extended his investigations of the French Revolution into its Napoleonic coda—which culminated in the assertion in 1989 that Napoleon pioneered a new type of monarchy, which Revunnenkov called, seemingly oxymoronically, a 'bourgeois monarchy'.[180] By this, Revunnenkov—who was always more inclined than other Soviet historians of his generation to test the limits of Marxist concepts and categories—meant a system in which the institution (monarchy) that under feudalism had served as the principal instrument of the aristocracy had somehow survived a bourgeois revolution intent on destroying it and lived on to serve the bourgeoisie under capitalism.

But idiosyncratic interpretations like Revunnenkov's would not be widely known or discussed until the Gorbachev era, when the freedom of expression Gorbachev allowed made possible public discussion of virtually all matters of opinion, even those concerning the prospects for Bonapartism in the Soviet Union, which, in and of itself, suggested the impermanence, even the fragility,

[178] Volgin, 'Lenin i revoliutsionnye traditsii frantsuzskogo naroda', pp. 13–14.
[179] Iu. A. Krasin, *Revoliutsiei ustrashennye. Kriticheskii ocherk burzhuaznykh kontseptsii sotsial'noi revoliutsii* (Moscow, 1975), pp. 122–3.
[180] Revunenkov, *Ocherki po istorii Velikoi frantsuzskoi revoliutsii*, p. 116.

of the Soviet system as a whole. Dmitrii Zatonskii, writing in 1988, compared Stalin to Napoleon, and concluded that the two rulers and the regimes they created were different politically and morally.[181] Perhaps the most obvious contrast he drew was in how each took power and consolidated it. Stalin inherited a political system Lenin had previously established and remoulded it to serve his own interests and objectives. Napoleon, by contrast, simply disbanded the Directory, and after an interregnum in which he ruled essentially as a military dictator, created a seemingly new and different kind of polity based on his own unique status as *imperator*—a concept Napoleon resurrected from the old Roman Empire in keeping with the fascination of the Enlightenment and the French Revolution with everything traceable to ancient Greece and Rome. Only considerably later in his rule did Napoleon, out of political necessity, revive certain practices of the (more recent) *ancien régime*.[182]

But Zatonskii also acknowledged similarities. Both Stalin and Napoleon were pragmatic, even cynical, in their political and ideological commitments. Stalin, in particular, thought nothing of altering Marxism-Leninism while simultaneously pledging fealty to Lenin. But Zatonskii's article was more concerned with explaining why the Soviet system under Stalin was not, strictly speaking, a species of Bonapartism if, by the term, one meant an actual military dictatorship—as opposed to a militarist system enforcing discipline and obedience within a rigid hierarchy based on a strict compartmentalization of functions. But even if the system Stalin created in the Soviet Union was truly militarized, a better, more descriptive term for it, in Zatonskii's considered opinion, was 'barracks socialism', a common term for the Soviet system, usually used derisively, during the Gorbachev era. In short, the barracks socialism Stalin caused to exist in the Soviet Union was not the same thing as Bonapartism. Indeed, for Zatonskii the more pressing question requiring historians' attention was why the Soviet Union, even under Stalin, never succumbed to a military dictatorship. His explanation was that civilians like Bukharin and Rykov, because they had helped Lenin establish the Soviet system, never tried to overthrow it either alone or in collaboration with the military. The same was true, he said, of Red Army generals, who for their own reasons might have preferred a military dictatorship to Stalin's, but took no action to create one.[183]

The fear of Bonapartism that existed among the Bolsheviks, and which achieved its fullest public expression in Zhukov's dismissal, was not limited, in the Gorbachev era, to historians. Even one of the Soviet dissidents—in the minds of many the most prominent and the most morally virtuous—publicly warned of the danger of Bonapartism in the form of a military dictatorship. When, in 1989, it seemed that Gorbachev had repudiated *perestroika* after appointing opponents of it to key

[181] Dmitrii Zatonskii, 'Pochemu oni ogovarivali sebia i drugikh', *Nedelia*, no. 28 (1988): pp. 6–7.
[182] Ibid., pp. 6–7.   [183] Ibid., p. 7.

THE PHANTOM OF THE RUSSIAN BONAPARTE

positions in the government and the police, Andrei Sakharov thought that that might prompt army generals to seek power themselves.[184] Sakharov's invocation of the danger reflected his fear—however unfounded it turned out to be—that a Bonapartist *coup d'état* was a real possibility.

But others less ethical than Sakharov, and with a more personal stake in the vicissitudes of high Soviet politics, used the threat of a Soviet 18 Brumaire for their own purposes, and with the same vigour and disregard for the actual chances of its occurring when it was used to discredit Kerensky in 1917, Trotsky in the early 1920s, and Zhukov in the late 1950s. In 1986 and 1987, after Boris Yeltsin had begun to criticize Gorbachev for not reforming the Soviet system sufficiently, Bonapartism was among the charges the general secretary levelled against his new rival. At a meeting of party functionaries in 1986, the specific charge was that Yeltsin harboured 'Napoleonic plans'.[185] In November 1987, at a meeting of the Moscow Party Committee, he was forced, in the manner of defendants in the show trials of the 1930s, to confess publicly to multiple violations of party discipline, decorum, and regulations; in the same venue, an obscure Moscow party member accused him of possessing 'elements of Bonapartism'.[186] Proof that Gorbachev approved of the latter accusation, irrespective of its empirical absurdity, was its inclusion in the article in *Pravda* describing the meeting two days later.[187] No less absurd was the accusation at a session of the Congress of People's Deputies in 1989 that Gorbachev resembled Napoleon just as much as Yeltsin did, the reason being that both men were susceptible to flattery; in the case of the general secretary, there was the lamentable fact that he usually did what his wife wanted him to do.[188]

On such an unedifying note, the debate about Bonapartism in the Soviet Union ended.[189] But for most of the union's existence, the chance of its emerging was considered seriously, even when the term was used as a pejorative to discredit political and personal enemies. The fear of Bonapartism was real. Not having first-hand experience in the military, Soviet leaders from Lenin to Gorbachev knew

---

[184] Andrei Sakharov, 'Stepen' svobody: Aktual'noe intrev'iu', *Ogonëk* (July 1989): p. 28.
[185] Quoted in 'Can Moscow Believe in Yeltsin?', *Détente* (Autumn, 1986): p. 4.
[186] At the meeting, twenty-three speakers denounced Yeltsin for one transgression or another or for many of them. Louis Sell, *From Washington to Moscow: U.S-Soviet Relations and the Collapse of the USSR* (Durham NC, 2016), p. 190.
[187] 'Energichno vesti perestroiku', *Pravda*, no. 317(25304) (13 November 1987): p. 2.
[188] Schoenfeld, 'Uses of the Past' (PhD dissertation), p. 229.
[189] Charges of Bonapartism continued in Russia after the Soviet Union's collapse. In the infighting around Yeltsin during his campaign for the Russian presidency in 1996, the Prime Minister, Viktor Chernomyrdin, called General Alexander Lebed, then Yeltsin's national security advisor, 'a little Napoleon'. Steven Lee Myers, *The New Tsar: The Rise and Reign of Vladimir Putin* (New York, 2016), p. 111. Whether the appellation contributed to Yeltsin's subsequent decision to fire Lebed is not clear.

little of its intimate workings. Trotsky, in that respect, was the exception, and it afforded him an advantage over his rivals. But the fear of military dictatorship was so pervasive among the Bolsheviks that Trotsky's military service and connections were actually more of a hindrance than a help, and the perception that he resembled Napoleon and might betray the October Revolution the way the emperor, in his last years in power, had betrayed the French, helped to seal Trotsky's political fate and, as it turned out, virtually guaranteed his physical destruction. Bonapartism was not the only reason Trotsky lost out to Stalin, but it was certainly one of them.

As a general whose achievements during the Second World War were real, Zhukov conformed more closely than Trotsky to the Bonapartist paradigm. But Zhukov's very involvement in military matters, seemingly to the exclusion of everything else, made him, in reality, less of a threat to the Soviet civilian leadership than a general or marshal who once had a career in politics and retained the instincts and abilities of a politician. Indeed, one is left with the conclusion that the Soviets' obsession with Bonapartism had less to do with the Trotskys and the Zhukovs who triggered it, and more to do with the two Napoleons, each of whose betrayal of an earlier and mostly virtuous revolution, from which they each had benefitted politically, encapsulated the very real fear among the Bolsheviks that their success in 1917 was an ideological anomaly, and that the regime that followed it was vulnerable to enemies at home and abroad. What is more, the whole notion of Bonapartism, in the context in which the Bolsheviks tried to deal with it, seemed to transcend the conceptual limits of their Marxist-Leninist ideology. For Marx and Engels, Bonapartism could only exist under capitalism. For that reason its emergence in a socialist society could plausibly be construed to mean that the society's socialism was fraudulent, that its socialist exterior concealed a core that was more capitalist than socialist, and with the passage of time might shed its socialist aspects entirely. Considered the way the Bolsheviks saw it, Bonapartism was the result of the Marxist dialectic reversing itself, so that history ran backwards instead of forward. This was truly the spectre that made Bonapartism, for the Bolsheviks, so fearsome.

Whether Bonapartism was ever a real possibility in the Soviet Union was irrelevant.[190] Most of the Bolsheviks believed that it was, and their fear that it existed or would soon come to exist was genuine. What they were unable to deal with was the reason for their fear, because by doing so they would be calling into question the very legitimacy of the whole Soviet Experiment. Conjuring phantoms such as Bonapartism was emblematic of what happens when revolutionaries wedded to a rigid ideology that tells them any revolution they make would be

---

[190]   Also irrelevant in this context is whether Bonapartism even constitutes a discrete political system and form of politics worthy of inclusion in any taxonomy or classificatory schemata that is empirically accurate and analytically useful.

premature and destined to fail nonetheless throw caution to the winds, as the Bolsheviks did in 1917 despite their knowing precious little about what the consequences of their own actions would be. The result, for the Bolsheviks, were new and unfamiliar realities that their ideology left them ill-equipped to understand, much less harness for their own political and ideological purposes. Because so much of what the Bolsheviks did after 1917 was improvised, they had no choice but to look to history, and to the tradition of revolutions in France in particular, for at least a modicum of the confidence that comes from relying on useful and relevant precedents. The trouble with the particular precedent, or series of precedents, personified historically in the two Napoleons, was that it was an unexpected aberration from a virtuous norm, a kind of coda that detracted from the progressive phenomena preceding it that, for the lack of a more descriptive term, was called Bonapartism.

In sum, Bonapartism was a very real potential impediment on the road to communism that should be avoided not just because it implied a regression delaying, or even obviating entirely, the triumphal march of history from capitalism and communism. By its instantaneous invocation of the Bonapartes themselves, it also personalized this regression, which might result in the very destruction of the Soviet state, in a way that only heightened the danger the term itself was meant to evoke. Both Napoleons gave a human face to a particular scenario resulting ultimately, perhaps, in the destruction of the Soviet Union and the demise of the entire enterprise of constructing socialism and communism. Each ended his political career, and his life, as a loser—Bonaparte a lonely exile on St Helena in the South Atlantic, Louis Napoleon in England three years after the humiliation of being captured by the Prussians at Sedan. This effectively disqualified them both from retroactive martyrdom. There was nothing terribly gallant or heroic or inspiring about Louis Napoleon's capture, deposition, and demise. About that of his uncle one could, to be sure, conceptualize a legend, namely that of the resplendent emperor and general who was the victim, after countless victories, of the sheer magnitude of the forces arrayed against him, first at Leipzig in 1813, and then at Waterloo in 1815. Viewed in this way, the first of the two Napoleons could qualify for martyrdom. But for the French, at least, it has been far more profitable, after the establishment of the Third Republic made a Napoleonic Restoration impossible, to memorialize and celebrate in a spirit of nationalism his many victories rather than to mourn ostentatiously his few defeats. In somewhat the same way, the Bolsheviks grudgingly admired Napoleon Bonaparte for his military prowess, and in any event never considered him or his nephew martyrs who had sacrificed their lives for their ideals. In fact, the Bolsheviks seemed to believe, perhaps correctly, perhaps not, that neither man had any ideals or permanent principles to begin with. Both Napoleons were defeated by superior military and political power, and neither ideology nor morality had anything to do with it.

Fortunately for the Bolsheviks, there occurred, after 1848, yet another revolution in France—as it happened, the last one in its Revolutionary Tradition—that *was* conducive of the martyrdom lacking in the lives—or more precisely the deaths—of the two Napoleons; indeed the depths of the martyrdom implicit in this last revolution far exceeded that produced by any of its predecessors. What this martyrdom clearly suggested was that defeats are often only temporary, that in defeat are often embedded the seeds of future triumphs, and that the nobility of character martyrdom demonstrates *post mortem* may even be transferable generationally from revolutionaries who try and fail to make a revolution to those of later generations, whose efforts are likely to be more successful precisely because they have absorbed the moral virtues of their predecessors; in addition, these later revolutionaries can avoid the mistakes to which earlier generations were understandably susceptible. In this way this last of the four revolutions in this tradition of revolutions, coming as it did after the partial success in 1830 and the abject failure in 1848, was truly a *deus ex machina*—atheists like the Bolsheviks preferred to consider it the result of impersonal forces driven by the dialectic—that would enable the Bolsheviks to end their lives neither as losers nor as martyrs but as the custodians of the most ethical and materially productive country in the world.

Louis Napoleon's deposition and the collapse of the Second Empire triggered a series of events, played out against a backdrop of chaos and uncertainty, from which emerged the Paris Commune in March 1871. The heroism and courage the Communards showed in defending it, and the suffering they endured when their efforts failed, soon became the absolute epitome of revolutionary virtue, and the basis for a mythology, to which the Bolsheviks would contribute significantly, that would not be nearly as powerful and appealing and inspiring if the Commune had somehow survived. It is this last manifestation of the French Revolutionary Tradition, ennobled by a martyrdom to which neither of the Napoleons could lay any plausible claim, that now commands our attention.

PART IV

1871

15

Revolution as Martyrdom

The Paris Commune was the stuff of genuine tragedy. Those who died defending it could easily be apotheosized for their martyrdom. Far from disqualifying the Commune as an object of veneration, its defeat had the paradoxical effect of making it more attractive, especially to revolutionaries like the Bolsheviks, who, prior to the October Revolution, were failures themselves, relegated by their powerlessness to the margins of Russian political life and saved from permanent oblivion only by the remarkable confluence of circumstances in 1917 that made the October Revolution possible. Because the Commune's defeat was so costly in human lives, one could plausibly compare the Communards to the earliest Christians in the Roman Empire—even though the Bolsheviks, as self-professed atheists could not do so themselves. That the Communards resisted their oppressors and killers instead of merely defying them, as the Christians did the Romans, in no way detracted from their moral virtue, and to hardened revolutionaries like the Bolsheviks it enhanced it.

At the same time, the Bolsheviks never romanticized the Communards in the way other lost causes in history, such as the restoration of the Stuart monarchy in England in the eighteenth century, have been extolled.[1] The Jacobites professed no ideology that claimed to guarantee success; nor did they inspire future generations of monarchists to consider their actions a harbinger of better things to come.[2] For the Bolsheviks, the Paris Commune was very different. Far from being a defeat from which no future rebirth or rejuvenation was possible, the failure of the Commune was bound, in dialectical fashion, to generate its antithesis: a glorious victory enabling the Bolsheviks to finish the task the Communards had begun of constructing a just and humane society in which all workers would be compensated fully and fairly for their labour. Even the Communards' mistakes served the useful purpose of showing the Bolsheviks what not to do. Indeed, the more mistakes the Communards made, the more relevant and useful their experiences became.

To be sure, the Commune included many non-Marxists among its leaders. But this did not preclude the Bolsheviks admiring them and, in certain ways,

---

[1] Moray McLaren, *Bonnie Prince Charlie* (New York, 1972); Carolly Erickson, *Bonnie Prince Charlie* (New York, 1989).

[2] George Hilton Jones notes in *The Mainstream of Jacobitism* (Cambridge MA, 1954), p. 246, that 'every factor influenced England and Scotland to forget the (Jacobite) cause'.

attempting to emulate them. In addition to the martyrdom that could fairly be imputed to the Commune's defenders, there was another aspect of the Commune that distinguished it from its predecessors in the French Revolutionary Tradition: in Marx's terminology, which the Bolsheviks used to explain virtually everything, the Paris Commune was the first revolution in France in which the haute-bourgeoisie did not participate; in fact it was the enemy of the revolution from the outset. For that reason, and notwithstanding numerous internal disagreements, no one betrayed the Paris Commune from within. In contrast to the Jacobins succumbing to Thermidorians who had once supported them but increasingly found their radicalism intolerable, and unlike the lower classes in the June Days in 1848 who were massacred by elements of the bourgeoisie that just four months earlier had been their allies, the Communards were never the remnant of any revolutionary coalition.[3] The Commune did not last long enough to generate any Thermidorian Reaction, and the *Versaillais* in uniform who destroyed it had never supported it. While the Commune was led by 'petit-bourgeois' professionals—journalists, lawyers, and teachers—who were prominent in earlier French revolutions, the remainder of the bourgeoisie stayed away. As a result, the Commune retained an ideological radicalism and a degree of socio-logical homogeneity, absent in earlier French revolutions, that enhanced its reputation among Marxists in Russia and elsewhere who believed their mission as revolutionaries was to continue what the Paris Commune began. The Paris Commune was the last revolution in the French Revolutionary Tradition, but it was also the first revolution in a new tradition that was predominantly the work of the lower classes; that these still were craftsmen and artisans like those of the French Revolution, rather than a modern, industrial proletariat, was a reality the Bolsheviks ignored.[4]

* * *

The Bolsheviks were not the first Russians to find meaning in the Commune. Several who did so before them had been Communards themselves; others, mostly *émigrés*, witnessed it as residents of Paris. Among the former were two women: Anna Krukovskaia and Elizaveta Dmitrieva. Krukovskaia, whose father was a general in the Russian army, rejected a proposal of marriage from Dostoevsky

---

[3] One might say that, in 1830, there was no betrayal because, in Marxist terms, the lower classes never held power long enough for the bourgeoisie or any part of it to betray them.

[4] The Commune could be considered a proletarian institution only if one defined the word proletarian so loosely that it loses its implication of workers performing unskilled labour in factories. That it was not is exemplified in the fact that there was not a single unskilled worker on the Commune's governing council. Robert Tombs, *The Paris Commune* (New York, 1999), p. 114. Tombs' larger conclusion that the Commune was the work of revolutionaries from the middle class and supported by a pre-industrial working class is reiterated in David Thomson, *Democracy in France since 1870* (New York, 1964), pp. 24–5; Edward S. Mason, *The Paris Commune: An Episode in the History of the Socialist Movement* (New York, 1967), p. 119; and Jacques Rougerie, *Procès des Communards* (Paris, 1964), p. 206.

before marrying a French Blanquist; Dostoevsky was so infatuated with her even after she rejected him that a character of uncommon beauty in his novel, *The Idiot*, was modelled on her.[5] Dmitrieva, who in March 1871 helped organize the Commune, was the only Russian to serve on the *Union des Femmes*, established in April, that helped doctors treat the wounded after the *Versaillais* attacked the Commune at the end of May. With a felt hat on her head and a scarf draped diagonally across her chest, Dmitrieva looked vaguely like the heroine in Delacroix's iconic painting 'Liberty on the Barricades'. Sentenced to hard labour for life after the Commune was suppressed, Dmitrieva escaped Paris before she could be arrested, and eventually found refuge in Switzerland.[6]

Among the Russian revolutionaries in Paris when the Commune began was Pëtr Lavrov, who was so infatuated by its emergence that it confirmed in his mind his longstanding belief, central to the populism he professed, that, if given power, the masses in Russia would govern responsibly and humanely.[7] Where the Communards were deficient, he believed, was in refusing to transform Parisian society after proclaiming that that was their intention. But this deficiency Lavrov ascribed entirely to the temperament of the Communards; with their principles and objectives he was in complete agreement. Nevertheless, it was not for any deficiency in temperament or personality that the Commune would have failed even if the assault of the *Versaillais* had somehow been repulsed. Rather, the Commune failed for lack of support from the French peasantry—an assertion consistent with Lavrov's belief that socialism was virtuous precisely in its fusion of the urban and the rural, in its vision of workers and peasants living harmoniously with one another in similar, if not exactly identical, ways.[8] Soviet historians, while praising Lavrov's assertion that the Commune was created in a proletarian revolution, also berated him for not considering the proletariat a class.[9] Nevertheless, they saw Lavrov's populism as a precursor, however imperfect, of Soviet Communism, and for that reason his lengthy analysis of the Commune, *Parizhskaia Kommuna 18 marta 1871 goda*, was published in several editions in the

[5] Edith Thomas, *The Women Incendiaries* (New York, 1966), pp. 89–90; Kenneth Lantz, The Dostoevsky Encyclopedia (Westport CT, 2004), p. 220. Dostoevsky did not let his feelings for Krukovskaia diminish his strong dislike of the Commune; he was especially distressed by the many fires that were set when the Commune was established, and slightly more than two months later when it was suppressed. This may be the reason he included in his novel *The Possessed*, which explores the corruptibility and criminality of revolutions, an act of arson that affected the plot. Ibid.

[6] Thomas, *Women Incendiaries*, pp. 67–75, 209–11; I. Knizhnik-Vetrov, *Russkie deiatel'nitsy Pervogo Internationala i Parizhskoi kommuny* (Moscow/Leningrad, 1964), pp. 74–101, 185–90.

[7] Philip Pomper, *Peter Lavrov and the Russian Revolutionary Movement* (Chicago IL, 1972), p. 120; Theodore Dan, *The Origins of Bolshevism* (New York, 1970), p. 63.

[8] P. L. Lavrov, 'Parizhskaia kommuna 1871 goda (1875)', in Lavrov, *Izbrannye sochineniia no sotsial'no-politicheskie temy*, vol. IV, pp. 24–5; 'Pis'mo P. L. Lavrov k E. A. Shtakenshneider (1871)', in *Golos minuvshago*, edited by S. P. Mel'gunov and V. I. Semevskii (The Hague, 1971), p. 125; McClellan, *Revolutionary Exiles*, p. 162.

[9] Lavrov, 'Parizhskaia kommuna', p. 25; B. S. Itenberg, *Rossiia i Parizhskaia kommuna* (Moscow, 1971), p. 149.

Soviet Union, and its author praised as second only to Marx and Engels in the perspicacity of his views on the Commune.[10]

For Mikhail Bakunin, the virtue of the Commune was bound up in its failure—an outcome Bakunin considered inevitable despite the bravery and heroism of its defenders.[11] In keeping with his comment in 1842 that 'destruction is a creative passion', Bakunin thought it would be a good thing if the Commune brought down with it the 'half of Paris' that was bourgeois: the more completely the corrupt society of the bourgeoisie was destroyed, the more morally pure its replacement would be.[12] The Commune, he wrote, was 'a bold and outspoken negation of the state'—even though he never described the Commune explicitly as an anarchist institution.[13] But looking back on the Commune late in life and with the benefit of hindsight, Bakunin acknowledged that the Communards had made mistakes, most notably relinquishing power to the 'Jacobins' among them, who were deluded by their 'the cult of unity and authority' and accordingly betrayed the noble aspirations of its mostly anarchist-minded creators.[14]

In Bakunin's writings on the Commune one senses a reluctance to acknowledge unpleasant truths, the most obvious of which was that the Communards were patriots and therefore hated the Prussians for trouncing French forces and controlling much of northern France as a result. The Commune, he affirmed in clear defiance of the facts, 'destroyed patriotism [and] inaugurated the new era, that of the final and complete emancipation of the masses of the people and their solidarity ... across state frontiers'.[15] But affirmations such as these did little to diminish his unhappiness after the Commune's suppression. Eventually, Bakunin made the best of a bad situation, claiming—several decades before the Bolsheviks existed—that the memory of the Commune, 'soaked in the blood of its most generous-hearted children', would inspire future revolutionaries to pick up the bloodstained banner the Communards had been forced to relinquish.[16]

Pëtr Kropotkin was not in Paris in 1871. But he met several Communards in Switzerland in the years that followed, and read avidly about their activities.[17] Like Bakunin, Kropotkin admired the Communards for the ad hoc manner in which they governed. But he also recognized that the spontaneity that made the Commune so appealing also had its limits. For example, instead of eliminating municipal government entirely, which is what Kropotkin's anarchism required the

[10] Lavrov's book was published in Petrograd/Leningrad twice in 1919, and in 1922 and 1925. McClellan, *Revolutionary Exiles*, p. 170, n. 42; I. Stepanov, *Parizhskaia kommuna 1871 goda i voprosy taktiki v proletarskoi revoliutsii* (Moscow, 1921), p. 114.
[11] E. H. Carr, *Michael Bakunin* (New York, 1975), p. 433.
[12] Mendel, *Michael Bakunin*, p. 370; Mikhail Bakunin, 'The Reaction in Germany', in *Michael Bakunin: Selected Writings*, edited by Arthur Lehning (London, 1973), p. 58.
[13] Michael Bakunin, *The Paris Commune and the Idea of the State* (London, 1971), p. 2.
[14] Bakunin, *Statism and Anarchy*, pp. 19–20; Bakunin, *Paris Commune*, p. 3.
[15] Bakunin, *Paris Commune*, p. 2.   [16] Ibid.
[17] N. K. Lebedev, *Kropotkin* (Moscow, 1925), pp. 34, 38–9.

Communards to do, they replaced it with one of their own, which 'neither boldly declared itself socialist nor proceeded to the expropriation of capital'.[18] This meant, as he finally admitted in 1913, that the Paris Commune was not a revolutionary entity at all. Indeed, because the influence of the Jacobins and Blanquists who organized it was far greater than that of the Proudhonists, whose anarchism was quickly marginalized and had little influence on actual policy, it could never have become one. The Commune, in short, was too centralized. The elections it held, irrespective of their fairness, perpetuated the apparatus of governance instead of eliminating it—a state of affairs Kropotkin believed made Paris somehow less able to withstand the *Versaillais* when they attacked in the third week in May.[19] In addition, Kropotkin pronounced the wage differentials between officials on the Commune Council and the so-called *fédérés* manning the barricades that protected it incompatible with anarchism.[20]

Nevertheless, Kropotkin considered the Commune a signal moment in the larger teleology he believed would culminate in the triumph of anarchism everywhere. For anarchists like Kropotkin, the Commune was valuable more for the possibilities it adumbrated than for the unpleasant, if perhaps unavoidable, realities of its actual existence.[21] For all its failings, the Paris Commune showed that 'the free commune', as Kropotkin called the generic category of polities to which the Commune belonged, was the most appropriate vehicle for providing the happiness, enlightenment, prosperity, and justice that would exist once centralized political authority had disappeared.[22] While the Commune itself was just a first attempt at the radical transformation of humanity, the revolutions Kropotkin was convinced would follow it 'would take up the work of the Paris Commune where it was interrupted by the massacres of the Versailles soldiery'.[23]

One might think that Marx, as an advocate of urban revolutions, would have praised the Commune more lavishly and consistently than did populists like Lavrov and anarchists like Bakunin and Kropotkin, of whose opinions Marx was well aware. But that was not the case. His view of the Commune was very much a function of circumstance: Marx argued against the idea of a commune before it existed, praised it fulsomely while it existed, and then mostly criticized it years later, when his memories had faded and his emotions had long since calmed. Incorporating Marx's views of the Commune in their own mythology was therefore no easy task for the Bolsheviks.

Prior to the Commune, Marx considered France unready for a proletarian revolution. For that reason any insurrection intent on establishing an institution that addressed workers' needs while also serving as a prototype for a socialist state

---

[18] P. A. Kropotkin, *The Paris Commune* (London, 1896), pp. 3–4, 6.
[19] Peter Kropotkin, *Modern Science and Anarchism* (1913), in *Kropotkin's Revolutionary Pamphlets*, pp. 163, 239–41.
[20] Kropotkin, *Conquest of Bread*, p. 151.   [21] Kropotkin, *Paris Commune*, pp. 7–8.
[22] Kropotkin, *Conquest of Bread*, p. 8.   [23] Kropotkin, *Paris Commune*, pp. 6–7.

was bound to fail. The Second Empire was too strong and the French working class not yet radical enough to challenge it successfully.[24] In April 1870 Marx stated in a private letter that England was 'the most important country for the workers' revolution, and moreover the only country in which the material conditions for this revolution have developed up to a certain point of maturity'.[25] By 1870 Marx had long since acknowledged that the French proletariat had shown its unreadiness for revolution in 1848, and in a letter to Engels in September of that year made clear that nothing that had happened since then had caused him to change his opinion.[26] In addition, Marx was fearful that the Prussians, whom he deemed incorrigible imperialists, would achieve an even more overwhelming victory over France in the event that the newly established Third Republic, which was still committed to resisting them, lost control of Paris. Any attempt to overthrow the new republic, in short, would be 'a desperate folly'.[27]

When the Commune was proclaimed, however, Marx realized the political necessity of blessing it publicly and supporting it wholeheartedly; whatever its deficiencies, it was the only revolution in Europe at the time, and the only one even remotely resembling the proletarian revolution Marx envisaged and still believed to be inevitable. As such, its mere existence was a form of vindication. What is more, the audacity of what the Communards were attempting appealed to his intuitive sense (well-developed despite the determinism in his ideology) of the role of contingency and individual will in history. Finally, one must remember that in 1871 Marx was fifty-three, an age then considered old, and perhaps for that reason likely to grasp at any straw in the wind, no matter how ephemeral, that seemed to prove his predictions about capitalism's collapse firmly grounded in reality.

While the Commune existed, Marx read the Parisian newspaper, the *Journal Officiel*, for information. He also corresponded with several Communards and members of the International in Paris who were assisting them.[28] Nonetheless, his descriptions of the Commune and the meanings he ascribed to it were largely self-generated, a reflection more of Marx's hopes and aspirations than of the empirical evidence he possessed. In his mind the Commune was a proletarian dictatorship— even though he never applied that appellation to it; rather, it was Engels, writing in 1891, who made the identification explicit, stating flatly in his introduction to Marx's pamphlet on the Commune, *The Civil War in France*, that anyone who

[24] K. Marx, 'Second Address of the General Council on the Franco-Prussian War (9 September 1870)', in Marx and Lenin, *Civil War in France*, p. 34. The General Council oversaw the activities of the (First) International, established in 1864.
[25] 'Letter, Marx to S. Meyer and A. Vogt (9 April 1870)', in Marx and Engels, *Selected Correspondence*, p. 290.
[26] Isaiah Berlin, *Karl Marx: His Life and Environment* (New York, 1963), pp. 187–8; 'Letter, K. Marx to F. Engels (6 September 1870)', in Marx and Engels, *Collected Works*, vol. XLIV, pp. 64–5.
[27] Marx, 'Second Address', p. 34.   [28] Mason, *Paris Commune*, p. 305.

'wants to know what a [proletarian] dictatorship looks like [should] look at the Paris Commune'.[29]

For Marx the Commune was 'the most glorious deed of our party since the June [1848] insurrection in France'.[30] The Communards, he stressed, were not content with inheriting the institutions the bourgeoisie had established. Instead, they would 'smash [the] bureaucratic-military machine' and the other institutions now at their disposal and replace them with new ones once the enemies that threatened them had been defeated.[31] Although Marx refrained in his contemporaneous analyses of the Commune from terming its ultimate objectives 'socialist', it was clear that this was what he considered them to be. Of course the premature destruction of the Commune rendered these objectives moot, and turned its defenders into martyrs. Nevertheless, *The Civil War in France* was as much a call for future revolutions as it was an elegy to a revolution that had failed. In Marx's estimation, the Commune will be 'forever celebrated as the glorious harbinger of a new society. Its martyrs are enshrined in the great heart of the working class.'[32]

Nevertheless, Marx was aware that many leaders of the Commune did not share his views. The Blanquists and Proudhonists were too numerous among the Communards to ignore. But that knowledge melted away in the excitement caused by the Commune's creation. It was a measure of Marx's emotional commitment that he supported the Commune even though his doing so lent credence to the sobriquet applied to him in reactionary circles in Europe as 'the Red Terrorist Doctor'.[33] If the only way Marx could claim paternity of the Commune was by distorting what it was and what it intended, that seemed a small price to pay for the psychological benefits it conferred.

[29] Frederick Engels, 'London, on the 20th Anniversary of the Paris Commune, 18 March 1891', in Marx and Engels, *Collected Works*, vol. XXVII, p. 191. Engels' words are also reprinted on the page preceding the first page of text of A. Slutskii, *Parizhskaia kommuna 1871 goda* (Moscow, 1925). Marx's essay was originally intended as an address to the American and European members of the General Council of the International. On his reluctance to term the Commune a proletarian dictatorship, see M. Johnstone, 'The Commune and Marx's Conception of the Dictatorship of the Proletariat and the Role of the Party', in *Images of the Commune*, edited by John A. Leith (Montreal, 1978), p. 204.
[30] K. Marx, 'Letter to Dr. Kugelmann on the Paris Commune (12 April 1871)', in Marx and Lenin, *Civil War in France*, p. 86.
[31] Ibid. Marx in this instance was paraphrasing his prediction in *The Eighteenth Brumaire* of what 'the next attempt of the French revolution' will involve. His phraseology suggested that the 1848 Revolution and the Paris Commune were really one revolution separated by twenty-three years or, more precisely, were part of a larger revolutionary tradition to which the original French Revolution, and probably also the Revolution of 1830, belonged. While the Paris Commune still existed, he would have rejected the fact, admittedly ascertainable only with the benefit of hindsight, that from 1789 to 1871 revolutions in France became not only shorter but less and less successful, because 'the civil society of property owners' that succeeded 'the society of orders' in the original French Revolution proved stronger as the nineteenth century progressed, rather than weaker, as revolutionaries like Marx imagined. Sperber, *Revolutionary Europe*, pp. 424, 431.
[32] Marx, 'Second Address', p. 81.
[33] P. Thomas, *Karl Marx and the Anarchists* (London, 1980), p. 333.

Even so, Marx was not uncritical of the Commune. In his opinion it suffered from an excess of caution, which he ascribed, albeit reluctantly, to its prematurity. Had the Parisian proletariat it represented been more advanced economically, and therefore more radical politically, the Commune, in his estimation, would not have allowed forces loyal to Thiers—whom Marx described with sadistic relish as 'that monstrous gnome'—to evacuate Paris and find safety at Versailles.[34] Instead, the Commune should have ordered its military arm, the National Guard, to pursue these forces, which Marx believed could easily have led to their destruction. Had that been done, the whole history of the Commune might have been different.[35]

Above and beyond these specific mistakes, the Commune, in Marx's contemporaneous analysis, failed ultimately because it tried to reason with its enemies, appealing to what it considered to be their self-interest, instead of destroying them. Even worse, the Communards suffered from the mistaken belief that 'the political instrument of the proletariat's enslavement—by which Marx meant the governing institutions the Communards had inherited when they took power—could serve as 'the political instruments of their emancipation'.[36] Nonetheless, he believed that the legacy the Commune left behind transcended its failings. Its defeat, far from delaying the ultimate victory of socialism and the proletariat, would accelerate it. Indeed, by supporting the Commune so emphatically and enthusiastically, Marx was helping to make his prediction come true. In reality, he so transmogrified the Commune into something larger and more portentous than it was that nearly every Marxist of any significance in Europe in the late nineteenth and early twentieth centuries felt compelled to pronounce judgement on it.

But as the passage of time caused the Commune to recede from his consciousness, Marx's opinion changed yet again. He did not even mention the Commune in the *Critique of the Gotha Programme*, his next major work following the demise of the Commune, which he finished writing in the spring of 1875. In 1881, in a letter to the Dutch socialist Ferdinand Domela Nieuwenhuis, Marx denigrated the Commune as 'merely the rising of a town under exceptional conditions', and the majority of the Communards as 'in no sense socialist'.[37] Moreover, were it not for their lack of common sense, they could have reached a compromise with the *Versaillais*.[38] What caused this inversion of Marx's opinion of the Commune was a recognition not merely of its failure in Paris and in France but also of its inability to inspire insurrections elsewhere in Europe. By the time he was writing to Nieuwenhuis, Marx had fastened his hopes on a very different object, namely

---

[34] Marx and Lenin, *Civil War in France*, pp. 39, 51.   [35] Ibid., pp. 50–1.
[36] K. Marx, 'Vtoroi nabrosok 'Grazhdanskoi voiny vo Frantsii', in *Arkhiv Marksa i Engel'sa* (Moscow, 1934), vol. III, p. 415.
[37] 'Letter, K. Marx to Domela Nieuwenhuis (22 February1881)', in Marx and Engels, *Selected Correspondence*, pp. 387.
[38] Ibid.

the peasant commune in Russia, which he had come to believe could be the instrument enabling that country, and possibly others, to skip the capitalist stage of history and progress directly from feudalism to socialism.[39] That the Russian terrorists in *Narodnaia volia*, who shared Marx's newfound belief in the possibilities of the peasant commune, were the only revolutionaries in Europe acting to bring about the socialism he favoured only heightened his commitment to their cause.

*   *   *

Marx's animadversions on the Commune had no utility for Lenin, who always valued the Commune for the lessons it taught, the legitimacy it conferred, and the fortitude and perseverance inherent in its existence, and even more so in its defeat. In 1924, after Lenin's death, Zinoviev described his commitment to the Commune as follows:

> On not one of the movements of the foreign proletariat did Vladimir Ilich lavish such attention as he did on the Paris Commune. Of not one of the movements of the foreign proletariat did Vladimir Ilich speak with such respect as he did of the movement of the Paris Workers [i.e. the Commune].[40]

In reality, Lenin's view of the Commune was more complicated than Zinoviev suggested. In nearly everything Lenin wrote and said about the Commune one finds an unresolved contradiction between straightforward assertions that the Commune—as Marx had insisted—was the first proletarian polity in history, and grudging acknowledgement that members of the petit-bourgeoisie—which was how Lenin characterized pejoratively the Blanquists, Jacobins, and Proudhonists—were nonetheless an integral part of it. Rather than denying this contradiction, Lenin turned it to his advantage. He considered the Marxist socialists in the Commune to have been responsible for its achievements, and blamed the non-Marxists in the Commune for its shortcomings. To be sure, Lenin coupled his attacks on these non-Marxists with ritualistic reiterations of Marx's arguments that the principal reason for the Commune's failure was its prematurity, by which he meant its emergence before class relations under capitalism had deteriorated in France to the point where institutions like the Commune would have a social base in the French proletariat large enough for it to endure. But one senses that, for Lenin, these underlying factors were less important than the fact of the Commune's existence and the opportunity it provided to attack his ideological opponents. As a result, Lenin praised the Commune for what it was, even as he criticized it for much of what it did. In short, Lenin tried to have it both ways.

---

[39] 'Letter, K. Marx to V. Zasulich (1 March 1881)', in Deich, *Gruppa 'Osvobozhdenie Truda'*, vol. II, pp. 223–4.

[40] Quoted in A. Gambarov, *Parizhskaia Kommuna* (Moscow, 1925), p. 331.

Before 1908 Lenin did not evaluate the Commune comprehensively. He devoted no work to it exclusively—not even an article—and his comments on it were sporadic and merely supportive of arguments on other matters. Nevertheless, they adumbrated fairly well the conclusions he fleshed out when conditions in Russia in 1917 gave the Commune a tactical relevance it had not had before. Lenin's first reference to the Commune was in a private letter of 1901, in which he criticized Plekhanov for denigrating the Commune as 'ancient history'.[41] One year later, Lenin wondered 'where we would be now without the gigantic impulse given especially by the Paris Commune'.[42] By his comment Lenin was effectively situating the Commune within the larger revolutionary teleology that he believed had begun in France with the French Revolution and would culminate in a successful revolution in Russia. In 1904, in notes prepared for a talk delivered to Russian émigrés in Geneva, he even called the Commune 'the greatest working-class uprising of the nineteenth century' and thus a forerunner of 'the world republic' that would exist once socialists had come to power everywhere.[43] In this instance, however, he also listed what he considered the most consequential mistakes and failings of the Commune. These included, most prominently, not taking over the Bank of France and its assets, which were in Paris when the Commune was declared, and not pursuing the Republican army loyal to Thiers after it had withdrawn from Paris, which ensured the survival of the newly established Republican government in Versailles; this in turn prevented the Commune from extending its sovereignty to other parts of France. Lenin ascribed the Commune's failure to take these actions to an insufficiency of political consciousness on the one hand, and an excess of nationalism on the other. But the Commune also warranted praise for its separation of Church and state; for the deference it showed to the National Guard, which for Lenin was nearly the equivalent of a people's militia; for its ending of workers' fines and night work in bakeries; and for its policy of placing empty factories under its own jurisdiction.[44]

By 1905 Lenin had read not only what Marx and Engels had written about the Commune, but also the memoirs of several Communards.[45] Moreover, by July of that year he had had time to reflect on the revolution in Russia that had begun in January, and without retracting his earlier statement in another talk to Russian émigrés in Geneva that 'we all stand on the shoulders of the Commune', he now made clear that a commune was precisely what socialists should *not* attempt to

---

[41] Quoted in V. A. Eremina, 'V. I. Lenin kak istorik Parizhskoi Kommuny', *Voprosy istorii*, no. 2 (1971), p. 36.

[42] Lenin, *What is to be Done?*, p. 28.

[43] V. I. Lenin, 'Tri konspektov doklada o parizhskoi kommune (9 March 1904)', in Lenin, *PSS*, vol. VIII, p. 487.

[44] Ibid., pp. 490–1.

[45] Among them were those of Gustave Paul Clusert, who had served as a general in the Union army in the American Civil War before becoming a Communard. Billington, *Fire in the Minds of Men*, p. 357.

replicate in Russia.[46] In a paragraph he appended to an article, written by someone else, that he was editing for publication, the future Soviet leader explained why he agreed with the author's views on the Commune:

This article teaches us, most of all, that the participation of the socialist prole-tariat in a revolutionary government that includes the petit-bourgeoisie' is entirely permissible in principle, and in certain conditions is obligatory. It shows us further that the real task the Commune had to perform was primarily the achievement of the democratic (but not the socialist) dictatorship, which is to say the implementation of our 'minimum programme'. Finally, the article reminds us that when we study the lessons of the Paris Commune we should not imitate the mistakes it made (not seizing the Bank of France, not launching an offensive against Versailles, the lack of a clear programme, and so on) but its successful practical measures, which indicate the correct route. It is not the word 'Commune' that we must adopt from the great figures of 1871; we should not blindly repeat each of their slogans. What we must do is point out those programmatic and practical slogans that are relevant to the state of affairs in Russia and can be formulated in the words 'a revolutionary democratic dictator-ship of the proletariat and the peasant dictatorship'.[47]

What Lenin appeared to be arguing was that while the relative moderation of the Commune was appropriate given the capitalist epoch in which it existed, its failure to defend itself economically and militarily made its emulation in Russia pro-foundly unwise. Nonetheless, Lenin strongly criticized Plekhanov in 1917 for citing the Commune's destruction as proof that it should never have been established: if the Commune had never existed, revolutionaries of later gener-ations would not learn from its mistakes.[48] In addition, the Commune had inspirational value, which Lenin ascribed to its defeat. There were moments in history, he said, 'when a desperate struggle of the masses, even for a hopeless cause, is necessary for the future schooling of these masses and their preparations for the next struggle'.[49]

---

[46] V. I. Lenin, 'Plan chteniia o kommune', in Lenin, PSS, vol. IX, p. 330; V. I. Lenin, Dve taktiki, ibid., vol. IX, p. 70.

[47] V. I. Lenin, 'Zakliuchitel'naia chast' k stat'e "Parizhskaia Kommuna i zadachi demokraticheskoi diktatury"', Proletarii, no. 2 (17 July 1905), ibid., vol. XI, p. 132.

[48] V. I. Lenin, Predislovie k russkom perevodu pisem K. Marksa k L. Kugel'manu (1907), ibid., vol. XIV, pp. 375–6, 378–9. What made Lenin's attack on Plekhanov ironic, and perhaps unfair, was that in March 1903 Plekhanov had written an article for Iskra that uncannily adumbrated the view of the Commune Lenin advanced later. Plekhanov criticized the Commune for its lack of toughness and ruthlessness. But he also qualified his criticisms by pointing out that by studying failed revolutions one learned how to carry out successful ones. And far from denigrating the Communards for their mistakes, Plekhanov stated that 'they covered themselves in everlasting glory'. G. V. Plekhanov,'Martovskiie idy', Iskra, no. 36 (March 15, 1903), in Plekhanov, Sochineniia, vol. XII, pp. 334–41.

[49] Lenin, Predislovie, in Lenin, PSS, vol. XIV, p. 379.

In 1908 Lenin delivered a public lecture on the Commune that in its tone, if not in its content, reflected the absence of any additional revolution in Russia since 1905. Indeed, the text of Lenin's lecture reads in places like a eulogy for a beloved comrade struck down at the height of his powers by a fatal and unavoidable disease.[50] By that time it was de rigueur for Marxist socialists to describe the Commune as a proletarian institution, and in that respect Lenin's lecture did not disappoint. The Commune, he said, was 'a superb example of the great proletarian movement of the nineteenth century'.[51] At the same time, Lenin acknowledged ruefully that in 1871 French capitalism was insufficiently advanced for the proletariat in France to be fully aware of its historical obligations; this was identical to what he had written in *What is to be Done?* in 1902 about Russian capitalism and its failure to radicalize the Russian proletariat sufficiently for it to lead a Russian socialist party, much less to carry out a proletarian revolution. While in Lenin's opinion the Communards had demonstrated unwavering courage in the face of overwhelming opposition, their patriotic hatred of the Prussians, which he now said was what caused them to refrain from taking over the Bank of France, had made the promulgation of socialist measures impossible.[52] Although the Commune, as such, had carried out 'democratic tasks' of which Lenin believed the bourgeoisie to be incapable, the Commune, as was evident by its many failings, left much to be desired. But it was the best Marxist revolutionaries could have hoped for given the stage history had reached when the Commune began.[53] Two years later, in 1910, Lenin made explicit his perception of the Commune as an integral component of a larger revolutionary tradition, arguing that it marked the end of 'the democratic revolution' in Europe that had begun in France in 1789.[54]

In 1911 Lenin again situated the Commune historically, this time in terms of the development of French capitalism.[55] But the conclusion he drew was the same: that the Commune, for all its undeniable achievements, was destined to fail. The specific catalyst for its failure was that the petit-bourgeoisie withdrew its support from the Commune when it realized it was doomed to defeat. Without a political party of the type Lenin favoured—a highly centralized one in which the lower echelons executed the directives of the party's leaders loyally and obediently— there was no means of compensating for the petit-bourgeoisie's defection. Given the absence of such a party, it was not at all surprising that the Communards lacked the necessary toughness and ruthlessness.[56] In the same article, however, Lenin cited approvingly a new generation of Marxist revolutionaries, both in France and elsewhere in Europe, who were not disillusioned by the Commune's

[50] V. I. Lenin, 'Uroki kommuny', *Zagranichnaia gazeta*, no 2 (23 March 1908), ibid., vol. XVI, pp. 451–4.
[51] Ibid., vol. XVI, p. 453.   [52] Ibid., vol. XVI, p. 451.   [53] Ibid., vol. XVI, p. 452.
[54] V. I. Lenin, 'Zametki publitsista', *Diskussionyi listok*, no. 1 (6 March 1910), ibid., vol. IXX, p. 247.
[55] V. I. Lenin, 'Pamiati kommuny', *Rabochaia gazeta*, no. 4–5 (April 1911), ibid., vol. XX, p. 219.
[56] Ibid., vol. XX, pp. 218–19.

failure and were intent on renewing the struggle the Commune had begun.[57] In 1913, Lenin went a step further, arguing now that the Commune marked not just the end of one stage of history, but the beginning of another, which would supersede all previous ones by prompting urban insurrections. The ultimate result would be the destruction of capitalism and the emergence of socialism.[58] Still, there was something formulaic in Lenin's statements prior to the First World War about the Commune as a proletarian state, and thus the first step in the emancipation of the proletariat everywhere. His praise, especially after 1905, seems forced and ritualistic, and the reader could easily conclude that behind his litany of the Communards' mistakes and personal failings—especially a lack of toughness that precluded the harsh measures Lenin believed to be essential to the Commune's survival—the Bolshevik leader was harbouring a deeper, if unacknowledged pessimism about the imminence of future revolutions not only in France but also, more importantly, in Russia.

All this changed, however, with the outbreak of the First World War. Because the Commune had emerged in the aftermath of a war (albeit one on a much smaller scale that also ended quickly), it was now, suddenly, relevant again. In an article written in the autumn of 1914, Lenin castigated European socialists who, instead of opposing the war in the name of 'proletarian internationalism', not only supported it rhetorically, but in some cases even enlisted in their own country's army.[59] In the article, Lenin again reserved his sharpest rhetorical fusillades for those French socialists, who, by supporting their country in 1914, were compounding their original betrayal of the working class in 1900 when they 'accepted ministerial posts in the government of that very bourgeoisie which [in 1871] had betrayed its country and joined with Bismarck to crush the Commune'.[60] What made Lenin's article remarkable was that at the end of it he prefigured what would be one of his most powerful arguments in 1917 for taking power in Russia:

The transformation of the present imperialist war into a civil war is the only correct proletarian slogan, one that follows from the experience of the [Paris] Commune and, as outlined in the Basle resolution of 1912, from the conditions of an imperialist war between highly developed bourgeois countries.[61]

[57] Ibid., vol. XX, pp. 221–2.
[58] V. I. Lenin, 'Istoricheskie sud'by ucheniia Karla Marksa', *Pravda*, no. 50 (1 March 1913), ibid., vol. XXIII, p. 2.
[59] V. I. Lenin, 'Voina i rossiiskaia sotsial-demokratiia', *Sotsial-demokrat*, no. 33 (1 November 1914), ibid., vol. XXVI, pp. 15–23.
[60] Ibid., vol. XXVI, p. 18.
[61] Ibid., vol. XXVI, p. 22. That France's government in 1871 was located somewhere other than in its longtime capital, thereby making the Commune's emergence a historical accident unlikely to occur again in Russia or France or in any other country, Lenin conveniently ignored. This unusual circumstance also helps to explain why the people who ran the Commune previously had no interest in governance, or even in politics, and very little idea of how they would use power should they ever possess it. All revolutions entail improvisation, but the Paris Commune seems to have generated more of it than others.

In 1915, in a pamphlet written with Zinoviev's assistance, Lenin described the Commune as marking the end of the epoch in human history that began with the French Revolution, when wars were fought mostly by the bourgeoisie for national liberation. He also reiterated his earlier argument that the Commune signified the beginning of a more progressive phase, in which war would be an instrument for the liberation of the proletariat, and ultimately of humanity itself. What was new—and a forerunner of one of the April Theses he would formulate in 1917 and use to considerable political advantage—was his praising the Commune for having established a precedent European workers should follow of converting wars between governments into civil wars that would give political power to the workers.[62] Two years later, in an article written just one month before the Russian monarchy collapsed, Lenin noted that the Paris Commune showed that 'militarism can never be eliminated' as long as 'one part of a people's army is waging a victorious struggle against another part of it'.[63] In the context of the Commune, Lenin was alluding here to the split in the French army in 1871 that caused recruits from the lower classes to leave their units and fight for the Commune while their officers, drawn mainly from the upper classes, led the *Versaillais* against them. The result was the Commune's demise. But Lenin also suggested in his article that while such an outcome was unavoidable in 1871, the First World War had altered the balance of power between social classes irreversibly: now that a far larger proportion of European armies consisted of conscripts, most of them workers and peasants, any mutinies that broke out were likely to escalate into full-scale revolutions that the bourgeoisie would be powerless to defeat.[64]

After the Russian monarchy collapsed, and taking power became a real, if still remote, possibility, the Paris Commune played a significant role in Lenin's estimation of the kind of state he hoped to establish in Russia, and of the ideological adaptations his doing so would require. In March 1917, when Lenin was conceptualizing the ideas he would encapsulate a month later in his so-called April Thesis—the serial exhortations, in the form of slogans, that enabled the Bolsheviks to come to power in October—'the thought of the Paris Commune, of utilising its experience...and avoiding its errors, occupied [his] mind a good deal'.[65] Also in March, in one of the 'Letters from Afar' written just prior to his return to Russia, Lenin stated that Russian workers could learn what to do from

[62] V. I. Lenin, *Sotsializm i voina* (Geneva, 1915), ibid., vol. XXVI, pp. 311–12, 325.

[63] V. I. Lenin, 'Doklad o revoliutsii 1905 goda (9 January 1917)', reprinted in *Pravda*, no. 18 (22 January 1925), ibid., vol. XXX, p. 319.

[64] Lenin stated in the article that in the 1905 Revolution in Russia the mutinies that occurred were a harbinger of those in the First World War. But while the mutinies in 1905 were the result of a revolution that failed, those in 1917 would spark a revolution that succeeded. Ibid., vol. XXX, pp. 317–18.

[65] N. K. Krupskaia, *Reminiscences of Lenin* (New York, 1970), p. 337.

the experiences of the Commune.[66] Their first task should be to arm themselves, which would enable them 'to take the organs of state power directly into their own hands'.[67] At first glance, this seems to suggest that the proletariat should take power immediately. But Lenin also included the crucial caveat that the process he was advocating had only just begun: the workers were organizing themselves in soviets and thereby creating the conditions for taking power at some point in the future. To clarify the relationship between the Commune and the soviets, Lenin declared on 4 April that the former was the only exception to his assertion that the latter were unprecedented.[68] To make certain the other Bolsheviks understood what he was calling for, in the letter of 11 March Lenin stated that only anarchists wanted to destroy the state before the state took the necessary steps, as prescribed by the socialists who presumably controlled it, to destroy itself.[69]

On 9 April Lenin came close to calling for polities similar to the Paris Commune to be established everywhere in Russia.[70] The communes he envisioned would resemble the soviets; at several points in the article he even described the two institutions as if they were identical. But the soviets, he admitted, were not yet ready to take power from the Provisional Government: not only did Marxists not yet comprise a majority in them; there was also the simple fact, according to Lenin, that the Bolsheviks, unlike the Parisian Blanquists who had provided the impetus to establishing the Commune, would never seize power without the support of the general population, or at least of the workers and peasants.[71] One must bear in mind that Lenin's admiration of the Commune was always selective. For every decision it made of which he was critical, there was another he found praiseworthy. Among the most laudable of the latter were the replacement of the army and the police by a militia, and the substitution of a self-contained and hidebound bureaucracy by 'direct rule by the people'—by which Lenin meant a government the leaders of which were subject to recall if the people found their performance unsatisfactory.[72] To prevent extravagances like those that occurred under capitalism, Lenin also stated that these leaders would not receive a salary higher than that of the highest-paid worker.[73]

In his April Theses Lenin did not merely call for a state of which the Paris Commune was a precursor; he now envisaged in Russia during its ongoing transition from capitalism to socialism nothing less than 'a state of the Paris Commune type'.[74] Moreover, by including his call for a commune state in the

[66] V. I. Lenin, 'Pis'ma izdaleka: o proletarskoi militsii (11 March 1917)', in Lenin, PSS, vol. XXXI, p. 38.
[67] Ibid., p. 40.
[68] V. I. Lenin, 'Doklad na sobranii Bol'shevikov—uchastnikov v vserossiiskogo soveshchaniia sovetov rabochikh i soldatskikh deputatov (4 April 1917)', ibid., p. 108.
[69] Lenin, 'Pis'ma izdaleka', ibid., pp. 162–3.
[70] V. I. Lenin, 'O dvoevlastii', Pravda, no.28 (9 April 1917), ibid., pp. 145–7.
[71] Ibid., pp. 146–7.   [72] Ibid., p. 146.   [73] Ibid., p. 146.
[74] V. I. Lenin, 'Zadachi proletariata v nashei revoliutsii (proekt platforma proletarskoi partii)', Pravda, no. 26 (17 April 1917), ibid., pp. 162–3.

changes he proposed in the Bolsheviks' declared objectives, Lenin indicated how central a role it played in the scenario for seizing power that was germinating in his mind. This, of course, implied that Russia was ready for a proletarian revolution, and thus in violation of the conviction, to which Marx had been faithful until the last years of his life, that such a revolution would be premature and therefore destined to fail. Other Bolsheviks, not surprisingly, found the ideological implications of Lenin's vision unacceptable, and in the summer of 1917 Zinoviev invoked the Commune in explaining his opposition. Like Lenin, Zinoviev believed that the political vacuum that existed in Petrograd resembled that in Paris just prior to the establishment of the Commune. But whereas for Lenin this similarity served to sanction seizing power, for Zinoviev it suggested that such an undertaking would fail; the best the Bolsheviks could hope for was to take power and then lose it, which seemed an argument for the Bolsheviks doing nothing instead.[75]

More than any of the French revolutions that preceded it, that of 1871 helped Lenin to legitimize the ideological heresies he knew his fellow Bolsheviks would have to accept before any revolution they attempted could succeed.[76] This, of course, required a determined policy of adaptation. The defeatism implicit in Lenin's call in the April Thesis for the imperialist war (i.e. the First World War) to be transformed into a civil war meant that the patriotism of the Communards, who with few exceptions had been willing to resume war with the Prussians, had to be played down or ignored.[77] Similarly, in his *Letters on Tactics*, written in response to Lev Kamenev's charge, which Plekhanov happily repeated, that Lenin was intent on merging the bourgeois and socialist revolutions, the future Soviet leader rejected Kamenev's criticism that the Commune had been wrong to make programmatic changes immediately, and that that was the principal reason it had failed. Rather, the Communards were too slow in putting their socialism into practice, and as a result the Commune had been destroyed quickly.[78] Both Lenin and Kamenev, in what they wrote about the Commune in 1917, were dealing with what to Marxists in Russia was a question none of them had considered relevant just a few months earlier: whether circumstances in Petrograd and in Russia could be conducive of a seizure of power that would be followed immediately by a counter-revolution in which the Bolsheviks lost not only power but also, very possibly, their lives. That Kamenev and Lenin both invoked the Commune in defending their answer indicates that they did so not just to score debating points, but to gain some inkling about what the future would bring should the

---

[75] G. Zinoviev, 'Chego ne delat', *Rabochii*, no. 8 (30 August 1917): p. 8.

[76] Geoffrey Hosking argues plausibly in *The First Socialist Society: A History of the Soviet Union from Within* (Cambridge MA, 1985), p. 46, that Lenin's vision of the commune state in 1917 was what gave him the confidence to take power when his chances of doing so seemed minimal.

[77] Lenin, 'Zadachi proletariata', p. 162.

[78] V. I. Lenin, *Pis'ma o taktike* (Petrograd, 1917), in Lenin, *PSS*, vol. XXXI: pp. 138–42.

Bolsheviks cross the ideological and psychological Rubicon and do what Lenin was recommending they do.

Lenin's task in 1917 was not an easy one, and it was complicated by the need to describe in some detail what a Bolshevik state would look like should the Bolsheviks take power and hold onto it. He did this most thoroughly in *State and Revolution*, a first draft of which he finished in January, even before the monarchy collapsed, but which he revised considerably while in Finland in the year later, after the Provisional Government had published evidence of his earlier collaboration with Germany, making him, to all intents and purposes, a traitor. That one of the two books he took with him into his semi-exile was Marx's *Civil War in France* was consistent with the prominent role the Commune assumed in shaping, explaining, and justifying his evolving views on seizing power in Petrograd.[79] What Lenin seemed most intent on demonstrating in the essay was that the proletariat, after taking power, had to do what the Communards had been unable to do: not only to replace the existing institutions of coercion with a people's militia, but also, more broadly, to create a genuinely proletarian state out of the remnants of the bourgeoisie state it had overthrown.[80] The Communards, he wrote, had started to do this, but they lost power before they could finish. Lenin explained his objective, and invoked the Commune to underscore how essential it was to the ultimate construction of socialism and communism, as follows:

> To destroy officialdom immediately, everywhere, completely—this cannot be thought of. That is a Utopia. But to break up at once the old bureaucratic machine and to start immediately the construction of a new one, which will enable us gradually to reduce all officialdom to naught—this is no Utopia. It is the experience of the Commune. It is the direct and urgent task of the revolutionary proletariat.[81]

At another point in the essay Lenin stated flatly that the practical measures the Communards had carried out enabled them 'to start building a new proletarian state machinery' within a few weeks.[82] Had it not been for their subsequent overthrow, they would have finished the task.

In *State and Revolution*, Lenin subtly changed what he considered the message and the legacy of the Commune. Whereas prior to the summer of 1917 Lenin

---

[79] Stites, *Revolutionary Dreams*, p. 43; M. Sawer, 'The Soviet Image of the Commune: Lenin and Beyond', in *Images of the Commune*, edited by J. A. Leith (Montreal, 1978), p. 246.

[80] Lenin, *State and Revolution*, pp. 10–11, 26, 83.

[81] Ibid., p. 42. Lenin wrote more or less the same thing in an article written just three weeks before the October Revolution. V. I. Lenin, 'Uderzhat li bol'sheviki gosudarstvennuiu vlast', *Prosveshchenie*, no. 1–2 (October 1917), in Lenin, *PSS*, vol. XXXIV, pp. 302–3. Lenin's argument, with its reference to the Commune, was an adumbration by several months of his well-known suggestion to Trotsky that the latter employ former tsarist officers in the Red Army because the new order the Bolsheviks were constructing could be built with bricks left over from the old one. Trotsky, *My Life*, p. 447.

[82] Lenin, *State and Revolution*, p. 98.

considered the Commune valuable in clarifying how to carry out a proletarian revolution, from that time onward, it was useful mostly for what its actions while in power revealed about creating a proletarian state. This did not mean that Lenin stopped criticizing the Communards' mistakes, only that his criticisms were different. Among the most relevant, given the practical and ideological dilemmas Lenin had to resolve if the Bolsheviks were to establish socialism in a predominantly agrarian society, was the Commune's failure, in his estimation, to achieve a 'free union' of the proletariat and the poor peasantry.[83] Another was that the Communards had acted prematurely, which Lenin now considered the principal reason for their failure—more significant even than their overwhelming inferiority in numbers and generalship when Thiers ordered the Republican army he commanded to attack the Commune and retake control of Paris.[84] This would seem to suggest that a Bolshevik revolution would fail for the same reason the Commune had failed. But Lenin quickly nullified the parallel he suggested by stressing what he saw as the critical difference between France in 1871 and Russia in 1917: while the former was not ready for even a proto-proletarian revolution, the latter was ready for a genuinely proletarian revolution as long as the bulk of the peasantry supported it. Moreover, this proletarian revolution in Russia would succeed because the Bolsheviks possessed all of the laudable personal characteristics of the Communards—most notably their heroism, perseverance, and courage—but none of their failings and inadequacies, as these related to politics.[85]

* * *

The successful seizure of power in 1917 did not diminish the relevance of the Commune. In January 1918 Lenin made a point of noting exactly when the Bolsheviks held power longer than the Communards were able to do, and in July 1920 he led representatives of the foreign communist parties attending the Second Comintern Congress in Petrograd to Palace Square, where they commemorated the Commune and praised the Communards lavishly.[86] But whereas before the October Revolution Lenin did not hesitate to criticize the Commune for its deficiencies, once the revolution ended, he did his utmost to minimize them. The only criticism he mustered in a report to the Seventh Congress of the Communist Party in March 1918 was that it did what it did without understanding its

[83] Ibid., p. 35.
[84] Ibid., p. 42. The reader will note that just a few weeks earlier, Lenin, in his response to Kamenev, had written the opposite—that the Commune failed because its leaders had not acted quickly enough.
[85] Ibid., p. 42.
[86] V. I. Lenin, 'Doklad o deiatel'nosti soveta narodnykh komissarov 11 (24) janvaria', *Tretii vserossiiskii s"ezd sovetov rabochikh soldatskikh i krest'ianskikh deputatov 10-18 (23-31) ianvaria 1918 g.*, in Lenin, *PSS*, vol. XXXV, p. 261; Eremina, 'V. I. Lenin kak istorik', p. 31. According to Zinoviev, Lenin devoted more attention to the Commune than to any other proletarian movement. Mason, *Paris Commune*, pp. viii–ix. Zinoviev was correct as long as one did not consider the Jacobins—about whom Lenin wrote much more than he did about the Communards—proletarian.

historical significance.[87] Instead Lenin focused on what he said were its virtues, which in an article in December 1917 he expanded to include its adoption of a form of democratic centralism, which in the Soviet lexicon was a euphemism for party dictatorship.[88] In January 1919, in a letter in *Pravda* addressed to the workers of Europe and America, he stated unambiguously that the Commune 'created a new type of state, a proletarian state, [which is] a machine for the suppression of the bourgeoisie by the proletariat'.[89] Two months later, in a report to the First Comintern Congress in Moscow, Lenin denied that the Commune was ever 'a parliamentary institution', which seemed to call into question his assurance prior to the October Revolution that the 'commune state' he envisaged would be akin to the original Commune in basing its legitimacy on majority rule.[90]

In the way that Lenin now described it, the Commune, while hardly a blueprint for establishing socialism, had much in common with the political system he was seeking to bring about in Russia. His promise in 1917 to eliminate the army and the police, which he claimed was inspired by the error the Communards made by not doing so, was forgotten after the Civil War began in Russia in 1918. The only instance after 1917 of Lenin distinguishing his regime from the Commune was his elliptical admission in April 1918 that paying 'bourgeois experts' wages higher than those of workers (as the Commune had done) was inconsistent with its principles.[91]

Lenin was not the only Bolshevik to pronounce judgement on the Commune. In April 1918 Stepan Shaumian modelled the commune he established in Baku on what he understood to have been the agenda and the aspirations of the earlier Parisian one.[92] For Kamenev, by contrast, the Commune foreshadowed dangers the Bolsheviks should avoid: in the context of criticizing Lenin's April Theses, Kamenev argued that both the French Revolution and the Revolution of 1848 were more relevant than the Commune, presumably because the earlier revolutions had involved the entire country of France rather than merely its capital.[93] A decade later Nikolai Bukharin was criticized for seeming to argue in 1928—in contrast to what many Bolsheviks believed—that proletarian revolutions were possible only after a war. In the course of defending his position, Bukharin argued that evoking the Commune—which of course had come into existence in the

[87] V. I. Lenin, 'Doklad o peresmotre programmy i izmenenii nazvaniia partii (8 March 1918)', in Lenin, *PSS*, vol. XXXVI, p. 50.

[88] V. I. Lenin, 'Kak organizovat' sorevnovanie (December 1917)'? *Pravda*, no. 17 (20 January 1929), ibid., vol. XXXV, p. 203.

[89] V. I. Lenin, 'Pis'mo k rabochim evropy i ameriki', *Pravda*, no. 16 (24 January 1919), ibid., vol. XXXVII, p. 457.

[90] V. I. Lenin, 'Tezisy i doklad o burzhuaznoi demokratii i diktature proletariata', ibid., vol. XXXVII, p. 493; Lenin, *State and Revolution*, p. 55.

[91] V. I. Lenin, *Ocherednye zadachi sovetskoi vlasti* (Petrograd, 1917), in Lenin, *PSS*, vol. XXXVI, pp. 179–90.

[92] A. E. Kadishev, *Interventsiia i grazhdanskaia voina v Zakavkaz'e* (Moscow, 1960), p. 96.

[93] Lenin, Pis'mo o taktike', p. 42; Keep, *Contemporary History in the Soviet Mirror*, p. 204.

immediate aftermath of a war—had no bearing, one way or another, on the relationship between revolutions and war. In fact, he insisted that his critics had misconstrued his position: revolutions could occur before wars as well as after them, and in the absence of military conflict altogether. Thus the Paris Commune, while worthy of praise, could not be used as evidence of any universal law of revolutions.[94]

In contrast to Bukharin, who seemed to believe there were limits to what the Commune could teach the Bolsheviks, Zinoviev and Trotsky claimed to have learned much from it, and that in addition to providing inspiration, it contained insights that would contribute to the success of any revolutionary enterprise. Zinoviev, as has been shown already, drew the conclusion from the similarities he saw between Paris in 1871 and Petrograd in 1917 that a Bolshevik insurrection would be premature and fail. But that did not stop him, in a speech to the Third Congress of Soviets in January 1918, from criticizing the Communards for not taking over the Bank of France, which he ascribed to a lack of discipline and ruthlessness comparable to the weakness in 1917 and earlier of Iulii Martov and the Mensheviks.[95] During the Kronstadt Revolt, when the very survival of the Bolshevik regime was at stake, Zinoviev again ascribed the Commune's demise to the personal deficiencies of its leaders, principally their unwillingness to treat their enemies with the requisite harshness. He then went on to claim that that was what had caused the Communards to refrain from organizing their own political party, the existence of which, in his opinion, would have saved them. This, of course, was to echo Lenin's well-known belief in a political party that was both conspiratorial and tightly organized.[96] It is difficult, in this instance, to suppress the suspicion that Zinoviev, who was a notorious sycophant, criticized the Communards as he did because he hoped to repair his relationship with Lenin after having nearly ended it in the early autumn of 1917 by arguing against Lenin's call for the Bolsheviks to stage an insurrection.

For Trotsky, the Paris Commune—like the other revolutions in France with which he had more than just a passing familiarity—was a useful vehicle for defending the choices and decisions he made at various junctures in his political career, and for confirming the emendations of Marxist ideology he made to justify them. The Commune, in short, confirmed Trotsky's belief that he was never wrong. In March 1917, for example, he wrote that, just as war had triggered the emergence of the Commune, so, too, would it eliminate among Russian workers the submissiveness often characteristic of the working class before it undertook

[94] *Stenograficheskii otchet: VI kongressa Kominterna* (Moscow and Leningrad, 1929), pp. 598–9.

[95] Mason, *Paris Commune*, p. 350.

[96] 'Iz stenograficheskogo otcheta o zasedanii Ispolnitel'nogo Komiteta Petrogradskogo Gubernskogo Soveta—informatsiia G. E. Zinov'eva o Kronshtadskikh sobytiakh i polozhenii Petrograda', in *Kronshtadskia tragediia 1921 goda: dokumenty v drukh knigakh* (Moscow, 1999), vol. I, p. 638.

the task of destroying its oppressors.[97] Russia, he wrote, was much like Paris in 1870–1: on the precipice of a revolutionary conflagration—but one that would yield more favourable results because the working class was more powerful in Russia than it was in France a half-century earlier. The link he drew between the two revolutions—the first one a failure, the second one destined to succeed—suggested a larger teleology, an inexorable sequence of historically progressive developments culminating in communism prevailing everywhere in the world, one that permeated his writings on all four French revolutions.[98]

In 1921 Trotsky analysed the Commune in greater detail. In his preface to a study of the Commune by Charles Talès that was published in Paris, Trotsky pronounced a mixed verdict on the Commune.[99] To its everlasting credit, the Commune was 'a harbinger of a universal proletarian revolution'.[100] But after lavishly praising the Communards for their heroism and capacity for self-sacrifice, he reproached them for 'their indecision in the direction of their movement [and] their fatal tendency to stop after initial success'.[101] This of course was consistent with the stated views of Lenin and other Bolsheviks. But Trotsky then went on to argue—in contrast not only to Zinoviev and Kamenev, but also to Lenin—that an infusion of Leninism, in the form of an 'action party' that eschewed elections, might have enabled the Commune to survive.[102] In stressing this, Trotsky was more of a Leninist than Lenin.

In the 1930s, after losing whatever chance he had of succeeding Lenin, Trotsky returned to the Commune. Like his evaluation of earlier French revolutions, Trotsky evaluated the Commune in ways that served both to justify retroactively choices others considered harmful both to himself and to the Soviet Union, and to clarify his diagnosis of what now ailed the Soviet Union under Stalin. In his *History of the Russian Revolution*, published in 1932, Trotsky insisted again that the Commune had failed for the lack of a Leninist party. Now, however, he included among the broader reasons for its failure the role of the French peasantry as a bulwark of the bourgeois order. In contrast to Russian peasants in 1917, who according to Trotsky had supported the proletarian revolution of the Bolsheviks, French peasants had opposed the no less proletarian revolution of the Communards, leaving the latter incapable of fashioning in France the synthesis of the hammer and the sickle, of the proletariat and the peasantry, that Lenin and Trotsky achieved (or believed they had achieved) in Russia a half-century later.[103]

[97] L. Trotsky, 'Pod znamenem Kommuny', *Novyi mir* (17 March 1917), in L. Trotsky, *Voina i revoliutsiia: krushenie vtorogo internationala i podgotovka tret'ego* (Moscow, 1923), vol. II, p. 412.
[98] Ibid., p. 414.
[99] 'Préface de Leon Trotsky', C. Talès, *La Commune de 1871* (Paris, 1921), pp. vii–xxii.
[100] Ibid., p. vii.   [101] Ibid., p. vii.
[102] Ibid., pp. xi, xx. Also noteworthy in the preface was Trotsky's overt hostility to the election of military officers serving in the National Guard. This was consistent with the strict discipline Trotsky instilled in the Red Army while serving as its commander.
[103] Trotsky, *History of the Russian Revolution*, unabridged edition, pp. 38, 746.

Three years later, in *The Revolution Betrayed*, Trotsky evoked the Commune as a way of clarifying—for himself as well as for his readers—the unusual hybrid he believed the Soviet Union had become, namely a regime that was socialist in its forms of property but bourgeois in its norms of distribution. In purely ethical terms, the Soviet Union had become retrograde in its politics and political institutions while remaining progressive in its economy and class relations.[104] What this meant, as far as the Commune was concerned, was that it was more different from Stalin's Soviet Union than from Lenin's. But in one very significant way the Commune and the Soviet Union were similar: both regimes were 'experiments in proletarian dictatorship' that never advanced beyond creating socialism in a self-contained entity—a city in the case of the Commune, an entire country in the case of the Soviet Union.[105] As such, both the Commune and the Soviet Union had the potential to evolve in more than one direction: either forwards towards socialism or backwards to a full restoration of capitalism. The Commune might have lasted longer and introduced socialism, but its failure to produce someone like Lenin to lead it, Trotsky implied, prevented it from doing so. The Soviet Union, by contrast, had once been socialist, but had since deteriorated into something less than that. Nevertheless, the Stalinist dictatorship that accounted for this degeneration was not necessarily permanent. To be sure, it could be replaced by a military dictatorship. But it could also be replaced by a regime that would make Russia once again the beacon of hope for humanity it had been when he and Lenin held power. And when that happened, the causal link between the Paris Commune and the October Revolution—which for Trotsky meant that without the Commune the October Revolution would not have happened—would be restored.[106]

The Bolsheviks claim to be the sole legitimate legatee of the Paris Commune did not go unchallenged. Especially after the October Revolution, the Mensheviks emphatically denied it, claiming that they, not the Bolsheviks, were its rightful successor, and that the latter were distorting for their own political purposes what the Commune was, what it did, and what it stood for. Responding to Lenin's claim at the Third Congress of Soviets in January 1918 that the new state he was creating was based on the Commune, Martov replied on behalf of the Mensheviks, arguing that because the Communards, in contrast to the Bolsheviks, upheld civil liberties, did not practise terror, and allowed all political parties to exist and to participate in elections irrespective of their particular objectives, the Commune and the Soviet state were morally and politically dichotomous.[107] In short, Martov used the Commune to draw larger distinctions between Menshevism and Bolshevism.

---

[104] Trotsky, *Revolution Betrayed*, pp. 86–114, 234–56, 273–90.   [105] Ibid., p. 297.
[106] Ibid., p. 303. The theme, very common among the Bolsheviks, that the Paris Commune had to fail for the October Revolution to succeed, is repeated by non-Marxist historians such as Alistair Horne, in *The Fall of Paris: The Siege and the Commune, 1870–71* (New York, 2007), p. 15.
[107] Getzler, *Martov*, p. 174.

Two months later, he acknowledged that the Commune had been a proletarian dictatorship—on this he agreed with Lenin and Trotsky—but quickly qualified his assertion by stating, somewhat confusingly, that it had been also a democracy.[108] The reason for this paradox was that the Commune, while exercising power without institutional restraints, nonetheless represented the working class, which in Paris comprised a majority of the population or something close to it; whatever the case, no other political party or organization commanded as much popular support. Martov acknowledged that some of the Communards were like the Jacobins in the French Revolution in seeking to centralize political power. Fortunately, however, they were not strong enough to achieve their objective, which Martov of course strongly opposed. Democracy, all things considered, was always preferable to the Jacobins' and the Bolsheviks' authoritarianism; its only drawback was the occasional inability of those practising it to act decisively.[109]

In 1921, in several articles published after the suppression of the Kronstadt Revolt, Martov elaborated on the tendency he saw among many of the Communards to temporize and to limit themselves, in military terms, to defensive measures; the Kronstadt rebels had shared these characteristics, and that was one reason for their defeat.[110] But however detrimental they were to the Commune's survival, these same attributes showed the institution to have been 'genuinely and consistently democratic [and] based entirely on popular sovereignty'.[111] Statements such as this showed how completely Martov's view of the Commune differed from Lenin's. While both men claimed to be perpetuating the legacy of the Commune, they differed starkly on its political utility: in Lenin's case the Commune helped to legitimize the repressive measures the Soviet state was taking to preserve itself, while in Martov's it justified the democratic socialism to which the Menshevik was increasingly inclined now that he found himself in opposition to the new regime and with no real hope of gaining power. Moreover, while the two men saw the Commune very differently, as Marxists they felt obliged to claim that their view was the only one of which Marx would have approved. According to Martov, Marx saw in the Commune 'the principles of popular rule and universal suffrage'.[112] Indeed, in Martov's formulation the Commune was not the Soviet Union in embryo; rather it was a precursor, however imprecise and imperfect, of a genuine workers' democracy. As such, it had international and even universal significance.[113]

---

[108] Iu.O. Martov, 'Marks i problema diktatury proletariata', *Rabochii internatsional*, no. 3–4 (1918): pp. 66–76.

[109] Ibid.   [110] Iu. O. Martov, 'Kronshtadt', *Sotsialisticheskii vestnik*, no. 5 (5 April 1921): p. 5.

[111] Iu. O. Martov, 'Razlozhenie gosudarstva ili ego zavoevanie', *Sotsialisticheskii vestnik*, no. 11 (8 July 1921): p. 4.

[112] Ibid., p. 7.

[113] Iu. O. Martov, 'Kommuna 1871 goda', in Martov, *Mirovoi bol'shevizm*, pp. 74–6.

In Germany Karl Kautsky weighed in on the debate concerning the Commune, and because his ostensible betrayal of socialism in 1914 still loomed large among the Bolsheviks, they could not ignore his contributions to it, any more than they could his opinions on Bonapartism and on the other revolutions in France since 1789. In 1918 Kautsky argued that the Commune, while 'the work of the whole proletariat', was nonetheless not monolithic ideologically.[114] Socialists of all tendencies had belonged to it. For this reason the Commune was superior to the new Bolshevik regime, which represented only a portion of the proletariat, and survived only by excluding non-Bolshevik socialists.[115] In 1920 he explicitly rejected any analogy between the Paris Commune and the October Revolution. The latter was fundamentally an urban insurrection, and while it garnered support from peasants, which to Kautsky was what enabled the Bolsheviks to extend their rule beyond Russia's major cities, this support corrupted it. The Commune, by contrast, had little or no support from peasants, which ensured it remained a proletarian enterprise, and thus from Kautsky's perspective a laudable one.[116] Also, the Commune was democratic, certainly more so than the regime the Bolsheviks established, and to its credit it never practised mass terror, as the Bolsheviks did; in its moral virtue, it was infused with 'a spirit of humanity'.[117] Not even pressure from the proletariat to resume hostilities with the Prussians after the emergence of a unified Germany diminished Kautsky's admiration. A decision to that effect, he strongly implied, would have won his approval.[118]

By extolling the Commune as he did, Kautsky was effectively rejecting not only the Soviet state but also the mythology the Bolsheviks were then creating to legitimize it. Even more damaging, from the Bolsheviks' perspective, was his insistence on defending the Commune for precisely one of the reasons the Bolsheviks gave for criticizing it. For Kautsky the democracy to which the Commune was committed was not a shortcoming to be avoided, as it was for the Bolsheviks, but a virtue to be emulated. The same was true of the personal attributes the Communards required of their leaders, in particular a willingness to compromise that was utterly antithetical to the toughness and penchant for conspiratorial tactics that Trotsky, no less than Lenin, admired once he no longer condemned the latter as a Russian Robespierre, as he had in the early 1900s.

Behind these arguments about the Commune lay a much broader challenge by Kautsky to the legitimacy of the October Revolution. For this reason Lenin and Trotsky responded to Kautsky's strictures on the Commune with the same ferocity with which they countered his imputations of their Jacobinism. In his 1918 polemic denouncing the German socialist, Lenin described as foolish the Commune's decision, while it was effectively deciding France's fate, not to

---

[114] Kautsky, *Dictatorship of the Proletariat*, p. 1.   [115] Ibid.
[116] Kautsky, *Terrorism and Communism*, p. 66.   [117] Ibid., pp. 73–4, 120.
[118] Ibid., p. 54.

disenfranchise the bourgeoisie; even better, in his opinion, would have been suspending the democratic process entirely.[119] That Kautsky supported the Commune's decision was just another manifestation of the same covert sympathy for the bourgeoisie that in Lenin's opinion explained his supporting Germany's participation in what to Lenin was always a war of imperialism. But there was a substantive reason for Lenin's *ad hominem* attack. By 1918 Lenin had realized that the centralization of political power in Russia was not merely a temporary necessity to be ended once the civil war was won. Rather, this was a permanent requirement in a country too large and diverse to be ruled in any other way. But Russia's size did not render the Commune, the jurisdiction of which was by comparison miniscule, totally irrelevant. Lenin argued that the Commune came to power and held on to it for as long as it did because its leaders were mostly immune to the democratic scruples he saw as the essence of Kautsky's cowardice. In fact, it was precisely the German socialist's personal qualities—his moderation, his softness, his aversion to violence no matter how necessary it might be—that in Lenin's jaundiced opinion made him not really a socialist at all. The role the Commune played in Lenin's evisceration was as Kautsky's antithesis: the Communards were not at all squeamish about using force, rather than polite persuasion or the cumbersome paraphernalia of elections, to achieve their objectives.[120] For that reason it was the Bolsheviks, not *faux* socialists like Kautsky, who were acting in a fashion consistent with the Commune and on behalf of objectives the Communards would surely have adopted had they taken power a half-century later than they did.

In his 1920 essay attacking practically everything Kautsky had written about the French Revolution, Trotsky was similarly forthright in denouncing Kautsky's ideas on the Commune. To Trotsky, Kautsky was not just factually inaccurate; his words were an unconscionable slur on both the Soviet state and the Communards, whom Trotsky now dubbed 'the heroic elder brother' of the Petrograd proletariat.[121] Infuriated by the German socialist's condemnation of the executions he had ordered during the Civil War, Trotsky justified the Commune's executions of hostages as a way of rebutting it. Similarly, he defended the political repression Lenin ordered by pointing to the Commune's denial of free speech to royalists and others intent on overthrowing it.[122] Trotsky was not uncritical of the Commune. He called attention to what he considered the Communards' passivity and softness—although he stopped short of ascribing these inadequacies to the historical prematurity of the Commune. To have done so would have called into question, by analogy, his own recommendation in 1905, adopted by Lenin in 1917, that by merging the bourgeois and socialist revolutions—Trotsky's so-called

---

[119] V. I. Lenin, *Proletarskaia revoliutsiia i renegat Kautskii*, in Lenin, *PSS*, vol. XXXVII, p. 248.
[120] Ibid., pp. 240–50.   [121] Trotsky, *Terrorism and Communism*, pp. 79, 86.
[122] Ibid., pp. 53–4, 74–5.

480 THE FRENCH REVOLUTIONARY TRADITION

Theory of Permanent Revolution—Marxist revolutionaries could come to power before the objective conditions conducive to their doing so existed. Moreover, whatever their political shortcomings, the Communards proved capable of learning from their mistakes; from this he concluded—with more conviction than is evident in the appraisals of the Communards in his earlier writings—that they did not entirely lack revolutionary consciousness. In fact, towards the end of the Commune's existence, the Communards rectified many of their mistakes by creating a Committee of Public Safety, deliberately modelled on the original institution in the French Revolution, to exercise power for the duration of the existing emergency. Not surprisingly, Trotsky also had nothing but praise for the Committee's policy of shooting three *Versaillais* it had in custody for every Communard or supporter of the Commune murdered by the *Versaillais*.[123]

Like Lenin, Trotsky condemned in the Commune what Kautsky had praised, and praised what Kautsky had condemned. But his polemic, like Lenin's, served a purpose larger than that of simply besmirching the reputation of a figure whom Trotsky had once admired but now detested. Implicit in the *ad hominem* attacks was justification of specific actions Trotsky had taken himself, and of policies he had carried out, in 1917 and afterwards. That was why, in his diatribe against Kautsky, Trotsky, yet again, vilified Miliukov, Tsereteli, and Chernov, whose criticisms of the Soviet regime he traced to the same moral depravity he ascribed to the executioner of the Commune, Adolph Thiers.[124]

* * *

Given the relevance the Commune was thought to possess for contemporary events, it made sense for the new leaders of the Soviet Union to inform the Soviet people of its most salubrious attributes in the expectation that the Soviet people would express their own admiration for the Commune, albeit in ways that were very different from how the intelligentsia and the educated elite customarily expressed themselves. For example, it was not uncommon for infants born in the early years of the Soviet Union to be named 'Parizhkommuna'.[125] Of course the regime's formal praise and numerous commemorations of the Commune, designed as they were for a mass audience, were not issued and performed in a vacuum; these were clearly a companion to the *fêtes* and other public events associated with the French Revolution the Bolsheviks staged to legitimize their own revolution and the state to which it had given birth. The various honoraria the Bolsheviks bestowed on the Commune after 1917 were also meant to underscore the notion central to the French Revolution that, like all revolutions, including and especially the October Revolution, it expressed a universal aspiration to social justice. The Commune, in fact, occupied something like a pride of place, second only to the Revolution of 1789, in this new-found Soviet mythology

---

[123] Ibid., pp. 75–6.   [124] Ibid., pp. 71–2.   [125] Stites, *Revolutionary Dreams*, p. 111.

linking the October Revolution and the revolutionary tradition in France that preceded it. Although the *Internationale*—which remained the official anthem of the Soviet Union until 1944—was not put to music until 1888, its lyrics had been written by a Communard, Eugène Pottier, not long after the Commune was destroyed, in order to honour the Communards' bravery and to express his belief that the principles they stood for would one day be triumphant.[126] After the October Revolution, the Bolsheviks changed parts of the first Russian translation in 1902 from the future tense to the present tense to show that they were now continuing what the Communards had begun.[127] A large number of histories of the Commune were published in the 1920s, not all of them works of government-inspired propaganda.[128] Much the same was true of the poetry that was produced.[129]

The Bolsheviks did not scant film and theatre as vehicles for the transmission of propaganda about the Commune. By far the most extravagant was a play, 'K Mirovoi Kommune' ('To the Global Commune'), which was performed only once, when the Second Comintern Congress was meeting in Petrograd in July 1920, to an audience of some 45,000, including Lenin, on the site of the former Stock Exchange. With a cast of 4,000, many of them soldiers, the play re-enacted the events of the Commune in such a way as to suggest that it had failed for lack of international support, and that in the future the entire world would be a single Commune, identical to the original one in Paris.[130] Another production eliciting admiration of the Commune was the Soviet film, *Novyi Vavilon* (*The New Babylon*), the musical score for which was supplied by Dmitrii Shostakovich. The negative reviews the film received following its premiere in 1929 may have been the consequence of the projectionist speeding up the film while the music continued at its original tempo.[131] Nevertheless, the film captured the Manichean polarities the Bolsheviks thought inherent in the struggle between the Commune and its enemies—a conflict the film personalized by the romance it depicted between Louise, a sales clerk, and Jean, a soldier, who is killed by members of the unrelievedly malevolent bourgeoisie. At the end, after digging Jean's grave, Louise herself is shot by bloodthirsty and vengeful *Versaillais*.

[126] Tombs, *Paris Commune*, p. 193; Billington, *Fire in the Minds of Men*, p. 363.
[127] *Russkaia literatura i fol'klor*, http://feb-web.ru/feb/litenc/encyclop/le4/le4-5401.htm?cmd=p&istext=1.
[128] In addition to Slutskii, *Parizhskaia Kommuna*, see Stepanov, *Parizhskaia kommuna 1871*. Large sections of M. Voimolovskii, ed., *Geroizm revoliutsii* (Moscow, 1925) are devoted to the Commune.
[129] B. Murin, V. Aronov, and N. N. Masienikov, *Parizhskaia kommuna: posobie dlia massovoi raboty v klube* (Moscow, 1921), p. 62.
[130] Corney, *Telling October*, pp. 74–5; Stites, *Revolutionary Dreams*, p. 96; Von Geldern, *Bolshevik Festivals*, pp. 185–6. For details of the performance, see *Istoriia sovetskogo teatra: Petrogradskie teatry na poroge Oktiabria i v epokhu voennogo kommunizma, 1917–1921* (Moscow, 1933), pp. 272–5.
[131] Laurel E. Fay, *Shostakovich: A Life* (New York, 2000), pp. 49–50.

The new Soviet government honoured the Commune in more formal ways. The day on which the Commune was proclaimed in 1871, 18 March, was marked throughout the 1920s by solemn commemorations in the Soviet press. A typical example was an article in 1926 that lauded the suicidal courage of Communards gunned down brutally by 'Theirs's mercenaries'.[132] Because martyrdom was a central element of the Commune's mythology, it was given tangible expression in posters displayed in cities and towns across the Soviet Union. That the Bolsheviks were self-professed atheists did not preclude their using Christian concepts to emphasize what they saw as their own unique relationship to the Commune: the caption of one poster stated that 'the martyrs of the Paris Commune were resurrected under the red banner of the Soviets'.[133] Renaming city streets '18 March'; assigning readings on the Commune at clubs formed in factories to bind workers to the regime; including 18 March among the *prazdniki* that were set aside for rest and reflection—these were just a few of the means by which the Bolsheviks used the Commune to enhance their legitimacy and increase their support.[134] For the same reason, the battleship *Sevastapol*, which had been taken over by rebellious sailors during the Kronstadt Revolt, was renamed *Parizhskaia Kommuna* shortly after the revolt was suppressed.[135] By far the most poignant expression of how much the Bolsheviks valued the Commune and considered its tragic conclusion, even more than its triumphant creation, a central element in their foundational mythology was demonstrated by their use, in 1924, of a red flag of the Commune that had been given to the Soviet Union by a visiting delegation of the French Communist Party. By placing the flag on Lenin's body after it was laid to rest, hermetically sealed in a glass case, in the first of what would be several mausoleums in Red Square in Moscow, the new Soviet leadership gave the flag iconic status as one of the enduring symbols of the Soviet state.[136] Zinoviev once referred to the flag as 'a holy relic', and for anyone viewing the flag with knowledge of where it came from, the implications of martyrdom were inescapable.[137] Lenin, one was meant to conclude, was a martyr to the cause of socialism whose premature death had been prefigured by the collective martyrdom of the Communards.

*   *   *

---

[132] 'Pamiati parizhskikh kommunarov', *Krasnaia panorama*, no. 12 (March 19, 1926): p. 1.

[133] Von Geldern, *Bolshevik Festivals*, p. 178 and figure 14.

[134] Mason, *Paris Commune*, pp. ix, 362. The other days of the year so designated were New Year's Day; 9 January (Bloody Sunday); 12 March (on which day in 1917 the monarchy was formally abolished); May Day; and 7 November (on which the anniversary of the October Revolution was celebrated after the Gregorian calendar was adopted in 1918). P. V. Gidulianov, *Tserkov' i gosudarstvo po zakonodatel'stvu R.S.F.S.R.* (Moscow, 1923), pp. 13–14.

[135] Avrich, *Kronstadt*, p. 213.

[136] Billington, *Fire in the Minds of Men*, p. 346; Tombs, *Paris Commune*, p. 202; 'Prazdnovanie dnia konstitutsii v Moskve i peredachi znameni Parizhskikh kommunarov', *Leningradskaia Pravda*, no. 8 (July 1924): p. 2.

[137] 'Prazdnovanie dnia konstitutsii', p. 2.

With Lenin's death and Stalin's rise to power, the relevance of the Commune diminished: after 1928, 18 March was no longer a day of rest.[138] Stalin's belief in the self-sufficiency of the October Revolution lessened the need for prior revolutions to legitimize it. In addition, Stalin's burgeoning 'cult of personality' allowed no other cults, not even Lenin's, to compete with it. Nevertheless, the Commune remained useful in other ways, as Stalin's comments on the institution and its leadership make clear.

From his earliest pronouncements on the Commune, Stalin emphasized the need for brute force to save it. In an article in January 1917, he pronounced a mixed verdict on the Commune: while the Communards had not been averse to using violence in taking power, their reluctance once in power to pursue Thiers's army when it was retreating from Paris to Versailles was the principal cause of their downfall. The bourgeoisie, he wrote, would never relinquish power when it considered itself politically dominant, and nothing less than the application of overwhelming counterforce would destroy it.[139] Nonetheless, the Commune, in his opinion, conformed sufficiently to Marx's expectations for him to paraphrase Engels's remark that the Paris Commune was the epitome of a proletarian dictatorship.[140] In November 1927, no longer a hunted revolutionary but now the virtual leader of a sovereign state, Stalin appended to his earlier comments on the Communards' aversion to violence that the lack of ruthlessness it implied was directly relevant to the current predicament of the Soviet Union:

> Comrades, we do not want to repeat the mistakes of the Paris Communards. The Paris Communards were too lenient in dealing with the *Versaillais*, for which Marx at the time rightly reproved them. They had to pay for their leniency by tens of thousands of workers being shot by the *Versaillais* when Thiers entered Paris. Do our comrades think that the Russian bourgeoisie and landlords are less bloodthirsty than the *Versaillais* were in France?...No, comrades, we do not want to repeat the mistakes of the Paris Communards. The revolution needs the GPU [the new abbreviation, as of 1922, for the secret police established in 1917]; and the GPU will continue to be the terror of the enemies of the proletariat.[141]

Also in 1927, just one day before the Soviet state celebrated its tenth anniversary, Stalin made clear he considered the Commune, in comparison to earlier revolutions in France, England, and Germany, *primus inter pares*. The Commune, he declared, was the result of the only revolution that did not merely substitute one form of exploitation for another.[142] In 1939, in the so-called *Short Course*

[138] I. Shilova, 'Building the Bolshevik Calendar through *Pravda* and *Isvestiia*', *Toronto Slavic Quarterly*, no. 19 (Winter 2007), http;//sites.utoronto.ca/tsq/19/shilova19.shtml.

[139] J. V. Stalin, 'Anarkhizm ili sotsializm', in Stalin, *Sochineniia*, vol. I, pp. 345, 363.

[140] Ibid., vol. I, pp. 345, 363.

[141] J. V. Stalin, 'Beseda inostrannymi rabochimi delegatsii (5 November 1927)', ibid., vol. X, pp. 236–7.

[142] J. V. Stalin, 'Mezhdunarodnyi kharakter Oktiabr'skoi revoliutsii: k desiatiletiiu Oktiabria (6 November 1927)', ibid., vol. X, pp. 238–9.

recounting the history of the Soviet Communist Party, the Commune was described as the only workers' revolution to have gained power prior to the October Revolution.[143] Taken together, these statements suggest that, of all the revolutions predating the Soviet Union, the Commune, in Stalin's opinion, was its most proximate precursor. But because, as stated in the Short Course, the Commune did not 'smash the fetters of capitalism', which was ascribed to the Communards' lack of time, rather than to any timidity or weakness, its resemblance to the Soviet Union was imperfect.[144] Only by destroying its enemies once and for all could a revolution committed to creating socialism and communism devote all of its energy and resources to creating 'the material conditions of a prosperous life for the people'.[145]

Soviet historians followed Stalin's lead. A. I. Molok, in a history of the Commune that appeared in 1927, criticized it for not centralizing power sufficiently—a claim more Leninist than Stalinist—and argued that that was the principal reason it had failed.[146] But by 1952, his perspective had become entirely Stalinist. After praising the Commune while simultaneously enumerating its failings, Molek linked Stalin's views on the Commune to 'the history of the struggle of our party against ... the traitors, the Trotskyites and the Bukharinists, these agents of the fascist espionage services'.[147] In less bombastic language, P. M. Kerzhentsev, in his own history of the Commune, like Molek reiterated what by then had ossified into Party orthodoxy: the Commune had been the first proletarian revolution, the first 'heroic, glorious attempt by the proletariat to turn history against capitalism'.[148] In this respect the Commune resembled the Soviet Union more than it did any of the governments of the French Revolution. But it also made mistakes: it failed to pursue Thiers's forces when it might have destroyed them; it did not seize the Bank of France; it refrained from seeking support from the peasantry; and it welcomed into its ranks nefarious elements of the petit-bourgeoisie committed to the perversion of its ideals and objectives. Without a dictator (presumably like Stalin) exercising power ruthlessly through a centralized party, these mistakes proved fatal.[149]

What made Kerzhentsev's analysis distinctively Stalinist was his argument that the threats to the Commune had been internal as well as external, and that they were inextricably intertwined: like the defendants in the show trials, who were alleged to be agents of foreign intelligence services, Thiers's spies in Paris

---

[143] J. V. Stalin, *History of the Communist Party of the Soviet Union (Bolsheviks): Short Course* (New York, 1939), p. 341. Although Stalin's claim to have written the history was false—in fact he merely edited it—it reiterated his views accurately.
[144] Ibid.   [145] Ibid.
[146] A. I. Molok, *Parizhskaia Kommuna 1871 g.* (Leningrad, 1927), p. 120.
[147] A. I. Molok, 'Staline et la Commune de Paris', *Cahiers du Communisme*, no. 3 (1952): p. 308.
[148] P. M. Kerzhentsev, *Istoriia Parizhskoi Kommuny 1871* (Moscow, 1959), p. 4. The book was first published in 1940.
[149] Ibid., pp. 189–91, 218, 356, 482.

transmitted sensitive information to the *Versaillais*—but, in contrast to Stalin, the Communards had showed insufficient vigilance in apprehending them.[150] Similarly, Kerzhentsev harshly criticized the generals commanding the Commune's military forces in their last stand against the *Versaillais* for not shooting all deserters and any others who had violated military discipline.[151]

After Stalin's death, the Soviet government continued to extoll the Commune for what it prefigured about the proletariat and the virtues of socialism. In 1959 it authorized publication of the formal protocols of the Commune's proceedings, and in 1964 the three cosmonauts on the Voskhod spacecraft that orbited the earth brought with them pictures of Marx and Lenin and a fragment from a banner of the Commune.[152] In 1970, on the occasion of the Commune's anniversary, Leonid Brezhnev made clear that he considered the Commune an inspiration for the Russian proletariat, without which it could not have brought the October Revolution to its triumphal consummation in the creation of a true workers' state:

> In 1871 the first proletarian revolution lit up our planet like a lightning bolt; the red flag of the Paris Commune was its banner. The Communards suffered defeat. But the cause for which they fought could not be defeated. The ranks of the proletariat multiplied; its consciousness and its organisational abilities increased; its hatred of its oppressors was magnified.[153]

On the centenary of the Commune in 1971, *Pravda* marked the occasion by including on the first page a declaration, in large letters, that 'the Soviet people and all progressive socialists in the world note the centenary of the Paris Commune'.[154] Directly below the declaration was a photograph of Brezhnev and other Soviet leaders literally applauding the occasion.

Not surprisingly, the Cold War imposed its own requirements. The liberation of Paris in 1944 was ascribed by one Soviet historian not to patriotism or hatred of the Nazis but to Charles de Gaulle's desire to prevent the establishment in the city of another Commune.[155] But the growing threat from Communist China in the 1960s and 1970s came to play an even larger role than the Cold War in the way the Soviets now conceptualized the institution. In China's claim to be the sole legitimate communist superpower in the world was implicit the notion that its revolution in 1949 was the culmination of the entire socialist tradition originating in Marx and Engels. By contrast—or so the Chinese Communists asserted—the Soviet Union, after Stalin, betrayed this noble tradition, and the result was its degeneration into fascism and a particularly disreputable form of state capitalism. For this reason, the Chinese Communists could claim sole proprietary rights to

---

[150] Ibid., pp. 143, 363–70.   [151] Ibid., p. 257.

[152] Shleev, *Revoliutsiia i izobrazitel'noe iskusstvo*, p. 6; Horne, *Fall of Paris*, p. 433.

[153] L. I. Brezhnev, *Delo Lenina zhivet i pobezhdaet* (Moscow, 1970), p. 12.

[154] 'Fotografiia', *Pravda*, no 77(192220) (18 March 1971), p. 1.

[155] A. I. Korolev, *Parizhskaia Kommuna i sovremennost'* (Moscow, 1971), p. 175.

the Commune, and that as far as the larger teleology of revolutions of which the Commune was an early expression was concerned, this teleology's alighting on Petrograd in 1917 was a regrettable, but remediable diversion.[156]

The Soviets contested the Chinese claim to the Commune differently from the way they did Kautsky's and Martov's in the 1920s. Then, they had stressed that rival claimants to the Commune were not real socialists. Now, however, they focused on the Commune itself, stressing its identity as the harbinger of a movement with universal aspirations—which mirrored nicely the concurrent argument the Soviets were making that they, not the Chinese, were the rightful leaders of the international communist movement.[157] The aforementioned claim to a kind of socialist universalism in the tribute in *Pravda* on the centenary of the Commune was one expression of this. Another was an article in *Izvestiia* commemorating the same occasion by noting the Commune's commitment to 'proletarian internationalism'.[158] An unsigned article in *Kommunist* in January of the same year claimed that while the Commune's leadership had not included a single Marxist, its lessons were nevertheless applicable, not just in France or in Europe, but everywhere.[159] Also in *Kommunist*, V. Chkhikvadze measured the transnational relevance of the Commune by the degree to which the ideological miscreants who either misunderstood it or maligned it unfairly were themselves of various nationalities, such as Germans like Kautsky and Bernstein and Frenchmen like Raymond Aron, whose anti-communism and contempt for Marx almost surely were what generated Chkhikvadze's scorn and condescension.[160]

During the Cold War, the Chinese were not the only ones the Soviets sought to discredit by invoking the Paris Commune. F. Ryzhenko began his article in *Pravda* in 1971 by arguing that both the Hungarian Revolution in 1956, which he termed 'counterrevolutionary', and the Prague Spring in 1968, which he deemed 'quietly counterrevolutionary', were the polar opposites of the Commune, which to its eternal credit 'dreamt about the new world, and about the just society' that 'free people' in the Soviet Union and Eastern Europe were now creating.[161] Among the bourgeois enemies of socialism he included in his litany were the Israelis and the Americans, whose aggression in the Middle East and Vietnam respectively made both of them successors of the *Versaillais*.[162]

---

[156] John Bryan Starr, 'The Commune in Chinese Communist Thought', in Leith, *Images of the Commune*, pp. 291–311; Maurice Meisner, 'Images of the Paris Commune in Contemporary Marxist Thought', in *Revolution and Reaction: The Paris Commune, 1871*, edited by John Hicks and Robert Tucker (Amherst MA, 1973), pp. 112–29.

[157] Fëdor Konstantinov and Inna Krylova, *Harbingers of a New Society: Centenary of the Paris Commune* (Moscow, 1971), p. 114.

[158] P. Pospelov, 'Predvestnik Oktiabria: k 100-letiu parizhskoi kommuny', *Izvestiia*, no. 64(16682) (18 March 1871): p. 4.

[159] 'Parizhskaia kommuna i sovremennost', *Kommunist*, no. 2 (January 1971), pp. 28–9.

[160] V. Chkhikvadze, in 'Parizhskaia kommuna—pervyi opyt proletarskoi diktatory', *Kommunist*, no. 1 (1971): pp. 98–100.

[161] F. Ryzhenko, 'Parizhskaia kommuna i sovremennost', *Pravda*, no. 7(19214) (12 March 1971): p. 4.

[162] Ibid.

After the Cold War ended, and as the new Gorbachev regime proclaimed its desire to co-exist peacefully in what Gorbachev himself called 'our common European home', the Commune retained its place of honour in Soviet mythology.[163] In September 1989, on the same occasion at which he told a visiting delegation from France that the roots of *perestroika* were traceable to the French Revolution, he also cited the Commune as a precursor.[164]

*   *   *

Because they believed the future was prefigured in the present, and the present prefigured in the past, the Bolsheviks always viewed the Communards as facing forwards. In that way the institution they had established served as a model for later generations of revolutionaries intent on establishing a new form of government and ultimately a new way of life, of which the Communards were only dimly and imperfectly aware. But to those less enamoured of this rather self-serving teleology, the Communards can also be considered the final personification of a self-contained tradition of revolutions in France that began in 1789 and ended in 1871. It is perfectly legitimate to view the Commune in this way, and many French historians have done so, arguing that the Communards, in their social origins, their ideology, and their actions while in power, were actually looking backwards to an epoch in the West that was ending, rather than forward to an epoch in the East—or at least east of Western Europe—that was about to begin. Most of the workers supporting the Commune were artisans and craftsmen, much like the so-called plebeians of the original French Revolution; in fact, Robert Tombs makes the argument that the workers in Paris in 1871 who most resembled a modern, industrial working class rejected the Commune and its policies when given the opportunity, in referenda and elections, to do so. What is more, the Commune Council, which exercised executive authority, was dominated not by unskilled workers—who were what a proletariat implied—but by skilled workers and persons in 'white collar' professions, such as law, journalism, and publishing, from which had come many of the leaders of the French Revolution and of the revolutions that followed it in 1830 and 1848. And what was true of the Council was also true of the Commune: both could be considered proletarian only if one considered everyone who worked for a wage a worker.[165]

To the extent that the artisans and craftsmen who supported the Commune or served on its Council had a coherent and definable vision of the future, it was of workers' cooperatives, rather than of a proletarian dictatorship.[166] In this respect the Commune was economically (and, one might also say ideologically and

---

[163] Mikhail Gorbachev, *Perestroika* (London, 1987), p. 195.
[164] 'Vstrecha M. S. Gorbacheva s predstaviteliami frantsuzskoi obshchestvennosti', p. 1.
[165] Tombs, *Paris Commune*, pp. 110–11, 114, 120–1.   [166] Lichtheim, *Marxism*, p. 114.

politically) retrograde, looking backward to a period in France's history (and also Europe's) that, with industrialization accelerating in the Second Empire, was rapidly receding and would soon be irretrievable.[167] It was no coincidence that the Communards, in the middle of May, adopted the old Jacobin calendar, and called the institution they established to deal harshly with internal enemies by the same name the Jacobins had used nearly eight decades earlier.[168] In short, the Commune was the last revolution in an age of revolutions in France and in Europe that began in 1789, rather than a harbinger of the industrialized and highly centralized states, many of them dictatorships, of the twentieth century.

That the Bolsheviks nonetheless incorporated the Commune into their revolutionary mythology testifies both to the emotive power of the Commune—the exhilaration its creation engendered no less than the despair that resulted from its destruction—and to the desire the Bolsheviks always harboured for antecedents in Europe's history to compensate for their absence in Russia's. That the Commune, like the other French revolutions that preceded it, was primarily an urban affair made it preferable—at least for Marxists like the Bolsheviks—to the peasantry in either France or Russia as an antecedent to honour and memorialize. For all the Bolsheviks' inducements in 1917 to the Russian peasants to support them, the proletariat was always the principal instrument of history's inexorable advance to the point at which communism is achieved, the dialectic magically stops, and all of humanity enjoys perpetual peace. While Soviet Communism had much in common with the tsarist autocracy it succeeded—certainly more than the Bolsheviks themselves were ever willing to acknowledge—it nonetheless relied for its mythology on analogies with revolutions in Europe, and specifically with revolutions in France.[169]

What were the larger lessons of these analogies is the last question in a study such as this one that needs to be answered.

---

[167] Wright, *France in Modern Times*, p. 212; François Caron, *An Economic History of Modern France* (New York, 1979), pp. 135–62.

[168] Horne, *Fall of Paris*, pp. 345–6.

[169] For some of the specific resemblances between tsarist and Soviet Russia, see Pipes, *Russia under the Old Regime*, which stresses how Russian rulers combined sovereignty and proprietary claims to the people and the natural resources of Russia, and used the coercive institutions of the state to enforce them. To comprehend the role that universal ethical principles, traceable ultimately to the Enlightenment, played in fuelling opposition to both the tsars and the Soviets—that of the intelligentsia in the case of the former and of the so-called Soviet dissidents in the case of the latter—see Shatz, *Soviet Dissent*, which shows how similar ideologically and sociologically the intelligentsia and the dissidents actually were.

PART V
CONCLUSION

Conclusion

Even if they had wanted to, the Bolsheviks could not have ignored the revolutions in France that collectively comprised a tradition of revolution. Too many within their political and ideological milieu had pronounced judgement on these revolutions for the Bolsheviks not to do the same. It mattered not at all that the judgements were favourable or unfavourable, or that they were offered by allies of the Bolsheviks or by their enemies. Nor did it make much difference whether those offering their opinions were contemporaries of the Bolsheviks or precursors of them. One must bear in mind that Bolshevism emerged in the early twentieth century out of the pre-revolutionary intelligentsia, which from its inception in the early nineteenth century considered the four French revolutions from 1789 to 1871 part of its own intellectual heritage; this was partly because Russia had nothing comparable in its own history. Radishchev, Herzen, Chernyshevskii, Lavrov, and Tkachev were just the most prominent of the *intelligenty* who considered the French revolutions they were familiar with sufficiently relevant to their own lives to draw lessons from them that bore directly on their political convictions. No less committed to doing this were Plekhanov and Axelrod and younger Mensheviks such as Martov, whose radicalism, moral absolutism, and alienation from the status quo—the essential attributes of the intelligentsia—were also informed by Marxist ideology.

The Bolsheviks, of course, considered themselves the rightful heirs of the intelligentsia, and formed strong opinions on matters on which the intelligentsia had previously rendered judgement. They did the same thing, albeit to a lesser extent, in the case of non-Russian socialists, whose views the Bolsheviks could not ignore as long as they remained part of the larger movement of international socialism; even after renouncing it in 1914 for the cowardice and opportunism its leaders showed in supporting their own country's declaration of war, Lenin and his followers felt compelled to respond to criticism from the likes of Karl Kautsky and Eduard Bernstein, whose apostasy preceded not only Kautsky's in 1914, but even the emergence of Bolshevism in 1903. Having unmasked such figures as 'renegades' was hardly a reason for the Bolsheviks to ignore them on the grounds that their views were unworthy of rebuttal. For secular theocrats like the Bolsheviks, heretics were more dangerous than non-believers. And so when non-Russian socialists like Kautsky invoked one or two or all four French revolutions in their indictment of the October Revolution, the Bolsheviks had no choice but to respond, and in doing so counter their critics' assessment of these French revolutions with assessments of their own.

Of course there were other, even more compelling reasons why the Bolsheviks expended so much energy and so much ink speaking and writing about these four French revolutions. Events in Russia in 1917 did not conform to the Bolsheviks' expectations; the downfall of the monarchy in February was as surprising as the relative ease with which they themselves' took power in October. In these instances their Marxism failed them. But this did not cause them to repudiate it. Instead, the Bolsheviks could not help but believe, after 1917, that their Marxism would guide them through any unexpected impediments encountered either in consolidating power or in the furtherance of their ultimate objective of establishing socialism and communism. But when necessary expedients like the NEP rendered their Marxism, once again and at least for the foreseeable future, irrelevant, they had no choice but to look elsewhere for guidance.

The Bolsheviks found what they were looking for in the French Revolutionary Tradition. Earlier, when the Bolsheviks had no power and were far from home in Western Europe and Siberia, it provided inspiration and legitimacy. And in the fever pitch of 1917, when Lenin had to stiffen the spines of his recalcitrant colleagues, and convince them they could replicate the heroics of the Jacobins and the Communards and all the other courageous instigators of radical transformation in France, it did exactly the same thing. Serendipitously, the French Revolutionary Tradition left behind a legacy that Lenin importuned his fellow Bolsheviks to continue.

Once the October Revolution had succeeded, however, the Bolsheviks looked to the French Revolutions of 1789, 1830, 1848, and 1871 more for guidance than for the psychological benefits inspiration and legitimacy had previously conferred. With their Marxism largely useless in providing a road map enabling the Bolsheviks to navigate their arduous journey to socialism, they had no other way of making sense of the course of events that followed in the 1920s, as the NEP, at the beginning of the decade, discombobulated expectations about the Soviet economy; by the end of it the Bolsheviks were genuinely frightened by the spectre the NEP had raised of a Soviet Thermidor. But the Bolsheviks could not openly and explicitly admit this, for to do so was tantamount to acknowledging either that their Marxism was deficient or that they had taken power in 1917 in defiance of it. For that reason—and also because the dictatorship they established disallowed dissent in 1921 by banning any 'factions' that might coalesce in the course of expressing it—they had no choice but to conclude that the difficulties they experienced were the result either of opposition from enemies outside the Communist Party or of betrayals by renegade communists inside it. 'The revolution betrayed' was more than the title of a book by Trotsky. It was also a convenient mantra of Bolshevism and Soviet Communism as a whole.

Indeed, it was in supplying analogies for these betrayals that the revolutions in France were perhaps most useful. The litany of Frenchmen who well before Bolshevism emerged had caused a noble enterprise to turn morally dubious, or simply rendered it ineffectual, was a long one. The Jacobins when they betrayed the Hébertists and their supporters among the *sans-culottes*; the Thermidorians after the Jacobins' demise; Georges Grisel, the member of Babeuf's conspiracy who betrayed it to the police; Napoleon Bonaparte after the coup of 18 Brumaire; the petit-bourgeoisie supporting Cavaignac during the June Days; Louis Napoleon after his replication of his uncle's rise to power; the duplicity of the Communards supposedly transmitting sensitive information to the *Versaillais*—in the minds of the Bolsheviks these were all instances in which a virtuous cause was betrayed by persons lacking virtue themselves.[1] Quite apart from the human drama entailed in these events, the betrayals they encapsulated proved supremely attractive to Marxist revolutionaries in Russia like the Bolsheviks, who could never acknowledge that the reason their own revolution did not turn out as they expected it would was because the socialist principles to which they were committed were incapable of organizing humanity in a way that ensured material security while also enabling every individual to achieve his full potential as a human being. Paraphrasing Martin Malia's summation of the seventy-four-year Soviet Experiment he believed to be doomed from the outset, 'socialism is impossible and yet the Soviets tried to build it'.[2] But rather than acknowledging the unworkability of their objectives, the Bolsheviks stressed their objectives' betrayal by internal and external enemies— while simultaneously scrambling to find temporary expedients to steady an unstable ship they were unable to admit was destined to sink on its own accord.

The Bolsheviks, in short, almost always had to improvise, and their improvisations depended for their plausibility on their finding precedents in the modern history of France. Why the French should have created a revolutionary tradition when other peoples with similar grievances failed to do so is a question beyond the purview of this study.[3] But that this tradition existed is undeniable. The French Revolution set forth fundamental principles on the basis of which politics and society should be organized, and the revolutions that followed it in the nineteenth century were arguably a lengthy commentary on these principles, sometimes, as in 1830, arguing for their sufficiency, other times for their radicalization, particularly in 1848 and 1871 by socialists who thought the French Revolution laudable but insufficient because it failed to nationalize private property; without it, the egalitarianism they favoured was impossible. Of course this tradition was perpetuated

---

[1] It is unclear if Grisel was acting in this instance as a government informer or had simply soured on Babeuf's communism and betrayed the conspiracy voluntarily. Birchall, *Spectre of Babeuf*, p. 70.

[2] Malia, *Soviet Tragedy*, p. 498.

[3] Robert Tombs has suggested that this was because the French Revolution politicized public life to the point where politics and governance assumed outsized importance. Tombs, *France 1814–1914*, pp. 1–3.

after the French Revolution had long ended for reasons other than a desire to bring to fruition the original revolutionary triad of *liberté* (that the French people should be free), *egalité* (that the French people should enjoy social justice), and *fraternité* (that all Frenchmen should live under the same government as members of the same nationality). There were also more prosaic reasons. This tradition was also a transgenerational phenomenon, its revolutions linked chronologically by the ties of family: Cavaignac's father had been a regicide in the French Revolution; Blanqui's had been elected to the Convention; Delescluze's had been a republican soldier and a commissioner under Napoleon.[4] What is more, many of the institutions and much of the functional vocabulary of the French Revolution were replicated in the revolutions that followed it: there was a Mountain in the 1848 Revolution, just as there was a Committee of Public Safety in the Paris Commune. Even in less tumultuous times, the images and symbols of the French Revolution were commemorated and perpetuated artistically: a statue of a typical *sans-culotte* with the indispensable Phrygian cap on his head was erected in Paris in 1883; elsewhere in the country were representations of Marianne, the iconic feminine personification of the revolution, sometimes adorned with the *bonnet rouge*, sometimes with 'the more bucolic and peaceable whitesheaf crown'.[5] And surely the establishment of an endowed chair for the study of the French Revolution at the Sorbonne in Paris in 1889 ensured that its message would be an ongoing influence on French politics and intellectual life.[6]

In short, a revolutionary tradition already existed in France when the Bolsheviks had to look for one outside Russia because none existed within their own history and culture. Neither the Decembrist revolt in 1825 nor the exploits of the *narodovol'tsy* later in the nineteenth century were sufficient to sustain a tradition of revolution, and in any case the Bolsheviks did not consider either phenomenon a precedent worth continuing. The former was a failed coup, not a revolution, and the latter, while heroic in personal terms, were counter-productive and destined to fail. But all was not lost. As the preceding chapters have shown, the Bolsheviks found what they needed in what this study has termed the French Revolutionary Tradition. The result was a Bolshevik tradition of its own, a mythology about the October Revolution and what followed it in the Soviet Union that based much of its legitimacy on analogies the Bolsheviks themselves had drawn with the four French revolutions—in 1789, 1830, 1848, and 1871—that preceded their own. Some of the analogies the Bolsheviks drew were meant to illustrate similarities

---

[4] Gildea, *Children of the Revolution*, p. 52.

[5] Christopher Prendergast, *The Fourteenth of July* (London, 2008), p. 136.

[6] The first incumbent of the chair was Alphonse Aulard. His successors included George Lefebvre and Albert Soboul. The prestige they enjoyed—according to one French historian, it made whoever held the chair 'the dean of French Revolutionary studies'—increased the likelihood of their works being known in Russia. Gary Kates, Introduction to *The French Revolution: Recent Debates and New Controversies*, edited by Gary Kates (New York, 1998), p. 1.

between Russia and France; others were intended to illuminate differences. But all were drawn because they were thought to be a source of wisdom, or at least of insights making the task of building socialism in Russia easier. In sum, the Bolsheviks drew analogies with French revolutions to make understandable everything about their own revolution and its aftermath that they found perplexing. Indeed, their puzzlement continued for the duration of the Soviet Union's existence because the task of constructing socialism and communism proved considerably harder than originally anticipated.

In his study of perception and misperception in international affairs, Robert Jervis has argued that analogies people make involving events they have lived through are more powerful in their minds than analogies that are temporally or geographically distant.[7] This may be true as a general rule, but for the Bolsheviks the opposite was the case. The very distance of the French Revolutionary Tradition—geographically, temporally, and ideologically—from the Bolsheviks *increased* its utility as a source of inspiration, moral legitimacy, fodder for political polemics, and specific lessons in what they should replicate on the one hand and avoid on the other. Being far away made these French revolutions more elastic, more flexible, more easily moulded than historical events in Russia or in countries more proximate to it geographically; and any analogies that might be drawn from the latter could be more easily refuted because much more was known about their factual basis. As a result, the Bolsheviks could easily change what they claimed to see in these revolutions to conform to their particular needs (as Trotsky did regarding Thermidor in 1935). Moreover, the fact that France experienced multiple revolutions, rather than only one revolution, was an additional attraction: if one French revolution did not provide what the Bolsheviks were looking for, there were always others that serve the same purpose.

What this study has been concerned with, in other words, is not the French revolutions themselves, but how they were perceived, misperceived, and at times distorted, sometimes deliberately, sometimes not, in accordance with the Bolsheviks' needs and objectives both prior to the October Revolution and after it. And if any of the Bolsheviks doubted their ability to comprehend events so distant from their own experiences—which prior to 1917 consisted mostly of engaging in interminable debates in unwanted solitude hundreds of miles from their homes—their Marxist ideology, which like its creator they considered universally valid, helped considerably—or so they said—in reassuring them. Lenin, for example, never admitted to disregarding Marxism, to which he always ascribed omniscience even when finding in French revolutions what he needed at any particularly moment in his career. Nor did he question his Marxism when he was actually revising it. The same was true, not surprisingly, for Trotsky, who never thought he

---

[7] Jervis, *Perception and Misperception*, pp. 239–40.

was revising Marxism when he grafted onto it his so-called Theory of Permanent Revolution. The only instance of his consciously questioning the ideology he professed for the entirely of his adult life was in 1939, when, in a single article, he speculated that the Soviet Union might currently be degenerating from the Bonapartism he thought descriptive of Stalinism into a form of bureaucratic collectivism more intractable than Bonapartism and even further removed from socialism.[8]

Thus armed with an ideology admitting neither error nor exceptions that nonetheless was unable to explain a proletarian revolution in a country that was as yet unready for it, the Bolsheviks vicariously transported themselves to France in 1789, 1830, 1848, and 1871 (with detours to visit Napoleon Bonaparte and Louis Napoleon), confident they would find there a veritable treasure trove of prospective wisdom that compensated for their ideology's deficiencies. And by their own reckoning, they found what they were looking for. But in the French Revolution, and in the Jacobin Terror in particular, the Bolsheviks discovered something else, which would be especially useful in justifying any bloodletting that enabled them to remain in power long enough to achieve their objectives. This was a moral calculus that did *not* sanction evil means to achieve virtuous ends. Rather what it held was that the moral virtue of an objective rendered morally virtuous the means that were used to achieve it. In short, the Machiavellian distinction between means and ends was an artificial one. Certainly it had no relevance to any revolutionary enterprise like that of the Jacobins or the Bolsheviks that, in their own considered opinion, was morally justified; the only imperative was the purely practical one that the methods they use should be the most efficient ones available.

What the Bolsheviks learned from the Jacobins, in other words, was that in achieving their goals, killing one person or a thousand persons was permissible, and no different in ethical terms from using non-violent methods and killing no one at all, because, in the Latin phrase Plekhanov cited in his 'neo-Jacobin' phase to legitimize the harsh measures he would inflict once he possessed the power to do so, *salus revolutiae supreme lex.*[9] In rough translation, this means that whatever the revolution demands is justified. But surely Plekhanov's maxim—which of course the Bolsheviks not only shared but made the basis of policy—is really nothing more a recipe for a particularly disquieting form of ethical nihilism: if in certain circumstances everything is permitted, then nothing is forbidden, and if nothing is forbidden, moral principles do not exist because they cannot exist.

This moral calculus might have been reason enough to avoid drawing analogies with the Jacobins and the French Revolution itself. Because the same calculus was evident in the three revolutions in France that followed it (albeit to a much lesser

---

[8] Leon Trotsky, 'The USSR in War', pp. 13–15.
[9] *Rossiskaia Sotsial-Demokraticheskaia Rabochaia Partiia, Vtoroi ocherednoi s"ezd. Polnyi tekst protokolov* (Geneva, 1903), p. 169.

degree because these revolutions lasted not nearly as long as the first one), the same prohibition would seem to apply. But even if one leaves aside the ethical dimension, which seems to suggest that all revolutions are corruptible, and perhaps for that reason should not be attempted under any circumstances, there were other reasons the Bolsheviks would have been better off ignoring the French Revolutionary Tradition. Instead of helping them in deciding what to do, the analogies it triggered in their minds had the opposite effect of immobilizing them until they came to a consensus on how the terms of these analogies, such as Jacobinism, Thermidor, and Bonapartism, should be defined. The Bolsheviks wasted an inordinate amount of time discussing all three concepts, straining to ascertain their meaning as if they were as real and as relevant as the conundrums they were intended to resolve.

The result was that the Bolsheviks distorted the history of France the way concave and convex mirrors in a funhouse distort the images of the persons looking at them; the results were insights, impressions, and ostensible antecedents that were misleading at best, and inaccurate and even counterproductive at worst. And because their Marxist mindset told them that to categorise something was to understand it, the Bolsheviks returned from their excursions into French history laden down with concepts—specifically Jacobinism, Thermidor, and Bonapartism—that proved incapable of explaining what more than anything else they wanted and needed to know, namely how to make a successful revolution in Russia and then to establish there a society that was just.

What ensued was not clarity but confusion. The debates on whether Jacobinism was a good thing or a bad thing, and whether its adoption and application would make a revolution easier or harder to achieve; on what Thermidor was and whether it existed in the Soviet Union or might emerge there in the future; on what Bonapartism implied as a form of governance and whether the Soviet Union was already showing signs of it—all of these debates, without exception, were never resolved, and the effect of this was that the Bolsheviks had no choice, really, but to improvise some more. The result was a duality between the short term and the long term that continued for the entirety of the Soviet Union's existence: in the short term its leaders devised policy consistent with Napoleon's famous maxim about acting without having at least some idea of what the consequences of one's actions will be, while in the long term remaining true to what they understood to be Marxist ideology. This, too, produced its own confusion, particularly in the last years of the Soviet Union, as *perestroika* became a series of frantic improvisations for the purpose of reforming it before the system itself imploded under the weight of its own contradictions.

In the case of the Bolsheviks, the cure for the uncertainty and indecision fostered by the irrelevance of their ideology was even worse than the disease itself. Analogies with the French Revolutionary Tradition were supposed to enable the Bolsheviks to act decisively and in ways that were politically useful. But this was almost always not the case. If the analogies the Bolsheviks drew between their own revolution and the four revolutions in France that predating it had generated a usable template for governance—instead of rhetorical fodder for intra-party polemics and attacks on ideological enemies outside the party such as Kautsky and the Mensheviks—the need to make policy 'on the fly' might not have been so pronounced. Then again, historical analogies may simply be incapable of providing the specific guidance the Bolsheviks needed. The history involved in them may be so complex, so multifarious in the variables that are inherent in even a single historical event, as to render analogies of any kind, not just those involving separate countries with very different cultures and national histories, a fool's gold the inauthenticity of which cannot be concealed indefinitely. James Bryce may well have been correct in claiming that 'the chief practical use of history is to deliver us from plausible historical analogies'.[10]

The Bolsheviks, in short, would have been better off had they known nothing of the French Revolution, and of the revolutions in France in 1830, 1848, and 1871 that followed it. If analogies still seemed necessary, confining them to Russian history would have had at least a chance of providing genuine assistance. For all their rhetoric about proletarian internationalism, the Bolsheviks were always a product of Russian national culture and knew more about their own country's history than they did about any other's. Whether such analogies would have saved the Soviet Union from collapse will forever remain an open question. But if this study has relevance beyond its specific subject matter, of one thing one can be certain. However alluring they might be for their ostensible powers of prognostication, historical analogies more often than not will confound expectations instead of confirming them, leaving those who look to them to bring the future into focus in most cases worse off than if they had ignored them entirely.

---

[10] James Bryce, *The American Commonwealth* (London, 1888), vol. I, p. 11.

Bibliography

'150-letie frantsuzskoi burzhuaznoi revoliutsii', *Pravda*, no. 193(7878) (14 July 1939): p. 1.

Abraham, Richard. *Alexander Kerensky: The First Love of the Revolution* (London, 1987).

Abramovich, R. 'Bol'shevizm v tupike. O knige Kautskogo togo zhe naznaniia'. *Sotsialisticheskii vestnik*, no. 20 (25 October 1930): pp. 3–10.

Abramovich, R. 'Bonapartizm i russkaia revoliutsiia'. *Sotsialisticheskii vestnik*, no. 523–4 (8 July 1943), pp. 145–7.

Abramovich, R. 'Martov i problemy russkogo bol'shevizma'. *Sotsialisticheski vestnik*, no. 8–9 (24 April 1923), pp. 10–11.

Abramovich, R. 'Termidor i krestianstvo'. *Sotsialisticheskii vestnik*, no. 7–8 (12 April 1929): pp. 5–8.

Ado, A. *Krestianskoe dvizhenie vo Frantsii vo vremia velikoi burzhuaznoi revoliutsii kontsa XVIII veka* (Moscow, 1971).

Ado, A. 'Zhivoe nasledie velikoi revoliutsii: Predislovie k serii knig "Velikaia frantsuzskaia revoliutsiia. Dokumenty i issledovaniia"'. In *Frantsuzskie rabochie: ot velikoi burzhuaznoi revoliutsii do revoliutsii 1848 goda*, edited by E. M. Kozhokin (Moscow, 1985), pp. 5–18.

Afanasiev Iu. N. and S. F. Blumenau. 'Diskussii vokrug Velikoi frantsuzskoi revoliutsii'. In *Frantsuzskii ezhegodnik: stat'i i materialy po istorii Frantsii 1989* (Moscow, 1989), pp. 10–33.

Afansiev, Yuri. 'The Agony of the Stalinist System'. In *Voices of Glasnost: Interviews with Gorbachev's Reformers*, edited by Stephen F. Cohen and Katrina vanden Heuvel (New York, 1989), pp. 97–114.

Agulhon, Maurice. *Marianne into Battle: Republican Imagery and Symbolism in France, 1789–1881* (London and New York, 1981).

Alexander, John T. *Catherine the Great: Life and Legend* (New York, 1989).

Alexeev-Popov, V. S. 'Znachenie opyta velikoi frantsuzskoi revoliutsii dlia russkogo rabochego dvizheniia nakanune i v period revoliutsii 1905-1907 gg.'. In *Frantsuzskii ezhegodnik stat'i i materialy po istorii Frantsii 1970* (Moscow, 1972), pp. 35–47.

Alexeev-Popov, V. S. and Iu. Ia. Baskin, 'Problemy istorii iakobinskoi literatury v svete trudov V. I. Lenina'. In *Iz istorii iakobinskoi diktatury 1793-1794*, edited by V. S. Alexeev-Popov, A. Ia. Gansov, and K. D. Petriaev (Odessa, 1962), pp. 21–154.

Alliluyeva Svetlana. *Twenty Letters to a Friend* (New York, 1967).

Amann, Peter. 'The Changing Outlines of 1848', *American Historical Review* 68, no. 4 (July 1963), pp. 938–53.

Andropov, Iu. O. *Kommunisticheskaia uvezhdennost'—Velikaia sila stroitelei novogo mira: Doklad na torzhestvennom sobranii v Moskve, posviashchennom 100 letiiu so dnia rozhdeniia F. E. Dzerzhinskogo* (Moscow, 1977).

Annenkov, P. V. *Extraordinary Decade* (Ann Arbor MI, 1968).

Antonov, N. [Lukin, N. M.]. *Karl I—Liudovik XVI—Nikolai II* (Moscow, 1918).

Aptekman, O. V. 'Pis'mo o byvshim tovarishcham (8 December 1879)'. *Chernyi peredel*, no. 1 (16 January 1880): pp. 121–41.

Arkhiv Marksa i Engel'sa (Moscow, 1934), vol. III.

Arkhiv Trotskogo. Kommunisticheskaia oppozitsiia v SSSR, 1923–1927 (Moscow, 1990), vol. IV.

Arkhiv Vorontsova (Moscow, 1876), vol. VIII.

Ascher, Abraham. *Pavel Axelrod and the Development of Menshevism* (Cambridge MA, 1972).

Ascher, Abraham. *The Revolution of 1905: Authority Restored* (Stanford CA, 1992).

Aulard, A. A. 'Dve revoliutsii (1789–1917)'. *Volia Rossii*, no. 20 (1923): pp. 14–21.

Aulard, Alphonse. *La Révolution française et la Révolution russe: letter aux citoyens de la libre Russie* (Paris, 1917). In *La Révolution française* 70 (1917): pp. 193–204.

Avrich, Paul. *Bakunin and Nechaev* (London, 1987).

Avrich, Paul. *Kronstadt 1921* (New York, 1974).

Avrich, Paul. *Russian Rebels: 1600–1800* (New York, 1976).

Axelrod, P. B. 'K voprosu ob istochnike i znachenii nashikh organizatsionnykh raznoglasii. Iz perepiska s Kautskim', *Iskra*, no. 68 (15 June 1904): pp. 2–3.

Axelrod, P. B. *Kto izmenil sotsializmu? (Bol'shevizm i sotsial'naia demokratiia v Rossii)* (New York, 1919), pp. 1–30.

Axelrod, P. B. *Narodnaia duma i rabochii s"ezd* (Geneva, 1905).

Axelrod, P. B. 'Ob"edinenie rossiiskoi sotsialdemokratii i eia zadachi'. *Iskra*, no. 55 (15 December 1903): pp. 1–4 and *Iskra*, no. 57 (15 January 1904): pp. 2–4.

Axelrod, P. B. *Perezhitoe i peredumannoe* (Berlin, 1923).

Axelrod, P. B. 'Sotsializm i melkaia burzhuaziia'. *Vestnik narodnoi voli*, no. 1 (1883): pp. 159–85.

Bakunin, M. A. *Sobranie sochineniia i pisem, 1828–1876*, edited by Y. M. Steklov (Moscow, 1934–6), vol. III.

Bakunin, Michael. *God and the State* (New York, 1970).

Bakunin, Michael. *Statism and Anarchy*, edited by Marshall Shatz (New York, 1990).

Bakunin, Michael. *The Paris Commune and the Idea of the State* (London, 1971).

Bakunin, Mikhail. 'The Reaction in Germany'. In *Michael Bakunin: Selected Writings*, edited by Arthur Lehning (London, 1973), pp. 37–58.

Baldwin, Roger S. ed. *Kropotkin's Revolutionary Pamphlets* (New York, 1927).

Banerji, Arup. *Writing History in the Soviet Union* (New Delhi, 2008).

Barber, John. 'Stalin's Letter to the Editors of *Proletarskaya Revolyutsiya*'. *Soviet Studies*, no. 1 (January 1976): pp. 21–41.

Baron, Samuel H. *Plekhanov in Russian History and Soviet Historiography* (Pittsburgh PA, 1995).

Baron, Samuel H. *Plekhanov: The Father of Russian Marxism* (Stanford CA, 1963).

Baturin, N. N. 'Eshche o tsvetakh russkogo iakobinstva'. *Proletarskaia revoliutsiia*, no. 8 (1925): pp. 97–109.

Baturin, N. N. 'O nasledstve russkikh iakobintsev'. *Proletarskaia revoliutsiia*, no. 7 (July 1924): pp. 82–9.

Beatty, Bessie. *The Red Heart of Russia* (New York, 1918).

Belinskii, V. G. *Pis'ma*, edited by E. A. Liatskago (St Petersburg, 1914), vol. II.

Belinskii, V. G. *Sobranie sochinenii* (Moscow, 1982), vol. IX.

Bergman, Jay. *Meeting the Demands of Reason: The Life and Thought of Andrei Sakharov* (Ithaca NY, 2009).

Bergman, Jay. 'Soviet Dissidents on the Russian Intelligentsia, 1956–1985: The Search for a Usable Past'. *Russian Review* 51, no. 1 (January 1992): pp. 16–35.

Bergman, Jay. 'The Idea of Individual Liberation in Bolshevik Visions of the New Soviet Man'. *European History Quarterly* 27, no. 1 (1997): pp. 57–92.

Bergman, Jay. 'Valerii Chkalov: Soviet Pilot as New Soviet Man'. *Journal of Contemporary History* 33, no. 1 (1998): pp. 135–52.

Bergman, Jay. *Vera Zasulich: A Biography* (Stanford CA, 1983).

Berlin, Isaiah. *Karl Marx: His Life and Environment* (New York, 1963).

Berlin, Isaiah. *Russian Thinkers* (New York, 1978).

Biblioteka V. I. Lenina v Kremle (Moscow, 1961).

Billington, James. *Fire in the Minds of Men: Origins of the Revolutionary Faith* (New York, 1980).

Binns, Christopher A. P. 'The Changing Face of Power: Revolution and Accommodation in the Development of the Soviet Ceremonial System: Part I'. *Man*, 14, no. 4 (1979): pp. 585–606.

Birchall, Ian H. *The Spectre of Babeuf* (London, 1997).

'Biulleten' no. 12 moskovskogo komiteta RSDRP o sobytiiakh v Moskve 17–19 Oktiabria'. In *Listovki moskovskikh Bol'shevikov v period pervoi russkoi revoliutsii* (Moscow, 1955), pp. 318–20.

Black, Cyril. ed. *Rewriting Soviet History* (New York, 1962).

Boffa, Giuseppe. *The Stalin Phenomenon* (Ithaca NY, 1992).

Bol'shaia sovetskaia entstiklopediia (Moscow, 1950), vol. V.

Bol'shaia sovetskaia entstiklopediia 3rd edition, 30 vols (Moscow, 1969–78).

Bolshakov, B. 'Nakanune Iubeleia'. *Pravda*, no. 195 (14 July 1989): p. 7.

Bonch-Bruevich, V. D. *Izbrannye sochineniia: Vospominaniia V. I. Lenine 1917–1924 gg.* (Moscow, 1963), vol. III.

Bonch-Bruevich, V. D. *Na boevykh postakh fevralskoi i oktiabrskoi revoliutsii* (Moscow, 1930).

Bonnell, Victoria. *Iconography of Power: Soviet Political Posters under Lenin and Stalin* (Berkeley CA, 1998).

Bouvier, Beatrix. 'On the Tradition of 1848 in Socialism'. In *Europe in 1848: Revolution and Reform*, edited by Dieter Dowe et al. (New York, 2001), pp. 891–915.

Bowlt, John E. 'Russian Sculpture and Lenin's Plan of Monumental Propaganda'. In *Art and Architecture in the Service of Politics*, edited by Henry Armond Millon and Linda Nochlin (Cambridge MA, 1978), pp. 182–93.

Breitman, George et al. eds. *Leon Trotsky: Collected Writings (1929–1940)*, 14 vols (New York, 1979).

Breyer, Siegfried. *Soviet Warship Development 1917–1937* (London, 1992), vol. I.

Brezhnev, L. I. *Delo Lenina zhivet i pobezhdaet* (Moscow, 1970).

Brinton, Crane. *A Decade of Revolution 1789–1799* (New York, 1934).

Brinton, Crane. *The Jacobins: An Essay in the New History* (New York, 1930).

Brissot, J. P. *Second discours sur la nécessité de faire la guerre aux Princes allemands* (Paris, 1791).

Brogan, D. W. *The Development of Modern France (1870–1939)* (New York, 1966).

Brubat, Jean. *Le châtiment des espions et des traîtres sous la Révolution française* (Paris, 1937).

Bryant, Louise. *Six Red Months in Russia* (New York, 1970).

Bryce, James. *The American Commonwealth* (London, 1888).

Buchanan, Meriel. *Petrograd: The City of Trouble, 1914–1918* (London, 1918).

Bukharin, N. 'Professor s pikoi'. *Pravda*, no. 249 (4081) (25 October 1928): p. 3.

Bukharin, N. 'The Russian Revolution and its Significance'. *The Class Struggle*, no. 1 (1917). https://www.marxists.org/archive/bukharin/works/1917/rev.htm.

Bukharin, N. 'Vystuplenie na VII rasshirennom plenume IKKI'. *Pravda*, no. 289 (14 December 1926): pp. 3–4.

Bukharin, N. and E. Preobrazhensky, *The ABC of Communism* (Monmouth, Wales, 2006).

Bukharin, N. I. 'Na poroge desiatogo goda'. *Pravda*, no. 258 (7 November 1926): p. 2.

Bukharin, N. I. 'Tsezarizm pod maskoi revoliutsii'. *Pravda*, no. 259(3190) (13 November 1925): pp. 2–4, and *Pravda*, no. 261(3192) (13 November 1925): pp. 2–3.

Bukharin, N. I. *V zashchitu proletarskoi diktatury: sbornik* (Moscow, 1928).

Bunyan, James and Harold Henry Fisher. eds. *The Bolshevik Revolution, 1917–1918: Documents and Materials* (Stanford CA, 1961).

Burbank, Jane. *Intelligentsia and Revolution: Russian Views of Bolshevism, 1917–1922* (New York, 1986).

'Can Moscow Believe in Yeltsin?', *Détente* (Autumn, 1986), p. 4.

Cantcuzene, Julia. *Revolutionary Days* (New York, 1970).

Caron, François. *An Economic History of Modern France* (New York, 1979).

Carr, E, H, *Michael Bakunin* (New York, 1975).

Carr, Edward Hallett. *Socialism in One Country, 1924–1926* (New York, 1958), vol. I.

Carter, Huntley. *The New Theatre and Cinema of Soviet Russia* (London, 1924).

Caute, David. *Communism and the French Intellectuals* (New York, 1964).

Chaadaev, P. Ia. *Polnoe sobranie sochinenii i izbrannye pis'ma* (Moscow, 1991).

Chaussinand-Nogaret, Guy. *The French Nobility of the Nineteenth Century* (Cambridge, 1984).

Cherniak, E. B. '1794-I god. Nekotorye aktual'nye problemy issledovaniia velikoi frantsuzskoi revoliutsii', *Novaia i noveishaia istoriia*, no. 1 (1989): pp. 77–95.

Chernov, Victor. *The Great Russian Revolution* (New Haven CT, 1936).

Chernov, Viktor. *Pered burei: vospominaniia* (New York, n.d.).

Chernov, Victor. *Rozhdenie revoliutsionnoi Rossii* (Paris, 1934).

Chernyshevskii, N. G. 'Iiul'skaia monarkhiia'. In N. G. Chernyshevskii, *Izbrannye sochineniia* (Moscow/Leningrad, 1928), vol. I, pp. 316–453.

Chkhikvadze, V. 'Parizhskaia kommuna—pervyi opyt proletarskoi diktatory'. *Kommunist*, no. 1 (1971): pp. 93–101.

Chudinov, A. V. 'Nazrevshie problemy izucheniia istorii velikoi frantsuzskoi revoliutsii (po materialam obsuzhdeniia v Institute vseobshchei istorii AN SSSR)'. *Novaia i noveishaia istoriia*, no. 2 (March–April 1989): pp. 65–74.

Cobban, Alfred. *The Social Interpretation of the French Revolution* (Cambridge, 1964).

Cohen, Stephen F. *Bukharin and the Bolshevik Revolution: A Political Biography, 1888–1938* (New York, 1973).

Coker, Adam Nathaniel. 'French Influences in Russia, 1780s to 1820s: The Origins of Permanent Cultural Transfer' (PhD dissertation, University of Exeter, 2015).

Colton, Timothy J. *Commissars, Commanders, and Civilian Authority: The Structure of Soviet Military Politics* (Cambridge MA, 1979).

Conquest, Robert. *Stalin and the Kirov Murder* (New York, 1989).

Conquest, Robert. *The Harvest of Sorrow: Soviet Collectivization and the Terror-Famine* (New York, 1986).

Corbesero, Susan M. 'The Anniversaries of the October Revolution, 1918–1927: Politics and Imagery', (PhD dissertation, University of Pittsburgh, 2005).

Corney, Frederick C. *Telling October: Memory and the Making of the Bolshevik Revolution* (Ithaca NY, 2004).

Courtois, Stéphane et al. *The Black Book of Communism* (Cambridge MA, 1999).

Crosley, Pauline. *Intimate Letters from Petrograd* (New York, 1920).

Dalin, V. M. *Istoriki Frantsii XIX–XX vekov* (Moscow, 1981).

Dalin, V. M. 'K istorii izucheniia Velikoi frantsuzskoi revoliutsii v SSSR'. In *Frantsuzskii ezhegodnik: stat'i i materialy po istorii Frantsii 1989* (Moscow, 1989), pp. 102–18.

Dallin, D. 'NEP i anti-NEP'. *Sotsialisticheskii vestnik*, no. 5(195) (8 March 1929): pp. 2–3.

Dallin, D. 'O termidore'. *Sotsialisticheskii vestnik*, no. 165 (1 December 1927): pp. 3–10.

Dan, F. 'Bol'shevistskii bonapartizm'. *Novaia zaria*, no. 3–4 (20 May 1918): pp. 12–18.

Dan, F. 'Protiv terrora – za revoliutsiiu'. *Sotsialisticheskii vestnik*, no. 1 (10 January 1935): pp. 2–4.

Dan, F. 'Puti vozrozhdeniia'. *Sotsialisticheskii vestnik*, no. 14–15 (14 August 1936): pp. 5–11.

Dan, Fëdor. 'Bol'shevistskii Bonapartizm'. *Novaia zaria*, no. 3–4 (20 May 1918): pp. 11–18.

Dan, Theodore. *The Origins of Bolshevism* (New York, 1970).

Daniels, Robert Vincent. *The Conscience of the Revolution: Communist Opposition in Soviet Russia* (New York, 1960).

Danilevskii, Nikolai. *Rossiia i Evropa. Vzgliad na kulturnye i politicheskie otnosheniia slavianskogo mira k germano-romanskomu* (St Petersberg, 1995).

David-Fox, Michael. *Showcasing the Soviet Experiment: Cultural Diplomacy and Western Visitors to the Soviet Union, 1921–1941* (New York, 2012).

Davidson, Ian. *The French Revolution: From Enlightenment to Tyranny* (New York, 2016).

De Coster, Michel. *L'analogie en sciences humaines* (Paris, 1978).

Deich, Lev. ed. *Gruppa 'Osvobozhdenie Truda': Iz arkhivov G. V. Plekhanova, V. I. Zasulich i L. G. Deicha* (Moscow/Leningrad, 1923–8), vol. II.

Denike, Iu. 'Revoliutsiia bez termidora'. *Novyi zhurnal*, no. 7 (1943), pp. 202–19.

Deutscher, Isaac. *Stalin: A Political Biography* (New York, 1967).

Deutscher, Isaac. *The Prophet Armed: Trotsky 1879–1921* (New York, 1954).

Deutscher, Isaac. *The Prophet Outcast: Trotsky 1929–1940* (London, 1963).

Deutscher, Isaac. *The Prophet Unarmed: Trotsky: 1921–1929* (London, 1963).

Diakov, V. A. *Osvoboditel'noe dvizhenie v Rossii 1825–1861 gg.* (Moscow, 1979).

Djilas, Milovan. *The New Class* (San Diego CA, 1983).

Dnevnik D. A. Miliutina, 1881–1882 (Moscow, 1950), vol. III.

Dobroliubskii, K. P. 'Novaia ekonomicheskaia politika termidorianskogo reaktsii'. In *Zapisky Odesskogo Instituti Narodnoi Osviti* (Odessa, 1927), vol. I.

'Doklad tv. Bukharina na sobranii partaktiva Leningradskoi organizatsii VKP (b) 9 avgusta 1927 goda'. *Pravda*, no. 186 (18 August 1927): p. 3.

Dolgorukov, P .V. *Petersburgskie ocherki: Pamflety emigranta. 1860–1867* (Moscow, 1934).

Doyle, William. *The Oxford History of the French Revolution* (New York, 2002).

Druzhinin, N. M. *Dekabrist Nikita Murav'ev* (Moscow, 1933).

Dukes, Paul. 'Russia and the Eighteenth Century Revolution'. *History* 118 (1971): pp. 371–86.

Dukes, Paul. *World Order in History: Russia and the West* (London, 2002).

Dülffer, Jost. 'Bonapartism, Fascism and National Socialism'. *Journal of Contemporary History*, no. 11 (1976): pp. 109–28.

Duncan, Peter J. S. 'Changing Landmarks? Anti-Westernism in National Bolshevik and Russian Revolutionary Thought'. In *Russian Nationalism Past and Present*, edited by Geoffrey Hosking and Robert Service (London, 1998), pp. 55–76.

Dunn, John. *Modern Revolutions: An Introduction to the Analysis of a Political Phenomenon* (Cambridge, 1989).

Dvinov, B. 'K partiinoi platforme'. *Sotsialisticheskii vestnik*, no. 6 (24 March 1940): pp. 71–5.

Dvinov, B. 'Na pochve deistvitel'nosti'. *Sotsialisticheskii vestnik*, no. 3 (15 February 1940): pp. 29–34.

Dzhedzhula, K. O. *Rossiia i velikaia frantsuzskaia burzhuaznaia revoliutsiia kontsa 18 veka* (Kiev, 1972).

Eastman, Max. 'Jacobinism and Bolshevism'. *Queen's Quarterly* 31 (1923): pp. 73–94.

Eisenstein, Elizabeth. *The First Professional Revolutionary: Filippo Michele Buonarroti (1761–1837)* (Cambridge MA, 1959).

Eisenstein, Elizabeth. 'Who Intervened in 1788? A Commentary on *The Coming of the French Revolution*'. *American Historical Review*, 71, no. 1 (October 1965): pp. 77–103.

Elton, Godfrey. *The Revolutionary Idea in France, 1789–1871* (New York, 1971).

'Energichno vesti perestroiku'. *Pravda*, no. 317(25304) (13 November 1987): p. 2.

Engels, F. Introduction to Karl Marx, *The Class Struggles in France 1848 to 1850* (New York, 1964), pp. 9–30.

Engels, Frederick. 'On the History of the Communist League'. In Karl Marx and Frederick Engels, *Selected Works*, vol. III (Moscow, 1968), pp. 173–90.

Engels, Friedrich. *Revolution and Counter-Revolution in Germany in 1848* (London, 1896).

Enteen, George M. 'Marxist Historians during the Cultural Revolution: A Case Study of Professional In-Fighting'. In *Cultural Revolution in Russia, 1928–1931*, edited by Sheila Fitzpatrick (Bloomington IN, 1984), pp. 154–68.

Eremina, V. A. 'V. I. Lenin kak istorik Parizhskoi Kommuny'. *Voprosy istorii*, no. 2 (1971): pp. 31–43.

Erickson, Ann K. 'E. V. Tarlé: The Career of a Historian under the Soviet Regime'. *American Slavic and East European Review* 19, no. 2 (April 1960): pp. 202–16.

Erickson, Carolly. *Bonnie Prince Charlie* (New York, 1989).

Evans, Michael. *Karl Marx* (London, 2004).

Fay, Laurel E. *Shostakovich: A Life* (New York, 2000).

Fervacque, Pierre. *La Vie Orgueilleuse de Trotski* (Paris, 1929).

Figes, Orlando. *A People's Tragedy: The Russian Revolution 1891–1924* (New York, 1998).

Figes, Orlando. *Natasha's Dance: A Cultural History of Russia* (New York, 2002).

Figes, Orlando and Boris Kolonitskii. *Interpreting the Russian Revolution: The Language and Symbols of 1917* (New Haven CT, 1999).

Figner, Vera. *Zapechatlennyi trud* (Moscow, 1932), vol. I.

Fisher, David James. *Romain Rolland and the Politics of Intellectual Engagement* (New Brunswick NJ, 2004).

Fitzpatrick, Sheila. *Education and Social Mobility in the Soviet Union 1921–1934* (Cambridge, 1979).

Fitzpatrick, Sheila. *Everyday Stalinism: Ordinary Life in Extraordinary Times: Soviet Russia in the 1930s* (New York, 1999).

Fitzpatrick, Sheila. *The Commissariat of Enlightenment: Soviet Organization of Education and the Arts under Lunacharsky, October 1917–1921* (Cambridge, 1970).

Fitzpatrick, Sheila. *The Russian Revolution* (New York, 1994).

Florinsky, Michael T. *Russia: A History and Interpretation* (New York, 1953), vol. I.

Forrest, Alan. *The Soldiers of the French Revolution* (Durham NC, 1990).

'Fotografiia'. *Izvestiia*, no. 197 (15 July 1989): p. 4.

'Fotografiia', *Pravda*, no 77(192220) (18 March 1971): p. 1.

Frankel, Jonathan. ed. *Vladimir Akimov on the Dilemma of Russian Marxism 1895–1903* (Cambridge, 1969).

Freiberg, N. P. 'Dekret 19 vandem'era i bor'ba beshenykh za konstitutsiiu 1793 goda'. *Istorik marksist* 6 (1927): pp. 142–74.

Frenkin, M. S. *Russkaia armiia i revoliutsiia 1917–1918* (Munich, 1978).

Fridliand, Ts. '9-e termidora'. *Istorik marksist* 7 (1928): pp. 159–88.

Fridliand, Ts. *Danton* (Moscow, 1965).

Fridliand, Ts. 'Klassovaia bor'ba v iiune–iiule 1793 goda', *Istorik marksist* 2 (1926): pp. 159–209.

Fridliand, Ts. 'Perepiska Robesp'era'. *Istorik marksist* 3 (1927): pp. 78–89.

Fridliand, Ts. *Zhan-Pol' Marat i grazhdanskaia voina XVIII v.* (Moscow, 1959).

Fritzsche, Peter. 'How Nostalgia Narrates Modernity'. In *The Work of Memory: New Directions in the Study of German Society and Culture*, edited by Alon Confino and Peter Fritzsche (Urbana IL and Chicago IL, 2002), pp. 62–85.

Fueloep-Miller, René. *The Mind and Face of Bolshevism: An Examination of Cultural Life in the Soviet Union* (New York, 1965).

Funck-Brentano, Frantz. *Legends of the Bastille* (London, 1899).

Furet, François. *Marx and the French Revolution* (Chicago IL, 1988).

Furet, François. *Revolutionary France 1779–1880* (New York, 1988).

'G. A. Lopatin – M. N. Oshaninoi', *Russkie sovremenniki o K. Markse i F. Engel'se* (Moscow, 1969), pp. 200–2.

Gambarov, A. *Parizhskaia Kommuna* (Moscow, 1925).

Garvi, P. 'Bonapartizm ili demokratiia'. *Sotsialisticheskii vestnik*, no. 23–4 (17 December 1923): pp. 2–7.

Garvi, P. 'Ot sud'by ne uidesh', *Sotsialisticheskie vestnik*, no. 161 (27 October 1927): pp. 5–7.

Garvi, P. 'P. B. Aksel'rod i Men'shevizm'. *Sotsialisticheskii vestnik*, no. 109–10 (1925): pp. 10–13.

Garvi, P. 'Pod znakom termidora'. *Sotsialisticheskii vestnik*, no 159–60 (22 September 1927): pp. 3–5.

Garvi, P. A. *Vospominaniia Sotsialdemokrata: stat'i o zhizni i deiatel'nosti* (New York, 1946).

Gavrilichev, V. A. 'Velikaia frantsuzskaia revoliutsiia v publitsistike revoliutsionnykh demokratov A. I. Gertsena, V. P. Popova, D. I. Pisareva (konets 50-x-60-e gody XIX v.)'. In *Frantsuzskii ezhegodnik: stat'i i materialy po istorii Frantsii 1989* (Moscow, 1989), pp. 374–89.

Gay, Peter. *The Party of Humanity: Essays in the French Enlightenment* (New York, 1963).

Gefter, Mikhail. 'Stalin umer vchera'. In *Inogo ne dano*, edited by Iu. N. Afanasiev (Moscow, 1988), pp. 297–322.

Getzler, Israel. *Martov: A Political Biography of a Russian Social Democrat* (London and New York, 1967).

Gidulianov, V. *Tserkov' i gosudarstvo po zakonodatel'stvu R.S.F.S.R.* (Moscow, 1923).

Gildea, Robert. '1848 in European Collective Memory'. In *Revolutions in Europe 1848–1849: From Reform to Reaction*, edited by R. J. W. Evans and Hartmut Pogge von Strandmann (New York, 2002), pp. 207–35.

Gildea, Robert. *Children of the Revolution: The French, 1799–1914* (Cambridge MA, 2008).

Glendon, Mary Ann. *A World Made New: Eleanor Roosevelt and the Universal Declaration of Human Rights* (New York, 2001).

Godechot, J. *La Grande Nation: expansion révolutionnaire de la France dans le monde de 1789 à 1799* (Paris, 1956).

Goldman, Emma. *My Disillusionment in Russia* (Garden City NY, 1923).

Goldstone, Jack. *Revolution and Rebellion in the Early Modern World* (Berkeley CA, 1991).

Golubeva, M. P. 'Vospominaniia o P. G. Zaichnevskom'. *Proletarskaia revoliutsiia*, no. 18–19 (1923): pp. 27–31.

Gorbachev, M. S. 'Ubezhdennost' – opora perestroika'. In *Izbrannye rechi i stat'i* (Moscow, 1987), vol. IV.

Gorbachev, Mikhail. *Perestroika* (London, 1987).

Gorev, B. 'Sotsializm ili Bonapartizm?' *Novaia zaria*, no. 5–6 (10 June 1918): p. 1420.

Gorev, B. I. *Iz partiinogo proshlogo: vospominaniia 1895–1905* (Leningrad, 1924).

Gorev, B. I. *Ogust Blanki* (Moscow, 1921).

Gorky, Maxim. *On Literature* (Seattle WA, 1973).

Gorky, Maxim. *Untimely Thoughts: Essays on Revolution, Culture and the Bolsheviks* (New York, 1968).

Gorky, Maxim. *Vladimir Il'ich Lenin* (Leningrad, 1924).

Gottschalk, Louis. 'Leon Trotsky and the Natural History of Revolution'. *American Journal of Sociology* 44 (1938): pp. 339–54.

Grey, Ian. *Stalin: Man of History* (Garden City NY, 1979).

Guérard, Albert. *Napoleon III* (Cambridge MA, 1943).

Guerman, Mikhail. *Art of the October Revolution* (New York, 1979).

Hardman, John. *Robespierre* (London and New York, 1999).

Hardy, Deborah. *Petr Tkachev, the Critic as Jacobin* (Seattle WA, 1977).

Hartley, Janet M., Paul Keenan, and Dominic Lieven. eds. *Russia and the Napoleonic Wars: War, Culture and Society, 1750–1850* (New York, 2015).

Haumant, Émile. *La culture française en Russie (1700–1900)* (Paris, 1913).

Heald, Edward T. *Witness to Revolution: Letters from Russia 1916–1919* (Kent OH, 1972).

Heenan, Louise Erwin. *Russian Democracy's Fatal Blunder: The Summer Offensive of 1917* (New York, 1987).

Herzen, A. I. *Polnoe sobranie sochinenii i pisem*, edited by M. K. Lemke, 22 vols (St Petersburg, 1915–25).

Herzen, A. I. *Sobranie sochineni*, edited by M. K. Lemke, 30 vols (Moscow, 1954–65).

Herzen, Alexander. *From the Other Shore* (New York, 1956).

Herzen, Alexander. *My Past and Thoughts* (New York, 1974).

Hibbert, Christopher. *The Days of the French Revolution* (New York, 1981).

Higonnet, Patrice. *Goodness Beyond Virtue: Jacobins During the French Revolution* (Cambridge MA, 1998).

Hoffmann, Stanley. 'A Note on the French Revolution and the language of Violence'. *Daedelus: Proceedings of the American Academy of Arts and Sciences* 116, no. 2 (Spring 1987): pp. 149–56.

Holden, Anthony. *Tchaikovsky: A Biography* (New York, 1995).

Hollander, Paul. *Political Pilgrims: Travels of Western Intellectuals in Search of the Good Society* (New York, 1981).

Horne, Alistair. *The Fall of Paris: The Siege and the Commune, 1870–71* (New York, 2007).

Hosking, Geoffrey. *The First Socialist Society: A History of the Soviet Union from Within* (Cambridge MA, 1985).

Houghteling, James L. *A Diary of the Russian Revolution* (New York, 1918).

Hughes, Lindsey. *Russia in the Age of Peter the Great* (New Haven CT, 1998).

Hunt, Lynn. *Politics, Culture and Class in the French Revolution* (Berkeley CA, 2004).

Huntington, Samuel. *Political Order in Changing Societies* (New Haven CT, 1968).

Hutton, Patrick H. *The Cult of the Revolutionary Tradition: The Blanquists in French Politics, 1864–1893* (Berkeley CA, 1981).

Il'ina, G. I. 'Obraz evropeiskikh revoliutsii i russkaia kul'tura'. In *Anatomiia revoliutsii 1917 goda v Rossii: massy, partii, vlast'*, edited by V. Iu. Cherniaev (St Petersburg, 1994), pp. 383–93.

Ioffe, Mariia. 'Nachalo'. *Vremia i my*, no. 20 (1977): pp. 163–92.

Israel, Jonathan. *Revolutionary Ideas: An Intellectual History of the French Revolution from* The Rights of Man *to Robespierre* (Princeton NJ, 2014).

Istoriia sovetskogo teatra: Petrogradskie teatry na poroge Oktiabria i v epokhu voennogo kommunizma, 1917–1921 (Moscow, 1933).

Itenberg, B. S. *Rossiia i Parizhskaia kommuna* (Moscow, 1971).

Itenberg, B. S. *Rossiia i velikaia frantsuzskaia revoliutsiia* (Moscow, 1988).

'Iz stenograficheskogo otcheta o zasedanii Ispolnitel'nogo Komiteta Petrogradskogo Gubernskogo Soveta—informatsiia G. E. Zinov'eva o Kronshtadskikh sobytiakh i polozhenii Petrograda'. In *Kronshtadskia tragediia 1921 goda: dokumenty v drukh knigakh* (Moscow, 1999), vol. I.

Jackson, George. 'The Influence of the French Revolution on Lenin's Conception of the Russian Revolution'. In *The French Revolution of 1789 and its Impact*, edited by G. M. Schwab and John R. Jeanneney (Westport CT, 1995), pp. 273–84.

Jervis, Robert. *Perception and Misperception in International Affairs* (Princeton NJ, 1976).

Johnson, Chalmers. *Revolution and the Social System* (Stanford CA, 1964).

Johnson, Christopher H. 'The Revolution of 1830 in French Economic History'. In *1830 in France*, edited by John M. Merriman (New York, 1975), pp. 139–90.

Johnstone, M. 'The Commune and Marx's Conception of the Dictatorship of the Proletariat and the Role of the Party'. In *Images of the Commune*, edited by J. A. Leith (Montreal, 1978), pp. 201–24.

Jones, George Hilton. *The Mainstream of Jacobitism* (Cambridge MA, 1954).

Kadishev, A. E. *Interventsiia i grazhdanskaia voina v Zakavkaz'e* (Moscow, 1960).

Kalpashnikoff, Andrew. *A Prisoner of Trotsky* (Garden City NY, 1920).

Kamenka, Eugene. 'Revolution – The History of an Idea'. In *A World in Revolution?* edited by Eugene Kamenka (Canberra, 1970), pp. 1–14.

Kaplan, Steven Laurence. *Farewell Revolution: Disputed Legacies: France 1789/1989* (Ithaca NY, 1995).

Kareev, N. I. '"Frantsuzskaia revoliutsiia v marksistskoi istoriografii v Rossii". Vstuplenie i publikatsiia D. A. Rostislavleva'. In *Frantsuzskii ezhegodnik: stat'i i materialy po istorii Frantsii 1989* (Moscow, 1989), pp. 196–209.

Kareev, N. I. *Frantsuzskie istoriki pervoi poloviny XIX veka* (Leningrad, 1924), vol. I.

Kareev, N. I. *Prozhitoe i perezhitoe* (Leningrad, 1990).

Kariakin, Iu. F. and E. G. Plimak. *Zapretnaia mysl' obretaet svobodu. 175 let bor'by vokrug ideinogo naslediia Radishcheva* (Moscow, 1966).

Karpovich, Michael. 'A Forerunner of Lenin: P. N. Tkachev'. *Review of Politics* 6, no. 3 (July 1944): pp. 336–50.

Kates, Gary. Introduction to *The French Revolution: Recent Debates and New Controversies*, edited by Gary Kates (New York, 1998), pp. 1–14.

Kautsky, K. *Dvizhushchie sily i perspektivy russkoi revoliutsii* (Moscow/Leningrad, 1926).

Kautsky, Karl. *Georgien, eine sozialdemokratische Bauernrepublik* (Vienna, 1921).

Kautsky, Karl. *Terrorism and Communism: A Contribution to the Natural History of Revolution* (London, 1920).

Kautsky, Karl. *The Dictatorship of the Proletariat* (Ann Arbor MI, 1964).

Kautsky, Karl. *Von der Demokratie zur Staats-Sklaverei. Eine Auseinandersetzung mit Trotzki* (Berlin, 1921).

Kazakov, N. I. 'Napoleon glazami ego russkikh soveremennikov'. *Novaia i novaeishaia istoriia*, no. 3 (1970): pp. 41–7.

Kedrov, Iu. [Martov, Iu.]. 'Obozrenie V. Ia. Bogucharskogo, *Markiz' Lafaiet: deiatel' trekh revoliutsii'. Zhizn'* 9 (September 1900): pp. 358–62.

Keep, J. L. H. *The Rise of Social Democracy in Russia* (London, 1963).

Keep, John. 'The Tyranny of Paris over Petrograd'. *Soviet Studies* 20, no. 1 (July 1968): pp. 22–35.

Keep, John. *Contemporary History in the Soviet Mirror* (New York, 1964).

Keep, John L. *The Debate on Soviet Power: Minutes of the All-Russian Central Executive Committee of Soviets: Second Convocation, October 1917–January 1918* (Oxford, 1979).

Kenafick, K. J. *Michael Bakunin and Karl Marx* (Melbourne, 1948).

Kenez, Peter. *Cinema and Soviet Society, 1917–1953* (Cambridge, 1992).

Kennedy, Michael L. 'The Best and the Worst of Times: The Jacobin Clubs from October 1791 to June 2, 1793'. *Journal of Modern History* 56, no. 4 (1984): pp. 635–66.

Kerensky, Alexander. *Russia and History's Turning Point* (New York, 1965).

Kerzhentsev, P. M. *Istoriia Parizhskoi Kommuny 1871* (Moscow, 1959).

Kheifets, F. 'Iakobinskaia diktatura'. *Pravda*, no. 193(7878) (14 July 1939): p. 3.

Khrushchev, Nikita S. *Khrushchev Remembers: The Last Testament* (New York, 1976).

Kirpotin, V. Ia. *Ideinye predshestvenniki marksizma-leninizma v Rossii* (Moscow, 1950).

Kiselev, E. V. 'Parizhskaia Kommuna i sektsii 9 Termidora'. In *Frantsuzskii ezhegodnik: Stat'i i materialy po istorii Frantsii 1981* (Moscow, 1983), pp. 106–26.

Kluchert, Gerhard. 'The Paradigm and the Parody: Karl Marx and the French Revolution in the Class Struggles from 1848 to 1851'. *History of European Ideas*, no. 14 (January 1992): pp. 85–99.

Knizhnik-Vetrov, I. *Russkie deiatel'nitsy Pervogo Internationala i Parizhskoi kommuny* (Moscow/Leningrad, 1964).

'Ko vsem sotsial-demokraticheskim rabochim Sovetskogo soiuza'. *Sotsialisticheskii vestnik*, no. 154 (20 June 1927): pp. 1–2.

Kobiakov, Sergei. 'Krasnyi sud: Vpechatel'niia zashchitnika revoliutsionnykh tribunalakh'. In *Arkhiv Russkoi revoliutsii* (Moscow, 1922), vol. VII, pp. 246–75.

Kolakowski, Leszek. *Main Currents of Marxism: Its Rise, Growth, and Dissolution* (Oxford, 1978), vol. II.

Kondratieva, Tamara. *Bol'sheviki-iakobintsy i prizrak termidora* (Moscow, 1993).

Konstantinov, Fëdor and Inna Krylova. *Harbingers of a New Society: Centenary of the Paris Commune* (Moscow, 1971).

Korolev, A. I. *Parizhskaia Kommuna i sovremennost'* (Moscow, 1971).

Kotkin, Stephen. *Stalin: Paradoxes of Power, 1878–1928* (New York, 2014).

Kotkin, Stephen. *Stalin: Waiting for Hitler, 1929–1941* (New York, 2017).

Kovalenko, Iu. 'Parizh, 14 iulia…: Frantsiia otmechaet 200-letie revoliutsii'. *Izvestiia*, no. 196 (14 July 1989): p. 4.

Kozhokin, Evgenii. 'Diktatura i demokrtiia'. *Novoe vremia*, no. 28 (1989): pp. 38–9.

Kozhukov, S. 'K voprosu osenke roli M. I. Kutuzova v obshestvennoi voine 1812 goda'. *Bol'shevik*, no. 15 (August 1951); pp. 21–35.

Krasin, Iu. A. *Revoliutsiei ustrashennye. Kriticheskii ocherk burzhuaznykh kontseptsii sotsial'noi revoliutsii* (Moscow, 1975).

Krasso, Nicolas. 'Trotsky's Marxism'. In *Trotsky: The Great Debate Renewed*, edited by Nicolas Krasso (St Louis MO, 1972).

Kropotkin, P. A. *The Great French Revolution 1789–1793* (New York, 1909).

Kropotkin, P. A. *The Paris Commune* (London, 1896).

Kropotkin, P. A. *Zapiski revoliutsionera* (Moscow, 1966).

Kropotkin, Peter. *The Conquest of Bread and Other Writings*, edited by Marshall S. Shatz (New York, 1995).

Krupskaia, N. K. *Reminiscences of Lenin* (New York, 1970).

Kuleshov, V. 'Otechestvennye zapiski' i literatura 40-kh godov XIX veka (Moscow, 1959).

Kumanev, G. A. *Riadom so Stalinym* (Moscow, 1991).

Kunitz, Joshua. 'A Biographical Sketch of Albert Rhys Williams'. In Albert Rhys Williams, *Through the Russian Revolution* (New York, 1967), pp. ix–cxxii.

Kuznetsov, F. F. *Russkoe slovo'* (Moscow, 1965).

L. D. Trotsky o partii v 1904 g. (Moscow/Leningrad, 1928).

Lacouture, Jean. *Ho Chi Minh: A Political Biography* (New York, 1968).

Lang, David Marshall. *The First Russian Radical: Alexander Radishchev 1749-1802* (London, 1959).

Lantz, Kenneth. *The Dostoevsky Encyclopedia* (Westport CT, 2004).

Lapidus, Gail Warshovsky. 'Educational Strategies and Cultural Revolution: The Politics of Soviet Development'. In *Cultural Revolution in Russia, 1928-1931*, edited by Sheila Fitzpatrick (Bloomington IN, 1984), pp. 78-104.

Laqueur, Walter. *The Age of Terrorism* (Boston MA, 1987).

Larin, Iu. 'Eshche o Kadetakh'. *Pravda*, no. 200(131) (9 December 1917): p. 1.

Lavrov, P. L. *Izbrannye sochineniia no sotsial'no-politicheskie temy*, edited by I. S. Knizhnik-Vetrov (Moscow, 1935), vol. III.

Lavrov, P. L. 'Rol' naroda i rol' intelligentsii'. *Vpered'*, no. 34 (1 June 1876): pp. 305-20.

Lavrov, P. L. *Vzgliad na proshedshee i nastoiashchee russkago sotsializma* (St Petersburg, 1906).

Lavrov, P. L. 'Zametki o novykh knigakh'. *Vestnik narodnaia volia*, no. 3 (1884): pp. 1-20.

Lebedev, N. K. *Kropotkin* (Moscow, 1925).

Leggett, George. *The Cheka: Lenin's Political Police: The All-Russian Extraordinary Commission for Combating Counter-Revolution and Sabotage, December 1917 to February 1922* (Oxford, 1981).

Lehning, Arthur. ed. *Archives Bakounine* (Leiden, 1977), vol. VI.

Lehning, Arthur. 'Buonarroti's Ideas on Communism and Dictatorship'. *International Review of Social History* 2, no. 2 (1957): pp. 266-87.

Lenin, V. I. *Collected Works*, 55 vols (Moscow, 1977).

Lenin, V. I. *Imperialism: The Highest Stage of Capitalism* (London, 2010).

Lenin, V. I. *Polnoe sobranie sochinenii*, 5th edition, 55 vols (Moscow, 1958-65).

Lenin, V. I. *Selected Works* (New York, n.d.), vol. II.

Lenin, V. I. *State and Revolution* (New York, 1969).

Lenin, V. I. *What is to be Done? Burning Questions of our Movement* (New York, 1969).

Lenoe, Matthew. 'Fear, Loathing, Conspiracy: The Kirov Murder'. In *The Anatomy of Terror: Political Violence under Stalin*, edited by James Harris (Oxford, 2013), pp. 195–215.

Lenoe, Matthew. *The Kirov Murder and Soviet History* (New Haven CT, 2010).

Lerner, Warren. *Karl Radek: The Last Internationalist* (Stanford CA, 1970).

Lesnodorski, B. *La Pologne au X-ieme Congrès International des Sciences Historiques à Rome* (Warsaw, 1955).

'Letter of the Revolutionary Committee to Alexander III (1881)'. In *Readings in Modern European History*, edited by James Harvey Robinson and Charles Beard (Boston MA, 1908), vol. II.

Lewis, Ben. *Hammer & Tickle: A Cultural History of Communism* (New York, 2009).

Liberman, Simon. *Building Lenin's Russia* (Chicago IL, 1945).

Lichtheim, George. *Marxism. An Historical and Critical Study* (New York, 1969).

Lieblich, André. *From the Other Shore: Russian Social Democracy after 1921* (Cambridge MA, 1999).

Limonov, Iu. A. 'Prazdnestva Velikoi frantsuzskoi revoliutsii v 1789-93 gg. i massovye prazdniki Sovetskoi Rossii v 1917-1920 gg.'. In *Frantsuzskii ezhegodnik: stat'i i materialy po istorii Frantsii 1989* (Moscow, 1989), pp. 390-412.

Linton, Marisa. *Choosing Terror: Virtue, Friendship and Authenticity in the French Revolution* (New York, 2013).

Linton, Marisa. 'Robespierre and the Terror'. *History Today* 56, no. 8 (August 2006): pp. 23-9.

'Listovki ob"edinennoi studencheskoi organizatsii pri Petersburgskom Komitete RSDRP s prizyvami k vooruzhdennomu vosstaniiu'. In *Listovki Peterburgskikh Bol'shevikov 1902-1917* (Moscow, 1939-57), vol. I.

Liubatovich, Olga. 'Dalekoe i nedavnee: vospominaniia iz zhizni revoliutsionerov 1878-81 gg.'. *Byloe*, no. 6 (1906): pp. 108-56.

Lobanov-Rostovsky, Andrei. *The Grinding Mill: Reminiscences of War and Revolution* (New York, 1935).

Lockhart, R. H. Bruce. *The Two Revolutions: An Eyewitness Study of Russia, 1917* (Chester Springs PA, 1967).

Lodder, Christina. 'Lenin's Plan of Monumental Propaganda'. In *Sbornik: Papers of the Sixth and Seventh International Conferences of the Study Group of the Russian Revolution* (Leeds, 1981), pp. 67-82.

Lotte, S. A. 'Protiv "matezovshchiny" i "ustrialovshchiny" v istoricheskoi literature'. *Problemy marksizma*, no. 2 (1931): pp. 210-14.

Lotte, S. A. *Velikaia frantsuzskaia revoliutsiia* (Moscow/Leningrad, 1933).

Loukomsky, General. *Memoirs of the Russian Revolution* (London, 1922).

Lucas, Colin. 'Nobles, Bourgeois, and the Origins of the French Revolution'. *Past & Present*, no. 60 (August 1973): pp. 84-127.

Lukin, N. 'Lenin i problema iakobinskoi diktatury'. *Istorik marksist* 1 (1934): pp. 99-146.

Lukin, N. M. 'Al'ber Mat'ez (1874-1932)'. *Istorik marksist* 3 (1932): pp. 60-86.

Lukin, N. M. *Izbrannye Trudy v trekh tomakh* (Moscow, 1960), vol. I.

Lukin, N. M. *Robesp'er* (Petrograd, 1919).

Lunacharskii, A. 'Ocherki po istorii revoliutsionnoi bor'by evropeiskogo proletariata'. *Vpered*, no. 2 (1 January 1905): pp. 4-8.

Lunacharskii, A. 'Ocherki po istorii revoliutsionnoi bor'by evropeiskogo proletariata'. *Vpered*, no. 9 (23 February 1905): pp. 2-3.

Lunacharskii, A. V. 'Lenin i isskustvo (1933)'. In *Lenin o kul'ture i iskusstve* (Moscow, 1956), pp. 524-9.

Luxemburg, R. 'Organizatsionnye voprosy russkoi sotsial demokratii'. *Iskra*, no. 69 (10 July 1904): pp. 2-7.

Luxemburg, Rosa. 'Blankizm i Socjaldemokracia'. *Czerwony Sztandar*, no. 86 (June 1906). https://www.marxists.org/archive/luxemburg/1906/06/blanquism.html.

Luxemburg, Rosa. *The Russian Revolution and Leninism or Marxism?* (Ann Arbor MI, 1972).

Lvov-Rogachevskii, V. L. ed. 'Predislovie', *Sotsialisty o tekushchem momente: materialy velikoi revoliutsii 1917 g.* (Moscow, 1917).

Lyons, Martyn. *France under the Directory* (Cambridge, 1975).

McClellan, Woodford. *Revolutionary Exiles: The Russians in the First International and the Paris Commune* (Totowa NJ, 1979).

McConnell, Allen. *A Russian Philosophe: Alexander Radishchev, 1749-1802* (The Hague, 1964).

McConnell, Allen. *Tsar Alexander I: Paternalistic Reformer* (Northbrook IL, 1970).

McDermott, K. and J. Agnew. *The Comintern: A History of International Communism from Lenin to Stalin* (New York, 1999).

McGregor, Richard. 'Zhou's Cryptic Caution Lost in Translation'. *The Financial Times* (11-12 June 2011): p. 8.

McLaren, Moray. *Bonnie Prince Charlie* (New York, 1972).

MacMillan, Margaret. *The War That Ended Peace: The Road to 1914* (New York, 2014).

McNeal, Robert. 'Trotsky's Interpretation of Stalin'. *Canadian Slavonic Papers*, no. 5 (1961): pp. 87-97.

McNeal, Robert. 'Trotskyist Interpretations of Stalinism'. In *Stalinism: Essays in Historical Interpretation*, edited by Robert C. Tucker (New York, 1977), pp. 30–52.

Mainz, Valerie. *Days of Glory? Imaging Military Recruitment and the French Revolution (War, Culture, and Society, 1750–1850)* (London, 2016).

Makhnovets, V. P. [V. Akimov]. *K voprosu o rabotakh II-go s"ezda* (Geneva, 1904).

Makhnovets, V. P. [V. Akimov]. *Ocherk razvitiia sotsialdemokratii* (St Petersburg, 1905).

Maletskii, A. 'Nasilovanie teorii ili teoriia nasiliia gospodina Olarda'. *Kommunisticheskii internatsional*, no. 7 (1925), pp. 68–83.

Malia, Martin. *Alexander Herzen and the Birth of Russian Socialism* (New York, 1965).

Malia, Martin. *History's Locomotives: Revolutions and the Making of the Modern World* (New Haven CT, 2006).

Malia, Martin. *The Soviet Tragedy: A History of Socialism in Russia, 1917–1991* (New York, 1994).

Malia, Martin. *Western Eyes from the Bronze Horseman to the Lenin Mausoleum* (New York, 2000).

Manfred, A. Z. 'O prirode iakobinskoi vlasti'. *Voprosy istorii*, no. 5 (1969): pp. 92–109.

Manfred, A. Z. *Ocherki istorii Frantsii XVIII–XX vv.* (Moscow, 1961).

Manfred, A. Z. *Velikaia frantsuzskaia revoliutsiia* (Moscow, 1983).

Marcosson, Isaac Frederick. *The Rebirth of Russia* (New York, 1917).

Maretskii, D. *Tak nazyvaemyi 'termidor'* (Moscow/Leningrad, 1927).

Maretskii, D. 'Tak nazyvaemyi "termidor" i opasnosti pererozhdeniia'. *Pravda*, no. 166 (3698) (24 July 1927): p. 3, and no. 170(3702) (29 July 1927): pp. 2–4.

Martov, Iu. O. *1917–1922. Pis'ma i dokumenty* (Moscow, 2014).

Martov, Iu. O. *Bor'ba s 'osadnym' polozheniem' v Rossiiskoi sotsial'demokratovskoi rabochei partii: otvet na pis'mo n. Lenina* (Geneva, 1904).

Martov, Iu. O. 'Kronshtadt'. *Sotsialisticheskii vestnik*, no. 5 (5 April 1921): pp. 2–5.

Martov, Iu. O. 'Marks i problema diktatury proletariata'. *Rabochii internatsional*, no. 3–4 (1918): pp. 66–76.

Martov, Iu. O. *Mirovoi bol'shevizm* (Berlin, 1923).

Martov, Iu. O. 'Na puti k likvidatsii'. *Sotsialisticheskii vestnik*, no. 18 (15 October 1921): pp. 2–4.

Martov, Iu. O. 'Problema "edinogo fronta" v Rossii'. *Sotsialisticheskii vestnik*, no. 13–14 (20 July 1922): pp. 4–6.

Martov, Iu. O. 'Razlozhenie gosudarstva ili ego zavoevanie'. *Sotsialisticheskii vestnik*, no. 11 (8 July 1921): pp. 4–7.

Martov, Iu. O. *Zapiski sotsial-demokrata* (Berlin, 1922).

Martynov, Alexander. *Dve diktatury* (Geneva, 1905).

Marx, K. 'Burzhuaziia i kontrrevoliutsiia (1848)'. In K. Marx and F. Engels, *Sochineniia*, 2nd edition (Moscow, 1955), vol. VI, pp. 109–34.

Marx, K. and F. Engels. *Izbrannye pis'ma* (Moscow, 1947).

Marx, K. and V. I. Lenin. *Civil War in France: The Paris Commune* (New York, 1968).

Marx, Karl. *Critique of Hegel's Philosophy of Right* (New York, 1970).

Marx, Karl. *Early Writings* (New York, 1975).

Marx, Karl. *The Class Struggles in France, 1848–1850* (New York, 1964).

Marx, Karl. *The Eighteenth Brumaire of Louis Bonaparte* (New York, 1968).

Marx, Karl and Frederick Engels. *Collected Works*, 50 vols (New York, 1975).

Marx, Karl and Frederick Engels. *Selected Correspondence 1846–1895* (Westport CT, 1942).

Marx, Karl and Frederick Engels. *The Holy Family, or Critique of Critical Criticism. Against Bruno Bauer and Company*, in Karl Marx and Frederick Engels, *Collected Works*, vol. IV (New York, 1975).

Mason, Edward S. *The Paris Commune: An Episode in the History of the Socialist Movement* (New York, 1967).

Mason, T. W. 'The Primacy of Politics—Politics and Economics in National Socialist Germany'. In *The Nature of Fascism*, edited by S. J. Woolf (New York, 1965), pp. 165–95.

Massino, Salvadori. *Karl Kautsky and the Socialist Revolution, 1880–1938* (London, 1979).

Mathiez, Albert. 'Robespierre et le culte de l'être suprême'. *Annales révolutionnaires* 3, no. 2 (April–June, 1910): pp. 209–38.

May, Ernest. *Lessons of the Past* (New York, 1973).

Mayer, Arno. *The Furies: Violence and Terror in the French and Russian Revolutions* (Princeton NJ, 2002).

Mayer, Robert. 'Lenin and the Jacobin Identity in Russia'. *Studies in Eastern European Thought* 51 (1999): pp. 127–54.

Mazour, Anatole. *Modern Russian Historiography* (Princeton NJ, 1958).

Mazour, Anatole. *The First Russian Revolution 1825: The Decembrist Movement* (Berkeley CA, 1937).

Medvedev, Roy. *Let History Judge: The Origins and Consequences of Stalinism* (New York, 1989).

Meisner, Maurice. 'Images of the Paris Commune in Contempoary Marxist Thought'. In *Revolution and Reaction: The Paris Commune, 1871*, edited by John Hicks and Robert Tucker (Amherst MA, 1973), pp. 112–29.

Melgunov, Sergei. *Kak Bol'sheviki zakhvatili vlast'; octiabr'iskii perevorot 1917 goda* (Paris, 1953).

Mendel, Arthur P. *Michael Bakunin: Roots of Apocalypse* (New York, 1981).

Merriman, John. *Massacre: The Life and Death of the Paris Commune* (New York, 2014).

Miliukov, P. N. *History of Russia: Reforms, Reaction, Revolutions (1855–1932)* (New York, 1968–9), vol. III.

Miliukov, Pavel N. *The Russian Revolution* (Gulf Breeze TX, 1978), vol. I.

Miller, Martin A. *The Russian Revolutionary Emigres 1825–1870* (Baltimore MD, 1986).

Mirskii, B. [Mirkin-Getsevich, M. V.]. '14 iiulia', *Poslednie novosti*, no. 330 (14 July 1921): p. 2.

Mirskii, B. [Mirkin-Getsevich, M. V.]. 'Put' termidora'. *Poslednie novosti*, no. 266 (3 March 1921): p. 260.

Mirsky, D. S. *Pushkin* (Moscow, 1926).

Mitskevich, S. I. 'K voprosu o korniakh bol'shevizma'. *Katorga i ssylka*, no. 3 (1925): pp. 92–101.

Mitskevich, S. I. 'Russkie iakobintsy'. *Proletarskaia revoliutsiia*, no. 6–7 (18–19) (1923): pp. 3–26.

Molchanov, N. 'Revoliutsiia na gil'otine: takov smysl diskussii v sviazi s priblizheniem 200-letiia vziatiia Bastilii'. *Literaturnaia gazeta*, no 28(5094) (9 July 1986): p. 14.

Molok, A. 'Obzor, *E. V. Tarlé, Taleiran* (Moscow/Leningrad, 1948)'. *Voprosy istorii*, no. 10 (1948): pp. 157–60.

Molok, A. 'Tribuny Konventa'. *Pravda*, no. 193(7878) (14 July 1939): p. 3.

Molok, A. I. *Parizhskaia Kommuna 1871 g.* (Leningrad, 1927).

Molok, A. I. 'Staline et la Commune de Paris'. *Cahiers du Communisme*, no. 3 (1952): pp. 288–309.

Montefiore, Simon Sebag. *Stalin: The Court of the Red Tsar* (New York, 2003).

Moore, Barrington. *Social Origins of Dictatorship and Democracy: Lord and Peasant in the Making of the Modern World* (Boston MA, 1967).

Mosse, George L. ed. *The Fascist Revolution: Towards a General Theory of Fascism* (New York, 1999).

Murin, B., V. Aronov, and N. N. Masienikov. *Parizhskaia kommuna: posobie dlia massovoi raboty v klube* (Moscow, 1921).

Myers, Steven Lee. *The New Tsar: The Rise and Reign of Vladimir Putin* (New York, 2016).

N. A. Dobroliubov v vospominaniakh sovremennikov (Moscow, 1986).

Naarden, Bruno. *Socialist Europe and Revolutionary Russia: Perception and Prejudice, 1848-1923* (New York, 2002).

Nabokov, Vladimir. *Speak, Memory: An Autobiography Revisited* (New York, 1999).

'Nakanune Uchreditel'nago Sobraniia vo Frantsii i v Rossii'. *Izvestiia*, no. 130 (29 July 1917): p. 2.

Namier, Lewis. *Avenues of History* (London, 1952).

Narochnitskii, A. L. 'Voprosy voiny i mira v politike iakobintsev nakanune 9 termidora'. In *Mezhdunarodnye otnosheniia politika, diplomatiia XVI–XX veka* (Moscow, 1964).

Naumov, V. ed. *Georgii Zhukov: Stenogramma oktiabr'skogo (1957g.) plenuma Tsk KPSS i drugie dokumenty* (Moscow, 2001).

Neustadt, Richard and Ernest May. *Thinking in Time: The Uses of History for Decision Makers* (New York, 1986).

Nikitenko, V. *Dnevnik* (Moscow, 1955), vol. II.

Nikolaevskii, B. '"Termidor" russkoi revoliutsii'. *Sotsialisticheskii vestnik*, no 15–16 (573–4) (6 September 1945): pp. 171–5.

Nilsson, Nils Ake. ed. *Art, Society, Revolution: Russia, 1917-1921* (Stockholm, 1979).

Novaia oppozitsiia: sbornik materialov o diskussii 1925 goda (Leningrad, 1926).

'O Staline i Stalinizme: beseda D. A. Volkogonym i R. A. Medvedevym'. *Istoriia SSSR*, no. 4 (1989), pp. 89–105.

Ogarev, N. P. *Konstitutsiia i zemskii sobor. Izbrannye sotsial'no-politicheskie i filosofskie proizvedeniia* (Moscow, 1952), vol. I.

Osinskii, V. V. 'Belyi i krasnyi terror'. *Pravda*, no. 192 (8 September 1918): p. 3.

'Otvet MK-RKP (b)—na pis'mo leningradskoi partkonferentsii'. In *Partiia i novaia oppozitsiia. Materialy k prorabotke resheniia i XIV s"ezda VKP (b)* (Leningrad, 1926).

'Otvet S. M. Kravchinskogo na pis'mo ispolnitel'nogo komiteta Narodnoi voli (March 1882)'. In S. M. Volk, *Revoliutsionnoe narodnichestvo: 70-x godov xix veka* (Moscow/ Leningrad, 1965), vol. II, p. 345.

'Otvet tov. Stalina na pis'mo tov. Razina'. *Bol'shevik istorii*, no. 3 (February, 1947): pp. 7–8.

Ozouf, Mona. *Festivals and the French Revolution* (Cambridge MA, 1988).

Paine, Thomas. *Common Sense*, edited by Isaac Kramnick (New York, 1976).

Palmer, R. R. *The Age of Democratic Revolution*, 2 vols (Princeton NJ, 1959-64).

Palmer, R. R. *The World of the French Revolution* (New York, 1971).

Palmer, R. R. *Twelve Who Ruled: The Year of the Terror in the French Revolution* (Princeton NJ, 1971).

'Pamiati parizhskikh kommunarov'. *Krasnaia panorama*, no 12 (March 19, 1926): p. 1.

'Parizhskaia kommuna i sovremennost''. *Kommunist*, no. 2 (January 1971): pp. 25–36.

Parker, Noel. *Revolutions and History: An Essay in Interpretation* (Oxford, 1999).

Paxton, Robert O. *The Anatomy of Fascism* (New York, 2005).

Payne, Howard C. 'Theory and Practice of Political Police during the Second Empire in France'. *Journal of Modern History* 30, no. 1 (March 1958): pp. 14–23.

Péchoux, P. 'Bakunin et la Révolution française'. *Revue des Études Slaves* 61, no. 1–2 (1989): pp. 161–8.

Pelshe, P. A. *Nravy i iskusstvo frantsuzskoi revoliutsii* (Petrograd, 1919).

Perepiska G. V. Plekhanova i P. B. Aksel'roda, edited by B. I. Nikolaevskii, P. A. Berlin, and V. S. Voitinskii (Moscow, 1925).

Pimenova, L. A. 'O sovetskoi istoriografii Velikoi frantsuzskoi revoliutsii (1979–1986 gg.)'. In *Frantsuzskii ezhegodnik: stat'i i materialy po istorii Frantsii 1989* (Moscow, 1989) pp. 119–32.

Pinckney, David H. 'The Crowd in the French Revolution of 1830'. *American Historical Review* 70, no. 1 (October 1964): pp. 1–17.

Pinckney, David H. *The French Revolution of 1830* (Princeton NJ, 1972).

Piontkovskii, S. A. *Ocherki istorii SSSR xix i xx vv.* (Moscow, 1935).

Pipes, Richard. 'The Origins of Bolshevism: The Intellectual Evolution of Young Lenin'. In *Revolutionary Russia: A Symposium*, edited by Richard Pipes (New York, 1969), pp. 33–66.

Pipes, Richard. *Russia under the Old Regime* (New York, 1974).

Pis'ma N. M. Karamzina k I. I. Dmitrievu (St Petersburg, 1886).

Pis'ma P. B. Aksel'roda i Iu. O. Martova, 1901–1916, edited by F. Dan, B. Nikolaevskii, and L. Tsederbaum-Dan (The Hague, 1967).

'Pis'mo P. L. Lavrov k E. A. Shtakenshneider'. In *Golos minuvshago*, edited by S. P. Mel'gunov and V. I. Semevskii (The Hague, 1971), pp. 124–7.

'Pis'mo Akselrodu (16 June 1918)'. In *Martov i ego blizkie: sbornik* (New York, 1959), p. 64.

'Pis'mo F. E. Dzerzhinskogo Stalinu i Orzhonikidze (5–6 October 1925)'. In *Politicheskii dnevnik* (Amsterdam, 1970), pp. 238–41.

'Pis'mo Izpolitel'nogo Komiteta "Narodnoi voli" zagranichnym tovarishcham'. In S. M. Volk, *Revoliutsionnoe narodnichestvo: 70-x godov xix veka* (Moscow/Leningrad, 1965), vol. II, pp. 315–21.

Pisarev, D. I. 'Istoricheskie eskizy'. *Russkoe slovo: zhurnal literaturno-politicheskii*, no. 2, sect. 1 (January 1864): pp. 1–79.

Pisarev, D. I. *Sochineniia* (St Petersburg, 1867), vol. IV.

Plamper, Jan. *The Stalin Cult: A Study in the Alchemy of Power* (New Haven CT, 2012).

Plekhanov, G. V. 'K voprosu roli lichnosti v istorii'. In G. V. Plekhanov, *Izbrannye filosofskie proizvedeniia* (Moscow, 1956), vol. II, pp. 317–26.

Plekhanov, G. V. 'Na poroge dvatsatago veka'. *Iskra*, no. 2 (February 1901): p. 1.

Plekhanov, G. V. *Sochineniia*, edited by D. Riazanov, 24 vols (Moscow, 1923–7).

Plekhanov, G. V. *Stoletie velikoi revoliutsii* (St Petersburg, 1906).

Plessis, Alain. *The Rise and Fall of the Second Empire 1852–1871* (Cambridge, 1985).

Plimak, E. G. and V. G. Khoros. 'Velikaia frantsuzskaia revoliutsiia i revoliutsionnaia traditsiia v Rossii'. In *Frantsuzskii ezhegodnik: stat'i i materialy po istorii Frantsii 1989* (Moscow, 1989), pp. 222–72.

Pogodin, M. P. *Istoriko-politicheskie pis'ma i zapiski v prodolzhenie Krymskoi voiny* (Moscow, 1874.

Pokrovskii, M. ed. *Vosstanie dekabristov; materialy po istorii vosstania dekabristov* (Moscow, 1925–31), vol. IV.

Pokrovskii, M. N. *Diplomatiia i voiny tsarskoi Rossii v xix stoletiia* (Moscow, 1923).

Pokrovskii, M. N. 'Lenin v russkoi revoliutsii'. *Vestnik kommunisticheskoi akedemii*, no. 7 (1924): pp. 8–21.

Polonskii, Viacheslav. 'Bakunin–Iakobinets'. *Vestnik Kommunisticheskoi akademii*, no. 18 (1926), pp. 42–62.

Pomper, Philip. *Peter Lavrov and the Russian Revolutionary Movement* (Chicago IL, 1972).

Poole, Ernest. *The Village: Russian Impressions* (New York, 1918).

Porshnev, B. F. 'V. I. Lenin o rannikh burzhuaznykh revoliutsiiakh'. *Novaia i noveishaia istoriia*, no. 2 (1960): pp. 50–66.

Pospelov, P. 'Predvestnik Oktiabria: k 100-letiu parizhskoi kommuny'. *Izvestiia*, no. 64 (16682) (18 March 1871): p. 4.

Possony, Stefan T. *Lenin: The Compulsive Revolutionary* (Chicago IL, 1964).

Power, Rhoda D. *Under the Bolshevik Reign of Terror* (New York, 1919).

'Prazdnovanie dnia konstitutsii v Moskve i peredachi znameni Parizhskikh kommunarov'. *Leningradskaia Pravda*, no. 8 (July 1924): p. 2.

'Préface de Leon Trotsky'. In C. Talès, *La Commune de 1871* (Paris, 1921), pp. vii–xxii.

Prendergast, Christopher. *The Fourteenth of July* (London, 2008).

Price, Philip M. *My Reminiscences of the Russian Revolution* (London, 1921).

Pushkin, A. S. *Polnoe sobranie sochinenii* (Moscow, 1965), vol. VIII.

Puti mirovoi revoliutsii. Sed'moi rasshirennyi plenum ispolnitel'nogo Komiteta Kommunis-ticheskogo internationala, 22 noiabria–16 dekabria 1926: stenograficheskii otchet, 2 vols (Moscow, 1927).

Rabinowitch, Alexander. *Prelude to Revolution: The Petrograd Bolsheviks and the July 1917 Uprising* (Bloomington IN, 1991).

Radek, K. ed. *Napoleon* (Moscow, 1936).

Radek, Karl. *Proletarian Dictatorship and Terrorism* (Detroit MI, n.d.).

Radishchev, Alexander. *A Journey from St. Petersburg to Moscow*, edited by Roderick Page Thaler (Cambridge MA, 1966).

Radkey, Oliver. *The Sickle under the Hammer: The Russian Socialist Revolutionaries in the Early Months of Soviet Rule* (New York, 1963).

Raeff, Marc. ed. *The Decembrist Revolt* (Englewood Cliffs NJ, 1966).

Raeff, Marc. *Michael Speransky: Statesman of Imperial Russia, 1772-1839* (The Hague, 1957).

Raeff, Marc. *Russia Abroad: A Cultural History of the Russian Emigration 1919-1939* (New York, 1990).

Raleigh, Donald G. *Revolution on the Volga: 1917 in Saratov* (Ithaca NY, 1986).

Ralli-Arbore, Zemfir. 'Sergei Gennadevich Nechaev (Iz moikh vospominanii)'. *Byloe*, no. 7 (July 1906): pp. 136–46.

Ransome, Arthur. *Russia in 1919* (New York, 1919).

Rapport, Mike. *1848: Year of Revolution* (New York, 2008).

'Rech' tovarishcha F. I. Golikova', *Pravda*, no. 304(15794) (31 October 1961): p. 3.

'Rech' Tsereteli'. *Izvestiia*, no. 176 (20 September 1917): p. 3.

Reed, John. *Ten Days That Shook the World* (New York, 1960).

Reeves, Nicholas. *The Power of Film Propaganda: Myth or Reality* (London, 1999).

Revunenkov, V. G. *Marksizm i problema iakobinskoi diktatury* (Leningrad, 1966).

Revunenkov, V. G. 'Novoe v izuchenii velikoi frantsuzskoi revoliutsii i vzgliad V. I. Lenina'. In *V. I. Lenin i istoricheskaia nauka*, edited by N. A. Zakher and V. V. Makarov (Moscow, 1969), pp. 117–49.

Revunenkov, V. G. *Ocherki po istorii Velikoi frantsuzskoi revoliutsii. Iakobinskaia respublika i ee krushenie* (Leningrad, 1983).

Revunenkov, V. G. *Problemy vseobshchei istorii: istoriograficheskii sbornik* (Leningrad, 1967).

Revunenkov, V. G. 'Velikaia frantsuzskaia revoliutsiia i traditsii izucheniia i novye podkhody'. *Voprosy istorii*, no. 5 (May 1989): pp. 98–116.

Riasanovsky, Nicholas. *Nicholas I and Official Nationality in Russia, 1825-1855* (Berkeley CA, 1969).

Riazanov, D. 'The Relations of Marx with Blanqui'. *Labour Monthly: A Magazine of International Labour* 10, no. 8 (August 1928), pp. 492–8.

Riazanov, David. *Karl Marx and Frederick Engels: An Introduction to their Lives and Work* (New York and London, 1973).

Ridley, Jasper. *Napoleon III and Eugénie* (New York, 1979).

Roberts, Andrew. *Napoleon: A Life* (New York, 2014).

Roberts, Geoffrey. *Stalin's General: The Life of Georgy Zhukov* (New York, 2012).

Rodichev, F. I. *Vospominaniia i ocherki o russkom liberalizme* (Newtownville MA, 1983).

Rolf, Malte. *Soviet Mass Festivals, 1917–1991* (Pittsburgh PA, 2013).

Romanova, Olga, 'Eisenstein's "October": Between Artistic Invention and the Myth of the Revolution, 2012'. http://urokiistorii.ru/en/taxonomy/term/200/2822.

Rosmer, Alfred. *Lenin's Moscow* (New York and London, 1971).

Rossiskaia Sotsial-Demokraticheskaia Rabochaia Partiia. Vtoroi ocherednoi s"ezd. Polnyi tekst protokolov (Geneva, 1903).

Rougerie, Jacques. *Procès des Communards* (Paris, 1964).

Rubel, Maximilien. 'The French Revolution and the Education of the Young Marx'. *Diogenes* 37 (Winter 1989): pp. 1–27.

Rudnitskaia, E. L. *N. P. Ogarev v russkom revoliutsionnom dvizhenii* (Moscow, 1969).

Rumii, V. 'Plekhanov i terror'. *Pod znamenem Marksizma*, no. 6–7 (June–July 1923): pp. 19–37.

Rusanov, N. S. *Na rodine 1859–1882* (Moscow, 1931).

Russkaia literatura i fol'klor. http://feb-web.ru/feb/litenc/encyclop/le4/le4-5401.htm?cmd=p&istext=1.

Ryzhenko, F. 'Parizhskaia kommuna i sovremennost'. *Pravda*, no. 7(19214) (12 March 1971): p. 4.

'S"ezd narodnykh deputatov SSSR'. *Pravda*, no. 160(25878) (9 June 1989): p. 2.

Sadoul, Jacques. *Notes sur la Révolution Bolchevique, Octobre 1917* (Paris, 1920).

Sakharov, Andrei. *Progress, Coexistence, and Intellectual Freedom*, edited by Harrison E. Salisbury (New York, 1968).

Sakharov, Andrei. 'Stepen' svobody: Aktual'noe intrev'iu'. *Ogonëk* (July 1989), pp. 26–9.

Salmin, Alexei. 'Zhazhda samoochishcheniia i terror'. *Novoe vremia*, no. 28 (1989): pp. 40–1.

Sanders, Thomas. ed. *Historiography of Imperial Russia: The Profession and Writing of History in a Multinational State* (New York, 1999).

Sawer, M. 'The Soviet Image of the Commune: Lenin and Beyond'. In *Images of the Commune*, edited by J. A. Leith (Montreal, 1978), pp. 245–63.

Schama, Simon. *Citizens: A Chronicle of the French Revolution* (New York, 1989).

Schapiro, Leonard. *The Communist Party of the Soviet Union* (New York, 1971).

Schapiro, Leonard. (Cambridge MA, 1977).

Schoenfeld, Gabriel. 'Uses of the Past: Bolshevism and the French Revolutionary Tradition' (PhD dissertation, Harvard University, 1989).

Schoenfeld, Gabriel. 'Uses of the Past: Bolshevism and the French Revolutionary Tradition'. In *The French Revolution of 1789 and its Impact*, edited by G. W. Schwab and John R. Jeanneney (Westport CT, 1995), pp. 285–303.

Schwarz, Solomon M. 'Populism and Early Russian Marxism on Ways of Historical Development in Russia'. In *Continuity and Change in Russian and Soviet Thought*, edited by Ernest J. Simmons (Cambridge MA, 1955), pp. 40–62.

Scott, Otto J. *Robespierre: The Voice of Virtue* (New Brunswick NJ and London, 2011).

Ségur, Count. *Memoirs and Recollections* (London, 1827), vol. III.

Selishchev, A. M. *Iazyk revoliutsionnoi epokhy: iz nabliudenii nad russkim iazykom (1917–1926)* (Moscow, 2003).

Sell, Louis. *From Washington to Moscow: U.S.–Soviet Relations and the Collapse of the USSR* (Durham NC, 2016).

Semenova, A. V. 'D. Diderot i dekabristy'. In *Frantsuzskii ezhegodnik: stat'i i materialy po istorii Frantsii 1989* (Moscow, 1989), pp. 366–73.

Sergeev, V. 'Tigr v bolote'. *Znanie-sila*, no. 7 (1988): pp. 65–74.

Shatz, Marshall. *Soviet Dissent in Historical Perspective* (New York, 1980).

Shatz, Marshall and Judith Zimmerman. eds. *Vekhi/Landmarks: A Collection of Articles about the Russian Intelligentsia* (Armonk NY, 1994).

Shchegolev, P. P. 'K kharakteristike ekonomicheskoi politiki termidorianskoi reaktsii'. *Istorik marksist* 4 (1927): pp. 73–100.

Shchegolev, P. P. *Posle termidora. Ocherki po istorii termidorianskoi reaktsii* (Leningrad, 1930).

Shchipanov, I. ed. *Izbrannye sotsial'no-politicheskie i filosofskie proizvedeniia Dekabristov* (Moscow, 1951), vol. I.

Shelgunov, N. V. 'Vnutrenee obozrenie'. *Delo*, no. 3 (1881), pp. 142–63.

Shilova, I. 'Building the Bolshevik Calendar through *Pravda* and *Isvestiia*', *Toronto Slavic Quarterly*, no. 19 (Winter 2007). http://sites.utoronto.ca/tsq/19/shilova19.shtml.

Shlapentokh, Dmitry. *The Counter-Revolution in Revolution: Images of Thermidor and Napoleon at the Time of the Russian Revolution and Civil War* (New York, 1999).

Shlapentokh, Dmitry. *The French Revolution and the Russian Anti-Democratic Tradition: A Case of False Consciousness* (New Brunswick NJ, 1997).

Shlapentokh, Dmitry. *The French Revolution in Russian Intellectual Life 1865–1905* (New Brunswick NJ, 2009).

Shlapentokh, Dmitry. 'The Images of the French Revolution in the February and Bolshevik Revolutions'. *Russian History* 16, no. 1 (1989): pp. 31–54.

Shleev, V. V. *Revoliutsiia i izobrazitel'noe iskusstvo* (Moscow, 1987).

Steinberg, I. N. *In the Workshop of the Revolution* (London, 1955).

Shtrange, M. M. *Russkoe obshchestvo i frantsuzskaia revoliutsiia 1789–1974 gg.* (Moscow, 1956).

Simpson, F. A. *The Rise of Louis Napoleon* (London, 1968).

'Sineira'. 'Est li v marksizme elementy blankizm?' *Pechat' i revoliutsii*, no. 5 (1923): pp. 112–15.

'Sineira'. 'Zakliuchitel'noe slovo k diskussii ob elementakh blankizma v marksizme'. *Pechat' i revoliutsiia*, no. 7 (1923), pp. 19–23.

Sisson, Edgar. *One Hundred Red Days: A Personal Chronicle of the Bolshevik Revolution* (New Haven CT, 1931).

Skariatina, Irina. *A World Can End: A Diary of the Russian Revolution* (New York, 1931).

Skocpol, Theda. *States and Social Revolutions: A Comparative Analysis of France, Russia, and China* (New York, 1979).

Slepkov, A. *Oppozitsionnyi neomen'shevizm. O novoi platforme* (Moscow, 1927).

Slutskii, A. *Parizhskaia kommuna 1871 goda* (Moscow, 1925).

Smirnov, V. 'Velikaia frantsuzskaia revoliutsiia i sovremennost'. *Mirovaia ekonomika i mezhdunarodnye otnosheniia*, no. 7 (1989): pp. 55–65.

Sogomonov, Alexander. 'Lafaiet ili Marat'. *Novoe vremia*, no. 28 (1989): pp. 39–40.

Solzhenitsyn, Alexander. *A World Split Apart* (New York, 1988).

Solzhenitsyn, Aleksandr Isaevich. *Krasnoe koleso* (Paris, 1988), knot III.

Solzhenitsyn, Alexander et al. *From under the Rubble* (New York, 1976).

Sorokin, Pitirim. *Leaves from a Russian Diary—and Thirty Years After* (Boston, 1950).

Sovet politicheskii plakat: iz kollektsii gosudarstvennoi biblioteki SSSR imeni V. I. Lenina (Moscow, 1984).

Sperber, Jonathan. *Karl Marx: A Nineteenth-Century Life* (New York, 2013).

Sperber, Jonathan. *Revolutionary Europe 1780–1850* (New York, 2013).

Sperber, Jonathan. *The European Revolutions, 1848–1851* (New York, 2005).

Stakhevich, S. G. 'Sredi politicheskykh prestupnikov'. In *N. G. Chernyshevskii v vospominanii sovremennikov*, edited by V. Ye. Vatsuro (Moscow, 1982).

Stalin, J. V. *History of the Communist Party of the Soviet Union (Bolsheviks): Short Course* (New York, 1939).

Stalin, J. V. 'O nekotorykh voprosakh istorii bol'shevizma'. *Proletarskaia revoliutsiia*, no. 6 (113) (October 1931): pp. 3–12.

Stalin, J. V. *Sochineniia*, vols 1–13 (Moscow, 1946–51), and vols 14–16 (Moscow, 1997).

Stalin, J. V. *The Foundations of Leninism* (New York, 1932).

Stanford, Doreen. *Siberian Odyssey* (New York, 1964).

Starosel'skii, Ia. 'Burzhuaznaia revoliutsiia i iuridicheskii kretinizm. O rechi Olara, 'Teoriia nasiliia i Frantsuzskaia revoliutsiia'. *Revoliutsiia pravda*, no. 2–3 (1927): pp. 95–7.

Starr, John Bryan. 'The Commune in Chinese Communist Thought'. In *Images of the Commune*, edited by J. A. Leith (Montreal, 1978), pp. 291–311.

Stasova, E. *Vospominaniia* (Moscow, 1969).

Stebling, E. P. *From Czar to Bolshevik* (London, 1918).

Steiner, George. *Tolstoy or Dostoevsky: An Essay in the Old Criticism* (New Haven CT, 1996).

Stenograficheskii otchet: VI kongressa Kominterna (Moscow/Leningrad, 1929).

Stepanov, I. *Parizhskaia kommuna 1871 goda i voprosy taktiki v proletarskoi revoliutsii* (Moscow, 1921).

Stites, Richard. *Revolutionary Dreams: Utopian Vision and Experimental Life in the Russian Revolution* (New York, 1989).

Stoecker, Sally W. *Forging Stalin's Army: Marshal Tukhachevsky and the Politics of Military Innovation* (New York, 2018).

Stokes, Gale. *The Walls Came Tumbling Down* (New York, 2011).

Stone, Bailey. *The Anatomy of Revolution Revisited: A Comparative Analysis of England, France, and Russia* (New York, 2014).

Stone, Lawrence. 'Theories of Revolution'. *World Politics* 18 (1965–6): pp. 159–76.

Strigalev, Anatolii. 'Sviaz' vremen'. *Dekorativnoe iskusstvo SSSR*, no 4 (1978): pp. 1–2.

Struve, P. 'Razmyshleniia o russkoi revoliutsii'. *Russkaia mysl'* (January–February, 1921): pp. 7–37.

Sukhanov, Nikolai Nikolaevich. *The Russian Revolution, 1917: A Personal Record* (New York, 1955), vol. I.

Sverdlov, Ia. M. *Izbrannye proizvedeniia* (Moscow, 1959), vol. II.

Talin, V. I. 'Ulitsy'. *Rabochaia gazeta*, no. 80 (14 June 1917): p. 2.

Talmon, Jacob. *The Origins of Totalitarian Democracy* (New York, 1952).

Tarasov-Rodionov, A. *February 1917: A Chronicle of the Russian Revolution* (Westport CT, 1931).

Tarlé, E. 'Bor'ba s interventsiei'. *Pravda*, no. 193(7878) (14 July 1939); pp. 3–4.

Tarlé, E. 'Mikhail Illarionovich Kutuzov—polkovodets i diplomat', *Voprosy istorii*, no. 3 (March 1952): pp. 34–82.

Tarlé, E. V. 'Pis'mo v redaktsii zhurnal "Bol'shevik"'. *Bol'shevik*, no. 19 (October 1951): pp. 71–7.

Tarlé, Eugene. *Bonaparte* (London, 1937).

Tarlé, Eugene. *Napoleon's Invasion of Russia* (New York, 1942).

Taylor, George V. 'Non-Capitalist Wealth and the Origins of the French Revolution'. *American Historical Review* 72, no. 2 (1967): pp. 469–96.

Taylor, Richard. *The Battleship Potemkin: The Film Companion* (New York, 2000).

Tchoudinov, Alexander. 'The Evolution of Russian Discourse on the French Revolution'. In *The Routledge Companion to the French Revolution in World History*, edited by Alan Forrest and Matthias Middell (New York, 2016), pp. 277–98.

Teodorovich, I. A. 'Iz epokhi "Narodnoi Voli"'. *Katorga i ssylka*, no. 57–8 (1929): pp. 7–44.

'The Beria Affair: Plenum of the Central Committee CPSU: The Fourth Session—July 4, 1953'. In *Political Archives of Russia* 3, no. 2–3 (1992), pp. 145–60.

Thomas, Edith. *The Women Incendiaries* (New York, 1966).

Thomas, P. *Karl Marx and the Anarchists* (London, 1980).

Thomson, David. *Democracy in France since 1870* (New York, 1964).

Tierso, Zh. *Pesni i prazdnestva frantsuzskoi revoliutsii* (Petrograd, 1919).

Tilly, Charles. *European Revolutions, 1492–1992* (New York, 1996).

Timasheff, Nicholas. *The Great Retreat: The Growth and Decline of Communism in Russia* (New York, 1946).

Tkachev, P. N. *Izbrannye sochineniia na sotsial'no-politicheskie temy*, edited by B. F. Kozmin (Moscow, 1932–6), vol. V.

Tkachev, P. N. 'Retsenziia no knigu A. Rokhau, "Istoriia Frantsii ot nizverzheniia Napoleona I do vosstanovleniia imperii (1866)"'. In *P. N. Tkachev, Izbrannye sochineniia na sotsial'no-politicheskie temy*, edited by B. F. Kozmin (Moscow, 1932–6), pp. 190–6.

Tolstoy, Leo. *Anna Karenina* (New York, 1961).

Tombs, Robert. *France 1814–1914* (New York and London, 1996).

Tombs, Robert. *The Paris Commune* (New York, 1999).

'Tov. P. B. Aksel'rod o bol'shevizme i bor'be s nim'. *Sotsialisticheskii vestnik*, no. 6 (20 April 1921): pp. 3–7, and no. 7 (4 May 1921): pp. 3–5.

Trotsky, L. '1905. Cherez dvadtsat' let'. *Pravda*, no. 6(3235) (8 January 1926): p. 5.

Trotsky, L. *Itogi i perspektivy* (Moscow, 1919).

Trotsky, L. *Nashi politicheskie zadachi* (Geneva, 1904).

Trotsky, L. 'Pod znamenem Kommuny', *Novyi mir* (17 March 1917). In Trotsky, L. *Voina i revoliutsiia: krushenie vtorogo internationala i podgotovka tret'ego* (Moscow, 1923), vol. II, pp. 412–14.

Trotsky, L. 'Rech' na parade v chest' krasnykh komandirov na Krasnoi ploshchadi'. In Trotsky, L. *Kak vooruzhalas' revoliutsiia (na voennoi rabote)* Moscow, 1924), vol. II, pp. 285–7.

Trotsky, L. *Sochineniia*, 23 vols (Moscow/Leningrad, 1924–7).

Trotsky, L. *The Military Writings and Speeches of Leon Trotsky*, 5 vols (Moscow, 1979).

Trotsky, L. *Vtoroi s"ezd RSDRP (Otchet Simbirskii delegatsii)* (Geneva, 1903).

Trotsky, Leon. *1905* (New York, 1971).

Trotsky, Leon. *Between Red and White: A Study of Some Fundamental Questions of Revolution* (New York, 1975).

Trotsky, Leon. 'Democracy, Pacifism, and Imperialism'. *Vpered* (30 June 1917). In Vladimir Lenin and Leon Trotsky, *The Proletarian Revolution in Russia*, edited by Louis B. Fraina (New York, 1918), pp. 193–200.

Trotsky, Leon. 'Hands Off Rosa Luxemburg!' *The Militant* (6 August and 13 August 1932), p. 4.

Trotsky, Leon. *History of the Russian Revolution*, unabridged edition (Chicago IL, 1932).

Trotsky, Leon. *In Defense of Marxism* (New York, 1973).

Trotsky, Leon. *Lenin: Notes for a Biographer* (New York, 1971).

Trotsky, Leon. *Literature and Revolution* (Ann Arbor MI, 1960).

Trotsky, Leon. *My Life* (New York, 1970).

Trotsky, Leon. 'Report on the World Economic Crisis and the New Tasks of the Communist International (June 1921)'. https://www.marxists.org/archive/trotsky/1924/ffyci-1/ch19b.htm.

Trotsky, Leon. *Terrorism and Communism: A Reply to Karl Kautsky* (Ann Arbor MI, 1969).

Trotsky, Leon. *The Challenge of the Left Opposition 1926–27* (New York, 1980).

Trotsky, Leon. The Only Road (New York, 1933).

Trotsky, Leon. *The Revolution Betrayed: What is the Soviet Union and Where is it Going?* (New York, 1972).

Trotsky, Leon. *The Russian Revolution: The Overthrow of Tzarism and the Triumph of the Soviets*, abridged edition (New York, 1959).

Trotsky, Leon. *The Stalin School of Falsification* (New York, 1972).

Trotsky, Leon. *The Struggle against Fascism in Germany* (New York, 1971).

Trotsky, Leon. *The War and the International 1915* (n.p. 1971).

Trotsky, Leon. *Where is Britain Going?* (Ann Arbor MI, 1960).

Trotsky, Leon. What Next? In Vladimir Lenin and Leon Trotsky, *The Proletarian Revolution in Russia*, edited by Louis B. Fraina (New York, 1918), pp. 263–7.

Trotsky, Lev. *Dnevnik i pis'ma*, edited by Iu. G. Fel'shtinskii (Moscow, 1986).

Tucker, Robert C. 'Stalin and the Uses of Psychology'. In *The Soviet Political Mind*, edited by Robert C. Tucker (New York, 1972), pp. 143–72.

Tucker, Robert C. *Stalin as Revolutionary 1879–1929* (New York, 1974).

Turgenev, Ivan. *A Nest of Gentlefolk and Other Stories* (London, 1959).

Turgenev, Nikolai. *Rossiia i russkie* (Moscow, 1915), vol. I.

Turner, Jr, Henry A. *German Big Business and the Rise of Hitler* (New York, 1985).

Ulam, Adam B. *Expansion and Coexistence: The History of Soviet Foreign Policy, 1917–1967* (New York, 1968).

Ulam, Adam B. *In the Name of the People: Prophets and Conspirators in Prerevolutionary Russia* (New York, 1977).

Ulam, Adam B. *Prophets and Conspirators in Pre-Revolutionary Russia* (New Brunswick NJ, 1998).

Ulam, Adam B. *The Bolsheviks: The Intellectual, Personal and Political History of the Triumph of Communism in Russia* (New York, 1965).

Unaniants, N. T. 'M. K. Sokolov. Tsikl "Velikaia frantsuzskaia revoliutsiia"'. In *Frantsuzskii ezhegodnik: stat'i i materialy po istorii Frantsii 1989* (Moscow, 1989), pp. 330–57.

Unaniants, N. T. 'Velikaia frantsuzskaia revoliutsiia v knizhnoi grafike. 1917–1940 gg.'. In *Frantsuzskii ezhegodnik: stat'i i materialy po istorii Frantsii 1989* (Moscow, 1989), pp. 413–26.

Unaniants, N. T. 'Velikaia frantsuzskaia revoliutsiia v programme monumental'noi propagandy'. In *Frantsuzskii ezhegodnik: stat'i i materialy po istorii Frantsii 1989* (Moscow, 1989), pp. 148–52.

Unaniants, N. T. 'Velikaia frantsuzskaia revoliutsiia v sovetskoi literature. 1917–1940 gg.'. In *Frantsuzskii ezhegodnik: stat'i i materialy po istorii Frantsii 1989* (Moscow, 1989), pp. 358–65.

Unaniants, N. T. 'Velikaia frantsuzskaia revoliutsiia v sovetskoi muzykal'noi zhizni. 1917–1940 gg.'. In *Frantsuzskii ezhegodnik: stat'i i materialy po istorii Frantsii 1989* (Moscow, 1989), pp. 441–5.

Unaniants, N. T. 'Velikaia frantsuzskaia revoliutsiia v sovetskom iskusstve i literature'. In *Frantsuzskii ezhegodnik: stat'i i materialy po istorii Frantsii 1989* (Moscow, 1989), pp. 504–9.

Unaniants, N. T. 'Velikaia frantsuzskaia revoliutsiia v sovetskom izobrazitel'nom iskusstve'. In *Frantsuzskii ezhegodnik: stat'i i materialy po istorii Frantsii 1989* (Moscow, 1989), pp. 261–70.

Unaniants, N. T. 'Velikaia frantsuzskaia revoliutsiia v spektaklaiakh sovetskogo teatra. 1917–1940 gg.'. In *Frantsuzskii ezhegodnik: stat'i i materialy po istorii Frantsii 1989* (Moscow, 1989), pp. 467–503.

Unaniants, N. T. 'Velikaia frantsuzskaia revoliutsiia v zhurnal'noi i prikladnoi grafike. 1917–1940 gg.'. In *Frantsuzskii ezhegodnik: stat'i i materialy po istorii Frantsii 1989* (Moscow, 1989), pp. 210–60.

Unaniants, N. T. 'Iu. P. Velikanov. Seriia "velikaia frantsuzskaia revoliutsiia"'. In *Frantsuzskii ezhegodnik: stat'i i materialy po istorii Frantsii 1989* (Moscow, 1989), pp. 271–2.

Ustrialov, N. 'Put' termidora'. In N. Ustrialov, *Pod znakom revoliutsii* (Harbin, 1927).

Ustrialov, N. V. 'Patriotika'. In *Smena vekh: sbornik statei* (Smolensk, 1922).

Utechin, S. V. 'Who Taught Lenin?' *Twentieth Century* (July 1960): pp. 8–16.

Utin, N. I. 'Staraia i novaia Frantsii'. *Vestnik evropy* (March 1871): pp. 12–40.

V. I. Lenin, Neizvestnye dokumenty: 1891–1922 (Moscow, 1999).

V. I. Lenin i A. V. Lunacharskii. Perepiska, doklady, dokumenty—Literaturnoe nasledstvo (Moscow, 1971), vol. LXXX, pp. 527–33.

Valentinov, N. 'Sut' bol'shevizma v izobrazhenii Iu. Piatakov'. *Novyi zhurnal*, 52 (1958): pp. 140–61.

Valentinov, Nikolai. *Encounters with Lenin* (New York, 1968).

Valentinov, Nikolai. *The Early Years of Lenin* (Ann Arbor MI, 1969).

Van Ree, Erik. *The Political Thought of Joseph Stalin: A Study in Twentieth Century Revolutionary Patriotism* (London, 2002).

Veber, B. G. 'V. I. Lenin i istoricheskoe nasledie iakobintsev'. In *Frantsuzskii ezhegodnik: stat'i i materialy po istorii Frantsii 1970* (Moscow, 1972). pp. 5–34.

Venturi, Franco. *Roots of Revolution: A History of the Populist and Socialist Movements in Nineteenth Century Russia* (New York, 1966).

Vertzberger, Yaacov Y. I. 'Foreign Policy Decision-Makers as Practical-Intuitive Historians: Applied History and its Shortcomings'. *International Studies Quarterly*, 30 (1986): 223–47.

Vinaver, M. *Nedavnee: vospominaniia i kharakteristiki, 1907* (Paris, 1926).

Vinogradov, V. *Ocherki po istorii russkogo literaturnogo iazyka XVII–XIX vv.* (Leiden, 1949).

Vneocherednoi XXI s"ezd Kommunisticheskoi Partii Sovetskogo Soiuza: Stenograficheskii otchet (Moscow, 1959), vol. II.

Vneocherednoi XXII s"ezd Kommunisticheskoi Partii Sovetskogo Soiuza: Stengraficheskii otchet (Moscow, 1961), vol. II.

Voimolovskii, M. ed. *Geroizm revoliutsii* (Moscow, 1925).

Voinov, Vsevolod. 'Zhivopos'. In *Oktiabr' v iskusstve i literature 1917–1927* (Leningrad, 1928).

Volgin, V. P. 'Lenin i revoliutsionnye traditsii frantsuzskogo naroda'. In *Frantsuzskii ezhegodnik: stat'i i materialy po istorii Frantsii 1958* (Moscow, 1959), pp. 7–18.

Volgin, V. P. 'O prirode iakobinskoi vlasti'. *Voprosy istorii*, no. 5 (1969): pp. 92–103.

Volkogonov, Dmitrii. *Stalin, Triumph and Tragedy* (New York, 1996).

Von Geldern, James. *Bolshevik Festivals, 1917–1920* (Berkeley CA, 1993).

Vosstanie dekabristov: materialy (Moscow/Leningrad, 1925), vol. I.

Vovelle, Michel. '1789–1917: The Game of Analogies'. In *The French Revolution and the Creation of Modern Political Culture*, edited by Keith Michael Baker (New York, 1994), pp. 349–78.

'Vstrecha M. S. Gorbacheva s predstaviteliami frantsuzskoi obshchestvennosti'. *Pravda*, no. 273 (30 September 1989): p. 1.

'Vystuplenie M. S. Gorbacheva v organizatsii Ob"ediennykh Natsii'. *Pravda*, no. 344 (9 December 1988): pp. 1–3.

Warnke, Martin. *Political Landscape: The Art History of Nature* (London, 1994).

Weber, Eugen. 'The Nineteenth-Century Fallout'. In *The Permanent Revolution: The French Revolution and its Legacy: 1789–1799*, edited by Geoffrey Best (London, 1988), pp. 155–82.

White, Stephen. *The Bolshevik Poster* (New Haven CT, 1988).

Whitley, M. J. *Battleships of World War Two: An International Encyclopedia* (Annapolis MD, 1998).

Wildman, Allan K. *The End of the Russian Army: The Old Army and the Soldiers' Revolt (March–April 1917)* (Princeton NJ, 1980), vol. I.

Williams, Albert Rhys. *Through the Russian Revolution* (New York, 1921).

Wilson, Edmund. *To the Finland Station: A Study in the Writing and Acting of History* (New York, 1972).

Woehrlin, William F. *Chernyshevskii: The Man and the Journalist* (Cambridge MA, 1971).

Wolfe, Bertram D. *Three Who Made a Revolution: A Biographical History* (New York, 1964).

Woloch, Isser. *Jacobin Legacy: The Democratic Movement under the Directory* (Princeton NJ, 1970).

Woronoff, Denis. *The Thermidorean Regime and the Directory: 1794–1799* (New York, 1984).

Wortman, Richard. *Scenarios of Power: Myth and Ceremony in Russian Monarchy from Peter the Great to the Abdication of Nicholas II* (Princeton NJ, 2006).

Wright, Gordon. *France in Modern Times: From the Enlightenment to the Present* (New York, 1981).

Writings of Leon Trotsky (1929–1940), 14 vols (New York, 1979).

XIV s"ezd vsesoiuznoi kommunisticheskoi partii (b). 18–31 dekabria 1925 g.: stenograficheskii otchet (Moscow, 1926).

XV konferentsiia vsesoiuznoi kommunisticheskoi partii (b). 26 oktiabria–3 noiabria 1926 g.: stenograficheskii otchet (Moscow, 1927).

Yakovlev, A. 'Velikaia frantsuzskaia revoliutsiia i sovremennost'. *Sovetskaia kultura* (15 July 1989): pp. 3–4.

Yarmolinsky, Avrahm. *Roots of Revolution* (New York, 1971).

Yuen, Foong Khong. 'From Rotten Apples to Falling Dominoes to Munich: The Problem of Reasoning by Analogy about Vietnam' (PhD dissertation, Harvard University, 1987).

'Za t. Zinov'evym—T. Trotskii', *Pravda*, no. 286(3515) (10 December 1926): p. 2.

Zaborov, P. 'Velikaia frantsuzskaia revoliutsiia v russkoi pechati 1905–1907 gg. (Bibliograficheskii materialy)'. *Revue des Études Slaves*, 61 (1989): pp. 143–6.

Zaichnevskii, P. 'Molodaia Rossiia'. In *Politicheskie protsessy v Rossii 1860-x gg (po arkhivnym dokumentam)*, edited by Mikhail Lemke (Moscow/Petrograd, 1923), vol. II, pp. 508–18.

Zaitsev, A. *Ob ustrailove, 'neonepe' i zhertvakh ustrialovshchiny* (Moscow/Leningrad, 1928).

Zakher, 'Problema "termidora" v svete noveishikh istoricheskikh rabot'. *Istorik marksist* 6 (1927): pp. 236–42.

Zakher, Ia. M. *Deviatoe termidora* (Leningrad, 1926).

Zakher, Ia. M. *M. Robesp'er* (Moscow/Leningrad, 1925).

Zakher, Ia. M. *Parizhskie sektsii 1790–1795 godov* (Petrograd, 1921).

Zapiski Dashkova (St Petersburg, 1907).

Zasulich, Vera. 'K istorii vtorogo s"ezda (5 November 1904)'. *Katorga i ssylka*, no. 7–8 (1926): pp. 128–30.

Zasulich, Vera. 'Kar'era nigilista'. *Sotsial-demokrat*, no. 4 (1892). In *Sbornik statei* (St Petersburg, 1907), vol. II, pp. 111–47.

Zasulich, Vera. 'Organizatsiia, partiia, dvizhenie'. *Iskra*, no. 70 (25 July 1904): pp. 4–6.

Zatonskii, D. V. 'Pochemu oni ogovarivali sebia i drugikh'. *Nedelia*, no. 28 (1988): pp. 6–7.

Zeldin, Theodore. 'The Myth of Napoleon III'. *History Today* 8, no. 2 (February, 1958): pp. 103–9.

Zeman, Z. A. B. and W. B. Scharlau. *The Merchant of Revolution: The Life of Alexander Israel Helphand (Parvus)* (London, 1965).

Zinoviev, G. 'Chego ne delat'. *Rabochii*, no. 8 (30 August 1917): p. 8.

Zinoviev, G. 'Filosofiia epokhi. K s"ezdu partii'. *Pravda*, no. 214(3145) (19 September 1925): pp. 2–3, and no. 215(3146) (20 September 1925): pp. 2–3.

Zinoviev, G. *Vtoroi international i problema voiny ot nazyvaemsia my ot nasledstva?* (Petrograd, 1917).

Index

perceive similarities with Jacobins 44
practise terrorism 41–2
Nash put' 202
Natanson, Mark 152
National Assembly in France 31–5, 46–8,
    53, 71, 248, 364
National Bolshevism 236
Naumov, V. 445nn169–70,172
Nazi, -s 240
    Germany 129n65, 146, 281n23, 290, 352n53,
    417n79, 419n85, 420, 436
    invasion of USSR 218, 276–7, 290n59, 292–3,
    431n125
    Nazism 280, 420
    Nazi–Soviet Pact 287
Nechaev, Sergei 29, 31, 73n70
Necker, Jacques 284
Nekrasov, Nikolai 149
Neue Rheinische Zeitung 60, 63, 364, 388
Neue Zeit 96
New Economic Policy (NEP) 170, 180, 232–3,
    238–44, 254–5, 263–4, 249–50, 417–18,
    421–3, 433, 437, 492
New Soviet Man 214, 219, 277
Nicholas I 13–14, 17, 21
Nicholas II 15–17, 72, 84, 115, 151, 184–5, 219,
    404, 425
Nieuwenhuis, Ferdinand Domela 462
Nikitenko, A. V. 32
Nikitenko, *Dnevnik* 32n4
Nikolaevskii, Boris 240, 380, 420
Nilsson, Nils Ake 141n19, 223n198
Novaia zhizn' 122
Novoe vremia 323
Novyi luch 199
Novyi Vavilon (film, *The New Babylon*) 481

Obozrenie teatrov (Survey of Theatres) 141
obshchina (peasants' commune) 72
October Revolution 28, 40, 79, 108, 127, 145–8,
    152, 165–71, 184–6, 199, 213, 221–3, 250,
    323–4, 353, 375, 380, 411–12, 432, 439
    and Paris Commune, analogy between
    476–8
    as Bolshevik myth 214–15
    emigration after 110n1
    legitimacy of 233, 478
    resembles *coup d'état* 212
Ogarev, Nikolai 22–3
Ol'minskii, M. S. 125
Orléanist, -s 341–7, 352–3, 361–2, 367,
    372, 387, 395
d'Orléans, Duc 339
Orthodox Church 7, 10

Oshanina, Maria 43
Osinskii, V. V. 185
Osvobozhdenie 105
Ozouf, Mona 148

Paine, Thomas 322
Palmer, R. R. 33n15, 297n86, 438n151
Paris Commune 39, 53, 124, 133,
    165, 342, 350–3, 378, 389, 452–9,
    468–76
    and October Revolution, analogy
    between 476–8
    as proletarian dictatorship 477, 483
    Bolshevik claim to be sole legitimate legatee
    of 476
    Bolshevik propaganda regarding 481
    destruction of 75, 345
    establishment of 72
    extolled and honoured by Soviet
    government 482–5
    last revolution in an age of revolutions 488
    led by 'petitbourgeois' professionals 456
    martyrdom 340
    suppression of 136, 385
Pasternak, Boris 216
patriotism, revolutionary 168, 278
Paul I 13
Paxton, Robert O. 431n125
peasants' commune (*obshchina*) 72
Péchoux, P. 28n121
Pelshe, P. A. 224n203
perestroika 300, 318–24, 423, 449
Permanent Revolution, Theory of 94,
    480, 496
Perovskaia, Sofiia 221
Pestel, Pavel 21, 47
Peter III 4
Peter the Great 7, 12, 53
Peter-Paul Fortress 147, 213, 230
Peters, Iakov 171n2
Petrograd Soviet 153
Petropavlovsk (Soviet battleship
    renamed *Marat*) 218
Petrovskii, P. G. 258
philosophical idealism, German,
    influence of 4
Pilsudskii, Józef Klemens (Trotsky's
    comments on) 428
Pimenova, L. A. 137n85, 333
Pinckney, David H. 339n1, 341nn9–12
Piontkovskii, S. A. 424
Pipes, Richard 5n6, 80n5, 297n87
Pisarev, Dmitrii 14, 34
Plavinskii, N. Iu. 333